mosaics FOCUSING ON ESSAYS

mosaics FOCUSING ON ESSAYS

Kim Flachmann

Wendy Wilson
Fanshawe College

Melissa Mackey
Fanshawe College

SECOND CANADIAN EDITION

PEARSON
Prentice Hall

Toronto

Library and Archives Canada Cataloguing in Publication

Flachmann, Kim
Mosaics : focusing on essays / Kim Flachmann, Wendy Wilson, Melissa Mackey.—2nd Canadian ed.

Includes index.
ISBN 978-0-13-205185-9

1. Report writing. 2. English language—Rhetoric. 3. English language—Grammar. I. Wilson, Wendy, 1946– II. Mackey, Melissa, 1973– III. Title.

PE1408.F476 2008 808'.042 C2007-907395-6

ISBN-13: 978-0-13-205185-9
ISBN-10: 0-13-205185-0

Vice President, Editorial Director: Gary Bennett
Acquisitions Editor: Christopher Helsby
Marketing Manager: Sally Aspinall
Senior Developmental Editor: Joel Gladstone
Production Editor: Avivah Wargon
Copy Editor: Claire Horsnell
Proofreaders: Sharon Kirsch, Karen Alliston
Production Coordinator: Avinash Chandra
Composition: Laserwords
Permissions Research: Christina Beamish
Art Director: Julia Hall
Cover Design: Anthony Leung
Interior Design: Anthony Leung
Cover Image: Veer Inc.

For permission to reproduce copyrighted material, the publisher gratefully acknowledges the copyright holders listed on pages 591–592, which are considered an extension of this copyright page.

1 2 3 4 5 13 12 11 10 09 08

Printed and bound in the United States of America.

PEARSON
Prentice Hall

For Michael.

—K.F.

For Ron, with thanks for all your support and patience.

—W.W.

For Emily Laura and Sarah Maree Mackey. Keep reading and writing, girls! You make Aunt Melissa very proud!

—M.M.

Brief Contents

PART IV ❖ THE HANDBOOK 385

Contents

PREFACE

Experience tells us that students have the best chance of succeeding if they learn how to respond productively to the varying academic demands made on them throughout the curriculum. One extremely important part of this process is being able to analyze ideas and think critically about issues in many different subject areas. *Mosaics: Focusing on Essays* is the first in a series of three books that teach the basic skills essential to all good academic writing. This series illustrates how the companion skills of reading and writing are parts of a larger, interrelated process that moves back and forth through the tasks of prereading and reading, prewriting and writing, and revising and editing. In other words, the *Mosaics* series shows how these skills are integrated at every stage of the writing process.

THE *MOSAICS* SERIES

The Mosaics series consists of three books, each with a different emphasis: *Focusing on Essays*, *Focusing on Paragraphs in Context*, and *Focusing on Sentences in Context*. The first book highlights the composition of essays; the second book, paragraph development; and the third, sentence structure. Each book introduces the writing process as a unified whole and asks students to begin writing in the very first chapter. Each volume also moves from personal to more academic writing. The books differ in the length and level of their reading selections, the complexity of their writing assignments, the degree of difficulty of their revising and editing strategies, and the length and level of their student writing samples.

This entire three-book series is based on the following fundamental assumptions:

- Students develop confidence in their ability to read and write by reading and writing.
- Students learn best from discovery and experimentation rather than from instruction and abstract discussions.
- Students need to discover and develop their personal writing process.
- Students learn both individually and collaboratively.
- Students profit from studying both professional and student writing.
- Students benefit most from assignments that integrate thinking, reading, and writing.
- Students learn how to revise their writing by following clear guidelines.
- Students learn grammar and usage rules by editing their own writing.

- Students must be able to transfer their writing skills to their other courses.
- Students must think critically and analytically to succeed in school.

HOW THIS BOOK WORKS

The second Canadian edition of *Mosaics: Focusing on Essays* teaches students how to read and write critically. For flexibility and easy reference, this book is divided into four parts:

Part I Reading and Writing: An Overview
Part II Reading and Writing Effective Essays
Part III The Research Paper
Part IV The Handbook

Part I: Reading and Writing: An Overview All seven chapters in Part I demonstrate the cyclical nature of the reading and writing processes. They begin with the logistics of getting ready to read and write and then move systematically through the interlocking stages of the processes by following a student from prereading to rereading and then from prewriting to revising and editing. Part I ends with four review practices that summarize the material and let students practice what they have learned.

Part II: Reading and Writing Effective Essays Part II, the heart of the instruction in this text, teaches students how to read and write essays by introducing the rhetorical modes as patterns of development. It moves from personal writing to more academic types of writing: describing, narrating, illustrating, analyzing a process, comparing and contrasting, dividing and classifying, defining, analyzing causes and effects, and arguing. Within each chapter, students learn to read critically and write their own essays, study the essay of another student, read professional essays with guidance, and finally revise and edit the essay they wrote earlier in the chapter. Two professional writing samples are now included in each rhetorical mode chapter so students can actually see the features of each strategy at work in different pieces of writing. Each professional essay is preceded by prereading activities that will help students focus on the topic at hand and then is followed by 10 questions that move students from literal to analytical thinking as they consider the essay's content, purpose, audience, and paragraph structure. By following specific guidelines, students learn how to produce a successful essay using each rhetorical mode.

Part III: The Research Paper The next section of this text helps students move from writing effective essays to writing a research paper by systematically illustrating the details of writing a paper with sources. Then it explains the paper through student examples. Part III ends with a series of writing assignments and workshops designed to encourage students to write, revise, and edit a term paper and then reflect on their own writing process.

Part IV: The Handbook Part IV is a complete grammar and usage handbook, including exercises, that covers eight units: Sentences, Verbs, Pronouns, Modifiers, Punctuation, Mechanics, Effective Sentences, and Choosing the Right Word. These categories are coordinated with the Editing Checklist that appears on the inside back cover of this text. Each chapter starts with five self-test questions so that students can determine their strengths and weaknesses in a specific area. The chapters provide at least three types of practice after each grammatical concept, moving the students systematically from identifying grammar concepts to filling in the blanks to writing their own sentences. Each chapter ends with a practical editing workshop that asks students to use the skills they just learned as they work with another student to edit their own writing.

APPENDICES

The appendices will help students keep track of their progress in the various skills they are learning in this text. References to these appendices are interspersed throughout the book so that students will know when to use them as they study the concepts in each chapter.

Appendix 1A: Revising Peer Evaluation Form
Appendix 1B: Editing Peer Evaluation Form
Appendix 2A: Your EQ (Editing Quotient)
Appendix 2B: Editing Quotient Error Chart
Appendix 3: Error Log
Appendix 4: Spelling Log
Appendix 5: Presentation Techniques
Appendix 6: Editing Symbols

Further appendices are available on the Text Enrichment Site for this book at **http://www.pearsoned.ca/flachmann/mosaics**. Web Appendices 7 and 8 consist of Revising and Editing Peer Evaluation Forms for the following types of writing:

Web Appendix 7A: Describing
Web Appendix 7B: Narrating
Web Appendix 7C: Illustrating
Web Appendix 7D: Analyzing a Process
Web Appendix 7E: Comparing and Contrasting
Web Appendix 7F: Dividing and Classifying
Web Appendix 7G: Defining
Web Appendix 7H: Analyzing Causes and Effects

Web Appendix 7I: Arguing
Web Appendix 8A: Revising a Research Paper
Web Appendix 8B: Editing a Research Paper

Finally, **Web Appendix 9**, referred to frequently in the text, provides answers to the Test Yourself questions.

OVERALL GOAL

Ultimately, each book in the *Mosaics* series portrays writing as a way of thinking and processing information. One by one, these books encourage students to discover how the "mosaics" of their own writing process work together to form a coherent whole. By demonstrating the relationships among thinking, reading, and writing on progressively more difficult levels, these books promise to help prepare students for success throughout the curriculum.

UNIQUE FEATURES

Several unique and exciting features separate this book from other basic writing texts:

- It moves students systematically from personal to academic writing.
- It teaches rhetorical modes as patterns of thought.
- It integrates reading and writing throughout the text.
- It uses both student and professional writing as models.
- It introduces and demonstrates reading as a process.
- It demonstrates all aspects of the writing process through student writing.
- It features culturally diverse reading selections that are of high interest to students.
- It teaches 10 effective reading strategies.
- It helps students discover their own reading and writing processes.
- It includes a complete handbook with exercises.
- It offers worksheets for peer- and self-evaluation.

CANADIAN FEATURES

This text has been changed to reflect the needs of Canadian students. Fifteen high-interest readings by Canadian authors include essays by Mordecai Richler, Wayne Johnston, Patricia Pearson, and Lawrence

Hill, among others. Examples throughout the text have been updated, and the grammar Handbook streamlined. At the same time, the integrity of the original text has been maintained. In the interests of keeping the book at a manageable size and providing electronic templates, some student material has been moved from the appendices to the Text Enrichment Site. The Revising and Editing Checklists now appear on the inside front and back covers and in Chapter 7.

Supplements

To help both instructors and students get the most out of *Mosaics: Focusing on Essays*, we have provided both an Instructor's Resource Manual and a Text Enrichment Site.

- The **Instructor's Resource Manual** (ISBN **978-0-13-515287-4**) provides over 350 pages of additional teaching strategies, collaborative activities, sample syllabi, chapter summaries, and two quizzes for each chapter. This supplement can be downloaded by instructors from a password-protected location on Pearson Education Canada's online catalogue. Simply search for the text, then click on "Instructor" under "Resources" in the left-hand menu. Contact your local sales representative for further information.
- The **Text Enrichment Site** (**www.pearsoned.ca/flachmann/mosaics**) offers students chapter objectives, quizzes, and internet activities, as well as further sample student essays.

ACKNOWLEDGMENTS

For the second Canadian edition, we would like to thank our colleagues in the General Studies Division at Fanshawe College, Brian, Andrew, Haythem, Joe, Jennie, Kim, Rita, Diana, and Tony, for their help with Canadian trivia.

The following individuals graciously gave up their time to provide constructive criticisms of various drafts of the revisions. We are grateful to these people, and a few who wish to remain anonymous, for their many useful comments and suggestions.

Jane Barley, Thompson Rivers University
Dave Buchanan, Grant MacEwan College
Patricia Campbell, Red Deer College
Brent Cotton, Georgian College
Adeesha Hack, Seneca College
Patricia Morgan, Humber College

Hamid Rezaeiyazdi, Seneca College
Gordon P. Turner, Selkirk College

Wendy Wilson and Melissa Mackey

I want to express my gratitude to my students, from whom I have learned so much about the writing process, about teaching, and about life itself, and to Cheryl Smith's students, who tested various sections of the books and gave me good ideas for revising them over the past three years. Thanks finally to the students who contributed paragraphs and essays to this series: Josh Ellis, Jolene Christie, Mary Minor, Michael Tiede, and numerous others.

Finally, I owe a tremendous personal debt to the people who have lived with this project for the last few years; they are my closest companions and my best advisers: Michael, Christopher, and Laura Flachmann. To Michael I owe additional thanks for the valuable support and feedback he has given me through the entire process of creating and revising this series.

Kim Flachmann

PART I

Reading and Writing: An Overview

There is an art of reading, as well as an art of thinking and an art of writing.

—Isaac D'Israeli

We have learned from experience that reading and writing are so closely related that succeeding in one is directly related to succeeding in the other. So the goal of this part is to help you develop self-confidence as a reader *and* writer. It will give you the basic tools you need to improve your reading and writing. Then, as you move through these seven chapters, you will discover how to adjust these processes to suit your own needs and preferences. As you become more aware of the choices available to you, you will also develop a better understanding of your strengths and weaknesses as a reader and writer. With practice, your personalized reading and writing processes will soon be a routine part of your academic life and will help you confirm your place in the community of college students.

CHAPTER

1

Reading and Writing in College

Words help us solve problems, discover new ideas, feel better, make people laugh, and understand the world around us. Reading and writing are companion processes for using words. They let us connect with our immediate environment—as we learn from our reading and contribute to society through writing.

WHY LEARN HOW TO READ *AND* WRITE WELL?

The better you read and write, the more completely you can connect with your environment and the more control you have over your daily routine. Reading and writing well let you understand precisely what issues are important and communicate exactly what you want to say about them. These companion skills actually help you get what you want out of life. So reading and writing well give you power—in a variety of ways.

Reading and Writing as Critical Thinking

Critical thinking is the highest form of mental activity that human beings engage in, and it is a major source of success in college and in life. Thinking critically involves grappling with the ideas, issues, and problems in your immediate environment and in the larger world. It means constantly questioning and analyzing different aspects of life. Since critical thinking is complex, it requires a great deal of concentration and practice. Once you have a sense of how your mind works at this level, you will be able to think critically whenever you want.

Reading and writing are companion activities that engage people in the creation of thought and meaning—either as readers interpreting a text or as writers constructing one. Clear thinking is the pivotal point that joins these two tasks. The traditional rhetorical strategies are presented in this text as ways of processing information that you can use in other academic assignments. We feature one strategy at a time in each chapter so you can understand how it works before you combine it with other strategies. In this way, you will be able systematically to improve your ability to think, read, and write critically.

With some guidance, learning how to read and write according to different rhetorical modes or strategies (such as describing, narrating, or dividing and classifying) can give you the mental workout you need to think critically in much the same way that physical exercise warms you up for various sports. As you move through the chapters in Part II, you will be asked to isolate each rhetorical mode—just as you isolate your abs, thighs, and biceps in a physical workout. Each rhetorical mode offers a slightly different way of seeing the world, processing information, and solving problems. So each rhetorical mode is really a different way of thinking and making sense of the world.

Reading and Writing as Discovery

In both reading and writing, we often start out not knowing specifically where we are going. As we read, we are following another person's line of reasoning and discovering our own thoughts and reactions in response to our reading material. Similarly, we often don't actually know the points we want to make until we start writing. As we write, we discover what we think and what we want to say.

The physical acts of reading and writing help your mind sort through lots of ideas and help you decide exactly what you think and feel about specific topics. Sometimes new ideas will come to you as a result of something you have read. Or alternatively, you might understand an idea better once you start writing about it. Whatever the case, the simple acts of reading and writing lead to understanding—of both the subject matter and of your own thought processes.

The more you read and write, the more ideas you generate. This is why your instructor might suggest that you read and/or start to write if you are stuck on a topic or don't know what to say next about it. Reading and writing help you discover and express the good ideas that are already in your mind.

Reading and Writing as Necessities

Most importantly of all, reading and writing are necessary for surviving both in college and on the job. On a daily basis, you have to read and respond to a multitude of documents, from endless emails to textbooks to professional reports. In addition, in today's electronic age, you will have to write more than any previous generation ever has. Some of your writing will take the form of reports or projects that extend over a long period of time. Other writing tasks will have to be completed immediately, such as responses to email messages. Whatever the terms, reading and writing will be significant parts of your life throughout college and beyond.

The better your reading and writing skills, the better grades you will make in college and the further you will get in your chosen career. Everything you learn about reading and writing in this text applies to all your courses. These strategies will also be helpful on the job, especially when you have to read a dense analysis, write that difficult report, or summarize your accomplishments for a professional evaluation. The same reading and writing guidelines apply to all communication tasks.

PRACTICE 1 Answer the following questions.

1. Why should you learn to read and write?

____

____

____

2. Why should you learn to read and write well?

____

____

____

3. How can reading and writing help you think critically?

____

____

____

4. In what ways are reading and writing processes of discovery?

____

____

____

5. Why are reading and writing necessary in today's world?

____

____

____

THINKING OF YOURSELF AS A READER AND WRITER

Part of this important process is thinking of yourself as both a reader and a writer. You perform these tasks—reading and writing—every day in a variety of ways. Yet many people don't actually envision themselves as readers and writers. How we use words tends to be the hallmark of our success—no matter what our field. So learning how to read and write critically—at the highest possible level of performance—is a basic requirement for a meaningful, successful life.

Words are a commodity that you use every day and that can help you get what you want out of life. If you want to enter an email conversation at work, you first need to read the words that have already been said. Then you must write your response. You will need to decide when to use conversational language or when to use academic language. In many of your courses, you will read academic reports and essays. You will need to know how to respond to these reports and essays in a formal, academic way. Remember, any word choices you put forward reflect on you as a person. They are the grounds on which others judge you constantly.

Whether you read email messages, the newest bestseller, or a credit card agreement you received in the mail, you are a reader. Conversely, if you write and leave a note on the refrigerator, email a friend, write a paper for economics class, or draft a report for your boss, you are a writer. Now that you are in college, you are part of a very special community of readers and writers who are trying to perfect these skills, and you will live your life at a more informed and intellectually stimulating level than your friends not attending college.

As you face more complex reading and writing tasks in college, you need to understand the sequence of activities that make up the reading and writing processes. Learning to use these processes so that the work you produce is the best you are capable of is what this book is all about.

You may be asked to write papers in a formal, academic style. This style of writing avoids the personal pronoun "I." It is traditional in academic writing to remove "I" from the expression of your opinions in the paper. You are still meant to have an opinion and to express it; however, you must express it in an objective, dispassionate, rational way. Avoiding the personal pronoun "I" will help you accomplish this goal. Not every instructor or writing situation will call on you to avoid "I." Therefore, it is very important to become flexible in being able to express your opinion using "I" or avoiding "I," depending on the situation or the assignment. Chapter 28, "Pronoun Problems," in the Handbook section will help you realize when personal pronouns are unacceptable in writing.

Even though each reader and writer is different, some general principles apply to everyone—students and professionals alike. Before you actually begin to read or write, a wise move is to get your surroundings ready. That involves setting aside a time and place to do your work, gathering supplies, and establishing a routine.

1. **Set aside a special time to read and write, and plan to do nothing else during that time.** When you first get a reading or writing assignment, a little procrastination is natural. In fact, procrastination can actually work in your favour when you are writing because your mind is working on the task subconsciously. The trick is to know when to quit procrastinating and get down to work so that you meet your deadlines with time to spare. The fish tank can wait until tomorrow to be cleaned; the furniture doesn't have to be dusted today; the DVDs can

be watched later; and your MSN or chatroom friends won't forget who you are overnight.

2. **Find a comfortable place with few distractions.** Joyce Carol Oates, a famous contemporary writer, claims that writing is a very private act that requires lots of patience, time, and space. The same principle applies to reading. First, you need to set up a place to read and/or write that suits your specific needs. It should be a place where you are not distracted or interrupted. Some people work best in a straight-backed chair sitting at a table or desk, while others do their best work sitting cross-legged in bed. The exact place doesn't matter, as long as you can think there.

   Even if you are fortunate enough to have a private study area, you may find that you still want to make some adjustments. You may decide to unplug your phone during your study time. Or you may discover that quiet background music helps you shut out all kinds of noises but doesn't distract you the way talk shows and rock stations would. One student may do her best studying after soaking in a hot tub; another might play jazz when he is getting down to work; and still another may have a pop on one side of his table and a chocolate bar on the other. Whatever your choices, you need to set up a comfortable working environment.

3. **Gather your supplies before you begin to study.** Don't risk losing your great ideas by not being able to find a pen and paper or a flash drive. Some students keep a yellow tablet and a mechanical pencil by their side as they study; others write directly in their books; others keep notes on their laptops. In like manner, with writing, some students draft their essays on paper, and others type directly onto their computers. One of the main advantages of writing on a computer is that once you type your ideas into it, changing them or moving them around is easy. As a result, you are more likely to make revisions when you work on a computer, and you will therefore turn in a better paper. Whatever equipment you choose, make sure it is ready at the time you have set aside to study.

4. **Establish a personal ritual.** As a member of the community of students, acknowledging your own study habits and rituals is a major part of discovering your reading and writing processes. These rituals begin the minute you are given an assignment. What activities help you get ready to read? Some people exercise, others catch up on email, and still others clean their rooms before they study. What activities prepare you to write? Most people perform certain activities when they face reading and writing tasks without even realizing why. But they are preparing their minds for studying. So in the course of validating yourself as a reader and writer, take a moment now to record some of your own preferences and rituals connected with your study time.

PRACTICE 2 Explain the rituals you instinctively follow as you prepare to study. How do you prepare your mind for reading? Where do you write? At what time of day do you do your best work? Do you like noise? Quiet? What other details describe your study environment? What equipment do you need to read and write?

KEEPING A JOURNAL

The word **journal** refers to a daily log of your thinking. It is a place where you can record ideas, snatches of conversation, dreams, descriptions of people, pictures of places, and thoughts about objects—whatever catches your attention. Keeping a journal to respond to your reading and writing tasks will be very beneficial to your progress as a critical thinker. The more you respond in writing to what you are reading, the more engaged you will be in your learning.

A good way to establish the habit of journal writing is to use your journal for answering the questions that accompany the instruction in Parts II and III of this text and the writing exercises in the handbook (Part IV). You should definitely use your journal to respond to your reading in this text, and you can also use it to jot down ideas and plans for essays as they occur to you. In addition, you might want to complete your prewriting activities in your journal. Keeping track of a journal is much easier than finding notes on assorted scraps of paper.

Keeping a section of your journal private is also a good idea. Sometimes, when you think on paper or let your imagination run free, you don't want to share the results with anyone. Yet those notes can be very important in finding a subject to write about or in developing a topic.

Your journal in college will essentially be a bank of thoughts and topics for you. If used thoughtfully, it can become an incredible resource—a place to generate, store, and reference your ideas. Writing in your journal can help you discover your thoughts and feelings about specific issues as well as let you think through important choices you may have to make. So writing can help you solve personal problems and work your way through various college projects.

If you use a notebook for your journal, choose one that you really like. You might even keep your journal on your computer. However, unless you have a laptop, you won't have your electronic journal with you all the time. The choice is yours (unless your instructor has specific requirements). Just remember that a journal should be a notebook you enjoy writing in and carrying with you.

The content of your journal entries depends to a great extent on your instructor's directions. But some basic advice applies to all entries, whether on paper or on a computer.

1. Date your entries, and note the time; you may find it useful to see when your best ideas occur.
2. Record anything that comes to your mind, and follow your thoughts wherever they take you (unless your instructor gives you different directions).

3. Glue or tape anything into your journal that stimulates your thinking, reading, or writing—cartoons, magazine ads, poems, pictures, advice columns, and URLs for useful websites.
4. Think of your journal as someone to talk to—a friend who will keep your cherished ideas safe and sound and won't talk back to or argue with you.

PRACTICE 3 Begin your own journal.

1. Buy a notebook that you like, and write in it.
2. Make at least two journal entries on your computer.
3. Which type of journal do you prefer—notebook or computer? Write an entry explaining your preference.

READING AND WRITING IN TANDEM WITH A STUDENT

In the rest of Part I, you will be reading and writing in tandem, or along with, another student, Beth Olson, who has already completed the assignments you will be doing. In other words, this student will be demonstrating her reading and writing processes as you work on your own. As you consider Beth's words and ideas, concentrate on discovering your own original thoughts as you do each assignment.

PRACTICE 4 Answer the following questions.

1. What does reading and writing in tandem mean in this text?

   ____

2. How can this approach help you?

   ____

3. Why is it important to discover your own original thoughts for each assignment?

   ____

CHAPTER

2

The Reading Process

The reading process, like the writing process, consists of "steps" or "stages" that overlap. But the process of reading, unlike writing, has to occur in a certain order or you will not be able to understand your material. As you write, you might decide to develop a paragraph for your second topic first, then go back to your first topic, and write your introduction and conclusion last. Reading, however, dictates its own order. To get the most out of the process, you have to start at the beginning and read to the end. What you do during the process, however, is what can raise your level of understanding to the analytical or critical level, which is where you want to be in order to succeed both in college and in life after college. This chapter will introduce you to the entire reading process, but keep in mind that you should adjust the options presented here to your individual preferences.

VISUALIZING THE READING PROCESS

Although we talk about reading in a fairly sequential way, the options you can pursue within the process of reading something from beginning to end can occur and reoccur in any order. The purpose of reading actively (rather than passively) is to make you a critical reader. Once you start to read critically, your writing will rise to a higher level as well.

Passive readers open a reading assignment, start at the first page, and read to the end without doing any recognizable activities as they read. Active readers are physically working with their reading material from beginning to end—making it their own, trying to understand it on a more sophisticated level, and constantly reacting to it as they read. Identifying your own opinions and thoughts in reference to your reading material is one of the essential parts of the reading process.

As you work with the reading process in this textbook, the following graphic might help you understand how various stages of the process can overlap. The rest of this chapter will explain each of these elements in detail.

The Cycle of Reading

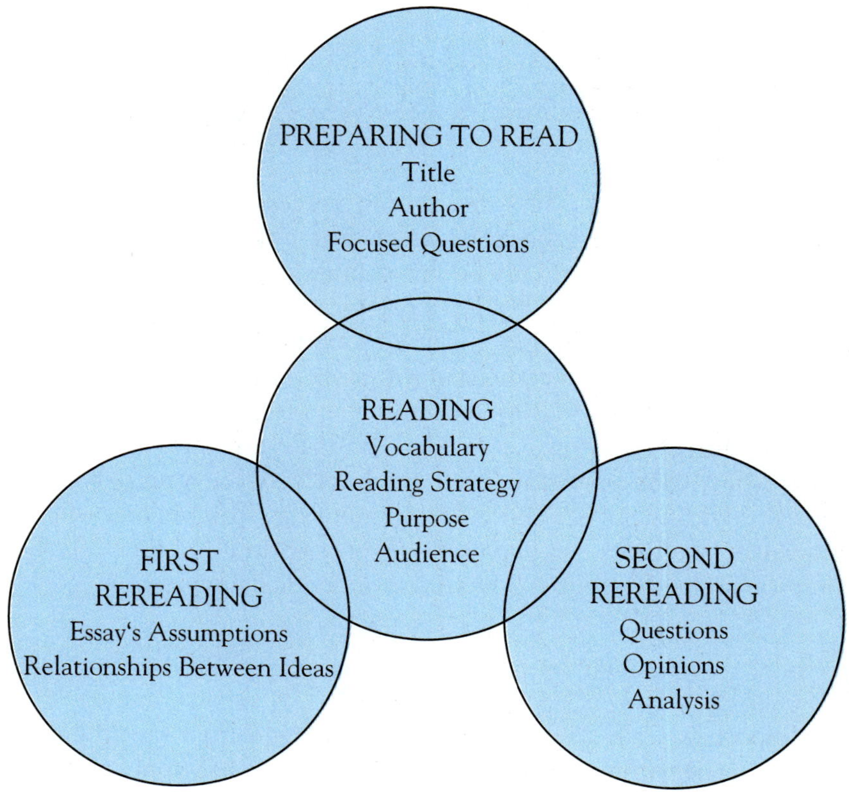

PRACTICE 1 Answer the following questions.

1. List the three elements of prereading.

____

2. List the four elements of reading.

____

3. List the two elements of first rereading.

____

4. List the three elements of second rereading.

____

THE READING PROCESS

The reading process, like the writing process, begins the minute you get a reading assignment. It involves all the activities you do, from finding your reading material to reading the entire piece, and includes trips to the library, text messages between you and your friends, and late-night snacks. Understanding the role these personal choices play in the reading process is just as important as knowing how the formal process works because all these personal rituals have to work together to help you complete your assignment on or before the assigned deadline. The main parts of the process are discussed in this section.

Preparing to Read

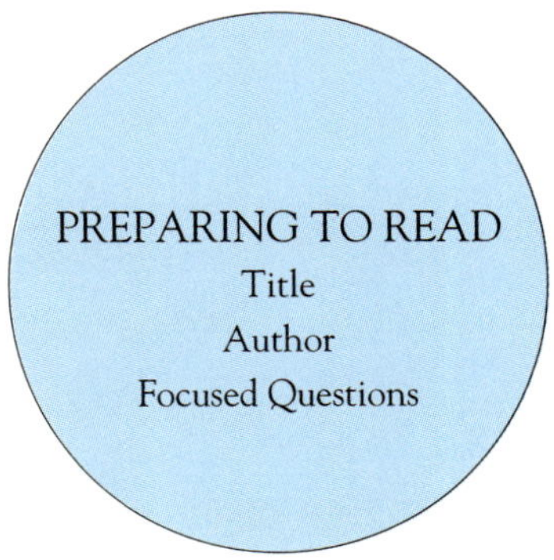

Prereading refers to activities that help you explore your reading material and its general subject so that you can read as efficiently as possible. It includes surveying your assignment and focusing on the task ahead of you. Your mission at this stage is to stimulate your thinking before and during the act of reading.

The most important tasks at this stage include looking closely at the title to see if it reveals any clues about the author and his or her attitude, finding out as much as you can about the author (background, profession, biases, etc.), and responding in this text to some preliminary questions that will focus your attention before you read. All of these activities will be demonstrated in Chapter 3 as Beth Olson approaches a reading assignment.

Reading

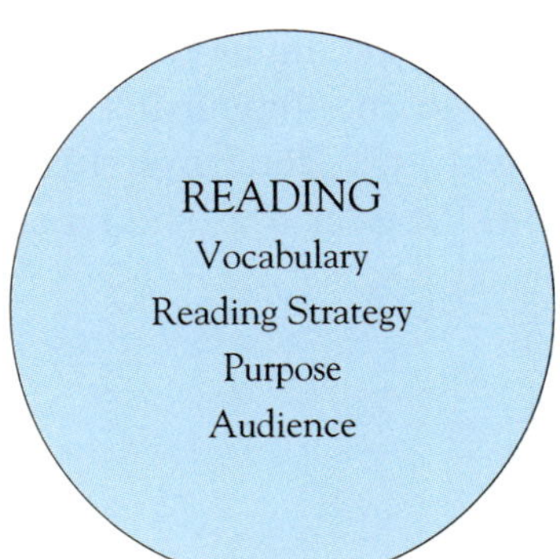

Once you have previewed your reading material, you can start reading at the beginning of the selection. As you read, you should mark or look up words that you can't understand from the context and annotate your reading material as you move through it. Writing on the material itself will keep you engaged in the process as the tasks become more difficult. You should also try to figure out the author's primary purpose for writing the selection.

Each chapter in Part II of this book will give you a specific reading strategy to master with a particular essay. These strategies can be applied to any reading material and are especially useful in helping you be an active reader. Once you learn different strategies that will improve your reading comprehension, you can choose your favourites to use in other courses.

First Rereading

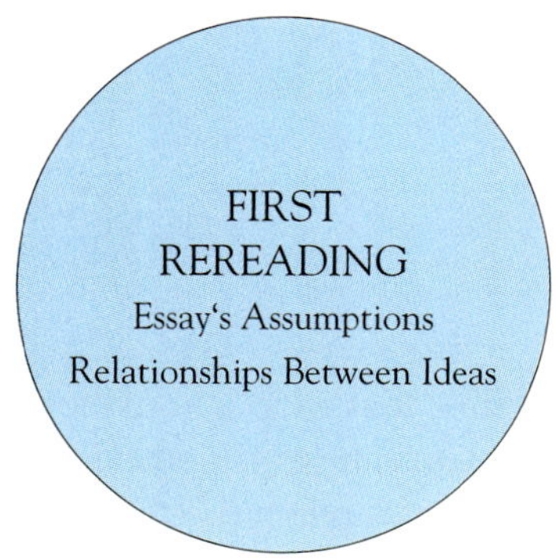

Most students don't want to read their assignments more than once, but the second and third readings are the ones that teach you how to read critically. Only after the first reading can you hope to understand your reading material at a deeper level. This second reading allows you to get to the assumptions that lie behind the words on the page and see relationships between ideas that you didn't notice in the first reading.

With this reading, you are closer to critical reading, but you are not there yet. This reading helps you dig more deeply into what the author is saying and prepares you to go one step further when you read the essay for the third time. Once again, the details of this reading will be demonstrated by Beth Olson in Chapter 3 as she records her reactions to her reading material.

Second Rereading

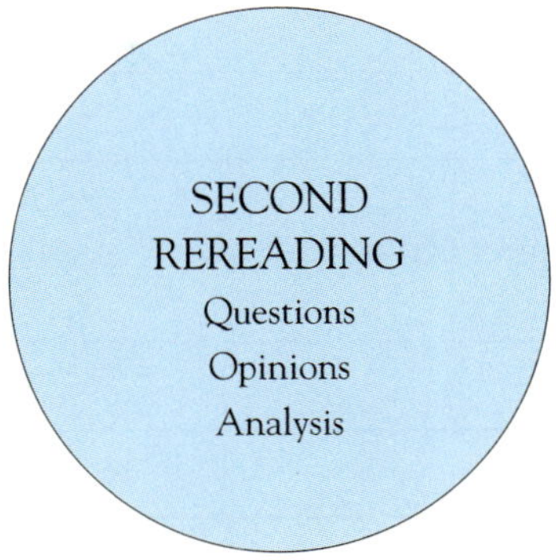

Now read the material one more time slowly and carefully to work out your opinions and analysis of the topic. This critical reading represents the highest level of comprehension, and that should be your goal with each essay that you approach in this book. To achieve this level of understanding, you must actually wrestle with the subject matter—ask questions, make associations of your own, and draw conclusions that capture your personal reaction to the reading material.

This reading requires the most energy on your part because you have to produce the questions and argue with the essay as it moves from point to point. Even though this third reading takes the most energy, it is also the most satisfying because your mind gets to exercise and grapple with ideas on a level that helps you understand both your reading and writing assignments more completely. Ultimately, this level of reading will raise your grades in all subjects.

Once you start reading and you understand where you are headed, these "stages" can occur in any order that you produce them. You may look up a word, argue with an idea in the first paragraph, and go back over a paragraph for a second reading—all in the first few minutes with an essay. Although you may never approach any two reading projects in the same way, the chapters in Part I will help you establish a framework for your personal reading process and guide you toward a comfortable ritual as a reader.

PRACTICE 2 Answer the following questions.

1. When does the reading process start for a writing assignment?

2. Explain "preparing to read" in your own words.

____

____

____

3. Describe your reading environment.

____

____

____

4. What does "reading" consist of?

____

____

____

5. What does rereading accomplish?

____

____

____

SAMPLE READING ASSIGNMENT

This first assignment is much like the reading tasks you will be asked to do throughout this book. As you learn some new techniques for reading at a higher level, you will follow the work of student Beth Olson so you can see how she approaches and completes the same assignment. If you work alongside her and mirror her actions, you too will understand the essay analytically and be able to apply it to all your work in college. By the end of Chapter 3, you will have a feel for the entire reading process, which is essential to strengthening your skills as a critical reader.

READING ASSIGNMENT

Read the essay in Chapter 3 entitled "I Just Wanna Be Average" by Mike Rose, following the guidelines in that chapter. Do the prereading activities and follow the directions for all three readings. Be aware of your level of understanding as you apply a specific reading strategy to the essay. Also, try to ask more complex questions with each reading.

CHAPTER 3

Reading Critically

Reading critically is the heart and soul of all successful communication. But unfortunately critical reading is often not taught. After elementary school, most teachers simply assume that students' reading abilities progress with the complexity of their assignments. But we are learning that this assumption is not true. We are living in an age of pictures, Xboxes, cell-phones with photo capabilities, and iPods, which has created a culture that does not naturally support reading. Reading requires time and reflection. Only then will your imagination be engaged so that you can read analytically and critically and be productive students and citizens in a very fast-moving world. But since our culture does not naturally promote reading as an activity, you have to work actively as an individual to become a critical reader. Reading critically will positively affect every aspect of your life in and out of college—especially your writing ability. As you read this chapter, record your responses to the exercises in your journal or on a separate piece of paper so that you can refer to them throughout the course.

PREPARING TO READ

Activities that take place before you actually start reading fall into the general category of **prereading** or **preparing to read**. This is a time when you should get your mind ready to interact with new information so that you can make meaning out of the text. You should also be thinking of using the right side (or the imaginative, creative side) of your brain over the left (more linear, sequential side). This is the part of your brain that thinks up new ideas and sees relationships among old ideas. More specifically, prereading consists of activities that help you do the following tasks:

- Survey and analyze the title
- Find out what you can about the author
- Focus your attention on the subject of the reading selection

Let's begin by looking at activities that many writers use to stimulate their minds as they approach a reading task. We will be following the thoughts and activities of a student named Beth Olson.

Title: I Just Wanna Be Average

Beth learned that the title of the essay she is about to read is "I Just Wanna Be Average." From the acknowledgments in the back of this book, she discovers that this selection is from a book called *Lives on the Boundary*. This is a surprising title because most people wouldn't admit their desire to be average even if it were true. They would say they want to be better than average. As Beth thinks about this title, she explores the following questions:

What does it mean at face value?

On what assumptions is it based?

Why would someone want to focus on this statement in an essay?

Author: Mike Rose

Beth then finds out the author's name (Mike Rose), but she doesn't know anything about him. So she does a web search of his name with the intention of trying to learn why he would write an essay on this topic. Here is a biography she found:

> Mike Rose is on the faculty of the UCLA Graduate School of Education and Information Studies and UCLA Writing Programs. He has written a number of books and articles on language and literacy and has received awards from the Spencer Foundation, the McDonnell Foundation, and the National Council of Teachers of English. He is the recipient of a Guggenheim Fellowship and is the author of *Lives on the Boundary: The Struggles and Achievements of America's Underprepared*.

One site Beth consulted was **www.nea.org/teacherexperience/divk040708.html.** This site and Mike Rose's book jacket told Beth that he is an immigrant who was singled out in school because he couldn't speak English. His experiences in school, in particular, taught him how to fight stereotyping and prejudice. He pushed through oppression and many hardships by continuing to push forward and by taking risks when he didn't know what the outcome would be. His story is one of determination and survival through education.

Focusing Your Attention

In this book, a set of questions will help you focus your attention on the material you are about to read. When you are reading material separate from this book, you should try to generate questions on your own—about the author, about the subject matter, about the title. In this way, you will begin all your reading with an inquiring mind, which is a basic necessity for active rather than passive reading.

Here are some questions to focus your attention on the Mike Rose essay. Writing your thoughts about these questions in a journal is the most beneficial approach to this exercise. Beth wrote her personal reactions to these questions before she started reading the essay.

1. What do you think about tracking, or separating students by ability level, in high school? What are the advantages and disadvantages of this system of teaching? How would it affect your learning? Did your high school track its students?
2. In the essay you are about to read, the writer claims that students use sophisticated defence mechanisms to get through high school. Have you ever used any defences in school? How did these defences make you act? Did they help or hinder your learning?

READING

As you approach a reading task, you should plan to read the material three times if you want to understand it critically. To get to the deeper levels of meaning, you need to work through literal and interpretive comprehension first. These three readings take time and reflection.

As you read, you need to realize that you are making meaning out of a text that someone else has written. You need to work in partnership with the author and his or her words to make sense of the material. Usually this does not happen in one reading. In like manner, when someone reads your writing, he or she must work with your words on the page to figure out what you are saying and what your words are implying.

Expanding Your Vocabulary

The first task you should undertake in a general first reading is to get the gist of the selection and look up vocabulary words that you don't understand. In this book, difficult vocabulary is identified and defined for you. You should keep this list handy and add other words to it as you read.

If you want to actually increase your vocabulary and take these words with you into your own speaking and writing, you need to interact with the text and highlight the words, compose your own lists, create index cards—complete some activity that will make the words your own. In this text, a specific task is suggested in each vocabulary section so you can try a few different activities and then choose those that work best for you to use in your reading outside this class.

Here is a list of difficult words you need to know for the first reading of "I Just Wanna Be Average." Beth looked at the words she knew and circled those that were new for her. Then she put each word she wanted to add to her vocabulary on an index card with the definition on the other side. That way, she can quiz herself on her new words as she accumulates cards.

vocational: focused on training for a job (paragraph 1)
Horace's Compromise: a novel by Theodore R. Sizer (paragraph 1)
hypotheses: educated guesses (paragraph 1)
disaffected: rebellious, uncooperative (paragraph 1)
skeletal: very basic (paragraph 1)
scuttling: moving quickly (paragraph 1)
somnambulant: walking while asleep (paragraph 2)
wherewithal: ability (paragraph 2)
prowess: strength (paragraph 3)
clique: exclusive social group (paragraph 3)
testament to: proof of (paragraph 3)
dearth: lack (paragraph 3)
much-touted: repeatedly praised (paragraph 4)
salubrious: socially or morally acceptable (paragraph 4)
equivocal: having two or more meanings (paragraph 4)
Argosy: a science-fiction magazine (paragraph 4)
Field and Stream: a hunting and fishing magazine (paragraph 4)
Daily Worker: a socialist newspaper (paragraph 4)
The Old Man and the Sea: a novel by Ernest Hemingway (paragraph 4)
rough-hewn: unsophisticated, unpolished (paragraph 4)
apocryphal: a story that is not true but is believed by some people anyway (paragraph 4)
ducktail: a hairstyle in which the hair is swept back at the sides to meet in an upturned point at the back (paragraph 5)
parable of the talents: a story from the New Testament (paragraph 5)
restive: restless, fidgety (paragraph 5)
affect: emotion (paragraph 5)
laryngectomize: surgically remove a person's larynx (paragraph 5)
platitudinous: dull, boring, full of unoriginal thoughts (paragraph 5)
melee: battle (paragraph 5)
dissonant: nonconforming, disagreeing (paragraph 6)
elite: privileged individuals (paragraph 6)
constrained: kept within limits (paragraph 6)
liberate: free (paragraph 6)
gray matter: brain (paragraph 7)
diffuse: scatter (paragraph 7)
cultivate: encourage (paragraph 7)
malady: illness (paragraph 7)

Using a Reading Strategy

As you begin to read, you will be prompted to use a reading strategy with each reading assignment. Here are the 10 reading strategies we introduce in this book:

Personal Annotations We all naturally make personal associations with our reading material. However, one person's associations are usually quite different from those of someone else. Recording the associations you make with a reading selection lets you "own" the essay, so to speak. It allows you to connect the author's ideas to your own experiences. To use this strategy, make notes in the margin that relate some of your specific memories to the details in this essay. Be prepared to explain the connection between your notes and the facts in the essay.

Think Aloud As we read and make meaning out of the author's words, we put a string of words together on a literal level, bring in any implications the author suggests, think about how the ideas relate to one another, and keep the process going until the entire essay makes sense. These are focused thoughts that will help you process the author's writing. On another level, however, we also stray from the essay in a wide variety of ways—thinking about chores we need to do, calls we forgot to return, and events we are looking forward to on the weekend. These are random ideas that are only loosely related to the reading. As you might suspect, focused reading is the most productive, but you can teach yourself to apply even your random ideas toward a better understanding of your reading material. To do this strategy, stop and "think aloud" about what is on your mind throughout the text. Point out places that are confusing to you, connections that you make, specific questions you have, related information you know, and personal experiences you associate with the text. In this way, you are able to hear what your mind does (both focused and random) as you read.

Chunking Reading illustration essays critically means looking closely at the selection to discover how it is structured. To understand how an essay works, circle the main idea or thesis. Then draw horizontal lines throughout the essay to separate the various topics that support the thesis. These lines may or may not coincide with paragraph breaks. Finally, label each "chunk" in the right margin. Be prepared to explain the divisions you made.

Graphic Organizers Students often find that making drawings of the ideas and details in their reading is a much more effective way than outlining to understand the material and see how it works. Graphic organizers, or concept maps, let you literally "draw" the relationship of ideas to one another. Figuring out what framework to use for this exercise is part of the process. You can make up a drawing of your own or do a web search for "graphic organizers" to see some options. For an essay, show the relationship of the ideas to one another in a graphic form that makes sense to you. Be prepared to explain your drawing.

Peer Teaching Teaching something to your peers is an excellent way to see if you understand it. To practise this technique, the class must first divide an essay into parts. The class members should then get into groups (one for each part of the essay) and choose one of the essay's sections to prepare for the rest of the class. After discovering the main ideas, the details, and their relationship to one another, each group should teach its section to the rest of the class.

Summarizing As you read more difficult essays, the ability to summarize is essential. A summary features the main ideas of a selection in a coherent paragraph. First, identify the main ideas in your reading; then fold them into a paragraph with logical transitions so your sentences flow from one to another. After you write your summary, draft three questions for discussion.

Critical Annotations Forming your own opinions and coming up with new ideas in response to your reading are very important parts of the reading process, but you need to learn how to produce these reactions. As you read an essay, plan to record your notes on a separate piece of paper. First, draw a vertical line down the centre of a sheet of paper. Then, as you read, write the author's main ideas on the left and your reactions to those ideas on the right side of the page. Be prepared to explain the connection between your notes and the material in the essay.

Lists Separating related ideas is an important part of understanding an essay. After a first reading, divide a sheet of paper into two parts with a vertical line. Then as you read the essay for a second time, record one set of ideas in the left column and related ideas from the essay on the right. Draw lines from one detail to another (if applicable). Be prepared to explain the connection between your lists and the details in the essay.

Highlighting Reading an argument critically calls for very high-level skills. You need to understand your reading on a literal level, know the difference between opinions and fact, and come up with your own thoughts on the topic by challenging the author's ideas. To do this strategy, highlight facts in one colour and the author's opinions in another colour. This activity works very well with the next strategy.

Reading with the Author/Against the Author This approach to reading is a very advanced form of reading. It asks you to recognize that you are consciously looking for ideas to agree with and then disagree with. By doing this, you will force yourself to form your own ideas. From the previous highlighting exercise, put an *X* by any facts or opinions that you do not agree with or want to question in some way. Then record your own thoughts and opinions on a separate sheet of paper. Be prepared to explain any marks you made on the essay.

Beth's Reading Beth read the following essay by Mike Rose. It stimulated her thoughts about learning in general because she believes that the most important part of learning is taking risks. She jotted several notes to herself in the margins as she read.

Yes I agree

But how does Gross do this?

three important skills

I know

1 Students will float to the mark you set. I and the others in the vocational classes were bobbing in pretty shallow water. Vocational education was aimed at increasing the economic opportunities of students who do not do well in our schools. Some serious programs succeed in doing that, and through exceptional teachers—like Mr. Gross in *Horace's Compromise*—students learn to develop hypotheses and troubleshoot, reason through a problem, and communicate effectively—the true job skills. The vocational track, however, is most often a place for those who are just not making it, a dumping ground for the disaffected. There were a few teachers who worked hard at education; young Brother Slattery, for example, combined a stern voice with weekly quizzes to try to pass along to us a skeletal outline of world history. But mostly the teachers had no idea of how to engage the imaginations of us kids who were scuttling along at the bottom of the pond.

Why defensive?

2 And the teachers would have needed some inventiveness, for none of us was groomed for the classroom. It wasn't just that I didn't know things—didn't know how to simplify algebraic fractions, couldn't identify different kinds of clauses, bungled Spanish translations—but that I had developed various faulty and inadequate ways of doing algebra and making sense of Spanish. Worse yet, the years of defensive tuning out in elementary school had given me a way to escape quickly while seeming at least half alert. During my time in Voc. Ed., I developed further into a mediocre student and a somnambulant problem solver, and that affected the subjects I did have the wherewithal to handle: I detested Shakespeare; I got bored with history. My attention flitted here and there. I fooled around in class and read my books indifferently—the intellectual equivalent of playing with your food. I did what I had to do to get by, and I did it with half a mind.

How did learning about people help Rose?

Max is like this

3 But I did learn things about people and eventually came into my own socially. I liked the guys in Voc. Ed. Growing up where I did, I understood and admired physical prowess, and there was an abundance of muscle here. There was Dave Snyder, a sprinter and halfback of true quality. Dave's ability and his quick wit gave him a natural appeal, and he was welcome in any clique,

though he always kept a little independent. He enjoyed acting the fool and could care less about studies, but he possessed a certain maturity and never caused the faculty much trouble. It was a testament to his independence that he included me among his friends—I eventually went out for track, but I was no jock. Owing to the Latin alphabet and a dearth of *R*'s and *S*'s, Snyder sat behind Rose, and we started exchanging one-liners and became friends.

There was Ted Richard, a much-touted Little League pitcher. 4
He was chunky and had a baby face and came to Our Lady of Mercy as a seasoned street fighter. Ted was quick to laugh, and he had a loud, jolly laugh, but when he got angry he'd smile a little smile, the kind that simply raises the corner of the mouth a quarter of an inch. For those who knew, it was an eerie signal. Those who didn't found themselves in big trouble, for Ted was very quick. He loved to carry on what we would come to call philosophical discussions: What is courage? Does God exist? He also loved words, enjoyed picking up big ones like *salubrious* and *equivocal* and using them in our conversations—laughing at himself as the word hit a chuckhole rolling off his tongue. Ted didn't do all that well in school—baseball and parties and testing the courage he'd speculated about took up his time. His textbooks were *Argosy* and *Field and Stream,* whatever newspapers he'd find on the bus stop—from the *Daily Worker* to pornography—conversations with uncles or hobos or businessmen he'd meet in a coffee shop, *The Old Man and the Sea.* With hindsight, I can see that Ted was developing into one of those rough-hewn intellectuals whose sources are a mix of the learned and the apocryphal, whose discussions are both assured and sad.

like Sam in Intro to Psych

And then there was Ken Harvey. Ken was good-looking in a 5
puffy way and had a full and oily ducktail and was a car enthusiast. . . . One day in religion class, he said the sentence that turned out to be one of the most memorable of the hundreds of thousands I heard in those Voc. Ed. years. We were talking about the parable of the talents, about achievement, working hard, doing the best you can do, blah-blah-blah, when the teacher called on the restive Ken Harvey for an opinion. Ken thought about it, but just for a second, and said (with studied, minimal affect), "I just wanna be average." That woke me up. Average?! Who wants to be average? Then the athletes chimed in with the clichés that make you want to laryngectomize

like Sasha in Orientation

What a great line, but why not "special"?

them, and the exchange became a platitudinous melee. At the time, I thought Ken's assertion was stupid, and I wrote him off. But his sentence has stayed with me all these years, and I think I am finally coming to understand it.

English 1A!!

Ken Harvey was gasping for air. School can be a tremendously disorienting place. No matter how bad the school, you're going to encounter notions that don't fit with the assumptions and beliefs that you grew up with—maybe you'll hear these dissonant notions from teachers, maybe from the other students, and maybe you'll read them. You'll also be thrown in with all kinds of kids from all kinds of backgrounds, and that can be unsettling—this is especially true in places of rich ethnic and linguistic mix, like the L.A. basin. You'll see a handful of students far excel you in courses that sound exotic and that are only in the curriculum of the elite: French, physics, trigonometry. And all this is happening while you're trying to shape an identity, your body is changing, and your emotions are running wild. If you're a working-class kid in the vocational track, the options you'll have to deal with this will be constrained in certain ways: You're defined by your school as "slow"; you're placed in a curriculum that isn't designed to liberate you but to occupy you, or, if you're lucky, train you, though the training is for work the society does not esteem; other students are picking up the cues from your school and your curriculum and interacting with you in particular ways. If you're a kid like Ted Richard, you turn your back on all this and let your mind roam where it may. But youngsters like Ted are rare. What Ken and so many others do is protect themselves from such suffocating madness by taking on with a vengeance the identity implied in the vocational track. Reject the confusion and frustration by openly defining yourself as the Common Joe. Champion the average. Rely on your own good sense. **** this bullshit. Bullshit, of course, is everything you—and the others—fear is beyond you: books, essays, tests, academic scrambling, complexity, scientific reasoning, philosophical inquiry. 6

I hate this feeling

so true

How?

putting down what you don't know or understand = a defence

The tragedy is that you have to twist the knife in your own gray matter to make this defense work. You'll have to shut down, have to reject intellectual stimuli or diffuse them with sarcasm, have to cultivate stupidity, have to convert boredom from a malady into a way of confronting the world. Keep your vocabulary simple, act stoned when you're not or act more stoned than you are, flaunt ignorance, materialize your dreams. It is a powerful 7

Why a tragedy?

Learning goes on hold so this "role" can succeed

Defence = Magic?

What price?

and effective defense—it neutralizes the insult and the frustration of being a vocational kid and, when perfected, it drives teachers up the wall, a delightful secondary effect. But like all strong magic, it exacts a price.

Your Reading Read Mike Rose's essay, and add your own notes to Beth's comments in the margins.

Discovering Purpose and Audience

Finally, at this stage of the reading process, you should determine the writer's purpose and audience. In Beth's case, she learns from the book jacket that Rose set out to write his autobiography, which ended up focusing on his educational experiences. Teachers had a great effect on Rose and his progress as a child trying to survive in American society. His initial audience was probably educators, but now he has a much broader appeal.

FIRST REREADING

Your first rereading must now focus on raising your level of thinking so that you have a deeper understanding of the essay you just finished. Looking again at the essay with an inquiring mind is the heart of this stage.

This book provides questions on progressively more difficult levels to help you accomplish this goal. But without these questions, you need to ask your own questions as you read. Focusing on questions that wonder "why" or "how" something happened will move you to these higher levels. You also want to focus on the assumptions that the writer bases his or her points on, and the relationship between ideas in an essay. These might be either stated or unstated. As you become a more proficient reader, you will be able to see both with ease.

Beth's First Rereading As Beth read Rose's essay a second time, she saw several relationships that she had not previously seen. She noted these relationships on the essay and then answered the following questions provided in the text. Her answers appear after each question.

Thinking Critically About Content

1. Who was vocational education aimed at in Rose's school? Who is this track for?

   Vocational training was aimed at students who were deemed "slow." They were "placed in a curriculum that isn't designed to liberate you but to occupy you, or, if you're lucky, train you" (para. 6).

2. What examples from this essay illustrate most clearly what Rose's academic life involved?

   The examples in paragraph 2 illustrate most clearly Rose's academic life. They point out his troubles with academics and his desire to retreat in part from the academic world.

3. Rose says the Voc. Ed. students "were bobbing in pretty shallow water" and then refers to them "scuttling along at the bottom of the pond" (paragraph 1). In these examples, he is comparing people trying to swim and stay above water to students on a vocational track in high school. This comparison is called a *metaphor*. Find another comparison like this in paragraph 7.

   Here are two examples: "The tragedy is that you have to twist the knife in your own gray matter to make this defense work" and "But like all strong magic, it exacts a price."

Thinking Critically About Purpose and Audience

4. What do you think Rose's purpose is in this essay? Explain your answer.

   Rose's purpose is to inform readers that teachers who expect mediocre work from students will receive just that. He wants teachers to set the mark higher so that students will reach it.

5. What type of audience do you think would most understand and appreciate this essay?

   Anyone can appreciate this essay, but students who are or have been perceived to be performing at low levels will understand it best.

6. What do you think Ken Harvey meant when he said, "I just wanna be average" (paragraph 5)?

   Harvey probably wanted to go unnoticed. He didn't want to stand out, but at the same time, he didn't want to fail. He was content to live his life somewhere in the middle.

Thinking Critically About Essays

7. Does Rose give you enough examples to understand his learning environment in high school? Explain your answer.

His examples do paint a picture about his learning environment because they show readers how teachers expected mediocrity from students who were more than willing to provide it.

8. Is this essay unified? Does each of the author's topic sentences support the essay's thesis statement? Explain your answer.

   The topic sentences do support Rose's thesis statement, and the essay is unified. All the paragraphs focus on proving that if teachers don't expect much from their students, they won't get much.

9. What is Rose's thesis in this essay? Where is it located?

   Rose's thesis is the first sentence in the essay: "Students will float to the mark you set."

10. Explain your opinion about tracking students. Is tracking a good idea? Does it help some students? Does it hurt anyone? Can you think of any alternatives to tracking? Respond to these questions in detail.

    I think tracking makes students feel bad. If they are in a low-level class, they know that teachers don't expect much from them. That feeling can stay with them forever. They may not be as strong as Mike Rose and will be marked by this label way beyond school.

Your First Rereading Read "I Just Wanna Be Average" a second time, and take more notes about assumptions and relationships between ideas in the margins as you read. Then, in your journal, generate five "why" or "how" questions about the ideas in this essay. Then, exchange questions with a classmate, and answer each other's questions in your journal.

SECOND REREADING

This final reading is the real test of your understanding. It has the potential to raise your grades in all subjects if you complete it for each of your reading assignments. It involves understanding the author's ideas as you also form your own opinions and analyze your thoughts.

To accomplish this reading, you should ask more questions that go beyond the words on the page and then answer them in writing. You should also bring your own opinions to the surface. Write them down as they occur to you. Finally, analyze your thoughts so that you end with some form of self-evaluation.

Beth's Second Rereading Beth took the following notes in her journal as she read Rose's essay for the third time. She asked herself some questions, answered those questions as best she could, recorded her opinions as they occurred to her, and analyzed her thoughts along the way. She covers all of these thought processes in the following journal entry.

> Opening yourself up to learning is tough. If you try and don't get it, you feel stupid. I guess that's the advantage of putting up defences when confronted with something to learn. With a defence, you don't look stupid—you just look cool because you are refusing to try.
>
> I know that feeling. I've dug my heels in before when I thought I wouldn't understand something. And it saved me from embarrassment, but I'm not sure I came out ahead. My feelings were intact/unruffled, but I realized with that behaviour I would be stuck in the mud forever. The only way to get ahead is to move forward (even a little bit) and the only way to move is to learn and the only way to learn is to take some risks—risk embarrassment, risk feeling stupid, risk your fragile ego. But defences are circular. Here's how they work—you get nervous or uncomfortable, you put up a defence of some sort, you save face, and you start all over again. You never learn anything that would help you get out of your rut. You only learn how to save your emotions. That's a form of survival. But I want more.

Your Second Rereading Take notes in your own journal as you read Rose's essay for the third time. Ask yourself more "how" and "why" questions, answer those questions, record your opinions, and analyze your thoughts as they occur.

CHAPTER

4

The Writing Process

The writing process consists of identifiable "stages" that overlap in a number of unique ways. No two people write in the same way, so it is important for you to find out exactly how your personal writing process works. In other words, you need to know how to arrange these stages to produce the best writing you can. Knowing each of the stages individually will help you organize them in a way that best suits your learning style and your lifestyle. This chapter will introduce you to the entire process in the hope that you will tailor it along the way to meet your individual needs.

VISUALIZING THE WRITING PROCESS

Even though we talk about the stages of writing, writing is actually a cyclical process, which means that at any point you may loop in and out of other stages. As you work with the writing process in this textbook, the graphic on the opposite page might help you understand how various stages of the process can overlap. The rest of this chapter will explain each of these elements in detail.

PRACTICE 1 After studying the graph on p. 29, answer the following questions.

1. List the two elements of prewriting.

2. List the four elements of writing.

3. List the six elements of revising.

4. List the three elements of editing.

The Cycle of Writing

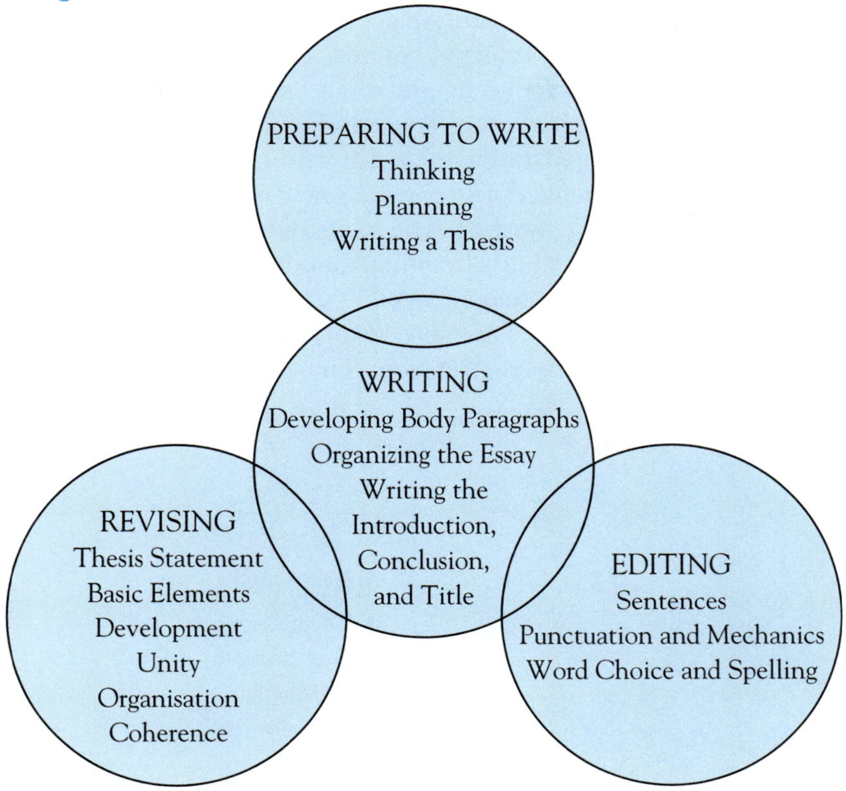

THE WRITING PROCESS

The writing process begins the minute you get a writing assignment. It involves all the activities you do, from choosing a topic to turning in a final draft, and includes computer searches, text messages, and late-night trips to Tim Hortons. Understanding these personal choices is just as important as knowing the details of the formal process because all these elements have to work together in order for you to produce a piece of writing on or before the assigned deadline. The main parts of the process are explained in this section.

Preparing to Write

Prewriting refers to activities that help you explore a general subject, generate ideas about it, select a specific topic, establish a purpose, and learn as much as possible about your readers. Chapter 5 will teach you different strategies for accomplishing these goals before you actually begin to write a draft of your essay. Your mission at this stage is to stimulate your thinking before and during the act of writing.

Whenever you generate new material throughout the writing process, you are prewriting. The most common prewriting activities are freewriting, brainstorming, clustering, questioning, and discussing. All of these activities will be demonstrated in Chapter 5 as Beth Olson approaches a writing assignment. The more ideas you generate now and throughout the entire writing process, the more you have to work with as you draft your essay.

Writing

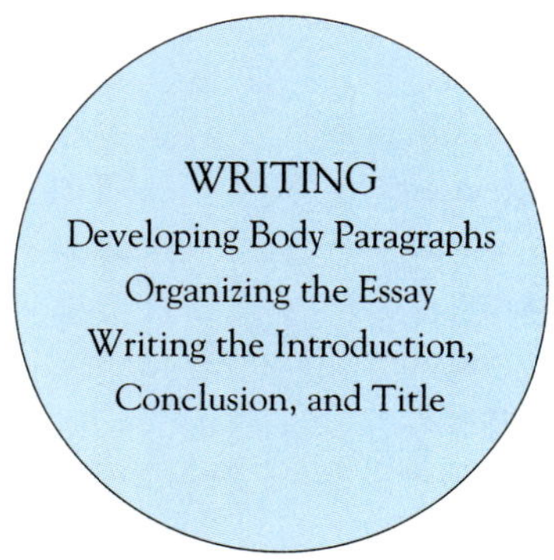

As you try to give your ideas shape, your thesis statement will give your writing focus. This statement or controlling idea, once written, should include your purpose for writing or an outline of what you want to accomplish in the essay. This "mission" will help you make important decisions as you begin to actually put your thoughts into essay form. Developing and organizing your ideas will come after you get your thoughts out on paper.

You can start writing after you have some ideas to work with. Writing includes developing some of your ideas further, organizing your thoughts with your purpose in mind, and writing a first draft. To begin writing, you should go back to your notes, journal entries, and other prewriting activities and then mould these ideas into a logical, coherent essay. As you write, you should concentrate on what you are saying and how your ideas fit together.

You might find it easier to add your introduction, conclusion, and title after you compose the body of your essay. Only after you actually generate a draft do you know what you are going to say in an essay. Don't let grammar and spelling distract you from your task at this point. You can correct your grammar and mechanical errors later.

Revising

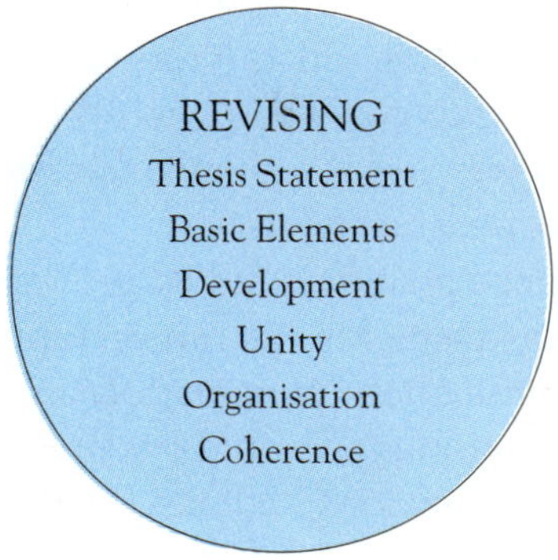

Most people do not want to take the time to revise their writing. But revising always pays off, because it will make your writing stronger. Revising involves rethinking your content and organization so that your words say exactly what you mean. (Editing, the last step, focuses on your grammar, punctuation, mechanics, and spelling.) Your main goal in revising is to make sure that the purpose of your essay is clear to your audience and that your main ideas are supported with adequate details and examples. In addition, you should check that your paper is organized logically and moves smoothly from one idea to the next.

The items listed in the circle above appear on the revising checklist throughout this text. We will explain each one of these elements so that you can use it effectively in the revisions of your own essays. If you go through this list each time you rewrite your essays, you will be creating a better draft with each change you make.

Editing

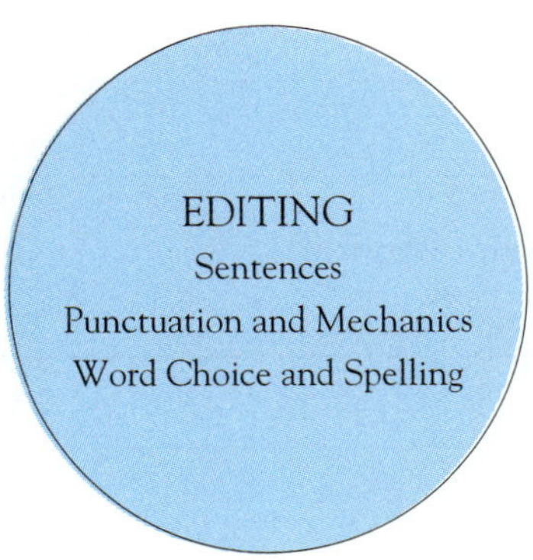

Editing is the final stage of the writing process. After you revise your content, read your writing slowly and carefully to find errors in grammar, punctuation, mechanics, and spelling. Such errors can distract your reader from the message you are trying to convey or can even cause communication to break down. Editing gives you the chance to clean up your draft so that your writing is clear, precise, and effective.

In this text, we have grouped grammar and usage errors into three categories: Sentence errors include fragments and run-on sentences that need to be corrected for clear communication; punctuation and mechanics cover end punctuation (periods, question marks, and exclamation points), internal punctuation (commas, semicolons, colons, apostrophes, quotation marks), capitalization, abbreviations, and numbers; and word choice and spelling ask you to check whether or not you have chosen the right word for what you mean and whether that word is spelled correctly. Checking all these features of your writing will give you the best chance possible to produce an effective essay.

Once you start writing, these "stages" do not necessarily occur in any specific order. You may change a word (revise) in the very first sentence that you write, then think of another detail that you want to add to your opening sentence (prewrite), and next cross out and rewrite a misspelled word (edit)—all in the first two minutes of writing. Although you may never approach any two writing projects in the same way, the chapters in Part I will help you establish a framework for your personal writing process and feel comfortable as a writer working within that framework.

PRACTICE 2 Answer the following questions.

1. When does the writing process start for a writing assignment?

____

____

____

2. Explain "prewriting" in your own words.

____

____

____

3. Describe your writing environment.

____

____

____

4. What does "writing" consist of?

____

____

____

5. What is the difference between "revising" and "editing"?

____

____

____

WRITING ON A COMPUTER

Many people—in school and at work—find that they write most efficiently directly on a computer. This strategy saves them time and energy and helps them meet deadlines. First of all, writing directly on a computer lets you change words and sentences as you go along. It also saves you time since you don't have to write out a draft by hand and then word-process it later. When you complete a first draft on a computer, you can move your ideas around without having to rewrite the whole paper. Finally, you can correct your grammar and spelling errors right on the final draft.

To compose on your computer, follow some simple rules so you don't lose your work or make word processing more complex than it is. Here are five essential guidelines for writing on a computer:

1. Give your document a name before you start writing.
2. Save your work often (or set the computer to save at short intervals). This will help you avoid losing your writing in a power failure or other accident.
3. Save your work in two different places—on your hard drive and on a flashdrive. Then if one becomes damaged, you always have the other.
4. Name and number each draft so that you can go back to earlier drafts if you want. For example, you might name and number an assignment this way: Description Essay D1, Description Essay D2, and so forth (D = draft).
5. Print out your work frequently so that you can refer to printed copies as well as electronic copies.

PRACTICE 3 Answer the following questions.

1. What are the advantages of writing directly on a computer?

____
____
____
____
____
____
____

2. What five guidelines should you remember if you write on a computer?

____
____
____
____
____
____
____

SAMPLE WRITING ASSIGNMENT

This first writing assignment is much like the writing tasks you will be asked to do throughout this book. You'll be working on this assignment yourself over the next three chapters as you apply what you are learning about the writing process to this task. At the same time, we will follow the work of student Beth Olson so you can see how she approaches and completes the same assignment. By the end of Chapter 7, you will have a feel for the entire writing process, which is essential to strengthening your writing and your identity as a writer.

Write Your Own Essay

We all learn about life in a variety of ways. These lessons help us become who we are. What have you learned over the years? How did you learn these lessons? What experiences have made you the person you are today? Based on a combination of your observations, your reading, and your personal experience, write an essay explaining how you learn best.

CHAPTER 5

PREPARING TO WRITE

Activities that take place before you actually start writing your paper fall into the general category of **prewriting** or **preparing to write**. This is a time when you should be generating as many new ideas on a topic as you can, using the right side of your brain over the left. This is the part of your brain that thinks up new ideas and sees relationships among old ideas. More specifically, prewriting consists of activities that help you do the following tasks:

- Explore a subject
- Generate ideas about the subject
- Settle on a specific topic
- Establish a purpose
- Analyze your audience

Let's begin by looking at activities that many writers use to stimulate their minds as they approach a writing task. You will get a chance to try each one. Record your responses to the following exercises in your journal or on a separate piece of paper so that you can refer to them throughout the course.

THINKING

Thinking is always the place to start any writing project. Thinking means exploring your topic and letting your mind run freely over the ideas you generate. We'll demonstrate five activities that students often use to stimulate their best thoughts: freewriting, brainstorming, clustering, questioning, and discussing. You will see how Beth Olson uses each strategy before you have a chance to try out the strategy yourself.

Freewriting

The strategy of freewriting involves writing about anything that comes to your mind. You should write without stopping for five to ten minutes because the act of writing alone will make you think of other ideas. Do not worry about grammar, punctuation, mechanics, or spelling. If you get stuck, repeat an idea or start rhyming words. Just keep writing.

Beth's Freewriting Beth had trouble freewriting, but she got going and then repeated some words to keep herself writing.

> My English teacher wants us to freewrite about whatever comes to our minds, but I can't think of anything to say. It's hard for me to just start writing. I still can't think of anything to say. And it's hard for me to just write. I don't even know what to write about. Everyone in here is writing furiously in their notebooks; I wonder what they're writing about. How many are writing about their girlfriends? their families? their dreams? I wonder what their dreams are. No one could ever guess that one of my dreams is to someday be my own boss in a company that will make enough money for my family to live comfortably. I suppose that's everyone's dream, really, but I don't think many people would think I had enough guts to go out on my own. But I will someday, and it's going to be a great life.

Focused freewriting is the same procedure focused on a specific topic—either one your instructor gives you or one you choose. Apply your guidelines for freewriting to a specific topic. Just write freely about a designated topic so that you find words for your thoughts and impressions.

Beth's Focused Freewriting Beth produced the following focused freewriting in her journal. She is trying to get her mind ready to write her essay about learning.

> People can learn about life from just about everything they do. It seems that every action can result in some sort of lesson. It's like all those fairy tales that have morals at the end of the story. If we keep our eyes open, everything we do can have a moral at the end. We can learn about how to study when we join a study group. We can decide how to treat our boyfriends or girlfriends when we watch our friends. And we can even learn from what's on the tube. I also like asking questions and talking to people about problems I'm having. I often get answers that way. Everywhere we look there's something to learn.

Your Freewriting Try a focused freewriting assignment to prepare for the essay you are going to compose by writing in your journal about ways that you learn.

Brainstorming

Like freewriting, brainstorming is based on free association. When you are brainstorming, you let one thought naturally lead to another, generally in the form of a list. You can brainstorm by yourself, with a friend, or with a group. Regardless of the method, list whatever comes into your mind on a topic—ideas, thoughts, examples, facts, anything. As with freewriting, don't worry about grammar, punctuation, mechanics, or spelling.

Beth's Brainstorming Here is Beth's brainstorming on learning about life:

- everyone learns about life through everyday lessons
- from my parents
- from my brothers and sisters
- from friends
- by watching our friends make mistakes
- by listening to others
- by listening to the radio
- by making my own mistakes
- by asking questions
- by listening to music
- by taking risks
- by succeeding and failing
- by reading books or newspapers
- by studying or going to school
- by observing

Your Brainstorming Brainstorm in your journal about how you think you learn.

Clustering

Clustering, like brainstorming, is based on free association, but it also shows how your thoughts are related. To cluster, take a sheet of blank paper, write a key word or phrase in the centre of the page, and draw a circle around it. Next, write down and circle any related ideas that come to mind. As you add ideas, draw lines to the thoughts they came from. After two or three minutes, you'll have a map of your ideas that can guide you toward a good essay.

Beth's Cluster Here is Beth's cluster on learning about life:

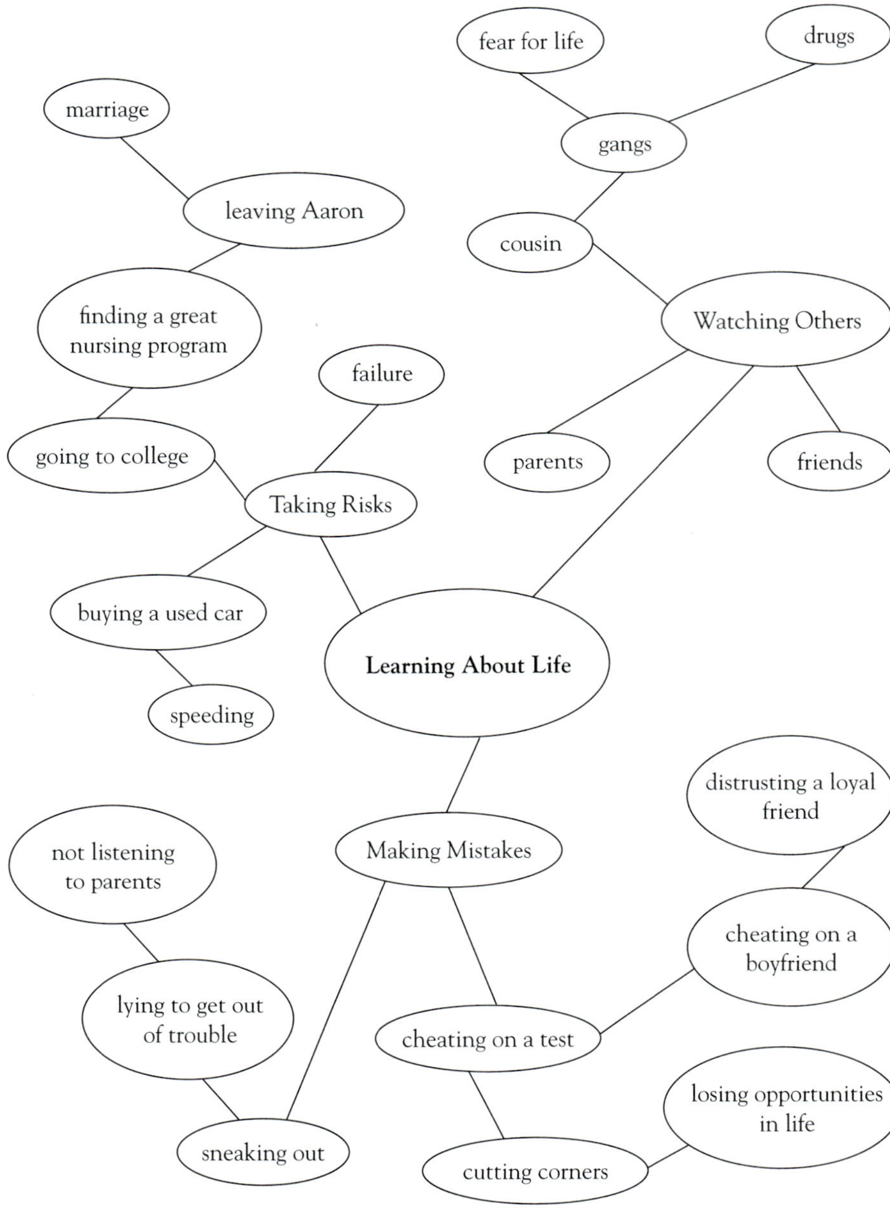

Your Cluster Write "Learning About Life" in the middle of a piece of paper, circle it, and create a cluster of your own associations with this concept.

Questioning

Journalists use the questions known as the "five *Ws* and one *H*"—*Who? What? When? Where? Why?* and *How?*—to check that they've covered all the important information in a news story. Other writers use these questions to generate ideas on a writing topic. Ask yourself each question as it relates to a particular topic. Then answer the questions one by one.

Beth's Questions Here is how Beth used questioning to generate ideas on her topic, learning about life:

Who?	everyone I know learns about life
What?	learning about life
When?	all day, every day
Where?	depends on what's being learned
Why?	to better themselves in life, for fun, for a variety of reasons
How?	by paying attention and taking action
	I guess we can even learn without realizing it.

Your Questions In your journal, answer these six questions about learning in preparation for your essay: Who? What? When? Where? Why? How?

Discussing

Discussing involves talking your ideas out with friends, relatives, classmates, tutors, or anyone who will listen. Often someone else will have a completely new perspective on your topic that will help you come up with even more ideas. Be sure to record your notes from these conversations so that you don't lose the ideas.

Beth's Discussion Here are Beth's notes from a conversation she had with her running partner about how we learn about life.

> When I spoke with my friend Alison, I realized that we all learn about life in just about everything we do. I guess it really depends on how much we want to pay attention. Alison talked about the risks I took when I decided to leave my hometown and study nursing at my current college. She also reminded me how much I learned from my cousin when she was involved in gangs. And we even reminisced about some of the bad choices I made and what they taught me. We talked about all the ways we learn in life, but realized we learn by watching what other people do, by taking risks throughout our lives, and by actually making mistakes. We figured these were the best ways to learn about life—for us.

Your Discussion Discuss learning about life with someone, and record notes from your conversation in your journal.

PRACTICE 1 Now that you have been introduced to several prewriting strategies, which is your favourite? Why do you like it best?

PRACTICE 2 Using two prewriting strategies on one assignment is often a good idea. What is your second favourite prewriting strategy? Why do you like this strategy?

PLANNING

In this course, you'll be writing essays. Although essays may differ a great deal in design, organization, and content, they share certain identifying features that distinguish them from other types of writing. At the simplest level, how an essay looks on the page tells its audience, "Here's an essay!" An essay usually has a title that names its broad subject. Many longer, more complex essays also have subtitles. When writers move from one topic to another, they indicate this shift by indenting a new paragraph. Most essays have a thesis that is either stated or implied in the introduction, several body paragraphs explaining or supporting that thesis, and a conclusion.

In content, essays are nonfiction, as opposed to short stories, poetry, or drama; that is, they deal with real-life subjects rather than made-up ones. Most essays concentrate on one specific subject and focus on a single purpose. For an essay to be successful, most writers choose methods of development that both suit their purpose and appeal to the audience they hope to inform or persuade. A successful essay gets the reaction from the readers that its author hopes for—whether this response is to appreciate a special scene, identify with someone's grief, or leap into action.

If you haven't already discovered it, you will learn in this book that writing an essay takes planning. If you make some decisions about your topic, audience, and purpose before you actually write, the job of writing will be much smoother and less stressful.

- **What is your subject (person, event, object, idea, etc.)?** An essay focuses on a single subject, along with related thoughts and details. In approaching an essay assignment, then, deciding what you are going to write about is very important. Sometimes your topic is given to you, as when your sociology instructor assigns a paper on abused children. But other times, you choose your own subject. In such cases, choosing a subject that interests you is best. You will have more to say, and you will enjoy writing much more if you know something about your topic.
- **What is your purpose?** Your purpose is your reason for writing an essay. Your purpose could be to explore your feelings on a topic (*to do personal writing*), to tell a friend about something funny that happened to you (*to entertain*), to explain something or share information (*to inform*), or to convince others of your position on a controversial issue (*to persuade*). Whatever your purpose, deciding on it in advance makes writing the rest of your essay easier.
- **Who is your audience?** Your audience consists of the people for whom your message is intended. The more you know about your audience, the more likely you are to accomplish your purpose. The audience for your writing in college is usually your instructor, who represents what is called a "general audience"—people with an average amount of knowledge on most subjects. A general audience is a good group to aim for in all your writing unless you are given other directions.

PRACTICE 3 Identify the subject, purpose, and audience of each of the following paragraphs.

1. Schools have been dealing with the issue of bilingual education for many years. The big debate is whether or not students should be allowed to study in their native language in order to learn English. Many people believe that students should be forced to learn in English, even if they don't know the language. Other people believe that this method of teaching will cause students not to learn, but they know bilingual education programs aren't teaching the students. Obviously, a compromise must be reached in order to help the students.

   Subject: ______________________________

   Purpose: ______________________________

   Audience: ______________________________

2. The world of computers has reached a point where people can conduct all of their business transactions from the comfort of their homes. Internet companies have made it possible for people to shop and do all of their business online. While most people using these services enjoy the convenience of being able to have a business meeting in their bathrobes, the idea of never having to leave the house worries other computer users. People will be able to do everything from home and won't have to interact with other people face to face. Eventually, the art of human interaction will be lost.

   Subject: ______________________________

   Purpose: ______________________________

   Audience: ______________________________

3. Playing sports came naturally to me and also taught me a valuable lesson. I began playing soccer and T-ball when I was five years old and continued playing all different types of sports through high school. I had times when I would get tired of constantly having to be at practice for one sport or another. Having a social life became very difficult because I was always busy with sports or trying to stay caught up in my classes. However, through the years of playing sports, I realized I had learned something that none of the teachers in my classes could ever teach me. I had learned how to deal with people. Competing against people taught

me how to play with a team and how to keep calm when something wasn't going my way.

Subject: ______________________________

Purpose: ______________________________

Audience: ______________________________

4. Reading a good book can be a fine substitute for a vacation. Every once in a while, people get the feeling that they need to get away from their normal routine and take a trip. Unfortunately, dropping everything and leaving town is not always possible. In this case, reading a book about somewhere far away can make people believe that they have really left their normal surroundings. People can become so involved in a book that they are completely oblivious to the world around them. Sometimes reading a book is just what people need to get away.

Subject: ______________________________

Purpose: ______________________________

Audience: ______________________________

5. Last summer, my family and I went on a two-day rafting trip. The morning our trip began, we loaded all the camping gear and food into the gear trailer and were on our way. The first day, the rapids were Class 2 and 3, which meant that they were moderate rapids and perfect for beginners. Everyone had fun playing in the rapids, swimming, and jumping off the rocks on the side of the river. That night in camp, the entire group was tired from such a full day on the river, so everyone was ready to go to bed early. The rapids the second day were Class 4, because they had large holes and waves, and were considered intermediate. I have to admit that the second day was more exciting than the first day. At the end of the trip, everyone was ready to get a good night's sleep but eager to come back and do it all again.

Subject: ______________________________

Purpose: ______________________________

Audience: ______________________________

Beth's Plans Beth made the following decisions before beginning to write on learning about life:

Subject: learning about life

Purpose: informative—to really talk about the different ways of learning

Audience: general—anyone from the general population

Your Plans Identify the subject, purpose, and audience of the essay you will write on learning about life.

Subject: ____

Purpose: ____

Audience: ____

WRITING A THESIS STATEMENT

By now, you have a subject (learning about life), and you have used several prewriting techniques with this subject, which means you have generated a number of thoughts that you can use in your essay. You have also decided on a purpose and an audience. Next, you will learn how to write a thesis statement, which you will develop into an essay in the next two chapters. Again, you will be writing alongside Beth Olson as she works through her writing process.

Writing assignments in college are most often on broad subjects. To compose a good essay, you need to narrow a broad subject to an idea that you can discuss in a limited number of pages. Your thesis statement is what puts limits on your essay. A **thesis statement** is the controlling idea of an essay. It is the main point that all other sentences relate to. Like a high-powered telescope, your thesis statement zooms in on the specific topic that you will discuss in the body of your essay. The decisions you made earlier in this chapter about subject, purpose, and audience will lead you to your thesis statement.

A thesis statement is usually in the first paragraph of an essay. It works best as the last sentence of the opening paragraph. Ending the introduction with the thesis statement lets the writer use the beginning of the paragraph to capture the reader's interest or give background information.

A thesis statement has two parts—a topic and an opinion you hold on that topic.

Subject	Limited Subject	+	Opinion	=	Thesis Statement
Sports	Playing a team sport		has lots of benefits		Playing a team sport teaches a person self-discipline, cooperation, and leadership.

Anger	Road rage	is very dangerous	Road rage is dangerous because it puts the driver, the victim, and the surrounding cars at risk.
Writing	College writing	is similar to writing in the business world	College writing is similar to writing in the business world in three important ways: Both types of writing must be logical, well developed, and clear.

PRACTICE 4 Fill in the blanks in this exercise.

1. A thesis statement is ______________________________

   ____
2. A thesis statement has two parts, a ______________________ and an ______________________________
3. Where should you put your thesis? ______________________

PRACTICE 5 Limit the following subjects that aren't already limited. Then add an opinion to all subjects, and make them into thesis statements.

Subject	Limited Subject	+	Opinion	=	Thesis Statement
1. Friendship	__________		______		__________
2. Work	Managers		______		__________
3. Winning	__________		______		__________
4. Love	Dating		______		__________
5. Winter	__________		______		__________

When you write a thesis statement, keep the following guidelines in mind:

1. **Your subject should not be too broad or too narrow.** A subject or topic that is too broad would need a book to develop it. One that is too narrow leaves you nothing to say. A manageable subject is one that you can write about in roughly three body paragraphs. You may find it necessary to limit your subject several times before you arrive at one that will work.

Subject:	Television
Too broad:	Prime-time TV
Still too broad:	Most popular TV shows
Good:	*CSI: Miami*
Too narrow:	Gil Grissom

2. **State your opinion clearly.** When you give your opinion on the topic, choose your words carefully. Be direct and take a stand. Opinions such as "is interesting," "are not good," "is a problem," or "can teach us a lot" are vague and boring. In fact, if you are specific enough about the opinion you hold, you will be very close to a thesis statement.

Vague opinion:	*CSI: Miami* is fun to watch.
Specific opinion:	*CSI: Miami* teaches us about forensics.

3. **Do not simply announce your topic.** Make an interesting statement about your topic.

Announcement:	My paper is going to be about *CSI: Miami*. *CSI: Miami* is the topic of this essay.
Statement:	*CSI: Miami* is a TV show that teaches us about forensics.

4. **Try your thesis statement (TS) as a question.** This does not mean that you should actually express your thesis statement as a question in your essay. Rather, you should try thinking of your thesis statement as a question that you will answer in the rest of your essay. You might want to write out your "TS question" and keep it in front of you as you draft your paper. It will help you keep your focus.

Thesis statement:	The television program *CSI: Miami* teaches us about forensics.
TS question:	How does *CSI: Miami* teach us about forensics?

PRACTICE 6 Which of the following are good thesis statements? Mark B for too broad, N for too narrow, MO for missing opinion, and C for complete. Test each thesis statement by turning it into a question.

_____1. Schools have good education programs.

_____2. In North America today, we face the problem of keeping our air clean.

_____3. Vehicles powered by natural gas will cut down on the pollution expelled by automobiles.

_____4. When using a computer, the user should know many things.

_____5. Human cloning is being studied to determine the scientific and moral consequences of the process.

_____ 6. Children are becoming desensitized to violence because of TV.

_____ 7. Many people do not eat meat because they cannot stand the thought of eating something that was once alive.

_____ 8. A lot of people avoid math because they have difficulty with analytical problem solving.

_____ 9. Our campus drama department will be performing *Noises Off* this spring.

_____10. Since the early 1980s, people have been on various health-craze diets and exercise programs.

PRACTICE 7 Complete the following thesis statements.

1. Marriage today______________________________.
2. ______________is my favourite class because______________.
3. Sleeping______________________________.
4. TV reality shows______________________________.
5. ______________________is a role model for college students today.

Beth's Thesis Statement Beth writes a thesis statement by stating her opinion about her subject.

Limited Subject	Opinion
I know that I learn	from many things in life.

Your Thesis Statement Write a thesis statement here that can serve as the controlling idea for your essay.

Limited Subject	Opinion
____________	______________________________

Thesis Statement

____

CHAPTER

6

Writing Effectively

The writing process is made up of several steps that lead you to your first draft. So far, you have been given a subject (learning about life) and worked through a number of prewriting techniques. You have generated ideas that you can use in your essay and have decided on a purpose and audience. In addition, you have composed a working thesis statement.

At this point, you are ready to write your essay. This chapter deals with the heart of the writing process: developing body paragraphs, organizing your essay, and writing the introduction, conclusion, and title. Once you work through this chapter, you will be more comfortable with these elements of the process and the way they function as part of the whole. Again, you will be writing alongside Beth as she works through the writing process with you.

As you learned in the first few chapters of this text, all stages of the writing process are part of a recurring cycle that you will mould into a routine to suit your lifestyle. The more you write, the more natural this process will become for you.

DEVELOPING BODY PARAGRAPHS

Now that you have written a thesis statement that comes at the end of your introduction, you are ready to write the body paragraphs of your essay. The body paragraphs explain and support the thesis statement.

Support for Your Thesis

What ideas will support the statement you are making in your thesis? This is the question you need to answer at this point. The supporting ideas are what make up the body of your essay. Each body paragraph covers one major idea of your thesis. The body paragraphs consist of a topic sentence and concrete details that support that topic sentence.

PRACTICE 1 For each of the following lists, cross out any ideas that do not support the thesis statement.

1. Thesis: Children are desensitized to violence by television, video games, and comic books.

   Children don't react to the violent acts they see on TV.

Children do not care when the heroes beat up the villains in comic books.

Many video games cost too much.

Children often want to be just like the sports figures they watch on TV.

Most children learn very early in life to shoot figures in video games.

2. Thesis: Starting your own business takes a lot of planning and work.

Prospective business owners must create a business plan in order to borrow money from a bank.

Owning your own business is rewarding.

People should research the current trends in the market for the type of business they plan to open.

Sometimes business owners can get their families to work for free.

People should determine how much money they will spend and how much money they will make so they can project possible earnings.

3. Thesis: To maintain a long-distance relationship, both people must be willing to sacrifice.

Couples often separate when they go to different universities.

Both parties must be sensitive to the other's needs—even at a distance.

People have to communicate often with each other, even if it's hard to find the time.

Both people must put extra effort into the relationship to make it work.

My parents had a long-distance relationship.

PRACTICE 2 For each of the following thesis statements, list three supporting ideas.

1. People should always look for three qualities when searching for a job.

____

____

____

2. Moving away from home for the first time can be hard.

____

____

____

3. Animals can help people live longer.

____

____

____

4. Vacations can often be more strenuous than restful.

____

____

____

5. Studying the right way can make a difference in a test grade.

____

____

____

Essays can be different lengths and often have a varying number of ideas that support their thesis statements. The thesis statement generally determines the length of an essay and the amount of support necessary to make a point. Some statements require very little proof and might need only one body paragraph; others require much more support and might need four or more body paragraphs for a complete explanation. An essay that falls somewhere in the middle has an introduction, three body paragraphs, and a conclusion.

Beth's Supporting Ideas Beth decided on three supporting ideas for her essay, which calls for three body paragraphs.

Thesis Statement: I know that I learn from many things in life.

Supporting Idea 1: Taking risks

Supporting Idea 2: Watching others

Supporting Idea 3: Making mistakes

Your Supporting Ideas Now list the support you might use for your thesis statement.

Your Thesis Statement: ______________________________

Supporting Idea 1: ______________________________

Supporting Idea 2: ______________________________

Supporting Idea 3: ______________________________

Outlining

At this stage of the writing process, many people benefit from putting their main ideas in the form of a rough, or working, outline. A rough outline can help you plan your essay and let you see the relationship of your ideas to one another. In this way, you can easily identify ideas that don't support your thesis and locate places where you need more information. A rough outline can evolve and become more detailed as your paper develops.

PRACTICE 3 Fill in the following rough outlines.

1. Subject: College life

   Limited Subject:

   Thesis Statement:______________________________

   Topic 1:______________________________

   Topic 2:______________________________

   Topic 3:______________________________

2. Subject: Summer jobs

   Limited Subject:______________________________

   Thesis Statement:______________________________

   Topic 1:______________________________

   Topic 2:______________________________

   Topic 3:______________________________

3. Subject: The Internet

   Limited Subject:______________________________

   Thesis Statement:______________________________

   Topic 1:______________________________

   Topic 2:______________________________

   Topic 3:______________________________

Beth's Rough Outline Here is a rough outline of Beth's ideas so far:

Thesis Statement: I know that I learn from many things in life.

A. I learn from taking risks.

B. I learn from watching others.

C. I learn from making mistakes.

Your Rough Outline Now put your ideas in outline form.

Thesis Statement:____________________________________

a. ____

b. ____

c. ____

d. ____

Topic Sentences

Now you need to state each of your supporting ideas in the form of a topic sentence that will be developed into a body paragraph. The decisions you made in Chapter 5 about subject, purpose, and audience will lead you to your topic sentences. Look back at your prewriting notes and think about which topics will best support your thesis statement. These will be the topics of your body paragraphs. These paragraphs will each include a topic sentence.

The **topic sentence** of a paragraph is its controlling idea. A typical paragraph consists of a topic sentence and details that expand on that topic sentence. A topic sentence performs two important tasks in its paragraph: (1) It supports the essay's thesis statement, and (2) it tells the reader what the paragraph will be about. It functions best as the first or last sentence in its paragraph. Beginning or ending a paragraph with the topic sentence gives direction to the paragraph and provides a kind of road map for the reader.

Like a thesis statement, a topic sentence has two parts—a topic and a statement about that topic. The topic should be limited enough that it can be developed in a paragraph. It should also be focused and not vague or scattered.

Topic	Limited Topic	Statement
Reading	Frequent reading	improves thinking skills.
Lotteries	Winning the lottery	will change a person's life forever.
Children	Having children	is a huge responsibility.
Hate	Hate crimes	are one of life's worst horrors.

PRACTICE 4 Limit the following topics. Then develop them into statements that could be topic sentences.

Topic	Limited Topic	Statement
1. Mondays	________________	________________
2. Hobbies	________________	________________
3. Theme parks	________________	________________
4. Writing	________________	________________
5. Summer	________________	________________

PRACTICE 5 Complete the following topic sentences. Make sure they are general enough to be developed into a paragraph but are not too broad.

1. Work-related injuries ______________________________.
2. ______________________________ is my favourite television show.
3. Sex education ______________________________.
4. Stray dogs and cats ______________________________.
5. ______________________ must be looked at on my college campus.

PRACTICE 6 Write topic sentences for the following paragraphs.

1. ____

   She watches the old ones like *Perry Mason* and can't get enough of the newer ones like *CSI*. But my mom really prefers the not-old and not-new mystery shows like *Matlock* and *Murder, She Wrote*. My mom will watch any of these shows for hours. My dad has a joke that she's watching all these TV shows so she can learn how to get rid of him and get away with it. I think she's just gathering information to write a book similar to these shows she loves to watch.

2. ____

   First, you must follow the directions to install it onto your computer. Then you must read the directions to learn what you should do first with the program. It's best to read all the directions first, but most of the time people just go straight to the program and try to navigate their way through it. Once you get a handle on how to work the program, it's best just to play around and use the book only when you have questions. Mastering computer programs can be hard, but once you've done it, you can be sure you'll never forget how to use them.

3. ____

   ____

   Because she wanted to save money for other parts of her wedding, the consultant was the first expense she cut. Everything went fine until the day of the wedding. My sister didn't get the flowers she ordered, but the ones that were delivered were okay. The cake arrived four hours late, and the reception hall wouldn't let us attach anything to the walls. And just before my sister walked into the church, she discovered that the train on her wedding dress was completely inside out. Luckily, no one but my sister and our family knew of the mishaps, but a consultant would have been worth every penny on the actual day of the wedding.

PRACTICE 7 Supply three topic sentences for each thesis statement.

1. Many people enjoy resting on Sundays.

 ____

 ____

 ____

2. Teachers should encourage all students to learn.

 ____

 ____

 ____

3. Computers will enable people to function more efficiently at work, at home, and at play.

 ____

 ____

 ____

4. Planning is the key to a successful vacation.

 ____

 ____

 ____

5. The abilities to think critically, act quickly, and communicate clearly are essential in the business world.

 ____

 ____

 ____

Beth's Topic Sentences Beth writes three topic sentences that she thinks will support her thesis statement.

> **Thesis Statement:** I know that I learn from many things in life.
>
> **Topic Sentence:** I have discovered that I learn a lot by taking risks.
>
> **Topic Sentence:** I also benefit from watching other people.
>
> **Topic Sentence:** I believe that I learn from making mistakes.

Your Topic Sentences Develop each of the ideas you listed on page 49 into a topic sentence that is directly related to your thesis statement. List your thesis first.

Thesis Statement: ______________________________

Topic Sentence: ______________________________

Topic Sentence: ______________________________

Topic Sentence: ______________________________

Specific Details

Now you are ready to generate the specific details that will make up the bulk of your body paragraphs. Later in this text, you will learn about different methods of developing your ideas, such as describing, comparing and contrasting, and analyzing causes and effects. For now, we are simply going to practise generating concrete supporting details and examples that are directly related to a specific topic. Concrete words refer to anything you can see, hear, touch, smell, or taste, such as *trees*, *boats*, *water*, *friends*, *fire alarm*, and *bread*. They make writing come alive because they help the reader picture what the writer is talking about.

PRACTICE 8 Put a check mark by the details and examples listed that support each topic sentence.

1. The members of every generation think they'll understand their kids' music—until they actually hear it.

    _____ parents don't appreciate today's rock music

    _____ parents who listened to rock and roll don't understand heavy metal

    _____ parents become wary of musicians like Kid Rock and Marilyn Manson

    _____ no parents understand new wave or punk music

    _____ Dick Clark has helped all kinds of music become established

    _____ parents have a hard time letting their kids listen to rap music

    _____ Elvis helped put rock and roll on the map

2. Students change their majors often throughout their academic careers.

    _____ general education courses allow students to learn about a variety of subjects

_____ in college, students discover new interests in subjects they have never been exposed to before

_____ professors bring new subjects to life for many students

_____ math is difficult for many students

_____ other students often influence a student's decision about a major

_____ the reality of the job market creates changes in majors

_____ academic performance sometimes makes students look for alternative interests

3. The best way to lose weight is through a good diet and exercise.

_____ snacking all day long can cause a person to eat more than usual

_____ people who exercise a lot need enough sleep

_____ skipping meals is counterproductive for people on diets

_____ people should exercise at least three times per week

_____ running is great exercise

_____ people should eat three sensible meals per day

_____ TSN has many exercise shows

PRACTICE 9 For each of the following topic sentences, list five details or examples to develop them.

1. Everywhere I go, I seem to see someone I know.

____

____

____

____

____

2. When I was in high school, I enjoyed many different extracurricular activities.

____

____

____

____

____

3. Friends and family are very important parts of life.

____

____

____

____

____

Beth's Development To come up with concrete details and examples that would support her topic sentence, Beth uses the brainstorming and focused freewriting techniques she learned in Chapter 5. This is what she wrote:

I have discovered that I learn a lot by taking risks.

- buying a used car
- quitting my new job
- leaving Aaron to come to this school
- driving way too fast
- trying new foods
- changing majors
- procrastinating in school

I also benefit from watching other people.

- moving in with roommates I don't know
- watching my friends make mistakes with their boyfriends
- looking at my parents make rules
- seeing my cousin ruin her life
- watching my brother mess up
- observing people around me get involved with drugs
- learning about other people's mistakes from my friends

I believe that I learn from making mistakes.

- cheating on the test
- believing the rumour about my best friend
- lying to my parents
- not believing my sister
- waiting too long to write a paper
- watching TV instead of studying

Here is Beth's new freewriting:

> I know I learn a lot by taking risks, watching other people, and making mistakes. I'm sure I learn in other ways too, but these are the ways that seem to give me the most information about life in general.
>
> Taking risks really helps everyone learn in life, but I think this is especially true for me. I mean, right now I'm sitting here in this class thinking about Aaron and how we want to get married someday. But I left my hometown and Aaron to come here for the nursing program. So far everything is great, but I knew it was a risk coming here. But how could I learn if I didn't?
>
> I also learn by watching other people. My parents are great role models, but it's hard to really learn because they are so much older. I mean, they tell me not to join a gang, but they're my parents. I learned more about gangs from my cousin than from my parents. Watching my cousin go through her experiences was way better than just listening to my parents. I definitely learn by watching others.
>
> And I definitely learn by making mistakes. And boy do I have tons of those. Most of my mistakes are pretty small, but I still learn from them. I think I learned the most from Mr. Turner, though, when he caught me cheating on his test. He talked to me, and that really helped. In fact, I think it's because of him that I started paying attention in class and decided to pursue nursing at this school.
>
> I will always learn about life from these sources. I guess I will always learn about life as long as I keep my eyes open, but these ways seem the most important to me right now.

Your Development Choose at least one of the prewriting strategies that you learned in Chapter 5, and use it to generate more specific details and examples for each of your topic sentences.

ORGANIZING YOUR ESSAY

You are moving along quite well in the writing process. You have determined your subject, purpose, and audience, and you have written your thesis statement. You have also written topic sentences for your body paragraphs and thought of details, examples, and facts to develop those topic sentences. You are now ready to organize your ideas. What should come first? What next?

To organize the ideas in your essay, you need to consider the purpose of your essay and the way each body paragraph serves that purpose. Then you should arrange your body paragraphs in a logical manner to achieve that purpose. If your essay's main purpose is informative—to describe the layout of a building, for example—you would probably arrange the details spatially. That is, you might begin with the entrance and move to the other parts of the building as if you were strolling through it. If, however, you want to persuade a reader to buy one type of car over another, you might arrange the essay so that it moves from one extreme to another—for example, from the least important feature of the car to the most important. Once you decide on the order of your paragraphs, you need to organize the details in each paragraph.

Most paragraphs and essays are organized in one of five ways:

1. From general to particular
2. From particular to general
3. Chronologically (by time)
4. Spatially (by physical order)
5. From one extreme to another

Let's look at these methods of organization one by one.

General to Particular

The most common method of organizing an essay or paragraph is from general to particular. This method begins with a general topic and becomes more specific as it progresses. A paragraph organized from general to particular might look like this:

Topic Sentence
  Detail
  Detail
  Detail
  Detail

Here is an example of a paragraph organized from general to particular:

> When I began attending college, I was very nervous because I was afraid I would not do very well in my classes. My first year, I took general education classes that reviewed a lot of the material I learned in high school. There was a lot of studying involved in these classes, but I was able to pass all of them. Soon I decided that my major would be business, so I began taking classes that dealt with business. All of the business classes were harder than the classes I had taken in general education. Just when I thought I would not pass a class, I would do well on a test, which would raise my confidence level again. I worked very hard in every class I took and was able to pass every one. Tomorrow I am graduating with my diploma in business.

This paragraph moves from the general idea of going to college to the specific notion of taking classes, graduating, and receiving a degree. Notice that it includes such transitions as *when, but, soon,* and *which.* They show the relationship among the writer's thoughts.

The skeleton of a general-to-particular essay looks like this, although the number of paragraphs and details will vary:

Introduction
- Topic sentence stating the most general point
  - Detail
  - Detail
  - Detail
- Topic sentence stating a more specific supporting point
  - Detail
  - Detail
  - Detail
- Topic sentence stating the most specific supporting point
  - Detail
  - Detail
  - Detail

Conclusion

PRACTICE 10 Write a topic sentence for the following group of sentences. Then organize the sentences into a paragraph using general-to-particular order. Add words, phrases, or sentences as necessary to smooth out the paragraph.

Topic Sentence: ______________________________

During these events, not only do you get to watch the athletes play their games, but you get to see former athletes announcing the action play-by-play.

Any time you turn on the TV, there are at least fourteen sporting events happening at one time.

You can see anything from basketball to golf to racing to fishing.

Let's face it; the likelihood of seeing a sports figure on TV is great.

And just when you think you've seen enough of the players, you are flooded with commercials that have athletes selling various products.

Particular to General

When you reverse the first method of organization, you arrange your material from particular to general. In this case, more specific ideas start the essay or paragraph and lead up to a general statement. This type of organization is particularly effective if you suspect that your reader might not agree with the final point you are going to make. With this method, you can lead your reader to your opinion slowly and carefully.

A paragraph organized from particular to general looks like this:

Detail
Detail
Detail
Detail
Topic Sentence

Here is a paragraph of particular-to-general organization.

The water is so crystal-clear that I can see every pebble settled on the bottom. A small sandy beach reaches the water's edge and makes a perfect spot to spend the afternoon. Across the water I can see the mountainside covered in the greenest trees imaginable. A log cabin also sits among the trees halfway up the mountain, so peaceful and secluded. The puffy white clouds make the sky appear to be a brighter blue, and the birds seem to enjoy floating on the soft breeze. I could sit all day next to the lake in the valley and just stare at my surroundings.

This paragraph starts with specific details about the area around the lake and ends with a topic sentence. Transitions such as *and*, *across the water*, and *also* move readers through the paragraph.

This is how a particular-to-general essay looks, though the number of details will vary:

Introduction
- Topic sentence stating the most specific point
  - Detail
  - Detail
  - Detail
- Topic sentence stating a less specific point
  - Detail
  - Detail
  - Detail
- Topic sentence stating the most general point
  - Detail
  - Detail
  - Detail

Conclusion

PRACTICE 11 Write a topic sentence for the following group of sentences. Then organize the sentences into a paragraph using particular-to-general order. Add words, phrases, or sentences as necessary to smooth out the paragraph.

Topic Sentence: ______________________________

My mom hopes I'll order something more grown-up, but I never will.

My family knew I loved pizza and always let me order one once a week.

I have always loved pepperoni, even on sandwiches and in soups.

I used to love pizza night when I lived at home.

I believe that pizza is the best food ever created.

Now when I go home, we just go to an Italian restaurant where I can order pizza.

Chronological Order

When you organize ideas chronologically, you are organizing them according to the passage of time—in other words, in the order in which they occurred. Most of the time, when you tell a story or explain how to do something, you use chronological order: First this happened, and then that. Or first you do this, next you do that, and so on.

A paragraph organized chronologically looks like this:

Topic Sentence
- First
- Then
- Next
- Finally

Here is an example of a paragraph organized chronologically:

> Preparing to go snowboarding for the first time can be a lot of fun. First of all, you must get into full gear when you arrive at the mountain. Then you ride a ski lift to the top of the mountain. Once at the top, it is time to buckle your boots into the bindings on the board. The bindings must be tight, but not so tight that they are uncomfortable. Next, you are ready to begin your descent. On the way down the mountain, pay attention to how the board moves when pressure is applied to the toes and heels of the feet. Finally, you need to learn which way to lean in order to turn right and left so you can fly down the mountain. Once you have mastered the basics, you will have fun perfecting your new hobby.

This paragraph is chronological because it explains snowboarding according to a time sequence and uses transitions such as *first of all*, *then*, *next*, and *finally*.

Here is what an essay organized chronologically looks like:

Introduction
- What happened first
  - Detail
  - Detail
  - Detail

What happened next
- Detail
- Detail
- Detail

What happened after that
- Detail
- Detail
- Detail

Conclusion

PRACTICE 12 Write a topic sentence for the following group of sentences. Then organize the sentences into a paragraph using chronological order. Add words, phrases, or sentences as necessary to smooth out the paragraph.

Topic Sentence: ____

Spread the jam on top of the peanut butter.

Unscrew the lid from a jar of peanut butter and from a jar of jam.

Using the knife again, remove a small amount of jam from the jar.

Place two slices of bread on a plate.

Using the knife, remove a small amount of peanut butter from the jar.

Place the second slice of bread on top of the slice with the peanut butter and jelly on it.

First, remove a butter knife from the drawer.

Spread the peanut butter on one slice of bread with the knife.

Spatial Order

Another method of arranging details is by their relationship to each other in space. You might describe the layout of your campus from its front entrance to its back exit or the arrangement of a beautiful garden from one end to the other. Explaining a homepage from top to bottom and describing a screened-in porch from inside to outside are also examples of spatial order. Beginning at one point and moving detail by detail around a specific area is the simplest way of organizing by space.

A paragraph organized spatially might look like this:

Topic Sentence
- Here
- There
- Next
- Across
- Beyond

Here is an example of a paragraph organized spatially:

It was the first football game of the season and her first football game ever as a cheerleader. Standing in front of the huge crowd made the butterflies in her stomach begin to flutter again. In the front row sat a group of her friends cheering her on. Two rows behind them sat her psychology professor. Next to her professor sat a few of her new sorority sisters. As the cheerleader looked across the aisle, she noticed a group of rowdy students screaming and cheering for their team. Beyond the crowd, the tall announcer's booth where all of the press people and the athletic director sat seemed to glare down at her. Any minute the music would begin to blare from that very booth, and she would begin her first half-time dance routine.

This paragraph is arranged spatially because it moves physically around the football stadium, using such words as *in front of*, *behind*, *next to*, and *beyond* as transitions.

Here is what an essay organized spatially looks like:

Introduction
- Here
  - Detail
  - Detail
  - Detail
- There
  - Detail
  - Detail
  - Detail
- Next
  - Detail
  - Detail
  - Detail
- Across
  - Detail
  - Detail
  - Detail
- Beyond
  - Detail
  - Detail
  - Detail

Conclusion

PRACTICE 13 Write a topic sentence for the following group of sentences. Then organize the sentences into a paragraph using spatial order. Add words, phrases, or sentences as necessary to smooth out the paragraph.

Topic Sentence: ______________________________

The hotel's check-in desk is located on the left side of the lobby.

Two little boys are sitting quietly on the couches next to the check-in desk, waiting for their parents to finish checking in.

In the centre of the lobby are four massive couches arranged in a conversational setting.

Directly across from the check-in desk is the activities counter, where people can plan their days.

Inside the front door, the guests' attention is immediately drawn to the ceiling.

Painted as a sky, the ceiling gives guests the feeling that they have never left the outdoors.

Framing the front door are two huge dolphins, each perched in the centre of a water fountain.

One Extreme to Another

Sometimes the best way to organize a paragraph is from one extreme to another: from most expensive to least expensive, from most humorous to least humorous, from most frustrating to least frustrating, and so on. (Of course, you can also move from least to most.) Use whatever extremes make sense for your topic. You might explain how to choose a pet by elaborating on the most important qualities of an animal and then considering the least important. For example, an apartment dweller's most important consideration would be the size of the pet and its need for exercise. Least important would be watchdog qualities. To accomplish another purpose, you might reverse this order and begin with the least important quality; this method is good in persuasive writing because you end with your most important idea.

This method of organization has one distinct advantage over the other four approaches: It is the most flexible. When no other method of organization works, you can always arrange details from one extreme to another.

Here is an outline of a paragraph organized from one extreme to another:

Topic Sentence
 Most
 Next most
 Somewhat
 Least

Here is an example of a paragraph that moves from one extreme to another:

> Ever since I was old enough to join Little League teams, I have played a variety of sports. I would have to say that my favourite sport has always been football. Absolutely nothing can top the feeling of

running for a touchdown and passing the defensive safety. My next favourite sport would have to be baseball. I used to love to pitch to catchers when we would work as though we were one athlete. My next favourite sport is basketball. As a teenager, I played guard in basketball, but eventually I got bored with the position. My least favourite sport is soccer. No matter how much I trained and ran before soccer season, I always got exhausted during the games—all we did was run up and down the field. Now that I'm in college, I'm grateful for the intramural teams that let me keep playing the sports that I love.

This paragraph moves from most to least preferred sports and is marked by such words as *favourite*, *next favourite*, and *least favourite*.

Here is what an essay organized according to extremes looks like:

Introduction
- Most
  - Detail
  - Detail
  - Detail
- Next most
  - Detail
  - Detail
  - Detail
- Somewhat
  - Detail
  - Detail
  - Detail
- Least
  - Detail
  - Detail
  - Detail

Conclusion

PRACTICE 14 Write a topic sentence for the following group of sentences. Then write a paragraph arranging the sentences from one extreme to another. Add words, phrases, and sentences as necessary to smooth out the paragraph. Also, label your system of classification (from most to least or from least to most).

Topic Sentence: ____

First, they have a hard time asking people for money.

Consequently, they allow debtors extra time to pay the bill.

But after a few months, the new employee has heard all the sob stories and is immune to their power.

That just makes it harder to get the money.

This may be because they believe the sob stories they hear, which probably aren't true.

Unfortunately, once the date has been extended, we all have to agree to it.

System of Classification: ______________________________

PRACTICE 15 List the best method of development for paragraphs on the following topics.

1. How to make homemade salsa.
2. I think I am going to rearrange my dorm room to create more space.
3. What I will have for dinner tonight.
4. Today, people question the ethics of capital punishment.
5. I lift weights for an hour and run five kilometres every day.

PRACTICE 16 Write a topic sentence that introduces the following details in a paragraph. Then arrange the details in logical order, and write a paragraph.

Topic Sentence: ______________________________

exercising three times a week
the advantages of aerobic exercise
exercising with a friend
the difficulty of starting an exercise routine

Beth's Organization Beth decided to organize her essay from one extreme to another—from the most important ways of learning for her to the least important. She first wants to introduce the idea of taking risks, which she believes is very important. Next she will discuss watching others and finally learning from mistakes because she thinks she learns a lot from her own mistakes. She thinks this order might work, so she lists as many concrete details as she can under each main idea.

Here is Beth's working outline at this point:

Thesis Statement: I know that I learn from many things in life.

Taking Risks (*most important*): taking risks and learning from them

Specific Details: finding a good nursing program
leaving my boyfriend back home
going to college

Watching Others (*less important*): learning from watching others

Specific Details: watching my cousin in gangs
living in fear
not in a gang because of her

Making Mistakes (*least important*): making mistakes and learning from those mistakes

Specific Details: cheating on test
talking with Mr. Turner
learning to pay more attention in school for a better future

Concluding Thoughts: people can learn from everything they do

Specific Details: taking risks
watching others
making mistakes

Does the method of organization that Beth has chosen suit her topic? Would any other method of organization work as well?

Your Organization What method of organization will work best for your ideas about learning? Why do you think this method will be best?

WRITING THE INTRODUCTION, CONCLUSION, AND TITLE

By now, you have written your thesis statement and topic sentences for your body paragraphs. You've thought of supporting details, facts, examples, and the most effective way of organizing your thoughts. At the end of this chapter, you will write a complete first draft of your essay. First, though, let's look at three important parts of your essay: the introduction, the conclusion, and the title.

You might have written some of these parts already. Some people write their introduction with their thesis; others write the introduction last. Some have an idea of how they want to conclude from the time they begin their papers; others write the conclusion last. Some struggle with a title; others write their titles as they generate their drafts. The order in which you write these three parts of an essay depends on your own personal writing process. All that matters is that your papers have a title, an introduction, several body paragraphs, and a conclusion that work together.

Introduction

The introduction to your essay—your first paragraph—should both introduce your subject and stimulate your audience's interest. The introduction of an essay captures the readers' interest, gives necessary background information, and presents your thesis statement. This paragraph essentially tells readers what the essay is going to cover without going into detail or discussing specifics.

Writers generally use the introduction to lead up to their thesis statement. As a result, the sentences at the beginning of the introductory paragraph need to grab your readers' attention. Some effective ways of capturing your audience's interest and giving necessary background information are to (1) furnish a vivid description; (2) tell a brief story; (3) give a revealing fact, statistic, or definition; (4) make an interesting comparison; (5) present a dramatic example; and (6) use an exciting quotation.

Also be sure that your introduction gives your readers any information they may need to follow your train of thought. One way to check that your readers have all the necessary background is to apply the five Ws and one H: who, what, when, where, why, and how. Any of this information that is important to your readers' understanding of your thesis statement should go in the introduction. You might also ask a friend to read your first draft and tell you if any background information is missing.

Beth's Introduction and Thesis Beth wrote a first draft of her introduction just to get started. She knew she would have to work with it later, but at least she was able to get some of her ideas down on paper.

> Everyone learns in different ways. Some people learn by watching, some by reading, and others by themselves. The way people learn is a part of who they are. Knowing how we learn can help us understand ourselves better. I know that I learn from many things in life.

Your Introduction Use the guidelines suggested here to capture your readers' interest and, if necessary, give them background information. Write two different introductions for your essay. End each with your thesis statement.

Conclusion

The concluding paragraph is the final paragraph of an essay. It draws your essay to a close, giving readers a sense of closure. That is, readers feel that all the loose ends are wrapped up and the point of the essay is clear. As with introductions, there are many good techniques for writing a conclusion. You might (1) summarize the main ideas, (2) highlight the most important issue, (3) ask a question that gets readers to think about something in particular, (4) predict the future, (5) offer a solution to a problem, or (6) call readers to action. In some cases, you might want to use several of these strategies.

You should avoid two common problems in writing a conclusion. First, try not to begin your conclusion with the words *in conclusion*, *in summary*, or *as you can see*. Your conclusion should show—not tell—that you are at the end of your essay. Second, do not introduce a new idea. The main ideas of your essay should be in your body paragraphs. The conclusion is where you finish your essay, leaving your readers with a sense of closure or completeness.

Beth's Conclusion Here is a rough outline of what Beth wants to include in her conclusion. These are the notes that she came up with at this point.

People can learn about life from just about anything.

- made me the person I am
- watching other people
- taking some risks myself
- making mistakes

Your Conclusion Sketch an outline or write a draft of a possible conclusion for your essay.

Title

A title is a phrase, usually no more than a few words, that gives a hint about the subject, purpose, or focus of what is to follow. For example, the main title chosen for this book, *Mosaics*, reflects a particular view of the writing process—as many bright pieces logically connected to complete a picture. In other words, that title expresses in capsule form this textbook's purpose, which is to guide writers through the process of fitting the separate pieces of their ideas into a single meaningful whole to make an essay. The title of this chapter, however, is a straightforward naming of its contents: "Writing Effectively."

Besides suggesting an essay's purpose, a good title catches an audience's attention or "hooks" readers so that they want to read more. Look at some of the essay titles in the readings in Part II. Which ones clearly tell you what the essay is about? Which ones attract your attention and make you want to read on? Do not underline or use quotation marks around your essay titles. Do not put a period at the end of your title, and be sure to capitalize your titles correctly. The first word and last word in a title are always capitalized. Capitalize all other words except articles (*a, an, the*) and short prepositions (such as *in, by, on,* or *from;* see page 391 for a more complete list of prepositions).

Beth's Title Beth has several possible titles for her essay. She doesn't really know which one to use.

Learning About Life

The Way We Learn

Everyone Can Learn

Your Title Write three titles for your essay: (1) one that gives a hint of your subject, (2) one that gives a hint of your purpose, and (3) one that gives a hint of your focus. Make each title as catchy as you can.

Beth's First Draft In Chapters 2 through 5, and again in this chapter, you have watched Beth thinking about, planning, developing, and organizing her essay. It is time now to get a complete first draft down on paper. Here is Beth's first draft.

The Way We Learn

Everyone learns in different ways. Some people learn by watching, some by reading, and others by themselves. The way people learn is a part of who they are. Knowing how we learn can help us understand ourselves better. I know that I learn from many things in life.

I have discovered that I learn a lot by taking risks. Being at this college was a risk. I have a boyfriend back home, we want to get married someday. We are hoping for a spring wedding with all of our friends and family. I left my boyfriend to come here. Coming here was a risk to our relationship. But if I am ever going to make it, I have to be willing to take risks.

I also benefit from watching other people. When my cousin became heavily involved with gangs, I watched my cousin live in constant fear. By watching my cousin, I made a conscious decision to be nothing like my cousin. By watching and understanding my cousin's life. I learned to live mine better.

I believe that I learn from making mistakes. When I was in high school, I didn't study for a major science test. So I cheated. My sister cheated once. I was so scared to do it. The teacher caught me. The teacher took the time to talk to me about the mistake I was making. This mistake made me reevaluate my education. I could have laughed off the cheating experience. I decided to slow down and learn from the experience.

People can learn about life from almost anything they do. They just have to be willing to do so. When I take risks, I think about what I will learn. I definitely try to learn as much as I can from watching others. When I make mistakes, I figure out why I made each mistake and how to avoid it a second time.

Your First Draft Now write a complete first draft of your essay on learning.

CHAPTER 7

Revising and Editing

No matter how hard you wish, writing does not end with your first draft. The fun of revising and editing still lies ahead of you. Revising has to do with the development and organization of your ideas, while editing focuses on correctness. Revising is **not** editing. **Revising** means "seeing again," and that is exactly what you should try to do when you revise to improve your writing—see it again from as many different angles as possible. **Editing** involves finding and correcting errors in grammar, punctuation, mechanics, and spelling. You have probably been revising and editing periodically through your entire writing process, but now is the time to perform these tasks systematically before you turn in your paper.

REVISING

More specifically, revising your writing means changing it so that it says exactly what you mean in the most effective way. Revision involves both *content* (what you are trying to say) and *form* (how you deliver your message). Having a friend or tutor read your paper before you revise it is a good idea so that you can see if you are communicating clearly.

Revising content means working with your words until they express your ideas as accurately and completely as possible. Revising form consists of working with the organization of your writing. When you revise, you should look closely at the six basic categories listed in the following checklist. Let's look at these revision strategies one by one.

REVISING CHECKLIST ✓

Thesis Statement

✔ Does the thesis statement contain the essay's controlling idea and an opinion about that idea?

✔ Does the thesis appear as the last sentence of the introduction?

Basic Elements

✔ Does the title draw in the readers?

✔ Does the introduction capture the readers' attention and build up to the thesis statement effectively?

- ✔ Does each body paragraph deal with a single topic?
- ✔ Does the conclusion bring the essay to a close in an interesting way?

Development

- ✔ Do the body paragraphs adequately support the thesis statement?
- ✔ Does each body paragraph have a focused topic sentence?
- ✔ Does each body paragraph contain specific details that support the topic sentence?
- ✔ Does each body paragraph include enough details to explain the topic sentence fully?

Unity

- ✔ Do the essay's topic sentences relate directly to the thesis statement?
- ✔ Do the details in each body paragraph support its topic sentence?

Organization

- ✔ Is the essay organized logically?
- ✔ Is each body paragraph organized logically?

Coherence

- ✔ Are transitions used effectively so that paragraphs move smoothly and logically from one to the next?
- ✔ Do the sentences move smoothly and logically from one to the next?

Thesis Statement

- ✔ Does the thesis statement contain the essay's controlling idea and an opinion about that idea?
- ✔ Does the thesis appear as the last sentence of the introduction?

As you learned in Chapter 5, every successful essay has a thesis statement that states the essay's controlling idea. This sentence gives direction to the rest of the essay. It consists of a limited subject and the writer's position on that subject. Although a thesis statement can appear anywhere in an essay, it is usually the last sentence of the introduction.

Here are two examples:

Limited Subject	+	Opinion	=	Thesis Statement
1. Children today		grow up too fast		Children today grow up too fast.
2. Children today		grow up too fast		Children today grow up too fast because of television, advertising, and working parents.

As in the second example, the thesis statement should introduce all the topics in its essay. The first example includes the limited subject and the writer's position on that subject but also needs to introduce its topics.

PRACTICE 1 Review the guidelines for developing a thesis statement in Chapter 5. Then write a thesis statement for each group of topic sentences listed here.

1. Thesis Statement: ____

   ____

   Everyone needs a friend who likes to do the same things.
   Everyone needs someone to share the good news with.
   Equally importantly, everyone needs a good listener during bad times.

2. Thesis Statement: ____

   ____

   Watching a movie on the big screen of a theatre makes the story and characters bigger and more interesting than life.
   The sound system in a movie theatre makes me feel that I'm right there in the action.
   The concession stand has all sorts of snacks and goodies, and I don't have to clean up my own mess afterward.

3. Thesis Statement: ____

   ____

   Being behind slow drivers can cause people to experience road rage.
   Tailgating can cause people to get angry.
   People who weave in and out of traffic at extreme speeds make many drivers furious.

4. Thesis Statement: ____

   ____

   Asking someone out on a first date can take a lot of courage.
   Suggesting places to go or things to do is harder than it sounds.
   It seems that there's always one very embarrassing moment on a first date that would never happen on a later date.

5. Thesis Statement: ____

   ____

   Signing up for a skydiving class is exciting, and all your friends think you're really cool.
   Boarding the plane for your first jump is a strong dose of reality, but not quite like getting up the nerve to actually jump.

Free-falling and landing safely provide a rush that skydivers never forget.

PRACTICE 2 Write thesis statements for the following introductions.

1. ____

____

No matter how much I tell myself I am going to get up in the morning and go, I cannot seem to do it. Every night before I go to bed, I lay out my sweats and shoes and set my alarm. In the morning when the alarm rings, I push the snooze button and promise myself that I will get up in 10 minutes. This routine goes on for the next hour until I have to get up in order to make it to work on time. Once again, I have failed to get up and go to the gym, and I have deprived myself of an hour of exercise.

2. ____

____

The most important detail is to determine the number of rooms in the house. A family must consider the needs of the people living in the house and their plans for the near future. Of course, don't forget the backyard. Does the family need a fenced yard for animals or an area for the kids to play? And the family must pay attention to how well the house has been kept up. All of these items are very important details when looking for a new home.

3. ____

____

Every morning, at precisely 8:00, the couple eats breakfast at the corner café. Afterward they go to the market for fresh fruit or vegetables and run errands. If they have no shopping to do, the couple goes home and does housework or yard work. Every afternoon at 1:00, they sit down to lunch and watch a little television. In the late afternoon, they go for a walk around the lake for a bit of exercise before preparing their dinner. After dinner, they watch the news and play a hand of cards. Soon the sun dips behind the mountain, and the couple retires for the night.

Beth's Revision When Beth looks back at her thesis statement, she realizes it does not completely introduce what she talks about in her essay. Her thesis tells readers only that she learns about life from different things, not that she has three important ways that she learns about life.

Thesis Statement: I know that I learn from many things in life.

She decides to expand her thesis statement so that it more accurately introduces the topics that will follow in her essay:

Revised Thesis Statement: I know that I learn ~~from many things in life~~ best from taking risks, watching others, and making mistakes.

She feels that this thesis statement introduces the notion of learning and the different ways that she has learned.

Your Revision With these guidelines in mind, revise your thesis statement.

Your Revised Thesis Statement: ______________________________

Basic Elements

- ✓ Does the title draw in the readers?
- ✓ Does the introduction capture the readers' attention and build up to the thesis statement effectively?
- ✓ Does each body paragraph deal with a single topic?
- ✓ Does the conclusion bring the essay to a close in an interesting way?

Now that you have written a complete draft of your essay, this is the time to review these basic elements. What changes do you want to make in your title? in your introduction? in your conclusion? Is your thesis statement at the end of your introduction? Do you need to split any body paragraphs? These revision items ask you to check that all the basic elements of the essay are present and are doing the jobs they are supposed to do.

Beth's Revision Beth sets out to answer each of these questions one by one. Here are her responses.

✓ Does the title draw in the readers?

No. It's kind of boring.

✓ Does the introduction capture the readers' attention and build up to the thesis statement effectively?

Not really—it's too short; I could use one of the ideas introduced in Chapter 6 to make it more interesting.

✓ Does each body paragraph deal with a single topic?

Yes. So I don't have to break any of them into two or more paragraphs.

✓ Does the conclusion bring the essay to a close in an interesting way?

Sort of. I guess I should look at it again and try to apply some of the material in Chapter 6 to my conclusion.

You saw Beth's first draft at the end of Chapter 6. Here is the second draft of her introduction, conclusion, and title with her changes highlighted.

Introduction

Everyone learns in different ways. Some people learn by watching, **while others learn by doing.** Some **learn** by reading, **while others learn by listening** ~~and others by themselves~~. **Some learn best when they work independently, while others do better in groups.** The way people learn is a **major** part of who they are. Knowing how we learn can help us understand ourselves better. I know that I learn best from taking risks, watching others, and making mistakes.

Conclusion

People can learn about life from almost anything they do. They just have to be willing to do so. When I take risks, I think about what I will learn. I definitely try to learn as much as I can from watching others, **which I believe, in the case of my cousin, has already saved my life.** When I make mistakes, I figure out why I made each mistake and how to avoid it a second time. **These three ways of learning are all part of who I am today. I know I'm not finished learning yet. In fact, I don't know if I ever will be.**

Title

~~The Way We Learn~~

The Learning Curve

Your Revision Apply these questions one by one to your essay.

☐ Does the title draw in the readers?

☐ Does the introduction capture the readers' attention and build up to the thesis statement effectively?

☐ Does each body paragraph deal with a single topic?

☐ Does the conclusion bring the essay to a close in an interesting way?

Development

✓ Do the body paragraphs adequately support the thesis statement?

✓ Does each body paragraph have a focused topic sentence?

✓ Does each body paragraph contain specific details that support the topic sentence?

✓ Does each body paragraph include enough details to explain the topic sentence fully?

When you develop an essay, you build the body paragraphs. Body paragraphs provide supporting evidence for the thesis statement. They are made up of a clearly focused topic sentence and details that support the topic sentence. Supporting details should be as specific as possible, and you need to provide enough details to support the point you are making in each paragraph.

Specific Details

An important part of developing a good essay is being able to recognize ideas that are more general (for example, *entertainment* and *exercise*) and more specific (the opening scene in *The Green Mile*). Two other essential terms to know in choosing details are *abstract* and *concrete*. As you learned in Chapter 6, concrete words refer to items you can see, hear, touch, smell, or taste—as opposed to abstract words, which refer to ideas and concepts, such as *entertainment*, *frustration*, and *peacefulness*. Look at the following examples, and notice how each line becomes more detailed.

entertainment (general, abstract)
movies
suspense films
Stephen King films
The Green Mile
opening scene in *The Green Mile* (specific, concrete)

Don't confuse levels of detail with examples. Compare the previous ladder with this one:

sports
team sports
hockey
NHL
Toronto Maple Leafs
Ottawa Senators
Montreal Canadiens
Vancouver Canucks

In this ladder, the four teams are at the same level of detail. One is not more specific than another. So these last four items are just a list of examples.

As a rule, your thesis statement should be the most general statement in your essay. Your topic sentences are more specific than your thesis, and the details in your body paragraphs are the most specific items in the essay. So an outline of these elements looks like this:

Thesis statement (general)
  Topic sentence
    Detail (specific and concrete)
    Detail (specific and concrete)
    Detail (specific and concrete)

PRACTICE 3 Underline the most specific word or phrase in each group.

1. books, library, shelves, page 42, stairs
2. computer, technology, software, power button, online help
3. backyard, swimming pool, Coppertone lotion, pool party
4. drinks, thirst, pop, Dr. Pepper, root beer in a frosty mug
5. pink candles on a birthday cake, dessert, dinner, sweets, chocolate

PRACTICE 4 Fill in each blank with a new level of concrete detail as indicated by the indentions.

1. ____________
    lottery
      ____
        ____

2. ____________
    brother
      ____
        ____

3. boat
      ____
        ____
          ____

4. ____________
    ____
      ____
        blue shirt with stripes

5. ____________
    ____
      Thursday's newspaper
        ____

Beth's Revision Making your essay more specific involves adding as well as rewriting words, phrases, and whole sentences. Here is one of Beth's body paragraphs with more specific details in bold type in her revision.

First Draft

I have discovered that I learn a lot by taking risks. Being at this college was a risk. I have a boyfriend back home, we want to get married someday. We are hoping for a spring wedding with all of our friends and family. I left my boyfriend to come here. Coming here was a risk to our relationship. But if I am ever going to make it, I have to be willing to take risks.

Revised with Specific Details

I have discovered that I learn a lot by taking risks. **If I didn't take risks, I think I'd never mature.** Being at this college was a risk. I have a boyfriend back home, we want to get married someday. We are hoping for a spring wedding with all of our friends and family. I left my boyfriend to come here. Coming here was a risk to our relationship. **Taking this risk taught me to be responsible and trust my boyfriend back home.** But if I am ever going to ~~make it~~ **reach my potential,** I have to be willing to take risks.

Enough Details

Not only should your details be specific and concrete, but you should furnish enough details to support your topic sentence. No matter how good one detail is, it is not adequate to develop a topic sentence. Without enough details, facts, or reasons, a paragraph can be too short and weak to support a thesis statement. So Beth needs to add more details to her paragraph.

PRACTICE 5 List three details that could support each of the following topic sentences.

1. My favourite pastime is swimming.

   ____

   ____

   ____

2. Eating a balanced diet is an important part of feeling good.

   ____

   ____

   ____

3. A simple gift is often the best.

   ____

   ____

   ____

4. Working for people you like is easy.

   ____

   ____

   ____

5. Spending time outside can change a person's mood.

____

____

____

PRACTICE 6 Develop the following topic sentences with enough specific details.

1. Before taking a test, take a moment to relax.
2. Always discuss major decisions with someone you trust.
3. When interviewing for a job, dress appropriately.
4. My roommate is a real neat freak.
5. When reading a book, think about what you are reading.

Beth's Revision Here is Beth's body paragraph with more details.

Revised with More Details

I have discovered that I learn a lot by taking risks. If I didn't take risks, I think I'd never mature. Being at this college was a risk. I have a boyfriend back home, we want to get married someday. We are hoping for a spring wedding with all of our friends and family. **But I knew that this school's nursing program was better than the one in my hometown.** I left my boyfriend to come here. Coming here was a risk to our relationship. **Not coming here would have been a risk to my career.** Taking this risk taught me to be responsible and trust my boyfriend back home. **I know that I will take many risks like this throughout my life and that not all of them will work out.** But if I am ever going to reach my potential, I have to be willing to take risks.

Your Revision Add more relevant details to your essay, making your explanations and descriptions as specific as possible. Also make sure all of your body paragraphs have focused topic sentences that support your thesis statement.

Unity

✓ Do the essay's topic sentences relate directly to the thesis statement?
✓ Do the details in each body paragraph support its topic sentence?

An essay is unified when its topic sentences are all related to the thesis statement and when each body paragraph discusses only one idea. Irrelevant paragraphs in essays are those that don't support their essay's thesis statement. They should be deleted or revised to fit into the essay's plan.

A paragraph's main idea is introduced in its topic sentence. All other sentences in a paragraph should expand on this idea and relate to it in some way. Information that is not about the topic sentence is irrelevant and does not belong in the paragraph.

PRACTICE 7 Cross out the topic sentences that don't support each thesis statement.

1. Thesis: Holidays are fun times in my family.

   My favourite holiday is Thanksgiving.
   The fireworks on July 1st always scare my dogs.
   Chanukah is a time of great celebration in my house.
   My boyfriend doesn't understand my family.

2. Thesis: I love working with children.

   Children's games still make me laugh.
   I hate foods that are good for me.
   I want a job that pays well.
   I have always liked babysitting.
   I have applied to work at the Children's Centre on our campus.

3. Thesis: Exercise is essential for good health.

   Exercise keeps our hearts in good shape.
   Exercise is fun.
   Exercise is difficult when you are on a tight schedule.
   Exercise is necessary for weight control.
   Exercise is good for us emotionally.

4. Thesis: I have learned over the years how to control my anger.

   One way is to count to 10 before I do anything.
   I get angry easily.
   Another solution is to take a deep breath before I act.
   The solution I use most often is to take a walk.

5. Thesis: I really like to cook, but I never have the time.

   I am most creative at breakfast.
   The dish I like to make the most is a frittata.
   My class schedule keeps me busy right through dinner.
   My philosophy class is my toughest class.
   I don't like spicy foods.

PRACTICE 8 Cross out the three irrelevant sentences in the following paragraph.

I have a very bad habit of waiting until the night before an exam to begin studying, so it is very important for me to have a well-planned and productive cramming session. One time during my first year of high school, I failed a test. I begin by putting on comfortable clothes so that when I begin to squirm and twist to try and get comfortable, I am able to move around. Next, I get a large glass of milk and several cookies to snack on. Peanut butter cookies have always been my favourite. Once I have my snack, I spread out all my books and study materials on the living room floor. I have a hardwood floor. Finally, I am ready to begin studying for the next few hours.

PRACTICE 9 Cross out the three irrelevant sentences in the following paragraph.

Most people wonder what it would be like to win the lottery and be able to spend money as they please. The odds are that even the people who buy a lottery ticket every day will never win the lottery. Winning the lottery would change most people's lives drastically. Many people say that they would begin by paying all their debts. There are people in the world who buy so many items on credit that they are constantly trying to get out of debt. Other people say that they would buy a new house or a new car to spoil themselves a little bit. Some people simply say that they would invest the money and use it when they retire so that they can live comfortably. Many elderly people are unable to continue the lifestyles they are accustomed to after retirement.

Beth's Revision When Beth reads her paper for unity, she sees that three sentences are off topic. So she deletes them.

In Paragraph 2: ~~We are hoping for a spring wedding with all of our friends and family.~~

In Paragraph 3: ~~My sister cheated once. I was so scared to do it.~~

Your Revision Read your essay carefully, and cross out any irrelevant sentences or paragraphs.

Organization

- ✓ Is the essay organized logically?
- ✓ Is each body paragraph organized logically?

In Chapter 6, you learned five ways to organize your paragraphs and essays:

1. From general to particular
2. From particular to general
3. Chronologically (by time)
4. Spatially (by physical arrangement)
5. From one extreme to another

The organization that you choose for your essay depends chiefly on your topic and overall purpose. What are you trying to accomplish? In what order should you present your evidence? Is point A the most important? Maybe it should be the last paragraph so you can build up to it.

After you put your paragraphs in order, you are ready to look at the organization of each individual paragraph. It's very likely that your essay will be organized one way (say, from least important to most important) and each of your body paragraphs will have its own method of organization. As you revise, you should check to see that your essay is organized as effectively as possible for what you are trying to accomplish and that each of your body paragraphs is arranged logically as well.

PRACTICE 10 Reorganize the following topics so that they are in a logical order. Then label your method of organization.

1. east at the mall to the stoplight
   west at the grocery store to the flower shop
   north at the flower shop until you get to Anita's
   south at the stoplight until you hit the grocery store

Method of Organization: ________________________________

2. sitcoms
   dramas
   documentaries
   musicals
   awards shows

Method of Organization: ________________________________

3. community servants
   police badges
   police officers
   police office staff
   police uniforms

Method of Organization: ________________________________

PRACTICE 11 Reorganize the following sentences so that they are in a logical order. Then identify your method of organization.

Next, I decide what I will have for dinner and begin to cook.
Then I change into comfortable clothes.
Before I completely wind down, I lay out my clothes for the next day and set my alarm clock.
This is always a good time to look at the mail or return phone calls.
While I am cooking, I listen to music or turn on the evening news.
First, I begin to relax by taking a shower.
When I return home in the evenings, I always follow the same routine.
After I eat, I do the dishes and sit down in the living room.
Finally I watch television or read a book until I fall asleep.

Method of Organization: ________________________________

PRACTICE 12 Reorganize the following sentences so that they are in a logical order. Then identify your method of organization.

Sweatshirts belong next to long-sleeved shirts, so they come next.
When I walk in the closet door, all of my T-shirts are hanging directly to my left in the closet.

My shoes follow the same pattern on the floor as the clothes on hangers.
Next to the T-shirts are my long-sleeved shirts.
Starting the summer clothes are the tank-tops, followed by summer dresses.
Everything in my closet must be in order, or I will never be able to find anything.
All of my sweaters can be found stacked neatly on the shelf just above my long-sleeved sweatshirts.
Jackets, of course, go along with sweatshirts, so they are hanging next to the sweatshirts.
I have winter shoes immediately as I walk in the door, with sandals for summer toward the back of the closet.
After the jackets come the summer clothes.

Method of Organization: ______________________________

Beth's Revision In Chapter 6, Beth decided that the best way to organize her essay was from one extreme to another (from most to least important). But now she needs to make sure that this is the most effective order for her ideas and that every paragraph is in the right place.

This is the order of the main ideas in her first draft:

Most important:	Taking risks
Next most important:	Watching others
Least important:	Making mistakes

After thinking about this order, Beth realizes that she learns more from making mistakes than from watching others. So she decides to reverse these two topics. She also remembers that she has to revise her thesis statement and her conclusion to reflect this new order.

Revised Thesis Statement:	I know that I learn best from taking risks, making mistakes, and watching others.
Revised Conclusion:	People can learn about life from almost anything they do. They just have to be willing to do so. When I take risks, I think about what I will learn. **When I make mistakes, I figure out why I made each mistake and how to avoid it a second time. I definitely try to learn as much as I can from watching others, which I believe, in the case of my cousin, has already saved my life.** These three ways of learning are all a part of who I am today. I know I'm not finished learning yet. In fact, I don't know if I ever will be.

Also in Chapter 6, Beth organized her three body paragraphs from general to particular. At this point, she checks to see if this is the most effective order for these ideas. She thinks that this order is a good choice for her body paragraphs.

Your Revision Double-check the method of organization you chose in Chapter 6 for your essay. Do you still think this is the most effective order for what you are trying to say? Then check each body paragraph to see that the details are arranged logically.

Coherence

- ✓ Are transitions used effectively so that paragraphs move smoothly and logically from one to the next?
- ✓ Do the sentences move smoothly and logically from one to the next?

A well-written paragraph is coherent—that is, its parts cohere or stick together. It is smooth, not choppy, and readers move logically from one thought to the next, seeing a clear relationship among the ideas. Here are four different strategies that writers use to help their readers follow their train of thought from one paragraph to the next and within paragraphs: *transitions*, *repeated words*, *synonyms*, and *pronouns*.

Transitions *Transitional words and phrases* provide bridges or links between paragraphs and ideas. They show your readers how your paragraphs or thoughts are related or when you are moving to a new point. Good use of transitions makes your writing smooth rather than choppy.

Choppy: I could have laughed off the cheating experience and the teacher. I decided to slow down and learn from the experience.

Smooth: I could have laughed off the cheating experience and the teacher. **However,** I decided to slow down and learn from the experience.

Transitions have very specific meanings, so you should take care to make logical choices that help you communicate your exact thoughts.

Confusing: I could have laughed off the cheating experience and the teacher. **In addition,** I decided to slow down and learn from the experience.

Here is a list of some common transitional words and phrases that will make your writing more coherent. They are classified by meaning.

Some Common Transitions

Addition:	*again, and, and then, also, besides, finally, first, further, furthermore, in addition, last, likewise, moreover, next, nor, second, third, too*
Comparison:	*in like manner, likewise, similarly*

Contrast:	*after all, and yet, at the same time, but, however, in contrast, nevertheless, on the contrary, on the other hand, otherwise, still, yet*
Emphasis:	*actually, after all, essentially, in any event, indeed, in fact, of course, to tell the truth*
Example:	*for example, for instance, in this case*
Place:	*adjacent to, beyond, here, near, nearby, opposite, there*
Purpose:	*for this purpose, to this end, with this objective*
Result:	*accordingly, as a result, consequently, hence, so, then, therefore, thus*
Summary:	*as I have said, in brief, in other words, in short, in sum, on the whole, that is, to conclude, to sum up, to summarize*
Time:	*after a few days, afterward, at length, (at) other times, immediately, in the meantime, later, meanwhile, now, sometimes, soon, still, then*

See page 418 in the Handbook (Part IV) for more information on transitions.

Sometimes longer phrases provide transitions between paragraphs or main ideas. See if you can find the long transition that Beth adds to the beginning of one of the paragraphs that she moved (pages 89–90). This phrase helps her readers shift gears to a new topic and makes her essay easier to follow.

PRACTICE 13 Fill in the blanks in the following paragraph with logical transitions.

> Today, an unlimited amount of information is available through the Internet. ______________, some of this information may not be suitable for younger audiences. Many concerned parents asked for a way to block Internet sites that they did not want their children to view. ______________, a system was developed by which a parent uses a password to choose which Internet sites the household computer will and won't access. ______________, children who do not know the password cannot access the blocked Internet sites. ________, parents have control over the technology in their homes and feel their children are safe when they use the Internet.

PRACTICE 14 Rewrite the following paragraph, adding at least three transitions to make it more coherent.

> In high school, I thought I had everything figured out. I never considered what I would do after graduation. I never made any plans. When I graduated, I was completely lost. I went to see a guidance counsellor at the local college. I decided to go to college. I am in college and have made many plans for the future.

Repeated Words *Repeating key words* is another way of binding the ideas of an essay together and guiding readers through the details. A key word is usually a main idea in an essay. You should also know that too much repetition becomes boring.

Effective Repetition: Coming here was a **risk** to our relationship. Not coming here would have been a **risk** to my career.

PRACTICE 15 Underline five effective repeated words in the following paragraph.

> All my life, I have gone to my grandmother's house near a lake out in farm country during the summer. This year, I'm taking my best friend from college with me. What I like most about summers at the lake is that the weather is so warm that I can swim all day long. I swim near the bridge and see the small fish swimming around the columns. Sometimes I even swim over to the docks where all of the people are loading and unloading their boats. I used to try to swim faster and faster to beat my own record. Now I just go to relax, forget about school, and think about the future.

PRACTICE 16 Underline at least five effective repeated words in the following paragraph.

> For many people, reading the daily newspaper is their main source of information about the world. The front page usually gives the national news or an international political event that affects Canadians. Major world events, such as an earthquake, always make front-page news. On the second page of the first section is the op-ed (opposite editorial) page, where editors and readers give their opinions on current news. The editorial and op-ed pages are among the few places in the newspaper where the writing is not objective, along with book and movie reviews and columnists such as Gwynne Dyer or Dear Abby. Most newspapers have separate sections for sports, business, entertainment, classified ads, and comics. All in all, a half hour spent with the newspaper over morning coffee keeps a person up to date on world affairs and local people, places, and events.

Synonyms *Synonyms* are another way to link your ideas and help you avoid ineffective repetition. Synonyms are words that have identical or similar meanings—*movie/film*, *feeling/emotion*, *fantastic/unbelievable*. They add variety and interest to your writing. A thesaurus, or book of synonyms, can help you choose synonyms for specific words. Be aware, however, that all the words in a thesaurus listing are not interchangeable. *Retreat*, for example, is listed as a synonym for *escape*, but the two words suggest two very different ways of leaving a place. In the following example from Beth's essay, Beth uses *incidents* in place of one of her references to *experiences*.

Boring Repetition:	She talked a lot to me about those **experiences.** By watching my cousin go through these horrible **experiences,** I made a conscious decision never to make the bad choices that my cousin made.
Synonym:	She talked a lot to me about those **experiences.** By watching my cousin go through these horrible ~~**experiences**~~ **incidents,** I made a conscious decision never to make the bad choices that my cousin made.

PRACTICE 17 Underline four different synonyms for *friend* in the following paragraph.

> My younger brother and his friends were always starting clubs when I was young. The clubhouse and the club name were very important. The pals usually decided on a name first. I think my favourite name that they had was "The Three Amigos," even though it was not very original. Every once in a while, an acquaintance of the boys would be allowed to join the club, and the name would have to be changed. Since the boys always thought that they were such sophisticated companions, they had a sign on the door that read "Associates Only—No Girls Allowed." The boys are all grown now, but I still smile every time I think about all of the meetings of "The Three Amigos" that I sat outside of and listened to.

PRACTICE 18 Replace two uses of the word *actor* with two different synonyms in the following paragraph.

> Being an actor seems like a glamorous career choice, but becoming famous is not easy. Many actors start out waiting on tables in restaurants, hoping to be discovered by agents dining there. Other actors go from bit part to bit part in movies and never really earn enough for a living. In the unlikely event that an actor makes it big, he or she suddenly loses all privacy. Still, there are advantages to fame, and most actors adjust quite well to the lifestyle.

Pronouns Finally, you can link your sentences with *pronouns.* Pronouns not only help you avoid needless repetition, but they also keep your writing moving at a fairly fast pace. Personal pronouns (*I, you, he, she, it, we, they*) and indefinite pronouns (*any, some, other, one*) are the ones most commonly used as replacements.

Beth can use a pronoun to get rid of her repetition of the words *my cousin.*

Repetition:	When my cousin became heavily involved with gangs and drugs, I watched my cousin live in constant fear.

Revision: When my cousin became heavily involved with gangs and drugs, I watched ~~my cousin~~ **her** live in constant fear.

For more information on pronouns, see pages 439–460 in the Handbook (Part IV).

PRACTICE 19 Underline 10 personal and indefinite pronouns in the following paragraph.

> The people down the street have a very large family, which means that there is always something going on in their house. Sometimes when I am at their house, I cannot keep up with everything that is happening. For example, when Sandy answers the phone, she yells that it's for Ryan. Of course, Ryan has to know who it is, and the yelling continues back and forth until Ryan decides to finally pick up the phone. Sometimes when the family members are really busy, they all make dinner individually. Everyone is in the kitchen at one time trying to find something to eat while trying not to step on one another. I'm not sure I could live at the Mitchells' house, but I definitely like visiting.

PRACTICE 20 Add five pronouns where appropriate in the following paragraph.

> A few days ago, Brian, Carol, Katie, and I went out to dinner. Brian, Carol, Katie, and I went to a new Italian restaurant on First Street. As soon as Brian, Carol, Katie, and I walked in the door, Brian, Carol, Katie, and I could smell the garlic, basil, and oregano in the rich tomato sauces of pizza, lasagne, and, of course, spaghetti and meatballs. Brian, Carol, Katie, and I couldn't stand it, so Brian, Carol, Katie, and I ordered immediately. The food was even better than it smelled. Before the dinner was over, Brian, Carol, Katie, and I set a date to return.

Beth's Revision When Beth checks her essay for coherence, she thinks her writing could be smoother if she used some of these techniques. So she makes the following revisions that help bind her sentences together and show the specific relationships between her ideas.

Here is Beth's essay with transitions, repeated words, synonyms, and pronouns highlighted.

The Learning Curve

Everyone learns in different ways. Some people learn by watching, while others learn by doing. Some learn by reading, and others learn by listening. Some learn best when they work independently, but others do better in groups. **In fact, t**~~T~~he way people learn is a major part of who they are. **So** knowing how we learn can help us understand ourselves better. I know that I learn best from taking risks, making mistakes, and watching others.

First, I have discovered that I learn a lot by taking risks. If I didn't take risks, I think I'd never mature. Being at this college was a risk. I have a boyfriend back home, we want to get married someday. But I knew that this school's nursing program was better than the one in my hometown~~.~~, **s**~~S~~o I left my boyfriend to come here. Coming here was a risk to our relationship. **However, n**~~N~~ot coming here would have been a risk to my career. Taking this risk taught me to be responsible and trust my boyfriend back home. I know that I will take many risks like this throughout my life and that not all of them will work out. But if I am ever going to reach my potential, I have to be willing to take risks.

Also, I believe that I learn from making mistakes. **For example, w**~~W~~hen I was a sophomore in high school, I didn't study for a major science test. I knew the test was important, but I decided to go to a party with my friends. I really needed the grade, so I cheated. I cut my notes into small strips of paper that I put in my desk, but the teacher caught me. Thank goodness ~~the teacher~~ **he** was a nice person. ~~The teacher~~ **He** took the time to talk to me about the mistake I was making, not only **cheating** for a grade, but **cheating** myself out of the knowledge that I could have. This mistake made me re-evaluate my education. ~~This mistake~~ **It** led me into nursing by making me ~~re-evaluate~~ **realize** what subjects I really enjoyed. I could have laughed off the cheating experience and the teacher. However, I decided to slow down and learn from the experience.

In addition to learning from my own actions, I also benefit from watching other people. **For instance, w**~~W~~hen my cousin became heavily involved with gangs and drugs, I watched her live in constant fear. She was worried that she would end up in jail, overdose on drugs, or become a "plaything" for other gang members. She worked hard to overcome that lifestyle. She talked a lot to me about those experiences. By watching my cousin go through these horrible incidents, I made a conscious decision never to make the bad choices that ~~my cousin~~ **she** made. I had plenty of opportunities to do so. Turning away from this life was difficult, but I did it. By watching and understanding my cousin's life. I learned to live mine better.

Essentially, p~~P~~eople can learn about life from almost anything they do. They just have to be willing to do so. **Now, w**~~W~~hen I take risks, I think about what I will learn. When I make mistakes, I figure out why I made each mistake and how to avoid it a second time. **Also,** I definitely try to learn as much as I can from watching others, which I believe, in the case of my cousin, has already saved my life. These three ways of learning are all part of who I am today. I know I'm not finished learning yet. In fact, I don't know if I ever will be.

Transitions In addition to *however*, Beth added 12 more transitions to her essay. What are they?

List the meaning of five of these transitions:

1. Transition: ____________________ Meaning: ____________________
2. Transition: ____________________ Meaning: ____________________
3. Transition: ____________________ Meaning: ____________________
4. Transition: ____________________ Meaning: ____________________
5. Transition: ____________________ Meaning: ____________________

Repeated Words When Beth checked her essay for repeated key words, she saw that she referred directly to *cheating* twice in the same sentence. She decided this was an effective repetition and chose to keep it in her essay.

Effective Repetition: He took the time to talk to me about the mistake I was making, not only **cheating** for a grade, but **cheating** myself out of the knowledge that I could have.

Synonyms When Beth looked at her essay again, she found another opportunity to use a synonym to link her ideas more clearly. Besides the addition of *incidents* for *experiences*, what other synonym does Beth use in her revision?

____________________ for ____________________

Pronouns Finally, in addition to substituting *her* for *my cousin*, Beth found four more places to use pronouns to bind key parts of her essay together. Where are these places in her essay?

____________________ for ____________________
____________________ for ____________________
____________________ for ____________________
____________________ for ____________________

Your Revision Now it's time to make your essay more coherent.

Transitions Check the transitions in your essay. Do you use enough transitions so that your essay moves smoothly and logically from one paragraph to the next and from one sentence to the next? Do you use your transitions logically?

Repeated Words Look at your essay to see when you might want to repeat a key word. Then revise your essay accordingly.

Synonyms Now look for places in your essay where you might add synonyms to link your sentences. Use a thesaurus (in book or electronic form) if you need help.

Pronouns Now check your essay for opportunities to use pronouns. Add appropriate pronouns.

Beth's Revised Essay After revising her thesis statement, her development of ideas, and the unity, organization, and coherence of her writing, Beth produced the following revised essay. All of her revisions are highlighted.

~~**The Way We Learn**~~

The Learning Curve

Everyone learns in different ways. Some people learn by watching, **while others learn by doing.** Some **learn** by reading, ~~**while**~~ **and others learn by listening** ~~**and others by themselves**~~. **Some learn best when they work independently,** ~~**while**~~ **but others do better in groups. In fact, t**~~**T**~~he way people learn is a **major** part of who they are. Knowing how we learn can help us understand ourselves better. I know that I learn ~~**from many things in life**~~ **best from taking risks, making mistakes, and watching others.**

First, I have discovered that I learn a lot by taking risks. **If I didn't take risks, I think I'd never mature.** Being at this college was a risk. I have a boyfriend back home, we want to get married someday. ~~**We are hoping for a spring wedding with all of our friends and family.**~~ **But I knew that this school's nursing program was better than the one in my hometown**~~**.**~~**,** ~~**S**~~so I left my boyfriend to come here. Coming here was a risk to our relationship. **However, n**~~**N**~~**ot coming here would have been a risk to my career. Taking this risk taught me to be responsible and trust my boyfriend back home. I know that I will take many risks like this throughout my life and that not all of them will work out.** But if I am ever going to ~~**make it**~~ **reach my potential,** I have to be willing to take risks.

Also, I believe that I learn from making mistakes. **For example, w**~~**W**~~hen I was **a sophomore** in high school, I didn't study for a major science test. **I knew the test was important, but I decided to go to a party with my friends. I really needed the grade,** ~~**S**~~so I cheated. ~~**My sister cheated once. I was so scared to do it**~~. **I cut my notes into small strips of paper that I put in my desk, but** ~~**T**~~the teacher caught me. **Thank goodness** ~~**the teacher**~~ **he was a nice person.** ~~**The teacher**~~ **He** took the time to talk to me about the mistake I was making**, not only**

cheating for a grade, but cheating myself out of the knowledge that I could have. This mistake made me re-evaluate my education. ~~This mistake~~ **It led me into nursing by making me** ~~re-evaluate~~ **realize what subjects I really enjoyed.** I could have laughed off the cheating experience **and the teacher. However,** I decided to slow down and learn from the experience.

In addition to learning from my own actions, I also benefit from watching other people. **For instance, w**~~W~~hen my cousin became heavily involved with gangs **and drugs,** I watched ~~my cousin~~ **her** live in constant fear. ~~My cousin~~ **She was worried that she would end up in jail, overdose on drugs, or become a "plaything" for other gang members. She worked hard to overcome that lifestyle. She talked a lot to me about those experiences.** By watching my cousin **go through these horrible** ~~experiences~~ **incidents,** I made a conscious decision ~~to be nothing like my cousin~~ **never to make the bad choices that** ~~my cousin~~ **she made. I had plenty of opportunities to do so. Turning away from this life was difficult, but I did it.** By watching and understanding my cousin's life. I learned to live mine better.

Essentially, p~~P~~eople can learn about life from almost anything they do. They just have to be willing to do so. **Now, w**~~W~~hen I take risks, I think about what I will learn. **When I make mistakes, I figure out why I made each mistake and how to avoid it a second time. Also, I definitely try to learn as much as I can from watching others, which I believe, in the case of my cousin, has already saved my life. These three ways of learning are all part of who I am today. I know I'm not finished learning yet. In fact, I don't know if I ever will be.**

Your Revised Essay Now that you have applied all the revision strategies to your own writing, rewrite your revised essay.

EDITING

After you have revised your writing, you are ready to edit it. Editing involves finding and correcting errors in grammar, punctuation, mechanics, and spelling. Correct writing is as important to communicating as well-chosen words. Nothing distracts readers from what you are saying more than editing errors. Editing is a two-part job: First, you must locate the errors. Then you must know how to correct them.

As the checklist here shows, we have divided the editing strategies into three categories: sentences, punctuation and mechanics, and word choice and spelling. This checklist doesn't cover all the grammar and usage problems you may find in your writing, but it focuses on the main errors college students make.

EDITING CHECKLIST ✓

SENTENCES

✓ Does each sentence have a main subject and verb?

✓ Do all subjects and verbs agree?

✓ Do all pronouns agree with their nouns?

✓ Are modifiers as close as possible to the words they modify?

PUNCTUATION AND MECHANICS

✓ Are sentences punctuated correctly?

✓ Are words capitalized properly?

WORD CHOICE AND SPELLING

✓ Are words used correctly?

✓ Are words spelled correctly?

Finding Your Errors

A major part of editing is proofreading. Proofreading is reading to catch grammar, punctuation, mechanics, and spelling errors. If you do not proofread carefully, you will not catch your errors and make the final changes that will improve your writing.

There are some specific techniques for finding errors. One good method is to read your essay backwards, sentence by sentence, starting with the last sentence. Taking sentences out of context lets you concentrate on individual sentences and not get caught up in reading for meaning.

Many students like to keep error logs like the one for grammar, punctuation, and mechanics in Appendix 3 and the one for spelling in Appendix 4. By the second or third paper you write, the logs will show you the types of errors you make most frequently. Then you can proofread your paper for one type of error at a time. For example, if you often write run-on sentences, you should read your paper once just to catch run-ons. Then read it again to find a second type of error, and so on. The error logs can help you reduce the number of errors in your writing. By recording the correction for each error you find, you will eventually learn the corrections.

You can also use the grammar-check or spell-check features on your computer. The grammar-check will point out possible grammar errors and suggest ways to reword sentences, but it is not foolproof. You need to decide if you want to accept or reject the grammar suggestions the computer makes. The spell-check is also not completely reliable because it misses errors. For example, it cannot tell the difference between *there* and *their*. So you should use it cautiously.

Asking a tutor or a friend to read your writing is also a good idea. A fresh pair of eyes may see errors you have missed. When others read your writing, they might want to use the editing symbols in Appendix 6 to highlight your errors for you. You can then use the page references on the chart to guide you to the part of this textbook that explains how to correct those errors.

PRACTICE 21 Find your Editing Quotient (EQ) by taking the EQ Test in Appendix 2A, on page 567. This test will help you learn what errors you have the most trouble identifying when you proofread someone's writing.

PRACTICE 22 Score your EQ Test by using the answer key that follows the test. Circle the errors you missed, and chart them in Appendix 2B. Do they fall into any clear categories?

Correcting Your Errors

Whenever you find errors, you need to correct them. To guide you through this phase of the writing process, Part IV of this text provides a complete handbook of grammar and usage. As you proofread, apply each question in the Editing Checklist to your essay. If you are not sure whether you have made an error, look up the problem in Part IV. Work with your writing until you can answer yes to every question on the checklist.

PRACTICE 23 Using the Handbook

Using the Handbook in Part IV, list the page references for the 15 different types of errors you worked with in Practices 21 and 22. This will help you learn to use the Handbook as a reference guide.

apostrophe	page ________
capitalization	page ________
comma	page ________
comma splice	page ________
confused word	page ________
dangling modifier	page ________
end punctuation	page ________
fragment	page ________
fused sentence	page ________
modifier error	page ________
pronoun	page ________
pronoun agreement	page ________
spelling	page ________
subject-verb agreement	page ________
verb form	page ________

Beth's Editing When Beth proofreads her paper for grammar, punctuation, mechanics, and spelling, she finds two errors that she looks up in Part IV and corrects. The first error is a comma splice:

Comma Splice: I have a boyfriend back home, we want to get married someday.

Beth realizes that this sentence has too many subjects and verbs without any linking words or end punctuation between them. She looks up "comma splice" on page 414 of Part IV and corrects the error by putting a coordinating conjunction (*and*) between the two clauses.

Correction: I have a boyfriend back home, **and** we want to get married someday.

Beth also finds a sentence that doesn't sound complete—it's not a sentence but a fragment:

Fragment: By watching and understanding my cousin's life.

When she looks up the problem in Part IV (page 404), she learns that a fragment is easily corrected by connecting it to another sentence.

Correction: By watching and understanding my cousin's life~~.~~, I learned to live mine better.

Beth's Edited Draft Both of these errors are corrected here in Beth's edited draft.

The Learning Curve

1 Everyone learns in different ways. Some people learn by watching, while others learn by doing. Some learn by reading, and others learn by listening. Some learn best when they work independently, but others do better in groups. In fact, the way people learn is a major part of who they are. Knowing how we learn can help us understand ourselves better. I know that I learn best from taking risks, making mistakes, and watching others.

2 First, I have discovered that I learn a lot by taking risks. If I didn't take risks, I think I'd never mature. Being at this college was a risk. **I have a boyfriend back home, and we want to get married someday.** But I knew that this school's nursing program was better than the one in my hometown, so I left my boyfriend to come here. Coming here was a risk to our relationship. However, not coming here would have been a risk to my career. Taking this risk taught me to be responsible and trust my boyfriend back home. I know that I will take many risks like this throughout my life and that not all of them will work out. But if I am ever going to reach my potential, I have to be willing to take risks.

3 Also, I believe that I learn from making mistakes. For example, when I was a sophomore in high school, I didn't study for a major science test. I knew the test was important, but I decided to go to a party with my friends. I really needed the grade, so I cheated. I cut my notes into small strips of paper that I put in my desk, but the teacher caught me. Thank goodness he was a nice person. He took the time to talk to me about the mistake I was making, not only cheating for a

grade, but cheating myself out of the knowledge that I could have. This mistake made me re-evaluate my education. It led me into nursing by making me realize what subjects I really enjoyed. I could have laughed off the cheating experience and the teacher. However, I decided to slow down and learn from the experience.

In addition to learning from my own actions, I also benefit from 4
watching other people. For instance, when my cousin became heavily involved with gangs and drugs, I watched her live in constant fear. She was worried that she would end up in jail, overdose on drugs, or become a "plaything" for other gang members. She worked hard to overcome that lifestyle. She talked a lot to me about those experiences. By watching my cousin go through these horrible incidents, I made a conscious decision never to make the bad choices that she made. I had plenty of opportunities to do so. Turning away from this life was difficult, but I did it. **By watching and understanding my cousin's life, I learned to live mine better.**

Essentially, people can learn about life from almost anything they 5
do. They just have to be willing to do so. Now, when I take risks, I think about what I will learn. When I make mistakes, I figure out why I made each mistake and how to avoid it a second time. Also, I definitely try to learn as much as I can from watching others, which I believe, in the case of my cousin, has already saved my life. These three ways of learning are all a part of what I am today. I know I'm not finished learning yet. In fact, I don't know if I ever will be.

Your Editing Proofread your paragraph carefully to find errors, using at least two of the methods described in this chapter. Record your grammar, punctuation, and mechanics errors in the Error Log (Appendix 3) and your spelling errors in the Spelling Log (Appendix 4).

Your Edited Draft Now write a corrected draft of your essay.

Review of the Reading and Writing Processes

Clues for Review

- **The reading process** is a series of tasks that involve prereading, reading, first rereading, and second rereading.

  Prereading: Thinking about the title, the author, and focused questions

  Reading: Focusing on vocabulary, a reading strategy, the author's purpose, the author's audience

  First Rereading: Understanding the essay's assumptions and relationships between ideas

  Second Rereading: Writing questions, forming opinions, analyzing

- **The writing process** is a series of tasks that involve prewriting, writing, revising, and editing. At any time, one activity may loop in and out of another.
- **Prewriting** consists of thinking about and planning your essay.

  Thinking: freewriting, brainstorming, clustering, questioning, discussing

  Planning: Deciding on a subject, purpose, and audience

  Writing a thesis statement: Stating a limited subject and an opinion about that subject
- **Writing** includes developing your ideas; organizing your essay; and writing your introduction, conclusion, and title.

  Developing: Explaining your ideas and adding specific details, examples, facts, and reasons

  Organizing: Arranging ideas from general to particular, particular to general, chronologically, spatially, or from one extreme to another

  Writing your introduction, conclusion, and title: Writing an introduction, conclusion, and title that support your thesis
- **Revising** means "seeing again" and improving all aspects of an essay's organization and development.

  Thesis statement

  Basic elements

  Development

  Unity

  Organization

  Coherence
- **Editing** involves proofreading and correcting your grammar, punctuation, mechanics, and spelling errors.

REVIEW PRACTICE 1

Answer the following questions.

1. What are the four main parts of the reading process?

   ____

   ____

2. What are the four main parts of the writing process?

   ____

   ____

3. What is your favourite reading strategy? Why is it your favourite?

____

____

4. What is your favourite prewriting activity? Why is it your favourite?

____

____

5. What personal rituals do you go through when you read?

____

____

6. What personal rituals do you go through as you write?

____

____

7. Where do you usually do your academic writing? Do you write your first draft on a computer? What time of day do you do your best writing?

____

____

8. What is a thesis statement?

____

____

9. What is the difference between topic sentences and details?

____

____

10. What are the five main methods of organization?

____

____

11. Do you usually ask a tutor or friend to look at your draft before you revise it?

____

____

12. What is the difference between revising and editing?

____

____

13. Draw a picture or graphic version of your own reading process. What happens first, second, third, and so on from the time you get a reading assignment? Don't use any words in your picture.

14. Draw a picture or graphic version of your own writing process. What happens first, second, third, and so on from the time you get a writing assignment? Don't use any words in your picture.

REVIEW PRACTICE 2 Write a thesis statement for five of the following topics. Then develop one thesis statement into a first draft of an essay.

1. My best friend
2. Politics
3. My best adventure
4. Animals
5. In the middle of the night
6. My family
7. My future career
8. The best car
9. Parents should never . . .
10. Sports

REVIEW PRACTICE 3 Revise the essay you wrote for Review Practice 2, using the checklist on pages 71–72.

REVIEW PRACTICE 4 Edit the essay you wrote for Review Practice 2, using the checklist on page 94.

PART II

Reading and Writing Effective Essays

Writing is not hard. Just get a paper and pencil, sit down and write it as it occurs to you. The writing is easy—it's the occurring that's hard.

—Stephen Leacock

In Part I of *Essays*, you learned about the various parts of the reading and writing processes. You discovered that you have to work with the author of an essay to create meaning when you read and with your potential reader to produce meaning when you write. Part II focuses on nine different ways of thinking or processing information, called *rhetorical modes*. In this section, you will concentrate on one mode at a time so you can understand in detail how a particular strategy actually works. In reality, however, although an essay may emphasize one mode, several rhetorical strategies function together to communicate a message.

Each chapter begins with an explanation of a rhetorical strategy and then provides specific guidelines for using that strategy in reading and writing. First, the chapter features the rhetorical strategy in a reading selection with specific guidelines for approaching this type of reading critically. Next, after furnishing specific guidelines for writing this type of essay, the chapter guides you through two writing samples to help you understand how this particular rhetorical strategy actually works: (1) a student essay and (2) your own essay. Students can usually see patterns in other students' writing more easily than they can in their own essays so you will work with someone else's writing before composing your own essay in a particular mode. Finally, the chapter introduces two essays written by professional writers. The questions framing these selections will help you process the content of the essays critically so you will ultimately be prepared to write a well–thought-out essay of your own at the end of each chapter.

Chapter 8

Describing

When you show, you get out of the readers' way and let them come right at the experience itself.

—Donald Murray

Description is an essential part of your life every day. Your friends might want to know what kind of car you just bought; your parents may ask what your new friend is like; your supervisor might need a description of the project you just finished. You constantly need to describe people, places, objects, and activities for different audiences if you want to communicate clearly and effectively.

In addition, you frequently use description when writing. Actually, description is a major part of our writing in our personal lives, at school, and at work:

You describe your new leather jacket in an email message to a friend.

You describe the damage to your car in an insurance report.

A student describes a cell and its parts on a biology exam.

A nurse describes the appearance of a wound in a patient report.

A landscape contractor describes a design for a rock garden.

Description creates a picture in words to help a reader visualize something a writer has seen, heard, or done. It helps the reader understand or share a sensory experience through "showing" rather than "telling." Description is one of our primary forms of self-expression.

At times, description is used as an end in itself. That is, you write a description for the sole purpose of telling what something looks, sounds, feels, tastes, or smells like. For instance, you might use pure description to tell a friend about your new apartment. More often, though, description is used to help accomplish another purpose—to explain a problem, to analyze the causes and effects of an event, or to persuade your readers to change their thinking or take some specific action.

READING AND WRITING A DESCRIPTION ESSAY

If you learn how to read a description essay critically, these skills will naturally transfer to your writing. But you need to be conscious of the process you use to understand your reading so you can use this strategy just as effectively in your writing. Reading and writing critically are demanding tasks in any mode, but they are necessary tools for succeeding in college and in life beyond college. Like two halves of a circle, these two processes complement each other and enhance your ability to perform many other tasks in all facets of life.

Reading a Description Essay

In his fictionalized account of the life of Newfoundland premier Joey Smallwood, Wayne Johnston describes the real-life seal hunt tragedy of March 1914. He imagines Smallwood on the S.S. *Newfoundland* as the men discover the fourth watch, which has been missing on the ice for three days.

First-hand accounts of natural disasters are common these days. In what ways has nature played a role in your life? Can you describe the role nature has played? Is it a positive or a negative one? What recent or ongoing natural events have dramatically changed our country? What natural events have affected the whole world?

READING CRITICALLY

We all naturally make personal associations with our reading material. However, one person's associations are usually quite different from those of someone else. Recording the associations you make with a reading selection lets you "own" the essay, so to speak. It allows you to connect the author's ideas to your own experiences. As you read the following essay, make at least five notes in the margin that relate some of your specific memories of the harshness of nature to the details in this essay. Be prepared to explain the connection between your notes and the facts in the essay.

WAYNE JOHNSTON

from *The Colony of Unrequited Dreams*

On the third day, when we looked through the porthole at mid-morning, we saw something other than the single shade of white we had become accustomed to—the many subtle shades of white that comprised the ice-field. 1

2 It was several hours more before the master watch came down and told me to go to my sleeping quarters.

3 I did as he said. I heard the boiler being fired up and felt the ship begin to move through the ice pack, which had loosened because the wind had changed.

4 About three o'clock in the afternoon, they found what they were looking for. Far off on the ice, I saw a couple of dozen men trudging about in a circle. The shout no sooner went up that the men of the *Newfoundland* were found than the ship's whistle shrieked in celebration. I looked out through the porthole, but that side of the ship was at too oblique an angle to the rescue site. As the ship ploughed on through the ice, however, the stem slowly drifted starboard and I was able to see round the curvature of the hull. The men were not a hundred feet away, still tramping in a circle as if even the ship's whistle had not roused them, each man with his hand on the shoulder of the man in front. They were so coated in snow I could not tell what they were wearing or make out their faces, which were rimed with frost. Most of them were limping badly; outside the circle was a man walking an even slower circle of his own and at the same time holding beneath the armpits another man whose feet made a feeble step now and then but otherwise dragged behind him on the ice.

5 As we drew closer to them, some of them at last noticed the ship and stopped walking. Some dropped to their knees or toppled over onto their backs, others stared as if they doubted that what they saw was real. The crew poured over the side and led the sealers or carried them on stretchers to the ship.

6 We moved on. I had counted twenty-three men. That left eighty unaccounted for. I stayed at the porthole. The ship came hard about, and for half an hour we crashed on through the ice, then stopped again.

7 My heart rose when I saw what looked to be the balance of the crew standing on a mile-wide ice pan in the near distance. From on deck, there were shouts of "Hurray" and footsteps thumped on the ceiling overhead as once again the ship's whistle sounded.

8 Gradually we drew up close to the ice pan. Mooring lines with grapnels on the end were cast onto the ice, and the pan was slowly pulled towards the ship until it thumped against it.

9 For several minutes after the ship stopped, no one disembarked. I saw what I had not been able to through my binoculars: that these were not survivors but a strange statuary of the dead. I was not repulsed by what I saw. I could not take my eyes away.

10 Two men knelt side by side, one man with his arm around the other, whose head was resting on his shoulder in a pose of tenderness between two men that I had never seen in life.

11 Three men stood huddled in a circle, arms about each other's shoulders, heads together like schoolboys conferring on a football field.

12 A man stood hugging himself, his hands on his arms, shoulders hunched, in the manner of someone who has momentarily stepped out of his house into the cold in shirtsleeves to bid a guest goodbye.

One man knelt, sitting back on his heels, while another stood behind him, his 13
hands on his shoulders, as if they were posing for a photograph.

Two sealers stood in a fierce embrace, the taller man with both arms wrapped 14
round the other, holding him against his chest, while the arms of the shorter man hung rigid at his sides.

Four men lay on their stomachs side by side, all facing the same way as if they 15
had lain down for some purpose or agreed together that they would.

Only a few men knelt or lay alone, perhaps those who had lasted longer than the 16
others.

One man sat by himself, his elbows resting on his drawn-up knees, his bare 17
hands frozen to his face.

The storm had started out as freezing rain. A man who must have been among 18
the first to fall lay encased within a mould of silver thaw.

I later learned that some who, in their delirium, thought they saw a light ran off 19
in pursuit of it and were never found.

Joined in some manner of embrace were men who before this journey to the ice 20
had never met, men who had outlasted those they knew best and for warmth or fellowship in death embraced some stranger.

They were all there, the boys too young and the men too old, who to get a berth 21
had lied about their ages or agreed to half a share; boys younger than me and men older than my father.

Perhaps, too tired to walk but still standing, they had been buried in snow that 22
had blown away when the storm let up, by which time they were rooted in the ice that lay like pedestals about their feet.

Some men lay in the lee of a low shelter they had managed to erect, a wall of ice 23
and snow that was barely three feet high.

I recognized a few of them, but only because of some distinctive article of 24
clothing, like the orange watch cap of the man who every morning made the tea. He lay on his side, his knees drawn up almost to his chest, his head resting on his hands, which were clasped in a prayer-like pillow, palm to palm.

They had been transformed by their passion on the ice. Each had assumed in 25
death some posture emblematic of his life. Or else they were refined to men that no one knew, as if in each face and posture was inscrutably depicted the essence of the person they had been.

Everywhere lay evidence of futile acts of courage and self-sacrifice. A man 26
stripped down to his undershirt and coveralls lay prone beside a boy bulked out in two sets of clothes.

In various places the snow was scorched where small fires had been lit. From 27
each a smudge of soot trailed out, a stain left from the smoke that had been flattened by the wind.

I did not want to see them moved or see the scene disturbed. I closed the porthole 28
and sat down on my bunk.

I heard above the wind and the droning of the ropes the sound of ice being hacked 29
and chopped. I heard the coal crank of the hatch at the far end of the ship lurch into

motion. The chopping and shouting and winching of the crank went on for hours. When it stopped, I considered opening the porthole but could not bring myself to do it.

30 I looked around the sleeping quarters at all the empty bunks. Not all the men had been lost. Not every bunk represented a man who would not be going home. It was impossible to tell which ones did. Three-quarters of them did, but I didn't know which ones. Except for the bunk of the man who made the tea.

31 Something deep within me, which I hadn't known was there, gave way. My body grieved but not my mind. I felt as though someone who was sitting right beside me was crying, and though I wanted to console him, I could not.

32 I felt the ship reach open water. The grinding of the ice against the hull ceased suddenly, the keel rocked from side to side until it balanced and we moved smoothly on. I got up and pounded on the door to be let out. As if, in all the commotion, I had been forgotten, I heard the sound of footsteps running. The hatch slid open and I saw the sky.

PREPARING TO WRITE YOUR OWN DESCRIPTION ESSAY

What are some memorable experiences you have had with nature (for example, a snowstorm, a sunny day, a drought, a tornado, a thunderstorm)? Why do you remember these experiences? Do any of them form a single impression when you think about them? Use one or more of the prewriting techniques that you learned in Chapter 5 to generate your thoughts about these memories.

Writing a Description Essay

Describing is a very natural process that is based on good observing. But some people describe things more vividly than others. When they describe an experience, you feel as though you were there too. We can all improve our skill at describing by following a few simple guidelines:

1. ***Decide on a dominant impression—the feeling or mood you want to communicate.*** How do you want your readers to feel after reading your description? Good about the characters in the scene? Angry at the situation? Satisfied with the outcome? Choosing a dominant impression gives your description focus and unity. You can't possibly write down everything you observe about a person, place, incident, or object. The result would be a long, confusing—and probably boring—list. But if you first decide on a dominant impression for your description, you can then choose the details that will best convey that impression.

The dominant impression Johnston's narrator conveys is his feeling of awe, both at the sight of the men frozen in the ice and the forces of nature that did this to them, and at the nobility depicted in the various human tableaux. This dominant impression gives his writing focus and helps him choose the details that will best communicate this feeling.

2. ***Decide how much of your description should be objective (factual) and how much should be subjective (personal reactions).*** An objective description is like a dictionary definition—accurate and without emotion. Scientific and technical writing are objective. If, for example, you are describing a piece of equipment used in a chemistry experiment or the packaging needed to ship a computer, you would be objective. Subjective description, in contrast, tries to produce a specific emotional response in the reader. It focuses on feelings rather than facts and tries to activate as many senses as possible. An advertisement describing a Caribbean cruise might be very subjective, as might a restaurant or movie review. Most descriptive writing has a combination of objective and subjective elements. The degree to which you emphasize one over the other depends on your purpose and your audience.

   Johnston's description demonstrates a good balance of objective and subjective writing. He presents the facts of what he sees through the porthole, vividly describing the image of the group of men walking in the unending circle, or the orange watch cap of the man who made the tea. Then he becomes more subjective, noting that some men seemed to be praying or huddled together in fellowship. At times he also becomes analytical, commenting that the men were frozen in a position that depicted their essence. This combination of objective and subjective elements makes the writing realistic and powerful at the same time. Note also how Johnston uses similes to create images familiar to the reader: "heads together like schoolboys conferring on a football field."

3. ***Draw on your five senses to write a good description.*** Although observing is at the heart of good description, limiting yourself to what you see is a mistake. Good description relies on all five senses: seeing, hearing, touching, smelling, and tasting. If you use all your senses to relay your description, your readers will be able to see, hear, touch, smell, and taste what you are describing as if they were there with you, participating in the same experience.

   Look again at Johnston's description. He draws primarily on sight throughout the essay, moving from a distant image seen through binoculars to a close-up view through the porthole of his cabin. When sight becomes too overpowering, the narrator closes the porthole and relies on sound—the droning of the ropes, the sound of the ice being hacked. As he *feels* the ship move, he *hears* the sound of running feet, and then the hatch opens and once more he sees outside, this time the open sky. The sensory details make the writing more vivid, but are also used in a literary way to create a changing sense of distance between the reader and the subject matter.

4. ***When you describe, try to show rather than tell your readers what you want them to know.*** Your ultimate goal in writing a description

essay is to give your readers an experience as close to yours as possible. Therefore, do not simply tell your readers what you saw or experienced; show them. Use your writing skills to re-create the event so that your readers can see, hear, feel, smell, taste, and understand as if they were there. For example, you can tell someone you bought a "terrific new car." But if you say you bought a "beautiful, new blue Mustang with a grey interior, custom wheels, and an awesome stereo," you're *showing* your readers why you are so excited about your purchase.

If Johnston had simply stated his dominant impression (that the young Joey Smallwood was awed by the sight of the sealers frozen on the ice pans) with no examples or details to support his statement, he would only be *telling* his readers how the narrator felt. Instead, he shows them. His sensory details demonstrate his main point.

5. ***Organize your description so that your readers can easily follow it.*** Most descriptions are organized from general to particular (from main idea to details), from particular to general (from details to main idea), or spatially (from top to bottom or left to right). Because the organization of your essay often depends on your point of view, you should choose a specific perspective from which to write your description. If your description jumps around your house, referring to a picture on the wall in your bedroom, then to the refrigerator in the kitchen, and next to the quilt on your bed, your readers are likely to become confused and disoriented. They will not be able to follow you. If, however, you move from room to room in a logical way, your audience will be able to stay with you. In fact, your vision will become their vision.

   Johnston organizes his description so that the narrator becomes a stand-in for the reader, looking through the porthole in the same way that the reader is looking into the pages of the book. The narrator becomes a guide for the reader, telling us exactly what to think, but also what to feel. The seal hunt has been the subject of much controversy throughout the world, and this description gives a sympathetic look at a group of men who are not often seen this way. They become real and honest and noble, even as "statuary" frozen on the ice pans of Newfoundland.

WRITING YOUR OWN DESCRIPTION ESSAY

What direct encounters have you had with nature? What are some of the details of these encounters? Was your general impression good or bad? Write an essay describing one of these encounters. Describe your experience through the senses, following the guidelines for writing a description essay. Remember to show rather than tell your readers about your memory. Begin by reviewing your prewriting notes. Then choose your dominant impression, and put it into a thesis statement.

A STUDENT'S DESCRIPTION ESSAY

In an essay about a fond memory, a student named Abby Reed reminisces about her grandfather. As you read this draft, ask yourself what dominant impression Abby is trying to communicate to her readers.

Grandma's House

My grandma lives in the country, near a large, blue lake and a small, green forest. I look forward to visiting her house. I think of my grandpa when I'm there. 1

Whenever I walk into my grandma's house, I always go directly to my grandpa's favourite room—the den. I am immediately reminded of my grandpa in this room. My grandma has a soft, brown sofa and a brown leather loveseat in this small, dark room, but all I see is the old, worn chair that was my grandpa's. The chair was re-covered in an itchy tweed fabric. I used to pretend to be asleep in his chair so my grandpa would gently lift me from the coarse fabric and place me on his lap. I would lie there even though I wasn't sleeping and enjoy the warmth of his body. I remember the times I sat on his sturdy lap in that chair while he read *One Fish, Two Fish, Red Fish, Blue Fish* or *The Cat in the Hat* in his deep voice. 2

Now when I sit in his chair, I look on the mantel and see an old Air Force picture of my grandpa and three of his Air Force buddies. They are all dressed in informal flight clothes and are standing in front of a World War II airplane. Next to this picture is a single portrait of my grandpa when he was 70. This picture represents the way I still see him in my mind. His grey hair is thin, his face has light brown sun spots on it that show his years of working outdoors. His gentle, light blue eyes sparkle in a way that usually meant he was up to something mischievous. But most of all. I love looking at his smile. The right side of his mouth always turned slightly downward, but it is a smile that I would give anything to see in person just one more time. 3

I also love to play with the pipe stand that sits on the table next to my grandpa's chair. I like the worn feeling of the pipe. It once was rough with ridges but is now smooth from use. When I quietly pick up his pipe and smell the sweet tobacco that was once housed in its shell, I think of all the times I knew my grandpa were near me because of this same aroma. 4

I have wonderful memories of my grandpa. When I go to my grandma's house, I can sit in my grandpa's old chair in my grandpa's favourite room and reminisce about all the times I felt safe when my grandpa was near. I will always treasure this one tiny room, with its smells from the past and its picture of my grandpa smiling. 5

Discovering How the Essay Works

1. This essay creates a certain mood. What is the dominant impression that Abby creates?

____

2. Is this description primarily subjective or objective? Explain your answer.

   ____

   ____

3. In this particular essay, the student writer describes her subjects mainly through the sense of sight, with a few references to hearing, touching, and smelling. Find at least one example of each of these senses in this essay.

   Seeing: ______________________________________

   Hearing: _____________________________________

   Touching: ____________________________________

   Smelling: ____________________________________

4. Abby works hard in this essay to show rather than tell us what she sees in the house. List three details that go beyond telling to show us what she observes.

   ____

   ____

   ____

5. How does Abby organize her essay? List the topics of each of her body paragraphs, and then identify her method of organization.

   ____

   ____

   ____

   Method of Organization: ______________________

REVISING AND EDITING THE STUDENT ESSAY

This essay is Abby's first draft, which now needs to be revised and edited. First, apply the Revising Checklist from the inside front cover to the content of Abby's draft. When you are satisfied that her ideas are fully developed and well organized, use the Editing Checklist in the inside back cover to correct her grammar and punctuation errors. Answer the questions below. Then write your suggested changes directly on Abby's draft.

Revision Questions

Thesis Statement

1. Put brackets around the last sentence in Abby's introduction. Does it contain her dominant impression?

   ____

2. Rewrite Abby's thesis statement if necessary so that it states her dominant impression as clearly as possible.

   ____

   ____

Basic Elements

1. Give Abby's essay an alternative title.

   ____

2. Rewrite Abby's introduction so that it captures the reader's attention and builds up to the thesis statement at the end of the paragraph.

   ____

   ____

   ____

   ____

3. Does each of Abby's body paragraphs deal with only one topic?

   ____

4. Rewrite Abby's conclusion, using at least one suggestion from Part I.

   ____

   ____

   ____

   ____

Development

1. Write out Abby's thesis statement (revised, if necessary), and list her three topic sentences below it.

Thesis statement: ____

____

Topic 1: ____

____

Topic 2: ____

____

Topic 3: ____

____

2. Do Abby's topics adequately support her thesis statement?

____

3. Does each body paragraph have a focused topic sentence?

____

4. Does the essay draw on all five senses?

____

5. Add at least one detail to Abby's essay that refers to a new sense. Label the detail you are adding.

   Sense: ____________________ Detail: ____________________

6. In what way does Abby's essay *show* rather than *tell* her readers about her memories of her grandfather?

____

____

Unity

1. Read each of Abby's topic sentences with her thesis statement (revised, if necessary) in mind. Do they go together?

____

2. Revise them if necessary so they are directly related.

3. Drop or rewrite any of the sentences in her body paragraphs that are not directly related to their topic sentences.

Organization

1. Read Abby's essay again to see if all the paragraphs are arranged logically.
2. Move any paragraphs that are out of order.
3. Look closely at Abby's body paragraphs to see if all her sentences are arranged logically within paragraphs.
4. Move any sentences that are out of order.

Coherence

1. Circle five transitions Abby uses.
2. Explain how two of these make Abby's essay easier to read.

For a list of transitions, see pages 85–86.

____

____

Now rewrite Abby's essay with your revisions.

Editing Questions

Sentences

Subjects and Verbs

1. Underline the subjects once and verbs twice in paragraphs 3 and 4 of your revision of Abby's essay. Remember that sentences can have more than one subject–verb set.

For help with subjects and verbs, see Chapter 23.

2. Does each sentence have at least one subject and verb that can stand alone?

____

3. Did you find and correct Abby's fragment? If not, find and correct it now.

For help with fragments, see Chapter 24.

4. Did you find and correct Abby's run-on sentence? If not, find and correct it now.

For help with run-ons, see Chapter 25.

Subject–Verb Agreement

1. Read aloud the subjects and verbs you underlined in your revision of Abby's essay.
2. Did you find and correct the subject and verb that do not agree?

For help with subject–verb agreement, see Chapter 27.

____

Pronoun Agreement

1. Find any pronouns in your revision of Abby's essay that do not agree with their nouns.
2. Correct any pronouns that do not agree with their nouns.

For help with pronoun agreement, see Chapter 30.

Modifiers

For help with modifier errors, see Chapter 33.

1. Find any modifiers in your revision of Abby's essay that are not as close as possible to the words they modify.
2. Rewrite sentences if necessary so that modifiers are as close as possible to the words they modify.

Punctuation and Mechanics

Punctuation

For help with punctuation, see Chapters 34–37.

1. Read your revision of Abby's essay for any errors in punctuation.
2. Find the fragment and the run-on sentence you revised, and make sure they are punctuated correctly.

Mechanics

For help with capitalization, see Chapter 38.

1. Read your revision of Abby's essay for any errors in capitalization.
2. Be sure to check Abby's capitalization in the fragment and run-on sentence you revised.

Word Choice and Spelling

Word Choice

For help with confused words, see Chapter 44.

1. Find any words used incorrectly in your revision of Abby's essay.
2. Correct any errors you find.

Spelling

For help with spelling, see Chapter 45.

1. Use spell-check and a dictionary to check the spelling in your revision of Abby's essay.
2. Correct any misspelled words.

Now rewrite Abby's essay again with your editing corrections.

REVISING AND EDITING YOUR OWN DESCRIPTION ESSAY

If you return to the description you wrote earlier in this chapter, you are now ready to revise and edit your own writing. Remember that revision involves reworking the content and organization of your essay, while editing asks you to check your grammar and usage. At this stage, you should repeat these processes over and over until you feel you have a draft that says exactly what you want it to say.

The checklists on the inside front and back covers will help you apply what you have learned in this chapter to your own essay.

WRITING CRITICALLY

As you begin to rework your essay, use the same technique you did in your reading. Just as you made personal associations with your reading to help you understand what the author was saying, expand your own writing with personal associations and sensory details that will help your readers understand your experience as if they were there. Work first with the content, making sure your thoughts are fully developed and organized effectively, before you start correcting your grammar and usage errors.

PRACTISING DESCRIPTION: FROM READING TO WRITING

Reading Workshop

Here are two essays that demonstrate good descriptive writing. The first essay, "Underground Toronto," was written by journalist Allen Abel. In it, he describes the diverse makeup of Toronto, as seen from its subway system. The second piece, "Dryden's Backyard," was written by Ken Dryden, ex-NHL goalie and current Member of Parliament. He describes playing hockey in his backyard as a child.

ALLEN ABEL
Underground Toronto

Focusing Your Attention

1. Think of a place you have lived in or visited that has special meaning for you. Where was this place? Why was it special?
2. In the essay you are about to read, the author describes the sights, sounds, smells, tastes, and textures of the Toronto subway. What sights, sounds, smells, textures, and tastes do you remember of the place you have lived in or visited? Can you describe that place for someone who has never been there?

Expanding Your Vocabulary

The following words are important to your understanding of this essay:

archipelago: a large group of islands (paragraph 6)
bilious: sickly (paragraph 7)

Chinese *erhu*: two-stringed fiddle (paragraph 8)
reveries: dreams (paragraph 9)
patrician: aristocratic (paragraph 12)
deduce: conclude (paragraph 20)
utilitarian: plain, practical (paragraph 21)
evocative: bringing to mind, calling to mind (paragraph 22)

READING CRITICALLY

As you learned at the beginning of this chapter, you should practise making connections with your reading by writing personal associations in the margins of this essay. Jot down anything that comes to mind. These notes will put your individual stamp on the essay with a set of memories that only you can recall. They will also help you understand the essay on an analytical level. Share your notes with someone in the class.

ALLEN ABEL

Underground Toronto

1 The slow train to China—and to Poland, Korea, Barbados, Greece, Peru and the Azores—slides with a screech from a fluorescent terminus, northbound on a weekday noon.

2 With me in the long, steel car are about 70 other passengers, most of them immigrants like me, strangers to each other and to this country, each of us making up less than a millionth of the great lakeside city beneath which we ride.

3 The car is rather crowded, yet nearly all of us today are riding alone. We are solitary travellers on a two-dollar, round-the-world ticket, our skins and stories far more colourful than the tired, tiled stations through which we pass.

4 I look at the faces around me, and I wonder—who has just landed the job of her dreams, and who has been let go? Who is newest to this cold, flat city, farthest from his home, farthest from her children, closest to a dream? Who is speeding toward a secret love affair, and who is running away?

5 But this is the subway. I keep my precious seat, flip through my paper, count off the stations and dare not ask. And no one asks me.

6 What are we doing as we stutter from stop to stop, and from nation to nation, below Toronto's ethnic archipelago? Drinking chocolate milk, studying *Parts of Speech* and the senior volleyball schedule of the Public School Girls Athletic Association, making a quick phone call when the train leaps from its tunnel for a two-stop breath of air. Or we are reading: Robert Heinlein, Ian McEwan, Mary Higgins Clark; *The Toronto Star*,

The Globe and Mail, The Korea Times; Memoirs of a Geisha, The Wandering Fire, Introduction to Microsoft Exchange Server, Your Wedding File, Steps to Christ.

The stations slip past in a blur of billboards: Jennifer Lopez's Still perfume, the ESP Psychic Expo, Parasuco Jeans. After a quarter-century on these trains, I need only glimpse the station walls for an instant to know exactly where we are: the brown bricks at King Street; the bilious green of Dundas; the murals of the Maple Leafs and Canadiens at College, where big-league hockey was played (at least by the visitors) for nearly 70 years. 7

Then suddenly, amid the bustle of the transfer point, where the two main lines meet at Bloor and Yonge streets, there is music—a two-stringed Chinese *erhu*, haunting and high-pitched above the rumbling and squealing of the trains—crying out a melody familiar, I suspect, to half the people in my car. 8

For me, this accidental concerto conjures other well-remembered reveries: standing stock-still amid the rush-hour madness at Union Station one winter morning, my eyes welling as a brilliant Russian violinist played the sweet, sad "Meditation" from Massenet's *Thaïs*; a guitarist at the Bay Street station one spring night singing Hank Williams' "I Saw the Light" with such joy and spirit that I had to run to phone the woman I loved. 9

If this is your city, every stop of every ride returns a memory. (The dentist's office at Davisville? A court date at Osgoode?) If it is not, then each opening of the doors invites the explorer to exit and taste what lies above. 10

So get out: 11

At patrician Rosedale, a neighbourhood so eager for its magnificence to be envied that it pulls the tracks out of the darkness and into the sun. 12

Or at Eglinton, where the smell of cinnamon buns from the bakery upstairs fills the cars with longing. 13

Or change trains with me at Bloor and Yonge, and head westward, just five stations, to another world—to Christie Street for a Korean lunch and the scorching stone bowl of rice and vegetables and chili paste that is known as bee-bim-bap. 14

For dessert, we can buy a bag of walnut cakes, tiny delights filled with sweet, creamy paste and baked on a long conveyor belt that passes through an oven imported, like almost everyone who gets off the train at Christie, from South Korea. 15

Then back on the subway: 16

"I'm hungry and you send me flowers. I cannot eat the iris." 17

"I wish I could walk around with my shirt off and feel comfortable." 18

I'm looking up at the advertising posters now and two quotations that face each other across the car. One is poetry ("Say It with Flowers" by Janice Kulyk Keefer) and the other is a placard for a hard-rock radio station that calls itself "The Edge." 19

I'll let you deduce which one is which. 20

Otherwise, there's not that much to see. There is no confusing Toronto's utilitarian tube with the grandeur of the Moscow subway, with its chandeliers and marble halls, or the silver-bullet rocketry of Hong Kong or the avant-garde (circa 1966) artistry of the Montréal Métro. Canada's oldest underground has been conveying commuters since 1954, which makes it far older than Toronto's new-found fascination with itself. 21

Newer stations such as Yorkdale, with an overarching rainbow of neon, and Eglinton West, with its giant murals of Toronto's beloved streetcars, offer some visual relief. There 22 are a few open-cut stretches, including a simultaneous vista of the Davisville yards and Mount Pleasant Cemetery, allowing us to see the eventual destination of both the cars and the people who ride in them. But the evocative elevated tracks of my New York City childhood exist only on a rapid-transit branch line in the far northeastern suburbs. To wreak havoc on Toronto rapid transit, King Kong would have to ride all the way out to Scarborough and change trains at Kennedy Station.

23 This hardly matters—the passengers provide fascination enough. The racial and linguistic diversity is astonishing, especially at the extremities of the long east-west line, where the tracks stab deeply into the low-rent, high-rise immigrant quarters that orbit the city's leafy European core. Fittingly, the map of the system closely resembles the Chinese character for "world."

24 It is up to each rider to decide what part of that world he or she wants to devour. Korean bee-bim-bap at Christie or Greek souvlaki at Pape. Polish tripe soup at Dundas West or Portuguese pork and clams at Ossington. Don Mills or York Mills; High Park or Queen's Park; St. George or St. Clair or St. Patrick.

25 Nowhere in the world does a two-dollar ticket offer such an amazing array. But there is one other station that the system serves. It is the most important destination of all, no matter where we board our train, no matter how long we ride.

26 And that's the stop called Home.

Thinking Critically About Content

1. The article contains several metaphors. To what does the author compare the Toronto subway? What other metaphors can you find?
2. List as many sensory details as you can from the essay, including seeing, hearing, touching, feeling, smelling, and tasting.
3. How does the author capture the essence of Toronto without actually describing the city?

Thinking Critically About Purpose and Audience

4. What dominant impression does the author have of the city he describes? Does it sound like another city you have visited in Canada? How is it similar? How is it different?
5. Do you think it is necessary to have visited Toronto to enjoy the essay? Why or why not?
6. How does the author use figurative language in this essay?

Thinking Critically About Essays

7. If an essay is unified, all of its paragraphs are related to one central idea. Based on this explanation, is this essay unified? Explain your answer.
8. How does Abel organize his ideas and observations in this essay? (Refer to pages 57–67 for information on essay organization.) Make a rough outline of this essay.

9. The organization of this essay follows a journey Abel makes in the train. Many literary works (*The Adventures of Huckleberry Finn*, for example) follow the same pattern. How is this journey pattern effective in this essay?
10. Abel ends his essay with the words "And that's the stop called Home." Is he referring literally to the stop where he is going to exit the train, or does he mean something more? What might he be trying to say? Explain your answer.

KEN DRYDEN
Dryden's Backyard

Focusing Your Attention

1. Think of a place where you played as a child. Does thinking about that place evoke your childhood for you? In what way?
2. In the essay you are about to read, the author describes the feeling of playing hockey as a boy in his family's backyard. He remembers that as a child he really became the hockey heroes of his day, rather than thinking he would ever be one of them. Have you watched young children play? What kind of future life do they seem to imagine in their play?

Expanding Your Vocabulary

The following words are important to your understanding of this essay:

agility: nimbleness, quickness (paragraph 4)
"billy" boots: rubber boots (paragraph 4)
duffel coat: a hooded winter cloth coat with toggles for buttons (paragraph 12)
euphoria: a state of elation, a high (paragraph 14)
unseverable: unbreakable (paragraph 16)

READING CRITICALLY

As you did with the previous essay, write any personal associations you make with this essay in the margins as you read. This process will give you some good insights into the author's approach to his topic and into his methods of developing his ideas. Write down anything at all that occurs to you. Then share your notes with one of your classmates.

KEN DRYDEN
Dryden's Backyard

1 I get out of bed and pull back the curtains. It has snowed overnight and traces are still gently falling. For several minutes I stand there, my forehead pressed to the window, watching the snow, looking out at the backyards of the houses behind, where the Pritchards, the McLarens, and the Carpenters lived, and down below at the winter's depth of snow, and at the backyard where I spent my childhood.

2 "Dryden's Backyard." That's what it was called in our neighbourhood. It was more than 70 feet long, paved curiously in red asphalt, 45 feet wide at "the big end," gradually narrowing to 35 feet at the flower bed, to 25 feet at the porch—our center line—to 15 feet at "the small end." While Steve Shutt and Guy Lafleur were in Willowdale and Thurso on backyard rinks their fathers built, while Larry Robinson was on a frozen stream in Marvelville and Réjean Houle on a road in Rouyn under the only street light that his street had, I was here.

3 It was an extraordinary place, like the first swimming pool on the block, except there were no others like it anywhere. Kids would come from many blocks away to play, mostly "the big guys," friends of my brother, a year or two older than him, seven or eight years older than me. But that was never a problem. It was the first rule of the backyard that they had to let me play. To a friend who complained one day, Dave said simply, "If Ken doesn't play, you don't play."

4 We played "ball hockey" mostly, with a tennis ball, its bounce deadened by the cold. A few times, we got out a garden hose and flooded the backyard to use skates and pucks, but the big end was slightly lower than the small end, and the water pooled and froze unevenly. More important, we found that the more literal we tried to make our games, the less lifelike they became. We could move across the asphalt quickly and with great agility in rubber "billy" boots; we could shoot a tennis ball high and hard. But with skates on, with a puck, we were just kids. So after the first few weeks of the first year, we played only ball hockey.

5 Depending on the day, the time, the weather, there might be any number of kids wanting to play, so we made up games any number could play. With four and less than nine, we played regular games, the first team scoring ten goals the winner. The two best players, who seemed always to know who they were, picked the teams and decided on ends. First choice of players got second choice of ends, and because the size of the big end made it more fun to play in, the small end was the choice to defend. Each team had a goalie—one with goalie pads, a catching glove, and a goalie stick; the other with only a baseball glove and a forward's stick. When we had more than eight players, we divided into three or more teams for a round-robin tournament, each game to five. With fewer than four, it was more difficult. Sometimes we attempted a regular game, often we just played "shots," each player being both shooter and goalie, standing in front of one net, shooting in turn at the other. Most often, however, we played "penalty shots."

6 In the late 1950s, the CBS network televised NHL games on Saturday afternoon. Before each game, there was a preview show in which a player from each of the

teams involved that day would compete in two contests, one of which was a penalty-shot contest. The goalie they used each week was an assistant trainer for the Detroit Red Wings named Julian Klymquiw. Short and left-handed, Klymquiw wore a clear plexiglass mask that arched in front of his face like a shield. None of us had ever heard of him, and his unlikely name made us a little doubtful at first. But it turned out that he was quite good, and most weeks he stopped the great majority of shots taken at him. So, during backyard games of "penalty shots," we pretended to be Julian Klymquiw, not Terry Sawchuk or Glenn Hall. And before each of our contests began, we would perform the ritual that Klymquiw and announcer Bud Palmer performed each week:

"Are you ready, Julian?" 7

"Yes, Bud." 8

But the backyard also meant time alone. It was usually after dinner when the 9
"big guys" had homework to do and I would turn on the floodlights at either end of the house and on the porch, and play. It was a private game. I would stand alone in the middle of the yard, a stick in my hands, a tennis ball in front of me, silent, still, then suddenly dash ahead, stickhandling furiously, dodging invisible obstacles for a shot on net. It was Maple Leaf Gardens filled to wildly cheering capacity, a tie game, seconds remaining. I was Frank Mahovlich, or Gordie Howe, I was anyone I wanted to be, and the voice in my head was that of Leafs broadcaster Foster Hewitt: ". . . there's ten seconds left, Mahovlich, winding up at his own line, at center, eight seconds, seven, over the blueline, six—he winds up, he shoots, *he scores!*" The mesh that had been tied to the bottoms of our red metal goalposts until frozen in the ice had been ripped away to hang loose from the crossbars, whipped back like a flag in a stiff breeze. My arms and stick flew into the air, I screamed a scream inside my head, and collected my ball to do it again—many times, for many minutes, the hero of all my own games.

It was a glorious fantasy, and I always heard that voice. It was what made my fan- 10
tasy seem almost real. For to us, who attended hockey games mostly on TV or radio, an NHL game, a Leafs game, was played with a voice. If I wanted to be Mahovlich or Howe, if I moved my body the way I had seen them move theirs and did nothing else, it would never quite work. But if I heard the voice that said their names while I was playing out that fantasy, I could believe it. Foster Hewitt could make me them.

My friends and I played every day after school, sometimes during lunch and 11
after dinner, but Saturday was always the big day. I would go to bed Friday night thinking of Saturday, waking up early, with none of the fuzziness I had other days. If it had snowed overnight, Dave and I, with shovels and scrapers, and soon joined by others, would pile the snow into flower beds or high against the back of the garage. Then at 9 a.m. the games would begin.

There was one team in the big end, another in the small; third and fourth teams 12
sat like birds on a telephone wire, waiting their turn on the wall that separated the big end from Carpenter's backyard. Each team wore uniforms identical to the other. It was the Canadian midwinter uniform of the time—long, heavy duffel coats in browns, grays, or blues; toques in NHL team colors, pulled snug over ears under the

watchful eye of mothers, here rolled up in some distinctive personal style; leather gloves, last year's church gloves, now curling at the wrist and separating between fingers; black rubber "billy" boots over layers of heavy woollen socks for fit, the tops rolled down like "low cuts" for speed and style.

13 Each game would begin with a faceoff, then wouldn't stop again. Action moved quickly end to end, the ball bouncing and rolling, chased by a hacking, slashing scrum of sticks. We had sticks without tops on their blades—"toothpicks"; sticks with no blades at all—"stubs." They broke piece by heart-breaking piece, often quickly, but still we used them. Only at the start of a season, at Christmas (Dave and I routinely exchanged sticks until one year he gave me a stick and I gave him a pair of socks) and once or twice more, would we get new ones. All except John Stedelbauer. His father owned a car dealership and during the hockey season gave away hockey sticks to his customers as a promotion. Stedelbauer got all the new sticks he needed, fortunately, as they weren't very good. One year he broke nineteen of them.

14 A goal would be scored, then another, and slowly the game would leapfrog to five. Bodies grew warm from exertion, fingers and toes went numb; noses ran, wiped by unconscious sleeves; coats loosened, toques fell off; steam puffed from mouths and streamed from toqueless heads. Sticks hacked and slashed; tennis balls stung. But in the euphoria of the game, the pain disappeared. Sitting on the wall that overlooked his backyard, Rick "Foster" Carpenter, younger and not very athletic, gave the play-by-play, but no one listened. Each of us had his own private game playing in his head. A fourth goal, then a fifth, a cheer, and the first game was over. Quickly, four duffel coats, four toques, four pairs of weathered gloves and rubber "billy" boots would jump from the wall to replace the losers; and the second game would begin. We paused at noon while some went home and others ate the lunch that they had brought with them. At 6 p.m. the two or three who remained would leave. Eighteen hours later, after church, the next game would begin.

15 When I think of the backyard, I think of my childhood; and when I think of my childhood, I think of the backyard. It is the central image I have of that time, linking as it does all of its parts: father, mother, sister, friends; hockey, baseball, and Dave—big brother, idol, mentor, defender, and best friend. Yet it lasted only a few years. Dave was already twelve when the backyard was built; I was six. He and his friends played for three or four years, then stopped; I played longer but, without them, less often. Yet until moments ago, I had never remembered that.

16 The backyard was not a training ground. In all the time I spent there, I don't remember ever thinking I would be an NHL goalie, or even hoping I could be one. In backyard games, I dreamed I *was* Sawchuk or Hall, Mahovlich or Howe; I never dreamed I would be like them. There seemed no connection between the backyard and Maple Leaf Gardens; there seemed no way to get to there from here. If we ever thought about that, it never concerned us; we just played. It was here in the backyard that we *learned* hockey. It was here we got close to it, we got *inside* it, and it got inside us. It was here that our inextricable bond with the game was made. Many years have now passed, the game has grown up and been complicated by things outside it, yet still the backyard remains—untouched, unchanged, my unseverable link to that time, and that game.

Thinking Critically About Content

1. In paragraph 3, Dryden says that his backyard was "like the first swimming pool." In what way does the backyard resemble "the first swimming pool" on the block? Explain your answer.
2. List as many sensory details as you can from the essay, including details of what the narrator is seeing, hearing, touching, feeling, smelling, and tasting.
3. What role does "the voice" play in Dryden's childhood fantasy world? Explain your answer.

Thinking Critically About Purpose and Audience

4. What dominant impression does the author create in this description? Explain your answer in detail.
5. Who do you think Dryden's primary audience is?
6. Do the examples Dryden uses evoke memories of the games you played growing up? What details in the essay sound most like your own childhood?

Thinking Critically About Essays

7. If an essay is unified, all of its paragraphs are related to one central idea. Based on this explanation, is this essay unified? Explain your answer.
8. How does Dryden organize his ideas and observations in this essay? (Refer to pages 57–67 for information on essay organization.) Make a rough outline of this essay.
9. The essay begins with Dryden looking out the window at his old backyard as an adult. How does the window function metaphorically in the essay? How does the atmosphere he describes at the start help in the look backward at his childhood?
10. Dryden ends his essay with the words "yet still the backyard remains." He has ended the essay physically where he started, but now he is referring to something that is inside him, and inside all Canadians. What is the effect of this change from external to internal in this essay? Explain your answer in detail.

Writing Workshop

This final section gives you opportunities to apply what you have learned in this chapter to another writing assignment. This time, we provide very little prompting beyond a summary of the guidelines for writing a description essay. This section will let you demonstrate that you can go through the entire writing process on your own with only occasional feedback from your peers. Loop back into the chapter as necessary when you have questions, so that this process becomes as automatic to you as possible before you move on to new material. Then pause at the end of the chapter to reflect briefly on what you have learned.

Guidelines for Writing a Description Essay

1. Decide on a dominant impression—the feeling or mood you want to communicate.
2. Decide how much of your description should be objective (factual) and how much should be subjective (personal reactions).
3. Draw on your five senses to write a good description.
4. When you describe, try to *show* rather than *tell* your readers what you want them to know.
5. Organize your description so that your readers can easily follow it.

Writing About Your Reading

1. In the first descriptive essay, Allen Abel draws on impressions from all the senses to describe the Toronto underground. Think of a place that is very important to you, a place that is a part of your life now or that was a part of your life in the past. Write a description of that place, drawing on as many of the senses as possible—seeing, hearing, touching, smelling, and tasting—so that your reader can experience it the way you did.
2. How well suited to you is the place where you live now? Write a description of the features of your house or apartment that make it most suitable or unsuitable for you.
3. What do you think are the most important features of a good description? Why are they important? What effect do they have on you?

Writing About Your World

1. Place yourself in the scene above, and describe it in as much detail as possible. Imagine that you can see, hear, touch, smell, and taste everything in this picture. What are your sensations? How do you feel? Before you begin to write, decide on the dominant impression you want to convey. Then choose your details carefully.
2. Describe for your classmates a class environment that is ideal for you. What kind of classroom atmosphere makes you thrive? What should the people in your class understand about you as a student? What kind of instructor brings out the best in you? Why?
3. A national travel magazine is asking for honest descriptions (positive or negative) of places people have visited. They are offering $100 to the writers of the essays chosen for publication. You may decide to write about a place with a marvellous beach or about an absolutely awful hotel. In either case, remember to begin with the dominant impression you want to create.
4. Create your own description assignment (with the help of your instructor), and write a response to it.

Revising

Small Group Activity (5–10 minutes per writer) Working in groups of three or four, each person should read his or her description essay to the other members of the group. Those listening should record their reactions on a copy of the Peer Evaluation Form in Appendix 1A. After your group goes through this process, give your evaluation forms to the appropriate writers so that each writer has two or three peer comment sheets for revising.

Paired Activity (5 minutes per writer) Using the completed Peer Evaluation Forms, work in pairs to decide what you should revise in your essay. If time allows, rewrite some of your sentences, and have your partner look at them.

Individual Activity Rewrite your paper, using the revising feedback you received from other students.

Editing

Paired Activity (5–10 minutes per writer) Swap papers with a classmate, and use the editing portion of your Peer Evaluation Form (Appendix 1B) to identify as many grammar, punctuation, mechanics, and spelling errors as you can. If time allows, correct some of your errors, and have your partner look at them. Record your grammar, punctuation, and mechanics errors in the Error Log (Appendix 3) and your spelling errors in the Spelling Log (Appendix 4).

Individual Activity Rewrite your paper again, using the editing feedback you received from other students.

CHAPTER

9

Narrating

There are things to confess that enrich the world, and things that need not be said.

—Joni Mitchell

Because we are constantly telling other people about various events in our lives, we all know how to use narration. Think of how many times a day you tell someone about an event that happened to you: your accident on the way to school; the conversation you had at the bus stop yesterday; your strange experience at the restaurant last night. Narration is an essential part of all of our lives. In fact, stories can teach us how to live our lives.

Narration also plays an important role in our writing. Think about how many times we tell a story when we write—in our personal lives, in classes, and at work:

You tell a friend in an email how you met the person you're now dating.

On a history exam, a student summarizes the chain of events that led to Newfoundland joining Confederation.

A student summarizes a short story in an English class.

An emergency medical technician gives an account of her 911 calls for the day.

A supervisor writes a report explaining an employee's accident on the job.

Narration, or storytelling, is an interesting way of getting someone's attention by sharing thoughts or experiences. Like description, narration is sometimes used as an end in itself (for example, when you tell a friend a joke or the plot of a movie). But very often it's used in conjunction with explaining or persuading. You might start a term paper analyzing drug abuse, for example, with a brief story of one addict's life. Basically, people use storytelling to help focus their readers' or listeners' attention.

READING AND WRITING A NARRATION ESSAY

Learning how to read narration essays critically gives you insight into the writing process in this particular rhetorical mode. Narration represents a way of thinking that you need to master so that you can use it in both your reading and writing. Approaching narration critically helps you raise your level of communication and function more successfully in college and in life. In this chapter, you will see again how the processes of reading and writing complement each other to form a whole. If you learn how to work with the author of a narration essay to understand how he or she makes meaning, your insights will transfer naturally to your writing so that you will also be improving your writing ability.

Reading a Narration Essay

Jane Maher, who teaches in New York City, wrote the following autobiographical essay to help her come to terms with the loss of her father. Can you think of an event that taught you something important about life? What was the event? What did you learn?

READING CRITICALLY

As we read and make meaning out of the author's words, we put a string of words together on a literal level, bring in any implications the author suggests, think about how the ideas relate to one another, and keep the process going until the entire essay makes sense. These are focused thoughts that will help you process the author's writing. On another level, however, we also stray from the essay in a wide variety of ways—thinking about chores we need to do, calls we forgot to return, and events we are looking forward to on the weekend. These are random ideas that are only loosely related to the reading. As you might suspect, focused reading is the most productive, but you can even teach yourself to apply your random ideas toward a better understanding of your reading material. As you read this selection, stop and "think aloud" about what is on your mind throughout the text. Point out places that are confusing to you, connections that you make, specific questions you have, related information you know, and personal experiences you associate with the text. In this way, you are letting others hear what your mind does (both focused and random) as you read.

JANE MAHER
Girl

I don't remember exactly when I began to be offended when my father called me, or other girls or women, "girl." I guess he always did it; at least I don't remember him ever not doing it. He'd often use it as a term of affection: "How's my girl today?" But just as often, he'd use it carelessly or callously, the way some men use the expression "sweetie." "Listen, girl," my father would say, "I make the rules around here." 1

Women, girls, were perceived by my father as less than men: less important, less intelligent, less capable, less in need of education or direction. In fact, for a long period of my life, I was so indoctrinated by my father's views, and by society's confirmation of those views, that I agreed with him. 2

But as I grew older, the term "girl" began to hurt me and make me angry. As my father became aware of my strong and growing aversion to the word, he'd use it even more often. "What's the matter," he'd ask. "You don't like it anymore when your old man calls you girl? You're my daughter; I'll call you whatever I want." Or he'd ask my mother, pretending I wasn't in the room, "What kind of daughter did you raise that she wants to become a man? Is she ashamed to be a girl?" The word took on stronger and stronger connotations for me as I began to realize how permanently, and adversely, my father's attitudes had affected my life. I had been sent to an all-girls commercial high school. "Listen, girl," my father declared, "as long as you know typing and stenography, you'll never starve." College was not mentioned very much in our house. I was one of three daughters. If one of us had a date, my father would tell my mother to remind us "what can happen to a girl if she's not careful." When I got married, I heard my father joking with my uncle: "One down, two to go." We were objects to be dispensed with, burdens of no conceivable use to him. 3

This does not mean that he did not love us or care for us; for my entire childhood, he worked two jobs so that he could afford to send us away to the country every summer. But it was the terms upon which he loved and cared for us which were so distressing to me. Nor did I always get angry when he used the term. When my first daughter was born, he arrived at the hospital carrying a silver dollar he had saved in his collection for many years as a gift for her. "Now I've got four of you girls instead of three," he said, knowing that I knew at this special time he was only teasing and did not intend to hurt me. 4

I saw less and less of my father after I moved to Connecticut in 1980. He and my mother kept their house in Brooklyn but spent most of the winter months in Florida. Sometimes when I called on the phone, I could tell how happy he was to hear my voice. "Hey, girl, is that husband of yours taking as good care of you as I did?" But other times, over Thanksgiving dinner or while opening Christmas presents, he'd use the term as he had when I was young. "Girl, get me a little more coffee will you?" Or when I enrolled my daughter in an expensive private school: "Why spend money you don't have to, girl? She's just going to get married the way you did." I'd keep my countenance at those times; I had grown wise to my father—I wouldn't give him the satisfaction of showing my anger. That's not to say he didn't keep trying: "So now 5 you like it when your old man calls you girl, huh? You're finally getting wise to the fact that men aren't so bad to have around when you need something."

6 And I suspected that secretly he was proud of me. Soon after I got married, I returned to college, part-time, in the evening, and graduated magna cum laude. By then, both of my daughters were in school, so I earned my master's degree from Columbia University, again part-time. It was my father who picked up my daughters from the school bus stop on the day I took my comprehensive exam. When I began to teach part time at a local community college, my father asked my mother, again pretending I wasn't in the room, "if there was a girl around here who thought her father was going to start calling her Professor."

7 My father had always had a heart condition, exacerbated by twenty-two years as a New York City fireman, two packs of cigarettes a day, and my mother's delicious Italian cooking. When he suddenly became seriously ill, my mother got him home from Florida and into a hospital in Brooklyn in less than 24 hours. But it still wasn't soon enough. My father died before they could perform a triple bypass, and before I got to say goodbye to him.

8 I had left Connecticut at nine in the morning, intending to wait out the surgery with my mother and to be with my father when he awoke. Instead, when I arrived at the hospital, one of my sisters and my mother were in a small, curtained-off section of the intensive care unit being told by a busy, preoccupied young resident that my father had experienced very little discomfort before he died. It sounded too pat, too familiar, too convenient to me. I was overcome with the fear that my father had been alone that entire morning, that no one in that overcrowded municipal hospital had even known that he was dead until they arrived to prepare him for surgery.

9 They left us alone to say goodbye to him, but I was so concerned over my mother's anguish that I didn't take the time I should have to kiss him or even to touch his forehead. A nurse came in and suggested, gently, that it was time to leave. She was right, of course; another moment and my mother would have collapsed.

10 I thanked the nurse and asked her, nonchalantly, if she knew exactly when my father had died, secretly convinced that she didn't have an answer, that he had been alone all morning. "I didn't see him this morning," she replied, "but I'll get the nurse who did."

11 A young, pretty nurse appeared several minutes later. "My shift is over," she said, "but I was waiting around to see the family."

12 "Was he in pain?" my mother asked.

13 "No, not at all. He even teased me a bit. I remember his exact words. 'Go take care of the patients who need you, girl,' he said. 'I'm perfectly fine.'"

14 I wasn't exactly fine, but I have never felt more comforted in my life than when I heard that word.

PREPARING TO WRITE YOUR OWN NARRATION ESSAY

We have all learned important lessons from various events in our lives. Over time, we find that some lessons are more worthwhile than others. What events in your life have taught you important lessons? What lessons did you learn? Use one or more of the prewriting techniques you learned in Chapter 5 to gather your thoughts on these events.

Writing a Narration Essay

Narrating involves telling a story about an experience—one of yours or someone else's. When you write a narrative essay, you focus on a particular event and make a specific point about it. You should provide enough detail so that readers can understand as completely as possible what your experience was like. Here are some guidelines to help you make your narrative interesting.

1. ***Make sure your essay has a point.*** The most important feature of a narrative essay is that it makes a point. Simply recording your story step by step is a boring exercise for both writer and reader. Writing an account of your walk to class in the morning might not be particularly interesting. But the walk becomes interesting when something important or significant happens on the way. An event is significant if it helps both writer and reader understand something about themselves, about other people, or about the world we live in. If you can complete one of the following sentences, you will produce a focused narrative:

   This essay shows that . . .

   This essay teaches us that . . .

   In Jane Maher's essay, the narrator focuses on the pain she felt, growing up, when her father referred to her as a "girl." She thought the term was degrading until she understood, after he died, that it was really a term of endearment. Maher is able to communicate the process of growing up through her experience with this one word. Her essay teaches us that the relationship between words and emotions is complex.

2. ***Use the five* Ws *and one* H *to construct your story.*** The five *W*s and one *H* are the six questions—*Who? What? When? Where? Why?* and *How?*—that journalists use to make sure they cover all the basic information when they write a news story. These questions can help you come up with details and ideas for a well-developed narrative essay. You should make sure that your essay answers all of these questions in detail.

   When you look at Maher's narrative again, you can see that she covered the answers to all these questions:

   Who was involved? Maher, her father, her mother, and the nurses

What was the central problem? Maher was offended by her father's use of the word "girl."

When did this story take place? As Maher was growing up

Where were they? At home and in a hospital

Why was Maher offended? Because she thought the word "girl" was degrading to her as a person and to other females

How did the author learn from this event? She finally understood that her father's use of "girl" wasn't as offensive as she thought it was.

Since Maher covers all these basic details, the reader can appreciate her full story and understand its significance.

3. ***Develop your narrative with vivid details.*** Your readers will be able to imagine the events in your narrative essay if you provide them with specific details. In fact, the more specific your details, the more vivid your essay will become. These details should develop the ideas you generated with the six journalistic questions. At the same time, you should omit any irrelevant details that don't support your thesis statement.

   Look again at Maher's essay. In this narrative, the author provides many vivid details about the narrator: She is a girl whose father thinks girls are less important than boys; he calls her "girl"; this term starts to bother the narrator as she is growing up; she gets married and moves to Connecticut; she has two daughters; she gets her master's degree at Columbia University and starts teaching at a local community college; and her father dies of a heart attack. The amount of detail in Maher's essay helps us participate in her narrative.

4. ***Build excitement in your narrative with careful pacing.*** To be most effective, narration should prolong the exciting parts of a story and shorten the routine facts that simply move the reader from one episode to another. If you were robbed on your way to work, for example, a good narrative describing the incident would concentrate on the traumatic event itself rather than on such boring details as what you had for breakfast or what clothes you were wearing. One writer might say, "I fell and hurt myself this morning." A better writer would draw out the exciting parts: "As I was running to my English class this morning, I slipped on a patch of black ice and landed flat on my back beside a group of smokers huddled by the entrance." The details themselves tell the story.

   Maher reveals the details in her story through some of her father's quotations that bothered her: "Listen, girl, I make the rules around here"; "Listen, girl, as long as you know typing and stenography, you'll never starve." She feels frustrated and belittled by her father, even as an adult: "Hey, girl, is that husband of yours taking as good care of you as I did?" Finally, she works through the hurtfulness when her father dies. At this point, Maher draws out the search for the nurse who could tell her if her father died alone. The pacing of her story holds our interest throughout the essay.

5. ***Organize your narration so that your readers can easily follow it.*** Most narrative essays follow a series of actions through time, so they are organized chronologically, or according to a time sequence. Once you choose the details you will use, you should arrange them so that your story has a clear beginning, middle, and end. If you add clear, logical transitions, such as "then," "next," "at this point," and "suddenly," you will guide your readers smoothly through your essay from one event to the next.

   Jane Maher organizes her narrative chronologically. It moves through time from her childhood to going to high school to getting married and having a baby as her father raises her, retires, and grows old. In other words, the two main characters—Maher and her father—move through normal life events. Because it follows a logical time sequence and does not jump around, Maher's narrative is easy to follow. She guides her readers through her essay with such transitions as "in fact," "as I grew older," "when," "sometimes," and "soon."

WRITING YOUR OWN NARRATION ESSAY

Choose one of the events from your prewriting notes that taught you an important lesson in life, and write a narrative essay explaining this incident and the lesson you learned. Follow the guidelines in this chapter to develop your essay.

A STUDENT'S NARRATION ESSAY

In an essay about a dramatic incident, student writer Tommy Poulos tells a story that taught him an important lesson in life. Here is his first draft. As you read this paragraph, try to figure out what Tommy's main point is.

"My Brother"

My family and I lead a fairly quiet life. My parents go to work, and my brother and I go to school. We never make headlines with sports events or science fairs. We essentially live a normal, average life out of the spotlight. It was quite a shock, then, when a lot of attention was focused on our family. 1

My brother, Wayne, was driving on a highway that is nicknamed "The Death Loop." It got its name because it's a two-lane highway that loops around the city, and many people have died because of drivers who take too many chances and cause head-on collisions. One afternoon, Wayne saw a woman's car wrecked into a guardrail with her passenger side of the car completely smashed in. The driver's side was mangled, and my brother could tell the woman inside was in trouble. Wayne didn't think twice about running up to help them. She was badly injured, but my brother knew not to move her! 2

3 The woman had not been wearing her seat belt. Her car was too old to have an airbag. She had obviously hit her head because she had blood gushing from a gaping wound in her forehead. She was conscious, so my brother sat with her, trying to keep her calm and awake. He kept asking her questions like if she had any children? Two other cars stopped, and my brother remembers telling one man to call 911. Wayne stayed with the woman until the paramedics arrived.

4 Wayne left the scene after giving a statement to the police. Later, he heard from the local newspapers and news stations that his heroic actions had saved the woman. In these stories, the woman's husband said he believed his wife was still alive because she had a guardian angel keeping her awake. Even the paramedics said Wayne probably kept her alive. By keeping her awake. In public, Wayne acts very humble, but in private, he is loving the attention.

5 Now my brother is the local hero. Our house used to be quiet, but since Wayne's act of heroism, it's become Grand Central Station. Everyone wants to talk to Wayne. I'm happy for him. But most of all, I'm glad Wayne realizes the importance of seat belts. He used to be macho and say seat belts were too uncomfortable to wear. Now he won't leave the driveway until everyone has buckled their seat belts. Perhaps the woman will save Wayne's life as well.

Discovering How the Essay Works

1. All the details in Tommy's essay lead to one main point. What is that point?

2. Tommy covers all the journalistic questions in his essay. Record at least one detail he uses for each question:

____

____

Who? ______________________________

What? ______________________________

When? ______________________________

Where? ______________________________

Why? ______________________________

How? ______________________________

3. In your opinion, which two details of Tommy's are the most vivid? What makes them so vivid?

____

____

4. How does Tommy pace his essay to build excitement?

____

____

5. How does Tommy organize his essay? List the topic of each of his body paragraphs; then identify his method of organization.

   Paragraph 2: ____

   Paragraph 3: ____

   Paragraph 4: ____

   Method of Organization: ________________________________

REVISING AND EDITING THE STUDENT ESSAY

This essay is Tommy's first draft, which now needs to be revised and edited. First, apply the Revising Checklist (inside front cover) to the content of Tommy's draft. When you are satisfied that his ideas are fully developed and well organized, use the Editing Checklist (inside back cover) to correct his grammar and mechanics errors. Answer the questions below. Then write your suggested changes directly on Tommy's draft.

Revision Questions

Thesis Statement

1. Put brackets around the last sentence in Tommy's introduction. Does it contain his main point? Does it express his opinion about that point?

____

____

2. Rewrite Tommy's thesis statement if necessary so that it states his main point and an opinion about that main point.

____

____

Basic Elements

1. Give Tommy's essay an alternative title. Also drop the quotation marks, since original titles should not be in quotation marks.

____

____

____

2. Rewrite Tommy's introduction so that it captures the reader's attention and builds up to the thesis statement at the end of the paragraph.

____

____

____

3. Does each of Tommy's body paragraphs deal with just one topic?

____

____

____

4. Rewrite Tommy's conclusion, using at least one suggestion from Part I.

____

____

____

Development

1. Write out Tommy's thesis statement (revised, if necessary), and list his three topic sentences below it.

   Thesis statement: ______________________________

   ____

   Topic 1: ______________________________

   Topic 2: ______________________________

   Topic 3: ______________________________

2. Do Tommy's topics adequately support his thesis statement?

____

3. Does each body paragraph have a focused topic sentence?

 ____

4. Add more specific information to two of Tommy's supporting details.

5. Add two new details to Tommy's essay that support his main idea.

Unity

1. Read each of Tommy's topic sentences with his thesis statement (revised, if necessary) in mind. Do they go together?

 ____

2. Revise them if necessary so they are directly related.

3. Drop or rewrite any of the sentences in his body paragraphs that are not directly related to their topic sentences.

Organization

1. Read Tommy's essay again to see if all the paragraphs are arranged chronologically.
2. Move any paragraphs that are out of order.
3. Look closely at Tommy's body paragraphs to see if all his sentences are arranged logically within paragraphs.
4. Move any sentences that are out of order.

Coherence

1. Circle five words or phrases Tommy repeats.

2. Explain how two of these make Tommy's essay easier to read.

 ____

 ____

Now rewrite Tommy's essay with your revisions.

Editing Questions

Sentences

Subjects and Verbs

1. Underline the subjects once and verbs twice in paragraph 4 of your revision of Tommy's essay. Remember that sentences can have more than one subject–verb set.

For help with subjects and verbs, see Chapter 23.

2. Does each sentence have at least one subject and verb that can stand alone?

____

For help with fragments, see Chapter 24.

3. Did you find and correct Tommy's fragment? If not, find and correct it now.

Subject–Verb Agreement

For help with subject–verb agreement, see Chapter 27.

1. Read aloud the subjects and verbs you underlined in your revision of Tommy's essay.
2. Correct any subjects and verbs that do not agree with each other.

Pronoun Agreement

For help with pronoun agreement, see Chapter 30.

1. Find any pronouns in your revision of Tommy's essay that do not agree with their nouns.
2. Did you find and correct the two pronouns that do not agree with their nouns? If not, find and correct them now.

Modifiers

For help with modifier errors, see Chapter 33.

1. Find any modifiers in your revision of Tommy's essay that are not as close as possible to the words they modify.
2. Rewrite sentences if necessary so that modifiers are as close as possible to the words they modify.

Punctuation and Mechanics

Punctuation

For help with punctuation, see Chapters 34–37.

1. Read your revision of Tommy's essay for any errors in punctuation.
2. Find the fragment you revised, and make sure it is punctuated correctly.
3. Did you find and correct Tommy's two other punctuation errors?

Mechanics

For help with capitalization, see Chapter 38.

1. Read your revision of Tommy's essay for any errors in capitalization.
2. Be sure to check Tommy's capitalization in the fragment you revised.

Word Choice and Spelling

Word Choice

For help with confused words, see Chapter 44.

1. Find any words used incorrectly in your revision of Tommy's essay.
2. Correct any errors you find.

Spelling

1. Use spell-check and a dictionary to check the spelling in your revision of Tommy's essay.

For help with spelling, see Chapter 45.

2. Correct any misspelled words.

Now rewrite Tommy's essay again, including your editing corrections.

REVISING AND EDITING YOUR OWN NARRATION ESSAY

Returning to the narration essay you wrote earlier in this chapter, you are now ready to revise and edit your own writing. Remember that revision involves reworking the content and organization of your essay, while editing asks you to check your grammar and usage errors. At this stage, you should repeat these processes over and over until you feel you have a draft that says exactly what you want it to say.

The editing and revising checklists on the inside front and back covers will help you apply what you have learned in this chapter to your essay.

WRITING CRITICALLY

As you begin your revision, apply the reading strategy that you used earlier to your writing. Read your essay aloud, and interrupt your reading regularly to talk about the focused or random thoughts going on in your head. Add to your essay any new material from your "think aloud" that you believe your readers will need to help them more fully understand your logic. Fill out your thoughts, and move them around until they communicate your full message to your readers.

PRACTISING NARRATION: FROM READING TO WRITING

Reading Workshop

Here are two essays that illustrate good narrative writing: "The Worth of Women's Work," in which Nina Lee Colwill tells the story of her grandmother and what she learned from her, and "In the Company of Soldiers" by Christie Blatchford, which talks about her experience in Afghanistan with Canadian soldiers. You might want to read these selections before writing another narration essay. As you read, notice how the writers cover the journalistic questions and use vivid descriptive details to pull you into their narratives, making the main point of the essays all the more meaningful.

NINA LEE COLWILL
The Worth of Women's Work

Focusing Your Attention

1. Can you recall visiting your grandparents when you were very young? Write down as many facts, impressions, and memories as you can of those visits.
2. In the essay you are about to read, the writer describes a person whose words stayed in her mind and shaped the way she thought. Has anyone had a similar impact on you? Have you found yourself, like the writer, thinking back to something someone said to you when you were younger and realizing how true it was?

Expanding Your Vocabulary

The following words are important to your understanding of this essay:

ruminating: thinking over (paragraph 6)
sombre: melancholy or sad (paragraph 8)
emulate: copy (paragraph 14)
lauded: praised (paragraph 18)
reconceptualized: formed a different concept or idea (paragraph 18)
derision: ridicule (paragraph 19)

READING CRITICALLY

As you learned at the beginning of this chapter, "think aloud" as you read. Interject personal references and focused ideas into your oral reading of the essay. The clearer you make your connections, the more deeply you will understand the essay. Read the essay at least two times. Discuss with a classmate the types of ideas you had as you read (focused or random). Which one of you did more focused reading?

NINA LEE COLWILL
The Worth of Women's Work

I was born during World War II into a fatherless world. Daddy was in Belgium and the Netherlands, fighting the war that would bring worldwide peace forever. Mum and I lived with her parents and sisters and brothers in Gaspé, Québec, in the little farming village of Wakeham. Central to that life was Grandma—Grandma, who, then as now, personified strength and wisdom. 1

My earliest memory is of creeping downstairs in the morning and hugging Grandma's legs as she lit the fire in the kitchen stove. Her braids hung freely then, and I'd play with them while she rocked me in the old green wooden rocking chair, waiting for the kitchen to warm for the day. She would scold me: "You should be in bed where it's warm, Nina Lee, not down here in this cold kitchen." But I always knew I was right where she wanted me, curled up on her lap. 2

Grandma could do anything. She baked the most delicious of breads, drawing sifter after sifter of flour from the deep bin that Grandpa had built under the kitchen counter—soft white bread with thick, hard, brown crusts. She made the most comforting of bedtime snacks—dried bread and cream and brown sugar. She taught me to play solitaire when I was two. She taught me not to cheat at solitaire when I was four. She solved an architectural problem that had plagued my grandfather and the other carpenters in the village for years. And she could kill a chicken in a trice. 3

Grandma belonged to the Women's Institute. Every couple of weeks she'd change from her housedress into her church dress and set a hat on her head, and off she'd go to the mysterious WI. 4

I'll never forget the day I discovered the photograph. Actually, I'd seen that group of women every day of my life, standing in four neat rows in their flowered dresses, right there in a black wooden frame in the livingroom. But one day, playing alone with a puzzle on the chesterfield, I looked up and spied Grandma in that group. It was then that she showed me her name printed neatly on brown paper on the back of the photograph: Ruby Jane Patterson, Wakeham. As we sat at the kitchen table eating blueberries and cream, she told me how she'd taken a train to Montreal to represent her district at the WI Convention. It was, I believed, the most worldly and sophisticated work a person could possibly undertake. 5

When I was older and the war was no longer foremost in our thoughts, when my parents and I had moved to another life and our family had grown to four, then five, then six, I would often visit my grandparents in Gaspé. Sometimes I'd sit cross-legged on the painted wooden floor and study that photograph, ruminating about the women and imagining their lives. All those women, all over Québec, with their own families and their own work. And Grandma was part of this illustrious band. 6

No one ever told me about the value of women's work. No one ever said, "To love your work is to love life." Yet a sisterhood of women, a mysterious train trip to Montreal, a grandmother with grey braids wound around her head, humming as she kneaded bread—these pictures arranged themselves into a complex collage of women and work. Grandma never told me that all work is a privilege, or that our integrity depends 7 on the value we place on our work. But she treated her work as a calling, and silently she taught me that my work is a calling, too—that I've been chosen.

8 Yet there's a sombre side of work. To study women and work is to face sadness, is to confront a belief shared by every culture in every country on this planet: the assumption that men, the things men do and all things masculine are more valuable than women, the things women do and all things feminine.

9 I remember the day it struck me, overwhelmed me: the work of women is less valued than the work of men. I suppose I'd always known it at an intellectual level, for I'd studied women and work for half my life. But on the day I truly understood, with a logic beyond logic, that women's work is valued less than men's, I wasn't collecting a paycheque or reading in a library or consulting for some organization. I was in the Rijksmuseum in Amsterdam with my husband, Dennis, and we were viewing the work of the Dutch Masters for the first time.

10 The Rijksmuseum has erected a veritable shrine to the Dutch Masters, where people the world over pay homage to the likes of Vermeer, de Hooch and Rembrandt. In every room is a guard, well-versed in the history of each painter and each painting, for many thousands of words have been written about these brilliant men and their work.

11 One passage leads from the chambers of the Dutch Masters into a quiet, darkened room; eventually we found ourselves there, in the needlework gallery. There we could browse without attending to the explanations of guides or the murmurs of worshippers. We saw crocheting, needlepoint, quilting, embroidery. Ancient works—works from the days of the Dutch Masters. Exquisite works—works of brilliant artists. And no names.

12 You can imagine Dennis' shock when he found me in the corner sobbing over a tablecloth, weeping for the woman who designed and created it without recognition, for the woman who didn't sign her name.

13 Yet, I like to believe they created with joy, these women. I like to believe their work was their calling, that they knew they'd been chosen. I hope their offerings were treated as precious, that people were generous with their praise and their payment. But most of all I hope they created with joy.

14 Because, when all is said and done, we must love our own work. If the historical and universal belief that men's work is more important than women's work is not to be perpetuated to yet another generation, we must judge our own work to be worthy. And we must value it so highly that we value the men who choose to emulate us.

15 Because women and men, who have much to learn from each other, do not imitate each other in equal numbers. For women to do the things men do, to do men's work, is for women to better themselves—a fine accomplishment in an achieving society. So women become ministers, fix their own cars and compete for Olympic medals in hockey, and most of us today consider such women to have achieved. But praise is not as loud for the men who become nurses or take on the family's housework and child care. To emulate one's superiors in an achieving society is to increase one's status. To emulate one's inferiors smacks of perversion.

No one ever told me that women would always be valued in proportion to the value we place on women's work. No one ever said that female physicians would never acquire the status of male physicians until secretaries are valued as highly as tool-and-die makers. No one ever explained that the father who needlepoints a birthday gift for his son must be accorded the same respect as the woman who wires her family cottage. But the status of women's work, I now know, is a measure of the value we place on women. 16

There's been monumental change in the past fifty years, in the past twenty years, even in the past year. It didn't occur because large groups of people decided simultaneously and unanimously that things must change. It occurred because you and I decided to change ourselves a little bit. We didn't change our spouses; we didn't change our children; we didn't change our co-workers. We addressed the only thing over which any of us has any direct control: we changed ourselves. We faltered, we backtracked and we hedged our bets, but we changed our beliefs about the worth of women and men. The rest followed. 17

We're placing higher value on women's traditional art forms, the fibre crafts: quilting, weaving, embroidery, smocking, tatting. Women's work. Honoured in ways it's never been honoured before in written history—in shops, in competitions, in art galleries, in homes. The entrepreneurial styles for which women have become famous are lauded today: start small, with as much of your own money as you can manage, and do what you love to do. As women feel free to be themselves, to lead as they are comfortable in leading, women's management styles are recognized and men are emulating those styles. More parents are steering their children away from violent, competitive sports and into lifetime, co-operative sports. And child care, the chronic issue of every employed mother, is slowly being reconceptualized as a family issue, a corporate issue, a community issue. 18

Of course there is more we can do. We can tell the world by word and by action that women and girls are valuable people and the things they do are valuable as well. We can refuse to participate in the derision of men and boys whose voices or gestures or interests are described as feminine. We can ensure that the family policies of our organizations and our governments are as supportive of fathers as they are of mothers. And if men who try to use these policies are ridiculed, we can be vocal in our protest of their treatment. For if we cannot imagine a world in which men choose to emulate women, we will never create a world in which women and men are equally valued. 19

When I finished my B.A. at the University of Western Ontario and was accepted into graduate school, Grandma sent me a note of praise and admiration—encouraging words, consistent with the support she'd given me all my life. But she closed her letter with a comment that enraged me: "Remember your husband and children and home." Thirty years later, I think I understand what she was telling me, and I now count these words among her wisest: "Never undervalue the work that your foremothers carved out as their special domain, for in doing so, you undervalue yourself." 20

Thinking Critically About Content

1. Colwill refers to "the mysterious WI" (Women's Institute). Why is it mysterious? Does this organization stand for more than simply a social group in the author's mind?
2. Notice the way the writer describes her feelings when she suddenly discovers that her grandmother is one of the women in the black-framed group photo. What does this discovery represent for her? How does the discovery relate to the rest of the essay?
3. Colwill describes herself "sobbing over a tablecloth." Why is she sobbing? What has she realized?
4. The image at the beginning of the essay of the author cuddling on her grandmother's lap permeates the rest of the essay. Why do you think the author began the essay with that image? Explain your answer in detail.

Thinking Critically About Purpose and Audience

5. What do you think Colwill's purpose is in writing this narrative essay? Explain your answer.
6. Colwill asks us to "imagine a world in which men choose to emulate women." In your opinion, what reader does she have in mind when she asks this question? Is that the same reader she is writing for in the rest of the essay?
7. Colwill writes about her grandmother. Do you think that she might be imagining her grandmother as a possible reader of the piece? Is she to some extent apologizing to her grandmother? Should she in fact be apologizing to her grandmother, or is she trying to rationalize what her grandmother has said to her? Explain your answer.

Thinking Critically About Essays

8. How does Colwill organize the details in this essay? Is this an effective order?
9. What perspective is the author writing from when she says, "Daddy was in Belgium and the Netherlands, fighting the war that would bring worldwide peace forever." Do you sense an ironic adult presence in the comment, or is she writing from a child's point of view? At what points in the essay is she writing from a child's viewpoint, and when is she writing from an adult viewpoint?
10. Explain in detail how this essay would be different if it were written by Colwill's grandmother.

CHRISTIE BLATCHFORD
In the Company of Soldiers

Focusing Your Attention

1. Can you remember a time in your life when you worked as part of a close-knit group? Did you feel that the group had an identity that was common to most of the members? Write down as many facts, impressions, and memories as you can about this feeling.
2. In the essay you are about to read, the writer describes the soldiers she is spending time with in Afghanistan. Why do you think these men and women decided to do what they are doing? Have you ever done a task that you felt had to be done, even though you may not have enjoyed the task? Explain your answer.

Expanding Your Vocabulary

The following words are important to your understanding of this essay:

rudimentary: basic or elementary (paragraph 4)

deprivations: going without, lack of basic needs (paragraph 7)

profanity: vulgar or abusive language (paragraph 10)

irreverent: disrespectful, satirical (paragraph 10)

metrosexualism: describes heterosexual men with interest in appearance and style (paragraph 11)

flourishing: growing vigorously, thriving (paragraph 12)

feigned: pretended, disguised (paragraph 14)

fidelity: loyalty or faithfulness (paragraph 15)

READING CRITICALLY

As you did with the previous essay, "think aloud" as you read this essay by Christie Blatchford. This process will give you some good insights into the author's approach to her topic. Write down any new ideas that you discover. As you continue to read critically, you will deepen your understanding of this essay. Read the essay at least two times. Discuss with a classmate the types of ideas you had as you read (focused or random). Which one of you did more focused reading?

CHRISTIE BLATCHFORD
In the Company of Soldiers

1 As I write this, I am for the first time in more than two weeks fully, completely warm.

I am dry. I am clean, having scrubbed myself in a long hot shower, even managing to unknit my hair from the threads of the filthy cap into which it had woven itself over the course of about 16 days of non-stop wear, often under a helmet. I have done a huge laundry, and washed the thick Afghan dust and mud from my clothes. I even spritzed on a little perfume.

2 I feel like a woman again, almost. No makeup, no heels, no skirt, but I am maybe halfway there, which come to think of it, may be as close as I ever get.

There's nothing like spending about three weeks in the company of several hundred soldiers to make you reflect upon the nature of men, and what it is to be a man and, as an afterthought, to wonder about what kind of a woman you are.

3 Since Dec. 12, Globe and Mail photographer Kevin Van Paassen and I have been in southern Afghanistan, and since Dec. 17 or 18, embedded with Charles Company of the 1st Battalion, The Royal Canadian Regiment.

4 After a few days at Kandahar Air Field, the big, safe warm NATO base to which we have now returned, we moved to a smaller, much more rudimentary base at Masum Ghar, and then out and into the Panjwai valley, where, if I were to put a romantic shine on it, I would say we slept on the ground under a brilliant carpet of stars in the black Afghan sky and where, if I were being whiny, I would say we froze our asses off. One night, as I was shivering myself to sleep, I noticed my head was lying in a pool of water (condensation from the frost on our pup tent) but was too tired and cold to care.

5 In summer, this plain is the garden patch of this part of Afghanistan, thick with grape vines and marijuana fields, the crops as if on steroids, but at this time of year, it is dull, drab, windy, frigid, with mists that roll in to cloak the mountains and low clouds that stay for days. It is like the red desert, not so far away, only wet, and thus charmless.

6 Anyway, from the moment we joined Charles Company, I was pretty much surrounded by men, most of them young enough to be my kids, but still for all that indisputably men.

7 The exceptions were two wonderful female medics, who on Christmas Day somehow managed to make us all a fully decorated gingerbread house and who remained so clearly girly (somehow, Angela still smelled of the cucumber face cream she uses, and this I know from the male medic who loved to catch a whiff of it every morning) despite the physical deprivations dear to the infantry heart, I was deeply envious and oddly shamed.

8 It is such a man's own world, the soldier's. As former U.S. Army Ranger Andrew Exum, as magnificent a writer as it appears he was an officer, wrote in *This Man's Army*, his intelligent account of his unit's year in post-9/11 Afghanistan, "The military—and the infantry especially—remains one of the last places where that most endangered of species, the alpha male, can feel at home."

Mr. Exum says that one of the big challenges any modern army faces is teaching young men who are in the main raised to apologize for their natural aggressiveness how to be warriors. I think he's right, but either this particular army, or the months of hard fighting the men of Charles Company have had, have done the trick, because these boys are certainly warriors, and they have the sort of self-confidence that comes from having nothing to prove. 9

Yet most of them are among the least showy, most modest and, despite their glorious profanity and wide-ranging irreverent skepticism about the world, the most curiously righteous and almost old-fashioned guys I think I've ever encountered. 10

I guess that's not surprising: If being a warrior goes against the modern grain—that is, runs contrary to the gender-bending of roles and the rise of what was briefly called metrosexualism—it only follows that such men may seem a bit out of their place and time. 11

Not outside of hockey arenas, and that was two or three decades ago, have I heard so many men, let alone so many young men, refer to "the wife," as in, "The wife won't like it if I deploy again," or, "I don't tell the wife anything." And yet, probe a little, and it turns out most of these young women back home have flourishing careers of their own (teacher, paramedic) and have carved for themselves pretty fiercely independent lives, if only of necessity. 12

And tender, are these men tender. 13

The oldest in our boat is 29, but of the five, only the two dimpled babies—22 and 23—aren't married or engaged. One night, to my astonishment, there were three of them keenly discussing the upcoming weddings of the two engaged fellows. They feigned hands-off nonchalance ("the wife is doing all the work") but were intimately aware of the details: the dinner; the ring; the honeymoon; the need for a wedding planner, or not; the cost; in one case, because the groom-to-be has asked all his army mates to be in the wedding party, the necessity for 11 bridesmaids ("I've told her, I don't care if she has to hire escorts, she has to find 11 single, good-looking girls"). 14

They seemed to me more grown up, more willing to embrace responsibility—marriage unto old age; children and parenthood; fidelity, and yes, they talked about that too—than men twice their age, than many of the men I know. 15

They made me wish my great niece, 25 and every bit as accomplished as the soldiers are, was single. But then her boyfriend, not in the military, is also a man rather like that, solid and smart and wonderful. 16

They made me wish I were 25 and single. But then, when I was, I didn't want those things. Ultimately, they made me wonder what kind of woman I am. 17

At night, in the dark, I would watch them walking, taking their turn on the unit's satellite phone, calling home, talking to their girls, telling them how much they loved them. 18

Thinking Critically About Content

1. How does the author characterize the nature of men?
2. What do you think the author means with her comments on the use of the expression "the wife"? Does she approve of the expression?
3. What is the author referring to in paragraph 17, when she says, "when I was, I didn't want those things"? Explain your answer.

Thinking Critically About Purpose and Audience

4. Explain your understanding of the writer's main point in this essay.
5. Who do you think Blatchford's primary audience is?
6. The reference to her niece's boyfriend in paragraph 16 seems somewhat out of place. Is it possible that the author is thinking of the two specific readers here? Should a writer be concerned about specific readers, such as family members? Explain your answer.

Thinking Critically About Essays

7. Describe Blatchford's point of view in this essay. Is she an observer or a participant in the story?
8. Blatchford uses many details to illustrate her admiration of Canadian soldiers. Which details communicate this admiration most clearly to you?
9. Blatchford ends her essay with a description of the soldiers talking on the unit's satellite phone to their girlfriends. Is this an effective ending? Why or why not?
10. Blatchford claims that young men are "raised to apologize for their natural aggression." Write a paragraph on why you agree or disagree with this statement.

Writing Workshop

This final section gives you opportunities to apply what you have learned in this chapter to another writing assignment. This time, we provide very little prompting beyond a summary of the guidelines for writing a narration essay. This section will let you demonstrate that you can go through the entire writing process on your own with only occasional feedback from your peers. Loop back into the chapter as necessary when you have questions, so that this process becomes as automatic to you as possible before you move on to new material. Then pause at the end of the chapter to reflect briefly on what you have learned.

Guidelines for Writing a Narration Essay

1. Make sure your essay has a point.
2. Use the five *W*s and one *H* to construct your story.
3. Develop your narrative with vivid details.
4. Build excitement in your narrative with careful pacing.
5. Organize your narrative so that your readers can easily follow it.

Writing About Your Reading

1. In "The Worth of Women's Work," Nina Lee Colwill writes of an epiphany she had when looking at pieces of embroidery and needlework in a Dutch museum. Many of us have had similar moments of enlightenment. Write an essay in which you recall the details of such a moment. Write what you learned from the experience.
2. Male-female relationships are very much on the minds of young people, especially when it comes to getting married. Explain how men and women approach marriage. Do they have the same approach to each other, or a different one? Is it fair to generalize? Write a narrative essay focusing on your own observations of a couple or couples who are about to get married.
3. What do you think are the most important features of a good story? Why are they important? What effect do they have on you?

Writing About Your World

1. Place yourself in the scene pictured below, and write a narrative about what is happening. How did you get here? Why are you here? Where are you going from here? Be sure to decide on a main point before you begin to write.

2. Your old high school has asked you, as a graduate, to submit an essay to the newsletter recalling a job or volunteer experience that you enjoyed. The editors want to inform current high school students about options for volunteer and paid work. Your purpose is to tell your story in enough interesting detail so that you convince the current high school students that the job you had is worth looking into.
3. Your college class is putting together a collection of essays that explain how classmates decided to go to their college. What happened first? When did you decide? What helped you decide? What activities or people influenced your decision the most? Tell your story in vivid detail.
4. Create your own narration assignment (with the help of your instructor), and write a response to it.

Revising

Small Group Activity (5–10 minutes per writer) Working in groups of three or four, each person should read his or her narration essay to the other members of the group. Those listening should record their reactions on a copy of the Peer Evaluation Form in Appendix 1A. After your group goes through this process, give your evaluation forms to the appropriate writers so that each writer has two peer comment sheets for revising.

Paired Activity (5 minutes per writer) Using the completed Peer Evaluation Forms, work in pairs to decide what you should revise in your essay. If time allows, rewrite some of your sentences, and have your partner look at them.

Individual Activity Rewrite your paper, using the revising feedback you received from other students.

Editing

Paired Activity (5–10 minutes per writer) Swap papers with a classmate, and use the editing portion of your Peer Evaluation Form (Appendix 1B) to identify as many grammar, punctuation, mechanics, and spelling errors as you can. If time allows, correct some of your errors, and have your partner look at them. Record your grammar, punctuation, and mechanics errors in the Error Log (Appendix 3) and your spelling errors in the Spelling Log (Appendix 4).

Individual Activity Rewrite your paper again, using the editing feedback you received from other students.

CHAPTER 10

ILLUSTRATING

When I began to write, I found it was the best way to make sense out of my life.

—John Cheever

Giving examples to make a point is a natural part of communication. For example, if you are trying to demonstrate how much time you waste, you can cite the fact that you talk on the phone for about two hours every day. Or to tell your friends how much fun you are having, you might say, "Residence is great because no one tells me what to do or when to go to bed. I am completely on my own." The message is in the examples you choose.

We also use examples every day to make various points in our writing. Think about the following situations that take place in our personal lives, at school, and at work:

In a letter to your parents, you tell them how hard you are studying by giving them examples of your weekend study schedule.

A student gives examples of gestures, facial expressions, and posture in a paper on nonverbal communication for a psychology course.

A student answers a sociology exam question by giving examples to show how children are integrated into society.

A human resources director of a large company writes a memo on sexual harassment in the workplace, including examples of inappropriate behaviour.

The owner of a catering business writes a brochure listing examples of dinners available in different price ranges.

An example is an **illustration** of the point you want to make. Well-chosen examples, then, are the building blocks of an illustration essay. You draw examples from your experience, your observations, and your reading. They help you show rather than tell what you mean, usually by supplying concrete details (what you see, hear, touch, smell, or taste) to support abstract ideas (such as hope, understanding, and love), by providing specifics ("I like chocolate") to explain generalizations ("I like sweets"), and by giving definite references ("Turn left at the second stoplight") to clarify vague statements ("Turn left in a few blocks").

Not only do examples help you make your point, but they also add interest to your writing. Would you like to read an essay stating that being a server in a restaurant is a lot harder than it looks? Or would you be more interested in reading an essay describing what it is like having to serve too many tables, carrying heavy trays, taking the wrong order to a table, and dealing with rude customers? The first statement *tells*, but vivid examples *show* your readers the point you want to make.

READING AND WRITING AN ILLUSTRATION ESSAY

Reading and writing are actually two halves of a whole process. For example, if you can see how a writer is accomplishing his or her purpose in a particular rhetorical mode, you will be more likely to use that same strategy effectively in your own writing. Being able to use these strategies critically or analytically is especially important for success in college and in life beyond college. This section will guide you to higher levels of thinking as you learn to use illustration.

Reading an Illustration Essay

In his essay "The Question," taken from his book *Black Berry, Sweet Juice: On Being Black and White in Canada*, Lawrence Hill writes about the insensitivity of Canadians who assume that if your skin is a different colour from theirs, you must be from somewhere else. Have you ever visited a foreign country where you stood out (or blended in) because of your appearance? Have you been part of a group that blended two or more cultures? What did you learn?

READING CRITICALLY

Reading illustration essays critically means looking closely at the selection to discover its purpose and then analyzing each example the author uses to prove his or her point. To understand how this essay works, circle the main idea or thesis. Then draw horizontal lines throughout the essay to separate the various examples Hill uses to support his thesis. These lines may or may not coincide with paragraph breaks. Finally, label each example in the right margin. Be prepared to explain the divisions you made.

LAWRENCE HILL
The Question

Canadians have a favourite pastime, and they don't even realize it. They like to ask—they absolutely have to ask—where you are from if you don't look convincingly white. They want to know it, need to know it, simply must have that information. They just can't relax until they have pinpointed, to their satisfaction, your geographic and racial coordinates. They can go almost out of their minds with curiosity, as when driven by the need for food, water, or sex, but once they've finally managed to find out precisely where you were born, who your parents were, and what your racial make-up is, then, man, do they feel better. They can breathe easy and get back to the business of living. 1

I don't have the math background of, say, an actuary, but I can manage the following calculation. I am forty-four years old. Since about age ten, I have been asked "So what are you, anyway?" and all its variations. ("Where are you from?" "Yes, but where are you really from?" "Yes, but where were your parents born?") That's thirty-four years I've been fielding The Question. 2

Let's assume I have been asked The Question once a day over these past thirty-four years. 34 x 365 = 12,410. But that would be an underestimation because it fails to factor in the two years I lived in Quebec. During those two years, I was most certainly asked The Question five times per day. (*"D'où viens-tu?" "Quelles sont tes souches?" "Tes parents sont de quel pays?"*) An extra four times per day for two years in Quebec City would add on another 2,920 questions. 12,410 + 2,920 = 15,330. 3

That, ladies and gentlemen, is the absolute minimum number of times Canadians have asked me either "Where are you from?" or *"D'où viens-tu?"* or any of the multitudinous variations. 4

Minelle Mahtani, whose doctoral thesis at the University of London examined identity among mixed-race Canadian women, tells a story of how she was walking alone one day in Toronto's St. Lawrence Market area, when someone tapped on her shoulder. Minelle turned around to find a woman who seemed motivated by a particular urgency—she had obviously been watching Minelle and just had to know where she was from. 5

"Ah," you may say, "but it's just curiosity. What's wrong with people being curious?" 6

I am a patient man. So patient that my children can confidently remove a chocolate chip cookie right from the edge of my fingers, or raid my dish of French vanilla ice cream and leave nothing but the cloudy bowl, and still know that I won't lose my cool. But even this patience was exhausted some time around the 5,000 mark of the 15,330 questions I have faced. 7

What is wrong with The Question? Nothing at all—when it is asked at the right time, when it results from a genuine interest in you as a person, and when the person asking the question actually accepts the answer. 8

Let's dissect the interrogation process. Imagine me at a party, sipping mineral water. A stranger walks up. 9

10 STRANGER: "Do you mind my asking where you are from?" [This is code for "What is your race?"]

11 Me: "Canada." [This is code for "Screw off."]

12 STRANGER: "Yes, but you know, where are you really from?" [This is code for "You know what I mean, so why are you trying to make me come out and say it?"]

13 Me: "I come from the foreign and distant metropolis of Newmarket. That's Newmarket, Ontario. My place of birth." [Code for "I'm not letting you off the hook, buster."]

14 STRANGER: "But your place of origin? Your parents? What are your parents?" [Code for "I want to know your race, but this is making me very uncomfortable because somehow I feel that I'm not supposed to ask that question."]

15 This exchange is like the opening of a chess game. The first few moves are pretty standard: White moves Pawn to King Four, Black responds with Pawn to King Four, White answers with Knight to King Bishop Three, and Black answers with Knight to King Bishop Three. From this point on, the possibilities multiply.

16 I can give a teaser, such as "My parents came up from the States," which frustrates the questioner, who really wants to know my parents' racial background.

17 I can give it all up and explain that I have a black father and a white mother.

18 I can invent an answer, such as "My father is a White Russian and my mother is an Ethiopian Jew."

19 Or I can turn the question around, as in "Why are you asking me this?"

20 And that is the nub of the issue. Why am I always asked that question? Why do people need to know the answer so desperately?

21 Have you ever noticed that black people rarely put other people of any race through the wringer like this? That's because many of them have been asked The Question more times than they care to count. They're sophisticated enough—by virtue of their own experiences—to understand that many people resent this line of interrogation.

22 Is it truly innocent? Can The Question be chalked up to basic curiosity? I don't think so. Children are the most innocent and curious of all human beings, yet they never hammer me with these questions. As a rule, adults aren't all that curious about other people. With me, they are generally interested in just one thing: my ancestry.

23 Do you suppose that—15,330 times in thirty-four years—strangers will ask an indisputably white Canadian with a traditional Anglo-Canadian accent where he is from, where he was born, or where his parents were born? Absolutely not. Strangers will assume that he is a true Canadian, and leave that part of his identity unmolested. The offence-causing kernel at the centre of this line of interrogation is its implication: "You are not white, you don't look like me, so you're clearly not Canadian." It also suggests "Since you're clearly not Canadian, and I am, I am within my rights to ask you just exactly where you're from."

24 We grow up learning that certain questions are off-limits in polite conversation. Any properly socialized Canadian knows, by the teenage years at the latest, that it would be considered grossly impolite to walk up to strangers and ask how much money they make, how they vote, whether they believe in God, or whether they sleep

with men, women, or both. These questions are deemed intrusive. But to my way of thinking, they are eminently preferable to "Where are you from?" After all, what is wrong with asking what people do or think? But to ask what they *are*, and to presume to know at least part of the answer—that they are not white and therefore are not Canadian—is very different.

Digging into someone's identity—especially a stranger's identity—is tricky 25
business. Hell, people can spend top dollar on psychotherapists to figure out their own identities and still fall short of satisfaction. When I wake up in the morning, stumble to the mirror, and brush my teeth, I'm certainly not saying to myself, "Hello, black man, how are you today?" Nor am I saying, "Hello, white and black mix-up, what are you doing today?"

Obviously, the blackness and the whiteness within me are reflected back at me 26
by society. But I don't care to have my identity boiled down to race. My identity may, at any given time, comprise a hundred elements.

I suppose the reason many of us mixed-race people find The Question offensive 27
is not just that it makes assumptions, which are often false, about our identity, but because it attempts to hang our identity on one factor: our race.

Not everybody I interviewed had the same take on this issue. Interestingly, two 28
of the strongest opposing views came from young men, both in their twenties, university-educated, and living in southern Ontario.

Stefan Dubowski, of Hamilton, told me The Question doesn't bother him. When 29
he is asked about his background, he just says he is part Ukrainian, part Barbadian. "Then we get into a discussion of what they thought I was. I've had Armenian, Egyptian, Pakistani, East Indian . . . It's just a question of curiosity. I've been asked so many times. If I got mad about it every single time, I'd just be this really angry person. I certainly don't feel any anger about it when people ask me about it, but my back does go up when I read it on an application form or on a government census."

Tyson Brown, who was raised in Burlington and now lives in Toronto, said he takes The 30
Question as an opportunity to educate people about issues of mixed race and blackness. "I say, 'I'm mixed, African Canadian and white Canadian.'" Tyson emerged from a largely white high school to embrace his black identity completely as a young man. He read black literature, listened to black music, wore funky black clothes, dated black women, and chose to immerse himself completely in the black student community at York University. Later, he lived with his girlfriend for a year in Barbados, and there the constant references to his race grated on him. "They called me 'red man' the whole time I was there," he complained.

However, my brother, Dan, described The Question as a painful experience, espe- 31
cially during childhood. "I was definitely asked that question a lot. And a lot of times, when I said part black, or half black, people would then decide to argue with me and tell me that no, I wasn't, 'cause I didn't look black enough. I can remember it happening a lot when I was a boy, at summer camp. When I went up to camp for the first time, I was sitting on the bus with this kid who was probably a year or two older than I was. And this kid was saying, 'You're not. You can't be.' So there I was arguing with him about this."

Like Dan, most of the people I interviewed—and virtually all of the women—expressed 32
impatience with constant questions about their racial background.

33 Karyn Hood, of Toronto, said, "People think I'm everything under the flipping sun, and it drives me insane. I get North African, Moroccan, Italian, Sicilian, Greek, Spanish, Jewish . . . Whenever I meet someone, I know it's going to be 'What are you? What background are you?' I usually try to put it to bed with one answer: 'My father is West Indian, my mother's Irish Canadian.' It's annoying. But life's a puzzle, and they want to know how you fit into their world." Karyn resents being perceived as "exotic," cultivates friendships in the black community, and prefers to date black men. "You can't live in two worlds. You have to make a choice. Saying you're white isn't really an option. So this makes it clear to people. If there's any doubt, that's the choice I'm making."

34 Natalie Wall, of Toronto, concurred. "I've been asked what I am so many times. It is the rudest question in the world. It's the basest form of labelling I've ever seen. People on the street are always guessing. 'You're Spanish, right? Indian? What the hell are you?' I tell them I'm Canadian. 'But where are you from?' 'Canada.' 'What about your parents?' 'My mom is from Nova Scotia, my dad is from Trinidad.' 'So what are you?' 'Black.' I get a surprised look. 'You *are*?'"

35 Jazz Miller, of Toronto, is so sick of The Question that when people ask her what she is, she has taken to answering "aardvark." "It is designed to embarrass the person asking the question. There's always a little bit of nervous laughter."

36 Aaron Cavon, who has a white father and a black mother, was a graduate student at Dalhousie University when I interviewed him. He said people always look astonished when he says that The Question irritates him and he won't answer it. He described the attitude of the questioner as unconsciously aggressive, a stance that suggests the person being questioned is inferior. Underneath The Question, Aaron argued, is this unarticulated belief: "It's not necessary for me to explain my origins, but it's necessary for you to tell me who you are." He told me, "The assumption behind The Question is, 'I'm just white. You are the person who answers the question because you are the one who is unknown.'"

37 Sara, one of my anonymous interviewees, fumed as she recalled the numerous times she had dealt with The Question.

38 "Sometimes I'm very rude. I don't give much information. I might just say, 'I'm from here.' Some days, if I don't feel like it, I just say, 'Africa.' And they're happy, not realizing that Africa's a continent and that there are fifty-two countries in it. It's just what they want to hear. They want to place you somewhere because it makes them feel comfortable, helps them compartmentalize you.

39 "Where the hell are they from? No one's from here unless they're First Nations peoples. But they're trying to make you feel strange. It's a displacement. They're just trying to let you know that you don't belong . . . They are not coming from a position of intelligence, asking those questions. White privilege doesn't operate from a level of consciousness. It operates from a position of privilege. Because they're privileged, they don't have to think about stuff. They really don't. Does it mean that they're not well intentioned? These can be people you love dearly, you know? But that's the way the world is. They're operating from a position of belligerent white privilege, and they don't have to look at stuff and think about stuff. So they ask these reckless questions."

PREPARING TO WRITE YOUR OWN ILLUSTRATION ESSAY

When did you last try something new in your life? Was it difficult? Did you plan this new experience, or did it just happen? Do you like new experiences, or do you prefer keeping your life routine? Use one or more of the prewriting strategies you learned in Chapter 5 to recall several times you tried something new, planned or not. Then think about the positive and negative aspects of trying new experiences. What value do they have in your life? What are the disadvantages of trying new experiences?

Writing an Illustration Essay

In the art world, a good illustrator is someone who makes an image or an idea come alive with the perfect drawing. The same principle applies in writing: someone who uses illustrations or examples effectively makes an essay or other piece of writing come alive. Moreover, in college, most essay exam questions are based on illustration—finding the best examples to support your main point. Here are some guidelines to help you use examples effectively:

1. ***State your main point and your opinion about that point in the last sentence of your introduction.*** Write a thesis statement that clearly and plainly states the main idea of your essay, and place it at the end of your introduction. This is the controlling idea of your essay and should consist of a limited subject and your opinion about that subject. You will explain this main point through the examples you furnish in the following body paragraphs.

   In the sample essay, Hill starts his essay with his main point in the second sentence of the introduction: "They [Canadians] have to ask where you are from if you don't look convincingly white." The essay that follows is a series of examples that illustrate that question and how those who are asked it react to it. He then closes the essay with Sara's opinion on the matter: "They're operating from a position of belligerent white privilege . . . so they ask these reckless questions." This movement of a thesis from general to specific is the inductive method of writing an essay. The more common method for students, which places the specific opinion first, is called the deductive method.

2. ***Choose examples that are relevant to your point.*** In an illustration essay, examples serve as the writer's explanation. Well-chosen examples are an essay's building blocks. They help you prove your point and must directly support the point you are trying to make. Examples that are not relevant are distracting, causing readers to lose their train of thought. Your readers will appreciate the point you are making not because you tell them

what to think but because you show them with relevant examples what you are trying to say. Keep in mind, too, that the more specific your examples are, the more likely your readers are to agree with your point.

Finding relevant examples is a fairly easy task. The best examples often come from your own experience and observation. You can also draw examples from your reading—books, newspapers, magazines. In addition, as technology advances, more and more information is available online, making the Internet a good place to find examples for an illustration essay.

In Hill's essay, all his examples focus on examples of The Question. Since his point is that Canadians of mixed race are always asked that question, he interviews several people and relates their experiences in addition to his own. Although not everyone he talks to finds The Question offensive, most of them do. He combines their speculations about the reasons people must have for asking The Question with his own. These focused examples make the essay coherent and unified.

3. ***Choose examples that your readers can identify with.*** To do this, you need to know as much as possible about your audience. Once you know who your readers are, you can tailor your examples to them. In this way, your readers are most likely to follow your line of reasoning. Suppose, for instance, that you want your parents to finance an off-campus apartment for you. You are not likely to make your point by citing examples of European universities that do not provide any student housing because this is not an example that Canadian parents can identify with. You need to furnish examples that address your specific situation.

   Hill's essay is a chapter in his book, *Black Berry, Sweet Juice: On Being Black and White in Canada*. He has two audiences: Canadians who ask The Question, and Canadians who are asked The Question. It is the first group he hopes will understand his point. His numerous examples make it clear that The Question is asked frequently. However, he also needs to convince his readers that it is offensive. For this reason he inserts a comment by an imagined reader: "'Ah,' you may say, 'but it's just curiosity. What's wrong with people being curious?'" As an answer, he can then give examples to show that it is indeed offensive to those who are asked.

4. ***Use enough examples to make your point.*** Nobody has a set formula for determining the perfect number of examples, because that depends on the point you are trying to make. Sometimes several short examples will make your point best. Or perhaps three or four fairly detailed examples—each in its own body paragraph—work best. At other times the most effective way to develop an essay is with a single extended example. Usually, however, three or four examples are sufficient. If you are in doubt whether to add another example or more

vivid details, you should probably do so. Most students err on the side of using too few examples or not adding enough detail to their examples.

In addition to his own experiences, Hill gives nine examples throughout his essay. The first example, Minelle Mahtani's story, sets up the opposing idea that it may just be curiosity. He then leads with two examples of people who are not offended, and follows with six examples of people who *are* offended. The variety of examples keeps the essay interesting and the reader engaged.

5. ***Organize your examples to make your point in the clearest, strongest way.*** When you have gathered enough relevant examples, you are ready to organize them into an essay. Most illustration essays are organized from general to particular (from a general statement—the thesis—to specific examples that support the general statement) or chronologically (according to a time sequence).

   The examples themselves must also be organized within their paragraphs in some logical way—chronologically, spatially, or by extremes. Which example should come first? Second? Last? The simple act of arranging examples can help you—and your reader—make sense of an experience or idea. Use basic logic to guide you to different patterns.

   Hill opens his essay with what Canadians will recognize as a rant. The rant is, however, presented in a semi-humorous way. Humour is also evident in the math, and in the totalling up of how many times the author may have been asked The Question. The first few examples give the reader a chance to express some polite Canadian doubts, and then Hill overwhelms the reader with the negative examples. Leading with the reader's question and the opposing views is a good persuasive technique, as it deals with any doubts the reader might have up front.

WRITING YOUR OWN ILLUSTRATION ESSAY

Based on the prewriting that you did earlier, write an essay about three new experiences you have had. Which were planned? Which were unplanned? Did they affect you in positive ways? In negative ways? Or were the outcomes mixed? What did you learn from these experiences? Draft a thesis statement. Then write a first draft of your essay, including an introduction and a conclusion. Use examples in your body paragraphs to support your thesis statement.

A STUDENT'S ILLUSTRATION ESSAY

In the following essay, student writer Taleah Trainor uses examples to explain her relationship with Murphy's Law. As you read this draft of her essay, try to find Taleah's main point.

Murphy's Law

1 Murphy's Law: If something can go wrong, it will. I have always been familiar with the concept of this law, but never from actual experience. It was not until the summer before my first year in college that different events taught me about Murphy's Law.

2 The first event was when my father informed me that on our family trip to Winnipeg we would be using my car. Since I had made previous plans I was not bubbling with enthusiasm. I had 14 "fun-filled" days in Winnipeg. And to top it all off, on the way home, my car decided to have a breakdown between two northern Ontario towns. Northern Ontario has a really long stretch of highway that driver's hate. People feel like they're on it forever. Luckily, my father had CAA, our delay was short.

3 This particular instance had familiarized me with Murphy's Law, and for the remainder of the summer, I began to notice it every time I turned around. At first it was little things like catching the flu just hours before a date. After a while, it turned into bigger hassles, like getting flat tires on the way to job interviews. I prayed my luck would take a turn for the better rather then the worse.

4 Murphy showed up again on August 29, when I left my home town to travel to my new school. Having to entrust my 397-mile journey to an old CAA map, I pictured getting sidetracked onto an out-of-the-way farm road leading me to an uncharted town. But I did not get lost until arriving at the infamous "traffic circle" in my new home town. Realizing my highway map was of know use in town, I frantically looked around and happened to catch a glimpse of the "I ♥ Ti-Cats" bumper sticker plastered on the car in front of me. I said to myself, "Now how many cars could have that sticker?" I convinced myself that I was in luck and that the car in front of me was headed toward campus. I decided to follow it. After arriving in a gruesome alley, which accurately resembled the pictures I had seen of a Third World country, I came to the conclusion the car was not headed toward campus but probably to the local chicken fights. Pulling in to the nearest Petro-Can station, directions were given to me. Three service stations later, their I was, at my new dorm on campus. Once again, I knew that Murphy's Law had decided to play with me.

5 I realized Murphy's Law was becoming a permanent part of my life. If something in my life could possibly go wrong, Murphy would be there to make sure of it. I had finally come to the conclusion that Murphy, and I would be friends for life—unless, of course, something went wrong.

Discovering How the Essay Works

1. What main idea do you think Taleah is trying to communicate in this essay?

   ____

   Does her thesis communicate this main idea?

   ____

2. How does each of Taleah's examples relate to her main point? List three examples she furnishes, and explain how they are related to her thesis statement.

3. Knowing that this essay was written for her college writing class, do you think Taleah's audience could identify with these examples? Explain your answer.

4. Does Taleah include enough examples to make her point? Explain your answer.

5. How are the examples in Taleah's essay arranged? List some of her examples in the order they appear; then identify her method of organization.

Method of Organization: ______________________

REVISING AND EDITING THE STUDENT ESSAY

This essay is Taleah's first draft, which now needs to be revised and edited. First, apply the Revising Checklist on the inside front cover to the content of Taleah's draft. When you are satisfied that her ideas are fully developed and well organized, use the Editing Checklist on the inside back cover to correct her grammar and mechanics errors. Answer the questions below. Then write your suggested changes directly on Taleah's draft.

Revision Questions

Thesis Statement

1. Put brackets around the last sentence in Taleah's introduction. Does it introduce her main point? Does it include her opinion about that point?

2. Rewrite Taleah's thesis statement if necessary so that it states her main point and her opinion about that point.

____

____

Basic Elements

1. Give Taleah's essay an alternative title.

____

2. Rewrite Taleah's introduction so that it captures the readers' attention and builds up to the thesis statement at the end of the paragraph.

____

____

____

3. Does each of Taleah's body paragraphs deal with only one topic?

____

4. Rewrite Taleah's conclusion, using at least one suggestion from Part I.

____

____

____

Development

1. Write out Taleah's thesis statement (revised, if necessary), and list her three topic sentences below it.

Thesis statement: ____

____

Topic 1: ____

____

Topic 2: ____

____

Topic 3: ____

____

2. Do Taleah's topics adequately support her thesis statement?

____

3. Does each body paragraph have a focused topic sentence?

____

4. Are Taleah's examples specific?

____

Add another, more specific, detail to one of the examples in her essay.

5. Does she offer enough examples to make her point?

____

Add at least one new example to strengthen Taleah's essay.

Unity

1. Read each of Taleah's topic sentences, keeping her thesis statement (revised, if necessary) in mind. Do they go together?

____

2. Revise them if necessary so that they are directly related.
3. Drop or rewrite the two sentences in paragraph 2 that are not directly related to their topic sentence.

Organization

1. Read Taleah's essay again to see if all the paragraphs are arranged logically.
2. Move any paragraphs that are out of order.
3. Look closely at Taleah's body paragraphs to see if all her sentences are arranged logically within paragraphs.
4. Move any sentences that are out of order.

Coherence

1. Circle five transitions, repetitions, synonyms, or pronouns Taleah uses.
2. Explain how two of these make Taleah's essay easier to read.

For a list of transitions, see pages 85–86.

For a list of pronouns, see pages 389–390.

____

____

Now rewrite Taleah's essay with your revisions.

Editing Questions

Sentences

Subjects and Verbs

For help with subjects and verbs, see Chapter 23.

1. Underline the subjects once and verbs twice in paragraph 2 of your revision of Taleah's essay. Remember that sentences can have more than one subject–verb set.

2. Does each one of Taleah's sentences have at least one subject and verb that can stand alone?

 ____

For help with run-ons, see Chapter 25.

3. Did you find and correct Taleah's run-on sentence? If not, find and correct it now.

Subject–Verb Agreement

For help with subject–verb agreement, see Chapter 27.

1. Read aloud the subjects and verbs you underlined in your revision of Taleah's essay.
2. Correct any subjects and verbs that do not agree.

Pronoun Agreement

For help with pronoun errors, see Chapter 28.

1. Find any pronouns in your revision of Taleah's essay that do not agree with their nouns.
2. Correct any pronouns that do not agree with their nouns.

Modifiers

For help with modifier errors, see Chapter 33. Did you find and correct her dangling modifier? If not, find and correct it now.

1. Find any modifiers in your revision of Taleah's essay that are not as close as possible to the words they modify.

Punctuation and Mechanics

Punctuation

For help with punctuation, see Chapters 34–37.

1. Read over your revision of Taleah's essay to find any errors in punctuation.
2. Find the run-on sentence you revised, and make sure it is punctuated correctly.
3. Did you find and correct Taleah's two comma errors?

Mechanics

For help with capitalization, see Chapter 38.

1. Read your revision of Taleah's essay for any errors in capitalization.
2. Be sure to check Taleah's capitalization in the run-on sentence you revised.

Word Choice and Spelling

Word Choice

1. Find any words used incorrectly in your revision of Taleah's essay.
2. Did you find and correct the three confused words in Taleah's essay? If not, find and correct them now.

For help with confused words, see Chapter 44.

Spelling

1. Use spell-check and a dictionary to check the spelling in your revision of Taleah's essay.
2. Correct any misspelled words.

For help with spelling, see Chapter 45.

Now rewrite Taleah's essay again with your editing corrections.

REVISING AND EDITING YOUR OWN ILLUSTRATION ESSAY

Returning to the illustration essay you wrote earlier in this chapter, you are now ready to revise and edit your own writing. Remember that revision involves reworking the content and organization of your essay, while editing asks you to check your grammar and usage. At this stage, you should repeat these processes over and over until you feel you have a draft that says exactly what you want it to say.

The editing and revising checklists on the inside front and back covers will help you apply what you have learned in this chapter to your essay.

WRITING CRITICALLY

Apply the reading strategy you learned earlier to your own essay. Circle your thesis or main idea; then draw horizontal lines between the examples you use to support your main idea. As you label these examples in the margin, decide whether they are the best choices to prove your point. Should you change any of them? Should you explain any of them further?

PRACTISING ILLUSTRATION: FROM READING TO WRITING

Reading Workshop

Here are two essays that use examples to make their point: "The Decorated Body" by France Borel uses examples to talk about the importance of altering our physical appearance, and "Wild Weather" by Chris Wood uses examples to talk about global "wettening." You might want to read these selections before writing another illustration essay. As you read, notice how the writers use examples to support and advance their ideas.

FRANCE BOREL
The Decorated Body

Focusing Your Attention

1. In what ways have you changed your natural appearance—hair colour, makeup, tattoos, piercings, and the like? Why do you make these alterations? What messages do they send to others?
2. The essay you are about to read deals with the ways we decorate our bodies. These methods vary according to someone's culture. Why do you think people change their appearance in North America? What physical decorations are appealing to you? Which are unappealing? Why do you think you have these various reactions?

Expanding Your Vocabulary

The following words are important to your understanding of this essay. Organize this list into two columns—words you know and words you don't know. Which of the words you don't know can you guess from their sentences?

unfathomably: impossible to measure (paragraph 1)

artifice: device used to trick people (paragraph 2)

millennia: thousands of years (paragraph 3)

prevalent: widespread (paragraph 3)

aesthetically: concerned with appearances (paragraph 4)

amorous: pertaining to love (paragraph 4)

scarification: scarring of the skin (paragraph 6)

pretexts: false justifications (paragraph 8)

malleable: easily influenced (paragraph 9)

eludes: evades or escapes from (paragraph 12)

homogenous: of the same kind (paragraph 12)

tacit: implied (paragraph 12)

adhere: stick to (paragraph 13)

READING CRITICALLY

As you did earlier, circle the thesis of the following essay, and then separate each example with horizontal lines. Share your marks with a classmate and justify each of your decisions.

FRANCE BOREL
The Decorated Body

Nothing goes as deep as dress nor as far as the skin; ornaments have the dimensions of the world.

—Michel Serres, *The Five Senses*

Human nakedness, according to social custom, is unacceptable, unbearable, and dangerous. From the moment of birth, society takes charge, managing, dressing, forming, and deforming the child—sometimes even with a certain degree of violence. Aside from the most elementary caretaking concerns—the very diversity of which shows how subjective the motivation is—an unfathomably deep and universal tendency pushes families, clans, and tribes to rapidly modify a person's physical appearance. 1

One's genuine physical makeup, one's given anatomy, is always felt to be unacceptable. Flesh, in its raw state, seems both intolerable and threatening. In its naked state, body and skin have no possible existence. The organism is acceptable only when it is transformed, covered with signs. The body only speaks if it is dressed in artifice. 2

For millennia, in the four quarters of the globe, mothers have molded the shape of their newborn babies' skulls to give them silhouettes conforming to prevalent criteria of beauty. In the nineteenth century, western children were tightly swaddled to keep their limbs straight. In the so-called primitive world, children were scarred or tattooed at a very early age in rituals which were repeated at all the most important steps of their lives. At a very young age, children were fitted with belts, necklaces, or bracelets; their lips, ears, or noses were pierced or stretched. 3

Some cultures have designed sophisticated appliances to alter physical structure and appearance. American Indian cradleboards crushed the skull to flatten it; the Mangbetus of Africa wrapped knotted rope made of bark around the child's head to elongate it into a sugar-loaf shape, which was considered to be aesthetically pleasing. The feet of very young Chinese girls were bound and spliced, intentionally and irreversibly deforming them, because this was seen to guarantee the girls' eventual amorous and matrimonial success.[1] 4

Claude Lévi-Strauss said about the Caduveo of Brazil: "In order to be a man, one had to be painted; whoever remained in a natural state was no different from the beasts."[2] In Polynesia, unless a girl was tattooed, she would not find a husband. An unornamented hand could not cook, nor dip into the communal food bowl. Pink lips were despicable and ugly. Anyone who refused the test of the tattoo was seen to be marginal and suspect. 5

Among the Tivs of Nigeria, women called attention to their legs by means of elaborate scarification and the use of pearl leg bands; the best decorated calves were known for miles around. Tribal incisions behind the ears of Chad men rendered the skin "as smooth and stretched as that of a drum." The women would laugh at any man lacking 6 these incisions, and they would never accept him as a husband. Men would subject themselves willingly to this custom, hoping for scars deep enough to leave marks on their skulls after death.

7 At the beginning of the eighteenth century, Father Laurent de Lucques noted that any young girl of the Congo who was not able to bear the pain of scarification and who cried so loudly that the operation had to be stopped was considered "good for nothing."[3] That is why, before marriage, men would check to see if the pattern traced on the belly of their intended bride was beautiful and well-detailed.

8 The fact that such motivations and pretexts depend on aesthetic, erotic, hygienic, or even medical considerations has no influence on the result, which is always in the direction of transforming the appearance of the body. Such a transformation is wished for, whether or not it is effective.

9 The body is a supple, malleable, and transformable prime material, a kind of modeling clay, easily molded by social will and wish. Human skin is an ideal subject for inscription, a surface for all sorts of marks which make it possible to differentiate the human from the animal. The physical body offers itself willingly for tattooing or scarring so that, visibly and recognizably, it becomes a social entity.

10 The absolutely naked body is considered as brutish, reduced to the level of nature where no distinction is made between man and beast. The decorated body, on the other hand, dressed (if even only in a belt), tattooed, or mutilated, publicly exhibits humanity and membership in an established group. As Theophile Gautier said, "The ideal disturbs even the roughest nature, and the taste for ornamentation distinguishes the intelligent being from the beast more exactly than anything else. Indeed, dogs have never dreamed of putting on earrings."

11 So, it is by their categorical refusal of nakedness that human beings are distinguished from nature. The "mark makes unremarkable"—it creates an interval between what is biologically and brutally given in the animal realm and what is won in the cultural realm. The body is tamed continuously; social custom demands, at any price—including pain, constraint, or discomfort—that wildness be abandoned.

12 Each civilization chooses—through a network of elective relationships which are difficult to determine—which areas of the body deserve transformation. These areas are as difficult to define and as shifting as those of eroticism or modesty. An individual alone eludes bodily modifications; they are the expression of a homogeneous collectivity which, at a chosen moment, comes to a tacit agreement to attack one or another part of the anatomy.

13 Whatever the choices, options, or differences may be, that which remains constant is the transformation of appearance. In spite of our contemporary western belief that the body is perfect as it is, we are constantly changing it: clothing it in musculature, suntan, or makeup; dying its head hair or pulling out its bodily hair. The seemingly most innocent gestures for taking care of the body very often hide a persistent and disguised tendency to make it adhere to the strictest of norms, reclothing it in a veil of civilization. The total nudity offered at birth does not exist in

any region of the world. Man puts his stamp on man. The body is not a product of nature, but of culture.

Notes

1. Of course, there are also many different sexual mutilations, including excisions and circumcisions, which we will not go into at this time as they constitute a whole study in themselves.
2. C. Lévi-Strauss, *Tristes Tropiques* (Paris: Plon, 1955), p. 214.
3. J. Cuvelier, *Relations sur le Congo du Père Laurent de Lucques* (Brussels: Institut royal colonial belge, 1953), p. 144.

Thinking Critically About Content

1. What does Borel mean when he says, "The body only speaks if it is dressed in artifice"?
2. According to Borel, what are the primary reasons people make changes in their appearance? Do you notice any common thread in these reasons?
3. In what ways is tattooing "a social entity" (paragraph 9)?

Thinking Critically About Purpose and Audience

4. What do you think France Borel's purpose is in this essay?
5. Do you think all students would be interested in this essay? What other groups would find this essay interesting? Why?
6. Do you think this essay might change someone's opinion about body decorations? Explain your answer.

Thinking Critically About Essays

7. What is the thesis of this essay?
8. Why do you think Borel divides this essay into two parts? What is the main idea of each part? Is this an effective way to break up this essay? Explain your answer.
9. In what way does the last sentence serve as a summary for the essay?
10. Were your views on any forms of body decoration changed as a result of reading this essay? If so, in what way? Explain your answer in detail.

CHRIS WOOD
Wild Weather

Focusing Your Attention

1. Think of your last experience with bad weather that broke records. What was it that made the weather so unusual? Was it the unusually high or low temperature, the amount of precipitation, or the inconvenience it caused?
2. In the essay you are about to read, the writer describes various cases of extreme weather. He points out that, according to experts, what is causing what we know as global warming is actually global wettening, as warm temperatures cause an increase in the amount of moisture the air can hold. Would you say that most of your experiences with extreme weather have involved an increase in either moisture or humidity? Did the extreme weather disrupt the way you worked or played?

Expanding Your Vocabulary

The following words are important to your understanding of this essay:

inundated: swamped, flooded (paragraph 2)
dislocation: put out of place (paragraph 2)
ratchets: increases incrementally (paragraph 4)
simulate: imitate (paragraph 5)
consensus: agreement (paragraph 5)
spawned: produced in large numbers (paragraph 9)
spate: sudden rush (paragraph 9)
wallop: punch (paragraph 13)

READING CRITICALLY

Once again, circle the thesis of the following essay, and draw horizontal lines in the text to show the different examples the author has chosen to support his thesis. Compare your marks with those of a classmate, and justify your decisions to each other.

CHRIS WOOD
Wild Weather

1 As a storm raged outside, the constantly ringing phones went unanswered at Environment Canada's Toronto offices last Thursday. Like many other workplaces in the city, it was shut down—by the worst series of blizzards ever to strike Toronto. As

heavy snow and bitterly cold temperatures swept along a corridor from Windsor, Ont., to the Maritimes, they snarled traffic, crippled public transportation and stranded thousands of commuters in Canada's largest city. Toronto Mayor Mel Lastman called in the Canadian Forces. In the northeastern United States, where the storm delivered heavy snow and freezing rain, it established a record low temperature in the state of Maine: –48°C.

Even so, Canada's first great storm of '99 paled beside other recent examples of nature's fury—last January's ice storm in Quebec, eastern Ontario and parts of the Maritimes, in particular. In economic and human terms, that blast, which disrupted electric power supplies to three million people and left more than 25 dead, was far more severe than last week's. Floods that inundated southern Manitoba in the spring of 1997 also produced greater dislocation—forcing 28,000 people from their homes and damaging hundreds of properties along the Red River. A year earlier, floods swept through Quebec's Saguenay region, leaving 10 dead and 2,000 families homeless. 2

Is it just our imaginations, or is the weather really getting worse? And if it is getting worse, just how bad can it get? 3

The answers, to the extent that science can provide them, are not comforting. For starters, it is not our imagination: the weather is indeed getting wilder. Researchers in the United States and Canada say extreme weather is not only becoming more frequent, it is getting more violent as well. The Ontario blizzard was typical, they say, of what Canadians can expect as Earth's temperature ratchets upward in the decades ahead. 4

As for how bad it could get, no one knows for sure. Computer models designed to simulate Earth's future climate hint at startling increases in snow and rainfall along with temperature shifts. But their reliability is unproven. And simulations designed to model large scale climate changes are unhelpfully imprecise about what may happen to local weather patterns in the 21st century. Still, there is a growing consensus among climate-watchers that worse, possibly far worse, weather lies ahead. As William Hsieh, head of the Climate Prediction Group at the University of British Columbia, put it: "You'll get more storms, and stronger storms." 5

The reason for that isn't the heat, it's the humidity. Along with global warming, scientists now forecast what might best be called global wettening. Warmer air is capable of holding more water vapour than cooler air. The warmth also increases the rate at which glaciers and polar ice melt, introducing yet more moisture into the environment. Taken together, the two effects will vastly increase the amount of water moving through the atmosphere, leading inevitably to heavier falls of both rain and snow. For Canadians there is an extra jolt in the global weather outlook. The greatest increases in precipitation are forecast to occur in the higher latitudes—those occupied by Canada—and in the winter. 6

Students of the world's climate have drawn another, sobering conclusion: the impact of global warming is already upon us. One of the world's most sophisticated computer models of Earth's atmosphere is at the Canadian Centre for Climate Modelling and Analysis in Victoria. "Changes," its researchers warned in a paper last September, "accelerate from the present into the next century." 7

8 In coming decades, their model suggests, Canada, and especially its central regions, can expect storms on the measure of last week's to become increasingly common. The number of extreme low pressure systems—the barometric engines that drive the most devastating storms—each winter could increase by more than 20 per cent by 2040. Precipitation—snow or ice in the winter and rain at other times—will become dramatically heavier. Other harsh weather patterns will also worsen: heat waves in some regions may become as much as 10 degrees hotter.

9 If human misery is the measure, the weather already seems bad enough. The last few years have produced a long list of unusual weather events:

- China's floods last summer, when the Yangtze River burst its banks and displaced millions of people from their homes, were some of the worst in that country's long history.
- The entire world sweltered through record heat last year—the hottest in 500 years.
- In Florida, forest fires during bone-dry heat last May destroyed 200,000 hectares before they were finally brought under control in July. Ferocious fires in British Columbia bumped the cost of fighting them from $40 million to $100 million.
- A heat wave in the U.S. South in July killed more than 100 people, as temperatures simmered above 38°C for more than two weeks. Other hot spells killed more than 2,500 people in India and spawned raging brushfires in Australia.
- The most devastating storm to strike Central America in 200 years—Hurricane Mitch—killed an estimated 11,000 people in October. And in the U.S. Midwest, a spate of tornadoes left 129 people dead—more than the toll from the previous three years combined.

10 Although it is hard to say just how extreme the weather may become, researchers at Environment Canada's Victoria Centre for Climate Modelling have some alarming predictions for the next half-century:

- Extremely violent winter storms that previously happened only once every 20 years will occur every 10 years, as the number of deep low-pressure systems generated each season increases.
- In some regions, including Canada's North, extreme daily maximum temperatures will peak at 10 Celsius degrees above present levels.
- Record rain and snow storms over Canada will deliver nearly 10 per cent more precipitation—and become more frequent. Vancouver's famous winter drizzle will become frequent torrential downpours. Blizzards in the East will last longer and dump more snow.

11 The changes, in fact, are already well under way. In a report released last month, the U.S. National Oceanic and Atmospheric Administration said the number of heat waves lasting three days or longer each summer has jumped 88 per cent between 1949 and 1995. The same agency's National Climatic Data Center reported that extreme snow and rainstorms became 20 per cent more frequent over the last century.

12 New research at the University of Victoria's School of Earth and Ocean Sciences points for the first time to similar findings for Canada. Graduate student Daithi

Stone, who is gathering data on extreme storms, has determined that current rain and snow falls are significantly heavier than those of decades past, especially in Eastern Canada. "Precipitation has been increasing steadily," says the 24-year-old researcher, "in Ontario, Quebec and the Maritimes for the last century, and in the North for about 40 years."

More snow means more avalanches like the one that killed nine people in a school gymnasium in Kangiqsualujjuaq, in northern Quebec, on New Year's Day. More winter precipitation will also mean more spring floods. And the presence of more heat and more water in the atmosphere means weather systems will hold more energy, giving them a bigger wallop when they touch down. 13

Some of the greatest changes will be felt in Central Canada, says Andrew Weaver, an atmospheric scientist at the University of Victoria's earth and ocean sciences school. "One of the misconceptions," he notes, "is that global warming means a slow, steady change in temperature. That is frankly not the issue. What will impact people most is the frequency of extreme events." Toronto's Storm of '99, like Montreal's Ice Storm of the Century and Winnipeg's Great Flood, could well turn out to be a mere overture to the far greater wrath of the weather to come. 14

Thinking Critically About Content

1. The author states that the weather is getting "wilder." Why does he use this word rather than saying it is getting worse? Explain.
2. What examples from this essay are the most persuasive? What makes an illustration persuasive?
3. In the opening of the essay, Wood describes the weather as moving along a corridor from Windsor to Toronto like a wild animal, snarling traffic and crippling transportation. This technique is a type of metaphor called a *personification*. Find other examples in the essay.

Thinking Critically About Purpose and Audience

4. What is Chris Wood's purpose in writing this essay? Why is the subject matter important?
5. Global warming is a popular topic, but global wettening may be a new term to many people. What are the effects of global wettening, and why is it important that Canadians, in particular, should be told about them?
6. You may have noticed that the essay was written in 1999 after a severe storm in Toronto. Is the essay still relevant today? Explain your answer. What examples would you use if you rewrote the essay today?

Thinking Critically About Essays

7. What is Wood's thesis in this essay? Where is it located?
8. Does Wood give enough examples to back up his thesis? Explain your answer. Are all the examples relevant? Why or why not?
9. The examples show what has happened in the past. What technique does the author use to relate these examples to future changes? How does he convince the reader that these changes indicate that future weather will continue to be unusual? Give examples.
10. In the final paragraph the author mentions a "Storm of the Century" and a "Great Flood." Do the author's examples seem to get more and more extreme throughout the essay? Do they change geographically? Look at the examples and see if there is a pattern. Why might the author be using a pattern?

Writing Workshop

This final section gives you opportunities to apply what you have learned in this chapter to another writing assignment. This time, we provide very little prompting beyond a summary of the guidelines for writing an illustration essay. This section will let you demonstrate that you can go through the entire writing process on your own with only occasional feedback from your peers. Loop back into the chapter as necessary when you have questions, so that this process becomes as automatic to you as possible before you move on to new material. Then pause at the end of the chapter to reflect briefly on what you have learned.

Guidelines for Writing an Illustration Essay

1. State your main point in the last sentence of your introduction.
2. Choose examples that are relevant to your point.
3. Choose examples that your readers can identify with.
4. Use enough examples to make your point.
5. Organize your examples so as to make your point in the clearest, strongest way.

Writing About Your Reading

1. What are some of the differences between the generations regarding body decorations? What do you think accounts for these differences? Give examples to support your claims.

2. How do you think extremes in weather will affect Canadians, specifically those involved in farming and tourism? Can you think of other examples?
3. What do you think writers should consider first when choosing examples in an essay? How should the examples be related to the thesis statement? Why are these criteria important when working with examples?

Writing About Your World

1. Identify some common themes in the news photo above. Then come up with a thesis statement that explains one of the themes. Write an essay to support your thesis statement that is developed with relevant examples from the picture and from your own experience.
2. Share with your classmates your opinion on salary caps for professional athletes or funding for non-professional Olympic athletes. Use examples in your body paragraphs to support your main point.
3. Why do you think Canadians are interested in exercise and weight loss? What actions illustrate your attitude? Use examples or illustrations to explain your observations on the current interest in health and weight.
4. Create your own illustration assignment (with the help of your instructor), and write a response to it.

Revising

Small Group Activity (5–10 minutes per writer) Working in groups of three or four, each person should read his or her illustration essay to the other members of the group. Those listening should record their reactions on a copy of the Peer Evaluation Form in Appendix 1A. After your group goes through this process, give your evaluation forms to the appropriate writers so that each writer has two or three peer comment sheets to use in revising.

Paired Activity (5 minutes per writer) Using the completed Peer Evaluation Forms, work in pairs to decide what you should revise in your essay. If time allows, rewrite some of your sentences, and have your partner look at them.

Individual Activity Rewrite your paper, using the revising feedback you received from other students.

Editing

Paired Activity (5–10 minutes per writer) Swap papers with a classmate, and use the editing portion of your Peer Evaluation Form (Appendix 1B) to identify as many grammar, punctuation, mechanics, and spelling errors as you can. If time allows, correct some of your errors, and have your partner look at them. Record your grammar, punctuation, and mechanics errors in the Error Log (Appendix 3) and your spelling errors in the Spelling Log (Appendix 4).

Individual Activity Rewrite your paper again, using the editing feedback you received from other students.

CHAPTER 11

ANALYZING A PROCESS

If you don't know where you are going, you will probably end up somewhere else.

—Laurence Peter

Process analysis satisfies our natural desire for basic information—how to be more assertive, how to invest in the stock market, how to eat more healthfully, or how to help your child do a better job in school.

Process analysis writing, more than other types of writing, helps you understand the world around you and improve yourself—in your personal life, in school, and in the workplace. Consider the following situations:

People who are coming to visit you from out of town email you for directions to your house.

A student needs to write a paper on how to improve employee morale for a course in business management.

A student needs to explain how to be a good listener for the midterm exam in speech communication.

The owner of an apartment building posts a notice in the laundry room explaining how to operate the new washers and dryers.

The manager of a shoe store has to write a memo reminding employees about the correct procedure for taking returns.

Process analysis is a form of explaining. Process analysis essays fall into one of two main types—giving directions or giving information. The first type, giving directions, tells *how to do something,* such as how to write a research paper or change the oil in your car. The second type, giving information, analyzes *how something works,* such as satellite TV or a bread machine, or *how something happened,* such as how the Soviet Union broke into separate nations. In each case, the explanation starts at the beginning and moves step by step, usually in chronological order, to the end result. Process analysis can be about something mental (how to solve a math problem) or something physical (how to pitch a tent).

READING AND WRITING A PROCESS ANALYSIS ESSAY

If you learn how to approach each rhetorical mode critically, these skills will transfer to your other college work. In fact, reading and writing are two parts of the same process. Reading process analysis essays critically involves understanding the steps of a process or sequence of an event and then going further to evaluate the steps or sequence. Are these steps the best way to create the final product or carry out the event? Would the results have been different with another approach? Dealing with this level of inquiry in both reading and writing will raise your level of thinking in all that you do.

Reading a Process Analysis Essay

In "Dare to Change Your Job and Your Life in 7 Steps," Carole Kanchier explains how to take the right risks in order to change jobs and improve your life. In other words, the essay demonstrates the first type of process analysis: how to do something. Kanchier tells you what to do first, then second, and so on until reaching the desired outcome—success in a job you like. Have you ever held a job that you intensely disliked? Were you able to quit? Why or why not? Do you know what career you want to follow? What steps are you taking to prepare for it?

READING CRITICALLY

Recently, students are finding that making drawings of the ideas and details in their readings is a much more effective way to understand them and see how they work than outlining. Graphic organizers, or concept maps, let you literally "draw" the relationship of ideas to one another. Figuring out what framework to use for this exercise is part of the process. You can make up a drawing of your own or do a web search for "graphic organizers" to see some options. After you read the following essay, show the relationship of the ideas to one another in a graphic form that makes sense to you. Be prepared to explain your drawing.

CAROLE KANCHIER

Dare to Change Your Job and Your Life in 7 Steps

1 Small, dark-haired, attractive, and warm, Melissa belies her 44 years. In a sharp gray suit and becoming blouse, she projects a professional yet approachable image. She is now director of training and development for a large retail outlet—and loves it.

"I feel good about myself," she says, "and at the end of the day, I have lots of energy left over." Melissa feels content because she believes she is doing something worthwhile. Her new position gives her life meaning and purpose. But getting there wasn't easy. 2

First a flight attendant, then a high school English teacher, then a manager in a retail store, Melissa stumbled about from what was for her one dead-end job to another. How did she finally find a meaningful, fulfilling, well-paid career? And how did she do what so many of us fail to do—dare to change? 3

A career change can take months or even years of soul-searching—10 months in Melissa's case. You need to know the steps, how to master the troublesome feelings that accompany change, where the possible dangers lie, and how to maximize your gains while minimizing your losses. While creating a life worth living isn't easy, Melissa and millions of others have shown that anything is possible. 4

In interviews and surveys with more than 30,000 people over the past 25 years, I have identified seven steps that are key to a successful career and life shift. 5

1. Become AWARE of Negative Feelings

Your body and mind may be sending you messages about your job satisfaction. The messages may be physical—lingering colds, flu or headaches—or verbal—"23 minutes till lunch!" or "One more day till Friday!" 6

Perhaps you've been working for several years in your job, and it appears to be going well. You've had steady promotions, praise from superiors, and admiration from colleagues. Then one day you get a queasy feeling that something is lacking. But what? You run the film of your life in reverse but you can't figure it out. These feelings may persist for months or even years, depending on your ability to tolerate them, but, sooner or later, you have to admit you have a problem. 7

2. DEFINE the Problem

A good written definition of your problem can help to put you on the road toward change. 8

First, ask yourself, "What's making me feel this way? What is it about my situation that is unpleasant? Does this job help me reach my goals?" If not, why? 9

Next, describe any barriers that may be blocking you from making a move—perhaps fear of change; fear of losing a secure income, pension or other benefits; fear that the change will interfere with your relationships; or fear that you'll lose power or status. 10

Fear is the result of conditioning, and because it is learned, it can be unlearned. Reprogram your old attitudes and beliefs with new ones by learning and practicing specific ways to overcome the fears blocking your path toward change. Think of FEAR as an acronym for "False Expectations Appear Real." Don't spend time worrying about what might happen. Focus on the now. 11

3. Listen to AMBIVALENCE

Milton, a rehabilitation counselor, was approached by a prospective partner to start an executive recruitment agency. For weeks before making the move, he went 12 straight to bed immediately after dinner and pulled the sheets up over his head. He tried to make light of this behavior, but he had undertaken many risks before and had never felt this way about them.

13 His underlying fears were prophetic. He later discovered that the hard-sell, aggressive style required for executive recruiting was not for him. The difference in basic values between Milton and his partner proved such a handicap that, within five months, the two parted ways.

14 The decision to change can provoke mixed feelings. A certain amount of ambivalence is natural. Inner emotional preparation—weighing losses as well as gains, fears as well as hopes—is a necessary prerequisite for successful risk taking.

15 But if the prospect of undertaking a change is so great that your stomach is churning, you can't sleep, you have constant headaches, or you feel you're developing an ulcer, your body, in its wisdom, is telling you to forgo the risk.

4. PREPARE for Risk

16 The key to avoiding potential potholes is to set tentative career goals before you explore new roads. Goals force you to focus on what you really want. Years from now, as you review your life, what would you regret not having done?

17 Fantasize about the ultimate goal, your shining star. If you could do anything in the world, what would it be? Write all of your ideas or fantasies in a notebook. Include everything you want to do, be, and have. The sky is the limit. Once you know what you want, you'll be more willing to take the risks necessary to achieve it.

18 Choosing a satisfying career and lifestyle also requires a basic understanding of yourself. A variety of exercises can help. To identify your strengths, for example, list some of the successes you've had—say, substituting for your son's soccer coach. Next to each success, identify what gave you the positive feelings. Did you contribute to the team's first win of the season?

19 Also list the skills and abilities you used to bring about that success. Were you well organized and adept at working with parents? Finally, decide how your interests, needs, accomplishments, and other personal strengths add up. What pattern do they form?

20 Self-exploration is just part of the process. You also need to take a careful look at your current situation, as well as the available alternatives. Some popular reference tools, available at your local library, can help. Check out the *Occupational Handbook*, the *Dictionary of Occupational Titles,* and the *Encyclopedia of Careers and Work Issues.* The Internet also offers excellent sites for exploring general occupational fields, job descriptions, and educational opportunities.

5. NARROW Your Options

21 Successful career management hinges on finding a position that's compatible with your personal qualities and goals. Do you have the necessary intelligence and skills to do the work? Can you afford the training required for the job? Might your shortcomings—health, vision, size, or strength, for example—pose a problem?

22 To help narrow your options, draw a series of vertical and horizontal lines so that your paper is divided into squares. Across the top of the page, list the most important

elements of your ideal job: income, responsibility, public image, creativity, challenge, and so on (one in each square). Down the left side of the page, list each occupational option you're considering.

Next, for each alternative, place a -1 in the appropriate box if that job option doesn't satisfy the criterion listed at the top of the page. If the criterion is met, but not as much as you'd like, record a 0. If the criterion is well met, record a +1. Add the points for each job option and place them in a column labeled "total" at the far right. The job with the highest score meets the greatest number of criteria that you have deemed important. 23

6. Take ACTION

Once you've determined your occupational goal, take steps to realize it. You'll need a well-planned campaign to market yourself for the job, establish your own business, or return to school. 24

Stay focused on your goals, and believe you will achieve them. View failures along the way as learning experiences—detours that might offer an unexpected dividend. 25

7. EVALUATE the Decision

When you have worked hard at making a decision, take the time not just to enjoy the outcome, but to evaluate it. Ask yourself: 26

- Do I feel good about the move?
- What other gains did I derive from the move? What did I lose?
- What factors contributed to the success of my move?
- If I could do it all over again, what would I do differently?
- Who was most helpful in the process? Who let me down?

Evaluation is a continuous process. Assess your needs, goals, and job satisfaction periodically to determine if your developing personality fits your position and lifestyle. Don't wait for a crisis to clear your vision. 27

There really is no substitute for risk as a way to grow. Knowing you have honestly faced the painful struggle and accepted the trade-offs, and yet proceeded in spite of them, is extremely gratifying. 28

Melissa learned that the tremendous investment of energy a successful job search demands is exactly what enables people to look back and say, "Win, lose, or draw, I gave it my everything." Being able to say with satisfaction that you risked all for a dream may be the biggest prize of all. 29

To remain fulfilled, however, you'll need to risk again and again until you've created a life in which you feel comfortable being yourself, without apology or pretense—a life in which you can continue to have choices. 30

PREPARING TO WRITE YOUR OWN PROCESS ANALYSIS ESSAY

Think of some advice that you would like to give to a friend or classmate—for example, how to survive your first year of college, how to find the partner of your dreams, how to buy a used car, or how to find good daycare for your child. Use one or more of the prewriting strategies you learned in Chapter 5 to generate ideas about advice you have for others.

Writing a Process Analysis Essay

Both types of process analysis call for careful step-by-step thinking, but especially the first—how to do something. If you leave out even one detail, you may confuse your reader or even endanger someone's life. If, for example, you forget to tell a patient who is coming to a doctor's office for some tests that she shouldn't eat after midnight and she has breakfast, the test results will not be accurate, and a serious medical condition might go unnoticed.

Good process analysis of the second type—how something works or how something happened—can help your reader see a product or an event in a totally new light. Someone looking at a product that is already assembled or at a completed event has no way of knowing how it got to the final stage without an explanation. Good process analysis gives the reader a new way of seeing something. The following guidelines will help you write clear and complete process analysis essays.

1. ***State in the thesis statement what the reader should be able to do or understand by the end of the essay.*** Stating the end result at the beginning, in the thesis statement, gives your reader a road map for what follows. The thesis statement in a process essay should also state the number of steps or stages in the process. For example, someone giving directions might start by saying, "It's easy to get to the library from here with just four turns." Even if a process involves many separate steps, you should divide the list into a few manageable groups: "Most experts agree that there are four stages in overcoming an addiction." Stating the end result and the number of steps or stages in the thesis statement helps the reader follow your explanation. These statements set up the tasks.

   Carole Kanchier's thesis statement, which appears in paragraph 5, at the end of her introduction, tells her readers exactly what they will be able to do by the end of her article: make "a successful career and life shift." She also tells them how many steps are involved—seven. In this way, she provides a very clear road map for reading her essay.
2. ***Know your audience.*** In a process analysis essay, more than in others, the success of your essay depends on how well you know your audience.

Knowing your audience helps you decide how much detail to include, how many examples to add, and which terms to define. Also keep in mind that your readers won't be able to ask you questions, so if they can't follow your explanation, they will become confused and frustrated. Whoever your audience is, explaining clearly is essential.

Kanchier's essay was first published in *Psychology Today*, which is read mostly by educated adults. The author's audience seems to be working adults of any age who are unhappy in their jobs. Kanchier addresses them in a very businesslike way; she doesn't talk down. Knowing that being unhappy in a job is very discouraging, she strives for an upbeat "you can do it" tone.

3. ***Explain the process clearly in the body of your essay.*** By the end of a how-to essay, the reader should be able to perform the activity. By the end of a how-something-works essay, the reader should understand what is going on behind the scenes, and by the end of a how-something-happened essay, the reader should understand more about a specific event.

   In writing the body paragraphs of a process essay, pay special attention to transitions. Use transitions such as *first, next, then, after that,* and *finally* to guide your reader through the process from beginning to end.

   Since Kanchier's process has seven parts, she numbers each step. This is a good idea if a process is complicated. If you are writing about a process with only three or four steps, you can use transitions to indicate to your readers where you are in the process.

4. ***Organize your material logically.*** Most process analysis essays are organized chronologically or according to a time sequence. The explanation starts at one point and progresses through time to the final point. If a process is complicated, figure out the most logical organization for the process you are explaining. For instance, playing the guitar involves pressing the strings with the fingers of one hand and strumming with the other hand. You might therefore explain each part of the process separately and then explain how the hands work together to make music.

   Kanchier's essay is organized chronologically. She moves from recognizing the problem to taking action and then to evaluating the action. To help readers follow along smoothly, she numbers the steps and uses transitions such as *first, next,* and *then.*

5. ***End your essay by considering the process as a whole.*** Don't just stop after you have explained the last step of a process. Instead, in the conclusion, look at the process as a whole. There are many ways to do this. You might state why knowing about this process is important: Knowing how to perform CPR (cardiopulmonary resuscitation) can save a life; knowing how your car runs might save you money in repair bills. Or you might review your introduction, summarize the steps of the process, call for action, or end with a fitting quotation. Whatever your method, leave your reader feeling that your essay has reached a natural close.

Kanchier concludes by returning to her introduction. She brings back Melissa, the person from the opening example, to emphasize the rewards of taking risks. She ends her essay by saying that a satisfying life requires taking risks over and over again.

> **WRITING YOUR OWN PROCESS ANALYSIS ESSAY**
>
> Look at the prewriting you did earlier on the topic of giving advice to a friend or classmate. If your directions involve many steps, divide them into three groups. Come up with a thesis statement that states the end result of the process and tells how many steps or stages are involved. Then write the first draft of your essay by following the guidelines for writing a process analysis essay. Make sure you have an introduction and a conclusion.

A STUDENT'S PROCESS ANALYSIS ESSAY

A student writer named Emily Bliss wrote the following essay about procrastination. See if you can follow her steps as you read her first draft.

You Too Can Procrastinate

1 My name is Emily, and I am a procrastinator. But I have discovered over the years that procrastination is not all bad. Especially when I have to write. At my college, the English instructors requires rough drafts. I have somehow mastered the art of procrastinating but still meeting deadlines with my papers. So I have perfected a successful plan for procrastinating that I now want to share with the world.

2 You will know the dreaded day you have to write has arrived when you wake up with a start. This day is different from the rest. You actually have to do something about your paper today. But whatever you do, resist the temptation to sit down and write early in the day by following two more steps. First (step 1), to avoid sitting down to write, you can clean, take a bike ride, do the laundry, rearrange the furniture, dust the light bulbs, and so on. But don't write. Then (step 2), when you finally think you are ready to start writing, call a friend. Talk about anything but your paper for about 15 or 20 minutes. This final delay is what creates the tension that a real procrastinator needs to do his or her best work.

3 Whether you want to or not, you will naturally think about the assignment from the moment you get it. If you have two weeks or two months, you will spend most quiet moments haunted by your paper topic. No matter what you do, your paper topic will be bouncing around in your head giving you headaches, making you worry, wanting attention. But that's OK. Don't give in and write. Ignore it until the day before it is due.

At this point, your third step is to prepare your immediate environment for work. 4
You need to get ready for serious business. Sharpen your pencils, and lay them in a row. Get out the white paper if you can't think on yellow, or get out the yellow paper if you can't think on white. Go to the kitchen for snacks. Whether or not you actually drink or eat these item's is irrelevant—as long as they are by your side. You can't be distracted if you don't have them next to you. My stomach growls really loudly when I'm hungry. Some sort of bread usually takes away the hunger pangs. Step 4 is to sit back in your chair and stare at the computer while you think long and hard about your paper. Fifth, brainstorm, list, or cluster your ideas on the coloured paper of your choice. Sixth, put all your procrastination strategies aside. Its finally time to write.

If you follow these six simple steps, you too can become a master procrasti- 5
nator. You can perform your very own procrastinating ritual and still get your first draft in on time. If you go through the same ritual every time you write. You can perfect it and get your own system for writing essays down to a science. The trick is just to make sure you start writing before you has to join Procrastinators Anonymous.

Discovering How the Essay Works

1. What should the reader be able to do by the end of this essay?

   ____

2. Who do you think Emily's audience is? Does she meet their needs?

   ____

   ____

3. Do you understand how to procrastinate and still meet your deadlines? If so, list the six steps of this process.

   Step 1: ________________________________

   Step 2: ________________________________

   Step 3: ________________________________

   Step 4: ________________________________

   Step 5: ________________________________

   Step 6: ________________________________

If you do not understand, what else do you need to know?

____

4. Are the details in the essay organized logically? Is this order effective for what the author is trying to say? Why or why not?

____

____

____

5. Does the essay conclude by considering the process as a whole? Explain your answer.

____

____

____

REVISING AND EDITING THE STUDENT ESSAY

This essay is Emily's first draft, which now needs to be revised and edited. First, apply the Revising Checklist on the inside front cover to the content of Emily's draft. When you are satisfied that her ideas are fully developed and well organized, use the Editing Checklist on the inside back cover to correct her grammar and mechanics errors. Answer the questions below. Then write your suggested changes directly on Emily's draft.

Revision Questions

Thesis Statement

1. Put brackets around the last sentence in Emily's introduction. Does it state her purpose?

____

2. Rewrite Emily's thesis statement if necessary so that it introduces her process and states her purpose.

____

____

Basic Elements

1. Give Emily's essay an alternative title.

____

2. Rewrite Emily's introduction so that it captures the reader's attention and builds up to the thesis statement at the end of the introduction.

   ___

   ___

   ___

3. Does each of Emily's body paragraphs deal with only one topic?

   ___

4. Rewrite Emily's conclusion, using at least one suggestion from Part I.

   ___

   ___

   ___

Development

1. Write out Emily's thesis statement (revised, if necessary), and list her three topic sentences below it.

   Thesis statement: ___

   ___

   Topic 1: ___

   ___

   Topic 2: ___

   ___

   Topic 3: ___

   ___

2. Do Emily's topics adequately support her thesis statement?

   ___

3. Do Emily's details in the essay explain the process step by step?

   ___

4. Where do you need more information?

   ___

5. Add at least two new details to make the steps clearer.

Unity

1. Read each of Emily's topic sentences with her thesis statement (revised, if necessary) in mind. Do they go together?

   ____

2. Revise them if necessary so that they are directly related.

3. Drop or rewrite the two sentences in paragraph 4 that are not directly related to their topic sentence.

Organization

1. Read Emily's essay again to see if all the paragraphs are arranged logically. Look at your list of steps in response to question 3 after Emily's essay (page 187).
2. Reverse the two paragraphs that are out of order.
3. Look closely at Emily's body paragraphs to see if all her sentences are arranged logically within paragraphs.
4. Move any sentences that are out of order.

Coherence

For a list of transitions, see pages 85–86.

1. Circle five transitions Emily uses.

2. Explain how two of these make Emily's essay easier to read.

   ____

   ____

   ____

Now rewrite Emily's essay with your revisions.

Editing Questions

Sentences

Subjects and Verbs

For help with subjects and verbs, see Chapter 23.

1. Underline the subjects once and verbs twice in paragraphs 1 and 5 of your revision of Emily's essay. Remember that sentences can have more than one subject–verb set.
2. Does each sentence have at least one subject and verb that can stand alone?

   ____

3. Did you find and correct Emily's two fragments? If not, find and correct them now.

For help with fragments, see Chapter 24.

Subject–Verb Agreement

1. Read aloud the subjects and verbs you underlined in your revision of Emily's essay.
2. Did you find and correct the two subjects and verbs that do not agree? If not, find and correct them now.

For help with subject–verb agreement, see Chapter 27.

Pronoun Agreement

1. Find any pronouns in your revision of Emily's essay that do not agree with their nouns.
2. Correct any pronouns that do not agree with their nouns.

For help with pronoun agreement, see Chapter 30.

Modifiers

1. Find any modifiers in your revision of Emily's essay that are not as close as possible to the words they modify.
2. Rewrite sentences if necessary so that modifiers are as close as possible to the words they modify.

For help with modifier errors, see Chapter 33.

Punctuation and Mechanics

Punctuation

1. Read your revision of Emily's essay for any errors in punctuation.
2. Find the two fragments you revised, and make sure they are punctuated correctly.
3. Did you find and correct Emily's two apostrophe errors? If not, find and correct them now.

For help with punctuation, see Chapters 34–37.

Mechanics

1. Read your revision of Emily's essay for any errors in capitalization.
2. Be sure to check Emily's capitalization in the fragments you revised.

For help with capitalization, see Chapter 38.

Word Choice and Spelling

Word Choice

1. Find any words used incorrectly in your revision of Emily's essay.
2. Correct any errors you find.

For help with confused words, see Chapter 44.

Spelling

For help with spelling, see Chapter 45.

1. Use spell-check or a dictionary to check the spelling in your revision of Emily's essay.
2. Correct any misspelled words.

Now rewrite Emily's essay again with your editing corrections.

REVISING AND EDITING YOUR OWN PROCESS ANALYSIS ESSAY

Returning to the process analysis essay you wrote earlier in this chapter, you are now ready to revise and edit your own writing. Remember that revision involves reworking the content and organization of your essay, while editing asks you to check your grammar and usage. At this stage, you should repeat these processes over and over until you feel you have a draft that says exactly what you want it to say.

The revising and editing checklists on the inside front and back covers will help you apply what you have learned in this chapter to your essay.

WRITING CRITICALLY

As you set out to revise and edit your essay, apply the strategy you learned for critical reading to your writing. Draw a picture of the relationship of your ideas to one another. In this way, you can check for logic and organization and make any changes that you think are necessary at this time. Then, you can turn to grammar and usage.

PRACTISING PROCESS ANALYSIS: FROM READING TO WRITING

Reading Workshop

Here are two essays that illustrate good process analysis writing: Chris Daniels's "Learn How to Negotiate Almost Anything," published in *Chatelaine* magazine, explains how to negotiate deals with airlines, hotels, and your boss, and Shanda Deziel's "How She Survived Freshman Year" explains one student's techniques for making it through her first year of university. You might want to read these selections before writing another process analysis essay. As you read, notice how the writers explain every step of the process carefully and completely.

CHRIS DANIELS

Learn How to Negotiate Almost Anything—an Airline Upgrade, a New Vehicle, Even a Raise

Focusing Your Attention

1. Think of your last experience flying home for the holidays, or away on a vacation. Were you cramped and uncomfortable? Did you envy the people you saw in business class? Did you ask for an upgrade, or would you feel that was inappropriate? Why?
2. In the essay you are about to read, the writer tells you how to negotiate deals. She points out that the most important thing you have to do to get a deal is to ask for it. Do you know people who always seem to get discounts at stores, or upgrades when they fly? Do you think the main reason you can't be like that is that you don't feel confident enough to ask?

Expanding Your Vocabulary

The following words are important to your understanding of this essay:

mediated: acted between parties to bring about an agreement (paragraph 1)

keynote: a speech containing central, important ideas (paragraph 5)

incentives: something that motivates effort (paragraph 8)

confrontational: a face-to-face meeting involving a clash of opinions (paragraph 13)

READING CRITICALLY

As you learned at the beginning of this chapter, practise drawing graphic organizers for the ideas in this essay. Exchange "pictures" with someone in your class, and write a brief statement of what your classmate's drawing communicates to you.

CHRIS DANIELS

Learn How to Negotiate Almost Anything—an Airline Upgrade, a New Vehicle, Even a Raise

1 You've mediated a truce between your two kids while manoeuvring your vehicle through rush-hour traffic. You've convinced your electronics-loving husband that, no, he actually wouldn't be better off with the newest iPod. And you've even convinced your dog that she doesn't control the pace of your morning jogs. But are your powers of persuasion restricted to warring children and a wayward canine? The truth is, armed with a few pointers, you can negotiate almost anything: an airline upgrade, a new vehicle, even a raise.

How to negotiate a raise

2 As a national recruitment consultant with more than 10 years experience, Shannon Jackson has heard a host of reasons why people want a raise ("I'm supporting an ill relative," "It's been over a year since my last one" and "So-and-so received a raise—I should too"). But really, only one approach works. "You need to demonstrate how you've carried out responsibilities outside the original expectations of your role," says Jackson.

3 Sounds easy enough, but you can't just say it; you have to prove it. That might mean highlighting—with actual dollar figures, if possible—how you saved or made the company money. Or it could mean pointing out you've taken on additional responsibilities. Jackson also recommends keeping a "happy file," an ongoing list of your accomplishments. That way, you can pull out information from the happy file to convince your boss (and yourself, too) that you're worth the money. A few other strategies can help improve your odds of a generous salary bump:

4 Watch your timing. If your performance review is not tied to an annual raise or if you've recently taken on new job responsibilities, you'll have to wait until the fall. Hit your boss up in October or November, when most employers plan for next year's budget. "It can be challenging from a budget perspective to significantly increase a salary mid-year," says Jackson.

5 Avoid uptalking. When nerves cause you to end every sentence as if asking a question, the rising inflection conveys insecurity. "Practise asking for a raise in a steady, confident tone of voice," says Nina Spencer, a keynote speaker, author and professional-development workshop facilitator. Simply put, don't sound like you're requesting a favour.

6 If you can, negotiate before you start a new job. According to new data from Statistics Canada, wives who were the breadwinners in 2003 earned on average $41,200. Husbands in the same position? $57,800. Jackson says that, in her experience, fewer women than men negotiate their starting salaries, believing they should first get in the door, wow their employer and then ask for a pay hike. Yet typically a company's first offer of employment isn't the only one. "And you know what? A two per cent raise of a $60,000 salary is a lot more than two per cent of a $50,000 salary," says Jackson.

How to negotiate the best price

In traditionally male environments such as car dealerships, salespeople hold the upper hand—or so it seems. They're trained to sweet-talk you so that, before you realize it, you're walking out with something that costs way too much. The truth is, you can level the playing field. 7

Buying a new vehicle? Find out through websites such as CarCostCanada.com, CarQuotes.ca or organizations such as the Automobile Protection Association how much the dealership actually paid for the car. (The APA charges $26.75 for this info.) Has the automaker offered the dealer any "hidden" incentives? A cash rebate, for instance, can shave $1,000 off the sticker price, yet many dealers will pocket the money themselves rather than pass the savings on to the buyer, warns Michael Turk, a lawyer for the Automobile Protection Association. 8

You can also negotiate—and save—while shopping for a new computer. Your best bet is to find a place where salespeople work on commission. It's not usually advertised (you can flat out ask, but even then they might not fess up), so it's a good idea to visit an independent store or Future Shop, where, unlike at Best Buy, the staff is motivated to close the deal. "I find when I say, 'Can you give me a better offer?,' they'll knock $50 to $100 off the retail price," says Amber MacArthur, new-media specialist for CityTV. Or, at the very least, ask them to throw in free software. 9

How to negotiate an upgrade

Don't want to be cramped on your next flight? Look sharp. "The agent will pick someone who looks presentable to upgrade to business class over someone who's lounging in their sweats," says Debbie Ross, president of the Women'sTravelNetwork.ca in Toronto. Arrive at the terminal early (as soon as you see an employee there) so your request is near the top, and travel solo. (Yes, travelling with kids is a deal breaker.) 10

Checking into a hotel? Roger Soane, general manager of the Fairmont Empress in Victoria, says hotels will negotiate upgrades with travellers on the day of check-in. "We've had people check in and upgrade for just $25," says Soane. "We've also had people pay $200 to $300 extra for the best suite in the hotel, which is a lot less than they would have paid for a general reservation the week before." 11

But be sure to figure out what an upgrade means to you. A jacuzzi tub? Pretty view? More space? Your definition determines how much—or how little—you negotiate to pay. 12

General tips

No matter what you're negotiating for, follow these laws of persuasion: 13

- Ask and ye shall (hopefully) receive. You'll never score a better price or an upgrade if you don't ask.
- State your case professionally and politely. No one wants to help out someone who's aggressive and confrontational.
- Do your homework—for instance, check online if you're in the market for a car (or even talk to your neighbour who just bought a new one). It can pay—literally—to be prepared.

Thinking Critically About Content

1. In the opening paragraph, Daniels describes a series of activities. How do these relate to the rest of the essay? Explain your answer.
2. What are the three main steps that apply to all negotiations?
3. In some ways, negotiating a raise is much like asking a teacher for a better mark. Could you apply the steps to the second activity? Would you expect it to work? Why or why not?

Thinking Critically About Purpose and Audience

4. When you read the first paragraph of this essay, what impression did you get of the intended reader? Why is Daniels aiming at that particular reader?
5. Is the information relevant only to the primary reader in this essay? Who else might find the information useful?
6. Do the examples Daniels uses help you in some of your own negotiating situations? When might you find the examples useful? Explain your answer.

Thinking Critically About Essays

7. If an essay is unified, all of its paragraphs are related to one central idea. Based on this explanation, is this essay unified? Explain your answer.
8. How does Daniels organize her information in this essay? Make a rough outline of this essay.
9. Choose a paragraph from this essay and explain how it is developed.
10. In paragraph 10, Daniels tells us that clothing makes a difference if you are trying to upgrade a flight. Does clothing make a difference when negotiating everything? Explain your answer in detail.

SHANDA DEZIEL

How She Survived Freshman Year: Facebook, MSN, the 4:20 and Day-old Bagels: A Day in the Life of a Frosh

Focusing Your Attention

1. Think of your experiences in first year of college or university. Do you think of your teachers and your courses, or does the social life come to mind first? Was it easy to be away from home for the first time? What problems did you run into?
2. In the essay you are about to read, the writer describes the first-year experiences of a student studying at York University in Toronto. By describing the events of a typical day, the author outlines the process a student might go through to survive the first year.

Expanding Your Vocabulary

The following words are important to your understanding of this essay:

aspirations: hopes and dreams (paragraph 2)

dismal: causing gloom or sadness (paragraph 4)

mandatory: compulsory (paragraph 5)

stimulating: energizing or exciting (paragraph 6)

READING CRITICALLY

As you did with the previous essay, draw a graphic organizer for the ideas in the following essay. Make the drawing so accurate that someone could look at the drawing and understand the basic concepts in the essay. Compare your drawing with someone else's in your class, and write a brief statement about the reading from the graphic organizer.

SHANDA DEZIEL

How She Survived Freshman Year: Facebook, MSN, the 4:20 and Day-old Bagels: A Day in the Life of a Frosh

When York University student Hailey Wojcik rolls out of bed, her first destination is Facebook.com. She takes the half-step to her desk and before her eyes are barely open she's logged onto the "totally addictive" online yearbook community that connects students from universities and colleges all over North America. "It's sad, I know, but I have to see, 'Did anyone post on my wall? Do I have any new friends?'" She checks to see if buddies from other schools have given her a "poke," sort of a virtual wave and nod. It's here she'll find out what pub all of her York friends are going to that night. And though she hates to admit it, she checks the profile of the guy she recently broke up with to see if he's added any female friends to his page. "You stalk people on it," Wojcik says of Facebook. "That's what it's known for." About now she notices that her roommate is already gone, which is a surprise. "She's an MSN freak. She's on the computer until five in the morning." 1

Wojcik's university experience sounds vastly different than it was for her parents' generation. But in other ways, the activities, anxieties and aspirations are the same. This 19-year-old sociology and communications major from Guelph, Ont.—and her fellow first-years—sleep, eat, go to class, go to the library, study, pull all-nighters, get homesick, hang out with friends, watch TV, drink, do drugs, date, have sex, get rejected, run out of money and worry about getting a job after it's all over. But the big picture has changed. University no longer seems like a privilege, but a right—and an expectation and a necessity. 2

3 After Wojcik finishes Facebook-ing, she wraps herself in a towel, takes her basket of beauty products and heads to the washroom, where she finds her friend Amanda—and her friend Adam. "I'm okay with coed washrooms," says Wojcik, "because I went backpacking before coming to university. And hostels are like that." Still, getting into the shower is tricky: doing that little dance of getting behind the curtain, taking off your wrap and stretching back out to hang it up without anyone sneaking a peek. And then there's that couple that has to ruin it for everyone. "There's some people on our floor who feel it's appropriate to shower together," says Wojcik. "You walk in, stop, think, 'What the hell is that noise?' And then, 'Ew, awkward.'"

4 Dressed and ready, Wojcik leaves Vanier College, her 13-storey residence in the heart of the campus, and ventures out into the concrete jungle that is York U. A wind-and-snow tunnel in the winter, and a hot-and-steamy oven in the summer. It's one of the country's biggest—and arguably most dismal—campuses. Classes can feel that way as well. In a hall that seats 500, Wojcik makes her way to the second row of her natural science lecture. "During orientation, someone said, 'Sit in the first five rows and you'll do well.'" At the back you can't hear a word the teacher says, so some students talk, others sleep. But Wojcik is enjoying the class. "We have a really good professor who cares," she says. "I like the way he structures his class. He writes on an overhead as he talks and then we copy it from the overhead. He kind of holds our hands, but for me that's a good learning strategy." It's one of the courses that has had an effect on her life outside of class. "I cared about the environment before, but because of this course I've become like a mini-environmentalist. I've changed a lot of what I do because I've realized how much trouble we're in."

5 Others are less moved. Wojcik's friend Amanda Canavan, bitter about the fact that a natural science course is mandatory for all non-science students, refuses to go to lectures. "I get the notes online," says Canavan, 19, "and just read up on them before the test. I have no desire to go or learn from that teacher. Basically, I pay 900 bucks to sit at my computer and print off stuff."

6 So classes aren't exactly as stimulating and inspiring as they are in Dead Poets Society. But students don't help the matter. Wojcik sits in her "brutal" communications class, frantically typing on her laptop. Turns out, she's on MSN—and one of the people she's messaging is sitting right beside her. "One of the reasons why the quality of education has gone down is we've let technology harm us in many ways," she acknowledges. "It's partly our fault."

7 On other occasions, Wojcik is happy to leave the laptop behind. In her dance class she was hoping for a more formal atmosphere. "But the dance courses here, for non-dance majors, are all about being weird, different, experimental," she says. "There's no emphasis on the technical. Instead of there being incredible jumps and leaps, it's a lot of heavy breathing, slapping arms, coming up with random faces and walking. Anyone can do that."

8 Dance is just a side interest for Wojcik—her plan is to move to Australia and open a traveller's hostel. She sees this bachelor of arts degree as something to broaden her horizons rather than a job training program.

Although, if her meal card is any indication, Wojcik could use an accounting 9
course before opening her own business. Come lunchtime, the choices at York are endless: coffee shops, fast food counters, a diner, cafeterias, a fresh fruit bar, a Falafel Hut, an Indian restaurant, an Italian eatery, a Taco Villa and a Japanese take-out. If this was the beginning of the year, she'd be having a huge meal, paying for her friends, and buying an extra bottle of water, even though she has a Brita filter in her room. But at the end of the year, all she's got left on her card is $15—down from $2,000. So she picks up a bag of day-olds from the Great Canadian Bagel and a container of cream cheese. "That's all I'll eat for three days straight," she says. "Until I'm forced to buy another bag." Wojcik does have a job at an American Eagle clothing store, but all her earnings are going toward a summer trip to England—and she's not about to go to her parents for money. "You have to learn to fend for yourself. I don't want to ask my dad. He's done his part, I need to grow up."

During the day, Wojcik looks for a quiet place to study, but it isn't easy. Her res- 10
idence room is too distracting: "computer desk, MSN, Internet, TV, phone, people knocking on your door." The library isn't much better. She bypasses the first couple of floors, where students come mainly to see and be seen. But even tucked into a corner cubicle on the fifth floor, there's no peace. "There's girls talking on their cellphones all day," she says. "Blah, blah, blah, blah—it's not cool." There's one last refuge, a study room at the bottom of her residence. It's a nice space with comfortable couches, but it has one downside. "There's this couple that comes in and hardcore makes out."

It's 4:20 p.m.: time to get high. Except Wojcik isn't a big pothead and only par- 11
takes about once every two months. Nonetheless, she explains that for reasons unknown to her, four-twenty has become a code word for pot and the designated time to smoke it. (The actual origins are debatable, ranging from a Bob Dylan song to a group of San Rafael, Calif., teens who used to meet every day after school at 4:20 p.m. to smoke marijuana.) "It's just widely known," says Wojcik. "It's especially huge on April 20, the actual four-twenty. It's like New Year's Eve. People go out and get drunk all the time, but they especially go out and get drunk on New Year's."

Wojcik says everyone in residence knows someone they could buy pot from, and 12
you don't have to go far to find harder stuff. "My cousin was here from Alberta, and he's got more of a gangsta look. He was here for not even five minutes and these guys who were out front smoking said to him, 'You wanna buy some pills?'"

Alcohol is Wojcik and company's substance of choice. After a day of classes, 13
drinks start flowing as early as eight—especially on Thursday, which is pub night. Everyone gathers in Wojcik's room for the pre-party because she has cable and they can watch *The O.C.* She also has a karaoke machine in case the mood strikes. Of Wojcik's group of girlfriends, three are of legal drinking age and three aren't. "At the beginning of the year," says friend Meghan Stone, 18, "all the pubs would let you in even if you were underage—you just had to wear a wristband. Now they're only letting five underage people in at a time. A lot of the younger students end up drinking in their dorms." Others, including Wojcik's friends, use fake IDs. Lots of 17- and 18-year-olds find their way into the bars—although many have trouble finding their way back

home. "There's drunk people in the bushes," says Wojcik of the post-pub-night scene, "shopping carts in the showers, people passed out in the bathroom and couches in the stalls."

14 After a night out, Wojcik arrives back in her shoebox of a room, where the walls are covered with pictures of friends, homemade posters from residence parties and trinkets like the lobster necklace from the night she splurged on a dinner at Red Lobster. Collapsing into bed, she has a direct view of her roommate's enormous collection of empty liquor bottles—proving that said roommate, an international student from Trinidad, doesn't do all of her socializing on MSN. The roommates get along great, respecting each other's space and privacy. With the exception of that one time: "I was sleeping," says Wojcik, "and then I heard her and this guy fooling around. Whatever. But then it turned into some X-rated activities. The guy's not even being quiet. If I was across the hall I'd hear it. Right after, I see this phone light go on and I hear him say, 'Your roommate's good-looking, we should invite her to have a threesome.' So like five minutes later I pretend to wake up and just ran. It's five in the morning, and I just hid in the stairwell."

15 It's a story she'll tell for years to come—remembering the sound of that dude's voice long after she's forgotten what her natural science teacher said about photosynthesis. Asked if all the social experiences, along with what she's learning in lectures, readings and tutorials, are worth the $15,000 a year she's spending, she concludes: "It's probably worth half of that." But she'll continue on. Wojcik wants the security of the degree, wants to make her parents and grandparents proud, and wants to spend three more years with the good friends she's made. Although she'll be happy if she never sees another bagel.

Thinking Critically About Content

1. In paragraph 2, Deziel lists all the things first-year students do, but then says that "the big picture has changed." How does she say it has changed? Do you agree that it has?
2. List the different stresses that the student in the essay faces, and give an example for each.
3. What techniques and experiences does the student in the essay use to cope with problems that arise?

Thinking Critically About Purpose and Audience

4. What do you think the purpose of this essay is?
5. How do you think a parent would respond to Deziel's essay?
6. Deziel walks us through a typical day of one student's life to help us understand the stresses a first-year student faces during the whole year. How do you respond to this technique?

Thinking Critically About Essays

7. Describe in a sentence the writer's point of view.
8. Deziel covers a number of different topics in her essay as she follows the student through her day. Is this the only way she could have written this essay? If you disagree, explain your answer.
9. What pattern does the author use? Is it chronological, spatial, or by topic? Defend your answer.
10. If Deziel were writing this essay as a report to university authorities, how would it be different? Explain your answer in detail.

Writing Workshop

This final section gives you opportunities to apply what you have learned in this chapter to another writing assignment. This time, we provide very little prompting beyond a summary of the guidelines for writing an illustration essay. This section will let you demonstrate that you can go through the entire writing process on your own with only occasional feedback from your peers. Loop back into the chapter as necessary when you have questions, so that this process becomes as automatic to you as possible before you move on to new material. Then pause at the end of the chapter to reflect briefly on what you have learned.

Guidelines for Writing a Process Analysis Essay

1. In the first essay, set out in the thesis statement what the reader should be able to do or understand by the end of the piece.
2. Know your audience.
3. Explain the process clearly in the body of your essay.
4. Organize your material logically.
5. End your essay by considering the process as a whole.

Writing About Your Reading

1. In the first essay, Chris Daniels tells us how to negotiate a deal. Explain how you would go about finding a bargain. Pick a specific item—a prom dress, a second-hand car, running shoes—and give the steps to finding and purchasing the best item for the lowest price.

2. Think of your first year (or semester) at college or university and explain how you managed to survive. Consider things like friendships and habits and explain how each one worked for you.
3. Which type of process analysis do you find most interesting—the how-to essays or the background explanations? Explain your answer.

Writing About Your World

1. Place yourself in a scene similar to the one in the photo, and write a process analysis essay explaining something that you find as interesting as this person finds this activity. Be sure to cover all steps or stages of the process you are discussing.
2. Choose an appliance or a piece of equipment that you understand well, and write a process analysis essay explaining how it works. Don't identify the item in your essay. Then see if the class members can guess what device you are talking about.
3. Research the history of your college or university, and write an essay explaining its background to prospective students. Be sure to give a focus to your study and decide on a purpose before you begin writing.
4. Write your own process analysis assignment (with the help of your instructor), and write a response to it.

Revising

Small Group Activity (5–10 minutes per writer) In groups of three or four, each person should read his or her process analysis essay to the other members of the group. Those listening should record their reactions on a copy of the Peer Evaluation Form (Appendix 1A). After your group goes through this process, give your evaluation forms to the appropriate writers so that each writer has two or three peer comment sheets for revising.

Paired Activity (5 minutes per writer) Using the completed Peer Evaluation Forms, work in pairs to decide what you should revise in your essay. If time allows, rewrite some of your sentences, and have your partner look at them.

Individual Activity Rewrite your paper, using the revising feedback you received from other students.

Editing

Paired Activity (5–10 minutes per writer) Swap papers with a classmate, and use the editing portion of your Peer Evaluation Form (Appendix 1B) to identify as many grammar, punctuation, mechanics, and spelling errors as you can. If time allows, correct some of your errors, and have your partner look at them. Record your grammar, punctuation, and mechanics errors in the Error Log (Appendix 3) and your spelling errors in the Spelling Log (Appendix 4).

Individual Activity Rewrite your paper again, using the editing feedback you received from other students.

CHAPTER

12 Comparing and Contrasting

The difference between the right word and the almost-right word is really a large matter—'tis the difference between the lightning-bug and the lightning.

—Mark Twain

Comparison and contrast are at the heart of our democratic society. Our competitive natures lead us to compare our lives to those of others so we can try to better ourselves. Even if we simply attempt to improve on our "personal best," comparison and contrast keep us striving for more. In school, we learn about different writers, different cultures, different musical instruments, and different political platforms by comparing them to one another. And every day we make decisions based on comparisons of one kind or another—which clothes to wear, which person to date, which apartment to rent, which job to take. Comparisons help us establish a frame of reference and figure out where we fit into the larger world around us.

On another level, comparison and contrast are also part of our writing. They play an important role in our personal lives, in our college courses, and in the workplace, as in the following situations:

Someone looking for a new car does comparison shopping on the Internet.

A student doing a report in a nursing course compares and contrasts traditional and alternative approaches to medical care.

A student compares and contrasts two cultures for an exam in anthropology.

An insurance agent prepares a report for a client that compares and contrasts several different insurance policies.

A travel agent compares and contrasts two vacation packages for a client.

Comparison and contrast help us understand one subject by putting it next to another. When we *compare,* we look for similarities, and when we *contrast,* we look for differences. Nearly always, however, comparison and contrast are part of the same process. For this reason, we often use the word *compare* to refer to both techniques.

READING AND WRITING A COMPARISON/ CONTRAST ESSAY

Looking closely at how a comparison/contrast essay works will improve your reading comprehension and transfer over time to your writing. Like two parts of a circle, the reading and writing processes function together and, as you learn how they operate, will serve you well in your college courses and in life. Reading and writing critically will help you succeed in all your life ventures.

Reading a Comparison/Contrast Essay

In the essay "D'oh! An Analysis of the Medical Care Provided to the Family of Homer J. Simpson," Robert Patterson and Charles Weijer compare and contrast two doctors from the television show *The Simpsons* to make a tongue-in-cheek case for the likely direction of medical care in Canada. What problems do you see as a consumer of medical care in Canada? Do the authors make a good case, even though they are using amusing examples?

READING CRITICALLY

We all naturally make personal associations with our reading material. However, one person's associations are usually quite different from those of someone else. Recording the associations you make with a reading selection lets you "own" the essay, so to speak. It allows you to connect the author's ideas to your own experiences. As you read the following essay, make at least five notes in the margin that relate to characters mentioned in the essay, or to your own health care experiences. Be prepared to explain the connection between your notes and the facts in the essay.

ROBERT PATTERSON AND CHARLES WEIJER

D'oh! An Analysis of the Medical Care Provided to the Family of Homer J. Simpson

These are hard times for physicians. Governments blame doctors for spiralling health care costs as they slash spending. Ethicists decry medical paternalism. Our patients—sorry, our clients—demand to be treated like consumers. And political 1 correctness has changed the way we speak. It's enough to give your average doctor an identity crisis. Who are we? Who should we aspire to be?

2 Working on the premise that life imitates art, we searched for and found a role model for physicians to follow in these difficult times. We found him in a long-running cartoon series, *The Simpsons,* and spent many hard hours in front of the television, collecting and collating data for analysis. We hope readers will give our conclusions the attention they deserve.

3 In the quiet town of Springfield,[1] noted for its substandard nuclear power plant and eccentric citizenry, Drs. Julius Hibbert and Nick Riviera frequently come in contact with Springfield's everyman, Homer J. Simpson, and his family. Homer, who works at the power plant, is known for his love of donuts and Duff's beer.

4 Like the forces of good and evil battling for the soul of medicine itself, these two physicians are polar opposites. Julius Hibbert is an experienced family physician with a pleasant, easygoing manner, while Nick Riviera is an ill-trained upstart who is more interested in money than medicine. Knowing that appearances can be deceiving (and first impressions rarely correct), we explored this question: Which of these two physicians should Canada's future physicians emulate?

5 We briefly entertained Hibbert as a potential role model. He is a trusted family physician who provides care not only to Homer but also to his spouse Marge and their three children: Bart, Lisa and Maggie. He delivered all of the children and has weathered many a Simpson medical crisis, from Bart's broken leg to Lisa's primary depression.

6 Generally the quality of care he provides is solid, although there was an incident when he accidentally left the keys to his Porsche inside a patient. We decided to ignore this incident, since such a mishap can befall any physician.

7 Hibbert has diagnostic acumen of Oslerian proportions. He uses this regularly to identify a variety of baffling conditions, from Marge's alopecia areata to Homer's unique form of hydrocephalus.

8 "Don't worry, it's quite beneficial," he told Homer about the latter condition. "Your brain is cushioned by a layer of fluid one-eighth of an inch thicker than normal. It's almost as if you're wearing a football helmet inside your own head. Why, I could wallop you all day with this surgical 2-by-4, without ever knocking you down."[2]

9 Another positive trait is Hibbert's sense of humour, which he uses to put patients and their families at ease. When Homer was critically injured and rushed to hospital after opening a can of beer that spent some time in a paint mixer thanks to Bart, Hibbert's levity helped relieve an otherwise tense situation.

10 "Mrs. Simpson, I'm afraid your husband is dead," he said.

11 "Oh my god!" Marge responded.

12 "April Fools!"

13 Deeper analysis, however, reveals that Hibbert is no Semmelweiss. He treats the health care system like his personal cash cow by taking time to talk to his patients and distributing lollipops to children. No wonder the U.S. system is so expensive.

Worse yet, he stocks his office with patient education materials that either contain value judgements or are poorly written.

When Homer first courted his bride-to-be, Hibbert gave a pamphlet entitled *So You've Ruined Your Life* to a pregnant but unmarried Marge. Fair enough. But later on, when Homer was poisoned after eating an incorrectly prepared blowfish at a Japanese restaurant, Hibbert handed him another brochure, *So You're Going to Die*. By giving away the conclusion in the title, Hibbert ruined the surprise ending. What fun is that? 14

Another gross violation of ethics occurred when Bart stuck various objects to his skin with Krazy Glue. In a scene reminiscent of the Spanish Inquisition, Dr. Hibbert showed him the instruments of surgery, thereby frightening the poor youngster so badly that he began to sweat, causing the objects to fall off. 15

Obviously, informed consent and truth-telling mean little or nothing to this medical Machiavelli. Any ethicist worth her salt would flail him for such an act of unbridled paternalism. Perhaps worst of all, Hibbert shows about as much sensitivity to politically correct language as Howard Stern, as demonstrated by this conversation with Lisa. 16

"Yes, I remember Bart's birth well," he said. "You don't forget a thing like Siamese twins!" "I believe they prefer to be called 'conjoined twins,'" Lisa replied. 17

"And hillbillies prefer to be called 'sons of the soil,'" Hibbert responded, "but it ain't gonna happen." 18

No, the true medical hero for whom we search is Julius Hibbert's foil, the enterprising Dr. Nick Riviera, an international medical graduate who attended the Club Med School. He practises with an enthusiasm that is matched only by his showmanship. Unfortunately, this has led to 160 complaints from Springfield's narrow-minded Malpractice Committee, but artists like Riviera are rarely understood in their time. Dr. Nick, as he is known, may be a tad weak on anatomy. "What the hell is that?" he asked after making the incision for Homer's coronary artery bypass. However, he does possess all the requisite traits for the doctor of tomorrow: he is resource conscious and he gives the customer what she wants. 19

Ever resourceful, Dr. Nick finds innovative new uses for underutilized medical materials, such as cadavers. By placing several of them in his vehicle, he can drive in the car-pool lane and get to work more quickly. This commendable behaviour is also environmentally conscious. 20

And he's no shill for the medical establishment. Knowing that physicians' fees are the real cause of the health care funding crisis, Dr. Nick produced a TV ad in which he offered to do any surgical procedure for just $129.95 (Can $193.95 at time of writing). Cost-effective and consumer conscious, Riviera would never let quality of care interfere with discount-rate fees. 21

His greatest asset, though, is his willingness—no, his mission—to satisfy every whim and fancy of his patients. 22

He is acutely aware that many patients actually want to be sick and, like Albert Schweitzer, he compassionately helps them. When Bart was run over by a car but 23 appeared unhurt, his parents considered a lawsuit against the driver. Dr. Nick was very eager to assist them. "Your son is a very sick boy," he said. "Just look at these X-rays! You see that dark spot there? Whiplash. And this smudge here that looks like my fingerprint? That's trauma."

24 In another touching moment, Homer discovered that he would qualify for disabled benefits and be able to work at home if he weighed more than 300 pounds, and immediately sought a way to increase his weight. Dr. Nick was there in his time of need.

25 "You'll want to focus on the neglected food groups, such as the whipped group, the congealed group and the choc-o-tastic," he advised. "Be creative. Instead of making sandwiches with bread, use Pop-Tarts. Instead of chewing gum, chew bacon."

26 Being so burdened with his patients' wishes, Riviera often sacrifices his personal needs. Every now and then, however, he manages to think of his own well-being. "The coroner—I'm so sick of that guy," he told Homer as he prepared to perform cardiac surgery on him. "Now if something should go wrong, let's not get the law involved. One hand washes the other."

27 In these turbulent times, we need a hero to guide us into the next millennium. As a profession, we must shed the dark past embodied by Dr. Hibbert—a wasteful, paternalistic and politically incorrect physician. Instead, the physician of the future must cut corners to cut costs, accede to the patient's every whim and always strive to avoid the coroner. All hail Dr. Nick Riviera, the very model of a 21st-century healer.

28 "See you at the operating place!"

References

1. It is unclear where Springfield is located. According to *Webster's Ninth New Collegiate Dictionary,* it could be in Illinois, Massachusetts, Ohio, Missouri or Oregon.
2. All quotations taken from our TV screens were checked against those from Richmond, R. (ed). *The Simpsons: A complete guide to our favorite family.* New York: HarperCollins Publishers; 1997.

PREPARING TO WRITE YOUR OWN COMPARISON/ CONTRAST ESSAY

Think of several ways you escape or relieve stress. What do you like about these methods of relaxation? Use one or more of the prewriting strategies you learned in Chapter 5 to generate ideas about these forms of relaxation. Why do they work for you?

Writing a Comparison/Contrast Essay

To write a comparison/contrast essay, you should consider two items that have something in common, such as cats and dogs (both are family pets), or cars and motorcycles (both are means of transportation). A discussion of cats and motorcycles, for example, would not be very interesting or useful because the two do not have common features. This is the basic rule underlying the following guidelines for writing a good comparison/contrast essay.

1. ***Decide what point you want to make with your comparison, and state it in your thesis statement.*** A comparison/contrast essay is usually written for one of two purposes: to examine the subjects separately or to show the superiority of one over the other. This purpose should be made clear in your thesis statement.

   In the sample essay, Patterson and Weijer outline the problems facing doctors today and look for a role model for the future in a cartoon: ". . . we searched for and found a role model for physicians to follow in these difficult times." The essay compares two doctors from the television show *The Simpsons* and finds that Dr. Nick Riviera is the superior role model. Of course, because the essay is ironic, the ideal role model is someone who is able to "cut corners to cut costs, accede to the patient's every whim and always strive to avoid the coroner." The authors use their sense of humour to make a point about government expectations of doctors in Canada today.

2. ***Choose items to compare and contrast that will make your point most effectively.*** Usually, the subjects you plan to compare and contrast have many similarities and differences. Your task, then, is to look over the ideas you generated in prewriting and choose the best points for making your comparison clearly and strongly.

   In their essay, the authors compare their subjects—Dr. Hibbert and Dr. Riviera—on two main points:

   - Positive traits
   - Faults

3. ***Use as many specific details and examples as possible to expand your comparison.*** The most common way of developing a comparison/contrast essay is to use description and example. Generate as many details and examples as you can for each of your subjects. Try to think of both obvious and not-so-obvious points of comparison.

   In "D'oh! An Analysis of the Medical Care Provided to the Family of Homer J. Simpson," Robert Patterson and Charles Weijer rely heavily on examples from the television show. The topics covered are summarized in the final paragraph. Instead of being wasteful, paternalistic, and politically incorrect, as they have been accused of being, doctors should cut corners, accede to patients' whims, and strive to avoid litigation. The examples are outrageous: Dr. Riviera makes practical use of cadavers by loading them into his car so he can drive in the car-pool lane and get to work sooner, for example. These specific examples draw the readers into the essay.

4. ***Develop your comparison in a balanced way.*** Having selected the points on which you will compare your two subjects, you are ready to develop the comparison in your body paragraphs. You should make sure that your treatment of each subject is balanced. That means that, first, you should cover the same topics for each subject. In other words, you should give equal coverage to both subjects, no matter what your conclusion is. In addition, you should spend the same amount of time on each point. If you describe one of your subjects in detail, you should describe the other in detail as well. In like manner, you should provide a similar number of examples for both subjects. In this way, your readers will feel that you have been fair to both subjects and that you are not presenting a biased discussion that favours one subject over the other.

   Patterson and Weijer spend approximately the same amount of time on each subject. They begin by discussing Dr. Hibbert's positive traits (undercutting each one), and then discuss his problems. Dr. Hibbert is greedy, unethical, and politically incorrect. The authors then turn to Dr. Riviera, beginning with his problems and concluding with his positive traits. He satisfies his customers, he is compassionate, and he sacrifices his own personal needs. By reversing the order of the points, the authors appear to indicate that Dr. Riviera is the superior role model.

5. ***Organize your essay subject by subject or point by point—or combine the two approaches.*** When you are ready to write, you have three choices for organizing a comparison-and-contrast essay: (1) subject by subject (AAA, BBB), (2) point by point (AB, AB, AB), or (3) a combination of the two.

   In the subject arrangement, you say everything you have to say about the first subject, A, before you move on to talk about the second subject, B. In a point-by-point arrangement, both subjects are compared on point 1; then both are compared on point 2; and so on through all the points.

   To choose which method of organization will be most effective, just use your common sense. If the subjects themselves are the most interesting part of your essay, use the subject pattern. But if you want single characteristics to stand out, use the point-by-point pattern.

   Patterson and Weijer's essay is organized subject by subject. Here is what the organization pattern looks like:

   Subject 1: Dr. Hibbert
   A. Positive traits
      a. trustworthy
      b. reliable
      c. good diagnostician
   B. Problems
      a. greedy
      b. unethical
      c. politically incorrect

Subject 2: Dr. Riviera

A. Problems
  a. opened himself to litigation
  b. doesn't understand anatomy

B. Positive traits
  a. resourceful
  b. satisfies customers' needs
  c. avoids litigation

WRITING YOUR OWN COMPARISON/CONTRAST ESSAY

Write an essay comparing and contrasting two methods of escape, based on the ideas you generated in your prewriting activities. How are they alike? How are they different? Decide what point you want to make before you start writing. Then spend some time choosing and organizing your topics and deciding on your method of organization (subject by subject, point by point, or a combination of the two). Form a clear thesis statement, and follow the guidelines for writing a comparison/contrast essay.

A STUDENT'S COMPARISON/CONTRAST ESSAY

Let's look at a student's management of a comparison/contrast essay. This next essay, called "The Truth About Cats and Dogs," was written by a student named Maria Castillo. See if you can identify her main point as you read this draft of her essay.

The Truth About Cats and Dogs

The majority of people in the world will say that dogs are man's best friends and that cats were put on this earth to aggravate dogs. Some people are closet cat lovers, meaning he or she is afraid to tell family and friends that they actually like cats. Others will proudly state, "I hate cats, except for yours." People who resist cats do so because they believe they are; aloof, self-centred, and dull. People prefer dogs because they are friendly, protective, and playful. However, cats exhibit these same qualities and deserve the same respect as dogs. 1

Dogs have always been considered to be friendly, but cats can also fit this description. Dogs stay by their owners' sides and live to make their masters happy. They are the first to greet their family at the front door, they want nothing more than to be praised by their owners. Yet cats are much the same way. They, too, will be at the front door when their family gets home and are always excited to see 2 them. They usually sit near their owners just to be by their sides. And despite what some people believe, a cat does come when they're called. Birds do not sit with their owners unless they are trained. Cats are very friendly to their owners.

3 As much as dogs love to play, so do cats. Most dogs love to play with chew toys, searching for the hidden-squeaker treasure. They often parade around with their "kill" until their masters notice their triumph. Some owners will awaken to find that their dogs have strewn all their toys all over the house. Dogs love the toys they know are theirs. However, so do cats. Cats will make a toy out of anything that will slide across a tile floor, whether it's a hair clip, a milk jug ring, a toy mouse, or a spool of thread. They can amuse themselves for hours. If the toy-of-the-day gets trapped under the refrigerator, cats will whine and wait for their owner to get the toy. Cats just love to play.

4 Even though dogs are great defenders, cats have been known to protect the family as well. Dogs bark or growl whenever they want to alert their owners to possible danger. They stand at the door and wait for their owners to check for danger. If they see their owner being attacked, they will attack the enemy. Most people think cats would just stand by and watch, but this simply isn't true. Cats also alert their owners of danger by growling or standing to stiff attention. They, too, stand near the door waiting for their owner to react. Cats have been known to bite people who harm their loved ones. Cats can be excellent watch animals.

5 Dogs and cats are a lot alike. People say cats are very different from dogs, but this is not the case. The truth is, most people love to hate cats. It's now an old established pastime. But it's time for all cat lovers to unite and prove that it can be a cat-eat-cat world too.

Discovering How the Essay Works

1. What is Maria's main point in this essay?

   ____

2. What exactly is Maria comparing or contrasting in this essay? List her points under the subjects below.

Dogs	Cats
____________	____________
____________	____________
____________	____________
____________	____________

3. Does Maria use as many specific details and examples as possible? List three of her specific references.

   ____

   ____

4. Does Maria develop her comparison in a balanced way? Explain your answer.

   ____

   ____

5. How does Maria organize her essay: subject by subject, point by point, or a combination of the two?

   ____

REVISING AND EDITING THE STUDENT ESSAY

This essay is Maria's first draft, which now needs to be revised and edited. First, apply the Revising Checklist on the inside front cover to the content of Maria's draft. When you are satisfied that her ideas are fully developed and well organized, use the Editing Checklist on the inside back cover to correct her grammatical and mechanical errors. Answer the questions below. Then write your suggested changes directly on Maria's draft.

Revision Questions

Thesis Statement

1. Put brackets around the last sentence in Maria's introduction. Does it contain her main point?

   ____

2. Rewrite Maria's thesis statement if necessary so that it states her main point and introduces her topics.

   ____

   ____

   ____

Basic Elements

1. Give Maria's essay an alternative title.

   ____

2. Rewrite Maria's introduction so that it captures readers' attention and builds up to the thesis statement at the end of the paragraph.

   ____

   ____

   ____

3. Does each of Maria's body paragraphs deal with only one topic?

   ____

4. Rewrite Maria's conclusion, using at least one suggestion from Part I.

   ____

   ____

   ____

Development

1. Write out Maria's thesis statement (revised, if necessary), and list her three topic sentences below it.

   Thesis statement: ______________________________

   ____

   ____

   Topic 1: ______________________________

   ____

   Topic 2: ______________________________

   ____

   Topic 3: ______________________________

   ____

2. Do Maria's topic sentences adequately support her thesis statement?

   ____

3. Does each body paragraph have a focused topic sentence?

____

4. Do Maria's details adequately characterize both cats and dogs?

____

5. Where do you need more information?

____

6. Make two of Maria's details more specific.
7. Add at least two new details to make her comparison clearer.

Unity

1. Read each of Maria's topic sentences with her thesis statement (revised, if necessary) in mind. Do they go together?
2. Revise them if necessary so that they are directly related.
3. Drop or rewrite the sentence in paragraph 2 that is not directly related to its topic sentence.

Organization

1. Read Maria's essay again to see if all the paragraphs are arranged logically.
2. Reverse the two paragraphs that are out of order.
3. Look closely at Maria's body paragraphs to see if all her sentences are arranged logically within paragraphs.
4. Move any sentences that are out of order.

Coherence

For the list of transitions, see pages 85–86.

1. Add two transitions to Maria's essay.
2. Circle five synonyms that Maria uses.
3. Explain how two of these make Maria's essay easier to read.

____

____

____

Now rewrite Maria's essay with your revisions.

Editing Questions

Sentences

Subjects and Verbs

For help with subjects and verbs, see Chapter 23.

1. Underline Maria's subjects once and verbs twice in paragraph 2 of your revision of Maria's essay. Remember that sentences can have more than one subject–verb set.
2. Does each of Maria's sentences have at least one subject and verb that can stand alone?

   ____

For help with run-ons, see Chapter 25.

3. Did you find and correct Maria's run-on sentence? If not, find and correct it now.

Subject–Verb Agreement

For help with subject–verb agreement, see Chapter 27.

1. Read aloud the subjects and verbs you underlined in your revision of Maria's essay.
2. Correct any subjects and verbs that do not agree.

Pronoun Agreement

For help with pronoun agreement, see Chapter 30.

1. Find any pronouns in your revision of Maria's essay that do not agree with their nouns.
2. Did you find and correct the two pronouns that do not agree with their nouns?

Modifiers

For help with modifier errors, see Chapter 33.

1. Find any modifiers in your revision of Maria's essay that are not as close as possible to the words they modify.
2. Rewrite sentences if necessary so that modifiers are as close as possible to the words they modify.

Punctuation and Mechanics

Punctuation

For help with punctuation, see Chapters 34–37.

1. Read your revision of Maria's essay for any errors in punctuation.
2. Find the run-on sentence you revised, and make sure it is punctuated correctly.
3. Did you find and correct Maria's semicolon error? If not, find and correct it now.

Mechanics

1. Read your revision of Maria's essay for any errors in capitalization.
2. Be sure to check Maria's capitalization in the run-on sentence you revised.

For help with capitalization, see Chapter 38.

Word Choice and Spelling

Word Choice

1. Find any words used incorrectly in your revision of Maria's essay.
2. Correct any errors you find.

For help with confused words, see Chapter 44.

Spelling

1. Use spell-check and a dictionary to check the spelling in your revision of Maria's essay.
2. Correct any misspelled words.

For help with spelling, see Chapter 45.

Now rewrite Maria's essay again with your editing corrections.

REVISING AND EDITING YOUR OWN COMPARISON/CONTRAST ESSAY

Returning to the comparison/contrast you wrote earlier in this chapter, you are now ready to revise and edit your own writing. Remember that revision involves reworking the content and organization of your essay, while editing asks you to check your grammar and usage. At this stage, you should repeat these processes over and over until you feel you have a draft that says exactly what you want it to say.

The revising and editing checklists on the inside front and back covers will help you apply what you have learned to your essay.

WRITING CRITICALLY

As you begin to rework your essay, use the same technique you did in your reading. Just as you made personal associations with your reading to help you understand what the author was saying, expand your own writing with personal associations and sensory details that will help your readers understand your experience as if they were there. Work first with the content, making sure your thoughts are fully developed and organized effectively before you correct your grammar and usage errors.

PRACTISING COMPARISON/CONTRAST: FROM READING TO WRITING

Reading Workshop

Here are two essays that illustrate good comparison/contrast writing. The first essay, written by Canadian Thomas Hayden, a journalist who works for *U.S. News and World Report*, was published in *The Globe and Mail*. It compares and contrasts Washington, D.C., and Saskatoon to make a point about the need to discuss the problem of racism. The second essay is taken from *The Truth About Stories: A Native Narrative*, by Thomas King, which was originally presented as part of the *2003 Massey Lectures*, sponsored by CBC Radio. You might want to read these selections before writing another comparison/contrast essay. As you read, notice how the writers make their points through well–thought-out, detailed comparisons and contrasts.

THOMAS HAYDEN

That Is Not the Image We Have of Canada

Focusing Your Attention

1. Do you feel that Native people are marginalized in Canadian society? How would you compare or contrast the way Canada has treated its earliest inhabitants with the way the United States has treated its African-American citizens?
2. In the essay you are about to read, the author compares and contrasts Saskatoon, the city he grew up in, with Washington, D.C., the city where he now lives. He looks at Saskatoon from an American point of view. What image do you think Americans might have of Canada? How accurate is that image, do you think? Explain.

Expanding Your Vocabulary

The following words are important to your understanding of this essay:

lynching: executing without trial (paragraph 3)

marginalized: relegated to the outer edge of a group (paragraph 7)

dilapidated: shabby and neglected (paragraph 8)

quadrant: one of four quarters (paragraph 8)

discourse: formal discussion (paragraph 9)

jibes: taunts (paragraph 12)
cacophony: harsh, discordant sounds (paragraph 12)
enclave: an enclosed area within another, larger area (paragraph 16)

READING CRITICALLY

As you learned previously, write any personal associations you make with this essay in the margins as you read. This process will give you some good insights into the author's approach to his topic and into his methods of developing his ideas. Write down anything at all that occurs to you. Then share your notes with one of your classmates.

THOMAS HAYDEN

That Is Not the Image We Have of Canada

When you live in Saskatoon, it's easy to forget how ugly it can be. The riverbank parks, tree-lined neighbourhoods and university campuses all are as lovely as any on the prairies, but drive in from Edmonton or the airport to the north and you get an entirely different impression. I prefer to just close my eyes as I pass the long, grey stretches of light industry and charmless cookie-cutter homes that crowd the city's flanks. 1

In the same way, it's all too easy to overlook the harder truths of life in Saskatoon. In the 11 years that I've lived in the United States, I've been a tireless, and sometimes I'm sure tiresome, booster of the city I left grudgingly and still consider home. But I'm finally opening my eyes more fully. Late last year the *Washington Post*, my new hometown newspaper, ran a front-page article datelined Saskatoon for the first time since the medicare debates of 1962: "Left for Dead in a Saskatchewan Winter." I knew immediately what it was about. 2

It's not hard to freeze to death in Saskatoon. When I was in high school there in the 1980s, we joked about who would get the yearbook dedication, a distinction too often claimed by a boozy grad who tried to wander home from a mid-winter party in only a jean jacket and running shoes. Easy enough to do, but from 1990 to 2000, several aboriginal men apparently had help from members of Saskatoon's police force—a particularly northern form of lynching. 3

With the final stage set to begin this week of a provincial inquiry into the death of Neil Stonechild, found frozen in a north Saskatoon industrial area in 1990, even the major American papers are starting to take notice. 4

"Okay, that is not the image we have of Canada," says Debra Dickerson, an American lawyer and journalist who writes regularly on race. She had never heard 5 about the infamous "starlight tours" in which aboriginal men were abandoned on the city's outskirts by police officers, and was understandably shocked. The image was as foreign to me as it is to Ms. Dickerson. I thought I knew which side of the border had the real race problem. But living in Washington, D.C., at the very centre of America's racial discord, I'm no longer sure whether the bigger trouble is in my old home or my current one.

6 On the surface, Saskatoon and Washington could not be more different. Almost three times as many people call the District home, and 60 per cent of them are black; Saskatoon is as out of the way as D.C. is central, and 85 per cent white. People die of the heat in Washington's summer, and of cold in the prairie winter.

7 Still, there are similarities that go beyond the fact that both are long on leafy parks and short on movie theatres and interesting restaurants: Both cities are the murder capitals of their respective countries; while Saskatoon's six homicides in 2002 can't compare to D.C.'s 264, the prairie town actually registered slightly more violent crimes per capita. And, most strikingly, much of Washington's African-American majority is as segregated and marginalized as Saskatoon's aboriginal minority is.

8 Like urban natives in Saskatoon's dilapidated core, working-class blacks in Washington, Ms. Dickerson says, "are living in a different city and a different reality." A reality that white residents like me rarely visit. Like Washington's primarily black South East quadrant, which I've seen only from the safety of a Habitat for Humanity work site, I pass through Saskatoon's largely aboriginal west-side neighbourhoods only to visit St. Paul's Hospital.

9 Though I pride myself on knowing my hometown well, I grew up without knowing a single aboriginal family. The geographical divide can be just as wide in American cities, but there's a critical difference. In the United States, race is a constant topic of conversation, and the discourse is opinionated, loud, and unmistakable. In the Saskatoon I grew up in, it simply didn't exist.

10 We didn't consider ourselves racist—who does?—but it can be tricky to draw a line between active oppression and passive ignorance. Ms. Dickerson, who spent her 20s in the military before heading to Harvard Law School, says it took that long to understand that she could be doing the same things as the white students she went to high school with. "History is taught so poorly here that it took me a long time to realize that the condition of black people in this country was anything but accidental," she says.

11 And that too, sadly, is not so different from back home. "Indians should just shut up" about treaty rights, I remember being told at the end of a heated argument in Saskatoon several years ago, "because we won the war." Maybe it was just the nearly empty beer keg between us, but I had no luck convincing my companion that the war he was thinking of happened in the country to the south. In high school, during a rare classroom discussion on racism, one student made the point that it was obviously unfair for Americans to be so racist against blacks. But here in Saskatoon, he said, it was another story. "It's different—Indians really are lazy."

Racism, it turns out, is easier to see from a distance. My first reaction to the *Post* headline was horror, not at what happened—it was old news back home—but that word was getting out. We're a protective bunch, Saskatoonians, too used to the slights and jibes of our fellow Canadians, and my immediate impulse was to pray that no one would notice. But they did. I spent weeks fielding uncomfortable questions from friends and colleagues. And through the cacophony of racial dialogue in the States, I've seen a hint of what might come next for Saskatoon. 12

Yelling at each other across the racial divide isn't a solution, of course. But that doesn't mean it can't be a promising sign. "Things are actually probably getting better" in Saskatoon, says John Lagimodiere, the Métis publisher and editor of *Eagle Feather News*, an aboriginal newspaper based in Saskatoon. More natives are educating themselves and joining professions, he says. "There are still incredible problems to overcome, but I think we're at a real turning point," he says, noting that "times of change always get a little ugly." 13

And noisy. Perhaps the angry shouts of urban America are the soundtrack of racial divides being breached. Which would make the silence of Saskatoon the sound of living too comfortably with an uncomfortable truth. 14

In her classic 1990 impressionistic survey of Canadian cities, *O Canada: Travels in an Unknown Country*, travel writer Jan Morris called Saskatoon "Canada's best surprise." That's how I've always liked to think of it. But Ms. Morris also hit on a more painful reality—residents told her tales of narrow-mindedness, prejudice and inequality. "No city is without its seamy side, of course, but in Saskatoon . . . it seems unfairly incongruous, like a lump in a particularly well-made bed, or slugs in a salad." 15

Racial inequality in Saskatoon, a centre of community spirit and an enclave of culture and learning with a strong progressive heritage, is most painful of all. When I spoke with Saskatoon mayor Don Atchison this past Christmas, he emphasized the city's civic pride, the links between the university and the broader community, and its unparalleled levels of volunteerism. That's all true. But it's also true that extreme acts of racial brutality don't come out of a void. 16

Saskatoon is still a wonderful place, its people generous and caring. But it's not wonderful enough for too many of its citizens. The Stonechild inquiry is exposing the darker sides of our city, but it also gives us an opportunity. Having bit into the slug in our civic salad, we can now either swallow it down and force a grin, politely pretending it never was there at all. Or we can clear our throats and join in the messy, difficult business of trying to spit it out. 17

Thinking Critically About Content

1. Notice how in the opening passage the writer describes how he closes his eyes against the ugliness of the industrial outskirts of Saskatoon. How does this image foreshadow the article that follows? What does it tell you about him, and about the people of Saskatoon?

2. Why does the author describe the practice of dropping aboriginal men outside the city limits as a "particularly northern form of lynching"? How is it different from the southern version?
3. Does this essay make you think about your own hometown and its prejudices? What kinds of prejudice exist? How are they evident? In what way is prejudice ignored?

Thinking Critically About Purpose and Audience

4. What do you think Hayden's purpose was in writing this essay? Give details from the article to back up your answer.
5. What readers might the essay affect? Would American readers and Canadian readers have something different to learn from the article? Explain your answer.
6. Should the writer have included a statement from the Saskatoon police? Why or why not?

Thinking Critically About Essays

7. Describe the writer's point of view in this essay. What comparison would you make between his physical and his emotional distance from the topic?
8. The comparison is confined to the centre of this essay. How is this effective in the development of the topic?
9. The title of the essay is taken from something someone said to the author. How is it effective?
10. Explain in detail how this essay might be different if it were written by someone who had not grown up in Saskatoon and moved away.

THOMAS KING
The Truth About Stories

Focusing Your Attention

1. Do you belong to a culture with a strong storytelling tradition? What kinds of stories does your family tell? How do the stories relate to cultural changes your family experienced?
2. The essay you are about to read begins with a reference to the Iroquoian story *The Woman Who Fell from the Sky*. As the story is not reproduced here due to lack of space, you might like to read it and other Iroquoian stories at **www.webwinds.com/yupanqui/iroquoisdreams3.htm**.

Expanding Your Vocabulary

The following words are important to your understanding of this essay:

decorum: appropriate behaviour (paragraph 1)
inherent: an essential part (paragraph 1)
exuberance: rich, excessive, usually applied to happiness (paragraph 1)
veracity: truthfulness (paragraph 1)
animism, polytheism, monotheism: types of religious beliefs (paragraph 3)
martial: warlike, from Mars, the Roman god of war (paragraph 9)
parlance: a manner of speaking, idiom (paragraph 9)
dichotomy: division into two opposing parts (paragraph 13)
honed: sharpened or ground, like a knife edge (paragraph 15)
Silko's witches in the cave: refers to *Ceremony*, a novel by Leslie Marmon Silko (paragraph 18)
rectitude: moral uprightness (paragraph 22)
platitude: trite or banal saying (paragraph 27)
insatiable: impossible to satisfy (paragraph 35)

READING CRITICALLY

As you did with the previous essay, write any personal associations you make with this essay in the margins as you read. This process will give you some good insights into the author's approach to his topic and into his methods of developing his ideas. Write down anything at all that occurs to you. Then share your notes with one of your classmates.

THOMAS KING
The Truth About Stories

Okay. Two creation stories. One Native, one Christian. The first thing you probably noticed was that I spent more time with the Woman Who Fell from the Sky than I did with Genesis. I'm assuming that most of you have heard of Adam and Eve, but few, I imagine, have ever met Charm. I also used different strategies in the telling of these stories. In the Native story, I tried to recreate an oral storytelling voice and craft the story in terms of a performance for a general audience. In the Christian story, I tried to maintain a sense of rhetorical distance and decorum while organizing the story for a knowledgeable gathering. These strategies colour the stories and suggest values that may be neither inherent nor warranted. In the Native story, the conversational voice tends to highlight the 1 exuberance of the story but diminishes its authority, while the sober voice in the Christian story makes for a formal recitation but creates a sense of veracity.

2 Basil Johnston, the Anishinabe storyteller, in his essay "How Do We Learn Language?" describes the role of comedy and laughter in stories by reminding us that Native peoples have always loved to laugh: "It is precisely because our tribal stories are comical and evoke laughter that they have never been taken seriously outside the tribe. . . . But behind and beneath the comic characters and the comic situations exists the real meaning of the story . . . what the tribe understood about human growth and development."[1]

3 Of course, none of you would make the mistake of confusing storytelling strategies with the value or sophistication of a story. And we know enough about the complexities of cultures to avoid the error of imagining animism and polytheism to be no more than primitive versions of monotheism. Don't we?

4 Nonetheless, the talking animals are a problem.

5 A theologian might argue that these two creation stories are essentially the same. Each tells about the creation of the world and the appearance of human beings. But a storyteller would tell you that these two stories are quite different, for whether you read the Bible as sacred text or secular metaphor, the elements in Genesis create a particular universe governed by a series of hierarchies—God, man, animals, plants—that celebrate law, order, and good government, while in our Native story, the universe is governed by a series of co-operations—Charm, the Twins, animals, humans—that celebrate equality and balance.

6 In Genesis, all creative power is vested in a single deity who is omnipotent, omniscient, and omnipresent. The universe begins with his thought, and it is through his actions and only his actions that it comes into being. In the Earth Diver story, and in many other Native creation stories for that matter, deities are generally figures of limited power and persuasion, and the acts of creation and the decisions that affect the world are shared with other characters in the drama.

7 In Genesis, we begin with a perfect world, but after the Fall, while we gain knowledge, we lose the harmony and safety of the garden and are forced into a chaotic world of harsh landscapes and dangerous shadows.

8 In our Native story, we begin with water and mud, and, through the good offices of Charm, her twins, and the animals, move by degrees and adjustments from a formless, featureless world to a world that is rich in its diversity, a world that is complex and complete.

9 Finally, in Genesis, the post-garden world we inherit is decidedly martial in nature, a world at war—God vs. the Devil, humans vs. the elements. Or to put things into corporate parlance, competitive. In our Native story, the world is at peace, and the pivotal concern is not with the ascendancy of good over evil but with the issue of balance.

10 So here are our choices: a world in which creation is a solitary, individual act or a world in which creation is a shared activity; a world that begins in harmony and slides toward chaos or a world that begins in chaos and moves toward harmony; a world marked by competition or a world determined by co-operation.

11 And there's the problem.

If we see the world through Adam's eyes, we are necessarily blind to the world that Charm and the Twins and the animals help to create. If we believe one story to be sacred, we must see the other as secular. 12

You'll recognize this pairing as a dichotomy, the elemental structure of Western society. And cranky old Jacques Derrida notwithstanding, we do love our dichotomies. Rich/poor, white/black, strong/weak, right/wrong, culture/nature, male/female, written/oral, civilized/barbaric, success/failure, individual/communal. We trust easy oppositions. We are suspicious of complexities, distrustful of contradictions, fearful of enigmas. 13

Enigmas like my father. 14

I have a couple of old black-and-white pictures of him holding a baby with my mother looking on. He looks young in those photos. And happy. I'm sure he didn't leave because he hated me, just as I'm sure that my mother didn't stay because she loved me. Yet this is the story I continue to tell myself, because it's easy and contains all my anger, and because, in all the years, in all the tellings, I've honed it sharp enough to cut bone. 15

If we had to have a patron story for North America, we could do worse than the one about Alexander the Great, who, when faced with the puzzle of the Gordian knot, solved that problem with nothing more than a strong arm and a sharp sword. 16

Perhaps this is why we delight in telling stories about heroes battling the odds and the elements, rather than about the magic of seasonal change. Why we relish stories that lionize individuals who start at the bottom and fight their way to the top, rather than stories that frame these forms of competition as varying degrees of insanity. Why we tell our children that life is hard, when we could just as easily tell them that it is sweet. 17

Is it our nature? Do the stories we tell reflect the world as it truly is, or did we simply start off with the wrong story? Like Silko's witches in the cave, conjuring up things to impress each other. 18

Making magic. 19

Making faces. 20

Making mistakes. 21

I'm dying to remind myself that the basis of Christian doctrine is rectitude and reward, crime and punishment, even though my partner has warned me that this is probably not a good idea. Tell a story, she told me. Don't preach. Don't try to sound profound. It's unbecoming, and you do it poorly. Don't show them your mind. Show them your imagination. 22

So am I such an ass as to disregard this good advice and suggest that the stories contained within the matrix of Christianity and the complex of nationalism are responsible for the social, political, and economic problems we face? Am I really arguing that the martial and hierarchical nature of Western religion and Western privilege has fostered stories that encourage egotism and self-interest? Am I suggesting that, if we hope to create a truly civil society, we must first burn all the flags and kill all the gods, because in such a world we could no longer tolerate such weapons of mass destruction? 23

No, I wouldn't do that. 24

25 Though certainly we understand that we clear-cut forests not to enrich the lives of animals but to make profit. We know that we dam(n) rivers not to improve water quality but to create electricity and protect private property. We make race and gender discriminatory markers for no other reason than that we can. And we maintain and tolerate poverty not because we believe adversity makes you strong, but because we're unwilling to share.

26 Ah. You've heard all this before, haven't you.

27 You may have already leaned over to a friend and whispered, Platitude. Platitude, platitude, platitude. Thomas King the duck-billed platitude.

28 But give this a thought. What if the creation story in Genesis had featured a flawed deity who was understanding and sympathetic rather than autocratic and rigid? Someone who, in the process of creation, found herself lost from time to time and in need of advice, someone who was willing to accept a little help with the more difficult decisions?

29 What if the animals had decided on their own names? What if Adam and Eve had simply been admonished for their foolishness?

30 I love you, God could have said, but I'm not happy with your behaviour. Let's talk this over. Try to do better next time.

31 What kind of a world might we have created with that kind of story?

32 Unfortunately, by the time we arrived in the wilderness, broke and homeless, the story of being made in God's image, of living in paradise, of naming the animals must have gone to our heads, for while we weren't the strongest or the fastest or the fiercest creatures on the planet, we were, certainly, as it turned out, the most arrogant.

33 God's Chosen People. The Alpha and the Omega. Masters of the Universe.

34 It is this conceit we continue to elaborate as we fill up our tanks at the gas station, the myth we embrace as we bolt our doors at night, the romance we pursue as we search our guidebooks for just the right phrase. The lie we dangle in front of our appetites as we chase progress to the grave.

35 Or as Linda McQuaig so delightfully puts it in her book *All You Can Eat: Greed, Lust and the New Capitalism*, "The central character in economics is Homo Economicus, the human prototype, who is pretty much just a walking set of insatiable material desires. He uses his rational abilities to ensure the satisfaction of all his wants, which are the key to his motivation. And he isn't considered some weirdo; the whole point of him is that he represents traits basic to all of us—Homo Economicus 'R' Us, as it were."[2]

36 It was Sir Isaac Newton who said, "To every action there is always opposed an equal reaction." Had he been a writer, he might have simply said, "To every action there is a story."

37 Take Charm's story, for instance. It's yours. Do with it what you will. Tell it to friends. Turn it into a television movie. Forget it. But don't say in the years to come that you would have lived your life differently if only you had heard this story.

38 You've heard it now.

References

1 Basil Johnston, "How Do We Learn Language?" in *Talking on the Page: Editing Aboriginal Oral Texts,* eds. Laura Murray and Keren Rice (Toronto: University of Toronto Press, 1999), 14.

2 Linda McQuaig, *All You Can Eat: Greed, Lust and the New Capitalism* (Toronto: Viking, 2001), 12.

Thinking Critically About Content

1. Explain the major differences between the two creation myths.
2. Why does King interject the story of his father into his discussion of the two creation myths? Is he momentarily getting off track, or is there a specific purpose to his use of this story? Explain.
3. According to King, "If we had to have a patron story for North America, we could do worse than the one about Alexander the Great." Why does King think the story of Alexander and the Gordian knot is appropriate for North America?

Thinking Critically About Purpose and Audience

4. What do you think Thomas King's purpose is in this essay?
5. Why do you think the writer phrases his comments in paragraph 23 in the form of questions? What effect might this form have on the reader?
6. The essay was originally delivered as a lecture. What elements of the essay do you think would work well in a lecture? Explain and illustrate your answer from the essay.

Thinking Critically About Essays

7. Can you locate a thesis statement in this essay? Where is it? How does the author lead up to the thesis?
8. Name three points of similarity and three points of contrast in this essay.
9. Is the essay organized by point, by subject, or by a combination of the two? Is the style he has chosen the most effective for this material? Explain your answer.
10. Are the details King uses persuasive? Does it matter that all the details of the stories of Charm and Genesis are not given here? What did you feel you had learned when you finished reading? Did you find yourself questioning previously held assumptions? Write a detailed response to the essay.

Writing Workshop

This final section gives you opportunities to apply what you have learned in this chapter to another writing assignment. This time, we provide very little prompting beyond a summary of the guidelines for writing a description essay. This section will let you demonstrate that you can go through the entire writing process on your own with only occasional feedback from your peers. Loop back into the chapter as necessary when you have questions, so that this process becomes as automatic to you as possible before you move on to new material. Then pause at the end of the chapter to reflect briefly on what you have learned.

Guidelines for Writing a Comparison/Contrast Essay

1. Decide what point you want to make with your comparison, and state it in your thesis statement.
2. Choose items to compare and contrast that will make your point most effectively.
3. Use as many specific details and examples as possible to expand your comparison.
4. Develop your comparison in a balanced way.
5. Organize your essay subject by subject or point by point—or combine the two approaches.

Writing About Your Reading

1. Thomas Hayden's article compares and contrasts Washington, D.C., and Saskatoon as part of an investigation of racism. Thomas King's essay compares Judeo-Christian creation myths with Native ones. Both, however, ultimately ask us to take a serious look at our attitude toward Native peoples. Write a comparison of the two essays, focusing on attitudes.
2. What process do you have to go through to come up with an interesting comparison or contrast? How is it different from the process you go through for other rhetorical modes?
3. Compare Canadian culture to that of another country you know well. Begin by creating a list of similarities and differences.

Writing About Your World

1. Compare and contrast the two buildings on this page. What details in both buildings are different? What are the same? What is the overall message you get from these two buildings? Look at both the obvious and the not-so-obvious.
2. Choose a job being advertised in your local newspaper's classified section, and write a cover letter to the employer comparing yourself to your probable competition. What are your best qualifications compared to others who might be applying for this job? What are your weaknesses in comparison to them? Why would you be the best candidate for the job?
3. Discuss the similarities and differences between two cities that you know well. How are they the same? How are they different? What do you think accounts for these similarities and differences? When you write your essay, consider whether a subject-by-subject or a point-by-point organization would be more effective.
4. Create your own comparison/contrast assignment (with the help of your instructor), and write a response to it.

Revising

Small Group Activity (5–10 minutes per writer) Working in groups of three or four, each person should read his or her comparison/contrast essay to the other members of the group. Those listening should record their reactions on a copy of the Peer Evaluation Form (Appendix 1A). After your group goes through this process, give your evaluation forms to the appropriate writers so that each writer has two or three peer comment sheets for revising.

Paired Activity (5 minutes per writer) Using the completed Peer Evaluation Forms, work in pairs to decide what you should revise in your essay. If time allows, rewrite some of your sentences, and have your partner look over them.

Individual Activity Rewrite your paper, using the revising feedback you received from other students.

Editing

Paired Activity (5–10 minutes per writer) Swap papers with a classmate, and use the editing portion of your Peer Evaluation Form (Appendix 1B) to identify as many grammar, punctuation, mechanics, and spelling errors as you can. If time allows, correct some of your errors, and have your partner look at them. Record your grammar, punctuation, and mechanics errors in the Error Log (Appendix 3) and your spelling errors in the Spelling Log (Appendix 4).

Individual Activity Rewrite your paper again, using the editing feedback you received from other students.

CHAPTER 13

Dividing and Classifying

Writing, like life itself, is a voyage of discovery.

—Henry Miller

Division and classification ensure that we have a certain amount of order in our lives. In fact, we constantly use these two processes to navigate through our days. Thanks to classification, you know where to find the milk in the grocery store and the chapter on the fur trade in your history textbook. Also, when you choose a major and a career, you use division and classification to make your choice. Division and classification are such a natural part of everyday life that we often don't even know we are using them.

In addition, we regularly use division and classification when we write. Actually, division and classification are a vital part of our written communication every day—in our personal lives, in school, and at work:

You divide your expenses into categories to create a budget.

A student explains three types of bacteria on a biology exam.

A student writes a report on types of hazardous materials for a science course.

A personal banker prepares a flyer about the types of savings accounts that are available.

The manager of a music store suggests a new system for arranging CDs to head office.

Like comparison and contrast, division and classification are really two parts of the same process. **Division** is sorting—dividing something into its basic parts, such as a home into rooms. Division moves from a single, large category (home) to many smaller subcategories (kitchen, bathroom, living room, bedroom, and so forth). **Classification,** grouping items together, moves in the opposite direction, from many subgroups to a single, large category. For example, several pieces of furniture in a home can be classified as living-room furniture or bedroom furniture. Division and classification help us organize information so that we can make sense of our complex world. Dividing large categories into smaller ones (division) and grouping many items into larger categories (classification) both help us put a lot of information into useful groups.

READING AND WRITING A DIVISION/ CLASSIFICATION ESSAY

Learning how to read division/classification essays critically will help you become a better writer. As you see how an essay is constructed and how a thesis is developed in this mode, you will be able to apply what you discover to your own writing. Reading and writing in any mode are demanding, but they are both necessary for success in college and in life. Like two halves of a circle, these two processes complement each other and enhance your ability to perform many other tasks.

Reading a Division/Classification Essay

Here is a sample division/classification essay by Roy Geiger called "On Being Persuaded." It classifies the various forms of persuasion as formulated by Aristotle more than 2000 years ago, including intellectual and emotional, but focusing particularly on the ethical. Have you ever wondered about the reasons behind a company making a case through an advertisement? Do you, for example, usually assume that the company is thinking mostly of the bottom line?

READING CRITICALLY

As you read more difficult essays, the ability to summarize is essential. A summary features the main ideas of a selection in a coherent paragraph. First, you identify the main ideas in your reading; then you fold them into a paragraph with logical transitions so your sentences flow from one to another. Write a summary of the following selection, and then draft three questions for discussion that come from your summary.

ROY GEIGER

On Being Persuaded

1 Why does anyone believe what he or she is told? It sounds suspiciously close to the kind of challenge familiar to all parents, grade school teachers, and gradeschoolers themselves—why are you right and I'm not? It's all too easy to dismiss the questioning as products of an ego screaming for power and control; that would deny the importance of the question, which ultimately lies behind just about everything.

In fact, when a ten- or twelve-year-old asks those kinds of questions, adults would do well to remember just how clearly young people can see the world.

Which brings us back to the question of why we accept some ideas and reject 2
others. Throughout the world, we see persuasion delivered by physical intimidation. People who know that opening their fat lips to argue or dissent will result in violence against themselves or their family are often inclined to silence. But even in the presence of fear and carnage, ideas survive, perhaps because we believe the world could be better for ourselves, for others. How, then, are we persuaded?

The business is ancient, but the basic principles of argument and persuasion 3
have remained constant. Aristotle, for one, some 2300 years ago, pointed out that arguments make three appeals to us, an appeal to reason, an appeal to emotions, and an appeal to ethics. Consider these three elements of an argument to examine the question of how we are persuaded, with special attention to the ethical appeal.

The appeal to reason asks us to use reason and logic, the mental operations that we 4
use to evaluate the sense of an idea. It is an area of study all to itself that aspires to a mathematical condition of proposition and proof. Generally we expect a series of propositions or examples, one logically developing out of another, that either lead us to a conclusion or support a conclusion already offered. To take an example, let's consider a recent video ad, "Evolution," part of Dove's ongoing Campaign for Real Beauty. This "75-second Internet ad uses time lapse photography to show an imperfect woman being transformed into a billboard model through makeup, lighting and digital photo editing" ("The best revealed"). The ad, apparently viewed over 4 million times on YouTube in 2006 and voted the best ad of the year in globeandmail.com's "Hard Sell" blog, brilliantly ends with a black screen on which appears the line "No wonder our perception of beauty is distorted."

As we see the frame-by-frame transformation of the subject into a stereotypical 5
billboard image, we are amazed. Intellectually, we can analyze how we are manipulated, particularly towards the end of the sequence when the image is Photoshopped and the neck is elongated and the eyes enlarged. The sequence of examples has us, as viewers, practically mouthing the conclusion before it appears on the screen. Our experience of the process, having been made to understand the way such images are produced and how far the images are from the flesh-and-blood they purport to represent, leaves us with virtually no choice but to accept the conclusion.

The second appeal an argument makes is emotional. We often dislike acknowledging 6
the role emotions like fear or desire play in our responses to argument. We may even feel sheepish or ashamed (Corbett 86), yet we cannot deny the visceral response. Rather than directly exhort us to accept an idea or position, emotional appeals often play on what we can see or imagine to instill or rouse feelings about that position. Further, a powerful piece like the Dove "Evolution" ad relies on the fact that exposure to marketing has trained us to accept and even be aroused by certain images of beauty. As with the work of the great American artist Cindy Sherman, the Dove ad catches us in the act of responding to the image of apparent beauty and makes us question ourselves. We watch the woman become more and more "beautiful," and we begin to think about just how fine she is starting to look. But then, aided by the increasing urgency of the soundtrack, we're caught short. We say, "Hey! I'm being shamelessly manipulated! And you're not allowing me to forget that fact!" In this ad, the appeals to emotions and reason work together in a cunning, irresistible way.

We respond emotionally until our reason takes over and analyzes what is happening to us as we watch. We respond emotionally a second time with a sense of disappointment and sheepishness (that word, again). By the end we accept the ad's point intellectually, but we also feel distaste towards the cynical process we've been forced to acknowledge. We can't pretend we haven't been influenced by a very manipulative process.

7 Finally, there is the ethical appeal which refers to "the persuasive value of the speaker's or writer's character" (Corbett 80), or, in the case of an ad, the character of the presenter, spokesperson, and company. Aristotle, in discussing this appeal, says that audiences are impressed by presenters with "sound sense," "high moral character," and "benevolence" or good will (Corbett 80). We determine these attributes by evaluating whether or not the presenter demonstrates expertise and knowledge, perspective, valid reasoning, good taste and judgment (Corbett 81). "Evolution" makes for an interesting case here. The campaign to massage the self-esteem of people who don't fit media-promoted images of beauty, which is almost every single person alive, cannot fail to strike a chord—as long as we don't detect insincerity. So far, despite the parodies readily available on the internet, the ongoing campaign seems direct and sincere, and this ad does as well. In fact, as one admiring ad executive commented, "Evolution" is almost like a public service announcement ("The best revealed"). Such a tribute would be most desired by advertisers and the companies they represent. Blurring the line between marketing and presenting the image of a firm that wants only what is good for people must be a kind of gold standard. We might accept that the people running Unilever, the company that makes Dove products, really do question the idea of using images of beauty that make us feel inadequate. However, we must have the slight suspicion that the company's real concern is profit margins. If the Campaign for Real Beauty didn't work to increase sales, we suspect the company would drop it in an instant. Therefore, when we consider the ethical appeal being made, we might be slightly suspicious and think, "Wait a minute. Your ad is not telling me anything I don't already know, really. Your bottom line is always to manipulate me into buying your products. Therefore, if I want to look at this idea of 'beauty' I'll do so independently, without reference to a soap company."

8 Since the tools of argument we've been discussing are, unfortunately, all too easily used by advertisers, propagandists, and liars, the ethical appeal can assume paramount importance; we need to see the intent of the presenter as clearly as possible. Paradoxically, as in the case of Dove's "Evolution," once we relieve a message of the dubious intent of its sponsor, we can sometimes find a good argument waiting to be considered.

Works Cited

Corbett, Edward P. J. *Classical Rhetoric for the Modern Student*. Toronto: Oxford UP, 1990.

"The best revealed: It's Evolution." "Hard Sell" blog. *globeandmail.com*. **http://www.theglobeandmail.com/blogs/thehardsell**. 6 Jan. 2007. 1 Jan. 2007.

"Evolution." Dove campaign for real beauty. 6 Jan. 2006. **http://www.campaignforrealbeauty.ca**.

PREPARING TO WRITE YOUR OWN DIVISION/CLASSIFICATION ESSAY

Many companies these days are going green, including even such unexpected businesses as oil companies like BP (British Petroleum), Chevron, and Mobil. What might the motivations for these companies be? Is it just about the bottom line, or could there be other reasons? Explore this topic using one or more of the prewriting strategies that you learned in Chapter 5.

Writing a Division/Classification Essay

To write a division/classification essay, keep in mind that the same items can be divided and classified in many different ways. Your friends probably don't all organize their closets the way you do, and no two kitchens are organized exactly alike. Similarly, in writing you can divide and classify a topic in different ways. Whatever your method of dividing or classifying, use the following guidelines to help you write an effective division/classification essay.

1. ***Decide on your purpose for writing, and make it part of your thesis statement.*** Dividing and classifying in themselves are not particularly interesting. But they are very useful techniques if you are trying to make a specific point. That point, or purpose, should be in your thesis statement. Look at these two examples:

   A. There are three types of dangerous drivers on the road today.

   B. Being aware of three types of dangerous drivers on the road today could save your life.

   Both thesis statements name a category—dangerous drivers—but only thesis statement B gives the reader a good reason to keep reading: Knowing the three types could save your life.

   In our sample essay, Geiger uses division and classification to outline the ways we are persuaded to believe an argument. Using a popular Internet ad, he divides persuasion into the three types of appeals originally advanced by Aristotle in ancient times, and still applicable today: appeals to reason, appeals to emotion, and appeals to ethics.

2. ***Divide your topic into categories that don't overlap.*** Since most subjects can be classified in different ways, your next task in writing a division/classification essay is to decide on what basis you will divide your subject into categories. First, gather information to come up with a list of all the possible topics. Second, decide on what basis you will put these topics into categories. Next, make sure that some of your topics don't fall into more than one category. Your categories should be separate enough that your topics fall into only one category. Also, don't add a category at the last minute to accommodate a topic. Keep adjusting your categories until they work with your thesis.

In the sample essay, the author begins by asking why anyone believes what they are told. He then answers that question by reminding us of the Aristotelian classification system, which divides argumentation into three categories or types of appeals: to reason, to emotion, and to ethics. He might have tried to classify forms of persuasion in other ways, such as spoken, written, and visual; types of audience or reader; and a combination of the two; or personal, cultural, and group-related. But none of these options would be as effective. The first two groupings are too broad to supply the detailed information that Geiger's categories give us. The third set of categories would force the author to classify many topics, like various cultures or types of groups, which would require a more in-depth analysis. Geiger's categories (actually Aristotle's), used in concert with the specific example of the Dove ad, are sufficient to explain how we are persuaded to believe an argument.

3. ***Clearly explain each category.*** With division, you are trying to show what differences break the items into separate groups or types. With classification, you let the similarities in the items help you set up categories that make sense. In either case, you need to explain each category fully and provide enough details to help your readers see your subject in a new way. To do this, use vivid description and carefully chosen examples. Comparison and contrast (Chapter 12) is also a useful technique because when you classify items, you are looking at how they are alike (comparison) and how they are different (contrast).

   Geiger uses comparison and contrast to place his ideas into categories. Then he describes each category using the SAME example, that of the Dove ad, and how we the viewers relate to it. As a result, the reader understands the categories fully and clearly.

4. ***Organize your categories logically.*** Your method of organization should make sense and be easy for readers to follow. Most often, this means organizing from one extreme to another. For example, you might organize your types from most obvious to least obvious. Or you might move from least important to most important, from least humorous to most humorous, from largest to smallest—or the other way around. In every case, though, try to end with the category that is most memorable.

   Roy Geiger's essay is arranged hierarchically, from the most easily understood appeal to the one that requires the most thinking—from logical to emotional to ethical, ending with the one that allows us to see the "intent of the presenter as clearly as possible." As he states at the conclusion of the essay, the tools can be used "by advertisers, propagandists, and liars," and therefore the "ethical appeal can assume paramount importance."

5. ***Use transitions to move your readers through your essay.*** Transitions will help your readers move from one category to another and follow your train of thought. They will also keep your essay from sounding choppy or boring.

Geiger moves the reader through his essay by using transitions at the start of several of his paragraphs, particularly the three that explain the three appeals: "The appeal to reason . . ." (paragraph 4); "The second appeal an argument makes . . . " (paragraph 6); and "Finally, there is the ethical appeal . . ." (paragraph 7). He also uses transitions within paragraphs. Here are some effective transitions from within Geiger's essay: "We watch," "we begin to think," "but then . . ." (paragraph 6), "We might accept," "however," and "therefore" (paragraph 7). These words and phrases serve as traffic signals that guide Geiger's readers through his essay.

WRITING YOUR OWN DIVISION/CLASSIFICATION ESSAY

Write an essay explaining why you believe some companies are going green, especially in their advertising. Begin by reviewing your prewriting notes. Next, divide your subject into distinct categories, and write a clear thesis statement. Then develop your essay with specific examples that explain each category.

A STUDENT'S DIVISION/CLASSIFICATION ESSAY

Sergio Mendola, a student writer, uses division and classification in an essay about neighbours. Called "Won't You Be My Neighbour?," it divides and classifies neighbours into specific categories to prove a point. See if you can identify his main point as you read this draft of his essay.

Won't You Be My Neighbour?

Neighbourhoods can be strange places. Every one is different, but they are all made up of the same ingredient—neighbours. In today's world, though, most people don't know there neighbours. It's not like the '50s. When people knew what their neighbours were doing. But in every neighbourhood today, you can find at least one Mystery Neighbour, one Perfect Cleaver Family, and one Good Neighbour Family. 1

The first type of neighbour everyone has is the Perfect Cleaver Family. This family has the perfect parents and the perfect children. They are the June and Ward Cleavers of today. They have 2.5 perfect children. Although these children get in their share of minor trouble, the children never repeat the same mistake after the parents express their disappointment. And then, to avoid future disappointments, the children always keep their parents' values in mind before making decisions. Eddie Haskell left a lot to be desired. I don't know what his values are. The Cleaver-type children later become heart surgeons or police chiefs in order to help the world around them. These neighbours are the role models for everyone else. 2

3 Then there is the Mystery Neighbour. The Mystery Neighbour remains aloof, and the only way the other neighbours know someone lives at the Mystery House is because the newspaper disappears sometime during the day and the lawn somehow gets mowed every week. Every once in a while, a car will sit in the driveway, but no one knows for sure if the car belongs to the people who own the house. Neighbourhood children make up stories about the Mystery Neighbour, which are based on nothing and compete with the best urban legends. The Mystery Neighbour is usually a workaholic or a travelling salesperson, but this doesn't stop the neighbours from wondering.

4 The best type of neighbour in any neighbourhood is the Good Neighbour Family. Made up of very reliable people. This family is always reaching out to other neighbours. Whenever something goes wrong, someone from the Good Neighbour Family is the first person at the doorstep to lend a helping hand. These neighbours will water the plants and feed the animals for people on vacation who always want to help others. They create the kinds of friendships that continue even when one family moves away. Sometimes the parents might try to "fix up" their boy and girl children so that the families relationship can be legally cemented for life. The Good Neighbour Family is one that everyone hopes to encounter at least once in a lifetime.

5 This mixture of neighbours makes up a very good neighbourhood. It creates a neighbourhood that functions smoothly and thoughtfully. And even though people don't no their neighbours like they used to 50 years ago, they will probably find at least three different types of neighbours if they look hard enough: the Perfect Cleaver Family, the Mystery Neighbour, and the Good Neighbour Family. It would be sad to be missing any one of them.

Discovering How the Essay Works

1. This essay doesn't simply classify neighbours for their own sake. It has a broader message. What is Sergio's general purpose in this essay?

____

____

2. Does Sergio divide his subject into categories that don't overlap?

____

____

3. Does Sergio clearly explain each of his categories? Explain your answer.

____

____

4. How does Sergio organize his categories? Is this the most logical order for this purpose? Explain your answer.

____

____

5. What transitions does Sergio use to move his essay along smoothly?

____

____

____

REVISING AND EDITING THE STUDENT ESSAY

This essay is Sergio's first draft, which now needs to be revised and edited. First, apply the Revising Checklist on the inside front cover to the content of Sergio's draft. When you are satisfied that his ideas are fully developed and well organized, use the Editing Checklist on the inside back cover to correct his grammatical and mechanical errors. Answer the questions below. Then write your suggested changes directly on Sergio's draft.

Revision Questions

Thesis Statement

1. Put brackets around the last sentence in Sergio's introduction. Does it introduce his purpose?

____

2. Rewrite Sergio's thesis statement if necessary so that it states his purpose and introduces his topics.

____

____

____

Basic Elements

1. Give Sergio's essay an alternative title.

____

2. Rewrite Sergio's introduction so that it captures the readers' attention and builds up to the thesis statement at the end of the paragraph.

____

____

____

3. Does each of Sergio's body paragraphs deal with only one topic?

____

4. Rewrite Sergio's conclusion using at least one suggestion from Part I.

____

____

____

Development

1. Write out Sergio's thesis statement (revised, if necessary), and list his three topic sentences below it.

   Thesis statement: ______________________________

   ____

   ____

   Topic 1: ______________________________

   ____

   Topic 2: ______________________________

   ____

   Topic 3: ______________________________

   ____

2. Do Sergio's topics adequately support his thesis statement?

____

3. Does each body paragraph have a focused topic sentence?

____

4. Do Sergio's details adequately explain his categories?

____

5. Where do you need more information?

____

6. Make two of Sergio's details more specific.
7. Add two new details to make his essay clearer.

Unity

1. Read each of Sergio's topic sentences with his thesis statement (revised, if necessary) in mind. Do they go together?

____

2. Revise them if necessary so that they are directly related.
3. Drop or rewrite the two sentences in paragraph 2 that are not directly related to their topic sentences.

Organization

1. Read Sergio's essay again to see if all the paragraphs are arranged logically.
2. Reverse the two paragraphs that are out of order.
3. Look closely at Sergio's body paragraphs to see if all his sentences are arranged logically within paragraphs.
4. Move any sentences that are out of order.

Coherence

1. Add two transitions to Sergio's essay.
2. Circle five transitions, repetitions, synonyms, or pronouns Sergio uses.
3. Explain how two of these make Sergio's essay easier to read.

____

____

For a list of transitions, see pages 85–86.
For a list of pronouns, see pages 389–390.

Now rewrite Sergio's essay with your revisions.

Editing Questions

Sentences

Subjects and Verbs

1. Underline the subjects once and verbs twice in paragraphs 1 and 4 of your revision of Sergio's essay. Remember that sentences can have more than one subject–verb set.
2. Does each sentence have at least one subject and verb that can stand alone?

____

For help with subjects and verbs, see Chapter 23.

For help with fragments, see Chapter 24.

3. Did you find and correct Sergio's two fragments? If not, find and correct them now.

Subject–Verb Agreement

For help with subject–verb agreement, see Chapter 27.

1. Read aloud the subjects and verbs you underlined in your revision of Sergio's essay.
2. Correct any subjects and verbs that do not agree.

Pronoun Agreement

For help with pronoun agreement, see Chapter 30.

1. Find any pronouns in your revision of Sergio's essay that do not agree with their nouns.
2. Correct any pronouns that do not agree with their nouns.

Modifiers

For help with modifier errors, see Chapter 33.

1. Find any modifiers in your revision of Sergio's essay that are not as close as possible to the words they modify.
2. Did you find and correct Sergio's modifier error? If not, find and correct it now.

Punctuation and Mechanics

Punctuation

For help with punctuation, see Chapters 34–37.

1. Read your revision of Sergio's essay for any errors in punctuation.
2. Find the two fragments you revised, and make sure they are punctuated correctly.
3. Did you find and correct the missing apostrophe in Sergio's essay?

Mechanics

For help with capitalization, see Chapter 38.

1. Read your revision of Sergio's essay for any errors in capitalization.
2. Be sure to check Sergio's capitalization in the fragments you revised.

Word Choice and Spelling

Word Choice

For help with confused words, see Chapter 44.

1. Find any words used incorrectly in your revision of Sergio's essay.
2. Did you find and correct his three confused words? If not, find and correct them now.

Spelling

For help with spelling, see Chapter 45.

1. Use spell-check and a dictionary to check the spelling in your revision of Sergio's essay.
2. Correct any misspelled words.

Now rewrite Sergio's essay again with your editing corrections.

REVISING AND EDITING YOUR OWN DIVISION/CLASSIFICATION ESSAY

Returning to the division/classification essay you wrote earlier in this chapter, revise and edit your own writing. The checklists in the front and back inside covers will help you apply what you have learned to your essay.

WRITING CRITICALLY

Now write a summary of your own essay. See if all your main ideas are clear and easy to identify. Make sure the connections between the ideas in your summary are logical and understandable. Are these connections also clear in your essay itself? Change any elements of your essay that will make your main ideas clearer and more logical to your readers.

PRACTISING DIVISION AND CLASSIFICATION: FROM READING TO WRITING

Reading Workshop

Here are two essays that illustrate good division and classification writing: "Bad Boys" by Mordecai Richler categorizes dating losers, while "Why You Think You're Wonderful" by Brian Bethune discusses different types of ways your brain deals with reality. You might want to read these selections before writing another division and classification essay. As you read, notice how the authors' categories support the points they are making.

MORDECAI RICHLER

Bad Boys

Focusing Your Attention

1. What dating fiascos have you heard about, or experienced yourself? What is your definition of a bad date? What are the female equivalents of the categories the author covers?
2. In the essay you are about to read, the writer divides and classifies young men that women should watch out for when they are dating. Do all bad dates fall into particular categories? What are they? Are there particular new problems with dating now that the Internet is so

prevalent? Could you classify the problems that might happen to someone using an online dating service?

Expanding Your Vocabulary

The following words are important to your understanding of this essay:

loping: running with a steady, even gait (paragraph 1)
seminal: the original basis for development, the seed (paragraph 2)
prescient: knowing what is coming (paragraph 3)
braggart: boaster (paragraph 3)
cherished: beloved (paragraph 7)

READING CRITICALLY

As you learned at the beginning of this chapter, practise your summary skills on the following essay. Then work with someone in the class, and write a single paragraph that represents both of your summaries.

MORDECAI RICHLER
Bad Boys

1 When we were horny teenagers, me and my bunch dreaded the coming of Saturday nights. Our anxieties, such as they were, struck as we left high school on Friday afternoons, loping home to begin to work the phones. Would we manage to get a date for the following night or would we be humiliated yet again? We were sixteen years old at the time, grade 11 students in Montreal, and the ungrateful girls we had invested in selflessly for years—treating them to double features at the Rialto, followed by toasted tomato and mayo sandwiches, washed down with Cokes or milkshakes at Ben Ash's, never mind the cost—had suddenly turned against us. Upwardly mobile in their nifty sweaters, tight skirts, nylons, and high heels, reeking of some cheap perfume shoplifted at Woolworth's, they now preferred the company of older guys, later to prosper as dentists or accountants, who were already at McGill. This being the case, we often had to put up with being men without women, as Mr. Hemingway had it, on Saturday nights, settling for going out together to shoot pool at the Park Billiards. However, there were Saturday nights when we did make out, repairing to neck on a bench in Outremont Park after the movie.

2 Be that as it may, I'm glad dating is no longer a problem for me and my bunch, because we would now all be classified as either the Show-Off, Know-It-All, Cheater, Sex Guzzler, Mr. Ego, Bug-Eyed Boy, or Boozer, dismissed as Losers to Watch Out For. I am indebted for this information to a fascinating book which recently came my way, *RED FLAGS! How to Know When You're Dating a LOSER,* published by Plume, the down-market imprint of Penguin Books. It is the seminal work of two eminent shrinks, doctors Gary S. Aumiller and Daniel A. Goldfarb. Aumiller is an "internationally known" lecturer and Goldfarb serves as

Webmaster to several psychology self-help sites on the Internet. Both authors have put in time as the prez of the Society of Police and Criminal Psychology and helped some 4,000 patients solve problems and make better decisions before combining to warn women about the 25 Losers to Watch Out For and How to Dump Them and Move On.

Consider, for instance, the Show-Off. In an idiom refreshingly free of academic prose, the authors warn, "If the man you are dating does more strutting than a rooster on Viagra in a brand-new hen house," this guy's a turkey. Cook his goose. The Show-Off, according to the prescient authors, can easily be recognized. He is a braggart, and a sharp dresser, who flexes his muscles a lot, and looks at himself frequently in the mirror, and, um, "other reflective substances" but is very insecure underneath his plumage. Reminds me of Hershel Greenbaum. Show him the Red Flag, girls. 3

"The Game for the Know-It-All is *Jeopardy!* Beat Him to the Buzzer," say Aumiller and Goldfarb. Signals to watch out for: his eyes dart, he namedrops, puts his friends down, and insists on ordering dinner for you. Yes, but like Arnie Debrofsky of blessed memory, he also showers a lot, and reads lots of non-fiction, which don't strike me as such bad things. But the doctors also adjudge him a Loser and highly recommend a clean break, goodbye: "Then go home and turn on the Discovery Channel and learn about the mating rituals of the giant Galapagos turtles. You too can know it all." 4

The Sex-Guzzler, as you might have expected, is very bad news. "The Way to Your Heart is Not Through Your Pants." Happily such villains can be easily spotted. They tend to wear gold jewellery, neck chains, bracelets, touch you very quickly on the first date, and talk about life being an adventure and about the need to take risks. Watch out, girls. If the sex is great, you could end up a Guzzler yourself. 5

With equal ease the doctors dispose of Mr. Ego ("If He Thinks He's God's Gift, Exchange Him!"); the Cheater, who tends to look at your breasts or legs and to invade personal space; the Bug-Eyed Boy, yet another eye-darter, who looks at body parts, not faces, when he is talking to you or other women (gosh, I used to know guys like that); and the Boozer, no eye-darter he, but he does tend to be restless, and at times has a rumpled look. Worse news. He has more than two drinks on the first date. Aumiller and Goldfarb recommend boozers to rely on the three Ms: meetings with Alcoholics Anonymous, meditation, and masturbation, "because he should not have a woman around." 6

RED FLAGS! takes no prisoners. It provides women with further good advice against Neglecters, Pleasers, Possessors, Abusers, and Loners, taking in just about all of my cherished male friends. Girls, beware of these two shrinks. Dump Them. Cook Their Goose. Lest you end up old maids. 7

Thinking Critically About Content

1. Richler divides and classifies dating losers into several categories. What are these categories?
2. What are the main differences in these categories? What phrase ties the categories together?
3. In the final paragraph, the author tells girls to beware of "these two shrinks." What indications has he given throughout the essay that he might disagree with the authors he is reviewing? Give examples.

Thinking Critically About Purpose and Audience

4. The essay is written as if it were a book review. Is this its main purpose?
5. Who do you think is Richler's main audience?
6. Is the author asking "girls" to accept any loser rather than "end up an old maid"? Is this a valid observation? Why or why not?

Thinking Critically About Essays

7. The paragraphs describing the different types of dating losers are organized in a similar pattern. Outline the pattern.
8. How do the descriptions of Richler's friends in the opening paragraph and the reference to "my cherished friends" in the last paragraph work in this essay?
9. Choose one of the central paragraphs from the essay and decide whether it is unified or not. Explain why.
10. Write a detailed description of one of the dating losers described in the final paragraph of the essay.

READING CRITICALLY

Once again, write a summary of the following essay, and exchange summaries with another person in your class. Then combine your two summaries into one summary that accurately represents the main ideas in this essay.

BRIAN BETHUNE

Why You Think You're Wonderful

Focusing Your Attention

1. Do you consider yourself more skilled in some areas than others? Are you better at hands-on work than you are at reading or writing? Or are you hopeless at working with your hands but a good reader? Which skill do you value most? The one that you are best at? Why do you think that is the case?
2. In the essay you are about to read, the writer summarizes a book on the way our brains play tricks on us and convince us that what we are good at is the most worthwhile ability to have. Do you think your brain is capable of playing tricks on you? Why or why not?

Expanding Your Vocabulary

The following words are important to your understanding of this essay:

objective: not influenced by emotions, fair and balanced (paragraph 2)
cognitive faculties: mental processes (paragraph 3)
antagonism: hostility, opposition (paragraph 4)
ameliorate: improve, make better (paragraph 5)

intolerable: unbearable, extremely hard to take (paragraph 5)
sombrely: seriously, gloomily (paragraph 7)

BRIAN BETHUNE
Why You Think You're Wonderful

There really isn't anything the human brain can't do, and that's aside from all that marvel-of-the-universe, super-computer stuff, like the ability to paint the *Mona Lisa*, or send a rocket to the moon or write *Hamlet*. No, the truly great stuff *your* brain does for *you* is to protect you from reality. Your mind loves you like a mother should: it convinces you that what you can do well (balloon animals, say) is important and what you're hopeless at (parallel parking, perhaps) is trivial; that you're better-looking and smarter than most and destined to stay that way forever. 1

Good thing too, as English psychologist Cordelia Fine explains in *A Mind of Its Own*, her lighthearted tour through recent research. The category of people who come closest to objective truth about themselves (as measured by outsiders) are the clinically depressed. Depression, of course, is an illness, but scientists have also learned that a more general sense of pessimism is dangerous to health. What Fine calls the "death-clock" only needs the answers to four questions to calculate how many years to shear off your life expectancy: sex, weight, smoking habits and "Are you a pessimist?" 2

Fine divides up the tricks played by our loving organ into various categories. The so-called vain brain, for instance, is so preening that research has shown it finds the very letters of your name more attractive than other letters. It obscures the statistical improbability of near-universal ideas about the self (almost 100 per cent of subjects rate themselves as better than average on any ordinary task like driving a car—a mathematically impossible outcome). Under the emotional brain, Fine cites tests that show how gut instinct makes many decisions that we think are reasoned. It's only after we've opted for one side of the question that our cognitive faculties—in a manner so smooth we don't notice which came first—provide the rationale. 3

The reason emotion speaks first is because it's so much quicker off the mark. Test subjects who pulled cards from four decks, two of which provided more rewards than the other two, developed an emotional antagonism to the penalty decks (as measured by skin receptors) long before they worked out why they felt the way they did. Conversely, people who have suffered subtle damage to the emotion-processing parts of their brains but whose intellects are otherwise unimpaired often lead chaotically indecisive lives, unable even to choose a brand of razor blades. 4

There is, sadly, much more from the cheerful Dr. Fine. The immoral brain is what propels our tendency to blame the victim. Faced with an injustice we cannot ameliorate, our brains desperately want to believe that bad things happened to bad people—otherwise we're faced with the intolerable idea that, through no fault of our own, we too could lose our health, our job, our child. There's the deluded brain. One of the trickiest topics in psychiatry is trying to find the dividing line between the seriously nutty (my wife has been replaced by a look-alike space alien) and the quite sane. Sometimes it's only a matter of how widespread the unproveable tenet is. That 62 per cent of Canadians believe in angels troubles few beyond particularly bloody-minded atheists, precisely because so many people do 5 and have done so for centuries. If belief in the continuing existence of Elvis suddenly spiked to that level, mental health professionals would be in full-blown panic mode.

6 Then there's the secretive brain (it's all right to let your subconscious take over walking, so you don't have to concentrate on sticking one foot in front of the other, but keep an eye on how it often rules your relationship with your parents); the weak-willed brain (the prima donna within); and the pigheaded brain, loftily unconcerned with mere proof. What the author likes best about that chapter is the fact, self-evident to the Fine brain, that anything the reader finds unconvincing in it merely proves the author's point.

7 It all adds up, Fine sombrely concludes, to a vulnerable brain. It's both disconcerting and bracing to learn all the ways our minds distort reality. But it's all in the cause of giving you a reason to get up in the morning, says the aptly named "terror management theory." Concocted by a dour psychologist named Tom Pyszczynski, that concept argues that the brain's tricks are a vital defence against any "awareness that we humans are merely transient animals groping to survive in a meaningless universe, destined only to decay and die." Yes, indeed, who could blame their mind for saving them from *that?* Far, far better to live in the comforting certainty that you're more than all right, no matter how many fools and knaves surround you—and that your poor brain only does what it does because it really, really loves you.

Thinking Critically About Content

1. How many types of brains does Bethune introduce? What are they?
2. What is the basis of these categories?
3. In what way is the brain vulnerable? (paragraph 7)

Thinking Critically About Purpose and Audience

4. Why do you think Bethune wrote this essay?
5. Who would be most interested in this essay?
6. Does this essay make you think you can't trust your own opinion about yourself?

Thinking Critically About Essays

7. How does Bethune organize this essay? Why do you think certain categories are chunked together?
8. The author uses quick examples to explain each category. Pick one example and expand on it. Write a paragraph with an introduction and topic sentence.
9. Explain the title of the essay.
10. Write a detailed description on how your own brain works, and how it sometimes seems to make you think and do things differently from your friends and family.

Writing Workshop

This final section gives you opportunities to apply what you have learned in this chapter to another writing assignment. This time, we provide very little prompting beyond a summary of the guidelines for writing a division/classification essay. This section will let you demonstrate that you can go through the entire writing process on your own with only occasional feedback from your peers. Loop back into the chapter as necessary when you have questions, so that this process becomes as automatic to you as possible before you move on to new material. Then pause at the end of the chapter to reflect briefly on what you have learned.

Guidelines for Writing a Division/Classification Essay

1. Decide on your purpose for writing, and make it part of your thesis statement.
2. Divide your topic into categories that don't overlap.
3. Clearly explain each category.
4. Organize your categories logically.
5. Use transitions to move your readers through your essay.

Writing About Your Reading

1. In the first essay, Richler writes about losers to avoid dating. Divide and classify classmates you have encountered in your courses.
2. Divide and classify your friends into meaningful categories, and write an essay explaining your classification system.
3. What process do you have to go through to come up with an interesting classification essay? How is it different from the process you go through for other rhetorical modes?

Writing About Your World

1. Looking at the picture on the preceding page, think of the types of activities students do in their spare time. Classify these activities into a few categories, and explain their advantages and disadvantages.
2. What are some rituals that you follow in your own life? Do these rituals serve a purpose in your life? Use division and classification to explain three rituals that you follow.
3. We all dream about trips we'd like to take. Sometimes we get to take one of these trips. Others have to remain dreams. What are your ideal trips? Discuss the types of trips you would like to take. What categories do they fall into? Why do you dream about these types of travel?
4. Create your own division/classification assignment (with the help of your instructor), and write a response to it.

Revising

Small Group Activity (5–10 minutes per writer) Working in groups of three or four, each person should read his or her division/classification essay to the other members of the group. Those listening should record their reactions on a copy of the Peer Evaluation Form (Appendix 1A). After your group goes through this process, give your evaluation forms to the appropriate writers so that each writer has two or three peer comment sheets for revising.

Paired Activity (5 minutes per writer) Using the completed Peer Evaluation Forms, work in pairs to decide what you should revise in your essay. If time allows, rewrite some of your sentences, and have your partner look at them.

Individual Activity Rewrite your paper, using the revising feedback you received from other students.

Editing

Paired Activity (5–10 minutes per writer) Exchange papers with a classmate, and use the editing portion of your Peer Evaluation Form (Appendix 1B) to identify as many grammar, punctuation, mechanics, and spelling errors as you can. If time allows, correct some of your errors, and have your partner look at them. Record your grammar, punctuation, and mechanics errors in the Error Log (Appendix 3) and your spelling errors in the Spelling Log (Appendix 4).

Individual Activity Rewrite your paper again, using the editing feedback you received from other students.

CHAPTER 14

DEFINING

Writers, most of all, need to define their tasks . . . their themes, their objectives.

—Henry Seidal Canby

All communication depends on our understanding of a common set of definitions. If we did not work from a set of shared definitions, we would not be able to carry on coherent conversations, write clear letters, or understand any form of media.

It's no surprise, then, that we regularly use definitions in writing as well—in our personal lives, in school, and in the workplace:

You email a friend to tell him or her about the equipment at the fitness centre you just joined.

A student has to define melody, harmony, and rhythm on a music appreciation quiz.

A student begins a report for a criminal justice course with a definition of criminal law.

A financial planner prepares a summary sheet defining the basic financial terms a client should know.

The manager of a sporting goods shop writes a classified ad for an opening on the staff.

Definition is the process of explaining what a word, an object, or an idea is. A good definition focuses on what is special about a word or an idea and what sets it apart from similar words or concepts. Definitions help us understand basic concrete terms (*cellphone, large fries, midterm exams*), discuss events in our lives (*baseball game, graduation, dentist appointment*), and grasp complex ideas (*friendship, courage, success*). Definitions are the building blocks that help us make certain both writer and reader (or speaker and listener) are working from the same basic understanding of terms and ideas.

Definitions vary greatly. They can be as short as one word (a "hog" is a motorcycle) or as long as an essay or even a book. Words or ideas that require such extended definitions are usually abstract, complex, and controversial. Think, for example, how difficult it might be to define an abstract idea like *equality* compared to concrete words such as *dog* or *cat*.

READING AND WRITING A DEFINITION ESSAY

Reading definition essays critically will help you write effective definition essays. You will find that the two processes of reading and writing work together to help you deal with information on a relatively high level. Like two halves of the same circle, these two skills will enhance your ability to perform a variety of other tasks in many other aspects of life.

Reading a Definition Essay

In the following essay, Patricia Pearson defines the term "bullying," comparing her own memories of bullies with her daughter's stories, and with the definitions currently used by experts. Have you ever been the subject of bullying? Have you ever watched someone else being bullied and stood by? How do you feel about bullying? What type of kids are bullies, in your experience?

READING CRITICALLY

Forming your own opinions and coming up with new ideas in response to your reading are very important parts of the reading process, but you need to learn how to produce these reactions. As you read the following essay, record your notes on a separate piece of paper. First, draw a vertical line down the centre of a sheet of paper. Then, as you read, write the author's main ideas on the left and your reactions to those ideas on the right side of the page. Be prepared to explain the connection between your notes and the material in the essay.

PATRICIA PEARSON
When Kids Are Cruel

1 I read my seven-year-old daughter a storybook the other day. It had been designed to address the question of bullying. Not a rip-roaring great story like *Walter the Farting Dog*, but, rather, one of those socially instructive tales that abound in children's literature, such as *Heather Has Two Mommies*, or *Everyone Poops*. Given the current near-obsession on childhood obesity, I reckon it's only a matter of time before we see *Emma's Roomy Pants*. Likewise, perhaps you've noticed that "bullying" has become a pervasive catchword of late. There've been newspaper headlines, school pamphlets, public seminars, government studies, all centred on what to do about bullying at school.

It is unclear, actually, whether incidents of bullying have increased since I attended elementary school in the 1970s. But certainly the concept has gained more urgency, and initiatives to combat bullying are flying out from every level of government, from municipal school boards putting on plays to the National Film Board producing a classroom short called *No More Bullies.* 2

In Clara's storybook, a little boy finds himself being tormented by a *taniwha*, a Maori monster with sharp teeth and wild eyes that's rampaging around the schoolyard. His grandfather urges him to befriend the *taniwha.* He shares his lunch; he invites the *taniwha* to play ball. Ultimately, they forge a happy friendship. The book's illustrations gradually shift, so that the *taniwha* looks less and less like a monster and more like an ordinary boy. "You see?" I said to Clara. "Bullies are really just insecure children trying to get attention. Instead of being scared of them, try to befriend them and see what happens." 3

My daughter chewed on her lip, looking decidedly unsure, and possibly wondering if I had a screw loose. Clara knows that there is an adult label for kids who bug you: "bully." And like other children, she is eager to put her knowledge of adult labels to use. But, in the highly complicated universe of her elementary school, it is difficult to picture what adults actually mean by bully. From Clara's point of view, all children pick on each other, in one way or another. That is her experience. I ought to know this, because whenever I listen to conversations between little girls in her class, I can't decide whether to laugh or cry, they're so outrageously cutting. 4

Some morning, one of them might come up to me and say: "Who's prettier, Zoe or me?" Unlike adults, who suppress their feelings and make nice, and would therefore say, "Oh, I think you both look lovely," young children insult one another with brutal frankness. "You're prettier, by far—Zoe's hair looks stupid," a kid might respond. 5

Under the circumstances, it is hard for children to pick out the "bullies" among all the garden-variety offenders who hurt their feelings—and whose feelings they hurt right back—on a daily basis. On reflection, Clara helpfully identified as "a bully" a boy who actually suffers from ADHD. He is hyperactive and impulsive, and will often throw chalk. In effect, he harasses her. Is that what adults mean by bullying? I asked the principal of Clara's school. She said she would dearly like to see more information out there for parents on "what bullying is not." In her view, bullying involves a powerful child picking on a weaker or less secure victim. She distinguishes this from peer aggression, which is also perceived to have increased in Canadian schools, although—again—there is little concrete data. 6

I seem to recall throwing a rock at someone when I was in elementary school. I also remember that bullying essentially involved the so-called cool kids picking on the nerd, or the fat girl, and this dynamic apparently persists. A study published last December in the journal *Pediatrics* reported that bullies were not like the *taniwha* in Clara's book. "Despite increased conduct problems," wrote author Jaana Juvonen of UCLA's psychology department, "bullies were psychologically strongest, and enjoyed high social standing among their classmates." 7

8 In other words, bullies are popular. They are not socially isolated or lonely. It is their victims—some of whom, the UCLA study points out, are aggressive or provocative themselves—who are more likely to have been demonized or rendered "monstrous," like the *taniwha*. That complicates our picture of the playground jungle.

PREPARING TO WRITE YOUR OWN DEFINITION ESSAY

What do you think of when you hear the word *harassment?* What associations do you make with this word? What examples does it bring to mind? Use one or more of the prewriting strategies you learned in Chapter 5 to generate ideas for writing an extended definition of *harassment.*

Writing a Definition Essay

Clear definitions give writer and reader a mutual starting point on the road to successful communication. Sometimes a short summary and an example are all the definition that's needed. But in the case of abstract and complex words or ideas, a writer may use several approaches to a definition. Use the following guidelines to help you write an extended definition essay.

1. ***Choose your word or idea carefully, and give a working definition of it in your thesis statement.*** First, you need to choose a word or idea that can be defined and explained from several angles, or you will end up with a short, lifeless essay. At the same time, you need to give your readers a working definition right at the start. Put that brief, basic definition in your thesis statement so that readers have a mental hook on which to hang the definitions and explanations in the rest of your essay. Also include the purpose of your essay in your thesis statement.

   Pearson does not give an initial definition of "bully," partly because it is a word that is all too familiar to most people. However, she notes that bullying has "become a pervasive catchword." The best definitions of bullying come in the last two paragraphs, which works best in this case because the essay follows the author's own investigation into bullying.

2. ***Decide how you want to define your term: by synonym, by negation, or by category.*** These are the three common ways to develop a definition.

When you define by using a *synonym*, you furnish readers with a similar word or a short explanation with synonyms. Pearson compares a bully to a character she finds in a child's book, a "*taniwha*," which she describes as "a Maori monster with sharp teeth and wild eyes that's rampaging around the schoolyard." This description is meant to evoke the emotion that bullies arouse in children, rather than their actual appearance. As the appearance of the *taniwha* changes, Pearson offers her daughter a definition: "Bullies are really just insecure children trying to get attention. Instead of being scared of them, try to befriend them and see what happens."

When you define a word by *negation*, you say what the term is not. That is, you define a term by contrasting it with something else. Pearson combines the use of negation with the use of expert opinion, quoting an expert who distinguishes bullying from peer aggression. She returns to definition by negation when she notes later in the essay that bullies are not like the *taniwha* in Clara's book. The principal of Pearson's daughter's school also tells Pearson that she would like to have more information out there for parents on "what bullying is not."

Defining a term by *category* is a more formal type of definition, as in a dictionary. Defining by category has two parts: the class or general category that the word belongs to and the way the word is different from other words in that group. For example, *heart* might be defined as "the organ that pumps blood through the body." The general category is *organ*, and it is different from other organs (brain, lungs, stomach, liver, and so on) because it pumps blood. Pearson does not use this type of definition directly. However, she does imply that bullying is part of a wider range of schoolyard aggression and problems. She also talks about "garden-variety offenders" as a larger group that includes bullies. She does not give information on this larger group, however, other than saying that they are people who "hurt feelings." This larger group could also be seen as existing in the "playground jungle" mentioned in the last paragraph.

3. ***Develop your definition with examples.*** Nearly every definition can be improved by adding examples. Well-chosen examples show your definition in action. Definitions can be *objective*—strictly factual, as in a dictionary definition—or *subjective*—combined with personal opinions. A definition essay is usually more subjective than objective because you are providing your personal opinions about a word or concept. You are explaining to your readers your own meaning, which is what makes your essay interesting. If your readers wanted an objective definition, they could go to a dictionary.

   Pearson uses examples throughout her essay to both expand and limit her definition. Clara's descriptions of the boy with ADHD who throws things and of the casual cruelty of children when asked who is prettier are examples of what bullying is not. Pearson combines the use of negation with the use of examples. She uses more general examples to explain her own idea of bullies: "the so-called cool kids picking on the nerd, or the fat girl . . ."

4. ***Use other rhetorical strategies, such as description, comparison, or process analysis, to support your definition.*** When you write a definition essay, you want to look at your word or idea from many different angles. The other techniques you have learned for developing body paragraphs can help you expand your definition even further. Perhaps a description, a short narrative, or a comparison will make your definition come alive.

   In addition to examples, Pearson uses comparison and contrast and narration to expand her definition. She uses comparison by looking at her own past experiences with bullying and comparing them to her daughter's experience. She also compares what adults will say when asked questions related to appearance with what children will say. She narrates short stories about her own experience of being a bully—"I seem to recall throwing a rock at someone."

5. ***Organize your essay in a logical way.*** Because a definition essay can be developed through several strategies and techniques, there is no set pattern of organization. So you need to figure out the most logical way to explain your word or idea. You might move from particular to general or from general to particular. Or you might arrange your ideas from one extreme to the other, such as from most important to least important, least dramatic to most dramatic, or most familiar to least familiar. In some cases, you might organize your definition chronologically or spatially. Or you might organize part of your essay one way and the rest another way. What's important is that you move in some logical way from one point to another so that your readers can follow your train of thought.

   Pearson organizes her essay by moving from specific examples to specific definitions, using what is called an inductive pattern. As noted above, this pattern follows her actual investigation of the word *bullying*. She questions people, from her own daughter to her daughter's principal to experts, until she finds a definition she can accept. The essay makes logical sense because it allows the reader to follow the same path of investigation as the writer.

WRITING YOUR OWN DEFINITION ESSAY

Bullying is one type of harassment. Write an essay defining "harassment." Begin by reviewing your prewriting notes. Then decide how you are going to approach your subject. Next, write your essay, starting with a clear thesis statement.

A STUDENT'S DEFINITION ESSAY

In the following essay, titled "True Friends," a student named Francine Feinstein defines friendship. See if you can identify her main point as you read this draft of her essay.

True Friends

Many people throw the term "friend" around loosely. They think they have friends 1
at work, friends at school, and friends from the Internet. But is all these people really friends? The word "friend" seems to be used today to refer to anyone from long-term to short-term relationships. However, a true friend is someone who will always be there in times of need, who will always be the best company, and who will always listen and give advice.

Without any questions asked, a good friend will always be there in times of 2
need. No matter how bad a problem is, a true friend will be the person who sits up nights and take days off work just to sit with a friend. If someone is in trouble with a difficult paper a friend will help brainstorm to figure out the problem. If someone is sick, a friend will be the first one at the door with chicken soup and will baby-sit the kids until the sick person feel better. I hate the feeling of being sick. If someone is stranded across town with a broken-down car, a friend will drop every thing to make a rescue and drive the person wherever he or she needs to go. Not everyone has a friend like this a true friend will always be the first one there, no matter what.

Most of all, a true friend is also someone who will listen and give reliable advice. 3
Some people will listen to problems and then give the advice that they think will work best for them, but that advice isn't necessarily best for their friend. Other people will listen but then interject personal stories that relate to the problem but don't solve it. But a true friend listens to a problem and gives suggestions to help a friend figure out the best solution for himself or herself. In other words, a true friend knows how to *listen* and help a person solve problems.

In addition, a friend is someone who is always great company, because friends 4
have so much in common with each other. Imagine working out together, grabbing a sandwich, and then spending the evening just talking—about life, about good times, about bad times, about classes at school. Right now my classes are really hard. At the end of the day, friends might rent their favourite DVD and make some fresh popcorn. Sometimes they even seem to be on the same biological clock, getting tired and waking up at the same time. Friends can always be themselves around each other.

The word "friend" may be misused in the English language, but at least we can 5
agree on what true friends are. True friends are hard to find. But once you find them, they will always be there, listen to you and be the best people to spend time with. No wonder true friends are so rare!

Discovering How the Essay Works

1. What is this essay defining?

2. Does this author define mainly by synonym, by negation, or by category in her essay? Explain your answer.

3. List three specific examples that Francine uses to develop her definition.

   Are her examples more objective or subjective?

4. What other techniques does Francine use to develop her definition?

5. How does Francine organize the examples in her essay?

   Explain your answer.

REVISING AND EDITING THE STUDENT ESSAY

This essay is Francine's first draft, which now needs to be revised and edited. First, apply the Revising Checklist on the inside front cover to the content of Francine's draft. When you are satisfied that her ideas are fully developed and well organized, use the Editing Checklist on the inside back cover to correct her grammatical and mechanical errors. Answer the questions below. Then write your suggested changes directly on Francine's draft.

Revision Questions

Thesis Statement

1. Put brackets around the last sentence in Francine's introduction. Does it state her purpose?

 ____

2. Rewrite Francine's thesis statement if necessary so that it states her purpose and introduces her topics.

 ____

 ____

 ____

Basic Elements

1. Give Francine's essay an alternative title.

 ____

2. Rewrite Francine's introduction so that it captures the reader's attention and builds up to the thesis statement at the end of the paragraph.

 ____

 ____

 ____

3. Does each body paragraph deal with only one topic?

 ____

4. Rewrite Francine's conclusion, using at least one suggestion from Part I.

 ____

 ____

 ____

Development

1. Write out Francine's thesis statement (revised, if necessary), and list her three topic sentences below it.

 Thesis statement: ______________________________

 ____

 ____

Topic 1: ______________________________

____

Topic 2: ______________________________

____

Topic 3: ______________________________

____

2. Do Francine's topic sentences adequately support her thesis statement?

____

3. Does each body paragraph have a focused topic sentence?

____

4. Do the examples in the essay help define "friend"?

____

5. Where do you need more information?

____

6. Make two of Francine's details more specific.

7. Add at least two new details to make her essay clearer.

Unity

1. Read each of Francine's topic sentences with her thesis statement in mind. Do they go together?

____

2. Revise them if necessary so that they are directly related.

3. Drop or rewrite the sentences in paragraph 2 and in paragraph 4 that are not directly related to their topic sentence.

Organization

1. Read Francine's essay again to see if all the paragraphs are arranged logically.

2. Reverse the two paragraphs that are out of order.

3. Look closely at Francine's body paragraphs to see if all her sentences are arranged logically within paragraphs.
4. Move any sentences that are out of order.

Coherence

1. Add two transitions to Francine's essay.
2. Circle five transitions Francine uses.
3. Explain how two of these make Francine's essay easier to read.

____

____

For a list of transitions, see pages 85–86.

Now rewrite Francine's essay with your revisions.

Editing Questions

Sentences

Subjects and Verbs

1. Underline the subjects once and verbs twice in paragraphs 1 and 2 of your revision of Francine's essay. Remember that sentences can have more than one subject–verb set.
2. Does each sentence have at least one subject and verb that can stand alone?

____

3. Did you find and correct Francine's run-on sentence? If not, find and correct it now.

For help with subjects and verbs, see Chapter 23.

For help with run-ons, see Chapter 25.

Subject–Verb Agreement

1. Read aloud the subjects and verbs you underlined in your revision of Francine's essay.
2. Did you find and correct the three subjects and verbs that did not agree?

For help with subject–verb agreement, see Chapter 27.

Pronoun Agreement

1. Find any pronouns in your revision of Francine's essay that do not agree with their nouns.
2. Correct any pronouns that do not agree with their nouns.

For help with pronoun agreement, see Chapter 30.

Modifiers

1. Find any modifiers in your revision of Francine's essay that are not as close as possible to the words they modify.
2. Rewrite sentences if necessary so that modifiers are as close as possible to the words they modify.

For help with modifier errors, see Chapter 33.

Punctuation and Mechanics

Punctuation

For help with punctuation, see Chapters 34–37.

1. Read your revision of Francine's essay for any errors in punctuation.
2. Find the run-on sentence you revised, and make sure it is punctuated correctly.
3. Did you find and correct the two comma errors in Francine's essay?

Mechanics

For help with capitalization, see Chapter 38.

1. Read your revision of Francine's essay for any errors in capitalization.
2. Be sure to check Francine's capitalization in the run-on sentence you revised.

Word Choice and Spelling

Word Choice

For help with confused words, see Chapter 44.

1. Find any words used incorrectly in your revision of Francine's essay.
2. Correct any errors you find.

Spelling

For help with spelling, see Chapter 45.

1. Use spell-check and a dictionary to check the spelling in your revision of Francine's essay.
2. Correct any misspelled words.

Now rewrite Francine's essay again with your editing corrections.

REVISING AND EDITING YOUR OWN DEFINITION ESSAY

Returning to the definition you wrote earlier in this chapter, you are now ready to revise and edit your own writing. Remember that revision involves reworking the content and organization of your essay, while editing asks you to check your grammar and usage. Repeating these processes again and again will ensure that you are producing the best draft possible.

Revise and edit your own writing using the checklists on the inside front and back covers of your text.

WRITING CRITICALLY

As you begin to rework your essay, use the same technique you did in your reading. Just as you identified the author's ideas and recorded your reactions to them to help you understand what the essay was saying, record the ideas from your own writing on the left side of a piece of paper and your reactions to them on the right. Expand your essay with any new ideas that surface from this exercise.

PRACTISING DEFINITION: FROM READING TO WRITING

Reading Workshop

Here are two good definition essays: "Google Never Forgets" by Max Fawcett defines the digital memory or shadow that users leave behind them on the Internet, and "What Is Intelligence, Anyway?" by Isaac Asimov defines intelligence with a humorous touch. You might want to read these selections before writing another definition essay. As you read, notice how the writers make their points through well-chosen examples and details.

MAX FAWCETT

Google Never Forgets: A Cautionary Tale

Focusing Your Attention

1. What kind of information have you posted about yourself online? Do you use MySpace or Facebook? Have you said anything on those sites that you later deleted? What would you think if someone told you that the information was not really gone?
2. In the essay you are about to read the author defines your "digital shadow." You leave information about yourself in many places. What might happen to that information? Could it be used by other people or organizations? Explain your answer.

Expanding Your Vocabulary

The following words are important to your understanding of this essay:

mitigated: made less severe (paragraph 1)
self-deprecating: modest, undervaluing self (paragraph 1)
ill-conceived: badly thought out or planned (paragraph 2)
implications: suggestions, things implied (paragraph 3)
tangential: slightly connected, a digression (paragraph 6)
quintessentially: the essence, a perfect example (paragraph 8)

READING CRITICALLY

As you learned at the beginning of this chapter, practise generating your reactions to your reading by recording the author's ideas on the left side of a piece of paper and your own reactions on the right. These notes will also help you understand the essay on an analytical level. Share your notes with someone in the class.

MAX FAWCETT

Google Never Forgets: A Cautionary Tale

1 We all have one, be it a mother, a well-meaning grandparent or a particularly mischievous college buddy. They're the people who insist on sharing embarrassing stories—which are invariably supported either by a gallery of photographs or a library of shaky home videos—with those you had foolishly hoped would never see them. For example, my mother enjoys producing the front page of the *Vancouver Sun*, circa 1981, on which I am pictured stark naked and sucking on my bottle while sitting on the edge of a public swimming pool on a particularly hot summer day. The upside was the fact that, like my naked baby picture, these embarrassing moments could be managed, the mortifying game of show-and-tell limited to small audiences, and its effects mitigated with healthy doses of self-deprecating laughter.

2 The internet, quite unintentionally, has changed that. Thanks to what amounts to a universally accessible photographic memory, the internet essentially creates the digital equivalent of an unauthorized biography for everyone who leaves a digital footprint. This biography is full of things you might like to share and others you might not, from your comments in an online discussion group to your Grade 12 graduation pictures or some ill-conceived poetry you submitted to an online journal a few years ago. Worse still is the fact that you have almost no control over the biography's content.

Douglas Coupland describes this as our digital "shadow," and he believes it has
3 dangerous implications. As he told a *Time* reporter last spring:

> You've got this thing that follows you no matter where you go. It's going to survive your real shadow long after you're dead. It's composed of truth, half-truth, lies, vengeance, wishful thinking, accuracy, inaccuracy. It grows and grows and gets bigger. It's you but it's not you.

4 It is, in other words, like having the details of a particularly nasty high-school rumour tattooed on your forehead for the rest of your life. Worse still to Coupland is the fact that these shadows are no longer limited merely to the famous and assorted minor celebrities: "Mine's pretty large at the moment but I think in a few years, everyone's is going to be huge. It won't be just people in the public light any more," he said in the same interview.

5 The ghost writer behind these increasingly common unauthorized biographies is none other than Google, that most trusted and financially successful search engine. Google, you see, has betrayed your trust. While it was guiding you to a particularly good restaurant or helping you find a long-lost high-school friend, it was also collecting the dirt on you and sharing it with anyone who would listen.

6 The search engine business used to be a competitive one, with rival engines like Lycos, HotBot and AltaVista battling Google for market domination. But Google's code won out, in large part because it was so good at finding a good bed and breakfast in Napa Valley instead of napalm manufacturers or articles on the dangers of breakfast in bed when you punched "bed and breakfast + Napa" into the search field. But that superior code is also ruthlessly efficient at finding every

reference, however obscure, tangential or dated it might be, when an individual's name is searched. As the *National Post*'s Samantha Grice wrote in March, "the internet's helpful librarian can become an embarrassing mom who insists on hanging your dorkiest kid photos above the mantel and incessantly gushing about your less-than-stellar achievements."

I learned this lesson first hand, thanks to an Angelfire/Geocities website that I 7
created in 1998. I was 18 years old, living in a student residence at UBC and, like many people at the time, relatively unfamiliar with the internet. One of my floormates, a computer science student, appealed to my vanity—a winning strategy to this day, unfortunately—by suggesting that I create a webpage. After all, he argued, what was the harm? It was free, and if I either got bored with it or didn't like what I had created I could just delete it and forget about the whole experience. He neglected to mention that I could also forget that it existed.

In 2004, I finally remembered. Vanity being one of my chief weaknesses, I was 8
Googling myself—a process in which you enter your own name as a search term on Google and discover your digital reflection—and I discovered, with no small degree of horror, the webpage that I had forgotten. Appropriately titled—appropriate in that it exacted the greatest amount of embarrassment—"Max Fawcett, this is your life," the page was a quintessentially amateurish presentation of my interests at age 18.

According to the site, "I'm an honours history student/freelance newspaper 9
writer. On this page you will find my collection of wrestling, southpark, and other cool links." Surf through and you could—and according to the ticker positioned at the bottom of the page, 670 people did—find a "shrine" to "the greatest wrestler of all-time, Chris Jericho" as well as "an extensive collection of *South Park* links, images, and episodes." The cherry in this cocktail of shame is the email address provided, greekgod@angelfire.com, a reference both to the summer I had spent in Greece and the fact that, I assume, I was fairly high on myself at the time of the page's construction. The cost of my "bad Google" has been limited to embarrassment, but for others the price of leaving a digital footprint can be much higher. Employers now routinely Google prospective hires, and one ill-considered comment on a weblog five years ago can mean the difference between making the final round of interviews and being passed over in favour of someone without an objectionable Google shadow. A recent Harris Interactive poll found that 23 percent of adult internet users in the United States had searched online for information about their clients, customers, workers and potential employees.

Worse still is the fact that these Google-happy bosses often find what they're 10
looking for. Nunavut Tourism employee Penny Cholmondeley—Polar Penny, to her online visitors—stumbled across this unfortunate reality on July 18, 2004, when she was terminated from her job for comments made on her weblog. Intended as a personal journal that would detail her summer in Canada's Arctic for her friends and family, the blog included the occasional unflattering picture of, or critical observation on Iqaluit. Without notice or an opportunity to defend herself, Cholmondeley was fired by Nunavut Tourism after it was tipped off about the existence of the blog by an anonymous source just before the end of her six-month probation period. Polar

Penny's experience isn't unique, either. Ironically enough, the next year Google employee Mark Jen was fired after blogging about his first few days at work. Delta Air Lines employee Ellen Simonetti was fired because the airline discovered photos of her in her uniform that she had posted on a website.

11 Perhaps the most infamous Google shadow in history belongs to Mike Klander, once a powerful organizer for former prime minister Paul Martin and the author of an ill-considered blog posting in which he compared federal NDP candidate Olivia Chow to a certain breed of dog. The post and blog were quickly taken down, but not before Google's robots—the architects of everyone's Google shadow—captured and archived it. Klander resigned, but the blog became a major news story and gravely harmed Klander's boss, then Trinity-Spadina Liberal MP Tony Ianno, who was trying to defeat Chow for a third consecutive time to retain his seat. I'm not sure what Mr. Klander is like as a person, but this seems like an awfully high price to pay for what amounts to a bad joke.

12 The lesson here—ironically, one I'm not heeding, as the publication of this piece will breathe new life into that darkest corner of my Google shadow—is to be careful of what you put on display. The internet, for all of its marvellous technological advances and still greater possibilities, is a more dangerous place than we'd like to admit, and that danger comes not from spam, viruses, worms or even those creepy old men who prowl chat rooms pretending to be 16-year-old girls, but instead from the fact that our every cyber-step, every cyber-thought and every search term is saved, sealed and put on display, without our consent and beyond our control. Consider yourself warned.

Thinking Critically About Content

1. Restate Max Fawcett's definition of a digital shadow in your own words. Does Fawcett's definition make sense to you?
2. What does the author say might be the outcome of his publishing his essay?
3. What does the author mean when he refers to a "universally accessible photographic memory"?

Thinking Critically About Purpose and Audience

4. Why do you think Fawcett wrote this essay?
5. Who do you think is his primary audience?
6. How do the examples work in this essay? Do they enhance the message of the essay? Explain your answer.

Thinking Critically About Essays

7. In paragraphs 5 and 6 the author describes Google as if it had human qualities and was capable of acting in a human way (ghost

writer, helpful librarian). How would you characterize Google if you thought of it as an evil human?

8. Choose one paragraph and explain its mood or humour.
9. Choose three transitions in Fawcett's essay and explain why they work.
10. Write your own example of a digital shadow in a paragraph.

ISAAC ASIMOV
What Is Intelligence, Anyway?

Focusing Your Attention

1. Do you ever feel smart in some subjects and not so smart in others? What do you think is the reason for these differences?
2. The essay you are about to read uses examples to explain different types of intelligence we all have. Do you think people can be intelligent in one area and not in another? How could this happen? Do you think these "intelligences" could be altered?

Expanding Your Vocabulary

The following words are important to your understanding of this essay. Highlight them throughout the essay before you begin to read. Then refer to this list as you get to these words in the essay.

aptitude: natural ability (paragraph 1)
KP: kitchen police or workers in the military (paragraph 1)
complacent: smug and satisfied (paragraph 2)
bents: angles (paragraph 2)
oracles: people with great wisdom (paragraph 3)
academician: someone connected to education (paragraph 4)
intricate: complicated or detailed (paragraph 4)
foist: impose something unnecessary (paragraph 4)
arbiter: person who settles a dispute (paragraph 4)
raucously: harshly or loudly (paragraph 6)

READING CRITICALLY

Once again, practise generating your reactions to your reading by recording the author's ideas on the left side of a piece of paper and your own reactions on the right. This activity will help you understand this essay at a deeper level than reading without annotating it. Share your notes with someone in the class.

ISAAC ASIMOV
What Is Intelligence, Anyway?

1 What is intelligence, anyway? When I was in the Army, I received a kind of aptitude test that all soldiers took and, against a normal of 100, scored 160. No one at the base had ever seen a figure like that, and for two hours they made a big fuss over me. (It didn't mean anything. The next day I was still a buck private with KP as my highest duty.)

2 All of my life I've been registering scores like that, so that I have the complacent feeling that I'm highly intelligent, and I expect other people think so too. Actually, though, don't such scores simply mean that I am very good at answering the type of academic questions that are considered worthy of answers by the people who make up the intelligence tests, people with intellectual bents similar to mine?

3 For instance, I had an auto repairman once, who, on these intelligence tests, could not possibly have scored more than 80, by my estimate. I always took it for granted that I was far more intelligent than he was. Yet, when anything went wrong with my car, I hastened to him with it, watched him anxiously as he explored its vitals, and listened to his pronouncements as though they were divine oracles—and he always fixed my car.

4 Well, then, suppose my auto repairman devised questions for an intelligence test. Or suppose a carpenter did, or a farmer, or, indeed, almost anyone but an academician. By every one of those tests, I'd prove myself a moron. And I'd be a moron too. In a world where I could not use my academic training and my verbal talents but had to do something intricate or hard, working with my hands, I would do poorly. My intelligence, then, is not absolute but is a function of the society I live in and of the fact that a small subsection of that society has managed to foist itself on the rest as an arbiter of such matters.

5 Consider my auto repairman, again. He had a habit of telling me jokes whenever he saw me. One time he raised his head from under the automobile hood to say, "Doc, a deaf-and-dumb guy went into a hardware store to ask for some nails. He put two fingers together on the counter and made hammering motions with the other hand. The clerk brought him a hammer. He shook his head and pointed to the two fingers he was hammering. The clerk brought him nails. He picked out the sizes he wanted and left. Well, doc, the next guy who came in was a blind man. He wanted scissors. How do you suppose he asked for them?"

6 Indulgently, I lifted my right hand and made scissoring motions with my first two fingers. Whereupon my auto repairman laughed raucously and said, "Why, you dumb jerk, he used his *voice* and asked for them." Then he said, smugly, "I've been trying that on all my customers today." "Did you catch many?" I asked. "Quite a few," he said, "but I knew for sure I'd catch you." "Why is that?" I asked. "Because you're so goddamned educated, doc, I knew you couldn't be very smart."

7 And I have an uneasy feeling he had something there.

Thinking Critically About Content

1. What is the main idea of this essay?
2. What does Asimov mean when he says his intelligence "is not absolute but is a function of the society I live in" (paragraph 4)?

3. Think of a synonym for "smart" in paragraph 6. What is Asimov implying about intelligence in this paragraph?

Thinking Critically About Purpose and Audience

4. What do you think Asimov's purpose is in this essay?
5. Who do you think is his primary audience?
6. What would Asimov's audience say education and intelligence have in common?

Thinking Critically About Essays

7. How does Asimov use examples in this definition essay?
8. What would Asimov say is his actual definition of *intelligence*?
9. Does this essay imply there are different types of intelligence? Explain your answer with details from the essay.
10. Write a paragraph defining *intelligence* from the auto repairman's point of view.

Writing Workshop

This final section gives you opportunities to apply what you have learned in this chapter to another writing assignment. This time, we provide very little prompting beyond a summary of the guidelines for writing a definition essay. This section will let you demonstrate that you can go through the entire writing process on your own with only occasional feedback from your peers. Loop back into the chapter as necessary when you have questions so that this process becomes as automatic to you as possible before you move on to new material. Then pause at the end of the chapter to reflect briefly on what you have learned.

Guidelines for Writing a Definition Essay

1. Choose your word or idea carefully, and give a working definition of it in your thesis statement.
2. Decide how you want to define your term: by synonym, by negation, or by category.
3. Develop your definition with examples.
4. Use other rhetorical strategies, such as description, comparison, or process analysis, to support your definition.
5. Organize your essay in a logical way.

Writing About Your Reading

1. In the first essay, Max Fawcett defines the term "Google shadow." Search for another new technology such as YouTube, blogging, social networking, or social bookmarking, find unusual words related to that technology, and write your own definition of one of those words.
2. In the second essay, Isaac Asimov defines *intelligence*. Write your own definition of another state of mind, such as *joy*, *fear*, *loneliness*, or *stress*.
3. Now that you have studied different approaches to the process of definition, what makes a definition effective or useful for you? Apply what you have studied about definition to your answer.

Writing About Your World

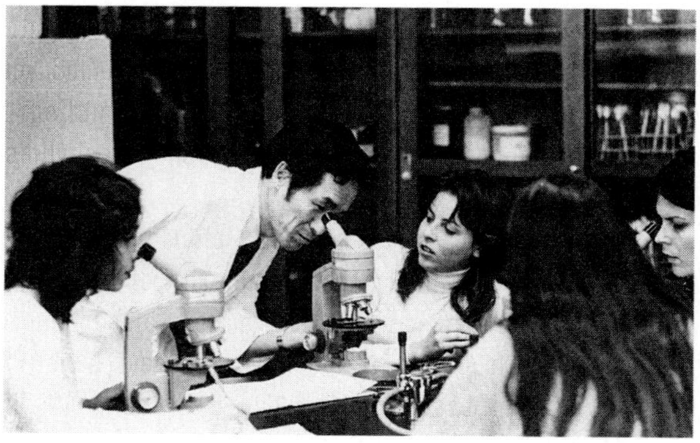

1. What does education mean to you? Define "education" as portrayed in this picture.
2. The concept of "family" has undergone a number of changes over the past few years. How would you define this term in our current society?
3. Define one of the following abstract terms: *fear, love, inferiority, wonder, pride, self-control, discipline, anger, freedom, violence, assertiveness, courtesy, kindness*.
4. Create your own definition assignment (with the help of your instructor), and write a response to it.

Revising

Small Group Activity (5–10 minutes per writer) Working in groups of three or four, each person should read his or her definition essay to the other members of the group. The listeners should record their reactions on a copy of the Peer Evaluation Form (Appendix 1A). After your group goes through this process, give your evaluation forms to the appropriate writers so that each writer has two or three peer comment sheets for revising.

Paired Activity (5 minutes per writer) Using the completed Peer Evaluation Forms, work in pairs to decide what you should revise in your essay.

If time allows, rewrite some of your sentences and have your partner look at them.

Individual Activity Rewrite your paper, using the revising feedback you received from other students.

Editing

Paired Activity (5–10 minutes per writer) Swap papers with a classmate, and use the editing portion of your Peer Evaluation Form (Appendix 1B) to identify as many grammar, punctuation, mechanics, and spelling errors as you can. If time allows, correct some of your errors, and have your partner look at them. Record your grammar, punctuation, and mechanics errors in the Error Log (Appendix 3) and your spelling errors in the Spelling Log (Appendix 4).

Individual Activity Rewrite your paper again, using the editing feedback you received from other students.

CHAPTER

15 Analyzing Causes and Effects

The act of writing is one of the most powerful problem-solving tools humans have at their disposal.

—Toni Fulwiler

We are born with a natural curiosity. Wanting to know why things happen is one of our earliest, most basic instincts; think of a toddler asking, "Daddy, why is the sky blue?" Closely related to this desire to understand *why* is our interest in *what* will happen as a result of some particular action: If I stay outside much longer, will I get a bad sunburn? But thinking about causes and effects is not only part of human nature; it is also an advanced mental process and the basis for most decisions we make. When faced with a decision, we naturally consider it from different perspectives. If we choose option A, what will happen? What if we choose B—or C? In other words, we look at the possible results—the effects—of the choices and then make up our minds.

Analyzing causes and effects is also an essential part of our writing lives. We use cause-and-effect writing in our personal lives, in school, and in the marketplace:

A volunteer for a mayor's campaign designs a poster telling how a vote for this candidate will benefit the city.

A student discusses the causes of schizophrenia in a paper for a psychology course.

A student explains the effects of repatriating the Constitution on a history exam.

A sales representative writes a report to her manager explaining why she didn't meet her sales projections.

The owner of a florist shop writes a letter of complaint to one of the suppliers about the negative effect of late deliveries on sales.

Analyzing causes and effects requires the ability to look for connections between two or more items or events and to analyze the reasons for those connections. As the name implies, this writing strategy is composed of two parts: cause and effect. To understand **causes,** we look in the past for reasons why something happened. To discover **effects,** we look to the future for possible results of an action. In other words, we break a situation into parts so we can look at the relationships between these parts and then reach conclusions that are logical and useful.

READING AND WRITING A CAUSE/EFFECT ESSAY

Learning how to read cause/effect essays critically will improve your writing. Understanding how a reading selection actually works (in both form and content) will show you how to develop your own writing assignments. Reading and writing critically in any mode are demanding, but they are necessary for success in college and in life beyond college. Like two parts of a whole, these two processes work together to increase your ability to perform other tasks in all facets of life.

Reading a Cause/Effect Essay

In "Why Do Schools Flunk Biology?" LynNell Hancock makes the point that education in the United States is stuck in the nineteenth century. She deals with both the causes and the effects of students' ability to learn. What do you think of our educational system at the high school level? How does the Canadian system compare to the U.S. system described here?

READING CRITICALLY

Separating causes from effects is an important part of understanding a cause/effect essay. After a first reading, divide a sheet of paper into two parts with a vertical line. Then as you read the essay for a second time, record the causes in the left column and the results on the right. Draw lines from each cause to its related effect (if applicable). Be prepared to explain the connection between your lists and the details in the essay.

LYNNELL HANCOCK

Why Do Schools Flunk Biology?

Biology is a staple at most American high schools. Yet when it comes to the biology of the students themselves—how their brains develop and retain knowledge—school officials would rather not pay attention to the lessons. Can first graders handle French? What time should school start? Should music be cut? Biologists have 1 some important evidence to offer. Not only are they ignored, but their findings are often turned upside down.

2 Force of habit rules the hallways and classrooms. Neither brain science nor education research has been able to free the majority of America's schools from their 19th-century roots. If more administrators were tuned in to brain research, scientists argue, not only would schedules change, but subjects such as foreign language and geometry would be offered to much younger children. Music and gym would be daily requirements. Lectures, worksheets, and rote memorization would be replaced by hands-on materials, drama, and project work. And teachers would pay greater attention to children's emotional connections to subjects. "We do more education research than anyone else in the world," says Frank Vellutino, a professor of educational psychology at State University of New York at Albany, "and we ignore more as well."

3 Plato once said that music "is a more potent instrument than any other for education." Now scientists know why. Music, they believe, trains the brain for higher forms of thinking. Researchers at the University of California, Irvine, studied the power of music by observing two groups of preschoolers. One group took piano lessons and sang daily in chorus. The other did not. After eight months the musical 3-year-olds were expert puzzlemasters, scoring 80 percent higher than their playmates did in spatial intelligence—the ability to visualize the world accurately.

4 This skill later translates into complex math and engineering skills. "Early music training can enhance a child's ability to reason," says Irvine physicist Gordon Shaw. Yet music education is often the first "frill" to be cut when school budgets shrink. Schools on average have only one music teacher for every 500 children, according to the National Commission on Music Education.

5 Then there's gym—another expendable hour by most school standards. Only 36 percent of school children today are required to participate in daily physical education. Yet researchers now know that exercise is good not only for the heart. It also juices up the brain, feeding it nutrients in the form of glucose and increasing nerve connections—all of which make it easier for kids of all ages to learn. Neuroscientist William Greenough confirmed this by watching rats at his University of Illinois at Urbana–Champaign lab. One group did nothing. A second exercised on an automatic treadmill. A third was set loose in a Barnum & Bailey obstacle course requiring the rats to perform acrobatic feats. These "supersmart" rats grew "an enormous amount of gray matter" compared with their sedentary partners, says Greenough. Of course, children don't ordinarily run such gantlets; still, Greenough believes, the results are significant. Numerous studies, he says, show that children who exercise regularly do better in school.

6 The implication for schools goes beyond simple exercise. Children also need to be more physically active in the classroom, not sitting quietly in their seats memorizing subtraction tables. Knowledge is retained longer if children connect not only aurally but emotionally and physically to the material, says University of Oregon education professor Robert Sylwester in *A Celebration of Neurons.*

Good teachers know that lecturing on the American Revolution is far less effective than acting out a battle. Angles and dimensions are better understood if children chuck their work sheets and build a complex model to scale. The smell of the glue enters memory through one sensory system, the touch of the wood blocks another, the sight of the finished model still another. The brain then creates a multidimensional mental model of the experience—one easier to retrieve. "Explaining a smell," says Sylwester, "is not as good as actually smelling it." 7

Scientists argue that children are capable of far more at younger ages than schools generally realize. People obviously continue learning their whole lives, but the optimum "windows of opportunity for learning" last until about the age of 10 or 12, says Harry Chugani of Wayne State University's Children's Hospital of Michigan. Chugani determined this by measuring the brain's consumption of its chief energy source, glucose. (The more glucose it uses, the more active the brain.) Children's brains, he observes, gobble up glucose at twice the adult rate from the age of 4 to puberty. So young brains are as primed as they'll ever be to process new information. Complex subjects such as trigonometry or foreign language shouldn't wait for puberty to be introduced. In fact, Chugani says, it's far easier for an elementary-school child to hear and process a second language—and even speak it without an accent. Yet most U.S. districts wait until junior high to introduce Spanish or French—after the "windows" are closed. 8

Reform could begin at the beginning. Many sleep researchers now believe that most teens' biological clocks are set later than those of their fellow humans. But high school starts at 7:30 a.m., usually to accommodate bus schedules. The result can be wasted class time for whole groups of kids. Making matters worse, many kids have trouble readjusting their natural sleep rhythm. Dr. Richard Allen of Johns Hopkins University found that teens went to sleep at the same time whether they had to be at school by 7:30 a.m. or 9:30 a.m. The later-to-rise teens not only get more sleep, he says; they also get better grades. The obvious solution would be to start school later when kids hit puberty. But at school, there's what's obvious, and then there's tradition. 9

Why is this body of research rarely used in most American classrooms? Not many administrators or school-board members know it exists, says Linda Darling-Hammond, professor of education at Columbia University's Teachers College. In most states, neither teachers nor administrators are required to know much about how children learn in order to be certified. What's worse, she says, decisions to cut music or gym are often made by noneducators, whose concerns are more often monetary than educational. "Our school system was invented in the late 1800s, and little has changed," she says. "Can you imagine if the medical profession ran this way?" 10

PREPARING TO WRITE YOUR OWN CAUSE/EFFECT ESSAY

What can be improved in our educational system at the high school level? What do you want to change? What would be the possible results of these changes? What do you want to keep the same? Use one or more of the prewriting techniques that you learned in Chapter 5 to generate ideas on this subject.

Writing a Cause/Effect Essay

When you write a cause/effect essay, your purpose is to give your readers some insight into the causes and effects of an event or a situation. Cause/effect writing is based on your ability to analyze. Good cause/effect essays follow a few simple guidelines.

1. ***Write a thesis statement that tells what you are analyzing.*** Cause/effect thinking requires that you look for connections between two or more situations. That is, you want to discover what caused an incident, or what its results might be. Then you can focus on the causes (what made something else happen) or the effects (the results), or some combination of the two.

   In her essay, Hancock puts her thesis statement at the end of her first paragraph: "Not only are they [biologists] ignored, but their findings are often turned upside down." She goes on to say that if school administrators paid attention to research (the cause), we would see many changes (the effects), which she names. The rest of the essay examines each effect in detail.

2. ***Choose facts, details, and reasons to support your thesis statement.*** Cause/effect essays are usually written to prove a specific point. As a result, your body paragraphs should consist mainly of facts, details, and reasons—not opinions. Your reader should be able to check what you are saying, and any opinions that you include should be based on clear evidence.

   Since Hancock sets out to prove that American education ignores research, she must name specific research studies that help her prove her point. She breaks her subject into five areas: music, gym, teaching methods, curriculum (subjects studied), and school hours. She then cites evidence in each area. For example, in the area of music, she describes research at the University of California, Irvine; for gym, she discusses rat studies from the University of Illinois; for curriculum, she describes research done at Wayne State University's Children's Hospital.

   Hancock also quotes many experts, such as Frank Vellutino, a professor of educational psychology at State University of New York at Albany (paragraph 2), and gives statistics from the National Commission on Music Education (paragraph 4). A reader could check every one of Hancock's research studies, quotations, statistics, and observations (such as when most high schools begin classes in the morning). By providing facts and reasons rather than opinions in her body paragraphs, Hancock proves her point—that American education is not paying attention to current research about learning.

3. ***Do not mistake coincidence for cause or effect.*** If you get up every morning at 5:30, just before the sun rises, you cannot conclude that the sun rises *because* you get up. The relationship between these two events is coincidence. Confusing coincidence with cause and effect is faulty reasoning—reasoning that is not logical. To avoid this kind of faulty reasoning, you can look more deeply into the issues connected with your subject. The more you search for real causes and effects, the less likely it is that you will be thrown off by coincidence.

   Hancock does not seem to mistake coincidence for cause or effect in any part of her essay. If, however, she had said that ignoring research on how teens learn has resulted in fewer students studying foreign languages today compared to 40 years ago, her reasoning would be faulty. She has no evidence to prove that the research about how students learn and the decline in students taking foreign languages in high school are related. It's only a coincidence that the research has been ignored and that fewer students study foreign languages today.

4. ***Search for the real causes and effects connected with your subject.*** Just as you wouldn't stop reading halfway through a good murder mystery, you shouldn't stop too early in your analysis of causes and effects. Keep digging. The first reasons or results that you uncover are often not the real reasons or results. Suppose that a character in a mystery dies by slipping in the shower. You should try to find out what caused the fall. A good detective who keeps digging might find that someone administered a drug overdose, which caused her to fall in the shower. In other words, you are looking for the most basic cause or effect.

   Hancock shows us through the large amount of evidence she presents that she has searched hard to discover the real causes and effects of education lagging behind the times. She names two causes—administrators ignore research and noneducators make decisions about education—and gives the effects of ignoring research in five areas of education.

5. ***Organize your essay so that your readers can easily follow your analysis.*** Though it may be difficult to think through the causes and effects of a situation, organizing this type of essay is usually straightforward. Your thesis statement tells what you are going to analyze. Then your body paragraphs discuss the main causes or main effects in the order they occurred, from one extreme to another, from general to particular, or from particular to general. You might, for example, use chronological order to show how one effect led to another and then to a third. Or you might move from the most important cause or effect to the least important. Your goal in a cause/effect essay is to get your readers to agree with

you and see a certain issue or situation the way you do. To accomplish this purpose, your readers need to be able to follow what you are saying.

Hancock discusses five effects of ignoring research on how students learn, moving from particular to general. First, she deals with the two subjects that school boards cut most often for budget reasons: music and gym. From these specific classes she moves to more general concerns—teaching methods and curriculum. Finally, she discusses high school hours, the most general topic of all. In other words, she organizes her essay from specific to general, moving from specific classes to the general logistics of the school day.

WRITING YOUR OWN CAUSE/EFFECT ESSAY

Write an essay analyzing one of the changes you think is needed in our high school educational system. What caused the current problem as you see it? Why is this change necessary? What will be the results of this change? Review your prewriting notes first. Then draft a thesis statement and write your analysis, following the guidelines for writing a cause/effect essay.

A STUDENT'S CAUSE/EFFECT ESSAY

Jefferson Wright, the student writer of the following essay, titled "The Budget Crisis," explores the problems of budget cuts at his local college. Can you find the points in this draft of his essay when he deals with causes? When does he focus on effects?

The Budget Crisis

1 The local community college has a budget crisis. Now, when a staff person quits their job or retires, no one is hired to replace that person. This wouldn't be of great concern to most students, except now the lack of money is starting to affect the campus grounds. The college no longer has the money to replace some of the maintenance and facilities crew, which means the campus grounds, classrooms, and offices are no longer well maintained.

2 A campus that used to be beautiful has turned into a wasteland because of the neglect in keeping up its grounds. The small maintenance crew simply cannot handle the workload necessary to maintain the campus. The flower beds in front of the buildings have not been weeded, so now it has more weeds than flowers. Garbage that is thrown around the campus has not been picked up. Around every doorway are cigarette butts ground into the concrete. People shouldn't smoke anyway. It's not a

great habit. There are old newspapers and candy wrappers caught on grass that has not been mowed in over two weeks, making the grounds look like the aftermath of a concert. Cans are overflowing with garbage and have colonies of flies circling them. The outside of the campus just looks unkempt and uncared for.

3 However, the campus grounds are not all that is ugly. The classroom buildings are also neglected. Everything inside is as messy as outside. The floors that used to shine are now covered with a sticky gray film. There are spills on the floors by all the soft drink machines. The bulletin boards are never cleaned off, so people just put new flyers over three or four layers of old flyers. On warm days, a strange smell overwhelms the classrooms, which the students have named "the biohazard." Washrooms are in desperate need of attention. And would probably fail any government check. The campus is really disgusting.

4 But the students aren't the only people suffering; the instructors are feeling the effects also. Their offices have ants crawling from various cracks in the walls. The dust in their offices is two inches thick. Spiders have woven cobwebs high in the windows and corners of the offices. Making both instructors and students wonder exactly where the insects hide during the day. Many light bulbs are broken near the offices, and the fluorescent bulbs flicker as if it is dancing to an unheard rhythm. The offices are as bad as the rest of the campus.

5 The condition of the campus can hardly be blamed on the maintenance crew. They are constantly working and trying to keep up with the workload. The problem lies in the fact that by the time they finish one job, two or more weeks pass by before they can get back to that job. There just isn't enough money to hire the necessary personnel to cover the demands of the job. The college should put money into hiring more maintenance personnel before students transfer to other colleges because of the condition of this one. Why can't the college just spend the necessary money to make the campus beautiful again.

Discovering How the Essay Works

1. What is Jefferson analyzing in this essay?

___

2. Do Jefferson's facts, details, and reasons support his thesis statement? Explain your answer.

___

___

3. Does Jefferson confuse any coincidences with causes and effects? Explain your answer.

___

4. Do you feel that Jefferson gets to the real problems connected with his college's budget crisis? Explain your answer.

____

____

5. How does Jefferson organize the topics in his essay?

____

REVISING AND EDITING THE STUDENT ESSAY

This essay is Jefferson's first draft, which now needs to be revised and edited. First, apply the Revising Checklist from the inside front cover to the content of Jefferson's draft. When you are satisfied that his ideas are fully developed and well organized, use the Editing Checklist on the inside back cover to correct his grammar and punctuation errors. Answer the questions below. Then write your suggested changes directly on Jefferson's draft.

Revision Questions

Thesis Statement

1. Put brackets around the last sentence in Jefferson's introduction. What does it say he is analyzing?

____

____

2. Rewrite Jefferson's thesis statement if necessary so that it states his purpose and introduces all his topics.

____

____

Basic Elements

1. Give Jefferson's essay an alternative title.

____

____

2. Rewrite Jefferson's introduction so that it captures the reader's attention and builds up to the thesis statement at the end of the paragraph.

___

___

3. Does each of Jefferson's body paragraphs deal with only one topic?

___

___

4. Rewrite Jefferson's conclusion using at least one suggestion from Part I.

___

___

Development

1. Write out Jefferson's thesis statement (revised, if necessary), and list his topic sentences below it.

   Thesis Statement: ___

   ___

   ___

   Topic 1: ___

   ___

   Topic 2: ___

   ___

   Topic 3: ___

   ___

2. Do the topics adequately develop the essay's thesis statement?

___

3. Does each body paragraph have a focused topic sentence?

___

4. Does Jefferson get to the real causes and effects in his essay?

____

5. Where do you need more information?

____

6. Make two of Jefferson's details more specific.
7. Add at least two new details to make his essay clearer.

Unity

1. Read each of Jefferson's topic sentences with his thesis statement. Do they go together?

____

2. Revise them if necessary so they are directly related.
3. Drop or rewrite the two sentences in paragraph 2 that are not directly related to their topic sentence.

Organization

1. Read Jefferson's essay again to see if all the paragraphs are arranged logically.
2. Move any paragraphs that are out of order.
3. Do you think his method of organization is the most effective one for his purpose? Explain your answer.

____

____

4. Look closely at Jefferson's body paragraphs to see if all his sentences are arranged logically within paragraphs.
5. Move the sentence in paragraph 2 that is out of order.

Coherence

For a list of transitions, see pages 85–86.

For a list of pronouns, see pages 389–390.

1. Add two transitions to Jefferson's essay.
2. Circle five pronouns Jefferson uses.
3. Explain how two of these make Jefferson's essay easier to read.

____

____

Now rewrite Jefferson's essay with your revisions.

Editing Questions

Sentences

Subjects and Verbs

1. Underline the subjects once and verbs twice in paragraphs 3 and 4 of your revision of Jefferson's essay. Remember that sentences can have more than one subject–verb set.
2. Does each of the sentences have at least one subject and verb that can stand alone?

____

3. Did you find and correct Jefferson's two fragments? If not, find and correct them now.

For help with subjects and verbs, see Chapter 23.

For help with fragments, see Chapter 24.

Subject–Verb Agreement

1. Read aloud the subjects and verbs you underlined in your revision of Jefferson's essay.
2. Correct any subjects and verbs that do not agree.

For help with subject–verb agreement, see Chapter 27.

Pronoun Agreement

1. Find any pronouns in your revision of Jefferson's essay that do not agree with their nouns.
2. Did you find and correct the three pronoun agreement errors in Jefferson's essay? If not, find and correct them now.

For help with pronoun agreement, see Chapter 30.

Modifiers

1. Find any modifiers in your revision of Jefferson's essay that are not as close as possible to the words they modify.
2. Rewrite sentences if necessary so that modifiers are as close as possible to the words they modify.

For help with modifier errors, see Chapter 33.

Punctuation and Mechanics

Punctuation

1. Read your revision of Jefferson's essay for any errors in punctuation.
2. Find the two fragments you revised, and make sure they are punctuated correctly.
3. Did you find and correct Jefferson's two errors in end punctuation? If not, find and correct them now.

For help with punctuation, see Chapters 34–37.

Mechanics

1. Read your revision of Jefferson's essay for any errors in capitalization.
2. Be sure to check Jefferson's capitalization in the fragments you revised.

For help with capitalization, see Chapter 38.

Word Choice and Spelling

Word Choice

For help with confused words, see Chapter 44.

1. Find any words used incorrectly in your revision of Jefferson's essay.
2. Correct any errors you find.

Spelling

For help with spelling, see Chapter 45.

1. Use spell-check and a dictionary to check the spelling in your revision of Jefferson's essay.
2. Correct any misspelled words.

Now rewrite Jefferson's essay again with your editing corrections.

REVISING AND EDITING YOUR OWN CAUSE/EFFECT ESSAY

Returning to the cause/effect essay you wrote earlier in this chapter, you are now ready to revise and edit your own writing. Remember that revision involves reworking the content and organization of your essay while editing asks you to check your grammar and usage. The more times you repeat these processes, the better your draft will be.

The checklists on the inside front and back covers will help you apply what you have learned to your essay.

WRITING CRITICALLY

As you begin to rework your essay, use the same technique you did in your reading. List the causes and effects that you discuss in your essay in two columns. Then draw lines from causes to related effects, making sure the relationship between these items is clear to your readers. Revise any connections that are unclear.

PRACTISING CAUSE/EFFECT: FROM READING TO WRITING

Reading Workshop

The two essays in this chapter show cause and effect at work: The first, "Happiness Is Catching: Why Emotions Are Contagious," by Stacey Colino, analyzes the roles of moods in our daily lives, and "Too Much Self-Esteem: The Blight of Modern Times," by Johanna Schneller, discusses the effect of excessive positive reinforcement. You might want to read these selections before writing another cause/effect essay. As you read, notice how the writers make their points through well–thought-out, detailed reasoning.

STACEY COLINO
Happiness Is Catching: Why Emotions Are Contagious

Focusing Your Attention

1. Are you easily influenced by other people's moods? How do you know this?
2. In the essay you are about to read, Stacey Colino explains how we "catch" the feelings of others. Think of someone who generally makes you happy and someone who usually makes you sad. What is the difference between these two people? How do they each approach life? How do they each relate to you?

Expanding Your Vocabulary

The following words are important to your understanding of this essay. As you read, circle any words you don't know beyond this list. Then break into groups, and help each other figure out the meanings of these unknown words.

elation: joy, happiness (paragraph 1)
euphoria: extreme happiness (paragraph 1)
inoculate against: become immune to, resist (paragraph 1)
milliseconds: thousandths of a second (paragraph 2)
synchronize: coordinate (paragraph 2)
extroverts: outgoing people (paragraph 4)
engulfed: completely surrounded, overwhelmed (paragraph 5)
introverts: shy, quiet people (paragraph 5)
susceptible to: easily influenced by (paragraph 8)
mimicry: copying (paragraph 9)

READING CRITICALLY

As you learned at the beginning of this chapter, practise recognizing causes and effects by listing them in the following essay. Put them in two columns on a separate sheet of paper. These lists will help you understand the essay on an analytical level. Compare your notes with someone in the class.

STACEY COLINO

Happiness Is Catching: Why Emotions Are Contagious

1 Researchers have found that emotions, both good and bad, are nearly as contagious as colds and flus. You can catch elation, euphoria, sadness, and more from friends, family, colleagues, even strangers. And once you understand how to protect yourself, you can inoculate yourself against the bad.

2 Mood "infection" happens in milliseconds, says Elaine Hatfield, Ph.D., a professor of psychology at the University of Hawaii in Honolulu and coauthor of *Emotional Contagion* (Cambridge University Press, 1994). And it stems from a primitive instinct: During conversation, we naturally tend to mimic and synchronize our facial expressions, movements, and speech rhythms to match the other person's. "Through this, we come to feel what the person is feeling," explains Dr. Hatfield. In other words, it puts us in touch with their feelings and affects our behaviour.

3 Not surprisingly, spouses are especially likely to catch each other's moods, but so are parents, children, and good friends. In fact, a recent study at the University of Texas Medical Branch at Galveston found that depression was highly contagious among college roommates. "The same thing can occur with a spouse or co-worker, where one person is moderately depressed," says study author Thomas E. Joiner Jr., Ph.D., assistant professor of psychiatry and behavioural sciences.

4 Dr. Hatfield's research shows that extroverts and emotionally expressive people tend to transmit their feelings more powerfully. There's also a breed of people who, consciously or not, may want or need you to feel what they feel; they're the ones who live by the adage "misery loves company." They manipulate other people's moods—perhaps without even realizing it—to gain the upper hand or to feel better about themselves. "They express emotion to get a response—perhaps attention or sympathy," says Ross Buck, Ph.D., professor of communication sciences and psychology at the University of Connecticut.

5 On the other hand, some personality types are more likely to be engulfed by others' moods. Introverts are vulnerable because they're easily aroused. So are highly sensitive individuals who react physically to emotionally charged situations—their hearts flutter before giving a speech, for example.

6 If anyone knows how quickly moods spread, it's Ginny Graves, 33, a San Francisco writer. Last year, when she was pregnant with her first child, her mood took a nosedive every time she saw a particular friend.

7 "Basically nothing good was going on in her life—she didn't like her job, and she was obsessed with her weight," recalls Ginny. "I tried to bolster her up, but whenever I talked to her, I'd feel tense and tired." Afterward, Ginny was left with a case of the moody blues that lingered a day or so.

8 Indeed, there's some evidence that women may be particularly susceptible to catching moods, perhaps because we're better able to read other people's emotions and body language, according to psychologist Judith Hall, Ph.D., professor of psychology at Northeastern University in Boston.

Since women perceive facial expressions so readily that we may be more likely to mimic them—and wind up sharing the feeling. Just how mimicry leads to catching a mood is not known, notes John T. Cacioppo, Ph.D., professor of psychology at Ohio State University and coauthor of *Emotional Contagion.* One theory holds that when you frown or smile, the muscular movements in your face alter blood flow to the brain, which in turn affects mood; another theory maintains that the sensations associated with specific facial expressions trigger emotional memories—and hence the feelings—linked with those particular expressions. 9

With any luck, we catch the happy moods—infectious laughter at a dinner party or a colleague's enthusiasm for a project, for instance. Some psychologists suspect, however, that negative emotions—especially depression and anxiety—may be the most infectious of all. "For women, stress and depression are like emotional germs—they jump from one person to the next," notes Ellen McGrath, Ph.D., a psychologist in Laguna Beach, California, and author of *When Feeling Bad Is Good* (Bantam, 1994). 10

Being susceptible to other people's moods does make for a rich emotional life. But let's face it: When you catch a happy mood, you don't want to change it. Downbeat emotions are harder to deal with. And who wants her life to be ruled by other people's bad moods? 11

Fortunately, there are ways to protect yourself from unpleasant emotions, while letting yourself catch the good ones. For starters, pay attention to how you feel around different people, suggests Dr. McGrath. Then label your emotions—noting, for example, whether you feel optimistic around your best friend or gloomy after seeing your aunt. Then ask yourself if you're feeling what you do because you actually feel that way or because you've caught a mood from the other person. Just recognizing that an emotion belongs to someone else, not you, can be enough to short-circuit its transmission. 12

Once you know how people affect you, you can be more selective about whom you spend time with. Instead of going on an all-day outing with family members who bring you down, for instance, try spending shorter periods of time with them. Another solution is to give yourself a time-out: It could be as simple as a restroom break during an intense dinner. 13

Putting up emotional barriers is not the answer, though. If the channels are open, both positive and negative influences flow in. Shutting out the bad precludes you from catching joyful moods, too. Instead, it's better to monitor the floodgates—and to come to your own rescue when you feel yourself catching other people's negativity. And if you get swept up in another person's excitement, sit back and enjoy the ride. 14

Thinking Critically About Content

1. What is Colino analyzing in this essay? How does her title help focus her analysis?
2. Name two causes and two effects of people's moods.
3. How does Colino suggest that you can protect yourself from unpleasant emotions?

Thinking Critically About Purpose and Audience

4. Why do you think Colino wrote this essay?
5. Considering that this essay was originally published in a magazine called *Family Circle*, who do you think Colino's intended audience is? Explain your answer.
6. Are you susceptible to other people's moods? Why or why not?

Thinking Critically About Essays

7. The author of this essay quotes many authorities in the field of psychology. Are these quotations convincing to you? Explain your answer.
8. Which of Colino's paragraphs deal primarily with causes? Which with effects? Do you think this is a good balance? Explain your answer.
9. Find five transitions in Colino's essay that work well, and explain why they are effective.
10. Discuss the emotional climate in the place where you live. Are you able to separate your emotions from those of the people you live with? Are you affected by the emotions of roommates, friends, and family? How might you manage emotional swings after reading this essay?

JOHANNA SCHNELLER

Too Much Self-Esteem: The Blight of Modern Times

Focusing Your Attention

1. What gives you a sense of self-esteem? Are you able to feel good about yourself without being told you are doing well?
2. In the essay you are about to read, Johanna Schneller writes about the effect the excessive reinforcement of self-esteem by baby-boomer parents has had on a generation of young people. Do you think that self-esteem should always be based on actual achievements? Is a sense of self-esteem necessary for happiness?

Expanding Your Vocabulary

The following words are important to your understanding of this essay:

chagrined: embarrassed (paragraph 2)

sashayed: flounced or strutted (paragraph 2)

fogey: an old-fashioned person (paragraph 2)

smitten: hit by a deep emotion (paragraph 3)
accolades: approval, praise (paragraph 3)
gorgons: ugly people, like Medusa, the mythological woman with snakes for hair (paragraph 6)
angst: anxiety (paragraph 8)
ilk: kind (paragraph 17)
simulacrum: a mockery or sham (paragraph 20)
travails: hard work (paragraph 24)
synapses: the pathway between nerves (paragraph 25)

READING CRITICALLY

As you did with the previous essay, list the causes and effects in the following essay on a separate sheet of paper. Then draw lines from specific causes to the related effects. This process will give you some good insights into the author's approach to her topic and her methods of developing her ideas. Compare your notes with those of one of your classmates.

JOHANNA SCHNELLER

Too Much Self-Esteem: The Blight of Modern Times

Earlier this season on *American Idol,* 19-year-old contestants were dolled up like children dressed as hookers for Halloween. Sometimes they sang, but sometimes their caterwauling was earsplitting. When the latter occurred, the show's three judges, music professionals all, proffered their opinions: "You are screaming, not singing," they said, again and again. 1

Were the children chagrined to be humiliated on TV? Did they vow to improve, sign up for singing lessons? No. Semi-nude, they sashayed straight up to the cameras, tossed their manes of hair and told those fogey judges, "You don't know anything about singing." 2

In the current reality movie *The Real Cancun*, a film spinoff of MTV's *Real World* series, fourteen 21-year-olds share a Mexican beach house for a week while cameras film their every move. "I am a very observant person," one young woman announces. Another says, "I am so good at figuring out people," while failing to pick up obvious signals from a smitten housemate. "You are so hot!" a boy says to a girl. "Thank you," she replies flatly, clearly accustomed to (and bored by) such accolades. 3

Remarkably, in the course of the entire week, only three of the 14 admit to any self-doubt. The rest are stunningly sure of themselves, particularly one young woman who is being pursued avidly by one of the guys. 4

5 On the dance floor, she gyrates her fanny against his crotch for hours. Clad in a minuscule bikini, she swims all over him in the pool. At the bar, she downs an oil drum's worth of tequila with him while discussing what she likes in bed. But she refuses his advances for five days. Finally, he has sex with someone else. She is furious. "I can do what I want," she shrieks at him. "The guys who like me are persistent. I play hard to get. I'm a mystery. It's your job to figure me out." He apologizes to her. Then she sleeps with him. Holy moly.

6 Watching these children—and the twentysomething contestants on *Survivor,* who are perfectly at ease telling the whole world that they don't have to collect firewood because they're too good-looking to have to; the young women on *The Bachelor* who hurl insults at one another and then explain blithely, "I know it's hurtful, but it's the way I feel, and I have to get my feelings out"; and the teenage clerk who recently waited on me at a gas station, overcharged me by $30, and then refused to apologize, because "it was the computer's fault for adding your bill wrong, and my manager's fault for programming the computer wrong"—what I want to know is, from where did these gorgons of self-confidence spring? How can they be so self-satisfied, so sure of themselves? Especially when their level of self-love appears to be in inverse proportion to their level of accomplishment?

7 Not all twentysomethings are egomaniacs, of course.

8 I know plenty who are plagued by anxiety, anorexia, alienation, angst; who are overwhelmed by how big and brutal this world of ours can be.

9 Hard as life is for them, they are my kind of kids. I can relate to them. I was them. But I'm fascinated by their opposite, this new breed of youth—ill-mannered, obnoxious, happy—that seems to be the unholy offspring of self-help books and shopping networks.

10 Their "issue" is to me unfathomable. They suffer from too much self-esteem.

11 Years ago, I attended a dinner party with old, very close friends. None of us had children yet. After a (large) number of bottles of wine, we went around the table and confessed the one thing we wished we could change about ourselves.

12 For all eight of us, it was some variation on our lack of self-confidence, our excess of self-loathing. Perhaps we—and our entire, therapy-happy generation—made the same silent vow: Whatever else we did to our kids, they would not hate themselves.

13 "We went to the other extreme," says Barbara Coloroso, the child-rearing expert and author (*Kids Are Worth It*).

14 "Instead of finding the middle ground, where a kid can genuinely assess herself, can strive to accomplish things, can make mistakes, admit them and learn from them, we went to the other extreme."

15 We told our kids that they are great no matter what they do. We hesitated to correct them for fear of damaging their fragile egos. We never wanted them to feel bad about anything, even if they did bad things.

16 And to our horror, we produced a population who cannot make change or point to Chad on a map, but who, when offered the slightest correction or criticism, turn away with a look of scorn which says, "We pity you—and we hate that."

The would-be Idols and their ilk think they deserve to be famous, feted and lauded, without bothering to actually do anything first. In fact, they think accomplishment is a chump's game. 17

"Earning money is good," goes the lottery ad pitched at twentysomethings. "Winning is better." 18

They don't want to be Mozart, writing symphonies at the age of 14. They want to go on the MuchMusic show *Becoming*, in which young adults recreate their favourite music videos shot by shot, move by move, sock by sock, hair by hair. 19

The perverse goal is to achieve a perfectly soulless copy, a simulacrum in which nothing is genuine or original. (An original moment would be a glitch, it would be wrong.) 20

The young girl who recreates Avril Lavigne's video for "Complicated"—ironically, the song repeats the line, "Promise me I'm never going to find you faking" several times—is pampered, primped and puffed up, for doing nothing other than taking orders and accepting favours. 21

At the show's end, she says, "I'm so proud of myself, I really did it." She really means it too—but what is it that she really thinks she did? 22

"Our original intent, to give our kids a strong sense of self, was good," Coloroso says. 23

"But self-esteem should be a by-product of other traits, of integrity, civility, compassion. Instead, we made self-esteem a goal. Now, we have a generation of big egos without a real sense of self, whose only question is, 'What's in it for me?'" My question is, where do the too-confident go from here? Will the travails of their 30s eventually humble them? 24

Or is humility, like language, something that has to be woven into one's brain while young or it's too late, the necessary synapses just aren't there? Will their children (if they can spare the time to birth and tend to them) rebel by becoming modest in the extreme? 25

"I now stay away from the word self-esteem in my lectures," Coloroso says. 26

"Instead, I say, 'We have to teach kids to have a strong sense of self.' If ever I do slip and say, 'We have to teach them self-esteem,' every parent in the place rolls their eyes." 27

Thinking Critically About Content

1. What is Schneller analyzing in this essay? How does the title help focus her analysis?
2. Name three possible effects of unearned positive reinforcement on a young person.
3. How does Schneller suggest parents change the way they speak to kids?

Thinking Critically About Purpose and Audience

4. Why do you think Schneller wrote this article?
5. Considering that this article was originally published in the newspaper *The Globe and Mail*, who do you think Schneller's intended audience is? Explain your answer.
6. Did you expect praise from your parents regardless of whether you had been successful at an activity? Were you ever told that all that was important was that you did your best? If so, how did that affect you?

Thinking Critically About Essays

7. The author of this article quotes expert Barbara Coloroso. Are you convinced by what Coloroso says?
8. Which of Schneller's paragraphs deal primarily with causes? Which with effects? Do you think this is a reasonable balance? Explain your answer.
9. Find five transitions in Schneller's article that work well, and explain why they are effective.
10. Discuss the effect of constant positive reinforcement on your generation. Did it affect everybody the same way? Will it affect your expectations of school and work?

Writing Workshop

This final section gives you opportunities to apply what you have learned in this chapter to another writing assignment. This time, we provide very little prompting beyond a summary of the guidelines for writing a description essay. This section will let you demonstrate that you can go through the entire writing process on your own with only occasional feedback from your peers. Loop back into the chapter as necessary when you have questions so that this process becomes as automatic to you as possible before you move on to new material. Then pause at the end of the chapter to reflect briefly on what you have learned.

Guidelines for Writing a Cause/Effect Essay

1. Write a thesis statement that tells what you are analyzing.
2. Choose facts, details, and reasons to support your thesis statement.
3. Do not mistake coincidence for cause or effect.
4. Search for the real causes and effects connected with your subject.
5. Organize your essay so that your readers can easily follow your analysis.

Writing About Your Reading

1. In "Happiness Is Catching," Stacey Colino talks about how contagious moods are. Do you think you might have been responsible for giving a good or bad mood to someone? What were the circumstances? How did someone "catch" your mood? Write an essay analyzing the causes and effects of the situation.
2. In "Too Much Self-Esteem: The Blight of Modern Times," Johanna Schneller writes about the dangers of boosting self-esteem without achievement. The same generation has been subject to zero tolerance for violence in school. How has that affected them? Write an essay analyzing the effects of zero-tolerance policies.
3. How would looking closely at causes and effects help you live a better life? How would the process of discovering causes and effects help you think through your decisions and problems more logically? Explain your answer.

Writing About Your World

1. Explain how the scene above got started. What caused this reaction? Why did it happen? What were the results of the actions pictured here? Write an essay focusing on either the causes or the effects of this scene.
2. We all deal with change differently, but it is generally difficult to accept change in our lives. Think of a significant change in your life, and write about its causes and effects. What was the incident? What were the circumstances connected with the incident?
3. Write an essay that analyzes a current social problem—homelessness, drug abuse, environmental concerns—including the reasons for its existence.
4. Create your own cause/effect assignment (with the help of your instructor), and write a response to it.

Revising

Small Group Activity (5–10 minutes per writer) Working in groups of three or four, each person should read his or her cause/effect essay to the other members of the group. Those listening should record their reactions on a copy of the Peer Evaluation Form (Appendix 1A). After your group goes through this process, give your evaluation forms to the appropriate writers so that each writer has two or three peer comment sheets for revising.

Paired Activity (5 minutes per writer) Using the completed Peer Evaluation Forms, work in pairs to decide what you should revise in your essay. If time allows, rewrite some of your sentences, and have your partner look at them.

Individual Activity Rewrite your paper, using the revising feedback you received from other students.

Editing

Paired Activity (5–10 minutes per writer) Swap papers with a classmate, and use the editing portion of your Peer Evaluation Form (Appendix 1B) to identify as many grammatical, punctuation, mechanical, and spelling errors as you can. If time allows, correct some of your errors, and have your partner look at them. Record your grammatical, punctuation, and mechanical errors in the Error Log (Appendix 3) and your spelling errors in the Spelling Log (Appendix 4).

Individual Activity Rewrite your paper again, using the editing feedback you received from other students.

CHAPTER 16

ARGUING

> Faced with the choice between changing one's mind and proving that there is no need to do so, almost everyone gets busy on the proof.
>
> —John Kenneth Galbraith

Argument may be our most important form of communication, because it helps us get what we want in life. The main reason people argue is to persuade someone of something. When you want to get a certain job, sell your car, or borrow some money, you need to present your request clearly and convincingly. On the flip side, others try to persuade you to do things all the time as well: Politicians make speeches trying to persuade you to vote for them; your friends try to persuade you to go to a movie when you know you should study for an exam; TV commercials, magazine ads, and billboards everywhere try to persuade you to buy this cereal or that car.

As you might suspect, your ability to argue in writing is also important in life. In fact, writing arguments is fundamental to your success on a personal level, in school, and in the workplace:

> The chairperson for your college reunion sends a letter with clear reasons why everyone should attend this year.
>
> A student writes an essay in an introductory composition course arguing for or against logging old-growth forests.
>
> A student writes a paper in a sociology course arguing that laws against hate crimes need to be stronger.
>
> A sales representative writes a letter arguing that customers should order supplies from him rather than from his competitor.
>
> A restaurant owner writes an advertisement to persuade people to eat at her restaurant.

The purpose of **arguing** is to persuade someone to take a certain action or to think or feel a specific way. You can use either logical arguments (based on facts and reasoning) or emotional arguments (based on vivid description and details) to achieve your purpose.

Some of the most important laws affecting people's lives in Canada are the result of arguments made to the Supreme Court. Lawyers argue such issues as child pornography, same-sex marriage, aboriginal fishing rights, and drunk driving. If, for instance, lawmakers are trying to get stricter jail sentences for drunk driving, they might rely heavily on facts and statistics (logical evidence). But then they might add an emotional element by describing the mangled bike, the bloodstained clothes, and the grief in the faces of the parents of a 12-year-old girl killed by a drunk driver as she rode her bike home from school. Such an appeal to feelings would create a much stronger argument than statistics alone.

The better you become at arguing—in both thinking and writing—the more you will get what you want out of life (and out of your studies). Arguing effectively means a better chance of getting the pay raise you hope for, the refund you deserve, and the grades you've worked hard for. Argumentation is a powerful tool.

READING AND WRITING AN ARGUMENT ESSAY

Reading arguments critically will help you write arguments critically, which are both necessary skills for success in college and in life beyond college. Like two halves of a whole, these processes work together to create a coherent approach to important tasks. Reading and writing arguments effectively calls for high-level thought processes that will ensure your success in all that you do.

Reading an Argument Essay

The following argument, "Let Boys Be Boys" by Robert Sibley, tries to persuade its readers that the reason boys aren't doing as well as girls at school is the "crisis of masculinity" brought about by a society that is suppressing masculinity. Have you found that boys don't do as well at school as girls? Why do you think this is happening? Should boys and girls be educated separately?

READING CRITICALLY

Reading an argument critically calls for very high-level skills. You need to understand your reading on a literal level, know the difference between opinions and fact, and come up with your own opinions on the topic by challenging the author's ideas. As you read the following essay for the first time, highlight facts in one colour and the author's opinions in another colour. Then, put an X by any facts or opinions that you do not agree with or want to question in some way. Be prepared to explain any marks you made on the essay.

ROBERT SIBLEY
Let Boys Be Boys

An academic acquaintance once told me how silence comes over his male stu- 1
dents when he lectures on Homer's *Odyssey* and describes how the character Telemachus was raised by his mother and grew up never knowing his father, Odysseus, the book's hero. "When I depict Telemachus as a boy from a broken home, forced at a too-early age to be his mother's protector, who has to bring himself up in a way that he hopes his absent father will be proud of," said my friend, "the young men in my undergraduate classes tend to become very quiet . . ."

I remembered this anecdote as I read Don Butler's insightful articles in the *Citizen*'s 2
series, "The Lost Boys," which concludes today. The series examined the demasculinization, as it were, of our universities, how women have become the majority on campuses. Mr. Butler cited various views on the phenomenon, but one in particular grabbed my attention: "'Every mother on Earth knows from day one that little boys and little girls are completely different animals,' American academic Thomas Mortenson said. 'Wouldn't you expect our universities of education to be preparing our teachers to teach our little boys and little girls differently?'"

The answer, it seems, is no. The education system works well for girls, says 3
Mr. Mortenson, but boys are "turned off." I'd like to suggest a connection between turned-off boys and the "crisis of masculinity." A spate of books—Waller Newell's *The Code of Man* and *What Is a Man?*; Leo Braudy's *From Chivalry to Terror: War and the Changing Nature of Masculinity;* Christina Hoff Summers's *The War Against Boys: How Misguided Feminism Is Harming Our Young Men*—testify to the fact of a crisis. (A crisis exists when once reliable ways of understanding the world no longer make sense.) But, as Mr. Mortenson suggests, we are now seeing its manifestations on the educational frontlines.

Indeed, Australian researchers report boys underachieving compared to girls. 4
British social scientists say crime rates show men less inclined to adopt "social behaviour"—obeying the law, maintaining a job, supporting a family. American and Canadian studies find that, academically, boys are falling behind girls when, 30 years ago, they achieved top grades. Males drop out of school at a higher rate than females. Male teen suicides outnumber female suicides by five to one.

Some blame a "boy culture" and out-of-date ideas about masculinity for 5
encouraging boys to live a slothful existence of television sports and computer games. I think not: It is not traditional maleness that is to blame for the "lost boys," but the debasement of masculinity. You might remember the movie *Fight Club*, starring Brad Pitt, in which young men relieve their boredom in basement fights. The film was denounced as a paean to fascism, but that judgment misses what's behind the nihilistic violence. The real "message" is delivered by Mr. Pitt's character, Tyler Durden: "I knew my dad for about six years, but I don't remember anything . . . What you see at fight club is a generation of men raised by women."

For four decades, our schools, courts and public institutions have engaged in a 6
vast social experiment to effeminize society. This effort is rooted in the assumption that males are inherently violent and therefore "masculinity" must be suppressed.

So the Boy Scouts are ordered by human rights tribunals to accept girls. The courts force little boys who sneak recess kisses to take sensitivity seminars. Drugs keep high-spirited boys in their seats.

7 The original goals of feminism—legal and political equality—were eminently reasonable. Today, though, the feminist agenda promotes a more extremist idea—eliminate all distinctions, psychological and physical, between men and women because the function and role of men and women, whether in the family or society, must be the same. Uproot traditional understandings of manhood, downgrade male virtues of courage, tenacity, pride and honour, and you'll produce "men" who have, well, "socially inclusive" habits. In other words, convert boys into girls, socially-speaking, and you'll have a kinder, gentler society.

8 It is a risky idea. Psychologically, young men need to undergo certain rites of passage to achieve a healthy maturity. Traditionally, these rites have been overseen by fathers or various father figures. But what happens to a society in which fatherhood is denigrated, where, in fact, many think fathers are no longer necessary for raising children? According to theorist Leon Podles, a society of absentee fathers leaves young males in a confused state of "hypermasculinity" in which they swing between the extremes of violence and hedonistic self-indulgence.

9 The ancient Greeks knew this, which was why they considered the education of young men so important. In the rush for the pacifist society, we have forgotten the Greek insight: The male instinct for violence has the same source as the impulse to protect children and rush into burning buildings. For the Greeks, a man's character was informed, for good and ill, by the spirited, or thymotic, part of his psyche. But *thymos* is not automatically rational; it has to be educated to reason. Hence, the central problem in Plato's *Republic*: Social order is at risk when the spirited psyches of young men are not directed to high purpose, so how do you educate young men to this purpose?

10 Homer certainly understood this, which is why in the Odyssey he sends Telemachus searching for his father to prevent his mother from marrying any of the evil suitors who want her to give up her husband for dead. As he wanders the world, Telemachus learns of Odysseus's struggles to return home, his fealty to home and hearth. Inspired by his father's example, Telemachus becomes a man himself.

11 What we see in *Fight Club* is young men who rightly don't want to be effeminized, but who lack worthy father figures to teach them about manhood. What we have in "The Lost Boys" series, perhaps inadvertently, is a consequence of the effeminization project—young men who lack healthy aggression and ambition, who've had their pride and sense of honour suppressed by their teachers. Barbarism, as Plato knew, can't be far behind.

PREPARING TO WRITE YOUR OWN ARGUMENT ESSAY

Choose a controversial issue on your campus or in the news that is important to you, and use one or more of the prewriting techniques that you learned in Chapter 5 to generate ideas on the issue. Consult your campus or local newspaper for ideas if you want. What is the exact issue? Why is it important? Why do people care about it? How do you think the issue should be resolved?

Writing an Argument Essay

When you write an argument essay, choose a subject that matters to you. If you have strong feelings, you will find it much easier to gather evidence and convince your readers of your point of view. Keep in mind, however, that your readers might feel just as strongly about the opposite side of the issue. The following guidelines will help you write a good argument essay.

1. ***State your opinion on your topic in your thesis statement.*** To write a thesis statement for an argument essay, you must take a stand for or against an action or an idea. In other words, your thesis statement should be debatable—a statement that can be argued or challenged and will not be met with agreement by everyone who reads it. Your thesis statement should introduce your subject and state your opinion about that subject.

   Robert Sibley's thesis is in his third paragraph: "I'd like to suggest a connection between turned-off boys and the 'crisis of masculinity.'" He follows this statement with an explanation of what the crisis of masculinity is, and then restates the thesis more fully: "For four decades, our schools, courts and public institutions have engaged in a vast social experiment to effeminize society." This is a debatable thesis. Some other statements on the topic would not be good topics:

   Not debatable: More women are attending law school now than 20 years ago.

   Not debatable: More men are in prison for violent crimes than women.

   Sibley sets up his essay with an anecdote about an acquaintance's experiences when teaching *The Odyssey* to a university class. He writes about the reaction of the male students to the story of Telemachus, son of Odysseus.

2. ***Find out as much as you can about your audience before you write.*** Knowing your readers' background and feelings on your topic will help you choose the best supporting evidence and examples. Suppose you want to convince people in two different age groups to quit smoking. You might tell the group of teenagers that cigarettes make their breath rancid, their teeth yellow, and their clothes smell bad. But with a group

of adults, you might discuss the horrifying statistics on lung and heart disease associated with long-term smoking.

Sibley's essay was first published in *The Ottawa Citizen*, where he is a member of the editorial board. The essay addresses a fairly educated audience. Many people in his original audience would have disagreed with him, so he chooses support that will persuade an educated audience, such as studies and expert opinions. He also makes reference to writers such as Homer and Plato that educated readers could be expected to be familiar with.

3. ***Choose evidence that supports your thesis statement.*** Evidence is probably the most important factor in writing an argument essay. Without solid evidence, your essay is nothing more than opinion; with it, your essay can be powerful and persuasive. If you supply convincing evidence, your readers will not only understand your position but perhaps agree with it.

   Evidence can consist of facts, statistics, statements from authorities, and examples or personal stories. Examples and personal stories can be based on your own observations, experiences, and reading, but your opinions are not evidence. You can also develop your ideas by using the writing strategies you've learned in Chapters 8 through 15. Comparison/contrast, definition, and cause/effect can be particularly useful in building an argument. Use any combination of evidence and writing strategies that will help you support your thesis statement.

   In his essay, Sibley uses several different kinds of evidence. Here are some examples:

   Facts

   The Boy Scouts were ordered by human rights tribunals to accept girls.
   The ancient Greeks considered the education of young men important.

   Statistics

   Males drop out of school at a higher rate than females.
   Male teen suicides outnumber female suicides by five to one.

   Statements from Authorities

   American academic Thomas Mortenson
   Australian researchers
   Theorist Leon Podles

   Examples and Personal Stories

   The acquaintance telling the story of Telemachus
   The references to the movie *Fight Club*
   The references to *The Odyssey*

4. ***Anticipate opposing points of view.*** In addition to stating and supporting your position, anticipating and responding to opposing views is important. Presenting only your side of the argument leaves half the story untold—the

opposition's half. If you admit that there are opposing arguments and answer them, you will move your reader further in your direction.

In paragraph 7, Sibley describes his opposition, which is the modern "feminist agenda." He undercuts the opposition with his use of quotation marks—you'll produce "men" who have "socially inclusive" habits. Be careful of this ironic use of quotation marks. It works for a professional writer but may fall flat in a student essay. However, by stating the opinion of the opposition, Sibley does set up an opportunity to rebut the opposite opinion, which he does in the following paragraph, partly by quoting an expert.

5. ***Find some common ground.*** Pointing out common ground between you and your opponent is also an effective strategy. *Common ground* refers to points of agreement between two opposing positions. For example, one person might be in favour of the gun registry and another strongly opposed. But they might find common ground—agreement—in the need to keep guns out of teenagers' hands. Locating some common ground is possible in almost every situation. When you state in your essay that you agree with your opponent on certain points, your reader sees you as a fair person.

   Sibley knows he is writing for an audience who has first-hand experience with education. He can expect that most people will have noticed that girls are doing better than boys in many educational settings. He can also assume that his readers have been following the series of articles published in the newspaper that he mentions several times. His job is to show the connection between the change in the level of achievement of boys and what he calls the effeminization of society.

6. ***Maintain a reasonable tone.*** Just as you probably wouldn't be convinced by shouting or by nasty or sarcastic comments, don't expect your readers to respond well to such tactics. Keep the "voice" of your essay calm and sensible. Your readers will be much more open to what you have to say if they think you are a reasonable person.

   Sibley maintains a reasonable, if somewhat sarcastic, tone throughout the essay. The argument is intellectual rather than emotional, and he maintains the tone of an expert quoting experts.

7. ***Organize your essay so that it presents your position as effectively as possible.*** By the end of your essay, you want your audience to agree with you. So you want to organize your essay in such a way that your readers can easily follow it. The number of your paragraphs may vary, depending on the nature of your assignment, but the following outline shows the order in which the features of an argument essay are most effective:

   Outline

   Introduction

   Background information

   Introduction of subject

   Statement of your opinion

Body Paragraphs

Common ground

Lots of evidence (logical and emotional)

Opposing point of view

Response to opposing point of view

Conclusion

Restatement of your position

Call for action or agreement

The arrangement of your evidence in an argument essay depends to a great extent on your readers' opinions. Most arguments will be organized from general to particular, from particular to general, or from one extreme to another. When you know that your readers already agree with you, arranging your details from general to particular or from most to least important is usually most effective. With this order, you are building on your readers' agreement and loyalty as you explain your thinking on the subject.

If you suspect that your audience does not agree with you, reverse the organization of your evidence and arrange it from particular to general or from least to most important. In this way, you can take your readers step by step through your reasoning in an attempt to get them to agree with you.

Outline

Robert Sibley's essay follows the general outline just presented. Here is a skeleton of his essay.

Introduction

Related anecdote detailing the reaction of young men hearing the story of a fatherless boy who must act to save his family honour leads to a question and answer about educating boys and girls differently.

Body Paragraphs

Subject introduced

Example: *Fight Club*

Opposing point of view

Theories, evidence, studies, statistics, and expert opinion

Traditions: Homer, Plato

Conclusion

Summary of argument

Reference to future

WRITING YOUR OWN ARGUMENT ESSAY

Write an essay that presents your opinion on the controversial issue you considered in your prewriting. Begin with a debatable thesis statement. Then follow the guidelines for writing an argument essay. As you write your essay, be sure you support your opinions with reasons. If a newspaper article inspired this assignment, attach it to your paper before you turn it in.

A STUDENT'S ARGUMENT ESSAY

Melinda Jackson, the student writer of the following essay, titled "A Call for Policies on Drinking," argues that drinking on college campuses is a serious problem. See if you can identify her main point and supporting evidence as you read this draft of her essay.

A Call for Policies on Drinking

College and drinking, drinking and college—most students believe the two go hand in hand. If asked, they would say that drinking in college is just a part of life, and it is not a major concern. However, when we examine drinking in college more closely, we see it is a serious problem that people on all levels are not facing. Drinking on college campuses is a bigger problem than parents and administrators realize, and something needs to be done about it—now. 1

No one would ever realistically believe that college students will never drink. In fact, most students, parents, and administrators are in favour of students taking a break and having fun. Studying during every available minute, parents and administrators realize the strain students are under. And they know that students will probably drink. What they don't understand is the trap students can fall into. 2

Jerry, a college student, explained how he got involved with alcohol and how it soon took over his life. Jerry went to a different fraternity party every weekend night, where his main goal was to get as drunk as possible. What he didn't know was that he was confrontational when he drank and that people didn't want to be around him. He didn't know his limit, so he often exceeded it. He usually passed out on someone's couch after drinking. In the morning he would wake up and find the next party. Jerry is just one of many students on every college campus. 3

Whereas most people think drinking occurs just during parties, it actually occurs for many students on a daily basis. Students like Jerry begin by drinking on weekends then they all too easily start drinking every day. They begin to need alcohol in order to feel normal. Once they fall into this pattern, several other serious problems can occur. Not only are they missing classes and falling behind in their coarses, but they are also endangering their lives. Drinking becomes the most important aspect in their lives. But it's not just the drinker who's life is 4 effected. Drinkers disrupt their roommates, who are either distracted from their studying or awakened from their sleep. When the roommate complains about being disturbed. The drinker gets angry. And so the pattern repeats itself again and again.

5 According to our dean of students, students who drink often take risks that endanger their lives and the lives of others. The most obvious risk involves a drinker who gets behind the wheel of a car. Drinkers also tend to get into more fights, because they mistakenly believe they are invincible. In this case, they risk harming the people they fight with and themselves, because they are in no condition to defend themselves. Everyone on the road is a potential victim of the drinker. Drinkers are also likely to have unprotected sex. This could lead to unwanted pregnancies, sexually transmitted diseases, or even AIDS. With the widespread drinking that occurs on college campuses, these consequences are very likely to occur to a student who drinks.

6 Drinking is a major problem on college campuses, but like every other controversial issue, some people say it has been given too much publicity by overzealous worriers. They believe that the college knows light drinking occurs and that the administration has control of the students who drink. They believe that kids will be kids, students will drink no matter what. These people say that letting students have fun is what's important. But to adopt this attitude is possibly placing someone's life in danger. If even one person is in danger from a drunken student. Then the college must take action.

7 Drinking in college is definitely going to happen, but there are measures that can be taken to prevent serious harm to students who do decide to drink. Campuses could have alcohol awareness programs and give students easy access to condoms. Campuses could set up a response team that would pick up any student who was incapable of driving. They could require all student union pubs to confiscate keys before anyone is given a drink to ensure that a person who has been drinking won't drive. They can offer literature on organizations that can help students who become addicted to alcohol. Its time for students, parents, and administrators to see the problem before them and take steps to fix it before it's too late.

Discovering How the Essay Works

1A. What is Melinda's thesis statement?

____

____

1B. Does it state her opinion clearly? Explain your answer.

____

____

1C. Is it debatable? (Does it have more than one side?)

____

____

2. Who do you think Melinda is addressing in this essay? How did you come to this conclusion?

____

____

3. What evidence does the author use to support her thesis statement? Find an example of each type of evidence in her essay.

   Facts: ______________________________________

   Statistics: __________________________________

   Statements from authorities: __________________

   Examples and personal stories: ________________

4. Does Melinda anticipate an opposing point of view? Explain your answer.

____

5. Did Melinda find some common ground with her readers? Explain your answer.

____

____

6. Does Melinda maintain a reasonable tone? Explain your answer.

____

7. How does Melinda organize the topics in her essay: general to particular, particular to general, or from one extreme to another?

____

REVISING AND EDITING THE STUDENT ESSAY

This essay is Melinda's first draft, which now needs to be revised and edited. First, apply the Revising Checklist on the inside front cover to the content of Melinda's draft. When you are satisfied that her ideas are fully developed and well organized, use the Editing Checklist on the inside back cover to correct her grammatical and mechanical errors. Answer the questions below. Then write your suggested changes directly on Melinda's draft.

Revision Questions

Thesis Statement

1. Put brackets around the last sentence in Melinda's introduction. Does it contain her opinion?

   ____

   Is it debatable?

   ____

2. Rewrite Melinda's thesis statement if necessary so that it states her opinion and is debatable.

   ____

Basic Elements

1. Give Melinda's essay an alternative title.

   ____

2. Rewrite Melinda's introduction so that it captures the reader's attention and builds up to the thesis statement at the end of the paragraph.

   ____

   ____

   ____

3. Does each of Melinda's body paragraphs deal with only one topic?

   ____

4. Rewrite Melinda's conclusion, using at least one suggestion from Part I.

   ____

   ____

   ____

Development

1. Write out Melinda's thesis statement (revised, if necessary), and list her topic sentences below it.

   Thesis Statement: ______________________________

   ____

   ____

   Topic 1: ______________________________

   ____

   Topic 2: ______________________________

   ____

   Topic 3: ______________________________

   ____

   Topic 4: ______________________________

   ____

   Topic 5: ______________________________

   ____

2. Do Melinda's topics adequately support her thesis statement?

   ____

3. Does each body paragraph have a focused topic sentence?

   ____

4. Does her evidence support her topic sentences?

   ____

5. What type of evidence does Melinda provide in each body paragraph?

   Paragraph 2: ______________________________

   Paragraph 3: ______________________________

   Paragraph 4: ______________________________

Paragraph 5: ______________________________

Paragraph 6: ______________________________

What type of evidence does she use the most? ______________

6. Is this a good choice for what she is trying to argue?

____

7. Where do you need more information?

____

Unity

1. Read each of Melinda's topic sentences with her thesis statement in mind. Do they go together?

____

2. Revise them if necessary so that they are directly related.

3. Drop or rewrite any sentences in her body paragraphs that are not directly related to their topic sentences.

Organization

1. Outline Melinda's essay to see if all her ideas are arranged logically.

____

____

____

____

____

____

____

____

2. Do you think her method of organization is the most effective one for her purpose? Explain your answer.

____

____

3. Move any paragraphs that are out of order.
4. Look closely at Melinda's body paragraphs to see if all her sentences are arranged logically within paragraphs.
5. Move any sentences that are out of order.

Coherence

1. Add two transitions to Melinda's essay.
2. Circle five transitions, repetitions, synonyms, or pronouns Melinda uses.
3. Explain how two of these make Melinda's essay easier to read.

For a list of transitions, see pages 85–86.

For a list of pronouns, see pages 389–39.

____

____

____

Now rewrite Melinda's essay with your revisions.

Editing Questions

Sentences

Subjects and Verbs

1. Underline the subjects once and verbs twice in paragraphs 4 and 6 of your revision of Melinda's essay. Remember that sentences can have more than one subject–verb set.

For help with subjects and verbs, see Chapter 23.

2. Does each of Melinda's sentences have at least one subject and verb that can stand alone?

____

3. Did you find and correct Melinda's two fragments and two run-on sentences? If not, find and correct them now.

For help with fragments and run-ons, see Chapters 24 and 25.

Subject–Verb Agreement

1. Read aloud the subjects and verbs you underlined in your revision of Melinda's essay.
2. Correct any subjects and verbs that do not agree.

For help with subject–verb agreement, see Chapter 27.

Pronoun Agreement

1. Find any pronouns in your revision of Melinda's essay that do not agree with their nouns.
2. Correct any pronouns that do not agree with their nouns.

For help with pronoun agreement, see Chapter 30.

Modifiers

For help with modifier errors, see Chapter 33.

1. Find any modifiers in your revision of Melinda's essay that are not as close as possible to the words they modify.
2. Did you find and correct Melinda's two modifier errors? If not, find and correct them now.

Punctuation and Mechanics

Punctuation

1. Read your revision of Melinda's essay for any errors in punctuation.
2. Find the two fragments and two run-on sentences you revised, and make sure they are punctuated correctly.

For help with punctuation, see Chapters 34–37.

Mechanics

For help with capitalization, see Chapter 38.

1. Read your revision of Melinda's essay for any errors in capitalization.
2. Be sure to check Melinda's capitalization in the fragments and run-on sentences you revised.

Word Choice and Spelling

Word Choice

For help with confused words, see Chapter 44.

1. Find any words used incorrectly in your revision of Melinda's essay.
2. Did you find and correct the four words Melinda used incorrectly? If not, find and correct them now.

Spelling

For help with spelling, see Chapter 45.

1. Use spell-check and a dictionary to check the spelling in your revision of Melinda's essay.
2. Correct any misspelled words.

Now rewrite Melinda's essay again with your editing corrections.

REVISING AND EDITING YOUR OWN ARGUMENT ESSAY

Returning to the argument you wrote earlier in this chapter, you are now ready to revise and edit your own writing. Remember that revision involves reworking the development and organization of your essay while editing asks you to check your grammar and usage. Repeating the revising and editing processes several times will ensure that you have written the best paper you can write.

The checklists on the inside front and back covers will help you apply what you have learned to your essay.

WRITING CRITICALLY

As you begin to rework your essay, use the same technique you did in your reading. Highlight your own opinions and facts in two different colours to demonstrate that you see the difference between the two. Then check to see that you support each of your main ideas with enough details to make your point.

PRACTISING ARGUMENT: FROM READING TO WRITING

Reading Workshop

Here are three examples of good argument essays: "We Are Training Our Kids to Kill" by Dave Grossman, which tries to persuade readers that our children are conditioned to kill from the violence they are exposed to through TV, movies, and video games, and two essays on spam, or junk email: "Ban Spam: E-Nough is E-Nough" by Rick Broadhead; and "Ban Spam? What, and Banish All the World?" by Doug Saunders. You might want to read these selections before writing another argument essay. As you read, notice how the writers make their points through well–thought-out, detailed reasoning.

DAVE GROSSMAN
We Are Training Our Kids to Kill

Focusing Your Attention

1. At what age or in what situation do you think children can handle violence in the media?
2. In the essay you are about to read, the writer discusses the dangers connected with violence on TV for children. What do you think some of these issues are?

Expanding Your Vocabulary

The following words are important to your understanding of this essay:

averted: avoided (paragraph 4)
phenomenally: amazingly (paragraph 6)
Draconian: harsh (paragraph 7)

indiscriminately: casually (paragraph 8)
pervasively: universally (paragraph 9)
anomaly: an exception from the normal (paragraph 15)
desensitization: numbed (paragraph 19)
epidemiological: referring to childhood behaviours (paragraph 25)
variable: element being compared (paragraph 25)
bayonet: stab (paragraph 28)
dismay: fear, dread (paragraph 32)
benign: good (paragraph 34)

READING CRITICALLY

As you learned at the beginning of this chapter, practise recognizing the facts and opinions in the following essay by highlighting them in two different colours. Then put an X by any points that you disagree with or want to challenge. These notes will give you insights into the topic and guide you to a deeper level of understanding. Compare your notes with someone else in the class.

DAVE GROSSMAN
We Are Training Our Kids to Kill

1 I am from Jonesboro, Arkansas. I travel the world training medical, law enforcement, and U.S. military personnel about the realities of warfare. I try to make those who carry deadly force keenly aware of the magnitude of killing. Too many law enforcement and military personnel act like "cowboys," never stopping to think about who they are and what they are called to do. I hope I am able to give them a reality check.

2 So here I am, a world traveler and an expert in the field of "killology," when the (then) largest school massacre in American history happens in my hometown of Jonesboro, Arkansas. That was the March 24, 1998, schoolyard shooting deaths of four girls and a teacher. Ten others were injured, and two boys, ages 11 and 13, were jailed, charged with murder.

Virus of Violence

3 To understand the why behind Littleton, Jonesboro, Springfield, Pearl, and Paducah, and all the other outbreaks of this "virus of violence," we need to first understand the magnitude of the problem. The per capita murder rate doubled in this country between 1957—when the FBI started keeping track of the data—and 1992. A fuller picture of the problem, however, is indicated by the rate at which people are

attempting to kill one another—the aggravated assault rate. That rate in America has gone from around 60 per 100,000 in 1957 to over 440 per 100,000 in 2002. As bad as this is, it would be much worse were it not for two major factors.

The first is the increased imprisonment of violent offenders. The prison population in America nearly quintupled between 1975 and 2002. According to criminologist John A. Dilulio, "dozens of credible empirical analyses . . . leave no doubt that the increased use of prisons averted millions of serious crimes." If it were not for our tremendous imprisonment rate (the highest of any industrialized nation), the aggravated assault rate and the murder rate would undoubtedly be even higher. 4

The second factor keeping the murder rate from being even worse is medical technology. According to the U.S. Army Medical Service Corps, a wound that would have killed nine out of ten soldiers in World War II, nine out of ten could have survived in Vietnam. Thus, by a very conservative estimate, if we still had a 1940-level medical technology today, our murder rate would be ten times higher than it is. The murder rate has been held down by the development of sophisticated lifesaving skills and techniques, such as helicopter medevacs, 911 operators, paramedics, CPR, trauma centers, and medicines. 5

Today, both our assault rate and murder rate are at phenomenally high levels. Both are increasing worldwide. In Canada, according to their Centre for Justice, per capita assaults increased almost fivefold between 1964 and 2002, attempted murder increased nearly sevenfold, and murders doubled. Similar trends can be seen in other countries in the per capita violent crime rates reported to Interpol between 1977 and 2002. In Australia and New Zealand, the assault rate increased approximately fourfold, and the murder rate nearly doubled in both nations. The assault rate tripled in Sweden and approximately doubled in Belgium, Denmark, England and Wales, France, Hungary, the Netherlands, and Scotland. Meanwhile, all these nations had an associated (but smaller) increase in murder. 6

This virus of violence is occurring worldwide. The explanation for it has to be some new factor that is occurring in all of these countries. There are many factors involved, and none should be discounted: for example, the prevalence of guns in our society. But violence is rising in many nations with Draconian gun laws. And though we should never downplay child abuse, poverty, or racism, there is only one new variable present in each of these countries that bears the exact same fruit: media violence presented as entertainment for children. 7

Killing Is Unnatural

Before retiring from the military, I spent almost a quarter of a century as an army infantry officer and a psychologist, learning and studying how to enable people to kill. Believe me, we are very good at it. But it does not come naturally; you have to be taught to kill. And just as the army is conditioning people to kill, we are indiscriminately doing the same thing to our children, but without the safeguards. 8

After the Jonesboro killings, the head of the American Academy of Pediatrics Task Force on Juvenile Violence came to town and said that children don't naturally kill. It is a learned skill. And they learn it from abuse and violence in the home and, 9 most pervasively, from violence as entertainment in television, the movies, and interactive video games.

10 Killing requires training because there is a built-in aversion to killing one's own kind. I can best illustrate this fact by drawing on my own military research into the act of killing.

11 We all know how hard it is to have a discussion with a frightened or angry human being. Vasoconstriction, the narrowing of the blood vessels, has literally closed down the forebrain—that great gob of gray matter that makes one a human being and distinguishes one from a dog. When those neurons close down, the midbrain takes over and your thought processes and reflexes are indistinguishable from your dog's. If you've worked with animals, you have some understanding of what happens to frightened human beings on the battlefield. The battlefield and violent crime are in the realm of midbrain responses.

12 Within the midbrain there is a powerful, God-given resistance to killing your own kind. Every species, with a few exceptions, has a hard-wired resistance to killing its own kind in territorial and mating battles. When animals with antlers and horns fight one another, they head-butt in a nonfatal fashion. But when they fight any other species, they go to the side to gut and gore. Piranhas will turn their fangs on anything, but they fight one another with flicks of the tail. Rattlesnakes will bite anything, but they wrestle one another. Almost every species has this hard-wired resistance to killing its own kind.

13 When we human beings are overwhelmed with anger and fear, we slam head-on into that midbrain resistance that generally prevents us from killing. Only sociopaths—who by definition don't have that resistance—lack this innate violence immune system.

14 Throughout all human history, when humans have fought each other, there has been a lot of posturing. Adversaries make loud noises and puff themselves up, trying to daunt the enemy. There is a lot of fleeing and submission. Ancient battles were nothing more than great shoving matches. It was not until one side turned and ran that most of the killing happened, and most of that was stabbing people in the back. All of the ancient military historians report that the vast majority of killing happened in pursuit when one side was fleeing.

15 In more modern times, the average firing rate was incredibly low in Civil War battles. British author Paddy Griffith demonstrates in his book *The Battle Tactics of the Civil War* that the killing potential of the average Civil War regiment was anywhere from five hundred to a thousand men per minute. The actual killing rate was only one or two men per minute per regiment. At the Battle of Gettysburg, of the 27,000 muskets picked up from the dead and dying after the battle, 90 percent were loaded. This is an anomaly, because it took 90 percent of their time to load muskets and only 5 percent to fire. But even more amazing, of the thousands of loaded muskets, only half had multiple loads in the barrel—one had 23 loads in the barrel.

16 In reality, the average man would load his musket and bring it to his shoulder, but he could not bring himself to kill. He would be brave, he would stand shoulder to shoulder, he would do what he was trained to do; but at the moment of truth, he could not bring himself to pull the trigger. And so he lowered the weapon and loaded

it again. Of those who did fire, only a tiny percentage fired to hit. The vast majority fired over the enemy's head.

During World War II, U.S. Army Brig. Gen. S. L. A. Marshall had a team of researchers study what soldiers did in battle. For the first time in history, they asked individual soldiers what they did in battle. They discovered that only 15 to 20 percent of the individual riflemen could bring themselves to fire at an exposed enemy soldier. 17

That is the reality of the battlefield. Only a small percentage of soldiers are able and willing to participate. Men are willing to die. They are willing to sacrifice themselves for their nation; but they are not willing to kill. It is a phenomenal insight into human nature; but when the military became aware of that, they systematically went about the process of trying to fix this "problem." From the military perspective, a 15 percent firing rate among riflemen is like a 15 percent literacy rate among librarians. And fix it the military did. By the Korean War, around 55 percent of the soldiers were willing to fire to kill. And by Vietnam, the rate rose to over 90 percent. 18

The method in this madness: desensitization. 19

How the military increases the killing rate of soldiers in combat is instructive because our culture today is doing the same thing to our children. The training methods militaries use are brutalization, classical conditioning, operant conditioning, and role modeling. I will explain each of these in the military context and show how these same factors are contributing to the phenomenal increase of violence in our culture. 20

Brutalization and desensitization are what happens at boot camp. From the moment you step off the bus, you are physically and verbally abused: countless push-ups, endless hours at attention or running with heavy loads, while carefully trained professionals take turns screaming at you. Your head is shaved; you are herded together naked and dressed alike, losing all individuality. This brutalization is designed to break down your existing mores and norms, and force you to accept a new set of values that embraces destruction, violence, and death as a way of life. In the end, you are desensitized to violence and accept it as a normal and essential survival skill in your brutal new world. 21

Something very similar to this desensitization toward violence is happening to our children through violence in the media—but instead of 18-year-olds, it begins at the age of 18 months when a child is first able to discern what is happening on television. At that age, a child can watch something happening on television and mimic that action. But it isn't until children are six or seven years old that the part of the brain kicks in that lets them understand where information comes from. Even though young children have some understanding of what it means to pretend, they are developmentally unable to distinguish clearly between fantasy and reality. 22

When young children see somebody shot, stabbed, raped, brutalized, degraded, or murdered on TV, to them it is as though it were actually happening. To have a child of three, four, or five watch a "splatter" movie, learning to relate to a character for the first 90 minutes and then in the last 30 minutes watch helplessly as that new friend is hunted and brutally murdered, is the moral and psychological equivalent of introducing your child to a friend, letting her play with that friend, and then 23 butchering that friend in front of your child's eyes. And this happens to our children hundreds upon hundreds of times.

24 Sure, they are told, "Hey, it's all for fun. Look, this isn't real; it's just TV." And they nod their little heads and say OK. But they can't tell the difference. Can you remember a point in your life or in your children's lives when dreams, reality, and television were all jumbled together? That's what it is like to be at that level of psychological development. That's what the media are doing to them.

25 The *Journal of the American Medical Association* published the definitive epidemiological study on the impact of TV violence. The research demonstrated what happened in numerous nations after television made its appearance as compared to nations and regions without TV. The two nations or regions being compared are demographically and ethnically identical; only one variable is different: the presence of television. In every nation, region, or city with television, there is an immediate explosion of violence on the playground, and within 15 years there is a doubling of the murder rate. Why 15 years? That is how long it takes for the brutalization of a three- to five-year-old to reach the "prime crime age." That is how long it takes for you to reap what you have sown when you brutalize and desensitize a three-year-old.

26 Today the data linking violence in the media to violence in society are superior to those linking cancer and tobacco. Hundreds of sound scientific studies demonstrate the social impact of brutalization by the media. The *Journal of the American Medical Association* concluded that "the introduction of television in the 1950s caused a subsequent doubling of the homicide rate, i.e., long-term childhood exposure to television is a causal factor behind approximately one half of the homicides committed in the United States, or approximately 10,000 homicides annually." The article went on to say that "if, hypothetically, television technology had never been developed, there would today be 10,000 fewer homicides each year in the United States, 70,000 fewer rapes, and 700,000 fewer injurious assaults" (June 10, 1992).

Classical Conditioning

27 Classical conditioning is like the famous case of Pavlov's dogs they teach in Psychology 101. The dogs learned to associate the ringing of the bell with food, and once conditioned, the dogs could not hear the bell without salivating.

28 The Japanese were masters at using classical conditioning with their soldiers. Early in World War II, Chinese prisoners were placed in a ditch on their knees with their hands bound behind them. And one by one, a select few Japanese soldiers would go into the ditch and bayonet "their" prisoner to death. This is a horrific way to kill another human being. Up on the bank, countless other young soldiers would cheer them on in their violence. Comparatively few soldiers actually killed in these situations, but by making the others watch and cheer, the Japanese were able to use these kinds of atrocities to classically condition a very large audience to associate pleasure with human death and suffering. Immediately afterwards, the soldiers who had been spectators were treated to sake, to the best meal they had in months, and to so-called comfort girls. The result? They learned to associate committing violent acts with pleasure.

The Japanese found these kinds of techniques to be extraordinarily effective at quickly enabling very large numbers of soldiers to commit atrocities in the years to come. Operant conditioning (which we will look at shortly) teaches you to kill, but classical conditioning is a subtle but powerful mechanism that teaches you to like it. 29

This technique is so morally reprehensible that there are very few examples of it in modern U.S. military training, but there are some clear-cut examples of it being done by the media to our children. What is happening to our children is the reverse of the aversion therapy portrayed in the movie *A Clockwork Orange*. In *A Clockwork Orange,* a brutal sociopath, a mass murderer, is strapped to a chair and forced to watch violent movies while he is injected with a drug that nauseates him. So he sits and gags and retches as he watches the movies. After hundreds of repetitions of this, he associates violence with nausea. And it limits his ability to be violent. 30

We are doing the exact opposite: Our children watch vivid pictures of human suffering and death, and they learn to associate it with their favorite soft drink and candy bar or their girlfriend's perfume. 31

After the Jonesboro shootings, one of the high-school teachers told me how her students reacted when she told them about the shootings at the middle school. "They laughed," she told me with dismay. A similar reaction happens all the time in movie theaters when there is bloody violence. The young people laugh and cheer and keep right on eating popcorn and drinking pop. We have raised a generation of barbarians who have learned to associate violence with pleasure, like the Romans cheering and snacking as the Christians were slaughtered in the Coliseum. 32

The result is a phenomenon that functions much like AIDS, a phenomenon I call AVIDS—Acquired Violence Immune Deficiency Syndrome. AIDS has never killed anybody. It destroys your immune system, and then other diseases that shouldn't kill you become fatal. Television violence by itself does not kill you. It destroys your violence immune system and conditions you to derive pleasure from violence. And once you are at close range with another human being, and it's time for you to pull that trigger, Acquired Violence Immune Deficiency Syndrome can destroy your midbrain resistance. 33

Operant Conditioning

The third method the military uses is operant conditioning, a very powerful repetitive procedure of stimulus-response, stimulus-response. A benign example is the use of flight simulators to train pilots. An airline pilot in training sits in front of a flight simulator for endless hours; when a particular warning light goes on, he is taught to react in a certain way. When another warning light goes on, a different reaction is required. Stimulus-response, stimulus-response, stimulus-response. One day the pilot is actually flying a jumbo jet; the plane is going down, and 300 people are screaming behind him. He is wetting his seat cushion, and he is scared out of his wits; but he does the right thing. Why? Because he has been conditioned to respond reflexively to this particular crisis. 34

When people are frightened or angry, they will do what they have been conditioned to do. In fire drills, children learn to file out of the school in orderly fashion. One day there is a real fire, and they are frightened out of their wits; but they do exactly what they have been conditioned to do, and it saves their lives. 35

36 The military and law enforcement community have made killing a conditioned response. This has substantially raised the firing rate on the modern battlefield. Whereas infantry training in World War II used bull's-eye targets, now soldiers learn to fire at realistic, man-shaped silhouettes that pop into their field of view. That is the stimulus. The trainees have only a split second to engage the target. The conditioned response is to shoot the target, and then it drops. Stimulus-response, stimulus-response, stimulus-response—soldiers or police officers experience hundreds of repetitions. Later, when soldiers are on the battlefield or a police officer is walking a beat and somebody pops up with a gun, they will shoot reflexively and shoot to kill. We know that 75 to 80 percent of the shooting on the modern battlefield is the result of this kind of stimulus-response training.

37 Now, if you're a little troubled by that, how much more should we be troubled by the fact that every time a child plays an interactive point-and-shoot video game, he is learning the exact same conditioned reflex and motor skills?

38 I was an expert witness in a murder case in South Carolina offering mitigation for a kid who was facing the death penalty. I tried to explain to the jury that interactive video games had conditioned him to shoot a gun to kill. He had spent hundreds of dollars on video games learning to point and shoot, point and shoot. One day he and his buddy decided it would be fun to rob the local convenience store. They walked in, and he pointed a snub-nosed .38 pistol at the clerk's head. The clerk turned to look at him, and the defendant shot reflexively from about six feet. The bullet hit the clerk right between the eyes—which is a pretty remarkable shot with that weapon at that range—and killed this father of two. Afterward, we asked the boy what happened and why he did it. It clearly was not part of the plan to kill the guy—it was being videotaped from six different directions. He said, "I don't know. It was a mistake. It wasn't supposed to happen."

39 In the military and law-enforcement worlds, the right option is often not to shoot. But you never, ever put your money in that video machine with the intention of not shooting. There is always some stimulus that sets you off. And when he was excited, and his heart rate went up, and vasoconstriction closed his forebrain down, this young man did exactly what he was conditioned to do: he reflexively pulled the trigger, shooting accurately just like all those times he played video games.

40 This process is extraordinarily powerful and frightening. The result is ever more "homemade" sociopaths who kill reflexively. Our children are learning how to kill and learning to like the idea of killing; and then we have the audacity to say, "Oh my goodness, what's wrong?"

41 One of the boys involved in the Jonesboro shootings (and they are just boys) had a fair amount of experience shooting real guns. The other one, to the best of our knowledge, had almost no experience shooting. Between them, those two boys fired 27 shots from a range of over 100 yards, and they hit 15 people. That's pretty remarkable shooting. We run into these situations often—kids who have never picked up a gun in their lives pick up a real gun and are incredibly accurate. Why? Video games.

Thinking Critically About Content

1. According to Grossman, what is the "virus of violence" (paragraph 3)?
2. What three methods does the military use to train its soldiers to kill?
3. What does Grossman mean when he claims that the media are presenting violence "as entertainment for children"?

Thinking Critically About Purpose and Audience

4. What do you think Grossman's purpose is in this essay?
5. Who do you think would be most interested in this essay?
6. What effect do you think this essay would have on parents?

Thinking Critically About Essays

7. Describe in a complete sentence the writer's argument.
8. Grossman's statistics on violent assaults and murders in Canada are not accurate. Knowing this, how convinced are you by the essay as a whole?
9. Explain the title of this essay.
10. This essay discusses the sensitive issues related to children and violence in the media and then ends abruptly. Add a paragraph to the essay making some concrete suggestions for solving the problem the author poses.

Arguing a Position

Focusing Your Attention

1. If you were asked to take a position for or against a topic that you knew people held a strong opinion on, what are some of the topics you would consider?
2. In the two essays you will be reading, the writer of the first claims that we should not tolerate junk email arriving in our email boxes. The other writer claims that banning spam would cut people off from the world.

RICK BROADHEAD
Ban Spam: E-Nough Is E-Nough

Expanding Your Vocabulary

The following words are important to your understanding of this essay:

proliferators: those who cause growth to increase rapidly (paragraph 2)
purveyors: those who provide supplies (paragraph 7)
cocoon: provide protective covering (paragraph 9)
concoctions: mixtures (paragraph 9)

READING CRITICALLY

Once again, highlight the facts and opinions in both of the following essays, put an X by ideas you disagree with, and form your own opinions about the issue of junk email. Be prepared to defend your thoughts with details from the essays and examples from your own experience.

RICK BROADHEAD

Ban Spam: E-Nough Is E-Nough

1 Imagine if a quarter of all the voice-mail messages left in homes and businesses across North America never reached their intended recipients. Imagine if mail delivered through Canada Post had only a one-in-five chance of getting to its destination. Would we tolerate such a ridiculous state of affairs? Absolutely not.

2 But on the Internet, we have let proliferators of electronic junk mail control our lives and wreak havoc with the economy. That's why, last week, the four biggest e-mail providers—Microsoft, Yahoo, America Online and Earthlink—filed lawsuits in the United States against hundreds of individuals (including several Canadians) for sending unsolicited e-mails and swamping strangers' mailboxes.

3 The extent of the problem has become evident with recent revelations that roughly one out of every five e-mail messages sent over the Internet never gets to its intended recipient. Thanks to the increasing usage of junk-mail filters, which have become a necessity for businesses and Internet service providers these days, there's a roughly 20-per-cent chance that your next e-mail message will mistakenly get tagged as spam and never reach its final destination. It's a shocking situation that should make every lawmaker and politician sit up and take notice.

4 I've experienced this new reality first-hand. In the past few weeks, I've received multiple calls from colleagues who have been unable to e-mail me because their messages were classified as junk mail and rejected by my Internet service provider. The only alternative was to have the filter turned off completely. A flood of junk mail now pours into my e-mail box every day, but at least I'm no longer missing any vital communications.

5 The writing is on the wall: If we continue on this dangerous path, sending an e-mail message on the Internet and hoping for a successful delivery will be no better than rolling the dice at a Las Vegas casino.

6 During the past decade, we've made real progress at transforming the Internet into a powerful tool that is responsible for substantial economic growth. But all that progress will quickly evaporate if the Internet becomes an anarchic frontier controlled by unapologetic e-mail bandits. According to recent estimates, spam now accounts for as much as 60 per cent of global e-mail traffic. America Online and Microsoft are fending off more than four billion spam messages a day. And the

global cost of spam to businesses has reached a staggering $20 billion (U.S.). How did we ever let it get this bad?

Purveyors of electronic junk mail are winning the war and sadly, we're going out 7
of our way to accommodate them. In an attempt to communicate with business colleagues on-line, I'm now encountering people who require me to go to a website and identify myself as a real person (as opposed to a computer sending junk mail) before my electronic mail message can be granted safe passage.

Users of this new technology automatically quarantine messages from unfamil- 8
iar recipients and presume them to be junk e-mail unless the senders prove otherwise. The technology obviously works, but it's brought a disturbing chill to the Internet reminiscent of crime-plagued neighbourhoods where fearful citizens lock their doors, pull down their shutters and retreat indoors.

The Internet is supposed to make it easier for us to communicate—not force 9
people to cocoon themselves from a hurricane of unwanted e-mail. E-mail marketers are controlling the Internet's streets, while we shield ourselves behind spam filters and other high-tech concoctions. It's time to take back our streets from the e-mail thugs who control them.

Immediate action is needed and it requires our lawmakers to recognize that 10
spam is no longer just a nuisance—it's a serious threat to the vitality of our economy. As long as peddlers of junk e-mail continue to believe they're safe from prosecution, they'll have the upper hand.

Critics argue that legislation is an ineffective weapon against senders of spam, 11
and they have a point. In the U.S., previous attempts to sue senders of spam at the state level have failed miserably. More tellingly, the amount of spam on the Internet has increased, not decreased, despite dozens of lawsuits filed in recent years by legal heavyweights such as Microsoft.

But one only need look at the recent lawsuits filed by the Recording Industry 12
Association of America as proof that the threat of legal action does act as an effective deterrent. The amount of file-sharing on file-sharing networks such as Kazaa dropped by 50 per cent after the music industry began suing people who were illegally swapping music on-line. Now that the United States has federal anti-spam legislation in place, spam distributors will have fewer places to hide.

It is appalling that the Canadian government has continued to sit on the side- 13
lines while other nations, most noticeably the United States, are cracking down on spam with renewed vigour.

The very nature of our global, interconnected economy means that the United 14
States cannot win this war on its own. Indeed, one of the U.S. lawsuits filed last week alleges that a father and two sons from Kitchener, Ont., were responsible for disseminating an astonishing 94 million junk e-mail messages to Internet users—and that's just in the month of January. The story made headlines around the world, casting a black eye on Canada as a breeding ground for spam.

It is time for Canadian legislators to act swiftly and forcefully to send a strong 15
message to the global community that Canada is not a safe haven for spam. The world is watching.

DOUG SAUNDERS
Ban Spam? What, and Banish All the World?

Expanding Your Vocabulary

The following words are important to your understanding of this essay:

pariahs: social outcasts (paragraph 2)
hapless: unfortunate (paragraph 4)
teeming: overflowing, abounding (paragraph 5)
souk: a market in an Arab city (paragraph 5)
interlopers: intruders (paragraph 6)
snake oil: a worthless or fraudulent cure (paragraph 6)
embellish: enhance (paragraph 6)
Amazon.com: an online bookstore (paragraph 8)
ad-hoc: formed for one purpose—a committee, for example (paragraph 8)
insidious: spreading harm stealthily (paragraph 9)
lumpen class: underclass of society (paragraph 10)
dubious: uncertain or questionable (paragraph 15)
pungent: sharp or biting (paragraph 16)
dissolute: lacking moral restraint (paragraph 16)

DOUG SAUNDERS
Ban Spam? What, and Banish All the World?

1 Since nobody else appears willing to do it, I have taken it upon myself, ladies and gentlemen of the jury, to come to the defence of junk e-mail.

2 These poor Canadians you see before you, fellow citizens, have become pariahs, all because their London, Ont., "spam factory" helped make our country the world's second-largest exporter of unsolicited e-mail.

3 Now, I am fully aware of the pain and unease inflicted by their acts. The e-mail address at the bottom of this column is attached to a spam-catcher program that currently has 2,276 items in its box. Sorry, it just grew to 2,310.

4 Yet I am not defending these hapless individuals out of sympathy for abstract principle or for personal gain. I am defending them because I have become a spam believer.

5 My life has been improved by its teeming souk of goods and services, much as my diet has been vastly improved by the flyers that arrive in my mailbox, much as my house is being expertly and affordably painted by the student who knocked on my door.

6 What should offend us about junk e-mail, my friends, is not its existence, but its quality. The spam that bothers you is the spam that sells plain old fraud, like those

polite interlopers from Nigeria, or snake oil, like the folks who promise to embellish your privates. I implore you all to put this corruption to an end, to shut down the illegitimate voices. But please, ignore the calls of those like Rick Broadhead, who asked the government in these pages the other day to "ban all spam." By doing that, you are cutting yourself off from the world.

By banning all spam, look what you are doing: 7

You're a corporate clone. There is a scent of hypocrisy here: Many of the peo- 8
ple who oppose spam most aggressively are those who frequent a community java shop and wouldn't be caught dead in a Starbucks, who prefer poky local bookshops to Amazon.com. Yet unsolicited e-mail is the electronic equivalent of that local coffee shop: It is an ad-hoc, community alternative to the monolithic, homogenizing voices of big-corporation marketing.

If you're against the corporatization of society, you should be in favour of junk 9
mail. The big companies reach you in far more insidious, unavoidable ways. The spammers are the entrepreneurs who are trying to give you an alternative. In fact, even if you're fully opposed to capitalism, you should be for spam. These people are merchants, not capitalists. They are engaged in the ancient craft of buying low and selling high—the heart of any system, even collective utopias.

Capital, and labour exploitation, is not involved. These folks are not, to put it in 10
Marxist terms, engaging in the extraction of surplus value from alienated labour—they are the lumpen class, exploiting nobody but themselves.

You're racist. One thing unites the people putting the flyers in your mailbox and 11
the people sending spam to your inbox: Many of them (the London case notwithstanding) are recent immigrants, pulling themselves up by their bootstraps and DSL lines, struggling in a minority culture.

The guy who sold me the $104 computer router the other day, because I had 12
noticed his appealing pitch in my spam-catcher box, had moved here from India two years ago. The man in Quebec who sold me the excellent Roland Kirk recordings, after pitching them to my home e-mail address (which gets a better class of spam because of its relative secrecy) was a first-generation Russian Jew. All the scores of people who have sold me things through flyers and spam letters have been new Canadians, whose entrepreneurial spirit has got me good stuff and cheap prices.

The "no flyers" signs that have polluted mailboxes in better-heeled neighbour- 13
hoods are essentially shouting "no truck nor trade with immigrants." Is it any coincidence that the people who put up those signs are usually white and well-established? They are the same ones calling for a ban on spam. It is their way of keeping their people in, and the horde of newcomers with their low-priced goods and handshake deals and neighbourly banter out.

"Our people do not do business that way. We keep to our own. Get the hell off my 14
doorstep." That is what "ban all spam" means.

You're boring. Yes, I know. Most spam is garbage. Of course it is. That is why it 15
is a true human venture. Pick a dozen recordings, at random, from a CD store and the whole idea of music will seem dubious. Pull a few random books from random shelves in a library, and you'll conclude that the printed word is a dull and wasteful enterprise. It is the one in a thousand that has any value—a truth that we are willing to

accept about other human beings (in love, employment and friendship)—so why can't we say it about their electronic output?

16 What kind of street do you want to live on? The one in the all-white, gated community, where the only merchants allowed are the Roto-Rooter guy and the Sears truck? Or the one with the colourful storefronts, the streetside stalls full of pungent scents and surprising deals in imported goods and, yes, the occasional obnoxious beggar or dissolute old perv? I've always chosen to live on those streets, because they offer real human life.

17 I would rather we all lived on that street. It would make us better people. We can police the content and legality of those market stalls, but not their very presence here. That street, my friends, is called spam.

18 The defence rests.

Thinking Critically About Content

1. Make a list of the reasons, evidence, and statistics each writer uses to convince the reader of his position.
2. Explain how each writer uses analogies.
3. Which essay contains the most convincing evidence in your opinion? Why is it so convincing to you?

Thinking Critically About Purpose and Audience

4. What do you think the writers' purposes are in these essays?
5. What type of audience would be most interested in the subject of these two essays? Explain your answer.
6. If you changed your mind as the result of reading one of these essays, what in the essay caused the change?

Thinking Critically About Essays

7. State both writers' point of view in a single sentence.
8. How have both writers organized their essays? Make a rough outline to demonstrate your answer. What is the effect of the three words at the end of the second article: "The defence rests"?
9. Which points, if any, do the two writers agree on? Which points do they disagree on? Explain your answer.
10. Both writers use physical analogies in their discussions. Write your own argument based on the similarities between real and virtual mail.

Writing Workshop

This final section gives you opportunities to apply what you have learned in this chapter to another writing assignment. This time, we provide very little prompting beyond a summary of the guidelines for writing an argument essay. This section will let you demonstrate that you can go through the entire writing process on your own with only occasional feedback from your peers. Loop back into the chapter as necessary when you have questions so that this process becomes as automatic to you as possible before you move on to new material. Then pause at the end of the chapter to reflect briefly on what you have learned.

Guidelines for Writing an Argument Essay

1. State your opinion on your topic in your thesis statement.
2. Find out as much as you can about your audience before you write.
3. Choose evidence that supports your thesis statement.
4. Anticipate opposing points of view.
5. Find some common ground.
6. Maintain a reasonable tone.
7. Organize your essay so that it presents your position as effectively as possible.

Writing About Your Reading

1. In "We Are Training Our Kids to Kill," Grossman tries to convince his readers that various forms of violence in the media teach our kids to kill. Argue for or against government control of violence on TV, in movies, and/or in video games.
2. The pro and con essays deal with the annoyances or the usefulness of junk email. Many young people now communicate with instant messaging programs. Write an argument for or against banning instant messaging on school computers. Gather as much evidence as you can before you begin to write.
3. How can being able to develop good arguments and persuade people of your point of view help you in life? How might this ability give you the edge over other people on the job market?

Writing About Your World

1. Explain what the photographer had in mind in creating this pictorial statement about littering. How does it appeal to its viewers? Write an essay explaining what the ad communicates.
2. Argue for or against a controversial political issue. Take a firm stand, and develop an essay supporting your position. You might want to look at some newspaper headlines to get ideas for this assignment.
3. Write a letter to a potential employer for the job of your dreams, arguing that you are the best candidate for the job. Try to convince the employer not only that you are the perfect person for the job but also that you can take the position forward in new directions. Follow the format for a well-developed argument essay.
4. Create your own argument essay assignment (with the help of your instructor), and write a response to it.

Revising

Small Group Activity (5–10 minutes per writer) Working in groups of three or four, each person should read his or her argument essay to the other members of the group. Those listening should record their reactions on a copy of the Peer Evaluation Form (Appendix 1A). After your group goes through this process, give your evaluation forms to the appropriate writers so that each writer has two or three peer comment sheets for revising.

Paired Activity (5 minutes per writer) Using the completed Peer Evaluation Forms, work in pairs to decide what you should revise in your essay. If time allows, rewrite some of your sentences, and have your partner look at them.

Individual Activity Rewrite your paper, using the revising feedback you received from other students.

Editing

Paired Activity (5–10 minutes per writer) Swap papers with a classmate, and use the editing portion of your Peer Evaluation Form (Appendix 1B) to identify as many grammatical, punctuation, mechanical, and spelling errors as you can. If time allows, correct some of your errors, and have your partner look at them. Record your grammar, punctuation, and mechanics errors in the Error Log (Appendix 3) and your spelling errors in the Spelling Log (Appendix 4).

Individual Activity Rewrite your paper again, using the editing feedback you received from other students.

PART III

THE RESEARCH PAPER

In order to understand complex issues and situations and events, we need to analyze them from multiple perspectives; every position or every viewpoint ought to have reasons to support it; and the quality of the conclusion is dependent on the quality of the reasoning that went before it.

—John Chaffee

Part III discusses the research paper from assignment to final draft. It explains not only what this type of essay is but also how to write one, step by step. It provides you with a student model of a research paper and then guides you through the process of writing one on a topic of your own.

CHAPTER

17

Recognizing a Research Paper

The content of a research paper—an essay with sources—is based mainly on facts, statistics, and the opinions of others. The main difference between a research paper and other essays is that writers use information from outside reading material when writing an essay with sources. In other words, writers consult books, periodicals, and the Internet to find facts, statistics, and other material or evidence to support their main point.

Just as you develop the body of most essays with common knowledge or personal experience, you develop this type of essay with trustworthy evidence from outside sources. To begin choosing appropriate sources, you must have a good sense of your thesis statement. Then you must set out to find information in various sources that will back up your thesis statement.

In a research paper, the title gives the reader a clue to the subject of the essay. The introduction gives some background for understanding the topic and states the purpose of the paper in a thesis statement. Body paragraphs provide evidence to back up the thesis statement. And the conclusion wraps up the essay by restating the thesis statement and bringing the paper to a close.

DOCUMENTATION FORMAT

In many cases throughout your college career, the documentation style you use will be determined by your instructor. Documentation requirements vary according to your field of study. Two of the major documentation styles are MLA and APA. Because you may have to write papers using each of these documentation styles, you should have an understanding of their differences.

MLA Versus APA

MLA	APA
• Author's full name is used	• Author's last name and first initial are used
• Dates don't necessarily have to be mentioned; however, citing the dates allows your readers to easily look up your sources.	• Dates follow the author's names in the sentence or appear in the parentheses after the sentence.

- A parenthetical citation includes the author's last name and page number: (Turner 49).
- A parenthetical citation following a direct quote includes the author's last name, date, and a page number: (Turner, 2007, p. 49).

The following essay by Mary Minor, a student, is a good example of a research paper. She has written her essay in both MLA and APA styles of documentation so you may see the differences between the two. She proves her thesis statement solidly, using books and articles from many different sources as evidence in her supporting paragraphs. As you read the first paragraph of this draft of her essay, notice her thesis statement. Then, in each supporting paragraph that follows the introductory paragraph, be aware of how the author develops her essay and supports her thesis statement with material from outside sources.

Children as Robots 1

Mary Minor
COMM1035
Professor Dunphy
October 25, 2007

Children as Robots (MLA Example)

When children are infants, there are certain "norms" they are measured by to see if they 1
are progressing through developmental stages at the rate of other infants their age. The "norms" are never clear-cut and leave room for individual differences. When a child hits the age of two or enters day care, "norms" become all-important. More than in any other time in history, the 1990s brought about a change in "norms" that left parents confused. The "terrible twos" and "trying threes" no longer seem to be the best descriptions of toddlerhood. Today children who are "too" terrible at the age of two or "too" trying at the age of three are diagnosed with either "Attention Deficit Disorder (ADD) or its more severe variation, Attention Deficit Hyperactivity Disorder (ADHD). Both neurological conditions seem to be the childhood plague of the '90s" (Higdon 84). Children are often misdiagnosed with ADD or ADHD and suffer unnecessarily when medicated for a disorder they may not have.

Because medical professionals cannot agree on "whether this is one disease with sub- 2
categories or two entirely different diseases" (Brink 80), the terms ADD and ADHD are often used interchangeably. Both terms, however, refer to "a short attention span" (Schmitt), with or without hyperactivity. The *Diagnostic and Statistical Manual of Mental Disorders*

(DSM-IV) (American Psychiatric Association, 1994) defines ADHD as a "persistent pattern of inattention and/or hyperactivity-impulsivity that is more frequent and severe than typically observed in individuals at a comparable level of development" (Kendall 839). What's more, the disease ADD has become "one of the most commonly diagnosed" childhood diseases in the United States today (LeFever, Dawson, and Morrow 1359), afflicting "approximately 4 to 7 percent" of American children (Durall 38). The National Institute of Mental Health (NIMH) claims that "differences do not a disorder make. The differences could simply be part of human variation. . . . We don't know if perhaps we shouldn't treat ADD as the far end of normal behaviour, just like height, weight, or muscle mass" (Koch 918). Given the fact that children are identified as having this disease based on what a person may consider "normal" behaviour, it is unfortunate for the children being diagnosed that nobody can agree on what "normal" means. So specialists need to be careful when recommending treatments for what could be everyday behaviour.

3 Many children today who do not fit the "norm" of adult expectations may be diagnosed with ADD. Labelling a child's behaviour based on a set of "norms" is ludicrous since these qualities cannot accurately be measured, let alone defined. According to Thomas Armstrong, author of *The Myth of the ADD Child*, "Once the influential American Psychiatric Association (APA) declared ADD a disorder in 1980, the DSM defined it more and more broadly. . . . Increasing numbers of children are caught in the ever-widening definition net and are then labeled ADD" (914). But even though we have a definition for this disorder, nobody really knows for sure what the disorder is. According to psychologist Stephen P. Hinshaw, "There's clearly not a single cause of all cases of well-diagnosed ADHD" (qtd. in Bower 343). Other professionals agree that accurate diagnosis "remains elusive and controversial" (Koch 907). If our leading professionals in the field don't know what a "well-diagnosed" case is, how can we be sure that they even know what any case of ADHD is?

4 Because there are no reliable tests for ADD, nobody is really able to tell if a child actually has the disorder. "Given the explosion in ADHD diagnoses . . . the disorder is surprisingly ill defined. . . . There is no blood test, no PET scan, no physical exam that can determine who has it and who does not" (Gibbs 90). Professionals in the field argue over what the disease is, what causes it, how it should be treated, or whether it is a disease at all (Bower 343). Yet numerous children are diagnosed with this disease and are medicated because of it.

5 There are as many speculations about the causes of ADD and ADHD as there are experts. Unfortunately, the ones lost in the confusion are the children, and this is due to one fact:

Children as Robots 3

Ritalin, the most widely used method of treatment for this disorder, works so well that additional medical tests are not done. According to Dr. Sydney Walker, neither doctors nor insurance companies want to take the time or spend the money to track down the "real" cause of the problem. Instead, they mask the symptoms with Ritalin (Barkley and Walker 921). While Ritalin seems to work for many children, nobody knows why or how it works, not to mention what the long-term effects of the drug might be (Gibbs 89). We have no absolute information about ADD, only a set of symptoms, which include excessive talking, fidgeting, and similar behaviours. In other words, parents face the decision of whether or not to put their child on strong drugs when nobody has yet proved that a disorder exists.

Unfortunately, teachers are often the first to be involved in diagnosing a child, and "sometimes the school systems insist on a brain-disorder label" (Brink 81). One parent describes his experience and feelings about the matter in a *U.S. News and World Report* article: 6

> First it was the teacher. Then the school counselor. Then the heavies in the school, the principal, start to show up. You go to meetings, and everybody thinks your child has a problem. . . . Doctors and therapists each had a different diagnosis—ADHD, anxiety disorder, obsessive-compulsive disorder, depression—and each diagnosis called for a different drug. . . . Social conformity and mental health are becoming the same terms. . . . The person with a different perspective is seen as a candidate for medication. (Brink 81)

Parents are often pressured into placing their children on drugs with the hope that their children will achieve "academic and social success" (Brink 76). However, this pressure may be unwarranted. "There is no solid evidence that stimulant medicine [such as Ritalin] has any impact on scholastic achievement. . . . Teachers and parents tend to approve of the drug because it makes unruly kids more manageable and more social" (Sheppard 46). So what may be disruptive to teachers or other students may simply be normal behaviour for some children.

Some children are so hard to control that mind-altering drugs such as Ritalin appear to be a blessing; but drugs, if used at all, should be used *only* for a short period of time—until the "real" cause of the problem behaviour is found. Pediatrician Lawrence Diller states his opinion on the subject well when he says, "I just don't believe a pill is the moral equivalent of good parenting and good schooling. . . . I prescribe it because . . . my job is to relieve suffering, and Ritalin, in the short term, will ease suffering" (qtd. in Brink 81). One 7 must wonder, however, whose suffering this doctor is relieving; is it the teachers' and parents' or the children's? Diller's good intentions demonstrate why children should not be medicated for an ill-defined disease.

8 Despite major controversy in the medical field, however, there has been no proof that drugs are being overprescribed for children. Some experts even feel that children may be under-treated (Koch 912). No studies have been found that would prove one claim over the other, which again means that each child is treated according to the most popular opinion. As a result, "Students who were younger than their classmates were *21* times more likely to be medicated" for ADD or ADHD (920). With a statistic like this, it's astonishing that experts disagree on this subject.

9 Even if drugs can be beneficial in some instances, long-term usage is potentially dangerous because these drugs are presently "classified as 'having a high potential for abuse with severe liability for physical and/or psychic dependence'" (Morrow, Morrow, and Haislip 1121). Also, "a very small percentage of children treated at high doses have hallucinogenic responses" (Gibbs 90). To give a prescription for drugs to a child without comprehensive medical testing is, as Walker states, "inexcusable" (Barkley and Walker 921). Doctors need to agree that children are overmedicated for a disease that may not exist and find more acceptable ways to curb "disruptive behaviour." Many children exhibit the symptoms of ADHD due to family problems or other environmental factors. Diet may also play a major role in this scenario. The removal of certain foods, especially those containing "allergenic food additives and dyes" (Koch 916), may very well eliminate the symptoms. When doctors quote the Hippocratic Oath, they say these words: "I will apply dietetic measures for the benefit of the sick according to my ability and judgment; I will keep them from harm and injustice" ("Hippocratic Oath"). Sworn to dietetically treat their patients, doctors should remember this oath before prescribing drugs for a disease that nobody can prove exists.

10 Perhaps these "diseases" are nothing more than a belief system in an ever-increasing "conformist" society. Every effort should be made to find the cause of the "real" medical problems underlying ADD and ADHD before we even think about giving our children drugs. A doctor who doesn't order medical tests for a child with symptoms of ADD is negligent, to say the least, and the failure of a doctor to discuss alternatives to drug therapy with parents when diagnosing ADHD is more than "inexcusable"; it's unforgivable. More parents would seek alternative treatments if they knew that their child was diagnosed on the basis of nothing more than a list of symptoms that cannot be defined or measured. After all, most parents

do not want their child placed on long-term stimulant drugs. It's time to say goodbye to "conformist" classrooms and diagnoses. People don't fit "norms"; they have personalities.

Works Cited

American Psychiatric Association. *Diagnostic and Statistical Manual of Mental Disorders.* 4th ed. Washington: APA, 1994.

Armstrong, Thomas. *The Myth of the ADD Child: 50 Ways to Improve Your Child's Behavior and Attention Span Without Drugs, Labels, or Coercion.* New York: Dutton, 1995.

Barkley, Russell, and Sydney Walker III. "At Issue: Are Attention Deficit Disorder (ADD) and Attention Deficit Hyperactivity Disorder (ADHD) Legitimate Medical Diagnoses?" *CQ Researcher* 9 (1999): 921.

Bower, Bruce. "Kid's Attention Disorder Attracts Concern." *Science News* 154 (1998): 343.

Brink, Susan. "Doing Ritalin Right." *U.S. News and World Report* 23 Nov. 1998: 76–81.

Durall, John. "Toward an Understanding of ADHD: A Developmental Delay in Self-Control." *Camping Magazine* Jan. 1999: 38–41.

Gibbs, Nancy. "The Age of Ritalin." *Time* 30 Nov. 1998: 86–96.

Higdon, Hal. "Getting Their Attention." *Runner's World* July 1999: 84–87.

"Hippocratic Oath." *World Book Encyclopedia.* Vol. 9. 1999 ed.

Kendall, Judy. "Outlasting Disruption: The Process of Reinvestment in Families with ADHD Children." *Qualitative Health Research* 8 (1998): 839–857.

Koch, Kathy. "Rethinking Ritalin." *CQ Researcher* 9 (1999): 907–918.

LeFever, Gretchen B., Keila V. Dawson, and Ardythe L. Morrow. "The Extent of Drug Therapy for Attention Deficit–Hyperactivity Disorder Among Children in Public Schools." *American Journal of Public Health* 89 (1999): 1359–1364.

Morrow, Robert C., Ardythe L. Morrow, and Gene Haislip. "Methylphenidate in the United States, 1990–1995." *American Journal of Public Health* 88 (1998): 1121.

Schmitt, B. D. "Attention Deficit Disorder (Short Attention Span)." *Clinical Reference Systems* 1 July 1999. 17 Feb. 2000 <http://www.epnet.com/ehpst/login.html>.

Sheppard, Robert. "Growing Up Hyperactive." *Maclean's* 7 Sept. 1998: 45–46.

Children as Robots
APA Example

Mary Minor
COMM1035
Professor Dunphy
October 25, 2007

Children as Robots

1 When children are infants, there are certain "norms" they are measured by to see if they are progressing through developmental stages at the rate of other infants their age. The "norms" are never clear-cut and leave room for individual differences. When a child hits the age of two or enters day care, "norms" become all-important. More than in any other time in history, the 1990s brought about a change in "norms" that left parents confused. The "terrible twos" and "trying threes" no longer seem to be the best descriptions of toddlerhood. Today children who are "too" terrible at the age of two or "too" trying at the age of three are diagnosed with either "Attention Deficit Disorder (ADD) or its more severe variation, Attention Deficit Hyperactivity Disorder (ADHD). Both neurological conditions seem to be the childhood plague of the '90s" (Higdon, 1999, p. 84). Children are often misdiagnosed with ADD or ADHD and suffer unnecessarily when medicated for a disorder they may not have.

2 Because medical professionals cannot agree on "whether this is one disease with subcategories or two entirely different diseases" (Brink, 1998, p. 80), the terms ADD and ADHD are often used interchangeably. According to Schmitt (1999), both terms, however, refer to "a short attention span," with or without hyperactivity (para. 3). The *Diagnostic and Statistical Manual of Mental Disorders* (DSM-IV) (American Psychiatric Association, 1994) defines ADHD as a "persistent pattern of inattention and/or hyperactivity-impulsivity that is more frequent and severe than typically observed in individuals at a comparable level of development" (Kendall, 1998, p. 839). What's more, the disease ADD has become "one of the most commonly diagnosed" childhood diseases in the United States today (LeFever, Dawson, and Morrow, 1999, p. 1359), afflicting "approximately 4 to 7 percent" of American children (Durall, 1999, p. 38). The National Institute of Mental Health (NIMH) claims that "differences do not a disorder make. The differences could simply be part of human variation. . . . We don't know if perhaps we shouldn't treat ADD as the far end of normal

Children as Robots 3

behaviour, just like height, weight, or muscle mass" (Koch, 1999, p. 918). Given the fact that children are identified as having this disease based on what a person may consider "normal" behaviour, it is unfortunate for the children being diagnosed that nobody can agree on what "normal" means. So specialists need to be careful when recommending treatments for what could be everyday behaviour.

3 Many children today who do not fit the "norm" of adult expectations may be diagnosed with ADD. Labelling a child's behaviour based on a set of "norms" is ludicrous since these qualities cannot accurately be measured, let alone defined. According to Thomas Armstrong (1995), author of *The Myth of the ADD Child*, "Once the influential American Psychiatric Association (APA) declared ADD a disorder in 1980, the DSM defined it more and more broadly. . . . Increasing numbers of children are caught in the ever-widening definition net and are then labeled ADD" (p. 914). But even though we have a definition for this disorder, nobody really knows for sure what the disorder is. According to psychologist Stephen P. Hinshaw, "There's clearly not a single cause of all cases of well-diagnosed ADHD" (qtd. in Bower, 1998, p. 343). Other professionals agree that accurate diagnosis "remains elusive and controversial" (Koch, 1999, p. 907). If our leading professionals in the field don't know what a "well-diagnosed" case is, how can we be sure that they even know what any case of ADHD is?

4 Because there are no reliable tests for ADD, nobody is really able to tell if a child actually has the disorder. Gibbs (1998) states that, "Given the explosion in ADHD diagnoses . . . the disorder is surprisingly ill defined. . . . There is no blood test, no PET scan, no physical exam that can determine who has it and who does not" (p. 90). Professionals in the field argue over what the disease is, what causes it, how it should be treated, or whether it is a disease at all (Bower, 1998, p. 343). Yet numerous children are diagnosed with this disease and are medicated because of it.

5 There are as many speculations about the causes of ADD and ADHD as there are experts. Unfortunately, the ones lost in the confusion are the children, and this is due to one fact: Ritalin, the most widely used method of treatment for this disorder, works so well that additional medical tests are not done. According to Dr. Sydney Walker, neither doctors nor insurance companies want to take the time or spend the money to track down the "real" cause of the problem. Instead, they mask the symptoms with Ritalin (Barkley and Walker, 1999, p. 921). While Ritalin seems to work for many children, nobody knows why or how it works, not to mention what the long-term effects of the drug might be (Gibbs, 1998, p. 89). We have no absolute information about ADD, only a set of symptoms, which include excessive

talking, fidgeting, and similar behaviours. In other words, parents face the decision of whether or not to put their child on strong drugs when nobody has yet proved that a disorder exists.

6 Unfortunately, teachers are often the first to be involved in diagnosing a child, and "sometimes the school systems insist on a brain-disorder label" (Brink, 1998, p. 81). One parent describes his experience and feelings about the matter in a *U.S. News and World Report* article:

> First it was the teacher. Then the school counselor. Then the heavies in the school, the principal, start to show up. You go to meetings, and everybody thinks your child has a problem. . . . Doctors and therapists each had a different diagnosis—ADHD, anxiety disorder, obsessive-compulsive disorder, depression—and each diagnosis called for a different drug. . . . Social conformity and mental health are becoming the same terms. . . . The person with a different perspective is seen as a candidate for medication. (Brink, 1998, p. 81)

Parents are often pressured into placing their children on drugs with the hope that their children will achieve "academic and social success" (Brink, p. 76). However, this pressure may be unwarranted. According to Sheppard (1998), "There is no solid evidence that stimulant medicine [such as Ritalin] has any impact on scholastic achievement. . . . Teachers and parents tend to approve of the drug because it makes unruly kids more manageable and more social" (p. 46). So what may be disruptive to teachers or other students may simply be normal behaviour for some children.

7 Some children are so hard to control that mind-altering drugs such as Ritalin appear to be a blessing; but drugs, if used at all, should be used only for a short period of time—until the "real" cause of the problem behaviour is found. Pediatrician Lawrence Diller states his opinion on the subject well when he says, "I just don't believe a pill is the moral equivalent of good parenting and good schooling. . . . I prescribe it because . . . my job is to relieve suffering, and Ritalin, in the short term, will ease suffering" (qtd. in Brink, 1998, p. 81). One must wonder, however, whose suffering this doctor is relieving; is it the teachers' and parents' or the children's? Diller's good intentions demonstrate why children should not be medicated for an ill-defined disease.

8 Despite major controversy in the medical field, however, there has been no proof that drugs are being overprescribed for children. Some experts even feel that children

Children as Robots 5

may be under-treated (Koch, 1999, p. 912). No studies have been found that would prove one claim over the other, which again means that each child is treated according to the most popular opinion. As a result, "Students who were younger than their classmates were *21* times more likely to be medicated" for ADD or ADHD (p. 920). With a statistic like this, it's astonishing that experts disagree on this subject.

9 Even if drugs can be beneficial in some instances, long-term usage is potentially dangerous because these drugs are presently "classified as 'having a high potential for abuse with severe liability for physical and/or psychic dependence'" (Morrow, Morrow, and Haislip, 1998, p. 1121). Also, "a very small percentage of children treated at high doses have hallucinogenic responses" (Gibbs, 1998, p. 90). To give a prescription for drugs to a child without comprehensive medical testing is, as Walker (1999) states, "inexcusable" (Barkley and Walker, p. 921). Doctors need to agree that children are over-medicated for a disease that may not exist and find more acceptable ways to curb "disruptive behaviour." Many children exhibit the symptoms of ADHD due to family problems or other environmental factors. Diet may also play a major role in this scenario. The removal of certain foods, especially those containing "allergenic food additives and dyes" (Koch 916), may very well eliminate the symptoms. When doctors quote the Hippocratic Oath, they say these words: "I will apply dietetic measures for the benefit of the sick according to my ability and judgment; I will keep them from harm and injustice" (Hippocratic Oath, 1999). Sworn to dietetically treat their patients, doctors should remember this oath before prescribing drugs for a disease that nobody can prove exists.

10 Perhaps these "diseases" are nothing more than a belief system in an ever-increasing "conformist" society. Every effort should be made to find the cause of the "real" medical problems underlying ADD and ADHD before we even think about giving our children drugs. A doctor who doesn't order medical tests for a child with symptoms of ADD is negligent, to say the least, and the failure of a doctor to discuss alternatives to drug therapy with parents when diagnosing ADHD is more than "inexcusable"; it's unforgivable. More parents would seek alternative treatments if they knew that their child was diagnosed on the basis of nothing more than a list of symptoms that cannot be defined or measured. After all, most parents do not want their child placed on long-term stimulant drugs. It's time to say good-bye to "conformist" classrooms and diagnoses. People don't fit "norms"; they have personalities.

Children as Robots 6

References

American Psychiatric Association. (1994). *Diagnostic and statistical manual of mental disorders.* (4th ed.). Washington: Author.

Armstrong, T. (1995). *The myth of the ADD child: 50 ways to improve your child's behavior and attention span without drugs, labels, or coercion.* New York: Dutton.

Barkley, R., & Walker, S. III. (1999). At issue: Are Attention Deficit Disorder (ADD) and Attention Deficit Hyperactivity Disorder (ADHD) legitimate medical diagnoses? *CQ Researcher, 9,* 921.

Bower, B. (1998). Kid's attention disorder attracts concern. *Science News,* 154, 343.

Brink, S. (1998, Nov. 23). Doing Ritalin right. *U.S. News and World Report,* 76–81.

Durall, J. (1999, Jan.). Toward an understanding of ADHD: A developmental delay in self-control. *Camping Magazine,* 38–41.

Gibbs, N. (1998, Nov. 30). The age of Ritalin. *Time,* 86–96.

Higdon, H. (1999, July). Getting their attention. *Runner's World,* 84–87.

Hippocratic Oath. (1999). In *World book encyclopedia* (Vol. 9, p. 239). Chicago: World Book, Inc.

Kendall, J. (1998). Outlasting disruption: The process of reinvestment in families with ADHD children. *Qualitative Health Research, 8,* 839–857.

Koch, K. Rethinking Ritalin. (1999). *CQ Researcher, 9,* 907–918.

LeFever, G. B., Dawson, K. V., & Morrow, A. L. (1999). The extent of drug therapy for Attention Deficit–Hyperactivity Disorder among children in public schools. *American Journal of Public Health, 89,* 1359–1364.

Morrow, Robert C., Morrow, A. L., & Haislip, G. (1998). Methylphenidate in the United States, 1990–1995. *American Journal of Public Health, 88,* 1121.

Schmitt, B. D. (1999, July 1). Attention Deficit Disorder (short attention span). *Clinical Reference Systems.* Retrieved Feb. 17, 2000 from http://www.epnet.com/ehost/login.html

Sheppard, R. (1998, Sept. 7). Growing up hyperactive. *Maclean's,* 45–46.

Before continuing, choose one of the following topics for your own work in the rest of Part III:

Bias in the media	Censorship	Cloning
Spinal cord research	Government spending	Date rape
Herbal medicine	Performance enhancing drugs	Child abuse
Assisted suicide	Pollution	Alcohol and crime
Nursing homes	Drug treatment programs	Bilingual education

CHAPTER 18

AVOIDING PLAGIARISM

Plagiarism is using someone else's words or ideas as if they were your own. It is a serious offence in school and in life after school because it is dishonest. When you work with outside sources, you must give credit to them. In other words, if you quote, paraphrase, or summarize from another source, you must provide your reader with information about that source, such as the author's name, the title of the essay, and the identity of the publisher. If you use other people's words without giving them credit, you are plagiarizing.

When you don't cite your sources properly, your readers will think certain words and ideas are yours when they actually came from someone else. When you steal material in this way in college, you can get dismissed from school. When you commit the same offence in the professional world, you can end up in court. So make sure you understand what plagiarism is as you move through this chapter.

COMMON KNOWLEDGE

If you are referring to information such as historical events and known facts, like the effects of ultraviolet rays or smoking, you do not have to cite a source. This material is called *common knowledge* because it can be found in many different sources. You can use this information freely because you are not dealing with anyone's original words or ideas.

ORIGINAL IDEAS

If, however, you want to use someone's words or ideas, you must give that person credit by recording where you found this information. This process is called *citing* or *documenting* your sources, and it involves noting in your paper where you found the idea. Since essays based on sources are developed around sources that support your position, citations are an essential ingredient in any source paper.

As you can see in Mary Minor's paper in Chapter 17, every source is acknowledged at least twice in her paper: (1) in the paper, right after a quotation or idea and then (2) at the end of the paper, in a list of sources used in the paper. At the note-taking stage, you simply have to make sure that you have all the information on your sources that you need to acknowledge them in proper form in your paper. Having to track down missing details when you prepare your lists of works cited is frustrating and time-consuming.

PRACTICE 1 Identify the following information as either common knowledge (CK) or original (O).

1. _____ In a typical day, for human beings to drink the equivalent of what the glassy-winged sharpshooter insect drinks, humans would have to drink half the amount in a standard swimming pool.
2. _____ William Shakespeare was born and died on the same day, April 23, 52 years apart.
3. _____ Mike Weir, from Bright's Grove, ON, won the Masters Golf Tournament in 2003.
4. _____ A human being cannot survive more than three days without water.
5. _____ The Paleozoic era produced the first shellfish and corals in the Cambrian period, the first fishes in the Ordovician period, and the first land plants in the Silurian period.
6. _____ Tom Hanks has won two Oscars, one for his role in *Philadelphia* and one for the title role in *Forrest Gump*.
7. _____ Aerobic respiration consists of oxygen plus organic matter that produces carbon dioxide, water, and energy.
8. _____ The success of *Survivor* caused many other reality shows to be produced.
9. _____ The longest palindromic word in the English language is *saippuakivikauppias*.
10. _____ AIDS is a disease that can be caught through unprotected sex and sharing needles.

USING AND SYNTHESIZING SOURCES

When writers use more than one source in an essay, they are *synthesizing* their sources. In other words, they are taking pieces of information from various sources and weaving them into an argument to form their own essay. If you've written any type of paper using outside sources, including a research paper, you were synthesizing material.

Once you have figured out your topics, you'll most likely start writing. You'll have done some prewriting to help you choose what method of organization to use. You may realize later that you'll have to change your organization around, but you can worry about that when you revise.

Once you have written the introduction, ending with a thesis statement, you will probably begin working with your sources. This doesn't mean that you shouldn't use any sources in your introduction, but you'll want to save the majority of them for the body of your paper. As you write the paper, you want to make sure that you develop your argument and use sources as evidence for your claims. You should *not* write your paper around your sources. If you do this, you may end up with a disjointed argument, and your readers will not be able to determine what you really think about the issue. So when you write with sources, be sure to use them to back up your own argument and not the other way around.

Look at one of Mary Minor's paragraphs from her first draft:

> Many children today who do not fit the "norm" of adult expectations may be diagnosed with ADD. Labelling a child's behaviour based on a set of "norms" is ludicrous since these qualities cannot accurately be measured, let alone defined. According to Thomas Armstrong, author of *The Myth of the ADD Child*, "Once the influential American Psychiatric Association (APA) declared ADD a disorder in 1980, the DSM defined it more and more broadly. . . . Increasing numbers of children are caught in the ever-widening definition net and are then labelled ADD" (914). According to psychologist Stephen P. Hinshaw, "There's clearly not a single cause of all cases of well-diagnosed ADHD" (qtd. in Bower 343). Other professionals agree that accurate diagnosis "remains elusive and controversial" (Koch 907).

As Mary was revising this paragraph, she realized she was forcing the reader to make connections between her sources and her argument because she was not providing explanations that made those connections. So she revised her paragraph, connecting her sources to her own ideas and making her argument clearer.

> (1) Many children today who do not fit the "norm" of adult expectations may be diagnosed with ADD. (2) Labelling a child's behaviour based on a set of "norms" is ludicrous since these qualities cannot accurately be measured, let alone defined. (3) According to Thomas Armstrong, author of *The Myth of the ADD Child*, "Once the influential American Psychiatric Association (APA) declared ADD a disorder in 1980, the DSM defined it more and more broadly. . . . (4) Increasing numbers of children are caught in the ever-widening definition net and are then labelled ADD" (914). (5) But even though we have a definition for this disorder, nobody really knows for sure what the disorder is. (6) According to psychologist Stephen P. Hinshaw, "There's clearly not a single cause of all cases of well-diagnosed ADHD" (qtd. in Bower 343). (7) Other professionals agree that accurate diagnosis "remains elusive and controversial" (Koch 907). (8) If our leading professionals in the field don't know what a "well-diagnosed" case is, how can we be sure that they even know what any case of ADHD is?

By adding the fifth sentence, "But even though we have a definition for this disorder, nobody really knows for sure what the disorder is," Mary explains the significance of the previous quotation and tells her readers what she wants them to be thinking about after they read it. Similarly, the last sentence in Mary's paragraph also clarifies the quotation before it. "If our leading professionals in the field don't know what a 'well-diagnosed' case is, how can we be sure that they even know what any case of ADHD is?" This sentence, which also acts as the paragraph's concluding sentence, shows readers that the professionals are arguing among themselves about the disease, so we should be careful about any diagnosis of it. Notice, also, how this last sentence provides a transition into Mary's discussion about the scarcity of reliable tests for ADHD.

To better understand how Mary's paragraph works, look at the following breakdown of her paragraph:

(1) Topic sentence

(2) Explanation of topic sentence

(3–4) Quotation from Source A, Thomas Armstrong (with Source A Works Cited information at end)

(5) Statement explaining the significance of Source A

(6) Quotation from Source B, Stephen P. Hinshaw (with Source B Works Cited information at end)

(7) Paraphrase and quotation from Source C, Kathy Koch (with Source C Works Cited information at end)

(8) Concluding sentence showing relevance of Sources B and C and providing a transition into the next paragraph

This outline of Mary's paragraph should help you see how her paragraph works as one unit that supports her main argument. If you get stuck writing your own paragraphs, referring back to this outline might help you see where you need to add information.

Before you get to this stage, however, you must think about what information you want to use from your sources and how you might present that information. The most difficult task when writing a research paper is deciding what to quote directly, what to paraphrase, and what to summarize. Once you have a tentative thesis statement, you can start working with your outside sources.

DIRECT QUOTATION, PARAPHRASE, AND SUMMARY

Now that you know how to incorporate your sources, you need to decide whether you will directly quote, paraphrase, or summarize them. This section explains these three options to you. We will begin with an original source and show how to take and acknowledge material from the original in different ways.

The following paragraph is from "When Kids Are Cruel" by Patricia Pearson. It was published in *Maclean's* magazine on May 3, 2004, on pages 49–53. The quoted passage is from page 49.

Original Source

> Clara knows that there is an adult label for kids who bug you: "bully." And like other children, she is eager to put her knowledge of adult labels to use. But, in the highly complicated universe of her elementary school, it is difficult to picture what adults actually mean by bully. From Clara's point of view, all children pick on each other, in one way or another. That is her experience. I ought to know this, because whenever I listen to conversations between little girls in her class, I can't decide whether to laugh or cry, they're so outrageously cutting.

Direct Quotation

If you use a direct quotation from another source, you must put the exact material you want to use in quotation marks:

> Patricia Pearson, in her essay "When Kids Are Cruel," states, "in the highly complicated universe of her elementary school, it is difficult to picture what adults actually mean by bully" (49).

Direct Quotation with Some Words Omitted

If you want to leave something out of the quotation, use three dots (with spaces before and after each dot). The omission of words is known as *ellipsis*.

> Patricia Pearson, in her essay "When Kids Are Cruel," states, "in. . . elementary school, it is difficult to picture what adults actually mean by bully" (49).

Paraphrase

When you paraphrase, you are restating the main ideas of a quotation in your own words. *Paraphrase* literally means "similar phrasing," so it is usually about the same length as the original. Paraphrasing is one of the most difficult skills to master in college, but one trick you can use is to read the material, put it aside, and write a sentence or two about what you think it said. Then compare what you wrote with the original to make sure they are relatively the same. If you look at the source while you are trying to paraphrase it, you might inadvertently take a word or phrase from the original.

Then, even though this information is in your own words, you still need to let your readers know where you found it. A paraphrase of our original source might look like this:

> Patricia Pearson, in her essay "When Kids Are Cruel," states that she could sense the confusion that her daughter has about bullying.

> Clara's elementary school world is a very complicated place where all the kids seem to pick on each other. The little girls in Clara's class often talk about each other, saying hurtful things (49).

Summary

When you summarize, you state the author's main idea in your own words. A summary is much briefer than the original or a paraphrase. As with a paraphrase, you need to cite in your paper where you found the information. Here is a summary of the original source:

> Patricia Pearson, in her essay "When Kids Are Cruel," describes several different perceptions of what bullying means to an adult and to a child (49).

TAKING NOTES ON SOURCES

As you consider using your sources as direct quotations, paraphrases, and summaries, you will need to keep careful track of them. For your Works Cited page (Modern Language Association documentation style), References page (American Psychological Association documentation style), or Bibliography page (*Chicago Manual of Style*), you will need to provide your reader with several items of information for each source you use. The best time to start keeping track of this information is when you are taking notes.

When you take notes, notecards are an excellent tool because you can move them around as your paper takes shape. Put only one idea on a notecard. Taking notes this way will save you a lot of time in the future because you won't be scrambling around looking for the information on the source you just quoted. Taking notes electronically is another option. Whatever your choice, if you cannot find the original source for some information that you used in your paper and therefore cannot tell your reader where you found the quotation, then you cannot use the material.

As you read your sources, you should consider whether you might want to directly quote, paraphrase, or summarize the material. A general rule to follow is that you never want to use more than 10 percent of directly quoted information, which means 90 percent of the outside information you use in your essay should be paraphrased or summarized. The best way to determine whether you should use direct quotations or not is by asking yourself a question: "Is this the best possible way to relay this information?" If the answer is yes, then you should use a direct quotation. In most cases, however, you should try to put your sources in your own words. Only occasionally should you use the author's exact words in your paper. So when you are reading and taking notes on your sources, you should keep this in mind.

To avoid plagiarism when taking notes and when writing your paper, write down all the information you need to cite a source both in your paper and on the Works Cited (MLA) or References (APA) page. For a book, you need the following information:

- Book title
- Author or authors
- City where the source was published
- Publisher
- Year of publication

For an article, you must include the following:

- Article title
- Author or authors
- Title of the magazine or journal
- Date of issue (for a magazine)
- Year and volume and issue number (for a journal)
- Pages on which the article appeared

If you put all this information on one card, you can use just the author's last name on all other cards from that source. If an author has more than one book or article, add the source's date to the card. For both books and articles, you should also always record the page where you found the information. That way you can find it again or cite it in your paper. The format in which this information should be presented may depend on the field of study. A good handbook will help you with the formats of the various documentation styles; these include Modern Language Association (MLA) style for the humanities, American Psychological Association (APA) style for the social sciences, and *Chicago Manual of Style* (CMS) style for humanities and science. Make sure you understand which documentation style your instructor wants you to use because they are all slightly different from each other.

In this book, we are illustrating both the Modern Language Association style of citation and the American Psychological Association style of citation. The Pearson essay in the MLA format looks like this:

Pearson, Patricia. "When Kids Are Cruel." Maclean's. 3 May 2004: 49–53.

Many professors also prefer that their students include the volume and issue number of the magazine, if available. With this information included, the Pearson essay in the MLA format looks like this:

Pearson, Patricia. "When Kids Are Cruel." Maclean's. 5 March 2004. 117:18. 49–53.

The Pearson essay in the APA format looks like this:

Pearson, P. (2004, March 5). When kids are cruel. *Maclean's 117*(18), 49–53.

PRACTICE 2 Quote from, paraphrase, and summarize the following original sources. Document the source correctly in each case by looking up the MLA or APA documentation style in a handbook.

1. The following paragraph is from "We Are Training Our Kids to Kill" by Dave Grossman. It was originally published in the *Saturday Evening Post* in July/August 1999 on pages 64–66, 68, 70, and 72. The quoted paragraph appeared on page 65.

    This virus of violence is occurring worldwide. The explanation for it has to be some new factor that is occurring in all of these countries. There are many factors involved, and none should be discounted: for example, the prevalence of guns in our society. But violence is rising in many nations with Draconian gun laws. And though we should never downplay child abuse, poverty, or racism, there is only one new variable present in each of these countries that bears the exact same fruit: media violence presented as entertainment for children.

    Quotation: ______________________________

    ____

    ____

    ____

    Paraphrase: ______________________________

    ____

    ____

    ____

    Summary: ______________________________

    ____

    ____

    ____

    Works Cited (MLA) or References (APA) Citation: ______________

    ____

    ____

    ____

2. The following paragraph is from "The Question" by Lawrence Hill. It was originally published in *Black Berry, Sweet Juice* by Vintage Canada/Random House. The quoted paragraph appeared on page 173.

    Canadians have a favourite pastime, and they don't even realize it. They like to ask—they absolutely have to ask—where you are from if you don't look convincingly white. They want to know it, need to know it, simply must have that information. They just can't relax until they have pinpointed, to their satisfaction, your geographic and racial coordinates. They can go almost out of their minds with curiosity, as when driven by the need for food, water, or sex, but once they've finally managed to find out precisely where you were born, who your parents were, and what your racial make-up is, then, man, do they feel better. They can breathe easy and get back to the business of living.

Quotation: ____

____

____

____

Paraphrase: ____

____

____

____

Summary: ____

____

____

____

Works Cited Citation (MLA) or References (APA) Citation: ______

____

____

____

3. The following paragraph is from "Why You Think You're Wonderful," by Brian Bethune. The quoted paragraph appeared in *Maclean's* magazine, October 5, 2006, on page 68.

    Fine divides up the tricks played by our loving organ into various categories. The so-called vain brain, for instance, is so preening that research has shown it finds the very letters of your name more attractive than other letters. It obscures the statistical improbability of near-universal ideas about the self (almost 100 percent of subjects rate themselves as better than average on any ordinary task like driving a car—a mathematically impossible outcome). Under the emotional brain, Fine cites tests that show how gut instinct makes many decisions that we think are reasoned. It's only after we've opted for one side of the question that our cognitive faculties—in a manner so smooth we don't notice which came first—provide the rationale.

Quotation: ____

____

____

____

Paraphrase: ____

____

____

____

Summary: ____

____

____

____

Works Cited (MLA) Citation or References (APA) Citation: ______

____

____

____

4. The following paragraph is from "Dare to Change Your Job and Your Life in 7 Steps" by Carole Kanchier. It was originally published in *Psychology Today*, in the March/April issue, in 2000, and the quoted passage appeared on page 64.

> A career change can take months or even years of soul-searching—10 months in Melissa's case. You need to know the steps, how to master the troublesome feelings that accompany change, where the possible dangers lie, and how to maximize your gains while minimizing your losses. While creating a life worth living isn't easy, Melissa and millions of others have shown that anything is possible.

Quotation: ____

____

____

____

Paraphrase: ____

____

____

____

Summary: ______________________________

____

____

____

Works Cited (MLA) Citation or References (APA) Citation: ______

____

____

____

5. The following paragraph is from "On Being Persuaded," an unpublished essay by Roy Geiger.

> The second appeal an argument makes is emotional. We often dislike acknowledging the role emotions like fear or desire play in our responses to argument. We may even feel sheepish or ashamed (Corbett 86), yet we cannot deny the visceral response. Rather than directly exhort us to accept an idea or position, emotional appeals often play on what we can see or imagine to instill or rouse feelings about that position. Further, a powerful piece like the Dove "Evolution" ad relies on the fact that exposure to marketing has trained us to accept and even be aroused by certain images of beauty. As with the work of the great American artist Cindy Sherman, the Dove ad catches us in the act of responding to the image of apparent beauty and makes us question ourselves. We watch the woman become more and more "beautiful," and we begin to think about just how fine she is starting to look. But then, aided by the increasing urgency of the soundtrack, we're caught short. We say, "Hey! I'm being shamelessly manipulated! And you're not allowing me to forget that fact!" In this ad, the appeals to emotions and reason work together in a cunning, irresistible way. We respond emotionally until our reason takes over and analyzes what is happening to us as we watch. We respond emotionally a second time with a sense of disappointment and sheepishness (that word, again). By the end we accept the ad's point intellectually, but we also feel distaste towards the cynical process we've been forced to acknowledge. We can't pretend we haven't been influenced by a very manipulative process.

Quotation: ______________________________

____

____

____

Paraphrase: ______________________________

____

____

____

Summary: ______________________________

____

Works Cited (MLA) Citation or Reference (APA) Citation: ______

____

____

____

CHAPTER 19

Finding Sources

No matter what you are studying, you should know how to find outside sources using the library through a computer. You can access an enormous amount of information that will help you generate paper topics, teach you new information, challenge your thinking, support your opinions, and make you smile. In today's electronic world, learning how to use the resources available through the library's services is a basic survival skill.

CREDIBILITY OF SOURCES

When you are looking for information to use in your essays, you must be careful about what you choose. Your sources must be relevant, reliable, and recent. This "three *R*s" approach to finding sources will help you locate convincing evidence to support your argument.

Since anyone can put material on the Internet, you need to make sure you are not using biased or unreliable information in your academic papers. To use websites intelligently, follow these four guidelines.

1. ***Check the end of a web URL address.*** It may be .com, .ca, .edu, .gov, or .org. The last four are generally reputable sources, but you must be very careful of .com sources because this stands for "communication," and anyone can purchase a .com site. For example, **www.primeministerhome.com** is *not* a site for the Prime Minister's home, as you might suspect. On the other hand, .edu stands for "education,".gov for "government," and .org for "organization." But any site has the potential for bias, and you should consider the material carefully.
2. ***Pay attention to the argument a site makes.*** Who is the author and what is his or her purpose for entering information on the site? If you log onto a Martin Luther King Jr. site and are inundated with racial slurs, chances are you've found a site that was created by a faction of the Ku Klux Klan. If the argument does not fit the site or if the author has an obvious agenda, avoid the site altogether.
3. ***Make sure the site is providing fact and not opinion.*** For academic purposes, facts and evidence are generally more useful than opinions. If you are looking for a site that deals with teen suicide, you'll want to avoid the site that tells you story after story about innocent children dying, but fails to give you any specific information. Instead, you'll want to find a site that gives you examples that can be verified and supported with statistics.

4. ***Does the site provide any information about the other side of the argument?*** If a site provides you with details only about its own viewpoint, you should wonder why it is omitting information. If you find a site on breakfast in schools and see opinions only about why breakfast should be provided in schools, you should be curious about why they don't present the other side's argument. Will facts about the other side make you change your mind? The best sites provide both sides of an argument that so the source can, in turn, show why one side is more valid than the other. If you find a website that does not offer balanced information, consider it biased, and avoid the site.

These four guidelines will help you determine whether or not you should use information you find on the web. But if you want to be certain the information you are using will be acceptable to your instructor, you should stick with academic sources. These sources are different from other sources because they have been "refereed" or "reviewed." This means the authors of the essays send them to the publication and the editors of the publication send the essays anonymously to readers for review. If the readers accept the pieces for publication, they consider the essays to be well-researched and worth reading. If you can, you should use only these sources. The best place to find them is also online, as you will see in the following section.

CONSULTING ONLINE DATABASES, FULL-TEXT INDEXES, AND ELECTRONIC JOURNAL COLLECTIONS

The best places to begin searching for outside sources are online databases, full-text indexes, and electronic journal collections. You should have access to these services from home through your library's homepage or from a computer in your library. We will discuss each type of source separately. You may need a reference librarian to help you find these for the first time.

Online Databases

Online databases can direct you to an incredible number of books and journals on a wide range of subjects. The following are some online indexes found in SilverPlatter's WebSPIRS database, which is an information retrieval system that contains indexes on many different subjects and is used by many libraries.

Index	Primary Use
Biological and Agriculture Index	Science
ERIC	Education
GeoRef	Geology
MLA	Literature, language, and linguistics
Philosopher's Index	Philosophy
Sociological Abstracts	Sociology

Full-Text Indexes

The following indexes take you directly to complete journal articles online. In other words, you can print out the journal articles you find, right from your own computer.

Index	Primary Use
ABI Inform	News and business
Dow Jones	News and business
EBSCOhost*	Many subject areas
Expanded Academic ASAP*	General information in several disciplines
HRAF	Ethnographies
Lexis-Nexis	News, business, and law
WilsonWeb*	Popular magazines and newspapers, social sciences, humanities, business, general science, and education journals

*Not all articles will be available in full text.

Electronic Journal Collections

Electronic journal collections are similar to online databases in that you can print out complete journal articles directly from your own computer. The following collections might help you find information on the topic you have chosen.

Collection	Primary Use
Academic Press's IDEAL	Articles published by academic publishers
American Chemical Society's Web Editions	American Chemical Society's 26 scientific journals
American Mathematical Journals	American Mathematical Society's proceedings and transactions
JSTOR	Back issues of core journals in the humanities, social sciences, and sciences
Project Muse	Humanities, social sciences, and math

Once you access an online database, index, or collection, you can easily find articles and books on your topic. You can do online searches by author, title, or subject; since you will most likely be looking for articles on a topic, you will use the subject function most often. When you are searching for a title by subject, you should be aware of *Boolean connectors* or *operators*, which are shortcuts to help you narrow the search field.

Using Boolean Connectors or Operators

The Boolean connectors or operators for requesting a search are *AND*, *OR*, and *NOT*. By using these words, you can limit the search and find information directly related to your topic. If you type "AND" between your key words (for example, *TV AND violence*), you are asking the computer to combine the key words for the search. If you put "OR" between the key words (*TV OR video games*), you are separating the words and asking the computer to find articles and books with either one of them. If you add "NOT" (*TV NOT video games*), you limit the search by excluding certain terms from the search.

Accessing Sources

Once you type your topic into the search function of a database, index, or journal collection, the computer will display the number of articles and books it has found in a "results list." Following are some examples of articles found on the topic of *television AND violence* in an online database, a full-text index, and an electronic journal collection.

From an Online Database

Record 40 of 313 in *Sociological Abstracts* [in WebSPIRS] 1986-2001/06
TI: The National Television Violence Studies
AU: Chaffee, -Steven
IN: Stanford U, CA 94305
SO: Journal of Communications; 1997, 47, 4, autumn, 170-173.
DT: aja Abstract-of-Journal-Article
AB: A review essay on books by four university research teams—U California (Santa Barbara), U North Carolina (Chapel Hill), U Texas (Austin), & U Wisconsin (Madison)—(1) National **Television Violence** Study, Vol. 1 (Thousand Oaks, CA: Sage, 1997); & National **Television Violence** Study, Vol. 1. & Vol. 2 (Thousand Oaks, CA: Sage, 1997 & 1998, respectively). These works report on recent university studies of TV **violence** in diverse sectors of the US. The Executive Summary provides an overview of the project & policy recommendations & is appropriate for parents & teachers. The two main volumes present the coding system for **violence,** the effects of ratings & antiviolence advertising, & content analysis based on earlier literature. It is concluded that this team effort offers much useful information for the study of TV **violence,** & presents the studies in such a way that they can be easily replicated. 3 References. M. Cella
DEM: ***Television** (D859500); *Mass-Media-**Violence** (D497700); *Communication-Research (D151900); *Programming-Broadcast (D668400)
AN: 9904482

From a Full-Text Index

Entry 17 of 99 (from the Social Science Index in WilsonWeb)
Formichelli, L. *Programming behavior* [restricting violent **television** programming during hours when children may be watching] *Psychology Today* v. 34 no. 1 (January/February 2001) p. 10

From an Electronic Journal Collection

2. Warning: The Surgeon General Has Determined That TV Violence Is Moderately Dangerous to Your Child's Mental Health

Leo Bogart

Public Opinion Quarterly, Vol. 36, No. 4. (Winter, 1972–1973), pp. 491–521.
[Citation/Abstract] [View Article] [Page of First Match] [Print] [Download]

Notice that these examples contain all the information you need for citing those works in the text and at the end of your paper. So make sure you keep lists like this when you print them so that you can cite your sources correctly.

PRACTICE 1 For each of the following topics, find a book from an online database, an article from a full-text index, and an article from an electronic journal source. Record the title and the database, index, or source where you found it.

Example: Topic: Violence and TV
Database: Sociological Abstracts—in WebSPIRS
Title: *The National Television Violence Studies*
Index: Social Science Index in WilsonWeb
Title: *Programming Behavior*
Electronic Journal: JSTOR
Title: *Warning: The Surgeon General Has Determined That TV Violence Is Moderately Dangerous to Your Child's Mental Health*

1. Topic: Drug testing in college sports

   Database: ______________________________

   Title: ______________________________

   Index: ______________________________

   Title: ______________________________

   Electronic journal: ______________________________

   Title: ______________________________

2. Topic: Overtime and the workforce

Database: ____________________

Title: ____________________

Index: ____________________

Title: ____________________

Electronic journal: ____________________

Title: ____________________

3. Topic: Fish farming

Database: ____________________

Title: ____________________

Index: ____________________

Title: ____________________

Electronic journal: ____________________

Title: ____________________

4. Topic: Women in combat

Database: ____________________

Title: ____________________

Index: ____________________

Title: ____________________

Electronic journal: ____________________

Title: ____________________

5. Topic: Using animals for testing

Database: ____________________

Title: ____

Index: ____

Title: ____

Electronic journal: ______________________________________

Title: ____

SEARCHING FOR WEBSITES

To find a website related to your topic, you should go to the Internet through whichever browser you have (Netscape Communicator or Navigator, Microsoft Internet Explorer, etc.). Your browser probably has a search engine of its own that will let you search the Internet. Or you might want to use a search engine that automatically refers you to sites related to your topic: Both **www.google.com** and **www.dogpile.com** are examples of search engines that can save you a lot of time. For example, **www.google.com** searches millions of websites in mere seconds and is an excellent source for research.

Once you access a search engine, type in your topic as if you were searching a database. Most search engines will then begin helping you narrow your search and will provide a list of other possible topics. Here are some examples for the topic of *violence and television.*

Topic	Other Possible Topics
Violence and television	Television programs and violence
	On TV violence
	Television violence
	TV violence and children
	Violence on television
	Causes of TV violence
	Media violence

When the search is complete, your search engine will list the different websites in the order it thinks they will be most helpful to you. It will also briefly describe each website. After the description, you will most often find the website address. The following are the first three "hits" or websites from **www.dogpile.com** for the topic *violence and television*.

1. National Coalition on TV Violence

    Learn about the effects of TV violence and facts about theV-Chip, and get ideas to help kids avoid violent entertainment.

    www.nctvv.org

2. American Psych. Association—Violence on Television

   Association investigates the effect of television violence on children and discusses ways parents can intervene to minimize its impact.

   www.apa.org

3. APA HelpCenter: Warning Signs of Teen Violence

   The American Psychological Association and MTV team up to get important information to the nation's youth about warning signs of violent behaviour, including violence in schools. The Warning Signs site provides a violence prevention guide and resource.

   helping.apa.org

PRACTICE 2 For each of the following topics, find a different webpage through a different search engine, and list the webpage title, the explanation, and the web address.

Example: Topic: Violence and television

Search engine: GoTo.com through dogpile.com

Webpage title: Center for Educational Priorities: Two Studies

Explanation: Read brief overview of the 1996 National Violence Study and the 1995 UCLA Television Violence Monitoring Report

Web address: **www.cep.org**

1. Topic: Bilingual education in Nunavut

   Search engine: ______________________________

   Webpage title: ______________________________

   Explanation: ______________________________

   Web address: ______________________________

2. Topic: Benefits of the Canadian space program

   Search engine: ______________________________

   Webpage title: ______________________________

   Explanation: ______________________________

   Web address: ______________________________

3. Topic: Legalizing marijuana

   Search engine: ______________________________

   Webpage title: ______________________________

   Explanation: ______________________________

   Web address: ______________________________

4. Topic: Homeopathic medicine

   Search engine: ______________________________

   Webpage title: ______________________________

   Explanation: ______________________________

   Web address: ______________________________

5. Topic: Women's soccer

   Search engine: ______________________________

   Webpage title: ______________________________

   Explanation: ______________________________

   Web address: ______________________________

USING THE LIBRARY

Once you have compiled a list of books and journals from databases and indexes or from websites, you should use your library to check out books or copy journal articles that were not available online. First, you need to access your library's online catalogue to see if your library has the book. (If your library does not have computers, use the traditional card catalogue.) Ask a librarian how to access your particular catalogue through your school. You might also ask if this information is available online. You can search for authors and subjects through your library's catalogue in much the same way as you would search online databases or program search engines. But since you have already done the preliminary research, all you have to do is search for the books and journals you need. Find the "title" section of the catalogue, and type in the title of the book or journal you need in this section. For help finding books and journals in the library, ask a librarian.

If you are searching for a chapter or an essay contained in a book, be sure to type in the main book title. For example, if you searched for "I Just Wanna Be Average" (by Mike Rose), your library computer will tell you that the library does not carry it. You must type in the title of the book it came from, *Lives on the Boundary*, to find the essay. Once you have located the titles of your books or journals in the library's catalogue, you should write down the call numbers so that you can find the sources in your library. Then it's just a matter of finding the book itself in the stacks of your library.

PRACTICE 3 Find five books from your research, and using the "title" portion of your library's catalogue, locate the call numbers.

Example: **Title:** *Youth Culture: Identity in a Postmodern World*

Call number: HV 1431 Y684 1998

1. Title: ______________________

   Call number: ______________________

2. Title: ______________________

   Call number: ______________________

3. Title: ______________________

   Call number: ______________________

4. Title: ______________________

   Call number: ______________________

5. Title: ______________________

   Call number: ______________________

CHAPTER 20

How to Write a Research Paper

A research paper is really just an essay with supporting material that comes from outside sources. This type of writing assignment has all the elements of a typical essay. The following chart compares a standard essay and a research paper.

Standard Essay		Research Paper
Introduction with thesis statement	⟷	Introduction with thesis statement
Body paragraphs with facts and personal experience to support thesis statement	⟷	Body paragraphs with documented evidence to support thesis statement
Concluding paragraph	⟷	Concluding paragraph

Keep this outline in mind as you read about how to construct a good research paper. Laying out some clear guidelines is the best place to start.

1. ***Choose a subject.*** You might be choosing a subject from infinite possibilities or working with an assigned topic. Doing some general reading online or in the library is often necessary to get you started. As you consider various topics, you must ask one very important question before you begin planning your essay: Will you be able to find enough information to back up your thesis statement? To make sure you will be able to find enough material to use as good evidence in the body paragraphs of your essay, you must do a good job of choosing a subject, narrowing down that subject, and then writing a working thesis statement. You will prove this thesis statement with the information you find when you search for sources on your topic. If you were writing a research paper on pursuing an applied degree in college, for example, your initial prewriting for the thesis statement might look like this:

    General Subject: College programs

    More Specific: Applied degree

    More Specific: Applied degree in land planning

This limited subject would be perfect for a research paper. You could search for books, catalogues, and periodicals on what it takes to earn a bachelor's degree in land planning from various colleges and universities. While you are looking, you could be thinking about how to narrow down your subject even further.

Mary Minor (in Chapter 17) might have started with a general topic like "childhood disorders," limited it to "childhood behavioural disorders," and finally settled on "ADD and ADHD as childhood behavioural disorders."

PRACTICE 1 Choose a topic from the list on page 340. Why did you choose this topic?

PRACTICE 2 Limit this topic so that you can write a paper about five pages long.

2. ***Write a good, clear thesis statement about your subject.*** Just as a thesis statement is the controlling idea of an essay, a thesis statement also provides the controlling idea for your argument in a research paper. This statement will guide the writing of your entire paper. Your course assignments will usually be broad topics. To compose a good research paper, you need to narrow a broad topic to an idea that you can prove within a limited number of pages. A working thesis statement will provide the direction for your essay, and the evidence you collect in your research is what proves the thesis statement.

   A good way to start your first draft is to read some general sources on your topic. This reading will help you discover the range of your subject and will guide you toward a thesis. Before you start writing the first draft of your paper, make sure you write a sentence that clearly states your topic and your position on that topic. This is your working thesis statement and will be the controlling idea for your entire paper. Your thesis statement may change several times before your essay is finished, but making this statement and taking a position is a necessary first step. It will help you move from the broad subject of your assignment to your own perspective on the topic. This will also help you focus your essay and save you time in your search for good resources to back up your thesis statement.

   Just as in a standard essay, the thesis statement in your research paper is a contract between you and your readers. The thesis statement tells your readers what the main idea of your essay will be and sets guidelines for the paragraphs in the body of your essay. If you don't deliver what your thesis statement promises, your readers will be disappointed. The thesis statement is usually the last sentence in the introduction. It outlines your purpose and position on the essay's general topic and gives the reader an idea of the type of resources that you will use to develop your essay.

Mary Minor's controlling idea or thesis statement appears at the end of her first paragraph:

> Children are often misdiagnosed with ADD or ADHD and suffer unnecessarily when medicated for a disorder they may not have.

Her entire essay is about children who are too readily diagnosed with ADD or ADHD simply because they do not fall into society's "norm" for children's behaviour. The paragraphs following this thesis statement supply evidence that proves that her claim is true.

PRACTICE 3 List your thoughts and opinions on the topic you chose in Practice 1.

PRACTICE 4 Put your topic and your position on that topic into a working thesis statement.

3. ***Find sources that are relevant, reliable, and recent to support your thesis statement.*** The thesis statement of a research paper is really only the beginning. To convince your readers that what you say in your essay is worth reading, you must support your thesis statement with evidence. The evidence of a research paper lies in the sources that you use to back up your thesis statement. The sources must be relevant, reliable, and recent. This "three *R*s" approach to supporting evidence in a research paper will help you write a solid essay with convincing evidence.

   Mary's thesis statement suggests that young children are being too readily diagnosed with ADD and ADHD. To convince her readers that her thesis is correct, she uses a book, scientific journals, an encyclopedia, online journal articles, and general-circulation magazines as sources of evidence. Here is a breakdown of how she used her sources.

   - **Book:** *The Myth of the ADD Child*

     This source provides well-researched information from an expert's point of view. Mary uses this source early in her paper to help define the scope of her study.

   - **Scientific journals:** *CQ Researcher, Science News, Qualitative Health Research, American Journal of Public Health*

     These sources supply the reader with specific evidence put forth by experts in the field of ADD and ADHD research and diagnosis. Mary uses this information to prove that her thesis statement is true.

   - **Encyclopedia:** *World Book Encyclopedia*

     Mary uses this source to provide the reader with an understandable definition of the Hippocratic Oath. This definition plays an important role in Mary's stance on her topic.

- **Online journal articles:** *Clinical Reference Systems*

  The article from this source was printed from WilsonWeb. The information in this article defines hyperactivity in children for the general reader.

- **General-circulation magazines:** *U.S. News and World Report, Camping Magazine, Time, Runner's World, Maclean's*

  These sources supply information readily available at a newsstand, yet highly informative and applicable to Mary's topic. Information from articles in these magazines speaks to the average citizen. Even though these magazines are not scientific journals, the evidence in them is extremely useful because it is intended to make specialized information understandable to the general reader.

Mary Minor uses sources in her essay that do a thorough job of supporting her thesis statement. The information from her chosen book, journals, encyclopedia, and magazines speaks to the average citizen. Even though they are not highly technical scientific sources, the evidence in them is relevant, reliable, and recent, which are the same guidelines you should use when looking for your sources.

PRACTICE 5 Review Chapter 18 to make sure that you understand the options available to you for finding sources to use in your essay.

PRACTICE 6 Find five sources that give you information about the limited topic that you chose. Make sure they are relevant, reliable, and recent.

4. ***Take notes to avoid plagiarism.*** Now is the time to read your sources and take careful notes—putting the ideas in your own words or putting the writer's words in quotation marks if you record the exact words. You should also note the page numbers of all information you take down. If you don't take notes carefully, you will never be able to trace information that you want to use in your paper to its original source. Also, trying to put someone's ideas into your own words is a very good skill that will help you as you are writing.

   Taking notes on notecards will allow you to move your cards around and put ideas into different paragraphs. When you rearrange cards, you can work with them until you think the order will support what you are trying to prove. This notecard method saves you time in the long run.

   Mary Minor had to read and take notes on all the sources she found. She first made a set of bibliography cards with a notecard for every source she found. For the books, she put book title, author, city where published, publisher, and year of publication on each card; for the articles, she recorded article title, author, title of the magazine or journal, date of issue or volume and issue numbers, and page numbers of the article on each card. Then she began to read her sources. She wrote only one idea or quotation on a notecard, and she remembered to record on each notecard the author's name and the page number on which she found the information. She also made sure, as she took notes, to restate information in her own words or else put the author's exact words in quotation marks.

PRACTICE 7 Review Chapter 18 to make sure you understand what plagiarism is and how to avoid it.

PRACTICE 8 Read and take notes on your sources using notecards. Make sure each of your cards has a source and page number on it.

5. ***Make a working outline of your paper.*** To do this, you just need to start rearranging the notecards you have made. Start by putting all your notecards into small stacks of related ideas. Which ideas will work well together? Which should you put in the introduction? Which do you want to save for your conclusion? When you get all your notecards in stacks, label each group of cards according to its topic. These labels will then become the topics of your paper. You are now ready to start your working outline.

   A good way to begin a working outline is to write your tentative thesis statement at the top of a page and then list the topics you have developed under that thesis. These topics should be arranged in some logical order that will help you prove your main point and is easy to follow. Each topic should also directly support your thesis statement. Leave room in your outline to add subtopics and details throughout the paper. This outline then becomes a guide for your writing. It will change and grow with every paragraph that you add to your paper.

   Mary started developing her paper by putting related notecards into stacks. Next, she labelled her stacks of notecards and started organizing these topics in different ways until they started making sense to her. Her list of topics, with her thesis statement at the top, became the bulk of her working outline. She eventually turned these topics into topic sentences for her body paragraphs. The stack of cards for each topic became the content of her body paragraphs.

PRACTICE 9 Divide your notecards into topics that logically support your thesis statement. Then label each stack of cards.

PRACTICE 10 Start a working outline of your paper by listing your thesis statement and your supporting topics.

6. ***Construct an introduction that leads up to your thesis statement.*** The introduction to a research paper is your chance to make a great first

impression. Just like a firm handshake and a warm smile in a job interview, an essay's introduction should capture your readers' interest, set the tone for your essay, and state your specific purpose. Introductions often have a funnel effect. They typically begin with general information and then narrow the focus to your position on a particular issue. Regardless of your method, your introduction should "hook" your readers by grabbing their attention and letting them know what you are going to try to prove in your essay.

To lead up to the thesis statement, your introductory paragraph must stimulate your readers' interest. Some effective ways of capturing your audience's attention and giving necessary background information are (1) to use a quotation; (2) to tell a story that relates to your topic; (3) to provide a revealing fact, statistic, or definition; (4) to offer an interesting comparison; or (5) to ask an intriguing question. Be sure your introduction gives readers all the information they may need to follow your train of thought through the rest of your paper.

Mary's introduction starts out by noting the shifting "norms" that exist around early childhood development. The paragraph then discusses parents' confusion with their children's behaviour and introduces ADD and ADHD. The last sentence of the first paragraph contains Mary's thesis statement and ends the introduction.

PRACTICE 11 Make a rough outline of your ideas for a possible introduction to your research paper.

PRACTICE 12 Write a rough draft of your introduction, ending with your thesis statement.

7. ***Develop as many supporting paragraphs or body paragraphs as you think are necessary to explain your thesis statement.*** Following the introductory paragraph, a research paper includes several body paragraphs that support and explain the essay's thesis statement. Each body paragraph covers a topic that is directly related to the thesis statement.

   Supporting paragraphs, or body paragraphs, usually include a topic sentence, which is a general statement of the paragraph's contents, and examples or details that support the topic sentence. (See Chapter 6 for methods to use when you develop and organize paragraphs.)

   To write your supporting paragraphs, you should first organize your notecards within each of your stacks. Next, add the details from these cards to your working outline. Then write your supporting paragraphs by following your working outline and your notecards. Make adjustments in your outline as you write so that you can keep track of your ideas and make sure you are developing them in a logical order. The body of the paper and your outline should change and develop together with each sentence that you write.

After you write your body paragraphs, you should look at your thesis statement again to make sure it introduces what you say in the rest of your paper. Your thesis statement should refer to all of your topics, even if only indirectly, in the same order you discuss them in. It should also prepare your readers for the conclusions you are going to come to.

Mary's paper contains eight body paragraphs, each making a separate point that is directly related to her thesis:

Paragraph	Point
2	ADD and ADHD are defined as "a short attention span" and are the most commonly diagnosed childhood diseases.
3	Diagnosing children who do not fit a "norm" is ludicrous, especially since there is no accurate definition or diagnosis of ADD or ADHD.
4	No physical exam can determine that a child has ADD or ADHD.
5	There are as many theories about the causes of ADD as there are experts, so we are only treating the symptoms of these disorders.
6	Teachers, parents, and students get caught up in the diagnosis.
7	Drugs should only be a short-term answer to the hyperactive child.
8	No proof is available that says we over-prescribe drugs for children.
9	Long-term use of drugs for ADD and ADHD is potentially dangerous.

Like the foundation of a solid building, these paragraphs provide support for the position Mary takes in her thesis statement. The stronger the supporting paragraphs are, the stronger the paper will be.

In addition to strong topic sentences, you should use concluding sentences in your body paragraphs to help reinforce your thesis statement or build a transition to the next paragraph. Concluding sentences wrap up a paragraph just as a conclusion wraps up an essay, and using concluding sentences lets you remind your readers what you are arguing and where you are in your reasoning.

PRACTICE 13 Organize the notecards within each of your stacks so that they make sense. Add these details to your working outline.

PRACTICE 14 Write a rough draft of your body paragraphs. Remember that you will be revising and editing this draft a little later, so just concentrate on getting your ideas written up in an organized way. Revise your thesis statement, if necessary, to introduce all your body paragraphs.

8. ***Make sure you use your sources as evidence for your argument.*** Although your argument will evolve as you read your sources, you should decide on a general position on your topic before you begin to take notes. Don't write your essay around your sources, because your essay may become very disjointed and difficult to follow if you do. You should find appropriate sources to help you develop your argument. To heighten their effect, tell your reader the significance of the direct quotations, paraphrases, or summaries that you use. Look, for example, at one of the paragraphs in Mary's paper:

> Despite major controversy in the medical field, however, there has been no proof that drugs are being over-prescribed . . . Some experts even feel that children may be under-treated (Koch 912). No studies have been found that would prove one claim over the other, which again means that each child is treated according to the most popular opinion. As a result, "Students who were younger than their classmates were 21 times more likely to be medicated" for ADD or ADHD (920). With a statistic like this, it's astonishing that experts disagree on this subject.

Notice how Mary does not stop with her source's remarks. Instead, she includes a point about the significance of what each source says. She reminds her readers that she is arguing against drugging young children unnecessarily.

If you simply provide a series of quotations and let them argue for you, you are not demonstrating your understanding of the quotations or showing how they fit into your argument. Make sure that you use the quotations as support for your argument and do not let them stand for the argument itself.

PRACTICE 15 Consider the different ways your sources will support your argument. Organize them in a way that best helps you prove your main point.

PRACTICE 16 Write your body paragraphs using your sources as evidence in your argument. Be careful not to choose sources haphazardly to include in your body paragraphs. You need to have a reason for using each of your sources.

9. ***Write a concluding paragraph.*** The concluding paragraph is the final paragraph of an essay. In its most basic form, it should summarize the main points of the essay and remind readers of the thesis statement.

The best conclusions expand on these two basic requirements and bring the essay to a close with one of these creative strategies: (1) Ask a question that provokes thought on the part of the reader, (2) predict the future, (3) offer a solution to a problem, or (4) call the reader to action. Each of these options sends a specific message and creates a slightly different effect at the end of the paper. The most important responsibility of the last paragraph is to bring the essay to an effective close. It is the last information that readers see before they form their own opinions or take action.

Mary's conclusion offers a solution to the problem raised in the second sentence of the paragraph:

> Every effort should be made to find the cause of the "real" medical problems underlying ADD and ADHD before we even think about giving our children drugs.

Toward the end of her conclusion, she calls the reader to action:

> It's time to say goodbye to "conformist" . . . classrooms and diagnoses.

She ends by reflecting on her thesis in one last, short line:

> People don't fit "norms"; they have personalities.

Her concluding paragraph refocuses the reader's attention on the problem, offers a solution to the problem, and then calls the reader to action.

PRACTICE 17 Make a rough outline of your ideas for a possible conclusion to your research paper. Choose a strategy that you want to use to bring your paper to a close.

PRACTICE 18 Write a rough draft of your conclusion, reminding your readers of your thesis statement.

10. ***Think of a catchy title.*** Your title is what readers see first in any essay. A title is a phrase, usually no more than a few words, placed at the beginning of your essay that suggests or sums up the subject, purpose, or focus of the essay. Some titles are very imaginative, drawing on different sources for their meaning. Others are straightforward, like the title of this chapter—"How to Write a Research Paper." These are just two of the many different approaches you can take to creating a title.

    Besides suggesting an essay's purpose, a good title catches an audience's attention. For instance, Mary Minor's title, "Children as Robots," will catch most readers' attention because referring to children as "robots" is intriguing, and readers will want to find out just how and why this might occur. That's exactly what a title should do—make your readers want to read your paper.

PRACTICE 19 Jot down some catchy titles for your paper.

PRACTICE 20 Choose a title for your paper.

11. ***Check your sources and documentation format throughout your paper and at the end.*** Finding and using good, solid sources for evidence in a research paper is important, and equally important is the acknowledgment of those sources. If you use a source and do not cite it correctly or forget to cite it altogether, you are guilty of plagiarism, which can lead to a failing grade on the paper. So you need to learn when to cite a source (see Chapter 18), what documentation style to use (MLA, APA, or other appropriate format), and how to cite sources. You should check with your instructor to find out which format you should use in a particular course.

    Citations are of two types: (a) The *in-text citation* indicates the source of a quotation or idea right after it appears in the essay; (b) then, at the end, a list of all the sources cited in the paper must appear on the Works Cited (MLA style) or References (APA style) page. Many textbooks demonstrate the various forms of documentation, so you should look up the format that your instructor wants you to use. Then keep this text handy when you write papers with sources.

    Mary's essay has been done in both the MLA and the APA style of documentation. Often, English instructors ask their students to use the MLA format because the date of the work studied is not important. English instructors often have their students writing about works that were done centuries ago, such as Shakespeare. Science and Social Science instructors often have their students write in APA format because the date of the publication is highlighted. Including the date in the in-text citations shows how current the research is. Data in Science and Social Science is constantly changing and may become outdated. Mary includes a variety of sources in her paper, which we can use to illustrate the two types of citations. Listed here are some sample entries at the end of Mary's paper, with the corresponding in-text citations in parentheses.

Book (MLA)—Author's surname, given name. *Title of Book.* City of publication: publisher, year of publication.

Works Cited (MLA):	**Armstrong, Thomas. *The Myth of the ADD Child: 50 Ways to Improve Your Child's Behavior and Attention Span Without Drugs, Labels, or Coercion.* New York: Dutton, 1995.**
In-Text Citation:	**(Armstrong 914).**

Book (APA)—last name, initial. (Year). *Title in sentence format: Subtitle too.* City of publication: publisher.

References (APA): Armstrong, T. (1995). ***The myth of the ADD child: 50 ways to improve your child's behaviour and attention span without drugs, labels or coercion.*** **New York: Dutton.**

In-Text Citation: **(Armstrong, 1995, p. 914).**

Note: Notice how Mary introduced Armstrong before providing readers with this page number, so she doesn't have to repeat the author's name in the citation.

Note: The APA style's title is done in sentence format. This means you capitalize only the first word and any proper nouns.

Journal (MLA)—Author's surname, given name. "Title of Article." *Name of Journal* vol. no. (year): page number.

Works Cited (MLA): **Bower, Bruce. "Kid's Attention Disorder Attracts Concern."** ***Science News*** **154 (1998): 343.**

In-Text Citation: **(Bower 343).**

Journal (APA)—Author's surname, first initial. (year). Title of article. *Name of journal, vol. no.,* page number.

References (APA): **Bower, B. (1998). Kid's attention disorder attracts concern.** ***Science News, 154,*** **p. 343.**

In-Text Citation: **(Bower, 1998, p. 343).**

Entry in Encyclopedia (MLA)—Author's surname, given name. "Title of Article." *Name of Encyclopedia.* Vol. number. Year ed.

Works Cited: **"Hippocratic Oath."** ***World Book Encyclopedia.*** **Vol. 9. 1999 ed.**

In-Text Citation: **("Hippocratic Oath").**

Entry in Encyclopedia (APA): —Author's surname, initial(s). (year). Title of Article. In *Title of encyclopedia.* (Vol. number, p. number[s]). City of publication: publisher.

References (APA): **Hippocratic Oath. (1999). In** ***World book encyclopedia*** **(Vol. 9, p. 239). Chicago: World Book, Inc.**

In-Text Citation: **(Hippocratic Oath, 1999).**

Note: If an entry is unsigned, begin with the title and year.

Online Database (MLA)—Author's surname, given name. "Title of article." *Name of Database.* Day month year of publication. Day month year you accessed the material. <url in angle brackets>.

Works Cited: **Schmitt, Barton. D. "Attention Deficit Disorder (Short Attention Span)."** ***Clinical Reference Systems.*** **1 July 1999. 17 Feb. 2000 <http://www.epnet.com/ehost/login.html>.**

In-Text Citation: **(Schmitt).**

Online Database (APA)—Author's surname, initial(s). (year, month day of publication). Title of article. *Name of Database.* Retrieved Month day, year from URL.

References (APA): **Schmitt, B. D. (1999, July 1). Attention Deficit Disorder (short attention span). *Clinical Reference Systems.* Retrieved Feb. 17, 2000 from <http://www.epnet.com/ehpst/login.html>.**

Note: If some information required in the citation is missing, include whatever is available.

General-Circulation Magazine (MLA)—Author's surname, given name. "Title of Article." *Name of magazine.* day month year of publication: page number(s), no "pp."

Works Cited: **Sheppard, Robert. "Growing Up Hyperactive." *Maclean's* 7 Sept. 1998: 45–46.**

In-Text Citation: **(Sheppard 45)**

General-Circulation Magazine (APA)—Author's surname, initial(s). (year, month day). Title of articlel. *Name of magazine. pp. numbers.*

References (APA): **Sheppard, R. (1998, Sept. 7). Growing up hyperactive. *Maclean's.* 45–46.**

Note: If an article is unsigned, begin with the title of the article.

These examples from Mary Minor's essay are just a few of the various types of sources that you will probably use in your essays with sources. Every source is cited in a slightly different way, depending on the type of source and the documentation style. Not even the best writers know the correct format for every source they use. So when you have chosen your sources and determined that they are relevant, reliable, and recent (the three *R*s), your last step is to consult an appropriate, current manual or website to make sure you cite each source correctly.

PRACTICE 21 Make sure that the material from every source in your essay has an in-text citation. Then create a Works Cited, References, or Bibliography page, following an approved documentation format.

PRACTICE 22 Check the format of your in-text citations and your list of works cited or references by consulting a current handbook.

Revising and Editing a Research Paper

CHAPTER

21

In this chapter, you will revise and edit a new student research paper and then revise and edit your own. Refer to the checklists on the inside front and back covers, and the chapter will guide you through this process step by step.

REVISING AND EDITING A STUDENT RESEARCH PAPER

Here is the first draft of an essay written by Rick Schroeder, a student. It demonstrates the guidelines for writing a successful research paper that you have learned in Chapters 17 through 20. He has used MLA format for his essay. If required by your instructor, what would you change to put the essay into APA style?

Space Bucks

1 Every year an enormous amount of money is poured into NASA for space exploration. Does this research justify the expense? Many people would gratefully sacrifice the money just to prove that Americans can compete in the space arena. An overwhelming force drives us into the unknown realms of our universe in the same way that Christopher Columbus was adventurously driven to search for what was once called the New World. On the other hand, many taxpayers believe that more justification is needed for the large amount of money put into NASA research. But what these "non-supporters" tend to overlook is NASA's chance "to lead the exploration and development of the space frontier, advancing science, technology, enterprise, and building institutions and systems that make accessible vast new resources" (United States). NASA is a worthwhile organization that many people benefit from.

2 Most significantly, technology research that results from space exploration greatly benefit the field of medicine. The International Space Station (ISS), which was built by 16 different nations, is one of the biggest and most costly projects that NASA has constructed and is essential for research in space technology. Scientists aboard the ISS have the opportunity to test various theories and conduct experiments in several different fields of science using the microgravity on this station in space (NASA *Space Station*). Some of the most important research that will be done onboard the ISS involves searching for cures for both osteoporosis and cancer (Von Brook, Siegel, and Foster 67). Also, according to Von Brook, Siegel, and Foster, the authors of *Space Exploration: The Dream and the Reality*, some additional examples of "space-pioneer medical technology include a cardiac pacemaker that can be automatically recharged without surgery, a human tissue simulator that relieves chronic pain, anti-contamination hospital garments, X-rays that can penetrate bone and produce pictures of body tissues and organs," and several other advances in autism, diabetes, heart disease, and premature birth (69). These are just a few of the contributions from space exploration that help improve the quality of life for humanity on a day-to-day basis. Without NASA's research, scientists would never have discovered these contributions. Therefore, we must continue to fund NASA and all its programs.

3 The vast number of effective medicines, treatments, and machines used to test for and treat illnesses would be enough to warrant the space exploration funds if they were the only benefits to society from the NASA research. But another benefit of NASA's research is their ability to monitor the environment to ensure continued life on Earth. Since the ISS is a permanent structure that will observe the earth for the next 30 years, scientists will be able to monitor the earth and distinguish changes that have been made over time to its environment (Von Brook, Siegel, and Foster 67). These studies could lead to more breakthroughs and solutions for many environmental problems. For example, the balance between farming and water conservation will soon be made vastly more efficient due to advancements made by NASA using satellite imaging to dettermine watering priorities for irrigated farm lands (Rumsfeld 11). This information will help both the farmers and the general population—especially in a state like California where water rights are a volatile issue.

4 Not only can the space exploration program help solve environmental problems, but it can also identify those problems. In fact, the space program gave us "our first real perspective on global warming, ozone layer depletion, deforestation, and other environmental scourges" (Von Brook, Siegel, and Foster 69). Yet not all environmental benefits are plans for the future. Von Brook, Siegel, and Foster state,

> we have already achieved very promising results with indoor air pollution and wastewater treatment using NASA technology. Today, NASA researchers are contributing steadily to our knowledge of landfill leachate treatment, hazardous waste disposal, tropical rainforest, and ground water pollution. (69)

Recently, astronauts aboard the space station spent ten days creating a topographic map of all locations on the world within 60 degrees of the equator. A topographic map of uniform scale circling the entire globe has never before been created, and NASA accomplished this feat in 10 days. This model of the Earth can now be used to monitor changes on the Earth's surface, providing a very useful tool humanity can use for many reasons, including fighting forest fires

(Jet Propulsion Laboratory). The environment must be preserved, and since this task is made easier with the benefits of space exploration, we must continue to fund research for NASA.

Science, however, is not the only aspect of life that NASA affects, for it also greatly 5
influences the economy. According to Von Brook, Siegel, and Foster, "Space exploration . . . is the best investment for our future because it sharpens the skills and harnesses the talents of all Americans involved" (70). Sharpening the talents of Americans is important, yet the real question at hand is the economics of space exploration. A single space shuttle costs, for example, from $10,000–$20,000 per kilogram (Alpert 93). This is definitely a substantial amount of money to pay for a single launch. In 1975, NASA sponsored a study to design a space station it was never funded. A group of scientists created a plan for a circular station that would provide room for 10,000 colonists. The station would have cost $500 billion. However, the station would have paid for itself within 30 years because of enormous solar-power satellites that would be installed. A solar-energy-collection satellite would receive eight times as much energy as a collector on earth. The satellite would also produce five billion watts of electricity. Which is approximately five times that of an average power plant (Alpert 93–94). The economic benefits of this power are enormous considering the energy crises that tend to afflict parts of the United States.

Given the proper chance, much of space exploration could pay for itself. Von Brook, 6
Siegel, and Foster claim that "the Apollo mission yielded a 7-to-1 return of every dollar invested" (70). This does not suggest enormous waste. As Rumsfeld speculates, "An international space industry has developed, with revenues exceeding $80 billion in 2000. Industry forecasts project revenues will more than triple in the next decade" (11). Not only could a space project pay for itself, but the ISS will provide "50,000 jobs directly associated with spin-off technology," which "means greater national pride and fewer Americans that will require public support for basic needs like food and housing."

One major problem of NASA's budget, however, is the cuts it will cause for other 7
programs. Unfortunately, NASA shares a budget with the Environmental Protection Agency (EPA), the Department of Housing and Urban Development (HUD), and the Veterans Administration (Von Brook, Siegel, and Foster 66). This means that budget cuts are mandatory for the other agencies if any one program requires more capital. Von Brook, Siegel, and Foster explain, "This puts some of the nation's most futuristic plans competing directly against some of America's most pressing social needs" (66). Nevertheless, Americans and humanity must look passed the present problems and see into the future for solutions. Social needs have plagued society for centuries. We have tried to throw money at these problems in the past, which has been ineffective, so new solutions must be sought. The answers can be found by looking beyond the problems that humanity faces today and into the future of space exploration.

NASA is an important and vital force in American society. As long as our desire to explore 8
space continues to exist, advances and discoveries will follow. The benefits come not only in the form of space exploration, but also in medical, environmental, and economic advances that are necessary to the survival and progress of humanity. But NASA cannot continue to provide these major discoveries with a diminishing budget. In fact, NASA's 2002 budget allocation was less than the money it received in 1994 (NASA *FY 2003 Budget*). This budget desicion will affect all of American society for hundreds of years to come. An agency with the potential of NASA that has proven its usefulness time and time again should not be inadequately funded. It needs a generous budget that will let it continue to improve the quality of life for all Americans.

Works Cited

Alpert, Mark. "Making Money in Space." *The Future of Space Exploration.* 1 Jan. 1999: 92–95.

Jet Propulsion Laboratory. "Earth Has a New Look." *NASA News.* Jet Propulsion Laboratory, California Institute of Technology, Pasadena, California. News Release: 2003-116. August 22, 2003.

National Aeronautical and Space Agency (NASA). Chart: *FY 2003 Budget vs. History* and *Background Material NASA FY 2003 Budget Briefing.* 5 Sept. 2003.

Space Station Benefits. 4 Oct. 2003.

Rumsfeld, Donald H. (chairman). *Report of the Commission to Assess United States National Security Space Management and Organization.* Pursuant to Public Law 106-65. January 11, 2001. 28 Sept. 2003.

United States. The Report of the National Commission on Space. *Pioneering the Space Frontier.* Toronto: Bantam Books, 1986.

Von Brook, Patricia, Mark A. Siegel, and Carol D. Foster. *Space Exploration: The Dream and the Reality.* Eds. Patricia Von Brook, Mark A. Siegel, and Carol D. Foster. Wylie, Texas: Information Plus, 1990.

Rick's first draft now needs to be revised and edited. First, apply the Revising Checklist (on the inside front cover of this book) to the content of Rick's draft. When you are satisfied that his ideas are fully developed and well organized, use the Editing Checklist on the inside back cover to correct his grammatical and mechanical errors. The questions below will guide you through this process. Then rewrite the essay with your suggested changes.

Revision Questions

Thesis Statement

1. What is the main idea in Rick's research paper?

____

2. Put brackets around Rick's thesis statement. Does it introduce his main point?

____

3. Rewrite it to introduce all the topics in his essay.

____

____

Basic Elements

1. Give Rick's essay an alternative title.

____

2. Rewrite Rick's introduction so that it captures the reader's attention in a different way and builds up to the thesis statement at the end of the paragraph.

____

____

____

____

3. Does each of Rick's body paragraphs deal with only one topic?

____

4. Rewrite Rick's conclusion with a twist of your own.

____

____

____

____

Development

1. Do Rick's topic sentences support his thesis statement? Write out your revision of Rick's thesis statement, and list his six topic sentences.

   Thesis: _______________________________________

   ____

   Topics: _______________________________________

   ____

   ____

   ____

   ____

   ____

   ____

2. Does your revised thesis statement accurately introduce Rick's topic sentences?

3. Are Rick's examples specific?

   Add an even more specific detail to one of his paragraphs.

4. Does he offer enough examples or details in each paragraph?

For help, see Chapter 19.

5. Are Rick's sources relevant, reliable, and recent?

For help, see Chapter 18.

6. Does he give references for all original sources in his paper?

   Find the one sentence in paragraph 6 that is plagiarized and needs the reference "(Von Brook, Siegel, and Foster 68)."

For help, see Chapter 20.

7. Is the documentation format correct in his paper?

For help, see Chapter 20.

8. Is the format on his Works Cited page correct?

Unity

1. Read each of Rick's topic sentences with his thesis statement in mind. Do they go together?

 ____

2. Revise any topic sentences that are not directly related to his thesis.

3. Read each of Rick's paragraphs with its topic sentence in mind. Drop or rewrite any sentences that are not directly related to the paragraph's topic sentence.

Organization

1. Review your list of Rick's topics in item 1 under "Development," and decide if they are organized logically.

2. What is his method of organization?

 ____

3. Read Rick's paper again to see if all his sentences are arranged logically.

4. Move any sentences that are out of order.

Coherence

1. Circle five transitions that Rick uses.

For a list of transitions, see pages 85–86.

2. Explain how three of these transitions make Rick's paper easier to read.

 ____

 ____

Now rewrite Rick's essay with your revisions.

Editing Questions

Sentences

Subjects and Verbs

1. Underline the subjects once and verbs twice in paragraph 4 of Rick's essay. Remember that sentences can have more than one subject–verb set.

For help with subjects and verbs, see Chapter 23.

2. Does each sentence have at least one subject and verb that can stand alone?

 ____

For help with fragments, see Chapter 24.

3. Did you find and correct Rick's fragment in paragraph 5? If not, find and correct it now.

For help with run-ons, see Chapter 25.

4. Did you find and correct Rick's run-on sentence in paragraph 5? If not, find and correct it now.

Subject–Verb Agreement

For help with subject–verb agreement, see Chapter 27.

1. Read aloud the subjects and verbs in paragraph 2 of Rick's revised essay.
2. Correct any subjects and verbs that do not agree.
3. Now read aloud the subjects and verbs in the rest of his revised essay.
4. Correct any subjects and verbs that do not agree.

Pronoun Agreement

For help with pronoun agreement, see Chapter 30.

1. Find any pronouns in your revision of Rick's essay that do not agree with their nouns.
2. Correct any pronouns that do not agree with their nouns.

Modifier Errors

For help with modifier errors, see Chapter 33.

1. Find any modifiers in your revision of Rick's essay that are not as close as possible to the words they modify.
2. Rewrite sentences if necessary so that modifiers are as close as possible to the words they modify.

Punctuation and Mechanics

Punctuation

For help with punctuation, see Chapters 34–37.

1. Read your revision of Rick's essay for any errors in punctuation.
2. Make sure any fragments and run-on sentences you revised are punctuated correctly.

Mechanics

For help with capitalization, see Chapter 38.

1. Read your revisions of Rick's essay for any errors in capitalization.
2. Be sure to check the capitalization in the fragments and run-on sentences you revised.

Word Choice and Spelling

Confused Words

For help with confused words, see Chapter 44.

1. Find any words used incorrectly in your revision of Rick's essay.
2. Did you find and correct the confused word Rick used?

Spelling

1. Use spell-check and a dictionary to check the spelling in your revision of Rick's essay.
2. Did you find and correct his two misspelled words?

For help with spelling, see Chapter 45.

Now rewrite Rick's essay again with your editing corrections.

REVISING AND EDITING YOUR OWN RESEARCH PAPER

Now revise and edit the essay that you wrote in Chapter 20. Use the techniques you used when revising and editing Rick's essay.

Guidelines for Writing a Research Paper

1. Choose a subject.
2. Do some general reading, and write a good, clear thesis statement about your subject.
3. Find sources that are relevant, reliable, and recent to support your thesis statement.
4. Take notes to avoid plagiarism.
5. Make a working outline of your paper.
6. Construct an introduction that leads up to your thesis statement.
7. Develop as many supporting paragraphs or body paragraphs as you think are needed to explain your thesis statement.
8. Make sure you use your sources as evidence for your argument.
9. Write a concluding paragraph.
10. Think of a catchy title.
11. Check your sources and documentation format throughout your paper and at the end.

1. Research the changes in anti-drug ads over the past five years. How have they changed? Are they more or less effective now? Write an essay explaining these changes.
2. Research a controversial political issue of your choice. Then take a firm stand on the issue, and develop an essay supporting your position. You might want to look at newspaper headlines to get some ideas for this assignment.
3. Research a special trip that you want to take. Get all the information you need. Then write a letter to a close friend, inviting him or her to join you.
4. Create your own assignment (with the help of your instructor), and write a response to it.

Revising Workshop

Small Group Activity (10 minutes per writer) In groups of three or four, each person should read his or her research paper to the other members of the group. The listeners should record their reactions on a copy of the Peer Evaluation Form (Appendix 1A). After your group goes through this process, give your evaluation forms to the appropriate writers so that each writer has two or three peer comment sheets for revising.

Paired Activity (5 minutes per writer) Using the completed Peer Evaluation Forms, work in pairs to decide what you should revise in your essay. If time allows, rewrite some of your sentences, and have your partner check them.

Individual Activity Rewrite your paper, using the revising feedback you received from other students.

Editing Workshop

Paired Activity (10 minutes per writer) Swap papers with a classmate, and use the editing portion of your Peer Evaluation Forms (Appendix 1B) to identify as many grammar, punctuation, mechanics, and spelling errors as you can. Mark the errors on the student paper, using the correction symbols on the inside back cover. If time allows, correct some of your errors, and have your partner check them.

Individual Activity Rewrite your paper again, using the editing feedback you received from other students. Record your grammar errors in the Error Log (Appendix 3) and your spelling errors in the Spelling Log (Appendix 4).

PART IV

THE HANDBOOK

This part of *Mosaics* provides you with a complete handbook for editing your writing. You can use it as a reference tool as you write or as a source of instruction and practice in areas where you need work.

This handbook consists of an introduction and eight units:

The chapters in each unit start with a self-test to help you identify your strengths and weaknesses in that area. Then the chapter teaches specific sentence skills and provides exercises so you can practise what you have learned. Each chapter also asks you to write your own sentences and then work with another student to edit each other's writing.

The Editing Symbols in Appendix 6 will give you marks for highlighting errors in your papers. In addition, the Error Log (Appendix 3) and Spelling Log (Appendix 4) will help you tailor the instruction to your own needs and keep track of your progress.

Introduction: Parts of Speech, Phrases, and Clauses

CHAPTER 22

This handbook uses very little terminology. But sometimes talking about the language and the way it works is difficult without a shared understanding of certain basic grammatical terms. For that reason, your instructor may ask you to study parts of this introduction to review basic grammar—parts of speech, phrases, and clauses. You might also use this introduction for reference. You can refer to the Text Enrichment Site for practice exercises.

This section has three parts:

Parts of Speech
Phrases
Clauses

PARTS OF SPEECH

Test Yourself

In the following paragraph, label the parts of speech listed here:

2 verbs (v)	2 adverbs (adv)
2 nouns (n)	2 prepositions (prep)
2 pronouns (pro)	2 conjunctions (conj)
2 adjectives (adj)	2 interjections (int)

Professional basketball is definitely one of the best spectator sports. The talented players move around the court so quickly that the audience never has a chance to become bored. Boy, I'll never forget that Saturday night last February when my favourite uncle took me to see the Raptors game against the Trailblazers. It was an important home game for Toronto, so the Air Canada Centre was packed. The Raptors were behind throughout most of the game, but they pulled through and won with a three-pointer in the last few seconds. Wow! I have never seen so many people on their feet, screaming at the top of their lungs.

(Answers are in Appendix 9 on the Text Enrichment Site.)

Every sentence is made up of a variety of words that play different roles. Each word, like each part of a coordinated outfit, serves a distinct function. These functions fall into eight categories:

1. Verbs
2. Nouns
3. Pronouns
4. Adjectives
5. Adverbs
6. Prepositions
7. Conjunctions
8. Interjections

Some words, such as *is*, can function in only one way—in this case, as a verb. Other words, however, can serve as different parts of speech, depending on how they are used in a sentence. For example, look at the different ways the word *show* can be used:

Verb: The artists **show** their work at a gallery.
(*Show* is a verb here, telling what the artists do.)

Noun: The **show** will start in 10 minutes.
(*Show* functions as a noun here, telling what will start in 10 minutes.)

Adjective: My aunt loves to sing **show** tunes.
(*Show* is an adjective here, modifying the noun tunes.)

Verbs

The **verb** is the most important word in a sentence because every other word depends on it in some way. Verbs tell what's going on in the sentence.

There are three types of verbs: action, linking, and helping. An **action verb** tells what someone or something is doing. A **linking verb** tells what someone or something is, feels, or looks like. Sometimes an action or linking verb has **helping verbs**—words that add information, such as when an action is taking place. A **complete verb** consists of an action or linking verb and all the helping verbs.

Action: The girl **wandered** too far from the campsite.

Action: Luca **ran** to the bus stop.

Linking: He **looks** very tired.

Linking: It **was** a real surprise to see you.

Helping: My aunt and uncle **will** be arriving tomorrow.

Helping: My grandmother **has** been very ill lately.

Complete Verb: My aunt and uncle **will be arriving** tomorrow.

Complete Verb: My grandmother **has been** very ill lately.

Nouns

People often think of **nouns** as "naming words" because they identify—or name—people (*student, Susan, mom, pilot*), places (*city, ocean, Kingston*), or things (*bush, airplane, chair, shirt*). Nouns also name ideas (*peace, justice*), qualities (*bravery, patience*), emotions (*sadness, happiness*), and actions (*challenge, compromise*). A **common noun** names something general (*singer, hill, water, theatre*). A **proper noun** names something specific (*Avril Lavigne, Niagara Falls, Canada Dry, The Bay*).

Hint: To test whether a word is a noun, try putting *a*, *an*, or *the* in front of it:

Nouns:	a squirrel, an orange, the hope
NOT Nouns:	a funny, an over, the eat

This test does not work with all proper nouns:

NOT	a Natalie, the Winnipeg
BUT	the Raptors

Pronouns

Pronouns can do anything nouns can do. In fact, pronouns can take the place of nouns. Without pronouns, you would find yourself repeating nouns and producing boring sentences. Compare the following sentences, for example:

George drove **George's** car very fast to **George's** house because **George** had to get home early.

George drove **his** car very fast to **his** house because **he** had to get home early.

There are many different types of pronouns, but you only need to focus on the following four types for now.

Most Common Pronouns

Personal (refer to people or things)

Singular:	First person:	*I, me, my, mine*
	Second person:	*you, your, yours*
	Third person:	*he, she, it, him, her, hers, his, its*
Plural:	First person:	*we, us, our, ours*
	Second person:	*you, your, yours*
	Third person:	*they, them, their, theirs*

Demonstrative (point out someone or something)

Singular:	*this, that*
Plural:	*these, those*

Relative (introduce a dependent clause)

who, whom, whose, which, that

Indefinite (refer to someone or something general, not specific)

Singular:	*another, anybody, anyone, anything, each, either, everybody, everyone, everything, little, much, neither, nobody, no one, nothing, one, other, somebody, someone, something*
Plural:	*both, few, many, others, several*
Either Singular or Plural:	*all, any, more, most, none, some*

Hint: When any of these words are used with nouns, they become adjectives instead of pronouns.

Adjective: He can have **some candy**.

Pronoun: He can have **some**.

Adjective: The baby wants **that** toy.

Pronoun: The baby wants **that**.

Adjectives

Adjectives modify—or describe—nouns or pronouns. Adjectives generally make sentences clear and vivid.

Without Adjectives: She took an umbrella, a towel, and an iPod to the beach.

Without Adjectives: She took a bright orange umbrella, a striped blue towel, and a waterproof iPod to the beach.

Adverbs

Adverbs modify—or describe—adjectives, verbs, and other adverbs. They do *not* modify nouns. Adverbs also answer the following questions:

How?	thoughtfully, kindly, briefly, quietly
When?	soon, tomorrow, late, now
Where?	inside, somewhere, everywhere, there
How often?	daily, always, annually, rarely
To what extent?	generally, specifically, exactly, very

Hint: Notice that adverbs often end in *-ly*. That might help you recognize them.

Prepositions

Prepositions indicate relationships among the ideas in a sentence. Something is *at, in, by, next to, behind, around, near,* or *under* something else. A preposition is always followed by a noun or a pronoun, which is called the **object of the preposition.** Together, they form a **prepositional phrase.**

Preposition	+	Object	=	Prepositional Phrase
near	+	the beach	=	near the beach
for	+	the party	=	for the party

Here is a list of some common prepositions.

Common Prepositions

about	*beside*	*into*	*since*
above	*between*	*like*	*through*
across	*beyond*	*near*	*throughout*
after	*by*	*next to*	*to*
against	*despite*	*of*	*toward*
among	*down*	*off*	*under*
around	*during*	*on*	*until*
as	*except*	*on top of*	*up*
at	*for*	*out*	*upon*
before	*from*	*out of*	*up to*
behind	*in*	*outside*	*with*
below	*in front of*	*over*	*within*
beneath	*inside*	*past*	*without*

Hint: *To* + a verb (as in *to go, to come, to feel*) is not a prepositional phrase. It is a verb phrase, which we will deal with later in this unit.

Conjunctions

Conjunctions connect groups of words. Without conjunctions, most of our writing would be choppy and boring. The two types of conjunctions are easy to remember because their names state their purpose. *Coordinating conjunctions* link equal ideas and *subordinating conjunctions* make one idea subordinate to—or dependent on—another.

Coordinating conjunctions connect parts of a sentence that are of equal importance or weight. Among other things, these parts can be **independent clauses,** a group of words with a subject and verb that can stand alone as a sentence (see page 394). There are only seven coordinating conjunctions:

Coordinating Conjunctions
and, but, or, nor, for, so, yet

Coordinating: Melvin's parents arrived late and left early.

Coordinating: My sister wanted to go shopping or see a movie.

Coordinating: The teacher was very demanding, but I learned a lot from him.

Subordinating conjunctions join two ideas by making one dependent on the other. The idea introduced by the subordinating conjunction becomes a **dependent clause,** a group of words with a subject and a verb that cannot stand alone as a sentence (see page 394). The other part of the sentence is an independent clause.

Dependent Clause ↓

Subordinating: I won't leave until he comes home.

Dependent Clause ↓

Subordinating: Unless you study more, you won't get a scholarship.

Common Subordinating Conjunctions

after	*because*	*since*	*until*
although	*before*	*so*	*when*
as	*even if*	*so that*	*whenever*
as if	*even though*	*than*	*where*
as long as	*how*	*that*	*wherever*
as soon as	*if*	*though*	*whether*
as though	*in order that*	*unless*	*while*

Interjections

Interjections are words that express strong emotion, surprise, or disappointment. An interjection is usually followed by an exclamation point or a comma.

Interjection: **Whoa!** You're going too fast.

Interjection: **Ouch,** that hurt!

Other common interjections include *aha*, *alas*, *great*, *hey*, *neat*, *oh*, *oops*, *well*, *wow*, *yay*, and *yippee*.

PHRASES

Test Yourself

Underline the phrases in the following sentences.

- Using the computer, I got most of the research done for my report.
- To be totally confident, I checked for spelling and grammar errors twice.
- Susan lives in the grey house at the end of Maple Avenue behind the bank.
- Tess is going to be a ballet dancer when she gets older.
- Do you want to join us for dinner this evening?

(Answers are in Appendix 9 on the Text Enrichment Site.)

A **phrase** is a group of words that function together as a unit. Phrases cannot stand alone, however, because they are missing a subject, a verb, or both.

Phrases: the silver moon, a boneless fish

Phrases: threw out the trash, navigated the river, floated to the top

Phrases: after piano lessons, in the crowded boat, by the beach

Phrases: jumping into the water, to be smart

Notice that all these groups of words are missing a subject, a verb, or both.

CLAUSES

Test Yourself

Underline the clauses in the following sentences.

- Magdalena will make a great attorney because she argues so well.
- You don't understand the math concept, so I will keep going over it with you.
- If Shane is going to drive, he must have car insurance.

- We finished the big test, and then we all went out for pizza.
- I enjoyed the vacation even though I had one really bad seafood dinner.

(Answers are in Appendix 9 on the Text Enrichment Site.)

Like phrases, **clauses** are groups of words. But unlike phrases, a clause always contains a subject and a verb. There are two types of clauses: *independent* and *dependent*.

An **independent clause** contains a subject and a verb and can stand alone and make sense by itself. Every complete sentence must have at least one independent clause.

Independent Clause: The doctor held the baby very gently.

Now look at the following group of words. It is a clause because it contains a subject and a verb. But it is a **dependent clause** because it is introduced by a word that makes it dependent: *because*.

Dependent Clause: **Because** the doctor held the baby very gently.

This clause cannot stand alone. It must be connected to an independent clause in order to make sense. Here is one way to finish the dependent clause and form a complete sentence.

Dependent ↓ Independent ↓

Because the doctor held the baby very gently, the baby stopped crying.

Hint: Subordinating conjunctions (such as *since*, *although*, *because*, *while*) and relative pronouns (*who*, *whom*, *whose*, *which*, *that*) make clauses dependent. (For more information on subordinating conjunctions, see page 392, and on relative pronouns, see page 390.)

CHAPTER REVIEW

You might want to reread the examples in this chapter before you do the following exercises.

REVIEW PRACTICE 1 Identifying Use the following abbreviations to label the underlined words in these sentences.

v	Verb	adv	Adverb
n	Noun	prep	Preposition
pro	Pronoun	conj	Conjunction
adj	Adjective	int	Interjection
ph	Phrase	cl	Clause

1. Wow, that man looks just like my uncle Bob.
2. Tiffany is going shopping at the new mall on Harbour Boulevard tomorrow.
3. Frank is truly my best friend, but sometimes he can't keep a secret.
4. Whenever Lindsay feels sad, she drives into the mountains and looks at the stars.
5. The most popular recording artist of the 1960s was definitely Elvis Presley.
6. Gee, are you sure we had to read the entire novel before class today?
7. Ryan wants to take piano lessons, so he can compose music for the poetry he has written.
8. Mikella took her dog to the vet and found out it has a lung infection.
9. Though I didn't want to accept the job, I felt pressured by my mother.
10. This morning was dark and cloudy, so I stayed in bed until noon.

REVIEW PRACTICE 2 **Completing** Fill in each blank in the following paragraph with an appropriate word, phrase, or clause, as indicated.

The most foolish purchase I ever made was a new (1) ____________ (noun) for my computer. When I went to the (2) ____________ (adjective) store, the salesman (3) ____________ (verb) that I needed this item. I asked him what the part would do (4) ____________ (preposition) my computer, and he promised it would make a big difference in the way the computer operated. (5) ____________ (interjection), did I believe him! I knew my computer was pretty old, (6) ____________ (conjunction) I really didn't want to spend a lot of money on it. Still, I (7) ____________ (adverb) bought the part and took (8) ____________ (pronoun) home to try it out. After (9) ____________ (clause), I turned on the computer, and it began to heat up. Suddenly, smoke began coming (10) ____________ (phrase), and I realized the computer had just crashed.

REVIEW PRACTICE 3 **Writing Your Own** Write your own paragraph about your favourite pet. What did you name it? What kind of animal was it?

REVIEW PRACTICE 4 **Editing Your Writing** Exchange paragraphs from Review Practice 3 with a classmate, and do the following:

1. Circle any words that are used incorrectly.
2. Underline any phrases that do not read smoothly.
3. Put an X in the margin where you find a dependent clause that is not connected to an independent clause.

Then return the paragraph to its writer, and use the information in the Introduction to edit your own paragraph. Record your errors on the Error Log in Appendix 3.

CHAPTER

23

SUBJECTS AND VERBS

CHECKLIST for Identifying Subjects and Verbs

- ✔ Does each sentence contain a subject?
- ✔ Does each sentence contain a verb?

Test Yourself

Underline the subjects once and the verbs twice in the following sentences.

- You are my best friend.
- Hang up your clothes.
- They really wanted to be here tonight.
- He made a sandwich and put it in a brown paper bag.
- Susie and Tom went to the dance.

(Answers are in Appendix 9 on the Text Enrichment Site.)

A sentence has a message to communicate, but for that message to be meaningful, the sentence must have a subject and a verb. The subject is the topic of the sentence, what the sentence is about. The verb is the sentence's motor or action. It moves the message forward to its destination. Without these two parts, the sentence is not complete.

SUBJECTS

To be complete, every sentence must have a subject. The **subject** tells who or what the sentence is about.

Subject ↓	
He	always came home on time.
Horror **movies**	appeal to teenagers.

Compound Subjects

When two or more separate words tell what the sentence is about, the sentence has a **compound subject.**

Compound Subject: **Painting** and **sewing** are my hobbies.

Compound Subject: **My brother** and **I** live with my grandmother.

Hint: Note that *and* is not part of the compound subject.

Unstated Subjects

Sometimes a subject does not actually appear in a sentence but is understood. This occurs in commands and requests. The understood subject is always *you*, meaning either someone specific or anyone in general.

Command: Get up now or you'll be late.

s

Unstated Subject: **(You)** get up now or you'll be late.

Request: Write me an email soon, please.

s

Unstated Subject: **(You)** write me an email soon, please.

Subjects and Prepositional Phrases

The subject of a sentence cannot be part of a prepositional phrase. A **prepositional phrase** is a group of words that begins with a **preposition,** a word like *in*, *on*, *under*, *after*, *from*, or *with*. Here are some examples of prepositional phrases:

in the yard
on the plane
under the rug
after school
from the grocery store

next to it
behind the chair
around the circle
into the boat
during the storm

before supper
instead of me
across the road
for the family
at school

(See page 391 for a more complete list of prepositions.)

If you are looking for the subject of a sentence, first cross out all the prepositional phrases. Then figure out what the sentence is about.

s s

~~During the game~~, the coaches and the players had a fight ~~with the other team.~~

s

The new store ~~around the corner~~ sells designer jeans.

S
Some ~~of our luggage~~ was lost ~~on the trip~~.

PRACTICE 1 Identifying Cross out the prepositional phrases in each of the following sentences, and then underline the subjects.

1. The golfer stood quietly in front of the ball.
2. Marty and Mike gave a presentation at the big convention.
3. Two of the graduates had perfect grade point averages.
4. Before I go to the store, I need to put on a jacket.
5. Get the mayonnaise out of the refrigerator.

PRACTICE 2 Completing Fill in each blank in the following sentences with a subject without using a person's name.

1. _____ was voted the best restaurant in this area.
2. Walking to class, _____ thought seriously about changing his major.
3. Sometimes, _____ is a great bargain.
4. _____ and _____ are two very positive personality traits.
5. _____ was late for work again.

PRACTICE 3 Writing Your Own Write five sentences of your own, and underline the subjects.

VERBS

To be complete, a sentence must have a verb as well as a subject. A **verb** tells what the subject is doing or what is happening.

	Verb ↓
He	always **came** home on time.
Horror movies	**appeal** to teenagers.

Action Verbs

An **action verb** tells what a subject is doing. Some examples of action verbs are *skip*, *ski*, *stare*, *flip*, *breathe*, *remember*, *restate*, *sigh*, *cry*, *decrease*, *write*, and *pant*.

Action Verb: The children **laughed** at the clown.

Action Verb: The car **crashed** into the tree.

Linking Verbs

A **linking verb** connects the subject to other words in the sentence that say something about it. Linking verbs are also called **state-of-being verbs** because they do not show action. Rather, they say that something "is" a particular way. The most common linking verb is *be* (*am, are, is, was, were*).

Linking Verb: The horses **are** in the stable.
Linking Verb: I **am** unhappy with the results.

Other common linking verbs are *remain, act, look, grow,* and *seem.*

Linking Verb: Ian **remains** enthusiastic about school.
Linking Verb: I **act** happy even when I'm not.
Linking Verb: The yard **looks** neglected.
Linking Verb: She **grew** fonder of her aunt.
Linking Verb: Nala **seems** happy with her new house.

Some words, like *smell* and *taste*, can be either action verbs or linking verbs.

Action Verb: I **smell** smoke.
Linking Verb: This house **smells** like flowers.
Action Verb: She **tasted** the soup.
Linking Verb: It **tasted** too salty.

Compound Verbs

Just as a verb can have more than one subject, some subjects can have more than one verb. These are called **compound verbs.**

Compound Verb: She **cooks** and **cleans** every day.
Compound Verb: He **runs** and **swims** twice a week in the summer.

Hint: A sentence can have both a compound subject and a compound verb.

S S V V
Joe and **Philip jumped** into the water and **swam** to the raft.

Helping Verbs

Often the **main verb** (the action verb or linking verb) in a sentence needs help to convey its meaning. **Helping verbs** add information, such as when an action took place. The **complete verb** consists of a main verb and all its helping verbs. Here, the helping verb is underlined.

Complete Verb: The children <u>**will**</u> return tomorrow.
Complete Verb: It <u>**might**</u> **rain** this weekend.
Complete Verb: We <u>**should have**</u> **gone** to the concert.
Complete Verb: My uncle <u>**has**</u> **given** me money for Christmas.

Complete Verb: My sister **will be coming** home for my wedding.

Complete Verb: You **should** not go home with them.

Hint: Note that *not* isn't part of the helping verb. Similarly, *never, always, only, just,* and *still* are never part of the verb.

Complete Verb: I **have** always **liked** history classes.

The most common helping verbs are

be, am, is, are, was, were
have, has, had
do, did

Other common helping verbs are

may, might
can, could
will, would
should, used to, ought to

PRACTICE 4 Identifying Underline the complete verbs in each of the following sentences.

1. The students seemed tired in class Monday morning.
2. One of my professors is a popular public speaker.
3. High school students must read *Who Has Seen the Wind?*
4. Timothy will go to the championships.
5. Get out of the rain.

PRACTICE 5 Completing Fill in each blank in the following sentences with a verb. Avoid using *is, are, was,* and *were* except as helping verbs.

1. Brendan _____ extreme pain after falling from the ladder and landing on his back.
2. The specialist _____ her client about the different options.
3. Both the parents and the teachers _____ about the need for more meetings.
4. My ill child _____ throughout the night.
5. Red stickers on the price tags _____ the sale items.

PRACTICE 6 Writing Your Own Write five sentences of your own, and underline all the verbs in each.

CHAPTER REVIEW

Subject: who or what the sentence is about

Compound Subject: two or more separate words that tell who or what the sentence is about

Unstated Subject: The subject does not appear in the sentence. It is implied or understood.

Preposition: a word such as *in*, *on*, *under*, *after*, *from*, or *with*

Prepositional Phrase: a phrase beginning with a preposition

Verb: tells what the subject is doing or what action is happening

Linking Verb: connects the subject to other words in the sentence

State-of-Being Verb: does not show action, but shows that something "is" a particular way (*am*, *are*, *is*, *was*, *were*)

Compound Verb: more than one verb for one or more subjects

Helping Verb: adds information, such as when the action took place

Complete Verb: includes the main verb and all its helping verbs

You might want to reread the examples in this chapter before you do the following exercises.

REVIEW PRACTICE 1 **Identifying** Underline the subjects once and the verbs twice in each of the following sentences. Cross out the prepositional phrases first.

1. The horses in the corral are being trained for racing.
2. Matilda received a scholarship for her biology research.
3. Salespeople can earn thousands of dollars in commissions every year.
4. Each month, my office pays us for overtime.
5. The bikes and the helmets are on sale right now.
6. I am going to the grocery store for dinner.
7. Tonya's computer crashed the other day, and she used mine for her homework.
8. Grandma will not join us for dinner.
9. Joe and Christine are building a new house.
10. The baby played with the blocks and stacked them on top of each other.

REVIEW PRACTICE 2 Completing Fill in the missing subjects or verbs in each of the following sentences.

1. Tonight's dinner _____ like leftovers.
2. _____ can't remember where we said we would meet.
3. Taking that midterm _____ my hardest challenge last week.
4. The catcher and the pitcher _____ with the referee.
5. If you want to go with us, you _____ to come along.
6. When Tiffany left this morning, _____ didn't know when she would be back.
7. _____ wear lab coats to set them apart from students.
8. Yesterday I _____ an old box of letters from my friends in high school.
9. (You) _____ your room before we leave.
10. _____ was the best entertainment of the evening.

REVIEW PRACTICE 3 Writing Your Own Write a paragraph about a major decision you made within the past three years. How has it affected your life? What did you learn from the process?

REVIEW PRACTICE 4 Editing Your Writing Exchange paragraphs from Review Practice 3 with another student, and do the following:

1. Underline the subjects once.
2. Underline the verbs twice.

Then return the paragraph to its writer, and edit any sentences in your own paragraph that do not have both a subject and a verb. Record your errors on the Error Log in Appendix 3.

CHAPTER

24

FRAGMENTS

CHECKLIST for Identifying and Correcting Fragments

✔ Does each sentence have a subject?
✔ Does each sentence have a verb?

Test Yourself

Put an X by the sentences that are fragments.

- _____ I wanted to go to the gym yesterday.
- _____ Whose tie doesn't match his suit.
- _____ Giving up his seat for an elderly woman.
- _____ Paul asked for the most popular menu item.
- _____ While the captain was away from the cockpit.

(Answers are in Appendix 9 on the Text Enrichment Site.)

One of the most common errors in student writing is the fragment. A fragment is a piece of a sentence that is punctuated as a complete sentence, but does not express a complete thought. Once you learn how to identify fragments, you will be able to avoid them in your writing.

ABOUT FRAGMENTS

A complete sentence must have both a subject and a verb. If one or both are missing, or if the subject and verb are introduced by a dependent word, you have only part of a sentence, a **fragment.** Even if it begins with a capital letter and ends with a period, it cannot stand alone and must be corrected in your writing. The five most common types of fragments are explained in this chapter.

Type 1: Afterthought Fragments
He goes to school during the day. **And works at night.**

Type 2: *-ing* Fragments
Finding no one at the house. Kenny walked back home.

Type 3: *to* Fragments
The school started a tutoring program. **To help improve math results.**

Type 4: Dependent-Clause Fragments
Because I decided to go back to school. My boss fired me.

Type 5: Relative-Clause Fragments
Last summer I visited Winnipeg. **Which is a beautiful city.**

Ways to Correct Fragments

Once you have identified a fragment, you have two options for correcting it. You can connect the fragment to the sentence before or after it or make the fragment into an independent clause.

Correction 1: *Connect the fragment to the sentence before or after it.*

Correction 2: *Make the fragment into an independent clause:*
(a) either add the missing subject and/or verb, or
(b) drop the subordinating word before the fragment.

We will discuss these corrections for each type of fragment.

IDENTIFYING AND CORRECTING FRAGMENTS

The rest of this chapter discusses the five types of fragments and the ways to correct each type.

Type 1: Afterthought Fragments

Afterthought fragments occur when you add an idea to a sentence but don't punctuate it correctly.

Fragment: He goes to school during the day. And works at night.

The phrase *And works at night* is punctuated and capitalized as a complete sentence. Because this group of words lacks a subject, however, it is a fragment.

Correction 1: *Connect the fragment to the sentence before or after it.*
Example: He goes to school during the day and works at night.

Correction 2: *Make the fragment into an independent clause.*
Example: He goes to school during the day. He works at night.

The first correction connects the fragment to the sentence before it. The second correction makes the fragment into an independent clause with its own subject and verb.

PRACTICE 1A **Identifying** Underline the afterthought fragments in each of the following sentences.

1. The men on the opposing team were very strong. Everyone was scared to play them. Especially me.
2. Mark peered into the window of his locked car and saw his keys. Stuck in the ignition.
3. I am thinking about buying a really special car next year. For example, a Chevy Tahoe.
4. Carlene turned in her paper on time and knew she would get a good grade. Because she really liked her topic.
5. "He shoots. He scores!" is an expression. That my friends use.

PRACTICE 1B **Correcting** Correct the fragments in Practice 1A by rewriting each sentence.

PRACTICE 2 **Completing** Correct the following afterthought fragments using both correction 1 and correction 2. Rewrite any corrected sentences that you think could be smoother.

1. The child drew in a colouring book. With brand new crayons.
2. I am going to buy some new books to read. For example, the Harry Potter books.
3. Jennifer usually drives very fast. Sometimes running stop signs.
4. My friends are going to the beach. In Grand Bend for the weekend.
5. He walked over to my desk very slowly. And smiled in a friendly way.

PRACTICE 3 **Writing Your Own** Write five afterthought fragments of your own, and correct them.

Type 2: *-ing* Fragments

Words that end in *-ing* are forms of verbs that cannot be the main verbs in their sentences. For an *-ing* word to function as a verb, it must have a helping verb with it (*be*, *do*, or *have*; see page 388).

Fragment: Finding no one at the house. Kenny walked back home.

Finding is not a verb in this sentence because it has no helping verb. Also, this group of words is a fragment because it has no subject.

Correction 1: *Connect the fragment to the sentence before or after it.*
Example: Finding no one at the house, Kenny walked home.

Correction 2: *Make the fragment into an independent clause.*
Example: He found no one at the house. Kenny walked home.

Hint: When you connect an *-ing* fragment to a sentence, insert a comma between the two sentence parts. You should insert the comma whether the *-ing* part comes at the beginning or the end of the sentence.

Kenny walked home**, finding no one at the house.**

Finding no one at the house, Kenny walked home.

PRACTICE 4A Identifying Underline the *-ing* fragments in each of the following sentences.

1. Driving to the store. I thought about all the things I needed to buy.
2. The baseball player dropped the ball. Tripping over his shoelaces while running to make the catch.
3. Mr. Holland was the best music teacher I ever had. Treating everyone with respect.
4. I plan to read at least one book each month. Challenging my brother to do the same.
5. Wanting to leave her parents' house. Marissa got married when she was 18 years old.

PRACTICE 4B Correcting Correct the fragments in Practice 4A by rewriting each sentence.

PRACTICE 5 Completing Correct each of the following *-ing* fragments using both methods. Remember to insert a comma when using correction 1.

1. Making the best grade in the class. Pasquale was excited to tell his parents about it.
2. I think I hurt my back. Trying to move the desk.
3. Looking back at my last year of high school. I can't believe I dated that guy.
4. Wondering whether he had left his car windows down. Julio saw the rain begin to fall.
5. Jamar was glad he had survived the accident. Seeing the damage to his car.

PRACTICE 6 Writing Your Own Write five *-ing* fragments of your own, and correct them.

Type 3: *to* Fragments

When *to* is added to a verb (*to see, to hop, to skip, to jump*), the combination cannot be a main verb in its sentence. As a result, this group of words is often involved in a fragment.

Fragment: The school started a tutoring program. **To improve math results.**

Because *to* + a verb cannot function as the main verb of its sentence, *to improve math results* is a fragment as it is punctuated here.

Correction 1: *Connect the fragment to the sentence before or after it.*
Example: The school started a tutoring program **to improve math results.**

Correction 2: *Make the fragment into an independent clause.*
Example: The school started a tutoring program. **It wanted to improve math results.**

Hint: A *to* fragment can also occur at the beginning of a sentence. In this case, insert a comma between the two sentence parts when correcting the fragment.

To improve math results, the school started a tutoring program.

PRACTICE 7A **Identifying** Underline the *to* fragments in each of the following sentences.

1. To make the crowd more excited. The rodeo clown came out and chased the bull around the arena.
2. To grow perfect roses. You should attend free classes at The Garden Centre.
3. The baby screamed loudly. To tell his parents he was hungry.
4. We stopped eating fried foods and sweets. To lose weight before summer.
5. To improve their chances at winning the Stanley Cup. The Toronto Maple Leafs signed Mats Sundin.

PRACTICE 7B **Correcting** Correct the fragments in Practice 7A by rewriting each sentence.

PRACTICE 8 **Completing** Correct the following *to* fragments using both correction 1 and correction 2. Try putting the fragment at the beginning of the sentence instead of always at the end. Remember to insert a comma when you add the *to* fragment to the beginning of a sentence.

1. Avoid driving faster than the posted speed limit. To get the best gas mileage.

2. He wanted to buy a new suit. To impress his boss.
3. Amber told Warren that she had a boyfriend. To avoid hurting his feelings.
4. The bank is closed on Labour Day. To give the employees time with their families.
5. I put the names and addresses in a mail merge. To make it easier to print labels.

PRACTICE 9 Writing Your Own Write five *to* fragments of your own, and correct them.

Type 4: Dependent-Clause Fragments

A group of words that begins with a **subordinating conjunction** (see the list below) is called a **dependent clause** and cannot stand alone. Even though it has a subject and a verb, it is a fragment because it depends on an independent clause to complete its meaning. An **independent clause** is a group of words with a subject and a verb that can stand alone. (See page 393 for help with clauses.)

Here is a list of some commonly used subordinating conjunctions that create dependent clauses.

Subordinating Conjunctions

after	*because*	*since*	*until*
although	*before*	*so*	*when*
as	*even if*	*so that*	*whenever*
as if	*even though*	*than*	*where*
as long as	*how*	*that*	*wherever*
as soon as	*if*	*though*	*whether*
as though	*in order that*	*unless*	*while*

Fragment: Because I decided to go back to school. My boss fired me.

This sentence has a subject and a verb, but it is introduced by a subordinating conjunction, *because*. As a result, this sentence is a dependent clause and cannot stand alone.

Correction 1: *Connect the fragment to the sentence before or after it.*
Example: **Because I decided to go back to school,** my boss fired me.

Correction 2: *Make the fragment into an independent clause.*
Example: ~~Because~~ I decided to go back to school. My boss fired me.

Hint: If the dependent clause comes first, put a comma between the two parts of the sentence. If the dependent clause comes second, the comma is not needed.

> **Because I decided to go back to school,** my boss fired me.
> My boss fired me **because I decided to go back to school.**

PRACTICE 10A Identifying Underline the dependent-clause fragments in each of the following sentences.

1. I love to eat sushi. Although it's sometimes very expensive.
2. It is good to know some trivia. So that you can participate in lots of conversations.
3. After the child finished riding on it. The rocking horse stood in the corner.
4. I will have Thanksgiving dinner at my house again. As long as my parents get along with my in-laws.
5. Before she goes to work in the morning. Margaret takes her children to school.

PRACTICE 10B Correcting Correct the fragments in Practice 10A by rewriting each sentence.

PRACTICE 11 Completing Correct the following dependent-clause fragments, using both correction 1 and correction 2. When you use correction 1, remember to add a comma if the dependent clause comes first.

1. Manny takes his basketball with him. Wherever he goes.
2. While I'm out of town. My mother will take care of my house.
3. The power bill is higher this month. Though we didn't run the air conditioner very often.
4. When she got home from work. Jamie made green beans for dinner.
5. Jean-Pierre always watches TV for an hour. After he finishes studying.

PRACTICE 12 Writing Your Own Write five dependent-clause fragments of your own, and correct them.

Type 5: Relative-Clause Fragments

A **relative clause** is a dependent clause that begins with a relative pronoun: *who, whom, whose, which,* or *that*. When a relative clause is punctuated as a sentence, the result is a fragment.

Fragment: Last summer I visited Winnipeg. **Which is a beautiful city.**

Which is a beautiful city is a clause fragment that begins with the relative pronoun *which*. This word automatically makes the words that follow it a dependent clause, so they cannot stand alone as a sentence.

Correction 1: *Connect the fragment to the sentence before or after it.*
Example: Last summer I visited Winnipeg, **which is a beautiful city.**

Correction 2: *Make the fragment into an independent clause.*
Example: Last summer I visited Winnipeg. **It is a beautiful city.**

PRACTICE 13A Identifying Underline the relative-clause fragments in the following sentences.

1. I made an appointment with the doctor. Whom my cousin recommended.
2. The child ate the pills. That the father left on the bathroom counter.
3. The fire station got a new captain. Who transferred from another department.
4. At the car wash, I talked to the man. Whose name tag said "Sylvester."
5. Karen got a job at the bakery. Which makes fresh doughnuts every morning.

PRACTICE 13B Correcting Correct the fragments in Practice 13A by rewriting each sentence.

PRACTICE 14 Completing Correct the following relative-clause fragments, using both correction 1 and correction 2.

1. Paul studied for the midterm with Charlotte. Who scored the highest on the first exam.
2. My girlfriend works at the bank. That is located on the corner of Front Street and Market Avenue.
3. I put more memory in my computer. Which cost me about $70.
4. My boss is the man with the goatee. Whose ties are usually very colourful.
5. Penny shops only at grocery stores. That offer double coupons.

PRACTICE 15 Writing Your Own Write five relative-clause fragments of your own, and correct them.

CHAPTER REVIEW

Fragment: an incomplete sentence. It is missing a subject or a verb. It cannot stand alone as a complete thought.

Afterthought Fragment: an added idea that is not punctuated properly

***-ing* Fragment:** An *-ing* verb must have a helping verb with it; otherwise, it will be a sentence fragment.

***to* Fragment:** When *to* is added to the verb, it cannot be the main verb.

Dependent-Clause Fragment: It cannot stand alone as a complete thought or sentence. It depends on a complete sentence for more information.

Independent Clause: a complete sentence. It has a subject and a verb and stands on its own as a complete thought.

Relative Pronouns: *who, whom, whose, which, that*

You might want to reread the examples in this chapter before you do the following exercises.

REVIEW PRACTICE 1 Identifying Underline the fragments in the following paragraph.

> Buying an old home can be a good experience. If the house is inspected thoroughly before any papers are signed. Thinking we were getting an incredible deal. We rushed into buying a 30-year-old house in an established neighbourhood. The house had lots of personality and big living rooms. To make it perfect for entertaining. Unfortunately, there were several problems with the house that we didn't see right away. For example, plumbing problems. Faulty wiring. Not enough insulation. We put thousands of dollars into repairs. Before we could even invite our friends over for dinner. Even though the house wasn't expensive to buy. It became very expensive for us to maintain. Eventually, we had to sell it. To keep from losing more money. The man who bought it was a contractor. Who could do most of the repairs himself. Which is a big advantage that we didn't have.

REVIEW PRACTICE 2 Correcting Correct all the fragments you underlined in Review Practice 1 by rewriting the paragraph.

REVIEW PRACTICE 3 Writing Your Own Write a paragraph about your dream vacation. Where would you go? How long would you stay? Who would go with you, or would you go alone?

REVIEW PRACTICE 4 **Editing Your Writing** Exchange paragraphs from Review Practice 3 with another student, and do the following:

1. Put brackets around any fragments that you find.
2. Identify the types of fragments that you find.

Then return the paper to its writer, and use the information in this chapter to correct any fragments in your own paragraph. Record your errors on the Error Log in Appendix 3.

CHAPTER

25 FUSED SENTENCES AND COMMA SPLICES

CHECKLIST for Identifying and Correcting Fused Sentences and Comma Splices

- ✔ Are any sentences run together without punctuation?
- ✔ Are any sentences incorrectly joined with only a comma?

Test Yourself

Mark any incorrect sentences here with a slash between the independent clauses that are not joined properly.

- The rainstorm washed out my garden, I had just planted spring bulbs.
- When we cleaned the house, we found the TV remote control it was between the couch cushions.
- People in authority are often criticized and seldom thanked.
- The kids didn't find all of the Easter eggs during the hunt, when we finally found them, they were rotten.
- You should ask Aubri to cut your hair she's been cutting mine for four years.

(Answers are in Appendix 9 on the Text Enrichment Site.)

When we cram two separate statements into a single sentence without correct punctuation, we create what are called *fused sentences* and *comma splices*. These run-on sentences generally distort our message and cause problems for our readers. In this chapter, you will learn how to identify and avoid these errors in your writing.

IDENTIFYING FUSED SENTENCES AND COMMA SPLICES

Whereas a fragment is a piece of a sentence, **fused sentences** and **comma splices** are made up of two sentences written as one. In both cases, the first sentence runs into the next without the proper punctuation between the two.

Fused Sentence: The bus stopped we got off.

Comma Splice: The bus stopped, we got off.

Both of these sentences incorrectly join two independent clauses. The difference between them is one comma.

A **fused sentence** is two sentences "fused" or jammed together without any punctuation. Look at these examples:

Fused Sentence: Rosa's favourite subject is math she always does very well on her math tests.

This example consists of two independent clauses with no punctuation between them:

1. Rosa's favourite subject is math.
2. She always does very well on her math tests.

Fused Sentence: My grandfather likes to cook his own meals he doesn't want anyone to do it for him.

This example also consists of two independent clauses with no punctuation between them:

1. My grandfather likes to cook his own meals.
2. He doesn't want anyone to do it for him.

Like a fused sentence, a **comma splice** incorrectly joins two independent clauses. However, a comma splice puts a comma between the two independent clauses. The only difference between a fused sentence and a comma splice is the comma. Look at the following examples:

Comma Splice: Rosa's favourite subject is math, she always does very well on her math tests.

Comma Splice: My grandfather likes to cook his own meals, he doesn't want anyone to do it for him.

Both of these sentences consist of two independent clauses—but a comma is not the proper punctuation to use to separate these two clauses.

PRACTICE 1 **Identifying** Put a slash between the independent clauses that are not joined correctly.

1. Paul plays hockey every Thursday he usually gets home after dark.
2. My mom always tucked me into bed at night, that's what I remember most about her.
3. Toni borrowed my pencil yesterday then she lost it.
4. My boyfriend made my favourite cake for my birthday, I had to eat the whole thing.

5. The child needed a bone marrow transplant, we raised $10,000 last night for her cause.

PRACTICE 2 **Identifying** For each incorrect sentence in the following paragraph, put a slash between the independent clauses that are not joined properly.

> The fitness craze is sweeping across Canada, it seems like everyone has a gym membership. The best-selling food items have "light," "lite," or "fat free" on the packaging, and people are watching their cholesterol and counting calories. Only the thinnest models are shown in food advertisements they symbolize good health, responsible eating habits, and overall physical attractiveness. Ironically, thin people are even used in ads for unhealthy food items, like candy and soft drinks, this sends a very confusing message to the consumer. The stereotypes are not fair not everyone can have the "perfect" body seen in the ads. Some people are just born with bigger body shapes, and there is nothing wrong or unattractive about that. These people should learn to eat healthy foods, they should not try to be unnaturally thin.

PRACTICE 3 **Writing Your Own** Write five fused sentences. Then write the same sentences as comma splices.

CORRECTING FUSED SENTENCES AND COMMA SPLICES

You have four different options for correcting your fused sentences and comma splices.

1. Separate the two sentences with a period, and capitalize the next word.
2. Separate the two sentences with a comma, and add a coordinating conjunction (*and, but, for, nor, or, so,* or *yet*).
3. Change one of the sentences into a dependent clause with a subordinating conjunction (such as *if, because, since, after,* or *when*) or a relative pronoun (*who, whom, whose, which,* or *that*).
4. Separate the two sentences with a semicolon.

Correction 1: Use a Period

Separate the two sentences with a period, and capitalize the next word.

Rosa's favourite subject is math. **She** always does very well on her math tests.

My grandfather likes to cook his own meals. **He** doesn't want anyone to do it for him.

PRACTICE 4 Correcting Correct all the sentences in Practice 1, using correction 1.

PRACTICE 5 Correcting Correct the paragraph in Practice 2, using correction 1.

PRACTICE 6 Writing Your Own Correct the sentences you wrote in Practice 3, using correction 1.

Correction 2: Use a Coordinating Conjunction

Separate the two sentences with a comma, and add a coordinating conjunction (*and*, *but*, *for*, *nor*, *or*, *so*, or *yet*).

Rosa's favourite subject is math, **so** she always does very well on her math tests.

My grandfather likes to cook his own meals, **and** he doesn't want anyone to do it for him.

PRACTICE 7 Correcting Correct all the sentences in Practice 1, using correction 2.

PRACTICE 8 Correcting Correct the paragraph in Practice 2, using correction 2.

PRACTICE 9 Writing Your Own Correct the sentences you wrote in Practice 3, using correction 2.

Correction 3: Create a Dependent Clause

Change one of the sentences into a dependent clause with a subordinating conjunction (such as *if*, *because*, *since*, *after*, or *when*) or a relative pronoun (*who*, *whom*, *whose*, *which*, or *that*).

Rosa's favourite subject is math **because** she always does very well on her math tests.

Since my grandfather likes to cook his own meals, he doesn't want anyone to do it for him.

For a list of subordinating conjunctions, see page 409.

Hint: If you put the dependent clause at the beginning of the sentence, add a comma between the two sentence parts.

Because she always does very well on her math tests, Rosa's favourite subject is math.

PRACTICE 10 **Correcting** Correct all the sentences in Practice 1, using correction 3.

PRACTICE 11 **Correcting** Correct the paragraph in Practice 2, using correction 3.

PRACTICE 12 **Writing Your Own** Correct the sentences you wrote in Practice 3, using correction 3.

Correction 4: Use a Semicolon

Separate the two sentences with a semicolon.

Rosa's favourite subject is math; she always does very well on her math tests.

My grandfather likes to cook his own meals; he doesn't want anyone to do it for him.

You can also use a **transition**, a word or an expression that indicates how the two parts of the sentence are related, with a semicolon. A transition often makes the sentence smoother. It is preceded by a semicolon and followed by a comma.

Rosa's favourite subject is math; **as a result,** she always does very well on her math tests.

My grandfather likes to cook his own meals; **therefore,** he doesn't want anyone to do it for him.

Here are some transitions commonly used with semicolons.

Transitions Used with a Semicolon Before and a Comma After

also	*however*	*furthermore*	*instead*
meanwhile	*consequently*	*for example*	*similarly*
in contrast	*therefore*	*for instance*	*otherwise*
of course	*finally*	*in fact*	*nevertheless*

PRACTICE 13 **Correcting** Correct all the sentences in Practice 1, using correction 4.

PRACTICE 14 Correcting Correct the paragraph in Practice 2, using correction 4.

PRACTICE 15 Writing Your Own Correct the sentences you wrote in Practice 3, using correction 4.

CHAPTER REVIEW

Fused Sentences: two or more separate sentences put into a single sentence without proper punctuation. A fused sentence is also called a run-on sentence.

Comma Splice: two or more separate sentences joined together with a comma. A comma splice is also called a run-on sentence.

Correct run-on sentences by using a period, a coordinating conjunction, or a semicolon.

Coordinating Conjunction: Words such as *and*, *but*, *for*, *nor*, *so*, or *yet* can join two complete sentences. A comma comes before the conjunction.

You might want to reread the examples in this chapter before you do the following exercises.

REVIEW PRACTICE 1 Identifying Label each of the following sentences as fused (F), comma splice (CS), or correct (C).

1. _____ My sister woke up late this morning, she made us late for school.
2. _____ River rafting can be dangerous you need an experienced guide.
3. _____ When I dyed my hair black, I didn't know it might turn my scalp black too, it did.
4. _____ People who compete in triathlons are excellent athletes because the events are very difficult.
5. _____ Mike made an ice sculpture in his art class it was a penguin with a fish in its mouth.
6. _____ Terry needed to mow his lawn, the grass was very high, and the neighbours were complaining.
7. _____ I drove my car without engine oil, and the repairs were incredibly expensive.
8. _____ The big earthquake was on the front page of the newspaper many homes and businesses were destroyed.
9. _____ We had the perfect beach vacation planned, but then it rained the whole time we were so disappointed.
10. _____ If you stay out in the sun very long, you should use sunblock, skin cancer is a horrible disease.

REVIEW PRACTICE 2 Completing Correct the fused sentences and comma splices in Review Practice 1.

REVIEW PRACTICE 3 Writing Your Own Write a paragraph about your favourite season of the year. Why do you enjoy it? What do you do during this time of year?

REVIEW PRACTICE 4 Editing Through Collaboration Exchange your paragraph from Review Practice 3 with another student, and do the following:

1. Put brackets around any sentences that have more than one independent clause.
2. Circle the words that connect these clauses.

Then return the paper to its writer, and use the information in this chapter to correct any run-on sentences in your own paragraph. Record your errors on the Error Log in Appendix 3.

CHAPTER

26

Regular and Irregular Verbs

CHECKLIST for Using Regular and Irregular Verbs

✔ Are regular verbs in their correct forms?
✔ Are irregular verbs in their correct forms?

Test Yourself

Underline the complete verb in each of the following sentences. Then mark an X if the form of the verb is incorrect.

- _____ The pipe has bursted.
- _____ Sim reacted to the scene calmly.
- _____ I bought my car at an auction.
- _____ We had hid in the basement.
- _____ Sorry, I eated all the cookies.

(Answers are in Appendix 9 on the Text Enrichment Site.)

All verbs are either regular or irregular. *Regular verbs* form the past tense and past participle by adding *-d* or *-ed* to the present tense. If a verb does not form its past tense and past participle this way, it is called an *irregular verb*.

REGULAR VERBS

Here are the principal parts (present, past, and past participle forms) of some regular verbs. **Regular verbs** form the past tense and past participle by adding *-d* or *-ed*. The past participle is the verb form often used with helping verbs like *have*, *has*, or *had*.

Some Regular Verbs

PRESENT TENSE	PAST TENSE	PAST PARTICIPLE (USED WITH HELPING WORDS LIKE *HAVE, HAS, HAD*)
talk	*talked*	*talked*
sigh	*sighed*	*sighed*
drag	*dragged*	*dragged*
enter	*entered*	*entered*
consider	*considered*	*considered*

The different forms of a verb tell when something happened—in the *present* (I *talk*) or in the *past* (I *talked*, I *have talked*, I *had talked*).

PRACTICE 1 Identifying Put an X to the left of the incorrect verb forms in the following chart.

	Present Tense	Past Tense	Past Participle
1.	________ clap	________ clapped	________ clapped
2.	________ help	________ helpt	________ helped
3.	________ watched	________ watched	________ watched
4.	________ gaze	________ gazed	________ gazd
5.	________ reclined	________ reclined	________ reclined

PRACTICE 2 Completing Write the correct forms of the following regular verbs.

	Present Tense	Past Tense	Past Participle
1. smoke	____________	____________	____________
2. create	____________	____________	____________
3. paste	____________	____________	____________
4. buzz	____________	____________	____________
5. pick	____________	____________	____________

PRACTICE 3 Writing Your Own Write five sentences using variations of the verbs in Practice 1.

IRREGULAR VERBS

Irregular verbs do not form their past tense and past participle with *-d* or *-ed*. That is why they are irregular. Some follow certain patterns (*spring, sprang, sprung; ring, rang, rung; drink, drank, drunk; sink, sank, sunk*). But the only sure way to know the forms of an irregular verb is to spend time learning them. As you write, you can check a dictionary or the following list.

Common Irregular Verbs

PRESENT TENSE	PAST TENSE	PAST PARTICIPLE (USED WITH HELPING WORDS LIKE *HAVE, HAS, HAD)*
am	*was*	*been*
are	*were*	*been*
begin	*began*	*begun*
bring	*brought (not brang)*	*brought (not brung)*
build	*built*	*built*
burst	*burst (not bursted)*	*burst*
buy	*bought*	*bought*
choose	*chose*	*chosen*
come	*came*	*come*
deal	*dealt*	*dealt*
do	*did (not done)*	*done*
draw	*drew*	*drawn*
drink	*drank*	*drunk*
drive	*drove*	*driven*
eat	*ate*	*eaten*
fall	*fell*	*fallen*
get	*got*	*got, gotten*

go	*went*	*gone*
is	*was*	*been*
know	*knew*	*known*
lay	*laid*	*laid*
leave	*left*	*left*
lie[1]	*lay*	*lain*
lose	*lost*	*lost*
meet	*met*	*met*
pay	*paid*	*paid*
prove	*proved*	*proved, proven*
ride	*rode*	*ridden*
ring	*rang*	*rung*
rise	*rose*	*risen*
run	*ran*	*run*
see	*saw (not seen)*	*seen*
shake	*shook*	*shaken*
shine[2] *(a light)*	*shone*	*shone*
shrink	*shrank*	*shrunk*
sink	*sank*	*sunk*
spring	*sprang (not sprung)*	*sprung*
stand	*stood*	*stood*
steal	*stole*	*stolen*
stick	*stuck*	*stuck*
stink	*stank (not stunk)*	*stunk*
strike	*struck*	*struck, stricken*

strive	*strove*	*striven, strived*
swear	*swore*	*sworn*
swell	*swelled*	*swelled, swollen*
swim	*swam*	*swum*
swing	*swung*	*swung*
take	*took*	*taken*
throw	*threw*	*thrown*
write	*wrote*	*written*

[1]*Lie* meaning "tell a lie" is regular: *lie, lied, lied.*
[2]*Shine* meaning "brighten by polishing" is regular: *shine, shined, shined.*

PRACTICE 4 Identifying Put an X to the left of the incorrect verb forms in the following chart.

	Present Tense	Past Tense	Past Participle
1.	_______ bear	_______ beared	_______ borne
2.	_______ shrink	_______ shrank	_______ shrank
3.	_______ swing	_______ swung	_______ swang
4.	_______ deal	_______ dealed	_______ dealt
5.	_______ chose	_______ chose	_______ chosen

PRACTICE 5 Completing Write the correct forms of the following irregular verbs.

	Present Tense	Past Tense	Past Participle
1. am	____________	____________	____________
2. write	____________	____________	____________
3. sweep	____________	____________	____________
4. fall	____________	____________	____________
5. swell	____________	____________	____________

PRACTICE 6 Writing Your Own Write five sentences using at least five of the words from the chart in Practice 5.

USING *LIE/LAY* AND *SIT/SET* CORRECTLY

Two pairs of verbs are often used incorrectly—*lie/lay* and *sit/set*.

Lie/Lay

	Present Tense	Past Tense	Past Participle
lie (recline or lie down)	lie	lay	(have, has, had) lain
lay (put or place down)	lay	laid	(have, has, had) laid

The verb *lay* always takes an object. You must lay something down:

Lay down *what?*

Lay down *your books*.

Sit/Set

	Present Tense	Past Tense	Past Participle
sit (get into a seated position)	sit	sat	(have, has, had) sat
set (put or place down)	set	set	(have, has, had) set

Like the verb *lay*, the verb *set* must always have an object. You must set something down:

Set *what?*

Set *the presents* over here.

PRACTICE 7 Identifying Choose the correct verb in the following sentences.

1. After I (sat, set) down, I felt much better.
2. All day I have (lain, laid) in my room watching TV.
3. He has (lay, laid) the blanket down for our picnic.
4. We had to (sat, set) our watches to exactly the same time.
5. (Lie, Lay) the pieces of the puzzle out on the table, please.

PRACTICE 8 Completing Fill in each blank in the following sentences with the correct form of *lie/lay* or *sit/set*.

1. Suzy has _____ in the bathtub for so long that her skin has wrinkled.
2. I could have _____ in the moonlight looking at the stars all night.
3. The cook _____ out all the ingredients.
4. Please _____ those heavy boxes down before you strain your back.
5. I think I will go and _____ down for a while.

PRACTICE 9 Writing Your Own Write five sentences using variations of *lie/lay* or *sit/set*.

CHAPTER REVIEW

Regular Verbs: form the past tense and past participle by adding *-d* or *-ed*.

Past Participle: verb form often used with helping verbs like *have*, *has*, or *had*.

Irregular Verbs: do not form the past tense or past participle by adding *-d* or *-ed*.

You might want to reread the examples in this chapter before you do the following exercises.

REVIEW PRACTICE 1 Identifying Write out the past tense and past participle of each verb listed here and then identify the verb as either regular or irregular.

Present Tense	Past Tense	Past Participle	Type of Verb
1. brush	________	________	________
2. fix	________	________	________
3. wear	________	________	________
4. buy	________	________	________
5. suffer	________	________	________
6. have	________	________	________
7. type	________	________	________
8. feel	________	________	________
9. touch	________	________	________
10. teach	________	________	________

REVIEW PRACTICE 2 Completing Fill in each blank in the following sentences with a regular or irregular verb that makes sense.

1. Yesterday, I ____________ at my computer and tried to write my essay.
2. Tilda ____________ over to my house last night.
3. I always smile and ____________ my hand to the people on the Mardi Gras floats.
4. Geraldo has ____________ his drink all over the waitress.
5. Carlos and Tom have ____________ class again.
6. You should never ____________ an infant; doing so can cause brain damage and death.
7. The groom smiled at his bride and ____________ the ring on her third finger.
8. The plumbing in the house has ____________ a leak.
9. Mary Ann ____________ the picture in her bedroom.
10. All cozy in my bed, I ____________ right through the earthquake.

REVIEW PRACTICE 3 Writing Your Own Write a paragraph explaining the most important parts of your daily routine. Be sure to explain why each activity is important.

REVIEW PRACTICE 4 Editing Your Writing Exchange paragraphs from Review Practice 3 with another student, and do the following:

1. Circle any verb forms that are not correct.
2. Suggest a correction for these incorrect forms.

Then return the paper to its writer, and use the information in this chapter to correct the verb forms in your own paragraph. Record your errors on the Error Log in Appendix 3.

Subject–Verb Agreement

CHAPTER

27

CHECKLIST for Correcting Subject–Verb Agreement Problems

✔ Do all subjects agree with their verbs?

Test Yourself

Underline the subjects once and the complete verbs twice in the following sentences. Put an X by the sentence if its subject and verb do not agree.

- _____ Neither the shorts nor the shirt fit me.
- _____ Chips and dip is my favourite snack.
- _____ There were a large storm last night.
- _____ Some of the soil along with the fertilizer are for the orchard.
- _____ Cotton and silk is more comfortable than wool.

(Answers are in Appendix 9 on the Text Enrichment Site.)

Almost every day, we come across situations that require us to reach an agreement with someone. For example, you and a friend might have to agree on which movie to see, or you and your manager might have to agree on how many hours you'll work in the coming week. Whatever the issue, agreement is essential in most aspects of life—including writing. In this chapter, you will learn how to resolve conflicts in your sentences by making sure your subjects and verbs agree.

SUBJECT–VERB AGREEMENT

Subject–verb agreement simply means that singular subjects must be paired with singular verbs and plural subjects with plural verbs. Look at this example:

Singular: **She works** in Halifax.

The subject *she* is singular because it refers to only one person. The verb *works* is singular and matches the singular subject. Here is the same sentence in plural form:

Plural: **They work** in Halifax.

The subject *they* is plural, referring to more than one person, and the verb *work* is also plural.

PRACTICE 1 **Identifying** Underline the verb that agrees with its subject in each of the following sentences.

1. In her free time, Cassie (are, is) a volunteer nurse.
2. The girls usually (store, stores) their gear in the lockers.
3. Rocky, my 80-pound dog, (eat, eats) more food in a day than I do.
4. I (do, does) all my reading for my classes at least a week ahead of time.
5. You (has, have) something green in your hair.

PRACTICE 2 **Completing** Fill in each blank in the following sentences with a present-tense verb that agrees with its subject.

1. Every evening, Michael ____________ by the fire.
2. They ____________ many questions.
3. Neil ____________ everything chocolate.
4. We rarely ____________ down that path, for it is always dark and eerie.
5. He ____________ to only classical music.

PRACTICE 3 **Writing Your Own** Write five sentences of your own, and underline the subjects and verbs. Make sure that your subjects and verbs agree.

WORDS SEPARATING SUBJECTS AND VERBS

With sentences that are as simple and direct as *She works in Halifax*, checking that the subject and verb agree is easy. But problems can arise when words come between the subject and the verb. Often the words between the subject and verb form a prepositional phrase. If you follow the advice given in Chapter 23, you will be able to find the subject and verb: *Cross out all the prepositional phrases in a sentence. The subject and verb will be among the words that are left.* Here are some examples:

Prepositional Phrases: The **notebook** (S) ~~for history class~~ is (V) ~~in my backpack~~.

When you cross out the prepositional phrases, you can tell that the singular subject, *notebook*, and the singular verb, *is*, agree.

Prepositional Phrases: The **roses** ~~in my garden~~ **bloom** ~~in April.~~

When you cross out the prepositional phrases, you can tell that the plural subject, *roses*, and the plural verb, *bloom*, agree.

PRACTICE 4 Identifying Cross out the prepositional phrase and underline the subject once and the verb twice in each of the following sentences. Cross out the prepositional phrases first. Put an X to the left of any sentence in which the subject and verb do not agree.

1. _____ Cindy, unlike many people today, do so much for others.
2. _____ That man in the blue pants think a lot about his social life.
3. _____ Frog legs, in spite of what most people say, tastes like frog legs.
4. _____ The flowers in the garden smell nice.
5. _____ The economy in Canada seem to be getting stronger.

PRACTICE 5 Completing Fill in each blank in the following sentences with a present-tense verb that agrees with its subject.

1. My little brother, despite being told otherwise, ____________ still in Santa Claus.
2. The train for Regina ____________ in the station at 7:45 p.m.
3. MuchMusic ____________ to air more music videos.
4. The boxes in the hallway ____________ in the moving van.
5. The wind during a thunderstorm always ____________ me.

PRACTICE 6 Writing Your Own Write five sentences of your own with at least one prepositional phrase in each, and underline the subjects and verbs. Make sure that your subjects and verbs agree.

MORE THAN ONE SUBJECT

Sometimes a subject consists of more than one person, place, thing, or idea. These subjects are called **compound** (as discussed in Chapter 23). Follow these three rules when matching a verb to a compound subject:

1. When compound subjects are joined by *and*, use a plural verb.

   Plural: **Thursday and Friday were** hot days.

   The singular words *Thursday and Friday* together make a plural subject. Therefore, the plural verb *were* is needed.

2. When the subject appears to have more than one part but the parts refer to a single unit, use a singular verb.

Singular: **Macaroni and cheese is** Eli's favourite food.

Macaroni is one item and *cheese* is one item, but Eli does not eat one without the other, so they form a single unit. Because they are a single unit, they require a singular verb—*is*.

3. When compound subjects are joined by *or* or *nor*, make the verb agree with the subject closest to it.

Singular: Neither hot dogs nor **chicken was** on the menu.

The part of the compound subject closest to the verb is *chicken*, which is singular. Therefore, the verb must be singular—*was*.

Plural: Neither chicken nor **hot dogs were** on the menu.

This time, the part of the compound subject closest to the verb is *hot dogs*, which is plural. Therefore, the verb must be plural—*were*.

PRACTICE 7 **Identifying** Cross out the prepositional phrases and underline the verb that agrees with its subject in each of the following sentences.

1. You and I (was, were) going the wrong way down a one-way street.
2. Chicken and dumplings (taste, tastes) better with a little salt and pepper.
3. Either the mosquitoes or the wind (cause, causes) my skin problems.
4. Celery and peanut butter (is, are) my favourite snack.
5. Neither the professor nor the students (knows, know) the answer to this question.

PRACTICE 8 **Completing** Cross out the prepositional phrases and fill in each blank in the following sentences. Use a present-tense verb that agrees with its subject. Don't use *is*, *are*, *was*, or *were*.

1. Either lilies or tulips ____________ well in the spring.
2. Pie and ice cream ____________ the best dessert.
3. The ants and flies in the house ____________ me.
4. The train and the passengers ____________ sometime this evening.
5. Neither the entrees nor the dessert ____________ appetizing tonight.

PRACTICE 9 **Writing Your Own** Write a sentence of your own for each of the following compound subjects. Make sure that your subjects and verbs agree.

1. either the handouts or the manuscript ________________________
2. brooms and brushes ________________________
3. neither the nurses nor the doctor ________________________
4. ham and cheese ________________________
5. the horse and her foal ________________________

VERBS BEFORE SUBJECTS

When the subject follows its verb, the subject may be hard to find, so making the subjects and verbs agree becomes more difficult. Subjects come after verbs in two particular situations—when the sentence begins with *here* or *there* and when a question begins with *Who*, *What*, *Where*, *When*, *Why*, or *How*. Here are some examples:

Verb Before Subject: Here **come** the **guests** for the party.

Verb Before Subject: There **is iced tea** in the refrigerator.

In sentences that begin with *here* or *there*, the verb always comes before the subject. Don't forget to cross out prepositional phrases to help you identify the subject. One of the words that's left will be the subject, and then you can check that the verb agrees with it.

Verb Before Subject: Who (V) is that tall **man** (S) in the blue suit?

Verb Before Subject: Where **are** (V) the watercolour **paintings** (S) **kept** (V)?

Verb Before Subject: When **are** (V) **you** (S) **flying** (V) to Whitehorse?

In questions that begin with *Who*, *What*, *When*, *Where*, *Why*, and *How*, the verb comes before the subject or is split by the subject, as in the last two examples.

PRACTICE 10 Identifying Cross out the prepositional phrases and underline the subject once and the verb twice in each of the following sentences.

1. Here lies the cause of the problem despite the evidence.
2. Who is the leader of your group?
3. How do you feel after your recent operation?
4. Where in the world are my keys?
5. There on the table are your books.

PRACTICE 11 Completing Cross out the prepositional phrases in each sentence. Fill in each blank in the following sentences with a verb that agrees with its subject.

1. Where ____________ the rest of the rhubarb pie?
2. Over the hill, there ____________ a great swimming hole.
3. Why ____________ their dirty clothes on the bathroom floor?
4. How many times ____________ your sister asked you to fix that hair dryer?
5. What ____________ this mess in the front yard?

PRACTICE 12 **Writing Your Own** Write a sentence of your own for each of the following words and phrases. Make sure that your subjects and verbs agree.

1. there may be ____________________
2. what has been ____________________
3. how did he ____________________
4. when is ____________________
5. here is ____________________

COLLECTIVE NOUNS

Collective nouns name a group of people or things. Examples include such nouns as *army*, *audience*, *band*, *class*, *committee*, *crew*, *crowd*, *family*, *flock*, *gang*, *jury*, *majority*, *minority*, *orchestra*, *senate*, *team*, and *troupe*. Collective nouns can be singular or plural. They are singular when they refer to a group as a single unit. They are plural when they refer to the individual actions or feelings of the group members.

Singular: The string **quartet**[S] **performs**[V] three times a year.

Quartet refers to the entire unit or group. Therefore, it requires the singular verb *performs*.

Plural: The string **quartet**[S] **get**[V] their new instruments on Monday.

Here *quartet* refers to the individual members, who will each get a new instrument, so the plural verb *get* is used.

PRACTICE 13 **Identifying** Underline the correct verb in each of the following sentences. Cross out the prepositional phrases.

1. The audience (listen, listens) intently to the guest speaker.
2. The majority (have, has) voted at different polling booths.
3. The orchestra (play, plays) different selections, depending on the concert.
4. Our high school cheerleading squad (is, are) all going to different colleges.
5. The litter of puppies (get, gets) a bath today.

PRACTICE 14 **Completing** Fill in each blank in the following sentences with a present-tense verb that agrees with its subject. Cross out the prepositional phrases.

1. A flock of geese always ____________ south for the winter.
2. The crew ____________ trouble making sure everyone has a good time.
3. The school orchestra ____________ this competition every year.
4. The army ____________ students who have degrees as officers.
5. The House of Commons ____________ according to individual beliefs.

PRACTICE 15 **Writing Your Own** Write a sentence of your own using each of the following words as a plural subject. Make sure that your subjects and verbs agree.

1. committee ____
2. gang ____
3. class ____
4. minority ____
5. group ____

INDEFINITE PRONOUNS

Indefinite pronouns do not refer to anyone or anything specific. Some indefinite pronouns are always singular, and some are always plural. A few can be either singular or plural, depending on the other words in the sentence. When an indefinite pronoun is the subject of a sentence, the verb must agree with the pronoun. Here is a list of indefinite pronouns.

Indefinite Pronouns

ALWAYS SINGULAR		ALWAYS PLURAL	EITHER SINGULAR OR PLURAL
another	*neither*	*both*	*all*
anybody	*nobody*	*few*	*any*
anyone	*no one*	*many*	*more*
anything	*nothing*	*others*	*most*
each	*one*	*several*	*none*
either	*other*		*some*
everybody	*somebody*		
everyone	*someone*		
everything	*something*		
little			
much			

Singular: **No one** ever **changes** at work. (s: No one; v: changes)

Everybody refuses to work harder. (s: Everybody; v: refuses)

Plural: **Many take** long lunches and **go** home early. (s: Many; v: take, go)

Others stay late but **are** tired and unmotivated. (s: Others; v: stay, are)

The pronouns that can be either singular or plural are singular when they refer to singular words and plural when they refer to plural words.

Singular: **Some** of Abby's day **was** hectic. (s: Some; v: was)

Some is singular because it refers to *day*, which is singular. The singular verb *was* agrees with the singular subject *some*.

Plural: **Some** of Abby's co-workers **were** late. (s: Some; v: were)

Some is plural because it refers to *co-workers*, which is plural. The plural verb *were* agrees with the plural subject *some*.

PRACTICE 16 **Identifying** Underline the verb that agrees with its subject in each of the following sentences. Cross out the prepositional phrases first.

1. All of my money (is, are) gone.
2. Both of the pools (was, were) treated with chlorine.
3. No one (do, does) more work than Pam.
4. Something (fly, flies) into my window every night and (buzz, buzzes) around my head.
5. Most of Omar's friends (seem, seems) friendly.

PRACTICE 17 **Completing** Fill in each blank in the following sentences with a present-tense verb that agrees with its subject. Cross out the prepositional phrases.

1. Most of the people ____________ to work in the mornings.
2. No one really ____________ if he will accept the job.
3. Both ____________ the consequences of their actions.
4. None of the fake contestants ____________ it was a joke.
5. Somebody ____________ moving my things off my desk.

PRACTICE 18 Writing Your Own Write a sentence of your own using each of the following words as a subject, and combining it with one of the following verbs: *is*, *are*, *was*, *were*. Make sure that your subjects and verbs agree.

1. anything ______________________________
2. others ______________________________
3. some ______________________________
4. any ______________________________
5. several ______________________________

CHAPTER REVIEW

Subject–Verb Agreement: Singular subjects must be paired with singular verbs. Plural subjects must be paired with plural verbs.

Prepositional Phrase: a group of words that begins with a preposition (*in*, *on*, *after*, *under*, *with*). The subject of a sentence cannot be in the prepositional phrase.

Compound Subject: a subject that consists of more than one person, place, thing, or idea.

Verbs Before Subjects: Place the verb before the subject in sentences that begin with *here*, *there*, *who*, *what*, *where*, *when*, *why*, or *how*.

Collective Nouns: a group of people or things.

Indefinite Pronouns: do not refer to anyone or anything specific.

You might want to reread the examples in this chapter before you do the following exercises.

REVIEW PRACTICE 1 Identifying Underline the subject once and the verb twice in each of the following sentences. Cross out the prepositional phrases first. Then put an X to the left of each sentence in which the subject and verb do not agree. Correct the subjects and verbs that don't agree by rewriting the incorrect sentences.

1. _____ There sit the man who will be the next Prime Minister of Canada.
2. _____ The moon and the stars in the evening sky shines brightly.
3. _____ The team usually practise off the track every Tuesday.
4. _____ Some of the fish in that tank seems to be sick.
5. _____ Doctor, how is the patient in room 204?
6. _____ Something very sharp keep punching me in the back.
7. _____ Sour cream and onion are my favourite type of dip.
8. _____ Here are the recipe from my grandmother.

9. _____ Neither the chairs nor the table match the decor in this room.
10. _____ My gang of artistic friends finds the new trends exciting.

REVIEW PRACTICE 2 **Completing** Fill in each blank in the following sentences with a present-tense verb that agrees with its subject.

1. My gang ____________ late for the show.
2. Neither wind nor rain nor snow ____________ us from going outside.
3. Here ____________ where Eugene's great-grandmother built her first house.
4. Several of the guests ____________ the secret code to the room backstage.
5. None of the water ____________ safe for drinking.
6. Where ____________ the tourists go for information about hotels?
7. Nothing ____________ to be wrong with the car.
8. The track team ____________ five kilometres every day, regardless of the weather.
9. Steven's mother and father ____________ planning a vacation to Paris.
10. There in that apartment building ____________ my former high school principal.

REVIEW PRACTICE 3 **Writing Your Own** Write a paragraph explaining why you did or did not join a committee, team, or other group. Make sure that your subjects and verbs agree.

REVIEW PRACTICE 4 **Editing Through Collaboration** Exchange paragraphs from Review Practice 3 with another student, and do the following:

1. Underline the subject once in each sentence.
2. Underline the verb twice.
3. Put an X by any verbs that do not agree with their subjects.

Then return the paper to its writer, and use the information in this chapter to correct any subject–verb agreement errors in your own paragraph. Record your errors on the Error Log in Appendix 3.

CHAPTER

28

PRONOUN PROBLEMS

CHECKLIST for Using Pronouns

- ✔ Are all subject pronouns used correctly?
- ✔ Are all object pronouns used correctly?
- ✔ Are all possessive pronouns used correctly?
- ✔ Are pronouns used in *than* or *as* comparisons in the correct form?
- ✔ Are the pronouns *this*, *that*, *these*, and *those* used correctly?
- ✔ Is the first person pronoun *I* avoided in formal academic writing?

Test Yourself

Correct the pronoun errors in the following sentences.

- The ball was their's to begin with.
- Tom told Valerie and I the most exciting story.
- James can type a lot faster than me.
- Those there running shoes are Kim's.
- Me and Julio are going to the movies tonight.

(Answers are in Appendix 9 on the Text Enrichment Site.)

Pronouns are words that take the place of nouns. They help us avoid repeating nouns. In this chapter, we'll discuss five types of pronoun problems: (1) using the wrong pronoun as a subject, (2) using the wrong pronoun as an object, (3) using an apostrophe with a possessive pronoun, (4) misusing pronouns in comparisons, and (5) misusing demonstrative pronouns.

PRONOUNS AS SUBJECTS

Single pronouns as subjects usually don't cause problems.

Subject Pronoun: **I** attended the opera with my aunt and uncle.
Subject Pronoun: **They** relocated to Calgary.

You wouldn't say "*Me* attended the game" or "*Them* went to Nunavut." But an error often occurs when a sentence has a compound subject and one or more of the subjects is a pronoun.

NOT **The boys and us** competed all the time.
Correct: **The boys and we** competed all the time.
Correct: **We and the boys** competed all the time.

NOT **Her and me** decided to go to Paris.
Correct: **She and I** decided to go to Paris.

To test whether or not you have used the correct form of the pronoun in a compound subject, try each subject alone.

Subject Pronoun? **The boys and us** competed for the trophy.
Test: **The boys** competed for the trophy. **YES**
Test: **Us** competed for the trophy. **NO**
Test: **We** competed for the trophy. **YES**
Correction: **The boys and we** competed for the trophy.
Correction: **We and the boys** competed for the trophy.

Here is a list of subject pronouns.

Subject Pronouns

SINGULAR	PLURAL
I	*we*
you	*you*
he, she, it	*they*

PRACTICE 1 **Identifying** Underline the pronouns used as subjects in each of the following sentences.

1. Diane and he will be gone for at least a week.
2. He is going to have to work faster if he wants to meet the deadline.
3. "I really don't want to go," he said.
4. We cannot use the elevator because it is not working.
5. She and I have been best friends since I can remember.

PRACTICE 2 Completing Fill in each blank in the following paragraph with a subject pronoun.

At first, my friends had me convinced that (1) _____ should go on the annual deep-sea fishing trip. (2) _____ spoke on and on about how much fun the last trip was. But before long, Brian admitted that (3) _____ got sick once the boat was out at sea. Then Misty described how the captain of the boat cut off the heads of the fish and gutted them. (4) _____ found the whole process exciting. (5) _____ can just imagine my reaction! I don't think I'll be joining my friends on their fishing trip.

PRACTICE 3 Writing Your Own Write a sentence of your own for each of the following subject pronouns.

1. they ____
2. you ____
3. he ____
4. it ____
5. I ____

PRONOUNS AS OBJECTS

One of the most frequent pronoun errors is using a subject pronoun when the sentence calls for an object pronoun. The sentence may require an object after a verb, showing that someone or something receives the action of the verb. Or it may be an object of a preposition that is required (see page 391 for a list of prepositions).

NOT She gave **Kenisha and I** some money.

Correct: She gave **Kenisha and me** some money.

NOT The secret is between **you and I.**

Correct: The secret is between **you and me.**

Like the subject pronoun error, the object pronoun error usually occurs with compound objects. Also like the subject pronoun error, you can test whether you are using the correct pronoun by using each object separately.

Object Pronoun?	She gave **Kenisha and I** some money.
Test:	She gave **Kenisha** some money. **YES**
Test:	She gave **I** some money. **NO**
Test:	She gave **me** some money. **YES**
Correction:	She gave **Kenisha and me** some money.

Here is a list of object pronouns:

Object Pronouns

SINGULAR	PLURAL
me	*us*
you	*you*
him, her, it	*them*

PRACTICE 4 Identifying Underline the correct object pronoun in each of the following sentences.

1. Natalie's grandmother had raised (her, she) since she was five.
2. The wonderful neighbours welcomed (we, us) to the community with a chocolate cake.
3. Corrina accidentally sprayed my sister and (I, me) with the hose.
4. All are going on the trip except for you and (him, he).
5. For (her, she), I will sit through this awful movie.

PRACTICE 5 Completing Fill in each blank in the following sentences with an object pronoun.

1. Between the two of _____, we should be able to fix the problem.
2. He asked you and _____ to the same dance.
3. Unlike _____, I am going to take emergency gear on this hiking trip.
4. According to you and _____, the test will take one hour.
5. The priest took _____ on a tour of the temple.

PRACTICE 6 Writing Your Own Write a sentence of your own for each of the following object pronouns.

1. us ______________________________
2. him ______________________________
3. me ______________________________
4. them ______________________________
5. her ______________________________

POSSESSIVE PRONOUNS

Possessive pronouns show ownership (***my*** *house*, ***her*** *hat*, ***our*** *family*). (See pages 389–390 for a list of pronouns.) An apostrophe is used with nouns to show ownership (***Jack's*** *dog, the* ***farmer's*** *barn, the* ***people's*** *opinions*). But an apostrophe is never used with possessive pronouns.

Possessive Pronouns

SINGULAR	PLURAL
my, mine	*our, ours*
your, yours	*your, yours*
his, her, hers	*their, theirs*

NOT That house is **their's.**
Correct: That house is **theirs.**

NOT The book on the table is **your's.**
Correct: The book on the table is **yours.**

NOT The dog chased **it's** tail.
Correct: The dog chased **its** tail.

PRACTICE 7 Identifying Underline the correct possessive pronoun in each of the following sentences.

1. The computer needs its monitor fixed.
2. Both of my aunts live in New Brunswick.
3. That piece of cake on the counter is hers.
4. The children left their toys in the driveway.
5. Hey! That was his.

PRACTICE 8 Completing Fill in each blank in the following sentences with a possessive pronoun.

1. These books aren't _____, so they must be _____.
2. _____ dogs bothered the neighbours so much that we had to move away.
3. The film crew left _____ equipment on the set.
4. Look at John's dog carrying _____ bowl in his mouth.
5. The car won't start because three of _____ tires are flat.

PRACTICE 9 Writing Your Own Write a sentence of your own for each of the following possessive pronouns.

1. mine ______________________________
2. theirs ______________________________
3. his ______________________________
4. its ______________________________
5. our ______________________________

PRONOUNS IN COMPARISONS

Sometimes pronoun problems occur in comparisons with *than* or *as*. An object pronoun may be mistakenly used instead of a subject pronoun. To find out if you are using the right pronoun, you should finish the sentence as shown here.

NOT She can analyze poems better than **me.**

Correct: She can analyze poems better than **I** [can analyze poems].

NOT Lilly is not as good a piano player as **him.**

Correct: Lilly is not as good a piano player as **he [is].**

Hint: Sometimes an object pronoun is required in a *than* or *as* comparison. But errors rarely occur in this case because the subject pronoun sounds so unnatural.

NOT Kay dislikes him more than she dislikes **I.**

Correct: Kay dislikes him more than she dislikes **me.**

PRACTICE 10 Identifying Underline the correct pronoun in each of the following comparisons.

1. Mark is much neater than (I, me).
2. Cindy, the head majorette at our high school, can twirl a baton as well as (we, us).
3. Simone is not as talented an artist as (him, he).
4. Those other puppies are much fatter than (they, them).
5. Tony is just as happy as (she, her).

PRACTICE 11 Completing Fill in each blank in the following sentences with an appropriate pronoun for comparison.

1. After he appeared in *Star Wars*, Harrison Ford became a bigger star than ____________.
2. Joey can throw a ball as far as ____________.
3. My friends managed to stay longer in the haunted house than ____________ did.
4. He makes you just as mad as he makes ____________.
5. Julia, whose parents are well-known artists, is a more talented painter than ____________.

PRACTICE 12 Writing Your Own Write a sentence of your own using each of the following pronouns in *than* or *as* comparisons.

1. I ____________________
2. she ____________________
3. they ____________________
4. we ____________________
5. he ____________________

DEMONSTRATIVE PRONOUNS

There are four demonstrative pronouns: *this*, *that*, *these*, and *those*. **Demonstrative pronouns** point to specific people or objects. Use *this* and *these* to refer to items that are near and *that* and *those* to refer to items farther away. Look at the following examples.

Demonstrative (near):	**This** is my room.
Demonstrative (near):	**These** are yesterday's notes.
Demonstrative (farther):	**That** is the town hall.
Demonstrative (farther):	**Those** are the cheerleaders for the other team.

Sometimes demonstrative pronouns are not used correctly.

	Incorrect	Correct
NOT	this here, that there	this, that
NOT	these here, these ones	these
NOT	them, those there, those ones	those
NOT	**Them** are the clothes she bought.	
Correct:	**Those** are the clothes she bought.	
NOT	I'd like to have **these here** books.	
Correct:	I'd like to have **these** books.	
NOT	I found **those ones** in the attic.	
Correct:	I found **those** in the attic.	
NOT	**Those there** are the ones I like.	
Correct:	**Those** are the ones I like.	

When demonstrative pronouns are used with nouns, they become adjectives.

Pronoun:	**That** is mine.
Adjective:	**That computer** is hers.
Pronoun:	**Those** are actions you may regret.
Adjective:	You may regret **those actions.**

The problems that occur with demonstrative pronouns can also occur when these pronouns act as adjectives.

NOT Please give me **that there** paper.

Correct: Please give me **that** paper.

PRACTICE 13A Identifying Underline the demonstrative pronoun errors in each of the following sentences.

1. The babies usually play with those there toys.
2. This here test is just too difficult.
3. I believe that there pair of shoes will do nicely for this outfit.
4. These ones should be brought in out of the rain.
5. I can carry this here if you'll take that there.

PRACTICE 13B Correcting Correct the demonstrative pronoun errors in Practice 13A by rewriting the incorrect sentences.

PRACTICE 14 Completing fill in each blank in the following sentences with a logical demonstrative pronoun.

1. _____ are the skates he wanted.
2. Would you like _____ curtains for your house?
3. _____ Corvette belongs to my uncle.
4. She baked _____ cookies herself.
5. I want _____ for my bathroom.

PRACTICE 15 Writing Your Own Write four sentences of your own, using each demonstrative pronoun. Be sure you don't use these pronouns as adjectives in your sentences.

CHAPTER REVIEW

Pronouns: take the place of nouns in a sentence

Subject Pronouns: take the place of the subject (*I*, *he*, *she*, *it*, *they*)

Object Pronouns: take the place of the object. One of the most frequent errors in pronoun usage is using a subject pronoun instead of an object pronoun (*him*, *her*, *me*, *them*).

Possessive Pronouns: show ownership. Never use an apostrophe with a possessive pronoun (*his*, *hers*, *ours*, *theirs*, *its*, *mine*, *yours*).

Demonstrative Pronouns: point to specific people or objects (*this*, *that*, *these*, *those*)

You might want to reread the examples in this chapter before you do the following exercises.

REVIEW PRACTICE 1 Identifying Underline the pronoun errors in each of the following sentences.

1. The football team and us went out for pizza after the game.
2. I think the fish is trying to tell you its' tank needs to be cleaned.
3. That secret was supposed to remain between you and I.
4. My brother at age four was as big as him at age six.
5. These here tarts are the best I've ever tasted.
6. Due to the power outage, him and me had dinner by candlelight.
7. I do believe you are stronger than him.
8. Hers' money is already spent even though she started out with $100.
9. One of my high school teachers taught me and she how to fly a plane.
10. I know that those there CDs belong to me.

REVIEW PRACTICE 2 Completing Correct the pronoun errors in Review Practice 1 by rewriting the incorrect sentences.

REVIEW PRACTICE 3 Writing Your Own Write a short paragraph about your most treasured object. Why is it your favourite possession?

REVIEW PRACTICE 4 Editing Through Collaboration Exchange paragraphs from Review Practice 3 with another student, and do the following:

1. Circle all pronouns.
2. Check that all the subject and object pronouns are used correctly. Also check that possessive pronouns, pronouns used in comparisons, and demonstrative pronouns are used correctly. Put an X through any that are not in the correct form.

Then return the paper to its writer, and use the information in this chapter to correct the pronoun errors in your own paragraph. Record your errors on the Error Log in Appendix 3.

CHAPTER

29 Pronoun Reference and Point of View

CHECKLIST for Correcting Problems with Pronoun Reference and Point of View

- ✔ Does every pronoun have a clear antecedent?
- ✔ Are pronouns as close as possible to the words they refer to?
- ✔ Do you maintain a single point of view?

Test Yourself

Underline the pronouns in these sentences. Then put an X over any pronouns that are confusing or unclear.

- It says to schedule your own appointments.
- Millie and Tanya were planning to go to Montreal, but her car broke down.
- I created a backup plan because you should always be prepared for the unexpected.
- You know they are covering up evidence of alien beings.

(Answers are in Appendix 9 on the Text Enrichment Site.)

Any time you use a pronoun, it must clearly refer to a specific word in the sentence. The word it refers to is called its **antecedent.** Two kinds of problems occur with pronoun references: The antecedent may be unclear, or the antecedent may be missing altogether. You should also be careful to stick to the same point of view in your writing. If, for example, you start out talking about "I," you should not shift to "you" in the middle of the sentence.

PRONOUN REFERENCE

Sometimes a sentence is confusing because the reader can't tell what a pronoun is referring to. The confusion may occur because the pronoun's antecedent is unclear or is completely missing.

Unclear Antecedents

In the following examples, the word each pronoun is referring to is unclear.

Unclear: A bucket and an oar lay in the boat. As Rachel reached for **it,** the boat moved.

(Was Rachel reaching for *the bucket or the oar?* Only Rachel knows for sure.)

Clear: A bucket and an oar lay in the boat. As Rachel reached for **the bucket,** the boat moved.

Clear: A bucket and an oar lay in the boat. As Rachel reached for **the oar,** the boat moved.

Unclear: Michael told Oliver that he should change jobs. (Does *he* refer to *Michael or Oliver?* Only the writer knows.)

Clear: Michael told Oliver that **Oliver** should change jobs.

Clear: Talking with Oliver, **Michael** said that he should change jobs.

How can you be sure that every pronoun you use has a clear antecedent? First, you can proofread carefully. Probably an even better test, though, is to ask a friend to read what you have written and tell you if your meaning is clear or not.

Missing Antecedents

Every pronoun should have a clear antecedent, the word it refers to. But what happens when there is no antecedent at all? The writer's message is not communicated. Two words in particular should alert you to the possibility of missing antecedents: *it* and *they*.

The following sentences have missing antecedents:

Missing Antecedent: In a recent political poll, **it** shows that many people consider their votes unimportant.
(What does *it* refer to? It has no antecedent.)

Clear: A **recent political poll** shows that many people consider their votes unimportant.

Missing Antecedent: **They** say that a fool and his money are soon parted.
(Who are *they?*)

Clear: **An old saying** states that a fool and his money are soon parted.

PRACTICE 1A Identifying Underline the pronouns in each of the following sentences. Then put an X next to any sentences with missing or unclear antecedents.

1. _____ According to recent surveys, it says that more people are walking to work.
2. _____ My red pen should be in my purse, but I can't find it.
3. _____ The sitting room must have its baseboards cleaned.
4. _____ Talking with Katrina and Mindy, I learned that she is moving to Saskatchewan!
5. _____ They say you can catch more flies with honey than with vinegar.

PRACTICE 1B Correcting Correct the sentences with pronoun errors in Practice 1A by rewriting them.

PRACTICE 2 Completing Correct the unclear or missing pronoun references in the following sentences by rewriting them. Pronouns that should be corrected are underlined.

1. <u>It</u> says that we are all required to be at the meeting.
2. <u>They</u> always told me to treat people the way I want to be treated.
3. According to Sue and Hannah, <u>she</u> has been accepted into Lakehead University.
4. We have chocolate and vanilla ice cream, but <u>it</u> tastes better.
5. <u>It</u> indicates that we should have turned left at the first light.

PRACTICE 3 Writing Your Own Write five sentences of your own using pronouns with clear antecedents.

SHIFTING POINT OF VIEW

Point of view refers to whether a statement is made in the first person, the second person, or the third person. Each person—or point of view—requires different pronouns. The following chart lists the pronouns for each point of view.

Point of View

First Person:	*I, we*
Second Person:	*you, you*
Third Person:	*he, she, it, one, they*

If you begin writing from one point of view, you should stay in that point of view. Do not shift to another point of view. For example, if you start out writing "I," you should continue with "I" and not shift to "you." Shifting point of view is a very common error in writing assignments.

Shift: If **a person** doesn't study, **you** will not do well in school.
Correct: If **a person** doesn't study, **he or she** will not do well in school.

Shift: **I** changed jobs because **you** have more opportunities here.
Correct: **I** changed jobs because **I** have more opportunities here.

PRACTICE 4A **Identifying** Underline the pronouns that shift in point of view in the following sentences.

1. If you don't eat a good diet, they may find their health suffering.
2. One can always find unique merchandise at the more exclusive stores, but you have to be willing to pay the price.
3. I hinted that I didn't want to take part in the play, but you never know if you've gotten the message across.
4. I see a couple of concerts a year because everyone needs a little culture in his or her life.
5. I've already started writing my research paper because you should never wait until the last minute.

PRACTICE 4B **Correcting** Correct the point-of-view errors in Practice 4A by rewriting the incorrect sentences.

PRACTICE 5 **Completing** Complete the following sentences with pronouns that stay in the same point of view.

1. I decided to pack lightly and carry my luggage on board the airplane, so _____ know my luggage will arrive when I do.
2. I should taste these dishes since _____ never know if I'm going to like them until I try them.
3. A person is expected to follow the rules of the road; otherwise, _____ may cause an accident.
4. I always wear a smile on my face since _____ never know who might be around.
5. One should pay attention; then _____ might not feel so confused.

PRACTICE 6 **Writing Your Own** Write a sentence of your own for each of the following pronouns. Be sure the pronouns have clear antecedents and do not shift point of view.

1. they ______________________________
2. you ______________________________
3. I ______________________________
4. it ______________________________
5. we ______________________________

CHAPTER REVIEW

Antecedent: the word that the pronoun refers to in the sentence.

Unclear Antecedent: the word each pronoun is referring to is unclear.

Missing Antecedent: If there is no word for the pronoun to refer to, then the meaning of the sentence will be unclear.

Point of View: refers to whether a statement is in first person (*I*, *we*), second person (*you*), or third person (*he*, *she*, *it*, *one*, *they*) point of view. Keep point of view consistent throughout your writing.

You might want to reread the examples in this chapter before you do the following exercises.

REVIEW PRACTICE 1 Identifying Label the following sentences U if the antecedent is unclear, M if the antecedent is missing, or S if the sentence shifts point of view. Then correct the pronoun errors by rewriting the incorrect sentences.

1. _____ If one forgets the answer, then you should look it up.
2. _____ They say you should never accept rides from strangers.
3. _____ Janie bought milk, bread, cheese, and lettuce at the grocery store, but she left it in the car.
4. _____ A person should always look both ways before crossing the street; otherwise, you might get hit by a car.
5. _____ Stacey and Myra have already left for the show, but she forgot her wallet.
6. _____ It explains that the majority of the citizens are in favour of the proposed freeway.
7. _____ I asked my friends about my decision because you always value your friends' advice.
8. _____ It pointed out that "every cloud has a silver lining."
9. _____ Steven told Jason that he was going to be late.
10. _____ I ordered two pairs of jeans, a pair of shorts, and a pair of shoes from a catalogue. I received it one week later.

REVIEW PRACTICE 2 Completing Correct the pronoun errors in the following sentences by rewriting each incorrect sentence.

1. I am going to purchase the most expensive champagne I can find, for you know that will impress the guests.
2. According to this announcement, it says we need to arrive no later than 2:00 p.m.
3. Jake and Dean will probably get into good colleges, even though he has a higher GPA.
4. A person should manage time wisely since you only have 24 hours in a day.
5. They are always carrying on about how bad the humidity is in Toronto.
6. Before Carla and Trisha left town, she bought a new swimsuit.
7. We were gossiping about Jarrett and Jeremy when he walked right by us.
8. One should study for the test if you want to pass it.
9. I had my hands full with a squirming puppy and a hissing cat until I decided to set him down.
10. You know what they say: "Never go to bed with a wet head."

REVIEW PRACTICE 3 Writing Your Own Write a paragraph about a new experience you have had. Include at least six different pronouns.

REVIEW PRACTICE 4 Editing Through Collaboration Exchange paragraphs from Review Practice 3 with another student, and then do the following:

1. Underline all pronouns.
2. Draw arrows to the words they modify.
3. Put an X through any pronouns that do not refer to a clear antecedent or that shift point of view.

Then return the paper to its writer, and use the information in this chapter to correct any pronoun reference and point-of-view errors in your own paragraph. Record your errors on the Error Log in Appendix 3.

CHAPTER

30 Pronoun Agreement

CHECKLIST for Correcting Pronoun Agreement Problems

- ✔ Do all pronouns and their antecedents agree in number (singular or plural)?
- ✔ Do any pronouns that refer to indefinite pronouns agree in number?
- ✔ Are any pronouns used in a sexist way?

Test Yourself

Underline the pronoun in each sentence, and draw an arrow to its antecedent. Put an X over any pronouns that do not agree with their antecedents.

- Somebody left his lights on in his car.
- A judge must put aside her bias.
- Each of the children needs their permission slip signed.
- None of the fans could keep their voices quiet.
- A motorcyclist must take care of her gear.

(Answers are in Appendix 9 on the Text Enrichment Site.)

As you learned in Chapter 27, subjects and verbs must agree for clear communication. If the subject is singular, the verb must be singular; if the subject is plural, the verb must be plural. The same holds true for pronouns and the words they refer to—their *antecedents*. They must agree in number—both singular or both plural. Usually, pronoun agreement is not a problem, as these sentences show:

Singular: **Dr. Wu** told **his** patient to stop smoking.

Plural: **Carlos** and **Gina** took **their** children to Canada's Wonderland.

INDEFINITE PRONOUNS

Pronoun agreement may become a problem with indefinite pronouns. Indefinite pronouns that are always singular give writers the most trouble.

NOT **One** of the students finished **their** test early.
(How many students finished early? Only one, so use a singular pronoun.)

Correct: **One** of the students finished **her** test early.

Correct: **One** of the students finished **his** test early.

NOT **Somebody** just drove **their** new car into a ditch.
(How many people just drove a car into a ditch? One person, so use a singular pronoun.)

Correct: **Somebody** just drove **her** new car into a ditch.

Correct: Somebody just drove his new car into a ditch.

Here is a list of indefinite pronouns that are always singular.

Singular Indefinite Pronouns

another	*either*	*much*	*one*
anybody	*everybody*	*other*	*neither*
anyone	*everyone*	*nobody*	*somebody*
anything	*everything*	*no one*	*someone*
each	*little*	*nothing*	*something*

Hint: A few indefinite pronouns can be either singular or plural, depending on their meaning in the sentence. These pronouns are *any*, *all*, *more*, *most*, *none*, and *some*.

Singular: **Some** of the money was left over, so we gave it to charity.

Plural: **Some** of the donations were left over, so we gave **them** to charity.

In the first sentence, *money* is singular, so the singular pronoun *it* is used. In the second sentence, *donations* is plural, so the plural pronoun *them* is used.

PRACTICE 1 **Identifying** Underline the correct pronoun from the choices in parentheses, and be prepared to explain your choices.

1. All of the infants had (his or her, their) footprints and handprints recorded at the hospital.
2. None of the cars needs (its, their) tires changed.
3. Anyone can get (his or her, their) high school diploma.
4. Before anybody can join the club, (he or she, they) must fill out an enrollment form.
5. The farmers and the farmworkers want (his or her, their) work hours reduced.

PRACTICE 2 Completing Fill in each blank in the following sentences with a pronoun that agrees with its antecedent.

1. Fabiola and Fabian asked _________ questions at the same time.
2. Everyone should listen more closely to _________ teacher.
3. Matt lost _________ backpack at the park.
4. Anyone who could do a thing like that should have _________ head examined.
5. Something in the car leaked all _________ fluids onto the driveway.

PRACTICE 3 Writing Your Own Write a sentence of your own for each of the following pronouns.

1. none ______________________________
2. other ______________________________
3. no one ______________________________
4. everything ______________________________
5. someone ______________________________

AVOIDING SEXISM

In the first section of this chapter, you learned that you should use singular pronouns to refer to singular indefinite pronouns. For example, the indefinite pronoun *someone* requires a singular pronoun, *his* or *her*, not the plural *their*. But what if you don't know whether the person referred to is male or female? Then you have a choice: (1) you can say "he or she" or "his or her"; (2) you can make the sentence plural; or (3) you can rewrite the sentence to avoid the problem altogether. What you should not do is ignore half the population by referring to all humans as males.

NOT If **anyone** wants to go, **they** are welcome to do so.
NOT If **anyone** wants to go, **he** is welcome to do so.

Correct: If **anyone** wants to go, **he or she** is welcome to do so.
Correct: **People** who want to go are welcome to do so.

NOT **Everyone** remembered to bring their lunch.
NOT **Everyone** remembered to bring his lunch.

Correct: Everyone remembered to bring **his or her** lunch.
Correct: All the students remembered to bring **their** lunch.

Sexism in writing can also occur in ways other than with indefinite pronouns. We often assume that doctors, lawyers, and bank presidents are men and that nurses, schoolteachers, and secretaries are women. But that is not very accurate.

NOT Ask a **fireman** if **he** thinks the wiring is safe.
(Why automatically assume that the person fighting fires is a male instead of a female?)

Correct: Ask a **firefighter** if **he or she** thinks the wiring is safe.

NOT The **mailman** delivered my neighbour's mail to my house by mistake.
(Since both men and women deliver mail, the more correct term is mail carrier.)

Correct: The **mail carrier** delivered my neighbour's mail to my house by mistake.

NOT An **assistant** cannot reveal her boss's confidential business.
(Why leave the men who are assistants out of this sentence?)

Correct: An **assistant** cannot reveal his or her boss's confidential business.

Correct: **Assistants** cannot reveal **their** bosses' confidential business.

PRACTICE 4A Identifying Underline the sexist references in the following sentences.

1. The chairperson should keep his board informed of new developments.
2. A nurse gives her time and patience freely.
3. Each person is responsible for make-up work if they miss an assignment.
4. Everybody must bring food if they plan to eat.
5. A good sailor knows his knots.

PRACTICE 4B Correcting Correct the sexist pronouns in Practice 4A by rewriting the incorrect sentences.

PRACTICE 5 Completing Fill in each blank in the following sentences with an appropriate pronoun.

1. A technician might become frustrated with __________ job.
2. A hairdresser who attracts celebrity customers can name __________ price.
3. An accountant needs help with __________ accounts.
4. Somebody wrote __________ phone number on the washroom wall.
5. Another child has forgotten __________ lunch.

PRACTICE 6 Writing Your Own Write a sentence of your own for each of the following antecedents. Include at least one pronoun in each sentence.

1. doctor ______________________________
2. politician ______________________________
3. police officer ______________________________
4. spokesperson ______________________________
5. astronaut ______________________________

PRONOUNS AND FORMAL ACADEMIC WRITING

Often your instructor will ask that you avoid using the first person pronoun *I* while writing an essay. The reason for avoiding the personal pronoun is to give your writing an objective tone, to appear dispassionate and unbiased. You must be able to tell your reader what you think, but present it as a rational, objective argument. One way to do this is to avoid emotive language such as the first person pronoun *I*. If you overuse *I*, the facts that you put forth in your writing may be overlooked by the reader. Throughout your college courses, you may have instructors who ask that you avoid *I* and ones who don't mind the use of *I*. You, as a writer, must develop the flexibility of being able to express your opinion with or without the first person pronoun.

Avoiding *I*:

NOT: I will show you in my report that option A is the best choice.
Correct: **The report** will show that option A is the best choice.

NOT: I believe that the results indicate option A is the best choice.
Correct: **The results** indicate that option A is the best choice.

NOT: I do not believe that option B is the best choice.
Correct: **Option B** is not the best choice.

PRACTICE 7 **Correcting** Rewrite the following sentences, avoiding the first person pronoun *I*.

1. I will discuss the effects of violence in video games in the following essay.

   ____

2. I believe that violent video games desensitize children to violence.

   ____

3. I think that parents should take a more active role in deciding which games are appropriate for their children.

   ____

   ____

   ____

4. I don't think that young children should be playing realistic war games such as *Call of Duty 3*.

   ____

   ____

   ____

5. I don't believe that placing warnings on video game packages works as well as it should to keep young kids away from the more violent games.

____

____

____

PRACTICE 8 Completing Write a sentence stating your opinion about the following topics. Be sure to avoid the first person pronoun *I*.

1. Dogs ____

____

2. Aliens ____

____

3. Reality TV ____

____

4. Tuition Fees ____

____

5. Reading ____

____

CHAPTER REVIEW

Pronoun Agreement: Pronouns must agree in number. The pronouns must be consistently singular or plural throughout the sentence.

Avoiding Sexism: Be aware of leaving out half the population by assuming the pronoun is only masculine or feminine. Don't forget that men can be nurses and women can be firefighters.

Avoiding the first person pronoun *I* in academic writing: Try to give your writing an objective tone by avoiding *I*.

You might want to reread the examples in this chapter before you do the following exercises.

REVIEW PRACTICE 1 Identifying Underline and correct the pronoun errors in the following sentences.

1. Anyone who wants their book signed should stand in this line.
2. A good assistant keeps her dictionary within easy reach.
3. A surfer can lose his wave.
4. Only one of the contestants turned in their enrollment form on time.
5. The politician who cares about his people will win the election.
6. Each of the photographers has their own camera.
7. Everyone needs their funny bone tickled every now and then.
8. A tattoo artist should always clean her equipment before each new client.
9. A teacher should always ask her students if they understand the assignment.
10. Someone that messy should clean their room more often.

REVIEW PRACTICE 2 **Completing** Fill in each blank in the following sentences with an appropriate pronoun.

1. Neither of the criminals wanted __________ picture taken.
2. A racecar driver depends on __________ car and skill to win the race.
3. A housecleaner brings __________ own supplies.
4. Each of the boys can do __________ own work.
5. None of the students wanted to disappoint __________ teacher.
6. At the reunion, everyone talked to __________ friends.
7. Another person left __________ homework behind.
8. Somebody needs to water __________ lawn.
9. Everyone should be nice to __________ neighbours.
10. Nobody should park __________ car in a no-parking zone.

REVIEW PRACTICE 3 **Writing Your Own** Write a paragraph describing your favourite type of music. Why is it your favourite? Are you able to argue it as your favourite type of music without using "I"?

REVIEW PRACTICE 4 **Editing Through Collaboration** Exchange paragraphs from Review Practice 3 with another student, and then do the following:

1. Underline any pronouns.
2. Circle any pronouns that do not agree with the words they refer to.
3. Double-underline the first person pronoun *I*. Suggest how it can be avoided.

Then return the paper to its writer, and use the information in this chapter to correct any pronoun agreement errors in your own paragraph. Record your errors on the Error Log in Appendix 3.

CHAPTER

31

ADJECTIVES

CHECKLIST for Using Adjectives

- ✔ Are all adjectives that show comparison used correctly?
- ✔ Are the forms of *good* and *bad* used correctly?

Test Yourself

Underline the adjectives in the following sentences. Then put an X over the adjectives that are used incorrectly.

- The kites were very colourful.
- She has the worstest hair colour that I have ever seen.
- We were more busier this week than last week.
- He is the oldest of the two brothers.
- The Ford Mustang is more better than the Nissan Sentra.

(Answers are in Appendix 9461 on the Text Enrichment Site.)

Adjectives are modifiers. They help us communicate more clearly (I have a *green* car; I want a *red* one) and vividly (the movie was *funny* and *romantic*). Without adjectives, our language would be drab and boring.

USING ADJECTIVES

Adjectives are words that modify—or describe—nouns or pronouns. Adjectives often tell how something or someone looks: *dark*, *light*, *tall*, *short*, *large*, *small*. Most adjectives come before the words they modify, but with linking verbs (such as *is*, *are*, *look*, *become*, and *feel*), adjectives follow the words they modify.

Adjectives Before a Noun: We felt the **cold, icy** snow.

Adjectives After a Linking Verb: The snow was **cold** and **icy**.

PRACTICE 1 Identifying In the following sentences, underline the adjectives, and circle the words they modify.

1. Michael left a shiny red apple on the wooden desk on Monday morning.
2. Mrs. Johnson gave the two-year-old boy a piece of hard candy.
3. Our family doctor wants us to come in for our annual checkups.
4. I read a great book by Rohinton Mistry last week.
5. Grandma's beautiful garden is a quiet place for me to read, draw, or take a quick nap.

PRACTICE 2 Completing Fill in each blank in the following sentences with logical adjectives.

During my (1) __________ year of high school, I asked the head cheerleader to go to the prom with me. I was (2) __________ when she agreed to be my date, and I really wanted to impress her. I rented an expensive tuxedo, bought a (3) __________ corsage for her to wear on her wrist, and made sure to pick her up on time. The (4) __________ price was worth it because when we arrived at the dance, all of my buddies patted me on the back and said, "You two look (5) __________ together!"

PRACTICE 3 Writing Your Own Write a sentence of your own for each of the following adjectives.

1. curious ______________________________
2. durable ______________________________
3. thirteen ______________________________
4. helpful ______________________________
5. short-tempered ______________________________

COMPARING WITH ADJECTIVES

Most adjectives have three forms: a **basic** form, a **comparative** form (used to compare two items or indicate a greater degree), and a **superlative** form (used to compare three or more items or indicate the greatest degree).

For positive comparisons, adjectives form the comparative and superlative in two different ways.

1. For one-syllable adjectives and some two-syllable adjectives, use *-er* to compare two items and *-est* to compare three or more items.

Basic	Comparative (used to compare two items)	Superlative (used to compare three or more items)
bold	bolder	boldest
warm	warmer	warmest

foggy	foggier	foggiest
cozy	cozier	coziest

2. For some two-syllable adjectives and all longer adjectives, use *more* to compare two items and *most* to compare three or more items.

Basic	**Comparative (used to compare two items)**	**Superlative (used to compare three or more items)**
friendly	more friendly	most friendly
peaceful	more peaceful	most peaceful
wonderful	more wonderful	most wonderful
appropriate	more appropriate	most appropriate

For negative comparisons, use *less* to compare two items and *least* to compare three or more items.

Basic	**Comparative (used to compare two items)**	**Superlative (used to compare three or more items)**
loud	less loud	least loud
funny	less funny	least funny
popular	less popular	least popular

Hint: Some adjectives are not usually compared. For example, one person cannot be "more dead" than another. Here are some more examples:

broken	*final*	*square*	*unique*
empty	*impossible*	*supreme*	
equal	*singular*	*unanimous*	

PRACTICE 4 Identifying Underline the adjectives, and note whether they are basic (B), comparative (C), or superlative (S).

1. ______ The most logical decision would be to appoint Sam to the position.
2. ______ Today the students showed how dedicated they can be.
3. ______ Mila was happier about the engagement than her father was.
4. ______ The strongest students always score the highest on the exam.
5. ______ The food Nora and Richard ate on vacation was less healthy than what they eat at home.

PRACTICE 5 Completing Fill in each blank in the following paragraph with the correct basic, comparative, or superlative form of the adjective in parentheses.

One summer afternoon, I was hiking high in the mountains when the sky above me grew suddenly (1) __________ (dark) than I have ever seen it. It looked like rain was going to fall soon, and I happened to be in an (2) __________ (unsheltered) place on the mountain. I looked around to find the (3) __________ (suitable) tree to sit under, but there weren't any that would protect me. Even the (4) __________ (thick) tree was very puny and wouldn't keep the rain off my head. Quickly, I realized I had no option but to run (5) __________ (fast) than the rain to find shelter farther down the hill.

PRACTICE 6 Writing Your Own Write a sentence of your own for each of the following adjectives.

1. a superlative form of *pretty* ______________________________
2. the basic form of *sensible* ______________________________
3. a comparative form of *talented* ______________________________
4. a superlative form of *disgusting* ______________________________
5. a comparative form of *tall* ______________________________

COMMON ADJECTIVE ERRORS

Two types of problems occur with adjectives used in comparisons.

1. Instead of using one method for forming the comparative or superlative, both are used. That is, both *-er* and *more* or *less* are used to compare two items or both *-est* and *most* or *least* are used to compare three or more items.

   NOT My youngest son is **more taller** than his brothers.
   Correct: My youngest son is **taller** than his brothers.

   NOT This is the **most happiest** day of my life.
   Correct: This is the **happiest** day of my life.

2. The second type of error occurs when the comparative or superlative is used with the wrong number of items. The comparative form should be used for two items and the superlative for three or more items.

   NOT Marina is the **smartest** of the two sisters.
   Correct: Marina is the **smarter** of the two sisters.

   NOT History is the **harder** of my four classes this semester.
   Correct: History is the **hardest** of my four classes this semester.

PRACTICE 7A Identifying Underline the adjectives in the following sentences that are used incorrectly in comparisons. Mark sentences that are correct C.

1. _______ The most rudest customers are usually the ones who are trying to get something for free.
2. _______ Bob and Chad are both good-looking, but Bob is smartest.
3. _______ This class would be more fun if we could meet outside sometimes.
4. _______ The most rainiest day of the year was April 15.
5. _______ The bigger house in town is at 1859 King Street.

PRACTICE 7B **Correcting** Correct the adjective errors in Practice 7A by rewriting the incorrect sentences.

PRACTICE 8 **Completing** Choose the correct adjective forms in the following paragraph to complete the sentences.

Giving the dog a bath is the (1) __________ (more difficult, most difficult) chore in our house, and somehow it always seems to be my job. My sister Stephanie and I share most of the chores, but I am definitely (2) __________ (more responsible, most responsible) than she is. Usually, I do my chores without complaining, but bathing the dog is just unfair. We have an Australian sheepdog, and he is the (3) __________ (clumsiest, most clumsiest) thing alive. He seems to find every puddle of mud and sticky stuff to step in, and it quickly gets all over his fur. Unfortunately, though, he has a great dislike for baths, so the struggle to wash him is (4) __________ (trickiest, trickier) than it should be. And Stephanie is no help at all. While I'm fighting to hose him down, she just stands back and laughs at me, which makes me even (5) __________ (madder, more madder).

PRACTICE 9 **Writing Your Own** Write a sentence of your own for each of the following adjectives.

strongest ______________________________

more truthful ______________________________

most gracious ______________________________

larger ______________________________

most frightening ______________________________

USING *GOOD* AND *BAD* CORRECTLY

The adjectives *good* and *bad* are irregular. They do not form the comparative and superlative like most other adjectives. Here are the correct forms for these two irregular adjectives:

Basic	Comparative (used to compare two items)	Superlative (used to compare three or more items)
good	better	best
bad	worse	worst

Problems occur with *good* and *bad* when writers don't know how to form their comparative and superlative forms.

NOT more better, more worse, worser, most best, most worst, bestest, worstest
Correct: better, worse, best, worst

These errors appear in sentences in the following ways:

NOT That is the **worstest** food I've ever tasted.
Correct: That is the **worst** food I've ever tasted.

NOT Air pollution is getting **more worse** every year.
Correct: Air pollution is getting **worse** every year.

PRACTICE 10A Identifying In the following sentences, underline the forms of *good* and *bad* used correctly, and circle the forms of *good* and *bad* used incorrectly.

1. Both options are good, but getting a raise is more better than getting time off from work.
2. Giving that presentation in my psychology class was the worstest experience of my college career.
3. Giving your time to a charity is more good than just giving your money.
4. Sean wanted to go to the University of Western Ontario, but his grades were worse than he thought.
5. Doing the laundry is more worse than getting a root canal.

PRACTICE 10B Correcting Correct the errors with *good* and *bad* in Practice 10A by rewriting the incorrect sentences.

PRACTICE 11 Completing Using the correct forms of *good* or *bad*, complete the following paragraph.

The (1) __________ day of my life was July 8, 2001. I will always remember it (2) __________ than any other. I had just bought a brand new convertible and was taking it to the beach for a couple of days of fun in the sun. Fortunately, my (3) __________ friend, Tara, was with me, because just 60 kilometres outside town, the engine of my dream car overheated! What was (4) __________ was neither of us had a cellphone, and the closest pay phone was more than three kilometres away. We finally found a phone and called another friend, and then we waited and waited for a tow truck. After spending more than $3,000 on repairs, I found that my dream car had become my (5) __________ nightmare.

PRACTICE 12 Writing Your Own Write a sentence of your own for each of the following forms of *good* and *bad*.

best ____

bad ____

worse ____

better ____

worst ____

CHAPTER REVIEW

Adjective: words that modify or describe the noun or pronoun

Basic Adjective: the adjective in its original form

Comparative Adjective: used to compare two items or indicate a greater degree

Superlative Adjective: used to compare three or more items or indicate the greatest degree

You might want to reread the examples in this chapter before you do the following exercises.

REVIEW PRACTICE 1 Identifying Label the following adjectives basic (B), comparative (C), superlative (S), or not able to be compared (X).

1. _____ sillier
2. _____ most ridiculous
3. _____ dead
4. _____ tempting
5. _____ more stubborn
6. _____ meatiest
7. _____ most appealing
8. _____ broken
9. _____ tired
10. _____ lovelier

REVIEW PRACTICE 2 Completing Supply the comparative and superlative forms (both positive and negative) for each of the following adjectives.

	Basic	Comparative	Superlative
1.	welcome	______________	______________
2.	justifiable	______________	______________
3.	scary	______________	______________
4.	kind	______________	______________
5.	mystical	______________	______________
6.	strong	______________	______________
7.	foolish	______________	______________
8.	confusing	______________	______________
9.	extraordinary	______________	______________
10.	loving	______________	______________

REVIEW PRACTICE 3 **Writing Your Own** Write a paragraph describing the first pet you ever owned. What kind of animal was it? What did it look like? How did it act? What did you name it, and why did you choose that name?

REVIEW PRACTICE 4 **Editing Through Collaboration** Exchange paragraphs from Review Practice 3 with another student, and then do the following:

1. Underline all the adjectives.
2. Circle those that are not in the correct form.

Then return the paper to its writer, and use the information in this chapter to correct any adjective errors in your own paragraph. Record your errors in the Error Log in Appendix 3.

CHAPTER

32

ADVERBS

CHECKLIST for Using Adverbs

- ✔ Are all adverbs that show comparison used correctly?
- ✔ Are *good/well* and *bad/badly* used correctly?

Test Yourself

Underline the adverbs in the following sentences. Then put an X over the adverbs that are used incorrectly.

- The pants fit me too loose, so I returned them to the store.
- Tori wasn't never so happy as after she won the lottery.
- When Madeline returned from Paris, she said she'd had a real good time.
- We happily made more ice cream when our first supply ran out.
- I wanted so bad to win the race, but I couldn't catch up.

(Answers are in Appendix 9 on the Text Enrichment Site.)

Like adjectives, adverbs help us communicate more clearly (she talked *slowly*) and more vividly (he sang *beautifully*). They make their sentences more interesting.

USING ADVERBS

Adverbs modify verbs, adjectives, and other adverbs. They answer the questions *How? When? Where? How often?* and *To what extent?* Look at the following examples.

How:	My grandfather walked **slowly** up the stairs.
When:	Classes **always** begin after Labour Day.
Where:	Music lessons are held **here**.
How often:	I shop at The Bay **regularly**.
To what extent:	The airport is **extremely** busy during the holidays.

Some words are always adverbs, including *here*, *there*, *not*, *never*, *now*, *again*, *almost*, *often*, and *well*.

Other adverbs are formed by adding *-ly* to an adjective:

Adjective	Adverb
dim	dimly
soft	softly
careless	carelessly

Hint: Not all words that end in *-ly* are adverbs. Some, such as *friendly*, *early*, *lonely*, *chilly*, and *lively*, are adjectives.

PRACTICE 1 Identifying In the following sentences, underline the adverbs, and circle the words they modify.

1. We drove quickly to Toronto so that we wouldn't miss the concert.
2. I never saw that girl again.
3. Alex suddenly changed his mind and agreed to host the party.
4. Stephen successfully completed the nursing program.
5. When the children became impatient during the drive, we continually told them, "We're almost there."

PRACTICE 2 Completing Fill in each blank in the following sentences with an adverb that makes sense.

Sam's mom (1) _____ drove him to the airport, where he caught a plane to Winnipeg, Manitoba. He was going to visit his grandparents. (2) _____ Sam was only 10 years old, but he had (3) _____ flown alone before. When the plane landed in Winnipeg, Sam (4) _____ grabbed his carry-on luggage and (5) _____ ran to meet "Papa" and "Nonny."

PRACTICE 3 Writing Your Own Write a sentence of your own for each of the following adverbs.

1. now ______________________________
2. briskly ______________________________
3. innocently ______________________________
4. lazily ______________________________
5. often ______________________________

COMPARING WITH ADVERBS

Like adjectives, most adverbs have three forms: a **basic** form, a **comparative** form (used to compare two items), and a **superlative** form (used to compare three or more items).

For positive comparisons, adverbs form the comparative and superlative forms in two different ways.

1. For one-syllable adverbs, use *-er* to compare two items and *-est* to compare three or more items.

Basic	Comparative (used to compare two items)	Superlative (used to compare three or more items)
soon	sooner	soonest
fast	faster	fastest

2. For adverbs of two or more syllables, use *more* to compare two items and *most* to compare three or more items.

Basic	Comparative (used to compare two items)	Superlative (used to compare three or more items)
strangely	more strangely	most strangely
carefully	more carefully	most carefully
happily	more happily	most happily

For negative comparisons, adverbs, like adjectives, use *less* to compare two items and *least* to compare three or more items.

Basic	Comparative (used to compare two items)	Superlative (used to compare three or more items)
close	less close	least close
quickly	less quickly	least quickly
creatively	less creatively	least creatively

Hint: Like adjectives, certain adverbs are not usually compared. Something cannot last "more eternally" or work "more invisibly." The following adverbs cannot logically be compared.

endlessly	*eternally*	*infinitely*
equally	*impossibly*	*invisibly*

PRACTICE 4 Identifying Underline the adverbs, and note whether they are basic (B), comparative (C), or superlative (S).

1. _____ When Jack joined the gym, he began to lose weight more quickly.
2. _____ The sun shone more brightly after the rain stopped.
3. _____ London is the most rapidly growing city in southern Ontario.
4. _____ People enroll less often in the morning classes than the afternoon classes.
5. _____ Priscilla rudely interrupted her mother and walked out of the room.

PRACTICE 5 Completing Fill in each blank in the following paragraph with the correct comparative or superlative form of the adverb in parentheses.

At one time, *Owl* was the (1) ____________ (widely) read children's magazine. It had (2) ____________ (simply) written stories for the younger readers and (3) ____________ (intellectually) challenging games for the older kids than any other magazine. Because of the wide variety of material in each issue, *Owl* was the (4) ____________ (highly) acclaimed publication for Canadian youth. Now, though, *Owl* has lots of competition, and big publishers are creating magazines for young readers (5) ____________ (often) than they used to.

PRACTICE 6 Writing Your Own Write a sentence of your own for each of the following adverbs.

1. a superlative form of *readily* ______________________________
2. a comparative form of *eagerly* ______________________________
3. the basic form of *unhappily* ______________________________
4. a superlative form of *angrily* ______________________________
5. a comparative form of *honestly* ______________________________

ADJECTIVE OR ADVERB?

One of the most common errors with modifiers is using an adjective when an adverb is called for. Keep in mind that adjectives modify nouns and pronouns, whereas adverbs modify verbs, adjectives, and other adverbs. Adverbs *do not* modify nouns or pronouns. Here are some examples.

NOT She spoke too **slow.** [adjective]
Correct: She spoke too **slowly.** [adverb]

NOT We were **real** sorry about the accident. [adjective]
Correct: We were **really** sorry about the accident. [adverb]

PRACTICE 7A Identifying Underline the adverbs in the following sentences. Write C next to the sentences that are correct.

1. _____ Mike Myers's character laughed loud in the movie *Austin Powers*.
2. _____ I rocked the baby gently to put her to sleep.
3. _____ Mr. Simpson talked too quick, and I didn't understand the assignment.
4. _____ Before we left the zoo, we checked the map careful to make sure we'd seen everything.
5. _____ Cook the beans slow so they don't burn.

PRACTICE 7B Correcting Correct the adverb errors in Practice 7A by rewriting the incorrect sentences.

PRACTICE 8 Completing Choose the correct adverb to complete the sentences in the following paragraph.

Zack and I went to Canada's Wonderland last weekend and had a (1) ______________ (real, really) good time. When we pulled into the parking lot, we could hear the roller coasters zooming (2) ______________ (loudly, loud) overhead, and we could smell the yummy junk food. After we got through the gates, we ran (3) ______________ (quick, quickly) to the line for the Ghoster Coaster. The line moved along (4) ______________ (smoothly, smooth), and we were on the ride within 20 minutes. When the ride was over, we (5) ______________ (glad, gladly) got in line to go on it again.

PRACTICE 9 Writing Your Own Write a sentence of your own for each of the following adverbs.

1. specifically ____
2. tightly ____
3. greatly ____

4. sadly ____________________

5. coldly ____________________

DOUBLE NEGATIVES

Another problem that involves adverbs is the **double negative**—using two negative words in one clause. Examples of negative words include *no, not, never, none, nothing, neither, nowhere, nobody, barely,* and *hardly*. A double negative creates the opposite meaning of what is intended.

Double Negative: She **never** had **no** time to rest.

The actual meaning of these double negatives is "She did have time to rest."

Correction: She had **no** time to rest.

Double Negative: My brother does **not** give me **nothing.**

The actual meaning of these double negatives is "My brother does give me something."

Correction: My brother does **not** give me **anything.**

Double negatives often occur with contractions.

Double Negative: There **aren't hardly** any apples left.

The actual meaning of these double negatives is "There are plenty of apples left."

Correction: There are **hardly** any apples left.

Using two negatives is confusing and grammatically wrong. Be on the lookout for negative words, and use only one per clause.

PRACTICE 10A **Identifying** Mark each of the following sentences as either correct (C) or incorrect (X).

1. _____ He didn't never study, but he always passed the tests.
2. _____ Tabitha wasn't hardly four years old when her mother passed away.
3. _____ Nobody showed up for none of the practices last week.
4. _____ Hawkins doesn't really know what he wants to do.
5. _____ I wouldn't go nowhere with him.

PRACTICE 10B **Correcting** Correct the double negatives in Practice 10A by rewriting the incorrect sentences.

PRACTICE 11 **Completing** Choose the correct negative modifiers to complete the following paragraph.

Last summer, I went to the beach and (1) ___________ (was hardly, wasn't hardly) prepared for the sunshiny weather. I didn't buy (2) ___________ (any, no) sunscreen before I left because I had a decent tan already. To my surprise, I started to burn after only three hours on the beach, and there (3) ___________ (wasn't nothing, wasn't anything) I could do about it. I thought the burning feeling wouldn't (4) ___________ (ever, never) go away. And no matter what lotions and ointments I put on, I couldn't get (5) ___________ (no, any) relief. Next time, I'll remember to take along an umbrella.

PRACTICE 12 **Writing Your Own** Write a sentence of your own for each of the following negative adverbs.

1. never ______________________________
2. not ______________________________
3. barely ______________________________
4. nobody ______________________________
5. nowhere ______________________________

USING *GOOD/WELL* AND *BAD/BADLY* CORRECTLY

The pairs *good/well* and *bad/badly* are so frequently misused that they deserve special attention.

Good is an adjective; *well* is an adverb. Use *good* with a noun (n) or after a linking verb (lv).

Adjective: Brian is a **good** boy. (n: boy)

Adjective: She looks **good**. (lv: looks)

Use *well* for someone's health or after an action verb (av).

Adverb: He is **well** again. [health] (lv: is)

Adverb: The baby sleeps **well** at night. (av: sleeps)

Bad is an adjective; *badly* is an adverb.

Use *bad* with a noun (n) or after a linking verb (lv). Always use *bad* after *feel* if you're talking about emotions.

n

Adjective: He seems like a **bad** person.

lv

Adjective: I feel **bad** that I got a ticket.

Use *badly* with an adjective (adj) or after an action verb (av).

adj

Adverb: The house was **badly** burned.

av

Adverb: He swims **badly.**

PRACTICE 13A Identifying Label each of the following sentences either correct (C) or incorrect (X).

1. ______ I want to do good in this job so my boss will like me.
2. ______ My favourite team is playing bad this week.
3. ______ Vilma sings well and is pursuing a career in opera.
4. ______ Rachel said she felt bad about Mr. Brown's accident.
5. ______ I wanted so bad to go diving, but I couldn't.

PRACTICE 13B Correcting Correct the adverb errors in Practice 13A by rewriting the incorrect sentences.

PRACTICE 14 Completing Choose the correct modifiers to complete the following paragraph.

When Scott was in high school, there was only one thing he could do really (1) ____________ (good, well). He struggled with academics, he played most sports very (2) ____________ (bad, badly), and he was never popular with the girls. But his one strength was music. From the moment he picked up his first guitar, he was always (3) ____________ (good, well) at creating songs. Fortunately, his natural talent earned him several (4) ____________ (good, well) scholarship offers from big-name universities. Unfortunately, his (5) ____________ (bad, badly) study habits in high school made university more difficult for him, but he survived.

PRACTICE 15 Writing Your Own Write a sentence of your own for each of the following modifiers.

1. well ____________________
2. badly ____________________
3. good ____________________
4. bad ____________________
5. well ____________________

CHAPTER REVIEW

Adverbs: words that modify verbs, adjectives, and other adverbs. They answer the questions *How? When? Where? How often?* and *To what extent?*

Comparative Adverb: used to compare two items

Superlative Adverb: used to compare three or more items

You might want to reread the examples in this chapter before you do the following exercises.

REVIEW PRACTICE 1 Identifying Underline the correct word in each of the following sentences.

1. Tia and Sue Ann studied together for the midterm, but Tia took notes (more, most) thoroughly.
2. We don't have (no, any) money for rent this month.
3. His speech seemed to go on (endlessly, more endlessly, most endlessly).
4. Of all the teachers at this school, Mrs. Thompson speaks the (more clearly, most clearly).
5. Jose drives (more fast, faster) than I do.
6. During the baseball game, I struck out (less, least) often than Jack did.
7. She plays the flute very (good, well) and is in the orchestra.
8. My senior year in high school, I was voted (less, least) likely to drop out of college.
9. He hurt his knee so (bad, badly) it required medical attention.
10. The children were (real, really) tired after spending the day at the lake.

REVIEW PRACTICE 2 Completing Fill in each blank in the following paragraph with an adverb that makes sense. Try not to use any adverb more than once.

Working as a food server can be very challenging. I take my job (1) __________ than the other servers, so I can (2) __________ count on coming home with better tips. But sometimes there are customers I just can't please, no matter how (3) __________ I want to. Also, there are the minor problems that happen (4) __________, like the kitchen running out of chicken or the bartender forgetting to make the drinks for my table. Because I'm determined to do my job (5) __________, though, my customers like me and keep coming back.

REVIEW PRACTICE 3 Writing Your Own If you could prepare anything you wanted for dinner tonight, what would you make? Write a paragraph about this meal. How would you prepare it? How would you serve it? How many courses would it consist of?

REVIEW PRACTICE 4 Editing Through Collaboration Exchange paragraphs from Review Practice 3 with another student, and then do the following:

1. Underline all the adverbs.
2. Circle those that are not in the correct form.
3. Put an X above any double negatives.

Then return the paper to its writer, and use the information in this chapter to correct any adverb errors in your own paragraph. Record your errors on the Error Log in Appendix 3.

CHAPTER

33

Modifier Errors

CHECKLIST for Identifying and Correcting Modifier Problems

- ✔ Are modifiers as close as possible to the words they modify?
- ✔ Are any sentences confusing because the words that the modifiers refer to are missing?

Test Yourself

Underline the modifier problem in each sentence.

- After studying together, his grades really improved.
- Before doing the laundry, the car needed to be washed.
- To get a good job, the interview must go well.
- The professor told the class he was retiring before he dismissed them.
- I wrote a letter to the newspaper that complained about rising power bills.

(Answers are in Appendix 9 on the Text Enrichment Site.)

As you know, a modifier describes another word or group of words. Sometimes, however, a modifier is too far from the words it refers to (*misplaced modifier*), or the word it refers to is missing altogether (*dangling modifier*). As a result, the sentence is confusing.

MISPLACED MODIFIERS

A modifier should be placed as close as possible to the word or words it modifies, but this does not always happen. A **misplaced modifier** is too far from the word or words it refers to, making the meaning of the sentence unclear. Look at these examples.

Misplaced: The instructor explained why plagiarism is wrong **on Friday.**

(Is plagiarism wrong only on Friday? Probably not. So the modifier *on Friday* needs to be moved closer to the word it actually modifies.)

Correct: The instructor explained **on Friday** why plagiarism is wrong.

Correct: **On Friday** the instructor explained why plagiarism is wrong.

Misplaced: In Ontario, it is illegal to carry liquor in a car **that has been opened.**

(It is the liquor, not the car, that must not have been opened. So the modifier *that has been opened* needs to be moved closer to the word it modifies.)

Correct: In Ontario, it is illegal to carry liquor **that has been opened** in a car.

Certain modifiers that limit meaning are often misplaced, causing problems. Notice how the meaning changes by moving the limiting word *only* in the following sentences:

Only Aunt Emily says that Lilly was a bad cook.
(Aunt Emily says this, but no one else does.)

Aunt Emily **only** says that Lilly was a bad cook.
(Aunt Emily says this, but she doesn't really mean it.)

Aunt Emily says **only** that Lilly was a bad cook.
(Aunt Emily says this but nothing more.)

Aunt Emily says that **only** Lilly was a bad cook.
(Lilly—and no one else—was a bad cook.)

Aunt Emily says that Lilly **only** was a bad cook.
(Aunt Emily says that there were some who were good cooks and Lilly was the only bad one.)

Aunt Emily says that Lilly was **only** a bad cook.
(Lilly was a bad cook, but she wasn't bad at other things.)

Aunt Emily says that Lilly was a bad cook **only.**
(Lilly was a bad cook, but she wasn't bad at other things.)

Here is a list of common limiting words.

almost	*hardly*	*merely*	*only*
even	*just*	*nearly*	*scarcely*

PRACTICE 1A **Identifying** Underline the misplaced modifiers in the following sentences.

1. Tina told Tom that to win the lottery she had a great chance.
2. The car leaked all its oil by the time I called a mechanic in the driveway.
3. Brittany went to the mall with Jim wearing her new hat.
4. I sold Luigi my old watch after I bought an expensive new one for $10.
5. We made a pie in the kitchen with lots of blueberries.

PRACTICE 1B **Correcting** Correct the misplaced modifiers in Practice 1A by rewriting the incorrect sentences.

PRACTICE 2 **Completing** Fill in each blank in the following paragraph with a modifier that makes sense. Include at least two phrases.

Several years ago, Rodger owned a (1) ________ farm in Saskatchewan where he grew corn and wheat. He also had (2) ________ orchards of apples that he (3) ________ harvested every September. His children had (4) ________ the farm. Shortly before Rodger died, he trained his children (5) ________ the family business.

PRACTICE 3 **Writing Your Own** Write a sentence of your own for each of the following modifiers.

1. before summer ____
2. since the company hired him ________________________________
3. while driving to the store ________________________________
4. after she bought the car __________________________________
5. though no one was there __________________________________

DANGLING MODIFIERS

Modifiers are "dangling" when they have nothing to refer to in a sentence. **Dangling modifiers** (starting with an *-ing* word or with *to*) often appear at the beginning of a sentence. Here is an example.

Dangling: Reaching the top of the hill, the view was beautiful.

A modifier usually modifies the words closest to it. So the phrase *Reaching the top of the hill* modifies *view*. But it's not the view that reaches the top of the hill. In fact, there is no logical word in the sentence that the phrase modifies. It is left dangling. You can correct a dangling modifier in one of two ways—by inserting the missing word that is being referred to, or by rewriting the sentence.

Correct: Reaching the top of the hill, we saw a beautiful view.

Correct: When we reached the top of the hill, **the view we saw was beautiful.**

Dangling: To get into the movie, **an ID must be presented.**

Correct: To get into the movie, **you must present an ID.**

Correct: **You must present an ID** to get into the movie.

Dangling: **The garage was empty** after moving the tools.

Correct: After moving the tools, **we had an empty garage.**

Correct: **The garage was empty after** we moved the tools.

PRACTICE 4A **Identifying** Underline the dangling modifiers in the following sentences.

1. To get a good deal, time must be spent comparing prices.
2. Screaming for help, the chair fell over with the little boy in it.
3. As an only daughter with four brothers, there was never enough food in the house.
4. To get a driver's licence, two tests must be passed.
5. Giving the dog a bath, the bathroom floor became flooded.

PRACTICE 4B **Correcting** Correct the dangling modifiers in Practice 4A by rewriting the incorrect sentences.

PRACTICE 5 **Completing** Fill in each blank in the following paragraph with a modifier that makes sense. Include at least two phrases.

(1) ____________ professional baseball teams begin spring training. The coaches plan on (2) ____________ weight lifting and lots of running. Hundreds of (3) ____________ athletes begin training each season, but within days, many get cut from the major league teams. These men usually get placed on (4) ____________ teams. These men hope to play well throughout the season and (5) ____________ move up.

PRACTICE 6 **Writing Your Own** Write a sentence of your own for each of the following phrases.

1. warm and bright ____
2. shaking my hand ____
3. to understand the opposite sex ____________________________
4. getting a chance to see the ocean __________________________
5. to win an argument ______________________________________

CHAPTER REVIEW

Modifier: describes another word or group of words

Misplaced Modifier: The modifier is placed too far away from the word it is modifying, causing confusion in the meaning of the sentence.

Dangling Modifier: The modifier has nothing to refer to, or modify, in the sentence.

You might want to reread the examples in this chapter before you do the following exercises.

REVIEW PRACTICE 1 **Identifying** Underline the modifier errors in the following sentences.

1. Turning in my essay late, my computer crashed.
2. I am flying to Vancouver on Friday and returning Monday to attend a wedding.
3. To make a perfect chocolate dessert, the oven temperature must be carefully watched.
4. I put away my clothes and then called some friends in the closet.

5. Throwing the ball across the room, the lamp fell over and broke.
6. Jennifer complained that she forgot to send out invitations in an angry voice.
7. I found a pressed flower in my Shakespeare textbook from my wedding.
8. Driving to the movie theatre, teenagers kept stepping out into the street in front of us.
9. Maria has a picture of her cousins at the beach in her locker.
10. To please your parents, good grades should be earned on every report card.

REVIEW PRACTICE 2 **Completing** Rewrite the sentences in Review Practice 1 so that the phrases you underlined are as close as possible to the words they modify.

REVIEW PRACTICE 3 **Writing Your Own** Write a paragraph about your greatest accomplishment. What did you do? How hard did you work for it? What was your reward?

REVIEW PRACTICE 4 **Editing Through Collaboration** Exchange paragraphs from Review Practice 3 with another student, and then do the following:

1. Underline any misplaced modifiers.
2. Put brackets around any dangling modifiers.

Then return the paper to its writer, and use the information in this chapter to correct any modifier problems in your own paragraph. Record your errors on the Error Log in Appendix 3.

CHAPTER

34

Commas

CHECKLIST for Using Commas

- ✔ Are commas used to separate items in a series?
- ✔ Are commas used to set off introductory material?
- ✔ Is there a comma before *and*, *but*, *for*, *nor*, *or*, *so*, and *yet* when they are followed by an independent clause?
- ✔ Are commas used to set off interrupting material in a sentence?
- ✔ Are commas used to set off direct quotations?
- ✔ Are commas used correctly in numbers, dates, addresses, and letters?

Test Yourself

Add commas to the following sentences.

- We drove to the beach and we had a picnic.
- Before I eat breakfast I take a multivitamin.
- "This is my favourite restaurant" said Matt.
- Email though makes corresponding easy and fast.
- They were married on May 26 2004 in Bright's Grove Ontario.

(Answers are in Appendix 9 on the Text Enrichment Site.)

The **comma** is the most frequently used punctuation mark, but it is also the most often misused. Commas make reading sentences easier because they separate the parts of sentences. Following the rules in this chapter will help you write clear sentences that are easy to read.

COMMAS WITH ITEMS IN A SERIES

Use commas to separate items in a series.

This means that you should put a comma between all items in a series.

Series: The house had three bedrooms, two bathrooms, and a pool.

Series: She caught the fish, cleaned it, and then cooked it.

Series: William can have a new car if his grades improve, if he gets a job, and if he does his chores at home.

Sometimes this rule applies to a series of adjectives in front of a noun, but sometimes it does not. Look at these two examples.

Adjectives with Commas: The **foggy, cold** weather is finally over.

Adjectives Without Commas: The **loose bottom** knob fell off my TV.

Both of these examples are correct. So how do you know whether or not to use commas? You can use one of two tests. One test is to insert the word "and" between the adjectives. If the sentence makes sense, use a comma. Another test is to switch the order of the adjectives. If the sentence still reads clearly, use a comma between the two words.

Test 1: The **foggy and cold weather** is finally over. **OK, so use a comma**

Test 2: The **cold, foggy** weather is finally over. **OK, so use a comma**

Test 1: The **loose and bottom** knob fell off my TV. **NO comma**

Test 2: The **bottom loose** knob fell off my TV. **NO comma**

PRACTICE 1 Identifying In the following sentences, circle the commas that are used incorrectly, and add any commas that are missing.

1. In my free time, I like to read sew, and make jelly.
2. My girlfriend is very good, at tennis volleyball and golf.
3. The best things, about gardening are the relaxation, the sense of accomplishment, and the feeling of being at one with nature.
4. To play professional basketball, one must practise regularly, play competitively and get a big break.
5. The couch the footstool and the computer desk are going to be donated to Goodwill.

PRACTICE 2 Completing Add the missing commas to the following paragraph.

We are flying to Halifax this weekend to attend a friend's wedding. Before we leave, I need to do the laundry pay the bills and arrange for a house sitter. My husband's childhood friend is the one getting married, so he also hopes to see some of his other friends there—especially Gene Brad and Dwayne. During the past two months, we bought airline tickets arranged for a rental car and reserved a hotel room. Now all we have to do is make it to the airport on time! I'm also trying to decide whether to wear navy pink or grey, and my husband is getting his best suit altered. Though it has required lots of time energy and money, we are really looking forward to this trip.

PRACTICE 3 **Writing Your Own** Write a sentence of your own for each of the following sets of items.

1. three things to do at the mall ______________________
2. three sports you like to play ______________________
3. three items on a to-do list ______________________
4. three popular magazines ______________________
5. three of your favourite snack foods ______________________

COMMAS WITH INTRODUCTORY WORDS

Use a comma to set off an introductory word, phrase, or clause from the rest of its sentence.

If you are unsure about whether to add a comma, try reading the sentence with your reader in mind. If you want your reader to pause after the introductory word or phrase, you should insert a comma.

Introductory Word:	**No,** it didn't rain.
Introductory Word:	**Really,** the weather wasn't as bad as we thought it would be.
Introductory Phrase:	**On the whole,** this is a great town to live in.
Introductory Phrase:	**To prove this to my relatives,** I took them for a tour of the town.
Introductory Clause:	**As the doors opened,** the light poured in.
Introductory Clause:	**When the movie was over,** everyone was silent.

PRACTICE 4 **Identifying** In the following sentences, circle the commas that are used incorrectly, and add any commas that are missing.

1. Three years, ago, we lived in Red Deer.
2. As the fire continued, to burn the firefighters feared it would get out of control.
3. Sure I can take you to the store.
4. After spilling the water the little boy began to cry.
5. The next time you go, to Indigo would you pick up a gift certificate for me?

PRACTICE 5 **Completing** Add the missing commas to the following paragraph.

When Terina was seven years old we took her to Disneyland. Since she was tall enough to go on all the rides she really enjoyed herself. First we had to take pictures with Mickey and Minnie. Of course we couldn't miss them! Next we got in line for Space Mountain, which turned out to be her favourite ride. By the end of the day we had ridden Space Mountain five times.

PRACTICE 6 **Writing Your Own** Write a sentence of your own for each of the following introductory words, phrases, or clauses.

1. well ______________________________
2. when we thought it was almost over ______________________________
3. yes ______________________________
4. as the mail carrier arrived ______________________________
5. wanting to win the lottery ______________________________

COMMAS WITH INDEPENDENT CLAUSES

Use a comma before *and*, *but*, *for*, *nor*, *or*, *so*, and *yet* when they join two independent clauses. (Remember that an independent clause must have both a subject and a verb.)

Independent Clauses: The boy flew to London, **and** he took a boat to France.

Independent Clauses: He enjoyed the flight, **but** he liked the boat ride more.

Hint: Do not use a comma when a single subject has two verbs.

s v no comma v

The **boy flew** to London and **left** for France the next day.

Adding a comma when none is needed is one of the most common errors in college writing assignments. Only when the second verb has its own subject should you add a comma.

s v comma s v

The **boy flew** to London, and **he left** for France the next day.

PRACTICE 7 **Identifying** In the following sentences, underline the subjects once and the coordinating conjunctions twice. Then circle any commas that are used incorrectly, and add any commas that are missing.

1. My computer crashed, so I lost my whole research paper.
2. The car looks great, and drives even better.
3. Going to the mountains was a good idea and we had a very nice time.
4. The cat will curl up on the chair, or the rug by the fireplace.
5. My cousin wants to get married but I think she's too young.

PRACTICE 8 Completing Add the missing commas to the following paragraph.

For my last birthday, my grandmother gave me $100 so I wanted to spend it on clothes. I went to the mall and I found three outfits that were perfect. I couldn't decide on just one but I didn't have enough money for them all. I needed the dressy outfit more yet the casual outfit was a great bargain. Finally, I settled on one pantsuit but I'm saving money to go back and get the others. I'll go back within a month or maybe I'll just wait until after my next holiday gift.

PRACTICE 9 Writing Your Own Write a sentence of your own using each of the following coordinating conjunctions to separate two independent clauses.

1. or ______________________________
2. and ______________________________
3. so ______________________________
4. but ______________________________
5. yet ______________________________

COMMAS WITH INTERRUPTERS

Use a comma before and after a word or phrase that interrupts the flow of a sentence.

Most words that interrupt a sentence are not necessary for understanding the main point of a sentence. Setting them off makes it easier to recognize the main point.

Word: My next-door neighbour, **Julio**, is from Portugal.

Word: I didn't hear the phone ring, **however**, because I was in the shower.

Phrase: My textbook, ***Ancient Rome***, is on the desk.

Phrase: One of the most popular vacation spots, **according to recent surveys**, is Cuba.

Phrase: Mr. Colby, **chair of the school board**, has been elected mayor.

A very common type of interrupter is a clause that begins with *who, whose, which, when,* or *where* and is not necessary for understanding the main point of the sentence:

Clause: The new mall, **which is downtown,** has three large restaurants.

Because the information "which is downtown" is not necessary for understanding the main idea of the sentence, it is set off with commas.

Clause: Carol Roth, **who has a Ph.D. in history,** is my new tutor.

The main point here is that Carol Roth is my new tutor. Since the other information isn't necessary for understanding the sentence, it can be set off with commas.

Hint: Do not use commas with *who, whose, which, when,* or *where* if the information is necessary for understanding the main point of the sentence.

My friend **who is a circus clown** just arrived in town.

Because the information in the *who* clause is necessary to understand which friend just arrived in town, you should not set it off with commas.

Hint: Do not use commas to set off clauses beginning with *that:*

The mall **that is downtown** has three large restaurants.

PRACTICE 10 Identifying Label each sentence C if commas are used correctly with the underlined words and phrases or X if they are not.

1. _____ Jaclyn Smith, <u>who used to be a model</u>, has a line of clothing at Kmart.
2. _____ My girlfriend <u>Cheri</u>, is almost 23 years old.
3. _____ The Cineplex theatre, <u>my hangout</u>, is located on Queen Street.
4. _____ Joe's leather jacket, <u>which he's had only four months</u> has a broken zipper.
5. _____ Rideau Hall, <u>the residence</u>, used by the Governor General, was built in 1838.

PRACTICE 11 Completing Insert commas around the interrupting words and phrases in the following paragraph.

> My favourite grandmother Gram turned 80 this year. My grandfather died last August, and we didn't want Gram living alone. She was able to take care of herself however and didn't want to go to a retirement home. Recently, we visited Rosewood which is a very popular retirement community and she was impressed with the facilities. There are group homes of course with "around the clock" care, but

there are also condominiums where residents can live alone or with roommates. The entire neighbourhood is monitored by security guards which is reassuring and the medical staff is always available. Gram's been there for three weeks now and said when we asked that she's never been happier.

PRACTICE 12 Writing Your Own Write a sentence of your own for each of the following phrases.

1. who is very brave ______________________________
2. which costs over $100 ______________________________
3. however ______________________________
4. the mayor's wife ______________________________
5. taking the keys ______________________________

COMMAS WITH DIRECT QUOTATIONS

Use commas to mark direct quotations.

A direct quotation records a person's exact words. Commas set off the exact words from the rest of the sentence, making it easier to understand who said what.

Direct Quotation: My friends often say, **"You are so lucky."**

Direct Quotation: **"You are so lucky,"** my friends often say.

Direct Quotation: **"You are so lucky,"** says my grandmother, "to have good friends."

Hint: If a quotation ends with a question mark or an exclamation point, do not use a comma. Only one punctuation mark is needed.

NOT **"What did he want?,"** she asked.

Correct: **"What did he want?"** she asked.

PRACTICE 13 Identifying In the following sentences, circle the commas that are used incorrectly, and add any commas that are missing.

1. Tonya noted "I want the Canucks to win tonight."
2. "If you go now" he said "don't come back."
3. "Are you absolutely sure?," David asked.
4. "That cat," Christine said "sets off my allergies."
5. Mr. Avery remarked "The paper will not be accepted late."

PRACTICE 14 Completing Add the missing commas to the following passage.

"Are you going to the game tonight?" Vijay asked Lonnie.

"Of course" she replied "I wouldn't miss it."

"But the Raptors will probably be slaughtered" Vijay said.

"What difference does that make?" she questioned.

Vijay answered "I just don't want to pay money to watch them lose."

"Well, I'm a real loyal fan!" Lonnie emphasized as she walked away.

PRACTICE 15 **Writing Your Own** Write five sentences of your own using commas to set off direct quotations.

OTHER USES OF COMMAS

Use commas in the following ways.

Numbers: What is **2,502,500** divided by **10,522?**

Dates: My great-grandfather was born in December 1888 in London and died on **July 23, 1972,** in Kingston.

Notice that there is a comma both before and after the year.

Addresses: Ashley moved from **Victoria, British Columbia,** to **1939 Queen St., Stratford, ON N6B 2C9.**

Notice that there is no comma between the province and postal code.

Letters: **Dear Alicia,**

Yours truly,

PRACTICE 16 **Identifying** In the following sentences, circle the commas that are used incorrectly, and add any commas that are missing.

1. The new Honda Accord costs more than $23000.
2. Chris Bosh plays basketball with the Raptors and lives in Toronto Ontario.
3. My five-year anniversary is June 16 2005.
4. Jamie lives in Dryden, Ontario with her two kids.
5. Yours truly Deena

PRACTICE 17 **Completing** Add the missing commas to the following paragraph.

Norma graduated from Fanshawe College in London Ontario on June 5 1999. There were more than 3000 people in the audience, including Norma's friends and family. Her parents drove all the way from Montreal Quebec and they stayed in London all weekend. After the graduation ceremonies, Norma and her loved ones spent the weekend visiting the Toronto area and other parts of Ontario that Norma didn't get to see while attending school.

PRACTICE 18 Writing Your Own Write a sentence of your own for each of the following items.

1. your date of birth

____

2. the city and province where you were born

____

3. your full address, including the postal code

____

4. the estimated number of people who attend your school

____

5. the amount of money you would like to make per year after graduation

____

CHAPTER REVIEW

Comma: separates items in a series; sets off an introductory word, phrase, or clause; joins independent clauses if used with a conjunction; sets off extra or non-essential information that interrupts a sentence; and differentiates a quote from the rest of the sentence

You might want to reread the examples in this chapter before you do the following exercises.

REVIEW PRACTICE 1 Identifying Add the missing commas to the following sentences.

1. When I was 12 years old, my father took me to Honolulu Hawaii.
2. Seth wanted more dessert but he was on a diet.
3. Although James read that book before he couldn't remember how it ended.
4. The Prelude is of course the best Honda vehicle.
5. I proudly cheered as Nick my best friend scored a touchdown.
6. "We will begin discussing genetics next Tuesday" said the professor.

7. Azaleas carnations and roses are my favourite flowers.
8. The beautiful tall brown-haired model walked down the catwalk.
9. There are 300400 people in this county.
10. Craig and I started dating on August 7 2001.

REVIEW PRACTICE 2 **Completing** Add the missing commas to the following paragraph.

> My only cat Mango is Siamese. I still remember when she was born; it was February 14 1997 Valentine's Day. There are more than 1000 different breeds of cats but the Siamese are the most strikingly beautiful. Mango is a friendly cat however unlike most Siamese. When I first brought her home my friends said "She'll be a spoiled brat" but I have come to love her.

REVIEW PRACTICE 3 **Writing Your Own** Write a paragraph about the importance of computer knowledge. What are the benefits of computer technology? Why should we be familiar with it?

REVIEW PRACTICE 4 **Editing Through Collaboration** Exchange paragraphs from Review Practice 3 with another student, and then do the following:

1. Circle any misplaced commas.
2. Suggest corrections for the incorrect commas.

Then return the paper to its writer, and use the information in this chapter to correct any comma errors in your own paragraph. Record your errors on the Error Log in Appendix 3.

CHAPTER

35

Apostrophes

CHECKLIST for Using Apostrophes

- ✔ Are apostrophes used correctly in contractions?
- ✔ Are apostrophes used correctly to show possession?

Test Yourself

Add an apostrophe or an apostrophe and *-s* to the following sentences.

- The flight crew was surprised by the pilots rudeness when he boarded the plane.
- Its important that the car have its engine checked every 5,000 kilometres.
- Whats going to happen after Dominic is gone?
- The mens washroom is located on the third floor.
- James house is the third one on the left.

(Answers are in Appendix 9 on the Text Enrichment Site.)

The **apostrophe** looks like a single quotation mark. Its two main purposes are to indicate where letters have been left out and to show ownership.

MARKING CONTRACTIONS

Use an apostrophe to show that letters have been omitted to form a contraction.

A **contraction** is the shortening of one or more words. Our everyday speech is filled with contractions.

I have	=	I've (*h* and *a* have been omitted)
you are	=	you're (*a* has been omitted)
let us	=	let's (*u* has been omitted)

Here is a list of commonly used contractions.

Some Common Contractions

I am	=	*I'm*	*we have*	=	*we've*
I would	=	*I'd*	*we will*	=	*we'll*
I will	=	*I'll*	*they are*	=	*they're*
you have	=	*you've*	*they have*	=	*they've*
you will	=	*you'll*	*do not*	=	*don't*
he is	=	*he's*	*did not*	=	*didn't*
she will	=	*she'll*	*have not*	=	*haven't*
it is	=	*it's*	*could not*	=	*couldn't*

Hint: Two words that are frequently misused are *it's* and *its*.

it's = contraction: it is (*or* it has) — **It's** too late to go to the movie.

its = pronoun: belonging to it — **Its** eyes are really large.

To see if you are using the correct word, say the sentence with the words *it is*. If that is what you want to say, add an apostrophe to the word.

? I think **its** burning.

Test: I think **it is** burning. **YES, add an apostrophe**

This sentence makes sense with *it is*, so you should write *it's*.

Correct: I think **it's** burning.

? The dog wagged **its** tail.

Test: The dog wagged **it is** tail. **NO, so no apostrophe**

This sentence does not make sense with *it is*, so you should not use the apostrophe in *its*.

Correct: The dog wagged **its** tail.

PRACTICE 1 **Identifying** In the following sentences, circle the apostrophes that are used incorrectly, and add any apostrophes that are missing.

1. Ive got to find a better job.
2. The attorney said shes working overtime on this case.
3. Theyll be glad to see you at the party.
4. It's a good thing they did'nt take their baby to the wedding.
5. Cameron doesnt get paid until Friday.

PRACTICE 2 Completing Write contractions for the following words.

1. she + would = ______________________________
2. did + not = ______________________________
3. will + not = ______________________________
4. they + will = ______________________________
5. should + have = ______________________________

PRACTICE 3 Writing Your Own Write a sentence of your own for each of the contractions you wrote in Practice 2.

SHOWING POSSESSION

Use an apostrophe to show possession.

1. For a singular word, use *'s* to indicate possession or ownership. You can always replace a possessive with *of* plus the noun or pronoun.

the soldier**'s** rifle	=	the rifle **of the soldier**
someone**'s** house	=	the house **of someone**
doctor**'s** office	=	the office **of the doctor**
yesterday**'s** paper	=	the paper **of yesterday**

2. For plural nouns ending in *-s*, use only an apostrophe.

the soldiers**'** rifles	=	the rifles **of the soldiers**
the doctors**'** office	=	the office **of the doctors**
the painters**'** studio	=	the studio **of the painters**
the students**'** grades	=	the grades **of the students**
the brothers**'** boat	=	the boat **of the brothers**

3. For plural nouns that do not end in *-s*, add *'s*.

the men**'s** pants	=	the pants **of the men**
the deer**'s** antlers	=	the antlers **of the deer**
the criteria**'s** importance	=	the importance **of the criteria**

PRACTICE 4 Identifying In the following sentences, circle the apostrophes that are used incorrectly, and add any apostrophes that are missing.

1. The boys bicycle had a flat tire.
2. The disaster was Jennifers' fault.
3. Our two cat's water bowl was empty.
4. We thought the airlines food would be tasty.
5. Todays' temperature reached 32 degrees.

PRACTICE 5 **Completing** Write a possessive for each of the following phrases.

1. the feet of Charles ______________________________
2. the guests of Dr. Blakeney ______________________________
3. the tide of the ocean ______________________________
4. the shirts of the men ______________________________
5. the assignment of the students ______________________________

PRACTICE 6 **Writing Your Own** Write a sentence of your own for each of the possessives you wrote in Practice 5.

COMMON APOSTROPHE ERRORS

Two common errors occur with apostrophes. The following guidelines will help you avoid these errors.

No Apostrophe with Possessive Pronouns

Do not use an apostrophe with a possessive pronoun.

Possessive pronouns already show ownership, so they do not need an apostrophe.

Error	Correct
his'	his
her's or hers'	hers
it's or its'	its
your's or yours'	yours
our's or ours'	ours
their's or theirs'	theirs

No Apostrophe to Form the Plural

Do not use an apostrophe to form a plural word.

This error occurs most often with plural words ending in *-s*. An apostrophe indicates possession or contraction; it does *not* indicate the plural. Therefore, a plural word never takes an apostrophe unless it is possessive.

NOT The **clothes'** are in the dryer.
Correct: The **clothes** are in the dryer.

NOT She bought three **DVD's** last week.
Correct: She bought three **DVDs** last week.

NOT Get your coffee and **doughnut's** here.
Correct: Get your coffee and **doughnuts** here.

PRACTICE 7 Identifying In the following sentences, circle the apostrophes that are used incorrectly, and add any apostrophes that are missing.

1. I've been to that store five time's, and I've never seen shoes like yours'.
2. My brother's are working for my father's company.
3. Sam left his' cars window's down, and it is starting to rain.
4. The soccer player's are meeting at noon.
5. The big story in the newspaper's is yesterday's flood.

PRACTICE 8 Completing Write a possessive for each of the following phrases.

1. the house belonging to them ______________________________
2. the pants she owns ______________________________
3. the pop you are holding ______________________________
4. the price of it ______________________________
5. the feet of him ______________________________

PRACTICE 9 Writing Your Own Write a sentence of your own for each of the possessives you wrote in Practice 8.

CHAPTER REVIEW

Apostrophe: indicates ownership or where letters were left out in a contraction. Apostrophes should not be used with possessive pronouns. Apostrophes do not show that a word is plural.

You might want to reread the examples in this chapter before you do the following exercises.

REVIEW PRACTICE 1 Identifying In the following sentences, circle the apostrophes that are used incorrectly, and add any apostrophes that are missing.

1. Mr. Thompson's diner serves many pasta entrée's.
2. Two plumber's came to fix the leaks.
3. I thought I picked up my purse, but it was really her's.
4. Naomi was'nt pleased with the restaurants service.
5. The rose's in my front yard havent bloomed yet.
6. Its amazing that Tricia cut her hair as short as yours.
7. His' new house is in Highland Park.
8. You've got to see Ming's new jet ski's.

9. Our high schools head cheerleader is getting a full athletic scholarship to college.
10. Marys parent's ordered four pizza's for her party.

REVIEW PRACTICE 2 Completing Add the missing apostrophes to the following sentences.

1. The trucks brakes went out while it was coming over the hill.
2. We havent heard from Ben since he left his father's ranch and headed for ours.
3. My next-door neighbours uncle is a big Hollywood actor.
4. Sarahs diet consisted of hot dogs and sodas.
5. The freeways are crowded because yesterdays fire still hasnt been contained.
6. I think its time for us to go to our house and for you to go to yours.
7. Devons kids were playing dominoes.
8. Maurice cant ever beat me at backgammon.
9. Stellas going to the game with us.
10. Both cars gas tanks are empty.

REVIEW PRACTICE 3 Writing Your Own Write a paragraph about your favourite teacher. What was his or her name? What was special about this person?

REVIEW PRACTICE 4 Editing Through Collaboration Exchange paragraphs from Review Practice 3 with another student, and then do the following:

1. Circle any misplaced or missing apostrophes.
2. Indicate whether they mark possession (P) or contraction (C).

Then return the paper to its writer, and use the information in this chapter to correct any apostrophe errors in your own paragraph. Record your errors on the Error Log in Appendix 3.

CHAPTER

36

QUOTATION MARKS

CHECKLIST for Using Quotation Marks

- ✔ Are quotation marks used to indicate someone's exact words?
- ✔ Are all periods and commas inside quotation marks?
- ✔ Are words capitalized correctly in quotations?
- ✔ Are quotation marks used to indicate the title of a short work, such as a short story or a poem?

Test Yourself

Add quotation marks where needed in the following sentences.

- Can we go out to dinner tonight? she asked.
- Jeri screamed, Don't go in there!
- If you can't find my house, Tom said, call me on your cellphone.
- My favourite poem is This Is a Photograph of Me by Margaret Atwood.
- David said, I'll fix your car this weekend.

(Answers are in Appendix 9 on the Text Enrichment Site.)

Quotation marks are punctuation marks that work together in pairs. Their most common use is to indicate someone's exact words. They are also used to mark the title of a short piece of writing, such as a short story or a poem.

DIRECT QUOTATIONS

Use quotation marks to indicate a **direct quotation**—someone's exact words.

Here are some examples that show the three basic forms of a direct quotation.

Direct Quotation: "I will not lend you the money," said the banker.

Here the quoted words come first.

Direct Quotation: The banker said, "I will not lend you the money."

Here the quoted words come after the speaker is named.

Direct Quotation: "I will not," the banker said, "lend you the money."

In this example, the quoted words are interrupted, and the speaker is named in the middle. This form emphasizes the first few words.

INDIRECT QUOTATIONS

If you just talk about someone's words, you do not need quotation marks. **Indirect quotations** usually include the word *that*, as in *said that*. In questions, the wording is often *asked if*. Look at these examples of indirect quotations.

Direct Quotation: "I lost my job at the supermarket," said Bob.

These are Bob's exact words, so you must use quotation marks.

Indirect Quotation: Bob **said that** he had lost his job at the supermarket.

This sentence explains what Bob said but does not use Bob's exact words. So quotation marks should not be used.

Direct Quotation: "The train trip took eight hours," said Kira.

Indirect Quotation: Kira **said that** the train trip took eight hours.

Direct Quotation: "Did you get the car fixed?" Mom asked.

Indirect Quotation: Mom **asked if** I had gotten the car fixed.

PRACTICE 1 Identifying In the following sentences, circle the quotation marks used incorrectly, and add any quotation marks that are missing.

1. "Help me! yelled the drowning woman.
2. "If you can't take the heat," my mom used to say, stay out of the kitchen."
3. Martina asked, "Have you found my jacket?"
4. Steffan said, My goal is to "get into the Olympics."
5. Chonda said that "she enjoyed the movie last night."

PRACTICE 2 Completing Add the missing quotation marks to the following paragraph.

When I went into the salon, my hairdresser asked, How do you want your hair cut today? I don't really know, I replied, but I brought in a couple of pictures of haircuts I like. Those are cute she said. Do you think my hair would look good like that? I asked. Absolutely! she exclaimed. Then she set to work with the scissors. When she was finished, I looked in the mirror in horror. That's not what I had in mind, I told her. But it looks just like the pictures, she said. How can you say that? I exclaimed. The haircuts I showed you are shoulder-length, and mine is now above my ears. Well, she said, it will always grow back.

PRACTICE 3 **Writing Your Own** Write a sentence of your own for each of the following expressions.

1. a question asked by Claudia ____________________
2. a statement spoken by the manager ____________________
3. an exclamation spoken by Becky ____________________
4. an indirect question that Jared asked ____________________
5. a statement spoken by the electrician ____________________

CAPITALIZING AND USING OTHER PUNCTUATION MARKS WITH QUOTATION MARKS

When you are quoting someone's complete sentences, begin with a capital letter and use appropriate end punctuation—a comma, a period, a question mark, or an exclamation point. You do not need to capitalize the first word of a quotation if it is only part of a sentence. Here are some examples.

Capitalize the first letter of the words being quoted, and put a comma or a period at the end of the quotation if it is a statement. Separate the spoken words from the rest of the sentence with a comma.

"He doesn't seem very nice," she said.

He said, "Turn off the music."

If the quotation ends with a question mark or an exclamation point, use that punctuation instead of a comma or a period.

"Why do you want to know?" she asked.

He yelled, "Turn off that music!"

In a quotation that is interrupted, capitalize the first word being quoted, but do not capitalize words in the middle of the sentence. Use a comma both before and after the interruption. End with a period if it is a statement.

"Yes**,"** said the bus driver**, "**this bus goes downtown**."**

You do not need to capitalize the first word of a quotation that is only part of a sentence.

I don't think that he will ever **"f**ind himself**."**

Hint: Look at the examples again. Notice when periods and commas go inside the quotation marks.

NOT	"Yes", he said, "we're ready to leave".
Correct:	"Yes," he said, "we're ready to leave."

PRACTICE 4 Identifying In the following sentences, circle the quotation marks, capital letters, and other punctuation marks that are used incorrectly, and add any missing quotation marks and punctuation.

1. "Is there a doctor in the house"? the man screamed.
2. "I can't believe", she said, "That you've never seen the ocean."
3. Margarita asked, "Are you ever going to meet me for coffee."?
4. "This is the last time", he promised, "that I come home late".
5. Garrett said, "I want to take the bus to the restaurant on the corner".

PRACTICE 5 Completing Add the missing quotation marks and punctuation to the following paragraph.

I was having car problems, so I drove to the garage on the corner. What do you think is wrong with my car? I asked the mechanic. I can't tell you he said, until I take a look at it myself. I replied, I'll leave it with you this afternoon, and you can tell me later today what you find out. That would be great, he said. Finally, around 4:00 p.m., he called me on the phone. Your car needs a new clutch, he said. No way! I exclaimed. Sorry, mister he calmly replied, but that's all I found to be wrong with it. I explained, But I just replaced the clutch four months ago. Well, he said I hope you saved your receipt and warranty paperwork.

PRACTICE 6 Writing Your Own Write a sentence of your own for each of the following direct quotations, punctuated correctly.

1. "No, I won't" ______________________________
2. "How are we going to do that" ______________________________
3. "This is the most important priority" ______________________________
4. "Yes" "you can come to the party" ______________________________
5. "Don't worry" "you didn't miss anything" ______________________________

QUOTATION MARKS AROUND TITLES

Put quotation marks around the titles of short works that are parts of larger works. The titles of longer works are put in italics (or underlined).

Quotation Marks	Italics/Underlining
"Last Snowstorm" (short story)	*Canadian Short Stories* (book)
"Song of Myself " (poem)	*Leaves of Grass* (book)
"My Girl" (song)	*The Temptations' Greatest Hits* (CD)
"Explore Canada's Territories" (magazine article)	*Canadian Geographic* (magazine)
"Convicts Escape" (newspaper article)	*The Globe and Mail* (newspaper)
"The Wedding" (episode on TV series)	*Friends* (TV series)

PRACTICE 7 Identifying Put an X in front of each sentence with errors in quotation marks or italics/underlining. Add any missing quotation marks and italics or underlining.

1. _____ My favourite song by the Beatles is *Yellow Submarine*.
2. _____ When Juliet was in high school, she read Shirley Jackson's famous short story The Lottery.
3. _____ Getting through *Moby Dick* by Herman Melville took me three weeks.
4. _____ My first boyfriend recited William Blake's poem *The Garden of Love* to me on my front porch.
5. _____ The "Globe and Mail" ran a long article called *Japan's Princess Gives Birth* about Crown Princess Masako.

PRACTICE 8 Completing Place quotation marks around the titles of short works, and underline the titles of long works in the following paragraph.

Mark got a great job with the Toronto Star last summer. He is now working as the editor of the entertainment section, and he writes a column called Making a Mark. In his column, he reviews celebrity events and activities, such as concerts, hit movies, and best-selling books. For one article, he interviewed several people from Survivor, the popular reality TV show. He also attended a Tragically Hip concert and quoted lines from the song Scared on their album Day For Night. Another article featured Nikki Giovanni, who read her poem Dream during their interview. Mark has become friends with some very interesting and well-known people, and he is now looking forward to speaking with Atom Egoyan on the set of the latest sequel to Ararat.

PRACTICE 9 Writing Your Own Write a sentence of your own for each of the following items. Make up a title if you can't think of one.

1. a short story ______________________________
2. a song ______________________________
3. a TV show ______________________________
4. a CD ______________________________
5. a magazine article ______________________________

CHAPTER REVIEW

Quotation Marks: indicate someone's exact words or mark the title of a short piece of writing

You might want to reread the examples in this chapter before you do the following exercises.

REVIEW PRACTICE 1 Identifying Add the missing quotation marks and punctuation to the following sentences.

1. Patty sang Fergie's London Bridge at the karaoke party.
2. Our next writing assignment is a critical review of Robert Browning's poem My Last Duchess.
3. You don't have to go to work today, I told Gerard.
4. Marjorie won the short story contest with a tale she wrote about her grandmother called It's a Happy Day.
5. Devonne asked Where does Jack live?
6. When Princess Diana died, the <u>Boston Globe</u> ran an article called Too Soon.
7. The scores came in, and our coach yelled, Great job, team!
8. I can't make it to the meeting, she said, but I'll call you tonight to find out what I missed."
9. What do you want to eat for breakfast? Charise asked.
10. I submitted an article to <u>Golf Magazine</u> called How to Swing like Tiger Woods.

REVIEW PRACTICE 2 Completing Add the missing quotation marks, commas, and underlining for italics to the following dialogue.

Hurry up, I said, or we're going to be late for the Beastie Boys concert.

I'm coming, John replied. Just hold your horses!

The write-up in USA Today said this was going to be their biggest concert ever, I told him. I asked John if he too had read that article, but he said that he hadn't.

I didn't have time to read today, he explained, because I was busy buying a CD of their greatest hits. Now, John said, I'm really excited about the concert tonight!

REVIEW PRACTICE 3 Writing Your Own In paragraph form, record a conversation you had this week. Who were you talking to? What did you talk about? What were your exact words?

REVIEW PRACTICE 4 Editing Through Collaboration Exchange paragraphs from Review Practice 3 with another student, and do the following:

1. Circle any incorrect or missing quotation marks.
2. Underline any faulty punctuation.
3. Put an X over any incorrect use of italics/underlining.

Then return the paper to its writer, and use the information in this chapter to correct any errors with quotation marks and italics/underlining in your own paragraph. Record your errors on the Error Log in Appendix 3.

CHAPTER

37 OTHER PUNCTUATION MARKS

CHECKLIST for Using Semicolons, Colons, Dashes, and Parentheses

- ✔ Are semicolons used to join two closely related complete sentences?
- ✔ Are long items in a series that already contain commas separated by semicolons?
- ✔ Are colons used correctly to introduce a list?
- ✔ Are dashes used to emphasize or further explain a point?
- ✔ Are parentheses used to include additional, but not necessary, information?

Test Yourself

Add semicolons, colons, dashes, or parentheses to the following sentences.

- Kris left for the dance Jean decided to stay home.
- We wanted to win therefore we practised every day.
- The computer's advertised price didn't include several important things a monitor, a printer, and speakers.
- Ray asked the best question during the interview "Why should we vote for you?"
- Bring the jelly to a "rolling boil" a boil that cannot be stirred down.

(Answers are in Appendix 9 on the Text Enrichment Site.)

This chapter explains the uses of the **semicolon, colon, dash,** and **parentheses.** We'll look at these punctuation marks one by one.

SEMICOLONS

Semicolons are used to join two closely related sentences. They are also used to avoid confusion when listing items in a series.

1. Use a semicolon to separate two closely related independent clauses.
   An independent clause is a group of words with a subject and a verb that can stand alone as a sentence. You might use a semicolon instead of a coordinating conjunction (*and*, *but*, *for*, *nor*, *or*, *so*, *yet*) or a period. Any one of the three options would be correct.

	independent / independent
Semicolon:	Sam never drove to school**; he** always rode his bike.
Conjunction:	Sam never drove to school**, for** he always rode his bike.
Period:	Sam never drove to school**. He** always rode his bike.

2. Use a semicolon to join two independent clauses that are connected by such words as *however*, *therefore*, *furthermore*, *moreover*, *for example*, or *consequently*. Put a comma after the connecting word.

	independent / independent
Semicolon:	Travelling can be expensive**; nevertheless,** it's always enjoyable.
Semicolon:	Brad is very smart**; furthermore,** he was offered seven scholarships.
Semicolon:	He has trouble in math**; therefore,** he hired a tutor.

3. Use a semicolon to separate items in a series when any of the items contain commas.

NOT	On the flight to Vancouver, Mei Lin read a popular new thriller with a surprise ending, took a long, relaxing nap, and watched an incredibly dull movie about a rock star.
Correct:	On the flight to Vancouver, Mei Lin read a popular new thriller with a surprise ending; took a long, relaxing nap; and watched an incredibly dull movie about a rock star.

PRACTICE 1 **Identifying** In the following sentences, circle the semicolons that are used incorrectly, and add any commas and semicolons that are missing.

1. The car needed new front tires the old ones were quite bald.
2. Lisa's 10-month-old son didn't take a nap today however; he was very pleasant.
3. I must have lost my keys I can't; find them anywhere.
4. Our team is the strongest; and we are prepared to win.

5. Mr. Banderas teaches Spanish; writes novels; books; and short stories; and reviews movies in his spare time.

PRACTICE 2 **Completing** Add semicolons, where needed, to the following paragraph.

> When I was in grade 9, my school had a big dance I dreaded it from the day it was announced. I didn't have a boyfriend I didn't have the right clothes, shoes, or hairstyle and I didn't have any money saved up for things like that. Even worse, I knew my parents felt I was too young to go nonetheless, I knew my friends would keep asking me if I was going. Finally, I thought of a good excuse: I told my friends my grandmother was having major surgery. My friends probably knew I was lying however, nobody said anything more to me about it.

PRACTICE 3 **Writing Your Own** Write five sentences of your own using semicolons correctly.

COLONS

1. The main use of the colon is to introduce a list or thought. Here are some examples:

   Colon: Buy the following items for the trip: toothpaste, toothbrush, razor, soap, and makeup.

   Colon: The fair had some new attractions: a double Ferris wheel, a roller coaster, and an antique merry-go-round.

   Colon: The choice was simple: return the merchandise.

   The most common error with colons is using one where it isn't needed.

2. Do not use a colon after the words *such as* or *including*. A complete sentence must come before a colon.

   NOT Cook only fresh vegetables, **such as:** green beans, broccoli, and spinach.

   Correct: Cook only fresh vegetables, **such as** green beans, broccoli, and spinach.

   NOT We went to many countries in Europe, **including:** Spain and Portugal.

   Correct: We went to many countries in Europe, **including** Spain and Portugal.

3. In addition, you should not use a colon after a verb or after a preposition. Remember that a complete sentence must come before a colon.

NOT	The movies to be reviewed **are:** *American Beauty* and *Wonder Boys.*
Correct:	The movies to be reviewed **are** *American Beauty* and *Wonder Boys.*
NOT	The box was full **of:** books, old dolls, and scrapbooks.
Correct:	The box was full **of** books, old dolls, and scrapbooks.

PRACTICE 4 **Identifying** In the following sentences, circle the colons that are used incorrectly, and add any colons that are missing.

1. The best things about summer are: swimming, biking, and picnics.
2. The man asked me for the following items my driver's licence, my Social Insurance number, and my credit cards.
3. We accidentally left many things at home, such as: my toothbrush, our hair dryer, and the baby's bottle.
4. I was most impressed by: the atmosphere, the prices, and the service.
5. The most expensive parts to repair were: the carburetor, the ignition system, and the fuel injector.

PRACTICE 5 **Completing** Add colons to the following paragraph.

Reading is an excellent way to spend free time. A good book can do many things take you to a faraway place, introduce you to different people, and expose you to extraordinary experiences. I especially like two kinds of books science fiction and romance novels. These genres are totally opposite, I know, but they have just what I like action, strange characters, and suspension of disbelief. When I am reading, I am in a world of my own. I escape all of my everyday problems my difficult job, my nagging mother, and sometimes even my homework.

PRACTICE 6 **Writing Your Own** Write five sentences of your own using colons correctly.

DASHES AND PARENTHESES

Dashes

1. Use dashes to emphasize or draw attention to a point.

   Dash: I know what I want to be—a doctor.

   In this example, the beginning of the sentence introduces an idea, and the dash then sets off the answer.

   Dash: Money and time—these are what I need.

In this example, the key words are set off at the beginning, and the explanation follows. Beginning this way adds some suspense to the sentence.

Dashes: I know what I want in a husband—a sense of humour—and I plan to get it.

The dashes divide this sentence into three distinct parts, which makes the reader pause and think about each part.

Parentheses

Whereas dashes set off material that the writer wants to emphasize, parentheses do just the opposite. They are always used in pairs.

2. Use parentheses to set off information that is interesting or helpful but not necessary for understanding the sentence.

   Parentheses: When in Rome **(as the saying goes)**, do as the Romans do.

   Parentheses: The MPP's position on the proposal **(Bill 193)** has changed several times.

3. Parentheses are also used to mark a person's life span and to number items in a sentence.

   Parentheses: Herman Melville **(1819–1891)** wrote the classic *Moby Dick*.

   Parentheses: My boss gave me three things to do today: **(1)** answer the mail, **(2)** file receipts, and **(3)** send out bills.

PRACTICE 7 Identifying Use dashes or parentheses with the underlined words in the following sentences.

1. One powerful tool for student research is becoming more popular than the library <u>the Internet</u>.
2. My brother <u>the police chief</u> keeps his phone number unlisted.
3. Nick <u>head of the math department</u> hires the new teachers.
4. I signalled the oncoming car <u>by flashing my lights</u> but it still didn't turn its headlights on.
5. Cheryl got her passport so that she can <u>1</u> visit other countries <u>2</u> go diving in all of the seven seas, and <u>3</u> photograph royalty.

PRACTICE 8 Completing Add dashes and parentheses to the following paragraph.

In high school, I volunteered to work on the yearbook. Mrs. Brady was our instructor a round lady with bright red cheeks and a strange laugh. She immediately set us to work on several things mostly after school, as we accumulated photos and news about the school's major events. I remember one lesson I learned in that class never procrastinate. If I failed to finish an assignment something that rarely happened, someone else would do it instead, and that person's work would be published instead of mine. I'll never forget my year with Mrs. Brady.

PRACTICE 9 Writing Your Own Write three sentences of your own using dashes and two using parentheses.

CHAPTER REVIEW

Semicolon: used to join two closely related sentences or to separate items in a complex list

Colon: used to introduce a list or a thought. A complete sentence must come before a colon.

Dash: used to emphasize or draw attention to a point

Parentheses: set off interesting or helpful information. They are always used in pairs.

You might want to reread the examples in this chapter before you do the following exercises.

REVIEW PRACTICE 1 Identifying Add semicolons, colons, dashes, and parentheses to the following sentences.

1. We are going to the grocery store we have nothing in the pantry.
2. There are only three people I trust Krista, Tanya, and Lucy.
3. He is always home however, he doesn't ever help out around the house.
4. I bought the car in my favourite colour neon yellow.
5. Put the flowers on the table outside the one by the wall, and the presents can go there too.
6. My favourite book was made into a movie *Beloved*.
7. There are many things to do today pick up the dry cleaning, vacuum the carpets, and wash the dishes.
8. The chicken coop needs to be cleaned out it is full of leaves and tree branches.
9. We will pick up Derek, Jenny, and Carmen load up with sunscreen and go to the beach.
10. I got your favourite ice cream for your birthday fudge ripple.

REVIEW PRACTICE 2 Completing Add semicolons, colons, dashes, and parentheses to the following paragraph.

Today was an extremely windy day, so we decided to fly kites. We drove to Kite Hill a place where I went as a kid, and we climbed to the very top. We took out the kites and other necessary things masking tape, string, and ribbons. This way we were prepared to repair our kites, if necessary. The wind was perfect we couldn't have asked for better weather. There was only one thing we forgot the picnic lunch! Fortunately, Lamar remembered to pack the cooler with sodas mostly Diet Coke for something to drink when we got thirsty. After about four hours of flying kites it felt like 14, the group decided to head back home.

REVIEW PRACTICE 3 Writing Your Own Write a paragraph explaining some of your five-year goals. What do you plan to be doing in five years? What do you want to have accomplished?

REVIEW PRACTICE 4 Editing Through Collaboration Exchange paragraphs from Review Practice 3 with another student, and then do the following:

1. Circle any incorrect or missing semicolons.
2. Circle any incorrect or missing colons.
3. Circle any incorrect or missing dashes.
4. Circle any incorrect or missing parentheses.

Then return the paper to its writer, and use the information in this chapter to correct any punctuation errors in your own paragraph. Record your errors on the Error Log in Appendix 3.

CHAPTER

38

CAPITALIZATION

CHECKLIST for Editing Capitalization

- ✔ Are all proper nouns capitalized?
- ✔ Are all words in titles capitalized correctly?
- ✔ Have you followed the other rules for capitalizing correctly?

Test Yourself

Correct the capitalization errors in the following sentences.

- According to uncle Bob, mother makes the best nanaimo bars.
- Antonio is a new canadian.
- "the shortest path," he said, "Is down baker street."
- Issa loves to go to walt disney world.
- Last year, I saw the red hot chili peppers in concert.

(Answers are in Appendix 9 on the Text Enrichment Site.)

Because every sentence begins with a capital letter, **capitalization** is the best place to start discussing the mechanics of good writing. Capital letters signal where sentences begin. They also call attention to certain kinds of words, making sentences easier to read and understand.

Correct capitalization coupled with correct punctuation adds up to good, clear writing. Here are some guidelines to help you capitalize correctly.

1. Capitalize the first word of every sentence, including the first word of a quotation that forms a sentence.

   My favourite city is Rome.

   "**R**ome is my favourite city," he said.

   He said, "**M**y favourite city is Rome."

Do not capitalize the second part of a quotation that is split.

"**M**y favourite city," he said, "is Rome."

2. Capitalize all proper nouns. Do not capitalize common nouns.

Common Nouns	Proper Nouns
person	Adrienne Clarkson
province	Newfoundland
building	CN Tower
river	St. Lawrence River

Here are some examples of proper nouns.

People:	**S**arah, **S**hania **T**wain, **M**ike **W**eir
Groups:	**A**ustralians, **M**ohawk, **E**uropeans, **B**ritish, **L**atino
Languages:	**R**ussian, **I**talian, **F**rench
Religions, Religious Books, Holy Days:	**C**atholicism, **B**uddhism, **K**oran, **B**ible, **Y**om **K**ippur, **K**wanzaa, **E**aster
Organizations:	**T**oronto **B**lue **J**ays, **N**ew **D**emocratic **P**arty, **C**anadian **L**abour **C**ongress, **K**iwanis **C**lub, **A**lpha **G**amma **D**elta
Places:	**B**anff **N**ational **P**ark, **A**ntarctica, **K**ingston, **M**iddlesex **C**ounty, **B**ay **S**treet, **H**ighway 401, **B**luewater **B**ridge, **L**ester **B.** **P**earson **A**irport
Institutions, Agencies, Businesses:	**O**akridge **S**econdary **S**chool, **D. B. W**eldon **L**ibrary, **U**nited **W**ay, **T**oronto **S**ick **C**hildren's **H**ospital, **P**etro-**C**anada
Brand Names, Ships, Aircraft:	**M**ustang, **T**ide, **P**epsi, **H.M.S.** *Toronto, Avro Arrow*

3. Capitalize titles used with people's names or in place of their names.

Mr. Ralph W. Gerber, **M**s. Rachel Lorca, **D**r. Letitia Johnson, **A**unt Jane, **G**randpa **B**ob, **C**ousin **M**aria, **S**is, **N**ana

Do not capitalize words that identify family relationships.

NOT	I saw my **G**randfather yesterday.
Correct:	I saw my **g**randfather yesterday.
Correct:	I saw **G**randfather yesterday.

4. Capitalize the titles of creative works.

Books:	*The Stone Angel*
Short Stories:	"The Sinking of the Mariposa Belle"
Plays:	*Goodnight Desdemona (Good Morning Juliet)*
Poems:	"In Flanders Fields"
Articles:	"Two New Inns Now Open for Business"
Magazines:	*Maclean's*
Songs:	"If I Had a Million Dollars"
Albums or CDs:	*Jagged Little Pill*
Films:	*The Sweet Hereafter*
TV Series:	*This Hour Has 22 Minutes*
Works of Art:	*Starry Night*
Computer Programs:	Create CD

Do not capitalize *a, an, the,* or short prepositions unless they are the first or last word in a title.

5. Capitalize days of the week, months, holidays, and special events.

    Monday, July, Canada Day, Thanksgiving, St. Jean-Baptiste Day

    Do not capitalize the names of seasons: *summer, fall, winter, spring.*

6. Capitalize the names of historical events, periods, and documents.

    the French Revolution, the Jurassic Period, World War II, the Sixties, the Battle of Vimy Ridge, the Magna Carta

7. Capitalize specific course titles and the names of language courses.

    Economics 201, Philosophy 101, Spanish 200, Civilizations of the Ancient World

    Do not capitalize a course or subject you are referring to in a general way unless the course is a language.

    my economics course, my philosophy course, my Spanish course, my history course

8. Capitalize references to regions of the country but not words that merely indicate direction.

    If you travel north from Toronto, you will end up in Northern Ontario, probably in Sudbury or Timmins.

9. Capitalize the opening of a letter and the first word of the closing.

    Dear Dr. Hamlin, Dear Sir,

    Best wishes, Sincerely,

    Notice that a comma comes after the opening and closing.

PRACTICE 1 Identifying Correct the capitalization errors in the following sentences.

1. Revenue canada is auditing aunt Joan.
2. Debbie and Sue bought their mother a bottle of chanel's coco perfume for mother's Day.
3. In our History class, we are studying the great wall of china.
4. This Winter, emilio will visit uncle Luis, who lives somewhere in the south.
5. David Bowie's song "changes" is a classic from the seventies.

PRACTICE 2 Completing Fill in each blank with words that complete the sentence. Be sure to capitalize words correctly. (You can make up titles if necessary.)

1. In my ______________ class, we had to read ______________.
2. Blanca bought a new truck, a ______________.
3. ______________ should be in charge of the charity drive.
4. I wish I could get tickets to see ______________ in concert.
5. We are going to ______________ for our vacation.

PRACTICE 3 Writing Your Own Write five sentences of your own that cover at least five of the capitalization rules.

CHAPTER REVIEW

Capitalize the first word of every sentence.

Capitalize all proper nouns.

Capitalize titles used with people's names.

Capitalize the titles of creative works.

Capitalize days of the week, months, holidays, and special events.

Capitalize historical events, periods, and documents.

Capitalize specific course titles and the names of language courses.

Capitalize references to regions of the country, but not mere directions.

Capitalize the opening of a letter and the first word of the closing.

You might want to reread the examples in this chapter before you do the following exercises.

REVIEW PRACTICE 1 Identifying Underline and correct the capitalization errors in the following sentences.

1. In April's edition of *people* magazine, LeAnn rimes talks about her love of Country music.
2. We decided to get married even though he's a member of the new democratic party and I am a member of the conservative party.
3. Raphael was born on October 31, 1972—he was a halloween baby.
4. Many Fathers, Sons, and Brothers fought against each other in the american civil war.
5. Ernesto's uncle has a beautiful statue of the buddha in his garden.
6. I watch *late night with David Letterman* for entertainment.
7. Christy can speak both english and spanish.
8. We celebrate both christmas and kwanzaa.
9. My Father used to drive me around town in his 1968 convertible ford mustang.
10. The spider said to the fly, "welcome to my home."

REVIEW PRACTICE 2 Completing Fill in each blank with words that complete the sentence. Be sure to capitalize words correctly.

1. Over the weekend, I watched my favourite movie, ______________.
2. In history, we are studying the ______________.
3. I was born on ______________.
4. Ashley wears nothing but ______________ clothes.
5. Fred and ______________ both plan to major in ______________.
6. He has an unusual accent because he's from ______________.
7. If you travel ______________ on the Trans-Canada Highway, you will eventually reach Vancouver.
8. My favourite relative, ______________, will visit soon.
9. Every summer, we go to ______________ to fish.
10. Even though she's a ______________ and I'm a ______________, we are still the best of friends.

REVIEW PRACTICE 3 Writing Your Own Write a paragraph about the most unusual person you've met or the most unusual place you've visited. What made this person or place unique?

REVIEW PRACTICE 4 **Editing Through Collaboration** Exchange paragraphs from Review Practice 3 with another student, and then do the following tasks:

1. Circle any letters that don't follow the capitalization rules.
2. Write the rule number next to the error for the writer to refer to.

Then return the paper to its writer, and use the information in this chapter to correct any capitalization errors in your own paragraph. Record your errors on the Error Log in Appendix 3.

CHAPTER

39

ABBREVIATIONS AND NUMBERS

CHECKLIST for Abbreviations and Numbers

- ✔ Are titles before and after proper names abbreviated correctly?
- ✔ Are government agencies and other organizations abbreviated correctly?
- ✔ Are numbers zero through nine spelled out?
- ✔ Are numbers 10 and over written as figures (10, 25, 1–20, 324)?

Test Yourself

Correct the abbreviation and number errors in these sentences.

- He earned two million three hundred thousand dollars last year.
- My cat had 5 kittens.
- Mandy moved from England to the U.S.
- Mister Johnson always drinks hot chocolate in the mornings.
- I work for the Royal Canadian Mounted Police.

(Answers are in Appendix 9 on the Text Enrichment Site.)

Like capitalization, **abbreviations** and **numbers** are also mechanical features of writing that help us communicate what we want to say. Following the rules that govern their use will make your writing as precise as possible.

ABBREVIATIONS

1. Abbreviate titles before proper names.

   Mr. Michael Charles, **Mrs.** Marschel, **Ms.** Susan Deffaa,
   Dr. Frank Hilbig, **Rev.** Billy Graham, **Sgt.** Arturo Lopez

   Abbreviate religious, governmental, and military titles when used with an entire name. Do not abbreviate them when used only with a last name.

NOT We thought that **Gov.** Peterson would be re-elected.

Correct: We thought that **Governor** Peterson would be re-elected.

Correct: We thought **Gov.** Richard Peterson would be re-elected.

Professor is not usually abbreviated: **Professor** Mya Belle is teaching this class.

2. Abbreviate academic degrees.

   B.Sc. (Bachelor of Science)

   R.N. (Registered Nurse)

3. Use the following abbreviations with numbers.

   a.m. or **A.M., p.m.** or **P.M., B.C., B.C.E., A.D.**

4. Abbreviate *United States* only when it is used as an adjective.

   NOT The **U.S.** is in North America.

   Correct: The **United States** is in North America.

   Correct: The **U.S.** Senate will consider this bill today.

5. Abbreviate only the names of well-known government agencies, businesses, and educational institutions by using their initials without periods.

   RCMP (Royal Canadian Mounted Police)

   UWO (University of Western Ontario)

6. Abbreviate province names when addressing mail or writing out the postal address. Otherwise, spell out the names of provinces.

   Maria's new address is 7124 Funston Street, Winnipeg,

   MB R3G 2W4.

   Maria has moved to Winnipeg, **Manitoba.**

PRACTICE 1 Identifying Correct the underlined words in each of the following sentences.

1. <u>Prof.</u> Smith said that I was a wonderful writer.
2. The <u>United States</u> economy has many markets.
3. When I can't sleep, I watch <u>Music Television</u>.
4. Last night, <u>Sergeant</u> David Montgomery devised the winning strategy.
5. Candice moved to 237 Bella Avenue, Mississauga, <u>Ontario</u> L5N 1A5.

PRACTICE 2 Completing In each sentence, write either an abbreviation or the complete word, whichever is correct.

1. We were caught speeding at 10 ____________________ (p.m., post meridian).
2. Alisha will be attending ____________________ (UBC, University of British Columbia) and will get her ____________________ (B.A., bachelor of arts) degree in English.
3. Darryl and Pat are visiting relatives in Stratford, ____________________ (ON, Ontario).
4. We moved to ____________________ (P.E.I., Prince Edward Island) when I was four years old.
5. (Rev., Reverend) ____________________ Matthews always has a kind word.

PRACTICE 3 Writing Your Own Write a sentence of your own for each of the following abbreviations.

1. Mr. ____
2. a.m. ____
3. CBC ____
4. A.A. ____
5. N.W.T. ____

NUMBERS

Most writers ask the same question about using numbers: When should a number be spelled out, and when is it all right to use numerals? The following simple rules will help you make this decision.

1. Spell out numbers from *zero* to *nine*. Use figures for numbers 10 and higher.

   I have **three** dogs.

   My mother-in-law has **19** grandchildren and **11** great-grandchildren.

   Do not mix spelled-out numbers and figures in a sentence if they refer to the same types of items. Use numerals for all numbers in that case.

   NOT I have **three** dogs, **18** goldfish, and **two** canaries.

   Correct: I have **3** dogs, **18** goldfish, and **2** canaries.

2. For very large numbers, use a combination of figures and words.

   The province's new budget is approximately **$32 million.**

   Computer sales for the company reached **2.1 million** units.

3. Always spell out a number that begins a sentence. If this becomes awkward, reword the sentence.

   Thirty-five people died in the crash.

   Approximately **260,000** people live in Kitchener, Ontario.

4. Use figures for dates, addresses, postal codes, telephone numbers, identification numbers, and time.

   On August **1, 1965,** my parents moved to **215** Circle Drive, Saskatoon, SK **PR5 2L7.**

   My new telephone number is **(555) 877-1420.**

   My Social Insurance number is **123-456-789.**

   My alarm went off at **5:00** a.m.

5. Use figures for fractions, decimals, and percentages.

   To make the dessert, you need **125** ml butter and **450** g of chocolate.

   His blood-alcohol level was **.09.**

   Over **35 percent** of Quebecers are of French background.

   Notice that *percent* is written out and is all one word.

6. Use figures for exact measurements, including amounts of money. Use a dollar sign for amounts over $1.

   The room measures **3** metres by **4** metres.

   She bought a bag of candy for **99** cents, **$1.20** less than it was yesterday.

7. Use figures for the parts of a book.

   Chapter **10,** page **120,** Exercise **8,** questions **1** and **7**

   Notice that *Chapter* and *Exercise* are capitalized, but *page* and *question* are not.

PRACTICE 4 Identifying Correct any errors with numbers in each of the following sentences.

1. On August third, 2001, sixteen dogs escaped from the kennel.
2. The park, which measures approximately 170 square metres, will cost five thousand dollars to landscape.
3. Mr. Thompson's old telephone number was three, nine, nine, four, two, zero, nine.
4. Almost twenty-five percent of my income comes from sales.
5. The earthquake that hit at six forty-five last night measured 6.0 on the Richter scale.

PRACTICE 5 Completing Fill in each blank in the following sentences with numbers in the proper form.

1. Please read Chapter ____________ and answer questions ____________ through ____________.
2. I have ____________ pencils, ____________ notebooks, and ____________ notecards; I am ready for this test.
3. ____________ percent of my time is spent doing homework.
4. Christmas is on ____________ every year.
5. He made $ ____________ million last year.

PRACTICE 6 Write Your Own Write a sentence demonstrating each of the following rules for numbers.

1. Spell out numbers *zero* through *nine*. Use figures for numbers 10 and higher.
2. For very large numbers, use a combination of figures and words.
3. Always spell out a number that begins a sentence.
4. Use figures for dates, addresses, postal codes, telephone numbers, identification numbers, and time.
5. Use figures for fractions, decimals, and percentages.

CHAPTER REVIEW

Abbreviate titles before proper names.

Abbreviate academic degrees.

Abbreviate names of well-known government agencies, businesses, and educational institutions.

Abbreviate province names when addressing mail or writing out the postal address.

Spell out numbers from *zero* to *nine*. Use figures for numbers 10 and higher.

For very large numbers, use a combination of figures and words.

Use figures for dates and addresses.

Use figures for fractions, decimals, and percentages.

Use figures for exact measurements and amounts of money.

Use figures for parts of a book.

You might want to reread the examples in this chapter before you do the following exercises.

REVIEW PRACTICE 1 Identifying Circle the abbreviation errors and underline the number errors in each of the following sentences. Some sentences contain more than one error.

1. According to Prof. Gleason, there is a process to writing.
2. At exactly 7:00 post meridian, everyone will jump out of his or her hiding place and yell, "Surprise!"
3. The crew will need explosives to blast the twenty-nine-ton boulder.
4. Gen. Brevington's retirement banquet will be held on January twenty-nine, 2007.
5. Only 2 of the 8 children remembered their permission slips.
6. Of all the people polled, only ten percent were in favour of the new law.
7. 9 days from now, Columbia Broadcasting System is airing a special on former United States President Bill Clinton.
8. You can receive an associate of arts degree from your local community college.
9. The answers to questions four and five are in Chapter 21.
10. After winning the lottery for two million five hundred thousand dollars, Janene moved to Beverly Hills, CA.

REVIEW PRACTICE 2 Completing Correct the errors in Review Practice 1 by rewriting the sentences.

REVIEW PRACTICE 3 Writing Your Own Write a paragraph describing the quickest route from your home to your school. Use numbers and abbreviations in your paragraph.

REVIEW PRACTICE 4 Editing Through Collaboration Exchange paragraphs from Review Practice 3 with another student, and do the following:

1. Underline all abbreviations, numbers, and figures.
2. Circle any abbreviations, numbers, or figures that are not in the correct form.

Then return the paper to its writer, and use the information in this chapter to correct any abbreviation and number errors in your own paragraph. Record your errors on the Error Log in Appendix 3.

CHAPTER

40

Varying Sentence Structure

CHECKLIST for Varying Sentence Patterns

- ✔ Do you add introductory material to vary your sentence patterns?
- ✔ Do you occasionally reverse the order of some subjects and verbs?
- ✔ Do you move sentence parts to add variety to your sentences?
- ✔ Do you sometimes use questions and exclamations to vary your sentence structure?

Test Yourself

Turn each of the following pairs of sentences into one sentence that is more interesting.

- I work too much. I am tired.
- My cat is very lazy. She sleeps more than 14 hours a day.
- He enjoys reading. He likes mysteries.
- I live in an old house. My family has lived here for generations.
- My brother loves to eat. He will eat anything.

(Answers are in Appendix 9 on the Text Enrichment Site.)

Reading the same sentence pattern, sentence after sentence, can become very monotonous for your readers. This chapter will help you solve this problem in your writing. Look at the following example.

> I have always loved animals. I am about to get my own dog for the first time. I am ready to be responsible enough to take care of it. I am excited about this new phase in my life. I got a part-time job. I can't wait to get my own dog.

This paragraph has some terrific ideas, but they are expressed in such a monotonous way that the readers might doze off. What this paragraph needs is variety in its sentence structure. Here are some ideas for keeping your readers awake and ready to hear your good thoughts.

ADD INTRODUCTORY WORDS

Add some introductory words to your sentences so that they don't all start the same way.

> **For as long as I can remember,** I have always loved animals. **Now** I am about to get my own dog for the first time. I am ready to be responsible enough to take care of it. I am excited about this new phase in my life. **To pay for my new friend,** I got a part-time job. I can't wait to get my own dog.

PRACTICE 1 Identifying Underline the sentence in each pair that could be turned into an introductory word, phrase, or clause.

1. Misty had a terrible stomachache. It was late last night.
2. We went to the river. We skipped over the rocks.
3. We went to McDonald's for breakfast. We saw our friends.
4. The sunsets are beautiful. It was spring.
5. He is afraid of dogs. He was bitten by a dog once.

PRACTICE 2 Completing Rewrite the sentences in Practice 1 by turning each sentence you underlined into an introductory word, phrase, or clause.

PRACTICE 3 Writing Your Own Write five sentences of your own with introductory elements.

REVERSE WORDS

Reverse the order of some subjects and verbs. For example, instead of *I am so excited*, try *Am I ever excited*. You can also add or drop words and change punctuation to make the sentence read smoothly.

> For as long as I can remember, I have always loved animals. Now I am about to get my own dog for the first time. I am ready to be responsible enough to take care of it. **Am I ever excited** about this new phase in my life. To pay for my new friend, I got a part-time job. I can't wait to get my own dog.

PRACTICE 4 Identifying Underline the words or phrases you could reverse in each of the following sentences.

1. I am happy to know you.
2. All the ingredients went into the pot.

3. The cat jumped out of the hat.
4. The children were happy.
5. A strange creature appeared out of nowhere.

PRACTICE 5 **Completing** Rewrite the sentences in Practice 4 by reversing the words you underlined.

PRACTICE 6 **Writing Your Own** Write five sentences of your own with subjects and verbs reversed.

MOVE SENTENCE PARTS

Move some parts of the sentence around. Experiment to see which order works best.

> For as long as I can remember, I have always loved animals. Now I am about to get my own dog for the first time. I am ready to be responsible enough to take care of it. Am I ever excited about this new phase in my life. **My part-time job can help me pay for my new friend.** I can't wait to get my own dog.

PRACTICE 7 **Identifying** Underline any parts of the following sentences that can be moved around.

1. To bake these cookies, you will need 500 ml of flour.
2. Finally, I knew the truth.
3. I was very full after lunch.
4. You will find your shoes underneath your bed.
5. If you enjoyed the film, you will probably like the book.

PRACTICE 8 **Completing** Rewrite the sentences in Practice 7, moving the words you underlined.

PRACTICE 9 **Writing Your Own** Write two sentences of your own. Then rewrite each sentence two different ways.

VARY SENTENCE TYPE

Use a question, a command, or an exclamation occasionally.

> For as long as I can remember, I have always loved animals. **Have you?** Now I am about to get my own dog for the first time. I am ready to be responsible enough to take care of it. **Am I ever excited about this new phase in my life!** My part-time job can help me pay for my new friend. I can't wait to get my own dog.

PRACTICE 10 Identifying Identify each of the following sentences as a statement (S), a question (Q), a command (C), or an exclamation (E).

1. _____ When is the meal being served
2. _____ Did you see that object flying in the sky
3. _____ Bring me a glass of iced tea and a bowl of grapes
4. _____ First do the prewriting exercises
5. _____ I just hate it when that happens

PRACTICE 11 Completing Complete the following sentences, making them into questions, commands, or exclamations. Then supply the correct punctuation.

1. Wow, I can't believe ______________________________
2. At the first intersection ______________________________
3. Why is ______________________________
4. Hand me ______________________________
5. Did you hear ______________________________

PRACTICE 12 Writing Your Own Write two statements, two questions, two commands, and two exclamations of your own.

USING THE ACTIVE VOICE

In the **active voice,** the subject performs the action. In the **passive voice,** the subject receives the action. Compare the following two examples:

Passive Voice: The mayor **was accused** of stealing **by the police.**

Active Voice: **The police accused** the mayor of stealing.

The active voice adds energy to your writing. Here is another example. Notice the difference between active and passive.

Passive Voice: **The cake was baked** for Tim's birthday **by my grandmother.**

Active Voice: **My grandmother baked the cake** for Tim's birthday.

PRACTICE 13 Identifying Write A if the sentence is in the active voice and P if it is in the passive voice.

1. _____ The astronauts landed on the moon and planted a flag.
2. _____ Flowers are being sent to the funeral home.

3. _____ Jordan hit the ball over the fence into the neighbour's yard.
4. _____ The experimental medicines were shipped to the laboratory for further testing.
5. _____ People who heckle the politicians will be escorted from the building.

PRACTICE 14 Correcting Rewrite the passive sentences in Practice 13 in the active voice.

CHAPTER REVIEW

Add some introductory words to sentences so that they don't all start the same way.

Reverse the order of some nouns and verbs.

Move parts of the sentences around.

Use a question, a command, or an exclamation occasionally.

Use the active voice to add energy to your writing.

You might want to reread the examples in this chapter before you do the following exercises.

REVIEW PRACTICE 1 Identifying Underline the words or groups of words that have been added or moved in each revised sentence. Then use the following key to tell which rule was applied to the sentence:

1. Add introductory words.
2. Reverse the order of subject and verb.
3. Move around parts of the sentence.
4. Use a question, a command, or an exclamation occasionally.

1. Eat your peas. You aren't finished with dinner yet.
   _____You aren't finished with dinner until you eat your peas.
2. He did what?
   _____What did he do?
3. You went to the store around the corner. You bought some milk and bread.
   _____ At the store around the corner, please buy some milk and bread.
4. To the park went he.
   _____ To the park he went.
5. The fireflies flew. They flew all around us.
   _____ All around us, the fireflies flew.
6. I believe that was mine.
   _____ Hey, that was mine!

7. How many times a day do you brush your teeth?
   _____ You brush your teeth how many times a day?
8. You are amazing!
   _____ Are you amazing or what?
9. Out of the darkness came a terrible noise.
   _____ Out of the darkness, a terrible noise came.
10. Carl does enjoy a good hamburger every now and then.
   _____ Every now and then, Carl does enjoy a good hamburger.

REVIEW PRACTICE 2 **Completing** Vary the structure of the following sentences with at least three of the four ideas you just learned.

> A good teacher should be encouraging toward students. He or she should understand when a student is having problems and spend some one-on-one time together. The teacher should then help the student identify problems and give helpful instruction to solve the problem. A good teacher never makes fun of a student.

REVIEW PRACTICE 3 **Writing Your Own** Write a paragraph about a good deed you have performed. What made you decide to do what you did? Try to use each of the four ways you have learned to make sentences interesting.

REVIEW PRACTICE 4 **Editing Through Collaboration** Exchange paragraphs from Review Practice 3 with another student, and then do the following:

1. Put brackets around any sentences that sound monotonous.
2. Suggest a way to vary each of these sentences.

Then return the paper to its writer, and use the information in this chapter to vary the sentence structure in your own paragraph. Record your errors on the Error Log in Appendix 3.

CHAPTER

41

PARALLELISM

CHECKLIST for Using Parallelism

- ✔ Can you use parallelism to add coherence to your sentences and paragraphs?
- ✔ Are all items in a series grammatically balanced?

Test Yourself

Underline the parts in each of the following sentences that seem awkward or unbalanced.

- Tony enjoys hockey, football, and runs.
- My mom and dad give money to help the homeless and for building new homes.
- I finished high school, started college, and I am beginning a new job.
- I love the mountains because they're cool, clean, and feel refreshing.
- Listening to music, watching television, or to read a book are good ways to relax.

(Answers are in Appendix 9 on the Text Enrichment Site.)

When sentences are **parallel,** they are balanced. That is, words, phrases, or clauses in a series start with the same grammatical form. Parallel structures make your sentences interesting and clear.

Following is a paragraph that could be greatly improved with parallel structures.

> My brother Ricardo was not excited when he was called in to work at the hospital today. He had been looking forward to this day off—his first in three weeks. He was planning to work out in the morning, swimming in the afternoon, and going to a movie in the evening. Instead he will be helping the patients, assisting the nurses, and will aid the doctors.

Words and phrases in a series should be parallel, which means they should start with the same type of word. Parallelism makes your sentence structure smoother and more interesting. Look at this sentence, for example.

NOT He had planned to **work** out in the morning,
swimming in the afternoon, and
going to a movie in the evening.

Parallel: He had planned to **work out** in the morning,
swim in the afternoon, and
go to a movie in the evening.

Parallel: He had planned on **working out** in the morning,
swimming in the afternoon, and
going to a movie in the evening.

Here is another sentence that would read better if the parts were parallel:

NOT Instead he will be **helping** the patients,
assisting the nurses, and
will aid the doctors.

Parallel: Instead he will be **helping** the patients,
assisting the nurses, and
aiding the doctors.

Parallel: Instead he will be helping **the patients,**
the nurses, and
the doctors.

Now read the paragraph with these two sentences made parallel or balanced.

> My brother Ricardo was not excited when he was called in to work at the hospital today. He had been looking forward to this day off—his first in three weeks. He had planned to work out in the morning, swim in the afternoon, and go to a movie in the evening. Instead he will be helping the patients, the nurses, and the doctors.

PRACTICE 1 **Identifying** Underline the parallel structures in each of the following sentences.

1. Scott plans to hide in his cottage, do some fishing, and work on his novel.
2. The car needs new windows, tires, and paint.
3. Georgia believes that she is the most wonderful person in the world and that she deserves everyone's love and attention.
4. They camped under the stars, swam in the cool lakes, and enjoyed the fresh air.
5. Because of the pouring rain, extreme cold, and bitter wind, we decided to stay inside.

PRACTICE 2 **Completing** Make the underlined elements parallel in each of the following sentences.

1. He will wear only clothes that have designer labels and they are expensive.

2. Regular exercise, drinking plenty of water, and eating lots of good food will help keep you healthy.

3. Deirdre went to the mall to get a bite to eat, to do some shopping, and will visit friends.

4. Please do not tap pens, talk to others, or eating food during the exam.

5. On his trip, he took pictures of mountains, fed animals, and some enjoyable people.

PRACTICE 3 Writing Your Own Write five sentences of your own using parallel structures in each.

CHAPTER REVIEW

Parallel Sentence: Words, phrases, or clauses in a series start with the same grammatical form.

You might want to reread the examples in this chapter before you do the following exercises.

REVIEW PRACTICE 1 Identifying Underline the parallel structures in each of the following sentences.

1. Football, basketball, and hockey are all competitive sports.
2. Because of the terrible weather, the horrible traffic, and the missed bus, we didn't make our flight.
3. When I'm in love, the sun always shines, the stars always sparkle, and the moon always glows.
4. Marilyn went to the city's annual air show because she wanted to see the jet planes and because she wanted to try the interesting foods.
5. The biting mosquitoes, barking dogs, and burning sun made me miserable.
6. Please feed, bathe, and change the baby before I get home.
7. If Harvey cleans the house, does his homework, and begs for forgiveness, he may get out of his punishment.

8. I believe that people should be treated fairly and that everyone should get a second chance.
9. He was suspended because he fought, cheated, and disrespected others.
10. Today Mother paid the bills, balanced the cheque book, and washed the car.

REVIEW PRACTICE 2 **Completing** Complete each of the following sentences with parallel structures.

1. I enjoy ____________, ____________, and ____________ in the summer.
2. Because of ____________ and because of ____________ , Miriam didn't go to the movies.
3. You can be successful in college if you ____________ , ____________, and ____________.
4. Even though Jeremy ____________, ____________, and ____________, he still can't find the problem.
5. ____________, ____________, and ____________ are essential items when hiking.
6. She cooks foods that ____________ and ____________.
7. My favourite foods are ____________, ____________, and ____________.
8. If I have to hear her ____________, ____________, and ____________ one more time, I'm going to scream.
9. The instructor has already explained _____, _____, and _____.
10. If you ____________, ____________, and ____________, you just might survive boot camp.

REVIEW PRACTICE 3 **Writing Your Own** Write a paragraph about the best holiday you've ever had. What was the holiday? Why was it the best? Use two examples of parallelism in your paragraph.

REVIEW PRACTICE 4 **Editing Through Collaboration** Exchange paragraphs from Review Practice 3 with another student, and then do the following:

1. Underline any items in a series.
2. Put brackets around any of these items that are not grammatically parallel.

Then return the paper to its writer, and use the information in this chapter to correct any parallelism errors in your own paragraph. Record your errors on the Error Log in Appendix 3.

CHAPTER

42

COMBINING SENTENCES

CHECKLIST for Combining Sentences

- ✔ Do you combine sentences to avoid too many short, choppy sentences in a row?
- ✔ Do you use different types of sentences?

Test Yourself

Combine each set of sentences into one sentence.

- My brother is taking tennis lessons. He takes his lessons from a professional player.
- The baby is crying. She's hungry.
- It's too hot outside. Let's go for a swim.
- We moved overseas when I was 11 years old. I learned a lot about different cultures.
- I like to travel. Africa has many interesting animals and plants. I want to go to Africa.

(Answers are in Appendix 9 on the Text Enrichment Site.)

Still another way to add variety to your writing is to combine short, choppy sentences into longer sentences. You can combine simple sentences to make compound or complex sentences. You can also combine compound and complex sentences.

SIMPLE SENTENCES

A **simple sentence** consists of one independent clause. Remember that a clause has a subject and a main verb.

In the following examples, notice that a simple sentence can have more than one subject and more than one verb. (For more on compound subjects and compound verbs, see Chapter 23.)

S V
I have several very good friends.

s v v
I have good friends and enjoy being with them.

s s v
Martin and Louis are good friends.

s s v v
Martin and I go to interesting places and do interesting things.

PRACTICE 1 Identifying Underline the subjects once and the verbs twice in each of the following sentences. Then label the simple sentences SS.

1. _____ Most cats don't like the water, but most dogs do.
2. _____ Tommy and I like listening to the same types of music and watching the same types of shows.
3. _____ I feel that our luck is about to change.
4. _____ We left quickly because of the smell.
5. _____ We have pictures of the family throughout the house.

PRACTICE 2 Completing Make simple sentences out of the sentences in Practice 1 that are not simple.

PRACTICE 3 Writing Your Own Write a simple sentence of your own for each of the following subjects and verbs.

1. Jessy and Leo ____________________
2. we're eating and drinking ____________________
3. the playful kittens ____________________
4. looking and listening ____________________
5. the hot pan ____________________

COMPOUND SENTENCES

A **compound sentence** consists of two or more independent clauses joined by a coordinating conjunction (*and*, *but*, *for*, *nor*, *or*, *so*, or *yet*). In other words, you can create a compound sentence from two (or more) simple sentences.

Simple: I can swim fast.

Simple: I am a good long-distance swimmer.

s v s v
Compound: I can swim fast, **and** I am a good long-distance swimmer.

Simple: She has a very stressful job.

Simple: She works out at the gym three times a week.

S V S V

Compound: She has a very stressful job, so she works out at the gym three times a week.

Simple: My parents are leaving for Hawaii on Tuesday.

Simple: They won't be here for my birthday party.

S V

Compound: My parents are leaving for Hawaii on Tuesday, so

S V

they won't be here for my birthday party.

Hint: As the examples show, a comma comes before the coordinating conjunction in a compound sentence.

PRACTICE 4 Identifying Underline the independent clauses in the following sentences, and circle the coordinating conjunctions.

1. I am not sick, and I feel fine.
2. You cannot bring food or drink into this building, but you can eat in the cafeteria.
3. We try not to gossip, for we know the damage rumours can cause.
4. I do not like raspberries, yet I do like raspberry pie.
5. Christy likes fast cars, so she is going to buy a sports car.

PRACTICE 5 Completing Combine each pair of simple sentences into a compound sentence.

1. I am leaving. I am late for an appointment.
2. Quickly, move out of the way. The angry elephant is going to charge us.
3. We usually take a month-long vacation. We are always happy to return home.
4. This food has been sitting out all day in the hot sun. It smells awful.
5. I have a lot of cousins. I haven't met them all.

PRACTICE 6 Writing Your Own Write five compound sentences of your own.

COMPLEX SENTENCES

A **complex sentence** is composed of one independent clause and at least one dependent clause. A **dependent clause** begins with either a subordinating conjunction or a relative pronoun.

Subordinating Conjunctions

after	*because*	*since*	*until*
although	*before*	*so*	*when*
as	*even if*	*so that*	*whenever*
as if	*even though*	*than*	*where*
as long as	*how*	*that*	*wherever*
as soon as	*if*	*though*	*whether*
as though	*in order that*	*unless*	*while*

Relative Pronouns

who	*whom*	*whose*	*which*	*that*

You can use subordinating conjunctions and relative pronouns to make a simple sentence (an independent clause) into a dependent clause. Then you can add the new dependent clause to an independent clause to produce a complex sentence that adds interest and variety to your writing.

How do you know which simple sentence should be independent and which should be dependent? The idea that you think is more important should be the independent clause. The less important idea will then be the dependent clause.

Following are some examples of how to combine simple sentences to make a complex sentence.

Simple: Myra has a large collection of movie videos.

Simple: Myra watches the same few films over and over.

dep

Complex: **Even though** Myra has a large collection of movie

ind

videos, she watches the same few films over and over.

This complex sentence stresses that Myra watches the same films over and over. The size of her collection is of secondary importance.

ind

Complex: Myra has a big collection of movie videos, though she

dep

watches the same few films over and over.

In the previous complex sentence, the size of the collection is most important, so it is the independent clause.

Simple: The winner of the lottery was Laura.

Simple: Laura is my cousin.

ind dep

Complex: The winner of the lottery was Laura, who is my cousin.

This complex sentence answers the question "Who won the lottery?" The information about Laura being the cousin is of secondary importance.

ind dep

Complex: My cousin is Laura, **who** won the lottery.

This complex sentence answers the question "Who is your cousin?" The information that she won the lottery is secondary.

PRACTICE 7 Identifying Label the underlined part of each sentence as either an independent (Ind) or a dependent (Dep) clause.

1. _____ Although I was tired, I still went to school.
2. _____ Here is the furniture that you ordered.
3. _____ Trish moved to the coast because she likes the beach.
4. _____ My doctor is Janet Wu, who is also my mom.
5. _____ If we cannot study at your house, then let's study at the library.

PRACTICE 8 Completing Finish each sentence, and label the new clause either dependent (Dep) or independent (Ind).

1. _____ Whenever John's face turns red, ____________________.
2. _____ ____________________ because he forgot to call home.
3. _____ Maya's mother, who ____________________, is a great cook.
4. _____ I like the blue one, ____________________.
5. _____ He climbed the mountain ____________________.

PRACTICE 9 Writing Your Own Write five complex sentences, making sure you have one independent clause and at least one dependent clause in each.

COMPOUND-COMPLEX SENTENCES

If you combine a compound sentence with a complex sentence, you produce a **compound-complex sentence.** That means your sentence has at least two independent clauses (to make it compound) and at least one dependent clause (to make it complex). Here are some examples.

Simple: My cousin likes scuba diving.

Simple: He is planning a trip to Hawaii.

Simple: He is excited about diving in Hawaii.

ind

Compound-Complex: My cousin likes scuba diving, so he

ind

is planning a trip to Hawaii, **which** he is

dep

very excited about.

Simple: She bought a new house.
Simple: It has a pool and a spa.
Simple: The house was very expensive.

Compound-Complex: She bought a new house, (ind) **which** has a pool and a spa, (dep) **but** it was very expensive. (ind)

Simple: Today's weather is very bad.
Simple: The rain could make it difficult to drive.
Simple: This could delay your departure for home.

Compound-Complex: Today's weather is very bad, (ind) and the rain could make it difficult to drive, (ind) which could delay your arrival home. (dep)

Hint: Notice that we occasionally have to change words in combined sentences so that the sentences make sense.

PRACTICE 10 Identifying Underline the clauses in each of the following compound-complex sentences. Then identify each clause as either independent (Ind) or dependent (Dep).

1. Whenever I travel, I set an alarm clock, and I arrange for a wake-up call.
2. Sandy likes Anthony because he is nice, but she also likes Mark.
3. After they fought, they decided to make up, and now they are inseparable.
4. The traffic, which is usually bad around noon, is very heavy today, so you'd better leave soon.
5. We went to the Virgin Islands because we love the sun, yet it rained the whole time.

PRACTICE 11 Completing Expand each sentence into a compound-complex sentence.

1. The boy likes oranges and pears.

____

2. The box was very heavy, but he lifted it anyway.

____

3. Jill says that she will never fly in a plane.

____

4. John will be 21 soon.

____

5. I am watching MuchMusic and getting some rest.

____

PRACTICE 12 Writing Your Own Write five compound-complex sentences of your own.

CHAPTER REVIEW

Simple Sentence: consists of one independent clause

Compound Sentence: consists of two or more independent clauses joined by a coordinating conjunction

Complex Sentence: consists of one independent clause and at least one dependent clause

Subordinating Conjunctions: make an independent clause a dependent clause. Add this dependent clause to an independent clause to create a complex sentence.

Compound-Complex Sentence: has at least two independent clauses and one dependent clause

You might want to reread the examples in this chapter before you do the following exercises.

REVIEW PRACTICE 1 Identifying Underline the independent clauses in each sentence. Then label the sentence simple (SS), compound (C), complex (CX), or compound-complex (CCX). The following definitions might help you.

Simple (SS)	=	one independent clause
Compound (C)	=	two or more independent clauses joined by *and, but, for, nor, or, so,* or *yet*
Complex (CX)	=	one independent clause and at least one dependent clause
Compound-complex (CCX)	=	at least two independent clauses and one or more dependent clauses

1. _____ Casey and Floyd have left the building.
2. _____ Even though he is quiet, he is very friendly.
3. _____ Marcy and David are boyfriend and girlfriend, and they are going to the prom together.
4. _____ The dog and cat ate my dinner last night.
5. _____ Mrs. Glancy is my close friend, and she visits me often.
6. _____ Marc is happy because Sheila is here, and he wants to ask her on a date.

7. _____ The folders are in the desk drawer.
8. _____ The dog needs to be fed, and he needs a bath.
9. _____ The gifts, which you bought yesterday, have been wrapped, and they are ready to be delivered.
10. _____ Because her alarm didn't go off, she was late for work.

REVIEW PRACTICE 2 **Completing** Combine each set of sentences to make the sentence pattern indicated in parentheses. You may need to change some wording in the sentences so that they make sense. The list of sentence types in Review Practice 1 may help you with this exercise.

1. Antoine bikes in the morning. He wants to stay in shape. He goes to the gym every weekend. (compound-complex)
2. I like to play in the mud. I always get dirty. (compound)
3. You should leave now. You should be at your appointment 15 minutes early to fill out paperwork. (complex)
4. Penny brought a stray dog home. Penny loves animals. Her mother wouldn't let her keep it. (compound-complex)
5. I slammed the car door on my thumb. I broke it. (complex)
6. I love to chew gum and pop bubbles. I can't chew gum in class. (complex)
7. The little girl lost her doll. She has looked everywhere for it. She is crying. (compound-complex)
8. The sun is shining. The birds are singing. (compound)
9. The reports are missing. I need them now. (compound)
10. It is October. The leaves are turning brown and falling from the tree. (complex)

REVIEW PRACTICE 3 **Writing Your Own** Write a paragraph about your fondest wish. What is it, and why do you wish for it?

REVIEW PRACTICE 4 **Editing Through Collaboration** Exchange paragraphs from Review Practice 3 with another student, and then do the following:

1. Put brackets around any sentences that you think should be combined.
2. Underline sentences that are incorrectly combined (for example, ones that have a weak connecting word or no connecting word).

Then return the paper to its writer, and use the information in this chapter to combine sentences in your own paragraph. Record your errors on the Error Log in Appendix 3.

Standard and Nonstandard English

Chapter 43

CHECKLIST for Choosing the Right Word

- ✔ Do you consistently use standard English in your paper?
- ✔ Is your paper free of nonstandard, ungrammatical words?
- ✔ Have you changed any slang to standard English?

Test Yourself

Label the following sentences as correct, incorrect, or slang.

- You shoulda seen Claudia's new hairstyle. _________
- Where are my friends at? _________
- Your new bike is really hot. _________
- Randy was enthused about his date. _________
- Fatboy Slim's new video rocks. _________

(Answers are in Appendix 9 on the Text Enrichment Site.)

Choosing the right words for what you want to say is an important part of effective communication. This chapter will help you find the right words and phrases for the audience you are trying to reach.

Look, for example, at the following sentences. They all have a similar message, expressed in different words.

I want to do good in college, being as I can get a good job.

I be studying hard in college, so I can get a good job.

I'm going to hit the books so I can rake in the bucks.

I want to do well in college so I can get a good job.

Which of these sentences would you probably say to a friend or to someone in your family? Which would you most likely say in a job interview? Which would be good for a college paper?

The first three sentences are nonstandard English. They might be said or written to a friend or family member, but they would not be appropriate in an academic setting or in a job situation. Only the fourth sentence would be appropriate in an academic paper or in a job interview.

STANDARD AND NONSTANDARD ENGLISH

Most of the English language falls into one of two categories—either *standard* or *nonstandard*. **Standard English** is the language of college, business, and the media. It is used by reporters on television, by newspapers, in most magazines, and on websites created by schools, government, business, and organizations. Standard English is always grammatically correct and free of slang.

Nonstandard English does not follow all the rules of grammar and often includes slang. Nonstandard English is not necessarily wrong, but it is more appropriate in some settings (with friends and family) than others. It is not appropriate in college or business writing. To understand the difference between standard and nonstandard English, compare the following paragraphs.

Nonstandard English

I was stoked to find out I would be getting a $300 refund on my taxes. My first thought was to blow it on a trip, maybe somewheres like Montreal. But none of my friends was enthused by that. Then I thought being as I watch television alot, I would buy a new TV with a built-in DVD player. My brother got hisself one last year. Then it hit me, hey, I'm gonna need some money to buy new duds for my job. Alright, I decided, I gotta buy clothes with the dough, irregardless of what I'd like to do with it.

Standard English

I was thrilled when I found out I would be getting a $300 refund on my taxes. My first thought was to spend it on a trip, maybe somewhere like Montreal. But none of my friends were enthusiastic about that. Then I thought that since I watch television a lot, I would buy a new TV with a built-in DVD player. My brother got himself one last year. Then I realized that I am going to need some money to buy new clothes for my job. All right, I decided, I have to buy clothes with the money, regardless of what I'd like to do with it.

In the rest of this chapter, you will learn how to recognize and correct ungrammatical English and how to avoid slang in your writing.

NONSTANDARD ENGLISH

Nonstandard English is ungrammatical. It does not follow the rules of standard English that are required in college writing. The academic and business worlds expect you to be able to recognize and avoid nonstandard English. This is not always easy because some nonstandard terms are used so often in speech that many people think they are acceptable in writing. The following list might help you choose the correct words in your own writing

ain't

NOT My economics professor **ain't** giving us the test today.

Correct My economics professor **isn't** giving us the test today.

anywheres

NOT Leah buys her clothes **anywheres** she can find them.

Correct Leah buys her clothes **anywhere** she can find them.

be

NOT I **be** so happy.

Correct I **am** so happy.

being as, being that, seeing as how

NOT Emilio will not get to go home over the weekend, **being as** he has to work.

Correct Emilio will not get to go home over the weekend **because** he has to work.

coulda/could of, shoulda/should of

NOT He **could of** earned a better grade on the test if he'd studied.

Correct He **could have** (or **could've**) earned a better grade on the test if he'd studied.

different than

NOT She is **different than** us.

Correct She is **different from** us.

drug

NOT She **drug** the mattress across the room.

Correct She **dragged** the mattress across the room.

enthused

NOT Mary was **enthused** about the wedding.

Correct Mary was **enthusiastic** about the wedding.

everywheres

NOT My dog follows me **everywheres** I go.

Correct My dog follows me **everywhere** I go.

goes

NOT Then Lori **goes,** "I'm leaving without you."

Correct Then Lori **said,** "I'm leaving without you."

Correct Then Lori **said** that she was leaving without me.

hisself

NOT Jerry made **hisself** a cheeseburger.

Correct Jerry made **himself** a cheeseburger.

in regards to

NOT We received a letter **in regards to** your complaint.

Correct We received a letter **in regard to** your complaint.

irregardless

NOT **Irregardless** of how long you study French, you'll never speak it like a native.

Correct **Regardless** of how long you study French, you'll never speak it like a native.

kinda/kind of, sorta/sort of

NOT The rooms smells **kinda** sweet, **sorta** like vanilla.

Correct The room smells **rather** sweet, **much like** vanilla.

most

NOT **Most** everyone accepted the invitation.

Correct **Almost** everyone accepted the invitation.

must of

NOT I **must of** lost my purse at the party.

Correct I **must have** lost my purse at the party.

off of

NOT Billy jumped **off of** the back of the truck.

Correct Billy jumped **off** the back of the truck.

oughta

NOT Sometimes I think I **oughta** watch less television.

Correct Sometimes I think I **ought to** watch less television.

real

NOT My boyfriend was **real** mad when I went out with another boy.

Correct My boyfriend was **really** mad when I went out with another boy.

somewheres

NOT Your jeans are **somewheres** in that pile of clothes.

Correct Your jeans are **somewhere** in that pile of clothes.

suppose to

NOT You were **suppose to** turn that paper in yesterday.

Correct You were **supposed to** turn that paper in yesterday.

theirselves

NOT They helped **theirselves** to the food in the buffet line.

Correct They helped **themselves** to the food in the buffet line.

use to

NOT I **use to** have a truck.

Correct I **used to** have a truck.

ways

NOT Curt's car broke down a long **ways** from home.

Correct Curt's car broke down a long **way** from home.

where . . . at

NOT	**Where** is the nearest bakery **at?**
Correct	**Where** is the nearest bakery?

youse

NOT	Can I get **youse** some coffee?
Correct	Can I get **you** some coffee?

PRACTICE 1A **Identifying** Underline the ungrammatical words or phrases in each of the following sentences.

1. Do you know where the children are at?
2. Then John goes, "There is no way I'm going to touch that."
3. Our production of *Romeo and Juliet* is kinda like the original, but sorta modern.
4. I coulda stayed at home instead of sitting here listening to this boring lecture.
5. Justin was suppose to mail the invitations.

PRACTICE 1B **Correcting** Correct the ungrammatical words and expressions in Practice 1A by rewriting the incorrect sentences.

PRACTICE 2 **Completing** Underline the ungrammatical word or words in each phrase, and change them to standard English.

1. Anywheres I go ________________
2. She drug it ________________
3. We are a long ways ________________
4. He made hisself ________________
5. Being that Susan ________________

PRACTICE 3 **Writing Your Own** Write five sentences of your own using the grammatical words and phrases you chose in Practice 2.

SLANG

Another example of nonstandard English is **slang,** popular words and expressions that come and go, much like the latest fashions. For example, in the 1950s, someone might have called his or her special someone *dreamy*. In the 1960s, you might have heard a boyfriend or girlfriend described as *groovy*, and in the 1990s, *sweet* was the popular slang term. Today your significant other might be *hot* or *dope*.

These expressions are slang because they are part of the spoken language that changes from generation to generation and from place to place. As you might suspect, slang communicates to a limited audience who share common interests and experiences. Some slang words, such as *cool* and *neat*, have become part of our language, but most slang is temporary. What's in today may be out tomorrow, so the best advice is to avoid slang in your writing.

PRACTICE 4 **Identifying** Underline the slang words and expressions in each of the following sentences.

1. *Return of the Mummy* rocks!
2. "Wassup?" I yelled to my homies.
3. This party is da bomb.
4. My mom tripped out when I got my tattoo.
5. Stewart is zoning on the video game.

PRACTICE 5 **Completing** Translate the following slang expressions into standard English.

1. Talk to the hand ______________________________
2. hella good ______________________________
3. flyboy ______________________________
4. right back atcha ______________________________
5. a wanna-be ______________________________

PRACTICE 6 **Writing Your Own** List five slang words or expressions, and use them in sentences of your own. Then rewrite each sentence using standard English to replace the slang expressions.

CHAPTER REVIEW

Standard English: the language of school, business, and the media

Nonstandard English: does not follow the rules of grammar and often includes slang

Slang: popular words and expressions that come and go in the English language

You might want to reread the examples in this chapter before you do the following exercises.

REVIEW PRACTICE 1 **Identifying** Underline the ungrammatical or slang words in the following sentences.

1. You really need to chill out.
2. He ain't going to know what's going on.

3. I was so enthused when I won the contest.
4. He's really jammin' to the music.
5. Hey, stop buggin' me.
6. Oops, I fell off of the ski lift.
7. He's no different than you or me.
8. She's thinks she's all that.
9. You oughta take art lessons.
10. Sandra is really phat.

REVIEW PRACTICE 2 **Completing** Correct any nonstandard English in each of the following sentences by rewriting the sentences.

1. I be wide awake and can't sleep.
2. Irregardless of them, Rufus is talking to hisself.
3. Tony's making big money at his new job.
4. Those singers are bad.
5. My girlfriend was real mad when I forgot Valentine's Day.
6. In regards to your question, I don't have an answer.
7. Watcha doin'?
8. Where's the party at?
9. Jane could of found extra blankets if you were cold.
10. You are solid, man.

REVIEW PRACTICE 3 **Writing Your Own** Write a paragraph on how you spend your free time. Do you spend it with your friends or alone? What do you do and why?

REVIEW PRACTICE 4 **Editing Through Collaboration** Exchange paragraphs from Review Practice 3 with another student, and then do the following:

1. Underline any ungrammatical language.
2. Circle any slang.

Then return the paper to its writer, and use the information in this chapter to correct any nonstandard or slang expressions in your own paragraph. Record your errors on the Error Log in Appendix 3.

CHAPTER

44

Easily Confused Words

CHECKLIST for Easily Confused Words

- ✔ Is the correct word chosen from the easily confused words?
- ✔ Are the following words used correctly: *its/it's*, *their/there/they're*, *to/too/two*, *who's/whose*, *your/you're*?

Test Yourself

Choose the correct word in parentheses.

- Miranda couldn't (choose, chose) a college.
- (It's, Its) time to leave for the show.
- I can't (hear, here) with all this noise.
- (Weather, Whether) you go or not, I'm still going to attend.
- (Who's, Whose) responsible for this mess?

(Answers are in Appendix 9 on the Text Enrichment Site.)

Some words are easily confused. They may look alike, sound alike, or have similar meanings, but they all play different roles in the English language. This chapter will help you choose the right words for your sentences.

EASILY CONFUSED WORDS, PART I

a/an: Use *a* before words that begin with a consonant. Use *an* before words that begin with a vowel (*a*, *e*, *i*, *o*, *u*).

> **a** bill, **a** cat, **a** zebra
>
> **an** artichoke, **an** island, **an** occasion

accept/except: *Accept* means "receive." *Except* means "other than."

> Mary will not **accept** the gift.
>
> Everyone went **except** Harry.

advice/advise: *Advice* means "helpful information." *Advise* means "give advice or help."

My mother usually gives me very good **advice.**

My parents **advise** me when I'm trying to make an important decision.

affect/effect: *Affect* (verb) means "influence." *Effect* means "bring about" (verb) or "a result" (noun).

She hopes having children won't **affect** her chance at promotion.

I believe that changes in the law will **effect** positive changes in society.

The weather had a bad **effect** on his health.

already/all ready: *Already* means "in the past." *All ready* means "completely prepared."

I have **already** taken that class.

We had packed the car and were **all ready** to go when the accident happened.

among/between: Use *among* when referring to three or more people or things. Use *between* when referring to only two people or things.

The students discussed the issues **among** themselves.

I can't decide **between** the two dresses.

bad/badly: *Bad* means "not good." *Badly* means "not well."

That meat is **bad,** so don't eat it.

He felt **bad** about the accident.

He was hurt **badly** in the accident.

beside/besides: *Beside* means "next to." *Besides* means "in addition (to)."

She sat **beside** him at lunch.

Besides sleeping, I can think of nothing else I want to do.

brake/break: *Brake* means "stop" or "the parts that stop a moving vehicle." *Break* means "shatter, come apart" or "a rest between work periods."

She didn't **brake** soon enough to avoid the other car.

I watched the limb **break** off the tree.

Can we take a **break?**

breath/breathe: *Breath* means "air." *Breathe* means "taking in air."

Take a long, slow **breath.**

The air we have to **breathe** is unhealthy.

choose/chose: *Choose* means "select." *Chose* is the past tense of choose.

> Please **choose** an answer.
> He **chose** the wrong answer.

PRACTICE 1 Identifying Underline the correct word in each of the following sentences.

1. I can (advice, advise) you on what courses to take.
2. The little boy behaved (bad, badly) when his father left.
3. We were (already, all ready) to leave the house when she realized she didn't have her purse.
4. (Among, Between) the three of us, we should have enough money to buy lunch.
5. The cold water took my (breath, breathe) away.

PRACTICE 2 Completing Complete the following sentences with a correct word from Part I of the list of easily confused words.

1. I __________ you to be on my team last year.
2. __________ for the humidity, we had a wonderful trip.
3. We have to keep the secret __________ you and me.
4. Corkey was a __________ dog; he chewed up my shoes.
5. Take my __________ and bring a jacket.

PRACTICE 3 Writing Your Own Use each pair of words correctly in a sentence of your own.

1. a/an ______________________________
2. breath/breathe ______________________________
3. affect/effect ______________________________
4. already/all ready ______________________________
5. beside/besides ______________________________

EASILY CONFUSED WORDS, PART II

coarse/course: *Coarse* refers to something that is rough. *Course* refers to a class, a process, or a part of a meal.

> This pavement is **coarse.**
>
> My **course** in math is very interesting.
>
> I will prepare a four-**course** meal.

desert/dessert: *Desert* refers to dry, sandy land or means "abandon." *Dessert* refers to the last course of a meal.

> It is difficult to live in the **desert.**
>
> He **deserted** his family.
>
> We had strawberry shortcake for **dessert.**

Hint: You can remember that *dessert* has two *s*'s if you think of *strawberry shortcake*.

does/dose: *Does* means "performs." *Dose* refers to a specific portion of medicine.

> My sister **does** whatever she wants.
>
> Children should have only a small **dose** of the medicine.

fewer/less: *Fewer* refers to things that can be counted. *Less* refers to things that cannot be counted.

> There are **fewer** cotton fields than there used to be.
>
> She has much **less** time now that she has a new job.

good/well: *Good* modifies nouns. *Well* modifies verbs, adjectives, and adverbs. *Well* also refers to a state of health.

> Bill looks **good** in his new suit.
>
> I'm afraid I didn't do **well** on the test.
>
> Kate isn't feeling **well** today.

hear/here: *Hear* refers to the act of listening. *Here* means "in this place."

> My father can't **hear** as well as he used to.
>
> **Here** is the book you asked for.

it's/its: *It's* is the contraction for *it is* or *it has*. *Its* is a possessive pronoun.

> The teacher said **it's** important to answer all the questions.
>
> The dog chased **its** tail.

knew/new: *Knew* is the past tense of *know*. *New* means "recent."

> I thought everyone **knew** I had a **new** boyfriend.

know/no: *Know* means "understand." *No* means "not any" or is the opposite of *yes*.

> We all **know** that we have **no** hope of defeating the other team.

lay/lie: *Lay* means "set down." (Its principal parts are *lay, laid, laid.*) *Lie* means "recline." (Its principal parts are *lie, lay, lain.*)

> He **lays** brick for a living.
>
> He **laid** down the heavy sack.

She **lies** down at 2 p.m. every day for a nap.

I **lay** in the grass.

(For additional help with *lie* and *lay*, see Chapter 26, "Regular and Irregular Verbs.")

loose/lose: *Loose* means "free" or "unattached." *Lose* means "misplace" or "not win."

Hal's pants are too **loose.**

If I **lose** another $10, I'm going to quit gambling.

passed/past: *Passed* is the past tense of pass. *Past* refers to an earlier time or means "beyond."

John **passed** by his old house on the way to school.

It is interesting to study the **past.**

The dog ran **past** me and into the street.

PRACTICE 4 Identifying Underline the correct word in each of the following sentences.

1. We (passed, past) Edward on the highway.
2. I think you have made a (good, well) choice.
3. With her second job, Marsha has (fewer, less) time to spend with her friends.
4. (It's, Its) going to be a beautiful day.
5. I cannot (loose, lose) this ring; it was given to me by my grandmother.

PRACTICE 5 Completing Complete the following sentences with a correct word from Part II of the list.

1. The restaurant served peach cobbler for _____.
2. How do you like my _____ car?
3. Mike _____ not want to go to the concert with us.
4. This business _____ will benefit me on the job.
5. I am not feeling _____ today.

PRACTICE 6 Writing Your Own Use each pair of words correctly in a sentence of your own.

1. fewer/less ______________________________
2. knew/new ______________________________
3. hear/here ______________________________
4. it's/its ______________________________
5. lay/lie ______________________________

EASILY CONFUSED WORDS, PART III

principal/principle: *Principal* means "main, most important," "a school official," or "a sum of money." A *principle* is a rule. (Think of *principle* and *rule*—both end in *-le*.)

> My **principal** reason for moving is to be closer to my family.
>
> Mr. Kobler is the **principal** at Westside Elementary School.
>
> He lives by one main **principle**—honesty.

quiet/quite: *Quiet* means "without noise." *Quite* means "very."

> The house was **quiet.**
>
> I am **quite** happy with my new car.

raise/rise: *Raise* means "increase" or "lift up." *Rise* means "get up from a sitting or reclining position."

> The province is going to **raise** the tax on cigarettes.
>
> Jane can **rise** slowly from her wheelchair.

set/sit: *Set* means "put down." *Sit* means "take a seated position."

> **Set** the vase on the table.
>
> I don't like to **sit** at a desk for long periods of time.

than/then: *Than* is used in making comparisons. *Then* means "next."

> My mother is younger **than** my father.
>
> I took piano lessons; **then** I took guitar lessons.

their/there/they're: *Their* is possessive. *There* indicates location. *They're* is the contraction of *they are*.

> **Their** house burned down last year.
>
> Too many people are living **there.**
>
> **They're** all going to London.

threw/through: *Threw*, the past tense of throw, means "tossed." *Through* means "finished" or "passing from one point to another."

> The pitcher **threw** the ball.
>
> I am **through** with dinner.
>
> My brother and I rode **through** the forest on our bikes.

to/too/two: *To* means "toward" or is used with a verb. *Too* means "also" or "very." *Two* is a number.

> I went to the store **to** buy some bread.
>
> I bought some artichokes **too,** even though they were **too** expensive for my budget.
>
> My mother has **two** sisters.

wear/were/where: *Wear* means "have on one's body." *Were* is the past tense of *be*. *Where* refers to a place.

> Can you **wear** shorts to school?
>
> **Where were** you yesterday?

weather/whether: *Weather* refers to outdoor conditions. *Whether* expresses possibility.

> No one knows **whether** the **weather** will get better or worse.

who's/whose: *Who's* is a contraction of *who is* or *who has*. *Whose* is a possessive pronoun.

> **Who's** going to decide **whose** car to take?

your/you're: *Your* means "belonging to you." *You're* is the contraction of *you are*.

> **Your** attention to details proves that **you're** a good worker.

PRACTICE 7 Identifying Underline the correct word in each of the following sentences.

1. Janice was (quiet, quite) pleased with your work.
2. (Your, You're) the best choice for this task.
3. Please (set, sit) here and wait for the doctor.
4. (Who's, Whose) planning on going to tonight's game?
5. Our (principal, principle) is retiring at the end of the year.

PRACTICE 8 Completing Complete the following sentences with a correct word from Part III of this list.

1. After the performance, the audience _____ flowers at the performer's feet.
2. Beatrice's _____ reason for quitting her job was the pay.
3. Finish your homework, and _____ you can watch television.
4. _____ are you going dressed like that?
5. Why did you _____ shorts in the winter?

PRACTICE 9 Writing Your Own Use each set of words correctly in a sentence of your own.

1. raise/rise ______________________________
2. their/there/they're ______________________________
3. your/you're ______________________________
4. set/sit ______________________________
5. who's/whose ______________________________

CHAPTER REVIEW

You might want to reread the examples in this chapter before you do the following exercises.

REVIEW PRACTICE 1 Identifying Underline the correct word in each of the following sentences.

1. Your influence is having a positive (affect, effect) on people's lives.
2. (Who's, Whose) that girl with Paul?
3. Jade needs to stand (hear, here) when her name is announced.
4. (Your, You're) the one for me.
5. There are many different plants that grow in the (desert, dessert).
6. Sydney (choose, chose) the smallest puppy of the litter.
7. The picture has come (loose, lose) from its frame.
8. Please sit (beside, besides) me during the ceremony.
9. Your counsellor gave you good (advice, advise), and you should take it.
10. Over (their, there, they're) is the house where I grew up.

REVIEW PRACTICE 2 Completing Complete the following sentences with a correct word from all three parts of the list.

1. We ________ each other when we were children.
2. Contestants should send in ________ photographs of themselves.
3. The ________ outside was so nice that we decided to walk.
4. If you leave now, you will ________ up our happy home.
5. The crowd was so ________ that you could hear people breathing.
6. Quantitative analysis is the most challenging ________ I have ever taken.
7. Jeffrey did not ________ the phone ringing.
8. I laughed so hard that I couldn't catch my ________.
9. Because of our uninvited houseguests, we have ________ food in the house.
10. Faith has ________ donated to the cause.

REVIEW PRACTICE 3 Writing Your Own Write a paragraph explaining the qualities of a good friend. What are the qualities, and why do you think they are important? Try to use some of the easily confused words from this chapter.

REVIEW PRACTICE 4 Editing Through Collaboration Exchange paragraphs from Review Practice 3 with another student, and then do the following:

1. Circle any words used incorrectly.
2. Write the correct form of the word above the error.

Then return the paper to its writer, and use the information in this chapter to correct any confused words in your own paragraph. Record your errors on the Error Log in Appendix 3.

CHAPTER

45

SPELLING

CHECKLIST for Identifying Misspelled Words

- ✔ Do you follow the basic spelling rules?
- ✔ Are all words spelled correctly?

Test Yourself

Correct the misspelled words in the following sentences.

- What is your new addres?
- Turn left on the third avenu.
- I was using the wrong calender when I made out the schedule.
- The dealer delt me a good hand.
- Please get all the items on the grocry list.

(Answers are in Appendix 9 on the Text Enrichment Site.)

If you think back over your education, you will realize that teachers believe spelling is important. There is a good reason they feel this way: spelling errors send negative messages. Misspellings seem to leap out at readers, creating serious doubts about the writer's abilities in general.

Because you will not always have access to spell-checkers—and because spell-checkers do not catch all spelling errors—improving your spelling skills is important.

SPELLING HINTS

The spelling rules in this chapter will help you become a better speller. But first, here are some practical hints that will also help you improve your spelling.

1. Start a personal spelling list of your own. Use the list of commonly misspelled words on pages 565–569 as your starting point.
2. Study the lists of easily confused words in Chapter 44.

3. Avoid all nonstandard expressions (see Chapter 43).
4. Use a dictionary when you run across words you don't know.
5. Run the spell-check program if you are writing on a computer. Keep in mind, however, that spell-check cannot tell if you have incorrectly used one word in place of another (such as *to*, *too*, or *two*).

PRACTICE 1A **Identifying** Underline the misspelled words in each of the following sentences. Refer to the list of easily confused words in Chapter 44 and to the spelling list in this chapter as necessary.

1. "We want to go to," cried the children.
2. The baloon floated away in the breeze.
3. With John's promotion came a better salry.
4. This vacation has had a relaxing affect on my attitude.
5. It was an akward situation when the bride wouldn't say, "I do."

PRACTICE 1B **Correcting** Correct the spelling errors in Practice 1A by rewriting the incorrect sentences.

PRACTICE 2 **Completing** Fill in each blank in the following sentences with hints that help with spelling.

1. Use a _____ to look up words you don't know.
2. You can always use the _____ on your computer, but you should remember that it cannot catch confused words, only misspelled words.
3. Start a _____ to help you remember words you commonly misspell.
4. Study the list of _____ in Chapter _____.
5. Try to avoid all _____ English.

PRACTICE 3 **Writing Your Own** Choose the correctly spelled word in each pair, and write a sentence using it. Refer to the spelling list on pages 565–569 if necessary.

1. concieve/conceive ______________________________
2. absence/absense ______________________________
3. vaccum/vacuum ______________________________
4. library/libary ______________________________
5. delt/dealt ______________________________

SPELLING RULES

Four basic spelling rules can help you avoid many misspellings. It pays to spend a little time learning them now.

1. **Words that end in *-e*:** When adding a suffix beginning with a vowel (*a, e, i, o, u*), drop the final *-e*.

achieve + -ing	=	achieving
include + -ed	=	included
value + -able	=	valuable

   When adding a suffix beginning with a consonant, keep the final *-e*.

aware + -ness	=	awareness
improve + -ment	=	improvement
leisure + -ly	=	leisurely

2. **Words with *ie* and *ei*:** Put *i* before *e* except after *c* or when sounded like *ay* as in *neighbour* and *weigh*.

c + ei	**(no c) + ie**
receive	grieve
conceive	niece
deceive	friend
	relief

3. **Words that end in *-y*:** When adding a suffix to a word that ends in a consonant plus *-y*, change the *y* to *i*.

happy + -er	=	happier
dry + -ed	=	dried
easy + -est	=	easiest

4. **Words that double the final consonant:** When adding a suffix starting with a vowel to a one-syllable word, double the final consonant.

big + -est	=	biggest
quit + -er	=	quitter
bet + -ing	=	betting

   With words of more than one syllable, double the final consonant if the word ends in a single vowel plus a single consonant.

begin + -ing	=	beginning
transmit + -ing	=	transmitting
excel + -ed	=	excelled

PRACTICE 4A Identifying Underline the spelling errors in each of the following sentences.

1. It's not like we're commiting a crime.
2. The boundarys have been clearly marked.
3. My suitcase wieghs too much.
4. Our bagage was lost somewhere in Calgary.
5. The facilitys are near one another.

PRACTICE 4B Correcting Correct the spelling errors in Practice 4A by rewriting the incorrect sentences.

PRACTICE 5 Completing Complete the following spelling rules.

1. When adding a suffix beginning with a vowel to a word that ends in *-e*, _____.
2. With words of more than one syllable, _____ the final consonant if the word ends in a single _____ plus a single _____.
3. Put *i* before *e* except after _____ or when sounded like _____ as in _____.
4. When adding a suffix starting with a _____ to a one-syllable word, _____ the final consonant.
5. When adding a suffix to a word that ends in a consonant plus *-y*, change the _____ to _____.

PRACTICE 6 Writing Your Own Make a list of words you commonly misspell. Then choose five of the words, and use each correctly in a sentence.

MOST COMMONLY MISSPELLED WORDS

Use the following list of commonly misspelled words to check your spelling when you write.

abbreviate
absence
accelerate
accessible
accidentally
accommodate
accompany
accomplish
accumulate
accurate
ache

achievement
acre
actual
address
adequate
advertisement
afraid
aggravate
aisle
although
aluminum

amateur
ambulance
ancient
anonymous
anxiety
anxious
appreciate
appropriate
approximate
architect
arithmetic

artificial
assassin
athletic
attach
audience
authority
autumn
auxiliary
avenue
awkward
baggage
balloon
banana
bankrupt
banquet
beautiful
beggar
beginning
behaviour
benefited
bicycle
biscuit
bought
boundary
brilliant
brought
buoyant
bureau
burglar
business
cabbage
cafeteria
calendar
campaign
canoe
canyon
captain

career
carriage
cashier
catastrophe
caterpillar
ceiling
cemetery
census
certain
certificate
challenge
champion
character
chief
children
chimney
coffee
collar
college
column
commit
committee
communicate
community
comparison
competent
competition
complexion
conceive
concession
concrete
condemn
conference
congratulate
conscience
consensus
continuous

convenience
cooperate
corporation
correspond
cough
counterfeit
courageous
courteous
cozy
criticize
curiosity
curious
curriculum
cylinder
dairy
dangerous
dealt
deceive
decision
definition
delicious
descend
describe
description
deteriorate
determine
development
dictionary
difficulty
diploma
disappear
disastrous
discipline
disease
dissatisfied
divisional
dormitory

economy
efficiency
eighth
elaborate
electricity
eligible
embarrass
emphasize
employee
encourage
enormous
enough
enthusiastic
envelope
environment
equipment
equivalent
especially
essential
establish
exaggerate
excellent
exceptionally
excessive
exhaust
exhilarating
existence
explanation
extinct
extraordinary
familiar
famous
fascinate
fashion
fatigue
faucet
February
fiery
financial
foreign
forfeit
fortunate
forty
freight
friend
fundamental
gauge
genius
genuine
geography
gnaw
government
graduation
grammar
grief
grocery
gruesome
guarantee
guess
guidance
handkerchief
handsome
haphazard
happiness
harass
height
hesitate
hoping
humorous
hygiene
hymn
icicle
illustrate
imaginary
immediately
immortal
impossible
incidentally
incredible
independence
indispensable
individual
inferior
infinite
influential
initial
initiation
innocence
installation
intelligence
interfere
interrupt
invitation
irrelevant
irrigate
issue
jealous
jewellery
journalism
kindergarten
knife
knowledge
knuckles
laboratory
laborious
language
laugh
laundry
league
legible
legislature

leisure
length
library
licence (n.)/license (v.)
lieutenant
lightning
likeable
liquid
listen
literature
machinery
magazine
magnificent
majority
manufacture
marriage
material
mathematics
maximum
mayor
meant
medicine
message
mileage
miniature
minimum
minute
mirror
miscellaneous
mischievous
miserable
misspell
monotonous
mortgage
mysterious
necessary
neighbourhood
niece
nineteen
ninety
noticeable
nuisance
obedience
obstacle
occasion
occurred
official
omission
omitted
opponent
opportunity
opposite
original
outrageous
pamphlet
paragraph
parallel
parentheses
partial
particular
pastime
patience
peculiar
permanent
persistent
personnel
persuade
physician
pitcher
pneumonia
politician
possess
prairie
precede
precious
preferred
prejudice
previous
privilege
procedure
proceed
pronounce
psychology
publicly
questionnaire
quotient
realize
receipt
recipe
recommend
reign
religious
representative
reservoir
responsibility
restaurant
rhyme
rhythm
salary
satisfactory
scarcity
scenery
schedule
science
scissors
secretary
seize
separate
significant
similar
skiing

soldier
souvenir
sovereign
spaghetti
squirrel
statue
stomach
strength
subtle
succeed
success
sufficient
surprise
syllable
symptom
technique
temperature
temporary
terrible
theatre
thief
thorough
tobacco
tomorrow
tongue
tournament
tragedy
truly
unanimous
undoubtedly
unique
university
usable
usually
vacuum
valuable
various
vegetable
vehicle
vicinity
villain
visible
volunteer
weather
Wednesday
weigh
weird
whose
width
worst
wreckage
writing
yacht
yearn
yield
zealous
zoology

PRACTICE 7A Identifying Underline any words that are misspelled in the following sentences.

1. This steak and lobster dinner is incredable.
2. You shouldn't condem others for doing what you do.
3. Valentine's Day is in Febuary.
4. How long have you been writting that novel?
5. I know you will suceed in college.

PRACTICE 7B Correcting Correct any spelling errors that you identified in Practice 7A by rewriting the incorrect sentences.

PRACTICE 8 Completing Correct the spelling errors in the following paragraph.

I was eating a plate of spagetti when the phone rang. It was my nieghbour. He said, "The big game is begining in 15 minutes, and my television screen just went out." He then beged me to let him come over and watch it at my house. So I told him that was fine. He neglected to tell me, however, that he wouldn't be alone. He and seven of his rowdy freinds invaded my house, ate my spagetti and drank my pop, and left a catastrophy behind. I think the next time I have a party, I'll have it at his house.

PRACTICE 9 Writing Your Own Write a complete sentence for each word listed here.

1. appreciate ______________________
2. laundry ______________________
3. marriage ______________________
4. excellent ______________________
5. opposite ______________________

CHAPTER REVIEW

You might want to reread the examples in this chapter before you do the following exercises.

REVIEW PRACTICE 1 Identifying Underline the misspelled words in each of the following sentences.

1. I'm trying to catch the rythm of this music.
2. You ate my desert.
3. This essay shows improvment.
4. Ramona is a genuis with figures.
5. The firy-hot peppers made my eyes water.
6. Most teenagers want their independance.
7. If we stick to the scedule, we should make it home before tomorow.
8. Breath deeply, and put your head between your legs.
9. My family lives in seperate states.
10. Dr. Murphy rides his bycicle to work every day.

REVIEW PRACTICE 2 Completing Correct the spelling errors in Review Practice 1 by rewriting the incorrect sentences.

REVIEW PRACTICE 3 Writing Your Own Write a paragraph explaining how to become a better speller. Are there any hints that may help?

REVIEW PRACTICE 4 **Editing Through Collaboration** Exchange paragraphs from Review Practice 3 with another student, and then do the following:

1. Underline any words that are used incorrectly.
2. Circle any misspelled words.

Then return the paper to its writer, and use the information in this chapter to correct any spelling errors in your own paragraph. Record your errors on the Spelling Log in Appendix 4.

APPENDIX 1A Revising Peer Evaluation Form

Use the following questions to evaluate your partner's essay. Direct your comments to your partner.

Writer: ______________________ **Peer:** ______________________

Describing

1. Is the dominant impression clearly communicated? Explain your answer.

Thesis Statement

2. Does the thesis statement contain the essay's controlling idea and an opinion about that idea?
3. Does the thesis appear as the last sentence of the introduction? Explain your answer.

Basic Elements

4. Does the essay have all the basic elements? Is each one effective? Explain your answer.

Development

5. Does each paragraph support the thesis statement? Does each paragraph contain enough specific details to develop its topic sentence? Explain your answer.

Unity

6. Do all the essay's topic sentences relate directly to the thesis statement? Do the details in each paragraph support its topic sentence? Explain your answer.

Organization

7. Is the essay organized logically? Is each body paragraph organized logically? Explain your answer.

Coherence

8. Are transitions used effectively so that paragraphs move smoothly and logically from one to the next? Do the sentences move smoothly and logically from one to the next? Explain your answer.

Forms for evaluating specific types of essays are available on the Text Enrichment Site.

APPENDIX 1B Editing Peer Evaluation Form

Use the following questions to help you find editing errors in your partner's essay. Mark the errors directly on your partner's paper using the editing symbols in Appendix 6.

Writer: ______________________ **Peer:** ______________________

Sentences

1. Does each sentence have a subject and verb?

   Mark any fragments you find with **frag**.

   Put a slash (/) between any fused sentences and comma splices.

2. Do all subjects and verbs agree?

   Mark any subject–verb agreement errors you find with **sv**.

3. Do all pronouns agree with their nouns?

   Mark any pronoun errors you find with **pro agr**.

4. Are all modifiers as close as possible to the words they modify?

   Mark any modifier errors you find with **ad** (adjective or adverb problem), **mm** (misplaced modifier), or **dm** (dangling modifier).

Punctuation and Mechanics

5. Are sentences punctuated correctly?

   Mark any punctuation errors you find with the appropriate symbol. You can find the editing symbols in Appendix 6.

6. Are words capitalized properly?

   Mark any capitalization errors you find with **lc** (lower case) or **cap** (capital).

Word Choice and Spelling

7. Are words used correctly?

   Mark any words that are used incorrectly with **wc** (word choice) or **ww** (wrong word).

8. Are words spelled correctly?

   Mark any misspelled words you find with **sp**.

APPENDIX 2A Your EQ (Editing Quotient)

A good way to approach editing is by finding your EQ (Editing Quotient). Knowing your EQ will help you look for specific errors in your writing and make your editing more efficient.

PRACTICE 1 EQ Test In each of the following paragraphs, underline the errors you find, and label them a, b, c, and so on. Then list them on the lines below the paragraph. The number of lines corresponds to the number of errors in each paragraph.

The possible errors are listed here:

apostrophe	end punctuation	pronoun agreement
capitalization	fragment	spelling
comma	fused sentence	subject–verb agreement
comma splice	modifier error	verb form
confused word	pronoun	

1. Many people seem to have a telephone permanently attached to one ear people have several phone lines going into their homes. And cellphones hanging off of their belts. People are talking on their cellphones in restaurants, in cars, and even in public washrooms. When they go home, they go online to check email. While the second line is ringing off the hook. Why would someone want to be available every second of the day? This rushed society will eventually have to slow down, people can't live at this pace for long.

   (a.) ______

   (b.) ______

   (c.) ______

   (d.) ______

2. Recently, a major computer software company was accused of being a monopoly. That is, it seemed to be trying to control the whole software industry. The company, reality software, sells many different types of software at reasonable prices. Which results in the company selling more products than its competitors. Reality Software also signed contracts with Computer Manufacturers that allow the manufacturers to install Reality programs on computers before they are sold. The courts, which guard against monopolies, say this is unfair to consumers, buyers should be able to choose their software. It is also unfair to other software companies. Because they are not given a fair chance to sell their products.

   (a.) ______

(b.) ____

(c.) ____

(d.) ____

(e.) ____

3. Public speaking is a valuable tool no matter what career path a person take. At some point in every career, if a person is going to advance, they will have to speak to a group. In fact, the higher up the career ladder a person climb, the more public speaking will be required. It is good preparation, therefore, to take a public speaking course in college, a public speaking course not only teaches the skills involved in making a presentation but also builds a person's confidence.

(a.) ____

(b.) ____

(c.) ____

(d.) ____

4. If I had my way, I would require every college student to take a course in geography. It is embarassing how little the average Canadian knows about his own country, to say nothing of other countries. For instance, do you know the capital of new brunswick? Could you name all the Great Lakes? On which continent is greece? If you can answer these questions you are one of very few people. People think geography is boring but it isn't. Its fascinating to learn about the world we live in.

(a.) ____

(b.) ____

(c.) ____

(d.) ____

(e.) ____

(f.) ____

(g.) ____

5. I believe that fast-food restaurants should change there names to "fast food sometimes, but at least faster than a sit-down restaurant." When I go through the drive-up window at a fast-food restaraunt, it is because I am in a hurry and want to get something to eat quickly, however, sometimes it would be quicker for me to go home and cook a three-course

meal. I do not understand what could take so long. I pull up to the intercom, order my food, procede to the window, and wait. If fast food always lived up to its name I would be able to get food fast.

(a.) ______________________________

(b.) ______________________________

(c.) ______________________________

(d.) ______________________________

(e.) ______________________________

6. Doing the family laundry used to be a chore for me but now I am a pro. First, I sort the clothes according to colours or whites. Before I learned this basic rule, my poor brother had to wear pink underwear from time to time. Next, I put the clothes in the washing machine, and add detergent. If I'm doing whites I also add bleach. I close the lid, turn the dial to hot wash and cold rinse, and push the "start" button. I allow the washing machine to do it's work while I read a magazine. When it's time to put the clothes in the dryer, I pay attention to the drying instructions on the tags. Once I neglected this step, and my favourite pants shrinked. When the dryer has done its work, I remove the clothes immediately so they do not become rinkled.

(a.) ______________________________

(b.) ______________________________

(c.) ______________________________

(d.) ______________________________

(e.) ______________________________

(f.) ______________________________

7. It's fun to watch a person with their animals. For instance, the lady down the street takes her dog for a walk every morning. The dog is a tiny rat terrier, it is really cute. The lady puts a little leash on the dog. To keep him from running away. Even though the dogs legs are short, he can run real fast. The dog seems so happy during his walks. He jumps and yips. The lady and her dog are a good pair they enjoy walking with each other and keeping each other company.

(a.) ______________________________

(b.) ______________________________

(c.) ______________________________

(d.) ____________________

(e.) ____________________

(f.) ____________________

PRACTICE 2 EQ **Answers** Score your answers in Practice 1 using the following answer key.

1. (a) Many people seem to have a telephone permanently attached to their ear people have several phone lines going into their homes. (b) And cellphones hanging off of their belts. People are talking on their cellphones in restaurants, in cars, and even in public bathrooms. When they go home, they go online to check email. (c) While the second line is ringing off the hook. Why would someone want to be available every second of the day? (d) This rushed society will eventually have to slow down, people can't live at this pace for long.

   a. *fused sentence or end punctuation*

   b. *fragment*

   c. *fragment*

   d. *comma splice or end punctuation*

2. Recently, a major computer software company was accused of being a monopoly. That is, it seemed to be trying to control the whole software industry. The company, (a) reality software, sells many different types of software at reasonable prices. (b) Which results in the company selling more products than its competitors. Reality Software also signed contracts with (c) Computer Manufacturers that allow the manufacturers to install Reality programs on computers before they are sold. (d) The courts, which guard against monopolies, say this is unfair to consumers, buyers should be able to choose their software. It is also unfair to other software companies. (e) Because they are not given a fair chance to sell their products.

   a. *capitalization*

   b. *fragment*

   c. *capitalization*

   d. *comma splice or end punctuation*

   e. *fragment*

3. Public speaking is a valuable tool no matter what career path (a) a person take. At some point in every career, if a person is going to advance, (b) they will have to speak to a group. In fact, the higher up the career ladder a

ⓒperson climb, the more public speaking will be required.ⓓ It is good preparation, therefore, to take a public speaking course in college, a public speaking course not only teaches the skills involved in making a presentation but also builds a person's confidence.

a. *subject–verb agreement*

b. *pronoun agreement*

c. *subject–verb agreement*

d. *comma splice or end punctuation*

4. If I had my way, I would require every college student to take a course in geography. It is ⓐembarassing how little the average Canadian knows about ⓑhis own country, to say nothing of other countries. For instance, do you know the capital of ⓒnew brunswick? Can you name all the Great Lakes? On which continent is ⓓgreece? If you can answer these questions ⓔyou are one of very few people. People think geography is boring ⓕbut it isn't.ⓖIts fascinating to learn about the world we live in.

a. *spelling*

b. *pronoun*

c. *capitalization*

d. *capitalization*

e. *comma*

f. *comma*

g. *confused word or apostrophe*

5. I believe that fast-food restaurants should changeⓐthere names to "fast food sometimes, but at least faster than a sit-down restaurant." ⓑWhen I go through the drive-up window at a fast-foodⓒrestaraunt, it is because I am in a hurry and want to get something to eat quickly, however, sometimes it would be quicker for me to go home and cook a three-course meal. I do not understand what could take so long. I pull up to the intercom, order my food,ⓓprocede to the window, and wait. If fast food always lived up to its nameⓔI would be able to get food fast.

a. *confused word*

b. *comma splice or end punctuation*

c. *spelling*

d. *spelling*

e. *comma*

6. Doing the family laundry used to be a chore for me ⓐ but now I am a pro. First, I sort the clothes according to colours or whites. Before I learned this basic rule, my poor brother had to wear pink underwear from time to time. Next, I put the clothes in the washing machine, ⓑ and add detergent. If I'm doing whites ⓒ I also add bleach. I close the lid, turn the dial to hot wash and cold rinse, and push the "start" button. I allow the washing machine to do ⓓ it's work while I read a magazine. When it's time to put the clothes in the dryer, I pay attention to the drying instructions on the tags. Once I neglected this step, and my favourite pants ⓔ shrinked. When the dryer has done its work, I remove the clothes immediately so they do not become ⓕ rinkled.

   a. *comma*

   b. *comma*

   c. *comma*

   d. *confused word or apostrophe*

   e. *verb form*

   f. *spelling*

7. It's fun to watch a person with ⓐ their animals. For instance, the lady down the street takes her dog for a walk every morning. ⓑ The dog is a tiny rat terrier, it is really cute. The lady puts a little leash on the dog. ⓒ To keep him from running away. Even though the ⓓ dogs legs are short, he can run ⓔ real fast. The dog seems so happy during his walks. He jumps and yips. ⓕ The lady and her dog are a good pair they enjoy walking with each other and keeping each other company.

   a. *pronoun agreement*

   b. *comma splice or end punctuation*

   c. *fragment*

   d. *apostrophe*

   e. *modifier error*

   f. *fused sentence or end punctuation*

APPENDIX 2B Editing Quotient Error Chart

Put an X in the square that corresponds to each question that you missed. Then record your errors in the categories below to find out where you might need help.

	a	b	c	d	e	f	g
1							
2							
3							
4							
5							
6							
7Z							

Fragments 1b ____ 1c ____ 2b ____ 2e ____ 7c ____

Fused sentences and comma splices 1a ____ 1d ____ 2d ____ 3d ____ 5b ____ 7b ____ 7f ____

Subject–verb agreement 3a ____ 3c ____

Verb forms 6e ____

Pronoun errors 4b ____

Pronoun agreement 3b ____ 7a ____

Modifiers 7e ____

End punctuation 1d ____ 2d ____ 3d ____ 5b ____ 7b ____ 7f ____

Commas 4e ____ 4f ____ 5e ____ 6a ____ 6b ____ 6c ____

Apostrophes 4g ____ 7d ____

Capitalization 2a ____ 2c ____ 4c ____ 4d ____

Confused words 4g ____ 5a ____ 5d ____

Spelling 4a ____ 5c ____ 5d ____ 6f ____

Appendix 3 Error Log

List any grammar, punctuation, and mechanics errors you make in your writing on the following chart. Then, to the right of this label, record (1) the actual error from your writing, (2) the rule for correcting t his error, and (3) your correction.

Error	**Example** I went to the new seafood restaurant and I ordered the lobster.
Comma	**Rule** Use a comma before *and*, *but*, *for*, *nor*, *or*, *so*, and *yet* when they join two independent clauses.
	Correction I went to the new seafood restaurant, and I ordered the lobster.
Error	**Example**
	Rule
	Correction
Error	**Example**
	Rule
	Correction
Error	**Example**
	Rule
	Correction
Error	**Example**
	Rule
	Correction
Error	**Example**
	Rule
	Correction
Error	**Example**
	Rule
	Correction
Error	**Example**
	Rule
	Correction

Error	Example
	Rule
	Correction
Error	Example
	Rule
	Correction
Error	Example
	Rule
	Correction
Error	Example
	Rule
	Correction
Error	Example
	Rule
	Correction
Error	Example
	Rule
	Correction
Error	Example
	Rule
	Correction
Error	Example
	Rule
	Correction
Error	Example
	Rule
	Correction

<table>
<tr><td rowspan="3">Error</td><td>Example</td></tr>
<tr><td>Rule</td></tr>
<tr><td>Correction</td></tr>
<tr><td rowspan="3">Error</td><td>Example</td></tr>
<tr><td>Rule</td></tr>
<tr><td>Correction</td></tr>
</table>

APPENDIX 4 Spelling Log

On this chart, record any words you misspell, and write the correct spelling in the space next to the misspelled word. In the right column, write a note to yourself to help you remember the correct spelling. (See the first line for an example.) Refer to this chart as often as necessary to avoid misspelling the same words again.

Misspelled Word	**Correct Spelling**	**Definition/Notes**
there	their	there = place; their = pronoun; they're = "they are"

APPENDIX 5 Presentation Techniques

The following guidelines will help you to prepare your oral presentation. They will help make your presentation a more enjoyable and less stressful experience. Good luck!

GUIDELINES FOR USING POWERPOINT

1. **Avoid having too much information on a slide.** If you type your whole speech onto the slide, your audience's attention will be divided. They won't know if they should listen to you, read the information on the slide, or write everything down. Use the main points of your topic on your PowerPoint slides. If you put the main points on the slide, the audience can see them and then listen to you discuss them. A good rule to follow is the six by six rule: Try to use no more than six words across and six words down on each side.
2. **Avoid using too many bells and whistles.** The swirling letters and dancing graphics are fun; however, can you imagine sitting through an hour-long presentation where each letter falls individually from the top of the screen and makes a typewriter sound as it reaches its place? Use these functions sparingly. You don't want to annoy your audience or have their attention pulled away from what you are saying.
3. **Always have a consistent background.** Your presentation will look more professional and will be seen as a united whole if you use the same background on every slide. This is important to remember if you are presenting with a group. Each presenter should have the same background slides. This consistency will help the audience link the group's topic together as a unified whole presentation.
4. **Always have a backup plan.** Sometimes the technology will fail on the day of your presentation. The computer may crash, the disk may be flawed, or the bulb on the projector may burn out. It's always a good idea to have a backup plan in case anything unforeseen happens. You might want to prepare a handout with your main points on it. You may want to put some of your slides on overhead to use in case there's an unfixable problem. It's a good idea to do a trial run with the equipment to make sure everything is in order. It's also a good idea to show up early enough to get things set up and to make sure everything is working.

GUIDELINES FOR PRESENTING

1. **Maintain eye contact with your audience.** By keeping eye contact, you will engage and interact with your audience. This interaction will help keep your audience's attention. It's difficult to daydream when the presenter is looking at you!
2. **Don't be afraid to move around.** Movement will engage your audience. If you are standing motionless behind a lectern, the audience's attention will wander. If you move around, you will look more comfortable and your audience will be more engaged with your presentation. If you are in a group, have another member click the mouse to change the PowerPoint slide. If you are presenting alone, and you don't have a portable mouse, put the mouse in a position where you can move around in front of the audience and still get back to reach the mouse.

3. **Be aware of your voice level.** Be sure to speak to the people in the back of the room. You want to make sure everyone can hear you. It's frustrating for the audience if they can't hear you, so they will stop listening. Sometimes you may mumble because you are nervous. Perhaps have someone sit in the back who can give you a visual clue to show that he or she can/cannot hear you. Another option may be to have a group member cue you. You are all members of a team, so don't be afraid to help each other out.
4. **Keep your notes organized.** Number your cue cards to keep them in order. This will help if you accidentally drop them and they get out of order. Have the main points in large type so they stand out; this will make them easy to follow even if you're nervous. Highlight information so that you can glance down and see it quickly. Write notes to yourself on your cue cards. Remind yourself to speak slowly, loudly, and clearly. Remind yourself to move around and look comfortable. Remind yourself to look up and keep eye contact with your audience.

HOW TO KEEP FROM READING YOUR MATERIAL

1. **Trust yourself and your knowledge of your topic.** You've spent a lot of time researching and preparing for your presentation. Do not wait until the day before to prepare your material! You know your topic. Trust that knowledge.
2. **Write only the main points on your cue cards.** If you have notes, don't write out your whole speech. This will only tempt you to read word for word what is on your page. It's hard for an audience to pay attention to someone who is reading the presentation. If you have only the main points, then you are forced to discuss your topic rather than read your topic to the audience. Again, trust your knowledge of the topic.
3. **Practise your presentation.** Rehearse what you want to say. If you can avoid reading, your presentation will be more interesting to listen to. Practising your presentation out loud will help you learn your material and get used to discussing it aloud at the same time. Say difficult words aloud a few times in order to get used to wrapping your mouth around them. The more you practise, the more comfortable you will become and the less you will need to rely on your notes.

GUIDELINES FOR FIGHTING NERVOUSNESS

1. **Be prepared.** If you are comfortable with your information, you will be less nervous. Try not to procrastinate and leave your presentation preparation until the day before. The longer in advance you are prepared, the more time you have to practise and rehearse your presentation. If you

can step in front of the audience confident that you know your material, you will be far less nervous.

2. **Take a drink of water.** If you are nervous and forget what you want to say, then take a drink of water. It's perfectly acceptable for a presenter to have water with him or her. If you get lost for a moment, take a drink of water. This will give you a moment to regain your thoughts or composure.
3. **Move around the room.** It's very difficult to be stiff and terrified if you walk or move around. The action of walking forces you to relax stiff leg and arm muscles. Once you are moving, your relaxed state will spread and you will find that your nervousness will dissipate.
4. **Remember that everyone gets nervous.** Even professional presenters get nervous. It's natural to be nervous when you are speaking in front of a group of people. Try to channel the nervous energy into your presentation. Use it to your advantage. Your mind can focus on the information. Focus the energy into your presentation. Move around. Make eye contact. Don't give in to the nervousness!

Appendix 6 Editing Symbols

Unit I	frag	fragment
	fs, cs	fused sentence, comma splice
Unit II	sv agr	subj–verb agreement error
	t	verb tense error
	v	verb form error
Unit III	pro ref	pronoun reference error
	pro agr	pronoun agreement error
Unit IV	ad	adjective or adverb error
	mm	misplaced modifier
	dm	dangling modifier
Unit V	p	punctuation error
	,/	comma error
	’/	apostrophe error
	“/”	quotation marks error
	;/	semicolon error
	:/	colon error
	—	dash needed
	( )	parentheses needed
Unit VI	cap	needs capital letter
	lc	needs lower case letter
	ab	abbreviation error
	n	number error
Unit VII	var	needs sentence variety
	//	faulty parallelism
Unit VIII	wc	word choice error
	ww	wrong word
	sp	spelling error

CREDITS ❖

CHAPTER 3

"I Just Wanna Be Average" by Mike Rose, from *Lives on the Boundary,* The Free Press © 1989. Reprinted with the permission of The Free Press, a Division of Simon & Schuster Adult Publishing Group, from 'Lives on the Boundary: The Struggles and Achievements of America's Unprepared' by Mike Rose. Copyright © 1989 by Mike Rose. All rights reserved.

CHAPTER 8

Extracted from *The Colony of Unrequited Dreams* by Wayne Johnston. Copyright © 1998 by Wayne Johnston. Reprinted by permission of Alfred A. Knopf Canada.

"Underground Toronto" by Allen Abel is reproduced by permission of the author.

"Dryden's Backyard" by Ken Dryden is excerpted from *The Game*, by Ken Dryden, and Copyright © (2003 Ken Dryden). Reprinted with permission from John Wiley & Sons Canada, Ltd.

Photo: Jim Mone/AP/Wide World Photos.

CHAPTER 9

"Girl" by Jane Maher. Reprinted by permission of the author.

"The Worth of Women's Work" by Nina Lee Colwill is reprinted by permission of the author.

"In the Company of Soldiers," originally published in *The Globe and Mail*, December 29, 2006, is reprinted courtesy of Christie Blatchford.

Photo: Kim Mould/Omni-Photo Communications Inc.

CHAPTER 10

"The Question" by Lawrence Hill is reprinted by permission of the author. Lawrence Hill is the author of five books, including the novel *Any Known Blood* and the nonfiction work *Black Berry, Sweet Juice: On Being Black and White in Canada*. He lives in Oakville, Ontario.

"The Decorated Body" by France Borel. "Le Vêtement incarne: Les Métamorphoses du Corps" by France Borel © Editions Calmann-Levy, 1992.

"Wild Weather" by Chris Wood, previously published in *Maclean's*, January 25, 1999, Vol. 112 Issue 4, page 16, is reprinted by permission of *Maclean's*.

Photo: CP Photo/Chuck Stoody.

CHAPTER 11

"Dare to Change Your Job and Your Life in 7 Steps" by Carole Kanchier, *Psychology Today*, March 2000. Reprinted by permission of Carole Kanchier, PhD.

"Learn How to Negotiate Almost Anything" by Chris Daniels is reprinted with permission of Chris Daniels, freelance writer, *Chatelaine*.

"How She Survived Freshman Year" by Shanda Dezeil, originally published in *Maclean's*, June 26, 2006, is reprinted by permission of *Maclean's*.

Photo: David Buffington/Getty Images, Inc. Photo Disc, Inc.

CHAPTER 12

"D'oh!" An analysis of the medical care provided to the family of Homer J. Simpson" by Robert Patterson and Charles Weijer is reprinted from CMAJ 15–Dec–98: 159(12), pages 1480–1481 by permission of the publisher. © 1998 Canadian Medical Association.

"That Is Not the Image We Have of Canada" by Thomas Hayden is reprinted with the permission of the author.

"The Truth About Stories" by Thomas King: Excerpt from *The Truth About Stories: A Native Narrative*, pages 22–29. Reprinted by permission of House of Anansi Press.

Photo: Massimo Mastrorillo, Corbis/Stock Market.

CHAPTER 13

"On Being Persuaded" by Roy Geiger is reprinted courtesy of Roy Geiger.

"Bad Boys" by Mordecai Richler, previously published in *Saturday Night*, March 2000, Vol. 115, Issue 2, page 78. © Mordecai Richler Productions Inc.

"Why You Think You're Wonderful" by Brian Bethune, originally published in *Maclean's*, October 5, 2006, is reprinted by permission of *Maclean's*.

Photo: CP Photo/Kitchener-Waterloo Record–Robert Wilson.

CHAPTER 14

Patricia Pearson, "When Kids Are Cruel," originally published in *Maclean's*, is reprinted with the permission of the author.

"Google Never Forgets: A Cautionary Tale" by Max Fawcett is reprinted by permission of the author. Max Fawcett is a contributing editor for Dooneyscafe.com, an alternative online news service. He lives in Toronto.

"What Is Intelligence, Anyway?" by Isaac Asimov. Published by permission of The Estate of Isaac Asimov c/o Ralph M. Vicinana, Ltd.

Photo: Laimute E. Druskis/Pearson Education/PH College.

CHAPTER 15

"Why Do Schools Flunk Biology?" by LynNell Hancock, *Newsweek*, 2/19/96, © 1996 Newsweek, Inc. All rights reserved. Reprinted by permission.

"Happiness Is Catching: Why Emotions Are Contagious," by Stacey Colino, *Family Circle*, 3/12/96. Reprinted by permission of Stacey Colino.

"Too Much Self-Esteem: The Blight of Modern Times" by Johanna Schneller is reproduced by permission of Johanna Schneller, *Globe and Mail* columnist.

Photo: Tony Freeman/PhotoEdit.

CHAPTER 16

"Let Boys Be Boys" by Robert Sibley. ("The Lost Boys. Let Boys Be Boys: The 'demasculinization' of society is doing more harm than good.") Material reprinted with the express permission of: "Ottawa Citizen Group Inc.," a CanWest Partnership.

"We Are Training Our Kids to Kill" by Dave Grossman, *Saturday Evening Post*, July 1999. Reprinted by permission of the author.

"Ban Spam: E-nough Is E-nough" by Rick Broadhead: Rick Broadhead is a best-selling author, technology analyst, public speaker, and literary agent. His most recent book is *Dear Valued Customer: You Are a Loser!—And Over 100 Other Embarrassing and Funny Stories of Technology Gone Mad* (Andrews McMeel Publishing, 2004). He can be reached by email at rickb@rickbroadhead.com © 2004 by Rick Broadhead. All rights reserved. No reproduction in any form without permission.

"Ban Spam? What, and Banish All the World?" by Doug Saunders is reprinted with permission from *The Globe and Mail*.

Photo: Charles Gatewood/Pearson Education/PH College.

INDEX

D

T